Hugh Johnson's

POCKET WINE BOOK

2009

GENERAL EDITOR MARGARET RAND

Acknowledgments

This store of detailed recommendations comes partly from my own notes and mainly from those of a great number of kind friends. Without the generous help and cooperation of innumerable winemakers, merchants, and critics, I could not attempt it. I particularly want to thank the following for help with research or in the areas of their special knowledge:

Sarah Ahmed
Geoff Adams
Helena Baker
Nicolas Belfrage
Phillip Blom
Charles Borden
Gregory Bowden
Stephen Brook
Jim Budd
Michael Cooper
Rupert Dean
Michael Edwards
Sarah Jane Evans MW
Rosemary George MW

Caroline Gilby MW
Robert Gorjak
James Halliday
Annie Kay
Chandra Kurt
Gareth Lawrence
James Lawther MW
Konstantinos Lazarakis
　　MW
John Livingstone-
　　Learmonth
Nico Manessis
Adam Montefiore
Jasper Morris MW

Shirley Nelson
Margaret Rand
Carlos Read
Daniel Rogov
Stephen Skelton MW
Paul Strang
Gabriella Szlovák
Bostjan Tadel
Marguerite Thomas
Larry Walker
Simon Woods
Philip van Zyl

Contents

Quantity v. quality

❝The rich want the best wine, the poor just lots of wine". So said the philosopher-poet Goethe, who came into the first category. Wine has always been a polarized market; luxury goods at one end, at the other a mere commodity. As every year now produces more eye-popping prices (at both ends) it may be time for a reality check. Two Buck Chuck (for non-Americans, a perfectly drinkable California varietal for $1.99) is so remote from a bottle of Romanée-Conti, released at $2,000, that the single category of table wine seems an odd place in which to find them both.

How do you make realistic price comparisons? One way is to ask how many bottles of a good, recognizable wine you could buy for the price of the most expensive. Clearly, in the case above, 1,000. In Bordeaux, where such comparisons are more readily and realistically made, the answer is about 50. A First Growth is about 100 euros, a petit château about 5. For a Super-Second classed growth you could buy about 15 of the petit château, for a regular reputable classed growth about 5, and for a good Cru Bourgeois maybe 2. In other words, the price accelerates alarmingly as you get more picky. Limit yourself to the few wines that all the world knows and expect to be taken to the cleaners.

Who coined the expression "world-class"? It has a lot to answer for. Have you noticed how it has crept into every field – taking the place, very often, of its worn-out predecessor, "award-winning"? Of course globalisation has its upside. There is no hiding place for incompetence these days: undrinkable wine is now unusual – though not as rare as many say. No one objects when standards go up and prices down. The downside? It starts a mad scramble for a handful of icons. Prepare to see it get madder as Asia joins the party. Château Lafite is becoming unobtainable since China learned it comes first in the 1855 (alphabetical) list of Bordeaux's First Growths. Apparently the name sounds good to Chinese ears too. The same goes – or soon will – for everything you could call an icon.

You can't clone First Growths. Until recently most people thought the supply of potential First Growths – or great vineyards of any kind – was finite too: that Bordeaux, Burgundy, and a handful of fortunate spots had terroir sewn up. The French, of course, did nothing to discourage the idea – indeed they tried to rubbish regions aspiring to high potential of their own. One advertisement for Burgundy showed a cartoon of a digger hunting for Côte d'Or soil in the Australian bush as though the poor man was nuts. Luckily for us he was only one of many who planted Pinot Noir with brilliant results thousands of miles from the Côte d'Or. Cloning is not necessary – or even desirable. It is only the market that is global: wine quality is so no longer – if it ever was. How do you detach fashion, though, from the world-class syndrome? With difficulty, I fear, but here's where you start.

Forget the "world's best" idea. Think locally. There is as much fun in learning your way round, say, Northern Italy or Northern Spain, Sonoma or South Australia, Austria or the Rhône Valley as treading the overcrowded roads of Pauillac and Pomerol, Vosne-Romanée, or the Napa Valley. The world of wine has infinitely more to offer than the auction rooms would have you believe. Is "world-class" really what you are looking for, or is it just a very expensive form of insurance? What you really want – if you are like me – is character and value, local (indeed personal) interest and the pleasures of variety. Variety comes horizontally between grape varieties, regions, vineyards and producers, and vertically between vintages. Even in a small region there is plenty of scope for comparisons and trying something new.

It is easy to be awestruck by a bottle of something you have read about as the greatest of its kind. We'd all like to taste it, once at least. "Great" is a big word to bandy about: will I really feel the earth move? You may well not, I fear, without the (very expensive) preparation of tasting comparable prodigies.

I confess I used, in the past, to urge readers to try everything from all over the world. Why not race Chilean and South African Sauvignons, or Syrahs from Australia and California? Pitting the world's fastest and strongest in every sport is, after all, the Olympic spirit; the spirit of our time. Or is it, just possibly, the spirit of past times? Doesn't the uneasiness of a world we know we cannot control tell us to look locally for pleasures and appreciate what we can reach without squandering air miles?

Goethe was right in his time, when only the best wine was even reliable, let alone very special. His thinking, though, needs correcting for today – and certainly for me. What I want is good, authentic, refreshing and interesting wine that goes well with what I like to eat, and preferably has a story to tell. And like the poor, lots of it.

[signature]

The memory lingers on...
In this edition I have indicated within entries 200 or so of the wines I remember having specially (and in some cases regularly) enjoyed over the past 12 months (that is mid '07–'08). It can be no guide to the future, but with so many alternatives on offer one has to start somewhere, and fragrant memories seem the best place. Lest anyone mistake these for "The World's 200 Best Wines" let me restate my fixed position: taste is personal. I like what I like – and so should you. The wines are indicated within entries in this way: ***Châteaux Aiguilloux***.

Agenda 2009

What's the rarest thing in wine today? A case of Le Pin? A case of magnums of Le Pin? Two cases of magnums of Le Pin? No, though few of us would turn these down if they were offered. The rarest thing in wine is something simple: it is authenticity.

But surely authenticity is easy to find, you say? Can't wine labels be trusted? If a wine says it comes from Sicily or Maipo, can't we rely on that? Yes, but that's not the authenticity I mean. What I am referring to is the picture of a place that a wine contains: a snapshot of sun, rain, and wind; of minerals and earth; of roots pushing deep down into layer after layer of soil. It's a sense of place; it's terroir.

Terroir is a well-trodden subject. We're all familiar with the definition: the combination of soil, exposure, and climate that makes one vineyard or region different to another. We're all used to adding the hand of man to the equation – without man's intervention there would be no vinyard. Too much intervention, though, and the terroir will not be heard above the noise of wine-making techniques, alcohol and strident varietal character. Too little intervention and the wine may not be good. Cabernet, say, planted in a site where Merlot would ripen better may express the terroir in its greeness and awkwardness, but it certainly wouldn't express the terroir to its best advantage. Authenticity can mean awkwardness, clumsiness, unripeness, and even faults in wine. But we are, as in all things, allowed to exercise discrimination. This book is all about sorting sheep from goats in all sorts of ways.

What makes a wine authentic? How wines reflect their terroir is something we don't yet understand. Wines grown on gravel don't taste of gravel. Wines grown on clay don't taste of clay. Yet if one compares Pinot Noirs from adjacent vineyards in Burgundy, made in the same way by the same people, there are still differences on the palate. The same goes for Rieslings from the Mosel. This is terroir at its truest: where it makes a difference in the glass. It may be scientifically unprovable as yet, and it's right to be sceptical; but if you can taste the difference in the glass, then there is a difference.

How to find it as a consumer is another matter. You don't necessarily find authenticity in wine by throwing money at your wine merchant; nor do you find it by reading the press releases of large wine companies. Sometimes you'll hit on it unexpectedly: in a glass, for example, of Grüner Veltliner from Schloss Gobelsburg in Austria. You don't have to have been to the vineyard to recognize that what you're tasting is something not just exceptional, but something utterly specific. Specificity is key. Wines that have the ring of authenticity call forth recognition in the taster, even if you've never tasted a wine before. A minerally note to the fruit is part of it; a range of aromatics that goes beyond simple fruit flavours is also part of it. Mostly it is that sense of specificity. You know the wine could only have come from a particular vineyard.

So yes, it is rare. Perhaps we shouldn't expect it in the wine we drink every day; most wines we drink will be well-made, enjoyable, and suited to the food we eat, but they won't have that arresting specificity. Maybe it's just as well: too much rarity cloys in the end. That shock of recognition is one of wine's most subtle pleasures.

How to use this book

The top line of most entries consists of the following information:

Aglianico del Vulture Bas | r dr (s/sw sp) | ★★★ | 96' 97 98 99' 00 01' 02 (03)

❶ ❷ ❸ ❹

❶ Wine name and the region the wine comes from.

❷ Whether it is red, rosé or white (or brown/amber), dry, sweet or
sparkling, or several of these (and which is most important):

r	red
p	rosé
w	white
br	brown
dr	dry*
sw	sweet
s/sw	semi-sweet
sp	sparkling

() brackets here denote a less important wine

* assume wine is dry when **dr** or **sw** are not indicated

❸ Its general standing as to quality: a necessarily rough-and-ready
guide based on its current reputation as reflected in its prices:

★	plain, everyday quality
★★	above average
★★★	well known, highly reputed
★★★★	grand, prestigious, expensive

So much is more or less objective. Additionally there is a subjective rating:

★ etc Stars are coloured for any wine which in my experience is usually
especially good within its price range. There are good everyday wines
as well as good luxury wines. This system helps you find them.

❹ Vintage information: which of the recent vintages can be recommended; of
these, which are ready to drink this year, and which will probably improve
with keeping. Your choice for current drinking should be one of the vintage
years printed in bold type. Buy light-type years for further maturing.

oo etc recommended years that may be currently available

96' etc vintage regarded as particularly successful for the property
in question

97 etc years in bold should be ready for drinking (those not in bold
will benefit from keeping)

98 etc vintages in colour are those recommended as first choice for
drinking in 2009. (See also Bordeaux introduction, p.72.)

(02) etc provisional rating

The German vintages work on a different principle again: see p.130.

Other abbreviations

DYA drink the youngest available

NV vintage not normally shown on label; in Champagne,
means a blend of several vintages for continuity

CHABLIS properties, areas or terms cross-referred within the section

Châteaux Aiguilloux type so styled within entries indicates wine
(mid '07–'08) especially enjoyed by Hugh Johnson.

Vintage Report 2007

"Saved from drowning." That was the verdict of Mumm Champagne on the 2007 vintage, and it sums up the experience of much of northern Europe. Spring was glorious, summer was filthy – cold, wet and horrible. Rot invaded the vineyards in region after region: it wasn't just growers who couldn't remember a year with more mildew; their fathers couldn't either. It was a year when some growers practising biodynamism but not certified as biodynamic felt obliged to reach for the chemical sprays – it was that or lose the whole crop. But if that warm April had raised false hopes it had also pushed the vines ahead, so that even with a cold, backward summer the vines had some time in hand. And at the end of August, hoorah! The rain stopped, the sun appeared and the grapes ripened in the nick of time. Will it be a great vintage? No, probably not. But providing growers kept the mildew at bay, and providing they selected very carefully in vineyard and winery, the wines should be pretty good.

In Bordeaux the Merlot is round and fruity, the Cabernet weightier. In the Médoc they're talking of finesse rather than power. Graves, too, seems to have made quite soft wines, though with more weight. The whites are well balanced. Pomerol and St-Emilion have made soft, forward wines. In Sauternes they're talking about purity – not much botrytis, in other words, although those who picked latest seem to have more power.

In Germany the talk is of aroma and tremendous fruit across the country, with the reds looking good as well as the whites – the run of good vintages continues unbroken. Somewhere between the raciness of 2004 and the ripeness of 2005 seems to be a fair assessment. At Dr Loosen in the Mosel they broke most records for "hang time": as a rule of thumb it's 105 days between flowering and picking in their part of the world. This year it was 130 days, and the wines have huge intensity. At Dr Loosen they measure the summer by barbecue days, and in 2007 they only managed two or three: not impressive. Later in the year they managed to make an Eiswein, but since the pickers had left by then the entire office and warehouse staff had to get up at 3 in the morning to get the job done.

In southern Europe the weather was the opposite: hot, with roasting sunshine all summer. Which climate worked better, that of the north or that of the south, is hard to say. Quantities were well down, and prices are on the up. (Well, where are they not?) Tuscany was lucky, as was Piedmont, albeit with relatively low acidity; in the Marche wines have more acidity than those of 2003, which the year it's being compared with, heatwise. In Spain it depends who you talk to. There was a small but decent crop in Catalonia but an officially 'excellent' vintage in Rioja; it should be noted that the Riojans never rate any vintage as lower than average.

It was a problem year in Australia, because of severe drought: many growers reported hardly any rain throughout the year, and water allocations for irrigation were cut right back. Some growers in the regions most heavily dependent on irrigation were having to abandon some of the vineyards and leave them to live or die. So quantities here, too, are low, and prices will have to rise.

A closer look at 2006

Oh, the cold, cold spring of 2006. In Bordeaux they were still waiting for a little warmth as late as May – but when it came, it really came. June and July were roasting, and very dry; and then, in some parts of France, it all ended with downpours in August and September. It was nobody's idea of an ideal growing season. And yet, somehow or other, some rather decent wines seem to have emerged from it. Cue a round of applause for the vignerons whose careful work in vineyard and cellar managed to balance the ups and downs of nature. In Bordeaux, to pick just one region, the same conditions 20 or 30 years ago would have produced wines of much less appeal.

The 2006 Bordeaux seem to be improving all the time. Tasted en primeur, in March 2007, they were a little unfriendly, a little mean and hard, but in the ensuing months they seem to have put on some flesh and started smiling. Whether you think them less good than the 2004s, or slightly better, is a matter of personal taste; and whether you can afford them is a matter of personal finance.

Some people are beginning to mutter that Burgundy begins to look better value than Bordeaux. If this proves so, the 2006 reds should be bought with an eye to drinking relatively soon: they're appealing, juicy, forward wines to be drunk young. The whites are delicious: ripe and full-bodied, the best of them combine the freshness of the 2004s with the concentration of the 2005s. It's definitely a white year.

It's definitely a Rhône year, too, with reds of richness and balance in both north and south. The wines have a lovely brightness of flavour and the whites are good, too: fresh, with some power. Champagne, too, seems to be looking better than it did initially, and no doubt the demand for vintage Champagne will mean that some houses will declare a vintage, even if it's generally a year for non-vintage.

Over in Germany it was a year for sweet wines – "even the Kabinetts were Auslese", as one wag put it. Some growers had a bit of a problem finding sufficient quantities of light dry wines, but for those who like botrytis richness and lushness, with excellent acidity, it's a wonderful year. It was good in Austria, too, where a hot summer produced tremendously exciting whites of great complexity, and ripe reds.

Italy was another of Europe's stars in 2006, especially in Tuscany, where the year enjoyed the sort of rational, balanced weather that much of France longed for. Piedmont was hot, and the Veneto suffered from August hail, but made very good wines nonetheless. And the south? Hot, hot, hot. But good.

In Australia it was a story of the wrong weather at the wrong times, at least in some places. The Adelaide Hills had spring frosts followed by rot later in the year; Western Australia had a cool summer followed by tropical cyclones in April. Not ideal. But Australia being what it is, plenty of good wines were made in spite of all this. And they're happy in New Zealand, too: even better than 2005, in some cases.

A safe pair of brands...

In an ideal world, all restaurants would have wine lists that make you rub your hands in glee. For a variety of reasons, however, they don't. Yet those who regularly eat in establishments that the Michelin inspectors prefer to bypass come to realise that even on a dismal wine list there are often wines that are reliable and affordable. Here are havens of drinkability in various countries around the world from contributors to this Guide (space precludes the inclusion of more countries, but the French, Italian, Spanish and Australian selections are available in many markets).

France
George Duboeuf Beaujolais-Villages Several different bottlings, at worst drinkable and at best a gloriously gluggable, raspberry-scented delight.
Guigal Côtes du Rhône Plump, plummy red with an enticing spicy finish.
Alsace Pinot Blanc Examples in humble restaurants will usually come from a cooperative, but since Alsace has some of the best co-ops in France, there are few duds. Creamy, textured, food-friendly white with an appley bite.

Italy
Santa Margherita Pinot Grigio, Valdadige Arguably the wine that began the Pinot Grigio phenomenon, a clean, nutty, white with its gentle apple flavours.
Frescobaldi Remole, IGT Toscana Soft, juicy blackcurrant and cherry are the hallmarks of this tangy Sangiovese/Cabernet blend.
Antinori Santa Cristina, IGT Toscana Like its big brother Villa Antinori, no longer a Chianti Classico, but still resembling one. Spicy, cherry fruit with a floral finish.

Germany
Robert Weil Riesling Trocken Pure, tangy Riesling with refreshing mineral character, from one of the Rheingau's best addresses.
Bernhard Huber Malterdinger Spätburgunder Baden Pinot of some class with a cool earthy side to its raspberry and cherry flavours.

Spain
Torres Sangre de Toro Fresh and herby with spicy, structured berry flavours. Other Torres reds are similarly reliable.
Tio Pepe Fino Still remarkably consistent and classic sherry brand, with that wonderful pungent nutty freshness.
Marques de Riscal Rioja Reserva Back on form, this lithe, fragrant red with its gentle wild-strawberry character and earthy finish is classic Rioja.

Portugal
Sogrape Gazela Vinho Verde Light, crisp, fresh and bracing, not hugely complex, but a refreshing citrussy drink.
José Maria da Fonseca Periquita, Terras do Sado More modern in style than in the past but still a plummy red with hints of fresh tobacco and orange peel.

Austria
Freie Weingärtner Wachau Grüner Veltliner Steinfeder Terrassen Crisp young wine, with the peppery, grapefruit flavours cut through with notes of minerals.
Lenz Moser Prestige Blauer Zweigelt Refreshing cherry and damson, well structured with earthy tannins.

Switzerland

Aigle les Murailles Chasselas Nicknamed "Eidächsliwy" after the lizard on the label, a light, crisp white wine, with aromatic fruit and minerally on the finish.

Greece

Strofilia white Light citrus wine; crisp, simple, seafood-friendly white.
Boutari Grand Reserve Hearty rustic red - wild herb and olive overtones on top of gamey berry and plum flavours, with a warm, nutty finish.

USA

Hogue Cellars Syrah, Washington State A reasonably new wine to the Hogue range, fruit-forward, with soft tannins, medium weight and finish.
Kenwood Sauvignon Blanc, California Typical California style, soft and easy drinking, with bright fruit and a lean, pithy finish.

Chile

Casillero del Diablo Casablanca Sauvignon Blanc The Casillero range from Concha y Toro is consistently good. This is supple, balanced Sauvignon with a zesty citrus and herb tang.
Santa Rita 120 Cabernet Sauvignon Santa Rita's excellent Cabernet range shows easy blackcurrant, black cherry and spice, with hints of mint and cloves.

Argentina

Trapiche Fond de Cave Chardonnay Gentle, juicy Chardonnay, apple and citrus to the fore, lightly spicy, honeyed characters behind.
Norton Malbec Soft, meaty wine that puts the accent on warm, spicy, berry fruit, but has a some of the Malbec violet edge, too.

Australia

Jacob's Creek Riesling Arguably the pick of a solid range of whites; lively, limey wine with a zesty, floral edge to the finish.
Penfolds Koonunga Hill Shiraz/Cabernet Notes of mocha, tobacco and spices add further interest to this plump, raspberry- and blackberry-rich red.

New Zealand

Church Road Hawke's Bay Chardonnay Ripe Chardonnay, with citrus and stone-fruit flavours, creamy notes, just a hint of oak and vibrant acidity on the finish.
Villa Maria Private Bin Marlborough Pinot Noir Juicy young Pinot, with rich plum/spice flavours, some savoury complexity and a rounded finish.

South Africa

Boschendal 1685 Shiraz Bumptious wine, with peppery blackcurrant and orange peel fruit propped up by soft tannins, with vanilla and liquorice finish.
Ken Forrester Petit Chenin Blanc Pure, clean unwooded Chenin with a musky bite and refreshing apple and lemon flavours.

India

Sula Chenin Blanc Off-dry luscious tropical fruit flavours and a musky finish.
Grover Cabernet Sauvignon/Shiraz Soft, Friendly red, with plum and berry fruit.

China

Wines from **Dynasty, Great Wall** and **Changyu** - are acceptable. With the rise of imports from Europe and Australia, many of the names above are safer bets.

Grape varieties

In the past two decades a radical change has come about in all except the most long-established wine countries: the names of a handful of grape varieties have become the ready reference to wine. In senior wine countries, above all France and Italy, more complex traditions prevail. All wine of old prestige is known by its origin, more or less narrowly defined, not just the particular fruit-juice that fermented.

For the present the two notions are in rivalry. Eventually the primacy of place over fruit will become obvious, at least for wines of quality. But for now, for most people, grape tastes are the easy reference-point – despite the fact that they are often confused by the added taste of oak. If grape flavours were really all that mattered this would be a very short book.

But of course they do matter, and a knowledge of them both guides you to flavours you enjoy and helps comparisons between regions. Hence the originally Californian term "varietal wine" – meaning, in principle, from one grape variety.

At least seven varieties – Cabernet Sauvignon, Pinot Noir, Riesling, Sauvignon Blanc, Chardonnay, Gewurztraminer and Muscat – taste and smell distinct and memorable enough to form international categories of wine. To these you can add Merlot, Malbec, Syrah, Sémillon, Chenin Blanc, Pinots Blanc and Gris, Sylvaner, Viognier, Nebbiolo, Sangiovese, Tempranillo. The following are the best and/or most popular wine grapes.

Grapes for red wine

Agiorgitiko (St George) Versatile Greek (Nemea) variety with juicy damson fruit and velvety tannins. Sufficient structure for serious ageing.

Baga Bairrada grape. Dark and tannic. Great potential but hard to grow.

Barbera Widely grown in Italy, at its best in Piedmont, giving dark, fruity, often sharp wine. Fashionable in California and Australia; promising in Argentina.

Blaufränkisch Mostly Austrian; can be light and juicy but at best (in Burgenland) a considerable red. LEMBERGER in Germany, KEKFRANKOS in Hungary.

Brunello Alias for SANGIOVESE, splendid at Montalcino.

Cabernet Franc, alias Bouchet (Cab Fr) The lesser of two sorts of Cabernet grown in Bordeaux but dominant (as "Bouchet") in St-Emilion. The Cabernet of the Loire, making Chinon, Saumur-Champigny, and rosé. Used for blending with CABERNET SAUVIGNON, etc., or alone, in California, Australia and South Africa.

Cabernet Sauvignon (Cab Sauv) Grape of great character: spicy, herby, tannic, with characteristic blackcurrant aroma. The first grape of the Médoc; also makes most of the best California, South American, East European reds. Vies with Shiraz in Australia. Its wine almost always needs ageing; usually benefits from blending with e.g. MERLOT, CABERNET FRANC, SYRAH, TEMPRANILLO, SANGIOVESE etc. Makes aromatic rosé.

Cannonau GRENACHE in its Sardinian manifestation: can be very fine, potent.

Carignan In decline in France. Needs low yields, old vines; best in Corbières. Otherwise dull but harmless. Common in North Africa, Spain, and California.

Carmènere An old Bordeaux variety now extremely rare in France. Widely used in Chile where until recently it was often mistaken for MERLOT.

Cinsault/Cinsaut Usually bulk-producing grape of S France; in S Africa crossed with PINOT NOIR to make PINOTAGE. Pale wine, but quality potential.

Dolcetto Source of soft seductive dry red in Piedmont. Now high fashion.

Gamay The Beaujolais grape: light, very fragrant wines, at their best young. Makes even lighter wine in the Loire Valley, in central France, and in

Switzerland and Savoie. Known as "Napa Gamay" in California.

Grenache, alias Garnacha, Cannonau Useful grape for strong and fruity but pale wine: good rosé and *vin doux naturel* – especially in the South of France, Spain, and California – but also the mainstay of beefy Priorato. Old-vine versions are prized in South Australia. Usually blended with other varieties.

Grignolino Makes one of the good everyday table wines of Piedmont.

Kadarka, alias Gamza Makes healthy, sound, agreeable reds in East Europe.

Kékfrankos Hungarian BLAUFRÄNKISCH; similar lightish reds.

Lambrusco Productive grape of the lower Po valley, giving quintessentially Italian, cheerful, sweet and fizzy red.

Lemberger See BLAUFRÄNKISCH. Württemberg's red.

Malbec, alias Côt Minor in Bordeaux, major in Cahors (alias Auxerrois) and the star in Argentina. Dark, dense, tannic wine capable of real quality.

Merlot Adaptable grape making the great fragrant and plummy wines of Pomerol and (with CABERNET FRANC) St-Emilion, an important element in Médoc reds, soft and strong (and à la mode) in California, Washington, Chile, Australia. Lighter but often good in North Italy, Italian Switzerland, Slovenia, Argentina, South Africa, New Zealand etc.. Grassy when not fully ripe.

Montepulciano A good central-eastern Italian grape, and a Tuscan town.

Morellino Alias for SANGIOVESE in Scansano, southern Tuscany.

Mourvèdre, alias Mataro Excellent dark aromatic tannic grape used mainly for blending in Provence (but solo in Bandol) and the Midi. Enjoying new interest in, for example, South Australia and California.

Nebbiolo, alias Spanna and Chiavennasca One of Italy's best red grapes; makes Barolo, Barbaresco, Gattinara, and Valtellina. Intense, nobly fruity, perfumed wine but very tannic: improves for years.

Periquita Ubiquitous in Portugal for firm-flavoured reds. Often blended with CABERNET SAUVIGNON and also known as Castelão.

Petit Verdot Excellent but awkward Médoc grape, now increasingly planted in Cabernet areas worldwide for extra fragrance.

Pinot Noir (Pinot N) The glory of Burgundy's Côte d'Or, with scent, flavour, and texture that are unmatched anywhere. Makes light wines rarely of much distinction in Switzerland and Hungary. Improving in Germany and Austria. But now also splendid results in California's Sonoma, Carneros, and Central Coast, as well as Oregon, Ontario, Yarra Valley, Adelaide Hills, Tasmania, New Zealand's South Island and South Africa's Walker Bay.

Pinotage Singular South African grape (PINOT NOIR X CINSAUT). Can be very fruity and can age interestingly, but often jammy. Good rosé.

Primitivo Southern Italian grape making big, rustic wines, now fashionable because genetically identical to ZINFANDEL.

Refosco In northeast Italy possibly a synonym for Mondeuse of Savoie. Deep, flavoursome and age-worthy wines, especially in warmer climates.

Sagrantino Italian grape found in Umbria for powerful cherry-flavoured wines.

Sangiovese (or Sangioveto) Main red grape of Chianti and much of central Italy. Aliases include BRUNELLO and MORELLINO. Interesting in Australia.

Saperavi Makes good, sharp, very long-lived wine in Georgia, Ukraine etc. Blends very well with CAB SAUV (e.g. in Moldova).

Spätburgunder German for PINOT N. Quality is variable, seldom wildly exciting.

St-Laurent Dark, smooth and full-flavoured Austrian speciality. Also in the Pfalz.

Syrah, alias Shiraz The great Rhône red grape: tannic, purple, peppery wine which matures superbly. Important as Shiraz in Australia, and under either name in California, Washington State, South Africa, Chile, and elsewhere.

Tannat Raspberry-perfumed, highly tannic force behind Madiran, Tursan, and other firm reds from Southwest France. Also rosé. Now the star of Uruguay.

Tempranillo Aromatic fine Rioja grape, called Ull de Llebre in Catalonia, Cencibel in La Mancha, Tinto Fino in Ribera del Duero, Tinta Roriz in Douro, Aragonez in southern Portugal. Now Australia, too. Very fashionable; elegant in cool climates, beefy in warm. Early ripening.

Touriga Nacional Top port grape grown in the Douro Valley. Also makes full-bodied reds in south Portugal.

Zinfandel (Zin) Fruity adaptable grape of California (though identical to PRIMITIVO) with blackberry-like, and sometimes metallic, flavour. Can be structured and gloriously lush, but also makes "blush" white wine.

Grapes for white wine

Albariño The Spanish name for North Portugal's Alvarinho, making excellent fresh and fragrant wine in Galicia. Both fashionable and expensive in Spain.

Aligoté Burgundy's second-rank white grape. Crisp (often sharp) wine needs drinking in 1–3 years. Perfect for mixing with cassis (blackcurrant liqueur) to make "Kir". Widely planted in East Europe, especially Russia.

Arinto White central Portuguese grape for crisp, fragrant dry whites.

Arneis Aromatic, high-priced grape, DOC in Roero, Piedmont.

Blanc Fumé Occasional (New World) alias of SAUVIGNON BLANC, referring to its smoky smell, particularly from the Loire (Sancerre, Pouilly). In California used for oak-aged Sauvignon and reversed to "Fumé Blanc". (The smoke is oak.)

Bourboulenc This and the rare Rolle make some of the Midi's best wines.

Bual Makes top-quality sweet madeira wines, not quite so rich as malmsey.

Chardonnay (Chard) The white grape of Burgundy, Champagne, and the New World, partly because it is one of the easiest to grow and vinify. All regions are trying it, mostly aged (or, better, fermented) in oak to reproduce the flavours of burgundy. Australia and California make classics (but also much dross). Italy, Spain, New Zealand, South Africa, New York State, Argentina, Chile, Hungary and the Midi are all coming on strong. Morillon in Austria.

Chasselas Prolific early-ripening grape with little aroma, mainly grown for eating. AKA Fendant in Switzerland (where it is supreme), Gutedel in Germany.

Chenin Blanc (Chenin Bl) Great white grape of the middle Loire (Vouvray, Layon, etc). Wine can be dry or sweet (or very sweet), but with plenty of acidity. Bulk wine in California, but increasingly serious in S Africa. See also STEEN.

Clairette A low-acid grape, part of many southern French blends.

Colombard Slightly fruity, nicely sharp grape, makes everyday wine in South Africa, California, and Southwest France. Often blended.

Falanghina Ancient grape of Campanian hills revived to make excellent dense aromatic dry whites.

Fiano High quality grape giving peachy, spicy wine in Campania, S. Italy.

Folle Blanche High acid/little flavour make this ideal for brandy. Called Gros Plant in Brittany, Picpoul in Armagnac. Also respectable in California.

Furmint A grape of great character: the trademark of Hungary both as the principal grape in Tokáj and as vivid, vigorous table wine with an appley flavour. Called Sipon in Slovenia. Some grown in Austria.

Garganega Best grape in the Soave blend. Top wines, esp sweet ones, age well.

Gewurztraminer, alias Traminer (Gewurz) One of the most pungent grapes, spicy with aromas like rose petals and grapefruit. Wines are often rich and soft, even when fully dry. Best in Alsace; also good in Germany (Gewürztraminer), East Europe, Australia, California, Pacific Northwest and New Zealand.

Grauburgunder See PINOT GRIS.

Grechetto or Greco Ancient grape of central and south Italy noted for the vitality and stylishness of its wine.

Grüner Veltliner Austria's favourite. Around Vienna and in the Wachau and

Weinviertel (also in Moravia) it can be delicious: structured, dry, peppery and lively. Excellent young, but the best age five years or so.

Hárslevelü Other main grape of Tokáj (with FURMINT). Adds softness and body.

Kéknyelü Low-yielding, flavourful grape giving one of Hungary's best whites. Has the potential for fieriness and spice. To be watched.

Kerner Most successful of recent German varieties, mostly RIESLING X SILVANER, but in this case Riesling x (red) Trollinger. Early-ripening, flowery (but often too blatant) wine with good acidity. Popular in Pfalz, Rheinhessen, etc.

Laski Rizling Grown in northern Italy and Eastern Europe. Much inferior to Rhine RIESLING, with lower acidity, best in sweet wines. Alias Welschriesling, Riesling Italico, Olaszrizling (no longer legally labelled simply "Riesling").

Loureiro The best and most fragrant Vinho Verde variety in Portugal.

Macabeo The workhorse white grape of north Spain, widespread in Rioja (alias Viura) and in Catalan cava country. Good quality potential.

Malvasia A family of grapes rather than a single variety, found all over Italy and Iberia. May be red, white, or pink. Usually plump, soft wine. Malvoisie in France is unrelated.

Marsanne Principal white grape (with ROUSSANNE) of the northern Rhône (e.g. in Hermitage, St-Joseph, St-Péray). Also good in Australia, California, and (as Ermitage Blanc) the Valais. Soft full wines that age very well.

Moschofilero Good, aromatic pink Greek grape. Makes white or rosé wine.

Müller-Thurgau (Müller-T) Dominant in Germany's Rheinhessen and Pfalz and too common on the Mosel. It was thought to be a cross between RIESLING and Chasselas de Courtellier, but recent studies suggests otherwise. Soft aromatic wines for drinking young. Makes good sweet wines but usually dull, often coarse, dry ones. Should have no place in top vineyards.

Muscadelle Adds aroma to white Bordeaux, esp Sauternes. In Victoria as 'Tokay' it is used (with MUSCAT, to which it is unrelated) for Rutherglen Muscat.

Muscadet, alias Melon de Bourgogne Makes light, refreshing, very dry wines with a seaside tang round Nantes in Brittany.

Muscat (Many varieties; the best is Muscat Blanc à Petits Grains.) Widely grown, easily recognized, pungent grapes, mostly made into perfumed sweet wines, often fortified (as in France's *vins doux naturels*). Superb in Australia. The third element in Tokáj Aszú. Rarely (e.g. Alsace) made dry.

Palomino, alias Listán Makes all the best sherry but poor table wine.

Pedro Ximénez, alias PX Makes very strong wine in Montilla and Málaga. Used in blending sweet sherries. Also grown in Argentina, the Canaries, Australia, California and South Africa.

Petit (and Gros) Manseng The secret weapon of the French Basque country: vital for Jurançon; increasingly blended elsewhere in the Southwest.

Pinot Blanc (Pinot Bl) A cousin of PINOT NOIR, similar to but milder than CHARDONNAY: light, fresh, fruity, not aromatic, to drink young. Good for Italian spumante. Grown in Alsace, northern Italy, south Germany, and East Europe. Weissburgunder in Germany.

Pinot Gris (Pinot Gr) Best in Alsace for full-bodied whites with a certain spicy style. In Germany can be alias Ruländer (sweet) or GRAUBURGUNDER (dry); the work horse Pinot Grigio Italy, where it is newly popular for rosé. Also found in Hungary, Slovenia, Canada, Oregon, New Zealand...

Pinot Noir (Pinot N) Superlative black grape used in Champagne and elsewhere (e.g. California, Australia) for white, sparkling, or very pale pink "vin gris".

Riesling (Ries) Making its re-entrance on the world-stage . Riesling stands level with Chardonnay as the world's best white wine grape, though diametrically opposite in style. Chardonnay gives full-bodied but aromatically discreet wines; Riesling offers a range from steely to voluptuous, always positively perfumed, and with more ageing potential than Chardonnay. Germany makes the greatest Riesling in all styles. Its popularity is being revived in S Australia, where this cool-climate grape does its best to ape Chardonnay. Holding the middle ground, with forceful but still steely wines, is Austria, while lovers of light and fragrant, often piercingly refreshing Rieslings have the Mosel as their exclusive playground. Also grown in Alsace (nowhere else in France), Pacific Northwest, Ontario, California, New Zealand and S Africa.

Roussanne Rhône grape of finesse, now popping up in California and Australia. Can age well.

Sauvignon Blanc (Sauv Bl) Makes distinctive aromatic grassy wines, pungent in New Zealand, often mineral in Sancerre, riper in Australia; good in Rueda, Austria, north Italy, Chile's Casablanca Valley, and South Africa. Blended with Semillon in Bordeaux. Can be austere or buxom (or indeed nauseating).

Savagnin The grape of *vin jaune* of Savoie: related to TRAMINER?

Scheurebe Spicy-flavoured German RIES X SILVANER (possibly), very successful in Pfalz, especially for Auslese. Can be weedy: must be very ripe to be good.

Semillon (Sem) Contributes the lusciousness to Sauternes and increasingly important for Graves and other dry white Bordeaux. Grassy if not fully ripe, but can make soft dry wine of great ageing potential. Superb in Australia; New Zealand and S Africa promising.

Sercial Makes the driest madeira (where myth used to identify it with RIESLING).

Seyval Blanc (Seyval Bl) French-made hybrid of French and American vines. Very hardy and attractively fruity. Popular and reasonably successful in eastern States and England but dogmatically banned by EU from "quality" wines.

Steen South African alias for CHENIN BLANC, not used for better examples.

Silvaner, alias Sylvaner Germany's former workhorse grape. Rarely fine except in Franken – where it is savoury and ages admirably – and in Rheinhessen and Pfalz, where it is enjoying a renaissance. Good in the Italian Tyrol; sadly declining in popularity in Alsace. Very good (and powerful) as Johannisberg in the Valais, Switzerland.

Tocai Friulano North Italian grape with a flavour best described as "subtle". Now to be called plain Friulano.

Tokay Supposedly Hungarian grape in Australia and a table grape in California. The wine Tokay (Tokáj) is FURMINT, HARSLEVELU and MUSCAT.

Torrontes Strongly aromatic, MUSCAT-like Argentine speciality, usually dry.

Trebbiano Important but mediocre grape of central Italy (Orvieto, Soave etc.). Also grown in southern France as Ugni Blanc, and Cognac as St-Emilion. Mostly thin bland wine; needs blending (and more careful growing).

Ugni Blanc (Ugni Bl) See TREBBIANO.

Verdejo The grape of Rueda in Castile, potentially fine and long-lived.

Verdelho Madeira grape making excellent medium-sweet wine; in Australia, fresh soft dry wine of great character. Worth trying elsewhere.

Verdicchio Potentially good dry wine in central-eastern Italy.

Vermentino Italian, sprightly with satisfying texture and ageing capacity.

Vernaccia Name given to many unrelated grapes in Italy. Vernaccia di San Gimignano is crisp, lively; Vernaccia di Oristano is sherry-like.

Viognier Ultra-fashionable Rhône grape, finest in Condrieu, less fine but still aromatic in the Midi. Good examples from California and Australia.

Viura See MACABEO.

Welschriesling See LASKI RIZLING.

France

**More heavily shaded areas are the
wine-growing regions**

The following abbreviations
are used in the text:

Al	Alsace
Beauj	Beaujolais
Burg	Burgundy
B'x	Bordeaux
Champ	Champagne
Lo	Loire
Prov	Provence
Pyr	Pyrenees
N/S Rh	North/South Rhône
SW	Southwest
AC	*appellation contrôlée*

France has become curiously divisive among wine-lovers: it's grown into a touchstone of where you stand on wine style. Are you for France? Then you're probably traditional, and favour tannin, fresh acidity, elegance; the attributes that make wines go so temptingly and digestibly with food. Are you against France? Then you must be for the New World and its fruit-forward, modern wines.

Black-and-white divisions like this are generally nonsense when it comes to wine, and it's a bit hard on France that it finds itself in this position. But it has been the touchstone of quality for so long that it's probably inevitable.

The truth is that France can produce wines as modern and fruit-driven as anywhere, and wines as tannic and traditional as anywhere. It's also

still intensely regional – a fact for which all wine-lovers should give thanks. Those different regions have inspired innumerable wine styles around the world – and curiously, if you ask a lover of, say, Cabernet, about their preferences they're far less likely to take a simple for-or-against-France position. Instead they'll pick out regions, or individual producers, around the world. And that's a much more logical way of thinking. It's not a question of France versus the rest of the world; instead we should see each French region in a global context.

Do the French see it like that? Well...

France entries also cross-refer to Châteaux of Bordeaux section.

Recent vintages of the French classics

Red Bordeaux

Médoc/red Graves For some wines bottle age is optional: for these it is indispensable. Minor châteaux from light vintages need only two or three years, but even modest wines of great years can improve for 15 or so, and the great châteaux of these years can profit from double that time.

2007 A miserable summer with a huge attack of mildew spelt a difficult year. Late-season sunshine offered some hope. Variable from one estate to the next. Be selective.

2006 A cool Aug with rain and rot during harvest meant Cabernet Sauvignon had difficulty ripening. Good colour and alcohol. Be selective.

2005 Perfect weather conditions throughout the year. Dry season and harvest. Rich, balanced, long-ageing wines from an outstanding vintage.

2004 Dry, sunny Sept and early Oct but rain during the Cabernet harvest. Mixed bag, but top wines good in a classic mould.

2003 Hottest summer on record. Cabernet Sauvignon can be tremendous (St-Estèphe, Pauillac). Atypical but rich, powerful wines at best (so keep), unbalanced at worst (already drinking). Yields right down.

2002 Saved by a dry, sunny Sept. Later-ripening Cabernet Sauvignon benefited most. Yields down. Some good wines if selective. Drink now–2018.

2001 A cool Sept and rain at vintage meant Cabernet Sauvignon had difficulty in ripening fully. Some fine fresh wines to drink now–2015.

2000 Late flowering and a somewhat damp start to the summer looked worrying, but the final product is outstanding – superb wines throughout. Start tentatively on all but the top wines.

1999 Vintage rain again diluted ripe juice, so-so wines to drink now–2010.

1998 Rain at vintage again. But Aug heat ripened (even roasted) grapes. Good (especially Pessac-Léognan), but the Right Bank is clearly the winner this year. Drink now–2015.

1997 Uneven flowering and summer rain were a double challenge. Top wines still of interest, but the rest have faded.

1996 Cool summer, fine harvest. Good to excellent. Drink now–2020.

1995 Heatwave and drought; saved by rain. Good to excellent. Now–2015.

1994 Hopes of a supreme year; then heavy vintage rain. The best good, but be careful. Drink now.

1993 Ripe grapes but a wet vintage. Most for drinking up.

1992 Rain at flowering, in Aug, and at vintage. A huge crop; light wines. Avoid.

1991 Frost in Apr halved crop and rain interrupted vintage. The northern Médoc did best. Drink up.

1990 A paradox: a drought year with a threat of over-production. Self-discipline was essential. Its results are magnificent. To 2015.

1989 Early spring, splendid summer. Top wines classics of the ripe, dark kind: elegance, length. Some better than 1990. Small chx uneven. To 2020.

Older fine vintages: 86 85 82 75 70 66 62 61 59 55 53 49 48 47 45 29 28.

St-Emilion/Pomerol

2007 Same pattern as the Médoc. Huge disparity in picking dates (up to five weeks). Extremely variable.

2006 Rain and rot at harvest. Earlier-ripening Pomerol a success but St-Emilion and satellites variable.

2005 Same conditions as the Médoc. An overall success.

2004 Merlot often better than 2003 (Pomerol). Good Cabernet Franc. Variable.

2003 Merlot suffered in the heat, but exceptional Cabernet Franc. Very mixed.

Some over-extraction again. Top St-Emilion on the plateau good.

2002 Problems with rot and ripeness; some over-extraction. Modest to good.

2001 Less rain than Médoc during vintage. Some powerful Merlot, sometimes better than 2000. Drinking now–2015.

2000 Similar conditions to Médoc. Less kind to Merlot, but a v.gd vintage.

1999 Careful, lucky growers made good wines, but rain was again a problem.

1998 Earlier-ripening Merlot largely escaped the rain. Some excellent wines.

1997 Merlot suffered in the rain. Only a handful of wines still of interest.

1996 Cool, fine summer. Vintage rain. Less consistent than Médoc. Now–2015.

1995 Perhaps even better than Médoc/Graves. Now–2015.

1994 Good, esp Pomerol. Drink now.

1993 Pomerol better than Médoc; good despite terrible vintage weather.

1992 Very dilute. Avoid.

1991 A sad story. Many wines not released.

1990 Another chance to make great wine or a lot of wine. Now–2015.

1989 Large, ripe, early harvest; an overall triumph. To 2020.

Older fine vintages: 85 82 71 70 67 66 64 61 59 53 52 49 47 45.

Red Burgundy

Côte d'Or Côte de Beaune reds generally mature sooner than bigger wines of Côte de Nuits. Earliest drinking dates are for lighter commune wines – *eg* Volnay, Beaune; latest for biggest wines of, *eg*, Chambertin, Romanée. Even the best Burgundies are more attractive young than equivalent red Bordeaux.

2007 Small crop of attractive, perfumed wines for the medium term.

2006 An attractive year, better in Côte de Nuits (less rain); some rot problems in Côte de Beaune but there are some gems.

2005 The best for a generation, potentially outstanding wines everywhere. Must be kept.

2004 Good, except where hail has caused significant damage. Can be herbaceous.

2003 Reds coped with the heat better than the whites. Muscular, rich wines. Best wines outstanding, others short and hot.

2002 Middleweight wines of great class with an attractive point of freshness. Best still to keep.

2001 Just needed a touch more sun for excellence. Starting to mature.

2000 Best Côte de Nuits wines still a pleasure. Drink up the rest.

1999 Big, ripe vintage; good colour, bags of fruit, silky tannins. Wines to keep.

1998 Ripe fruit but dry tannins. Those in balance starting to come round.

1997 Time to finish up these attractive wines from a sunny year.

1996 Fine summer and vintage. Top wines must be kept. 2008–2020.

1995 Small crop, potentially fine but not yet showing its expected class.

1994 Compromised by vintage rain. Drink up.

1993 Impressive fruit to balance the tannins in Côte de Nuits; mostly drying out in Côte de Beaune.

1992 Ripe, plump, pleasing. No great concentration. Drink up.

1991 V. small harvest; some wines v. tannic. Côte de Nuits best. Drink soon.

Older fine vintages: 90 88 85 78 71 69 66 64 62 61 59 (all mature).

White Burgundy

Côte de Beaune Well-made wines of good vintages with plenty of acidity as well as fruit. Will improve and gain depth and richness for some years – up to 10. Lesser wines from lighter vintages are ready for drinking after two or three.

2007 Big crop – those who picked late did very well.

2006 Plentiful crop of charming, aromatic wines – 1992-plus.

2005 Small but outstanding crop of dense, concentrated wines.

2004 Promising for aromatic, balanced wines. Beginning to show their paces.

2003 Hot vintage; all but the best are falling over fast.

2002 Stylish wines, starting to show very well.

2001 Sound but anonymous. Drink soon.

2000 A big crop of ripe, healthy grapes. Exciting wines.

1999 Generous vintage of good, well-balanced wines now hitting their stride.

1998 Difficult year for white. Chassagne was successful. Drink up rapidly.

1997 Attractive plump wines now passing their best.

1996 Not developing as well as hoped. Over-acidic.

1995 A potentially great vintage, diluted in places. Now–2010.

The white wines of the Mâconnais (Pouilly-Fuissé, St-Véran, Mâcon-Villages) follow a similar pattern, but do not last as long. They are appreciated more for their freshness than their richness.

Chablis *Grand cru* Chablis of vintages with both strength and acidity can age superbly for up to ten years; *premiers crus* proportionately less.

2007 Hail damage wiped out much of the crop. To monitor.

2006 An early harvest of attractive, aromatically pleasing wines.

2005 Small but outstanding crop of dense, concentrated wines.

2004 Difficult vintage, with mildew a problem. Not for keeping.

2003 Small crop of ripe wines, but acidity is low and balance in question.

2002 Delicious wines developing well.

2001 Too much rain. Relatively weak. Drink up.

2000 A great vintage for Chablis. Keep the *grands crus*, drink the rest.

1999 Attractive but now want drinking up.

1998 Cool weather and some hail. Wines fair to good: not for long keeping.

1997 Another fine vintage; *grands crus* excellent now.

Beaujolais 07: attractive but without the heart of a really great year. **06**: tricky vintage with some rot compromising the fruit. **05**: concentrated wines. **04**: light, some weak, some pretty. **03**: too much heat on the grapes, some excellent. **02**: drink up fast. **01**: very good if picked before rain. **00**: excellent, but drink up. **99**: splendid, rich, and deep. Older wines should be finished.

Southwest France

2007 Uniformly disastrous, though some growers claim that the late autumn sunshine partially saved their crop, esp in Jurançon and Monbazillac.

2006 A capricious and variable summer. Some wines may be better than expected. Tip: taste before you buy.

2005 Best year of the decade so far.

2004 Spoiled for many by bad Aug. Better than usual acidity suggests keeping potential. Excellent in Jurançon.

2003 The Ribena year. Small quantities of unbalanced wines, heavy in sweet fruit and alcohol, but often with stalky tannins. Drink up.

2002 For those who prefer elegance and finesse to brute force. Good Cahors, Madiran, and Jurançon (late pickers).

2001 Generally v. successful. Reds now at their best, and top *cuvées* will keep.

The Midi

2007 A damp spring and a cooler than average summer, with a fine Sept producing some beautifully balanced wines, with some ageing potential.

2006 Scorching Jun and Jul, followed by cooler Aug and some rain around harvest, but the best winemakers had fine results.

2005 A beautifully balanced year, with sunshine and rain at the right times throughout the region.

2004 Marked by Aug storms and a fine Sept. Wines are elegantly balanced, with lower alcohol than 03 or 01.

2003 The year of the heat-wave, in sharp contrast to 02, often resulting in a greatly reduced crop, but also many fine wines from skilled winemakers.

2002 Heavy rain in early Sept causing problems. Varies widely from AC to AC, and grower to grower. Good in the Minervois; diluted in Pic St-Loup.

2001 Quantity lower than average. Quality generally very good with a hot summer making for ripe, concentrated wines, drinking well now.

Northern Rhône

2007 Agreeable but not very profound reds. They will drink well quite young, and a 15–20-year horizon beckons for the best. The whites are good +.

2006 Big, healthy crop with wines showing plenty of clear fruit and sound stuffing. Can evolve consistently. Good acidity in quite robust whites.

2005 A great vintage, with wonderful Syrah. Keep the Hermitage, Côte-Rôtie and Cornas for 5+ years. St-Joseph reds have very bright fruit. Whites are full – good for mid-term drinking.

2004 Mid-weight, mid-term year, with Côte-Rôtie showing well over time; best reds are from top v'yds. Superb whites.

2003 A half-sized crop. Intense sun gave cooked "southern" flavours. Best reds show genuine richness, and are coming together.

2002 If you must, try before you buy. Best growers abandoned half their crop. Decent red St-Josephs, Cornas, light Hermitage, Côte-Rôtie. Good whites, especially Condrieu.

2001 Very good, lively year if picked before Sept rain. Fresh fruit, good acidity, ageing well. Top year at Côte-Rôtie. Often very good whites.

2000 Decent density, quite warm and rich. Some stewed flavours. Hermitage good in parts, Cornas did well, Côte-Rôtie variable. Good Condrieu, sumptuous. Reds simpler than 99/01.

1999 Very successful. Delicious, likely to live long. More balance than the 98s. Harmony a key word. Ace Côte-Rôties. Sound whites.

1998 Big, robust vintage. More overt tannins than 99, but have fused well, with rich, oily textures, now starting a second, gamey phase of life. Good Marsanne-based whites.

Southern Rhône

2007 Remarkably similar in its youth to 06: ripe, overtly fruited wines at Châteauneuf-du-Pape, adequate depth at Gigondas and Vacqueyras. Drink younger than the staying classics like 05 and 01. Côtes du Rhônes – choose best names. Openly fruited, aromatic whites.

2006 Rich, ripely fruited wines at Châteauneuf-du-Pape. More open than the 05s, the rounded fruit style shows up across the southern Rhône. Tannins are ripe and well fused. Good for the simple wines – Côtes du Rhône, Ventoux. Good, well-balanced whites.

2005 V. good from top sites and old vines. Intense wines with greater balance than the 03s, tannins need leaving until 2010, eg Gigondas. Whites best drunk young.

2004 Uneven ripening until a stable Sept. Some Côtes du Rhônes are sharp, drink them up. Good sinew and freshness in Châteauneufs will suit European palates. Gigondas not always rounded. Be patient. Good fresh whites.

2003 A chunky, potent, and warm year from the best, eg, Châteauneuf – better than Gigondas, Vacqueyras. Two-speed ripening, so not all balanced. Tannins starting to fuse, a relief. Go for the best names, best areas.

2002 Nature's payback: 66 cm of rain in a day. Floods around Châteauneuf. Simply fruited, early reds, acceptable whites. Gigondas did best.

2001 Excellent classic vintage, where grape, not oak, tannins prevail. Complex reds, lots of life ahead, be patient for top areas. Cracking Châteauneufs.

2000 Tasty wines, led by fruit. Not a long-lived year. Go for leading names. Gigondas may edge Châteauneuf in quality. Best reds are singing now.

1999 Very good overall. Ripe, open fruit with correct structure in the best wines. Châteauneuf reds have moved up a gear with age, very fine fruit.

1998 Very good. Big, warm wines, starting to emerge into a more integrated middle age after a mineral, funky stage.

Champagne

2007 Bizarre. Hottest Apr on record but miserable wet July and Aug. Harvest began too early before full benefit of Sept sun. Average.

2006 Topsy-turvy growing season but fine Sept: made for ripe, expressive wines, esp Pinot Noir. Could be underrated by some houses.

2005 Unlike Bordeaux and (red) Burgundy, not a great year in Champagne: a bit hot for real class, wines lacking dash and verve.

2004 Exactly what was needed. Record bumper crop giving Champagnes of classic finesse and "tension". Vintage year.

2003 Torrid, difficult year. Tiny harvest, esp from hail-struck Chardonnay. Wines lack acidity – most will be for NV blends.

2002 Undoubtedly a great, graceful year for Pinot Noir: selectively good Chardonnay. Best vintage of early 21st century.

2000 Harvest sun produced decent wines, ageing well. The best have zip and grip; others can be short on palate. Not a great vintage year.

1999 Warm summer with breaks of refreshing rain. Ripe, showy wines, ready soon. Grandstanding Dom Pérignon.

1998 Best are classic wines, some superior to 96, especially Chardonnay *cuvées* of Pol Roger and Billecart-Salmon. Great Clicquot Grande Dame.

Older fine vintages: 96 95 90 89 88 85 82

The Loire

2007 Very difficult summer – mildew rife. Vintage saved by fine Sept and Oct. Producer's name crucial. Fine dry whites and good Anjou sweets. Reds for early drinking.

2006 Challenging vintage in which only the conscientious succeeded. Dry whites fared well, reds nearly as attractive. Not great for sweet whites.

2005 Excellent across the board. Buy without fear. The sweet wines are more likely to be the product of shrivelled grapes than noble rot.

2004 Huge crop. In general better for reds than whites. Few or no sweet wines in Vouvray/Montlouis. Anjou's whites fewer and less sweet than usual.

2003 Heatwave vintage. Some areas hit by spring frost. Wines are big and supple, though not flaccid. Will they last? Excellent year for sweet wines.

2002 Best since 97 – wonderful balance. Vivid fruit and vibrant acidity in the dry whites. Some fine sweet Chenins. Where yields were kept low, the reds are juicy with good colour.

2001 Warm, wet winter left soils gorged with water. Best wines are from those who harvested late. But Muscadet perfect. Taste before buying.

Alsace

2007 As throughout France, hot spring, cold, wet summer but sunny autumn weather allowed picking of healthy, ripe grapes. Promising.

2006 Hottest recorded July followed by coolest Aug. Top producers like Faller and Koehly made subtle, fine Riesling.

2005 A large crop of healthy grapes harvested after an Indian summer. Ripe and well-balanced wines of character, minerality and strength.

2004 Despite it being a difficult year, growers who picked early and kept yields low produced classic wines. Subtle year, esp for Riesling.

2003 Earliest harvest since 1893. Small crop of variable wines. Best are ripe, but with low acidity (hence acidification allowed for the first time ever).

2002 Better than most of France. In *grand cru* sites, some beautiful wines – lots of personality, class, complete.

2001 Unsettled weather in Sept. Well-balanced wines, good but not great.

2000 Superb – probably best since 90. Very good for Vendanges Tardives and Sélections des Grains Nobles.

Abel-Lepitre Middle-rank CHAMPAGNE house. v.gd BRUT Millésimé **96'** 98 **00** 02. Excellent BLANC DE BLANCS Cuvée 134 (blend of two gd yrs).

Abymes Savoie w ★ DYA Hilly area nr Chambéry; light, mild Vin de Savoie AC from Jacquère grape has alpine charm. SAVOIE has many such *crus*.

Agenais SW France r p w ★ DYA VDP of Lot-et-Garonne, rapid burst of gd independents alongside co-ops, esp DOMS Lou Gaillot and Campet.

Aligoté DYA Fresh, thirst-quenching secondary grape from Burgundy with own appellation at BOUZERON. Base wine for apéritif *crème blanc* CASSIS (Kir).

Alliet, Philippe Lo r w ★★→★★★ Top-quality Chinon and one of the Loire's leading producers. Best CUVÉES include barrel-aged Coteau du Noire and VIEILLES VIGNES and a new hill v'yd L'Huisserie. Also a small amount of white.

Aloxe-Corton Burg r w ★★→★★★ **96'** 97 98 **99' 02' 03** 05' 06 Village at north end of CÔTE DE BEAUNE famous for 2 *grands crus*: CORTON (red), CORTON-CHARLEMAGNE (white). Village wines are lighter but to try.

Alquier, Jean-Michel Midir w Leading FAUGÈRES producer. White Roussanne/ Marsanne blend; red CUVÉES Maison Jaune and Les Bastides.

Alsace Al w (r sp sw) ★★→★★★★ 00 01 02 04 05' The sheltered east slope of the Vosges Mts makes France's Rhine wines: aromatic, fruity, full-strength, mostly dry and expressive of variety. Sugar levels vary widely: dry wines now easier to find. Much sold by variety (Pinot Bl, Ries, Gewurz). Matures well (except Pinot Bl, MUSCAT) 5–10 yrs; GRAND CRU even longer. Gd quality and value CRÉMANT. Formerly feeble Pinot N improving fast. See VENDANGES TARDIVE, SELECTION DES GRAINS NOBLES.

Alsace Grand Cru W ★★★ ·★★★★ 90 95 96 97 98 99 00 01 02 04 05' AC restricted to 51 (KAEFFERKOPF added in 2006) of the best-named v'yds (approx 1,600 ha, 800 in production) and 4 noble grapes (Ries, PINOT GR, Gewurz, MUSCAT) mainly dry, some sweet. Controversial classification now widely respected.

Why do Alsace wines vary so much?
Partly because of the convoluted geology of the region, most wine villages have at least 5 different types of soil. You'll find chalk and limestone, sandstone and schist, clay, loess, even volcanic sediment – each fabulous terroir tailor-made for finest Riesling, MUSCAT, PINOT GRIS, and Gewurz. Five soils or more, plus 4 grape varieties, plus umpteen different altitudes and exposures, equals enormous variety. Sweetness is another variable.

Amiel, Mas Midi r w sw The key DOMAINE MAURY. Warming CÔTES DU ROUSSILLON Carerades red, white Altaïr, VIN DE LIQUEUR Plénitude from Maccabeu. Vintage and cask-aged VDNs. Prestige 15 yrs a star.

Amirault, Yannick Lo r ★★→★★★ Meticulous, first-rate producer of both BOURGUEIL and ST-NICOLAS DE BOURGUEIL. Top CUVÉES incl La Petite Cave and Les Quartiers in BOURGUEIL, and Malagnes and Graviers in ST-NICOLAS.

Ampeau, Robert Burg ★★★ Exceptional grower and specialist in MEURSAULT and VOLNAY; also POMMARD. Unique in releasing only long-matured bottles.

André, Pierre Burg ★ NÉGOCIANT at Ch Corton-André, ALOXE-CORTON; 38 ha of v'yds in CORTON (gd Corton-Charlemagne, Corton Blanc), SAVIGNY, GEVREY-CHAMBERTIN, etc. Definite signs of improvement. Also owns REINE PÉDAUQUE.

d'Angerville, Marquis Burg ★★★★ One of Volnay's superstar DOMS with brilliant premier crus Clos des Ducs (monopole), Champans, and Taillepieds.

Anjou Lo p r w (sw dr sp) ★→★★★★ Both region and umbrella Loire AC covering Anjou and SAUMUR. Many styles: Chenin Bl-based dry whites range from light quaffers to potent agers; juicy reds incl rich Gamay; juicy Cab Fr-based Anjou rouge; and structured ANJOU-VILLAGES; also strong, dry SAVENNIÈRES; luscious COTEAUX DU LAYON Chenin Bl; dry sweet rosé, and sparkling.

Anjou-Coteaux de la Loire Lo w s/sw SW ★★→★★★ 02 03 04 05 Tiny westernmost Anjou AC for sweet whites made from Chenin Bl that tend to be less rich but nervier than COTEAUX DU LAYON. Esp Doms du Fresche, de Putille, Musset-Roullier, Ch de Putille.

Anjou-Villages Lo r ★→★★★ 02 03 04 05 06 Superior central ANJOU AC for reds (Cab Fr, but a few pure Cab Sauv). Usually ambitious, quality tends to be high and prices reasonable, esp Dom de Brize, Dom Philippe CADY, Ch de Coulaine, Philippe Delesvaux, Dom les Grandes Vignes, Ogereau, Ch PIERRE-BISE. Sub-ac Anjou-Villages-Brissac covers the same zone as Coteaux de l'Aubance; look for Bablut, Dom de Haute Perche, Montigilet, Richou, Rochelles, Ch de Varière.

Appellation Contrôlée (AC or AOC) Government control of origin and production (not quality) of all the best French wines.

Apremont Savoie w ★★ DYA One of the best villages of SAVOIE for pale, delicate whites, mainly from Jacquère grapes, but recently inc CHARD.

Arbin Savoie r ★★ Deep-coloured lively red from MONDEUSE grapes, rather like a gd Loire Cab Sauv. Ideal après-ski. Drink at 1–2 yrs.

Arbois Jura r p w (sp) ★★→★★★ Various gd and original light but tasty wines; speciality is VIN JAUNE. On the whole, DYA except excellent VIN JAUNE.

l'Ardèche, Coteaux de r p (w) ★→★★ Hilly area west of Rhône, buzzing along. New DOMS; fresh reds, some oaked; Viognier (eg Mas de Libian) and Marsanne. Best from pure Syrah, Gamay, Cab Sauv (Serret). Powerful, nr Burgundian CHARD *Ardèche by Latour;* Grand Ardèche mature vines but oaked. Also Doms du Colombier, Durand, Favette, Flacher, Mazel, Vigier.

Ariège SW r ★ 04 05' 06 Growing VDP from nr the Pyrenees. Note esp Dom des Coteaux d'Engravies. Production still not enough to quench the thirst of the Toulousains. Will keep.

l'Arlot, Domaine de Burg ★★★ Leading exponent in CÔTE DE NUITS of whole-bunch fermentation. Wines pale but aromatic and full of fruit. Best v'yds ROMANÉE-ST-VIVANT and NUITS-ST-GEORGES, esp Clos de l'Arlot.

Armagnac SW The alternative to COGNAC, and increasingly popular – *certainly chez moi*; tasty, rustic, and peppery. New AC for young white (colourless) Armagnac. Table wines: CÔTES DE GASCOGNE, GERS, TERROIRS LANDAIS.

Armand, Comte Burg ★★★ Excellent POMMARD wines, esp Clos des Epéneaux. Esp brilliant since 1999.

Aube Southern extension of CHAMPAGNE. Now known as Côte des Bar.

Aujoux, J-M Beauj Substantial grower/merchant of BEAUJOLAIS. Swiss-owned.

Auxey-Duresses Burg r w ★★→★★★ 99' 02' **03** 05' 06 07 Second-rank (but v. pretty) côte de beaune village: affinities with volnay, meursault. Best examples (red) comte armand, hospices de beaune (cuvée boillot), leroy, Prunier; (white) comte armand, Fichet, leroy (Les Boutonniers).

Avize Champ One of the top Côte des Blancs villages. All chard.

Aÿ Champ One of the best Pinot N-growing villages of champagne.

Ayala Revitalized aÿ-based champagne house, owned by bollinger. First-rate brut Majeur Zéro Dosage and racy Rosé. Prestige Perle d'Ayala (**99**).

Bandol Prov r p (w) ★★★ 95 96 97 **98** 99 **00** 01 02 03 04 05 06 Small coastal ac; provence's best. *Long-lasting reds* mainly from Mourvèdre; elegant rosé from young vines, and a splash of white. Stars include Doms Lafran Veyrolles, La Suffrène, tempier, Chx Pibarnon, Pradeaux, Mas de la Rouvière.

Banyuls Pyr br sw ★★→★★★ One of the most original vdns, mainly Grenache (Banyuls grand cru: over 75% Grenache, aged for 2 yrs+). Vintage style resembles ruby port but far better are rancios, aged for yrs in large casks. Think fine old tawny port. Best: Doms du Mas Blanc (★★★), la Rectorie, Vial Magnères, at 10–15 yrs old.

Barrique The bordeaux (and cognac) term for an oak barrel holding 225 litres. Barrique-ageing to flavour almost any wine with oak was craze in late 1980s, with some sad results. Current oak prices should urge discretion.

Barsac B'x w sw ★★→★★★★ 83' 86' 88' 89' 90' 95 96 97' 98 99' 01' **02** 03' 05' Neighbour of sauternes with similar superb golden wines from lower-lying limestone soil; generally less powerful with more finesse. Repays long ageing. Top: climens, coutet, doisy-daëne, doisy-védrines.

Barthod, Ghislaine Burg ★★★→★★★★ Impressive range of *archetypal Chambolle-Musigny*. Marvellous poise and delicacy yet with depth and concentration. Les Cras, Fuées, and Beauxbruns best.

Barton & Guestier bordeaux négociant now part of massive Diageo group.

Bâtard-Montrachet Burg w ★★★★ 89' 90' 92 93 95 96 97' 99' 00 02' **03** 04' 05' 06' 07 12-ha grand cru downslope from Le montrachet itself. Rich, fat wines, sometimes four-square. Also worthy siblings Bienvenues-B-M and Criots B-M. Seek out: bouchard père & fils, boillot, carillon, drouhin, gagnard, latour, dom leflaive, morey, Pernot, Ramonet, sauzet.

Baudry, Domaine Bernard Lo r p w ★★→★★★ Superb chinon in every style, from Chenin Bl-based whites to Cab Fr-based rosés and excellent chinon cuvées of red, from juicy Les Granges to structured Clos Guillot and Croix Boissées.

Baumard, Domaine des Lo ★★→★★★★★ Important family producer of anjou wine, esp Chenin Bl-based whites, inc savennières (Clos St Yves, Clos du Papillon) and quarts de chaume. Baumard makes crémant de loire and a tangy vin de table from Verdelho. The Loire's brave screwcap pioneer.

Béarn SW r p w ★→★★ w p DYA r **03** 04 05' 06 Pyrenean wine from madiran and jurançon producers. Also from Dom Lapeyre/Guilhémas and Béarn Co-op.

Beaujolais r (p w) ★ DYA The most basic appellation of the huge Beaujolais region, producing 5million cases a yr. Some from the hills can be excellent.

Beaujolais Primeur (or Nouveau) The Beaujolais of the new vintage, made in a hurry (often only 4–5 days' fermenting) for release at midnight on the third Wednesday in Nov. Ideally soft, pungent, fruity, and tempting; too often crude, sharp, too alcoholic. More of an event than a drink.

Beaujolais-Villages r ★★ 05' **06** 07 Wines from better (northern) half of beaujolais; should be much tastier than plain beaujolais. The 10 (easily) best villages are the *crus*: fleurie, st-amour, juliénas, chénas, moulin-à-vent, chiroubles, morgon, regnié, côte de brouilly, brouilly. Of the 30 others the best lie around Beaujeu. *Crus* cannot be released en primeur before 15 Dec. Best kept until spring (or considerably longer).

Beaumes-de-Venise S Rh br r (p w) ★★ →★★★ 01' 03 **04** 05' **06 07** for reds. DYA for MUSCAT. Long regarded as France's best dessert MUSCAT, from south CÔTES DU RHÔNE; can be honeyed or muskily scented, overtly flavoured, subtle, lingering (*eg* Doms Beaumaric, Bernardins, Durban, JABOULET, Pigeade, VIDAL-FLEURY, co-op). Midweight, slightly austere reds (Ch Redortier, Dom Cassan, du Fenouillet, Durban, Les Goubert, co-op) leave for 2–3 yrs. Own AC since 04 vintage. White and rosé are CÔTES DU RHÔNE.

Beaumont des Crayères Champ Bijou Côte d'Epernay co-op making excellent Pinot Meunier-based Grande Réserve NV and v. fine Fleur de Prestige **99** 00 02. Exceptional CHARD-led Cuvée Nostalgie 98'. Fleur de Rosé 02' **03** 04.

Beaune Burg r (w) ★★★ **90' 95 96** 99' 02' 03 05' 06 07 Historic wine capital of Burgundy and home to many merchants: BOUCHARD, CHAMPY, DROUHIN, JADOT, LATOUR as well as HOSPICES DE BEAUNE. No GRAND CRU v'yds but sound PREMIERS CRUS: *eg*, Cras, Grèves, Teurons, Cent Vignes, Clos du Roi, Bressandes for red and an increasing amount of white, of which Drouhin's CLOS DES MOUCHES stands out.

Becker, Caves J Al ★→★★ An organic estate. Stylish, well-balanced wines inc exceptional MUSCAT GRAND CRU Froehn.

Bellet Prov p r w ★★★ The local wine of Nice; fashionable, expensive, original and unknown in the city. White is best, with unexpected ageing potential. A few small producers, esp Ch de Bellet, Clos St Vincent, Les Coteaux de Bellet.

Bellivière, Domaine de Lo r w sw ★★→★★★ Eco-friendly grower: precise Chenin Bl in JASNIÈRES and COTEAUX DU LOIR and eye-opening PINEAU d'Aunis.

Bergerac Dordogne r w p dr sw ★→★★★ 01' 04 05' 06 Gd-value look-alike Bordeaux neighbour using B'x grape varieties. Top properties include ★★★ Dom l'Ancienne Cure, Clos des Verdots, Les Hauts de Caillevel, Ch Masburel, La Tour des Gendres. Otherwise ★★ Les Marnières, Chx Belingard-Chayne, Clos de la Colline, Les Eyssards, Les Fontenelles, Grinou, Jonc Blanc, de la Mallevieille, Les Miaudoux, le Paradis, Pion, le Raz, Thénac. See also MONBAZILLAC, ROSETTE, SAUSSIGNAC, PÉCHARMANT, MONTRAVEL.

Bertrand, Gérard Midi r p w One of biggest v'yd owners in South, with 325 ha; Villemajou in CORBIÈRES *cru* Boutenac, Laville-Bertou in MINERVOIS LA LIVINIÈRE, l'Hospitalet in LA CLAPE, l'Aigle in LIMOUX, and VDP d'Oc.

Besserat de Bellefon CHAMPAGNE house in Epernay. Lightish wines, not to keep.

Beyer, Léon ★★ →★★★ ALSACE specialist: v. fine, intense, dry wines often needing 10 yrs+ bottle age. Superb Ries. Comtes d'Eguisheim, but no mention on label of GRAND CRU PFERSIGBERG, its originating v'yd. Gd Gewurz.

Bichot, Maison Albert Burg ★★→★★★ Dynamic merchant and owner/distributor of LONG-DEPAQUIT (CHABLIS), Clos Frantin, and more. Quality on the rise.

Billecart-Salmon Exemplary family CHAMPAGNE house makes exquisite long-lived wines, vintage CUVÉES wholly fermented in wood from 2000. Superb Clos St-Hilaire BLANC DE NOIRS (96' **98**) and top BLANC DE BLANCS (98' **00**).

Bize, Simon Burg ★★★ Excellent range of SAVIGNY PREMIERS CRUS, plus LATRICIÈRES-CHAMBERTIN; ever better whites in CORTON-CHARLEMAGNE.

Blagny Burg r w ★★→★★★ (r) 99' 02' 03' 05' 06' 07 Austere reds sold as Blagny; fresh whites, mostly PREMIER CRU, borrow names of neighbouring MEURSAULT and PULIGNY. AMPEAU, LATOUR, Matrot, and Martelet-Cheresey are gd.

Blanc de Blancs Any white wine made from white grapes only, esp CHAMPAGNE. An indication of style, not of quality.

Blanck, Paul & Fils ★★→★★★ Grower at Kientzheim, ALSACE, producing huge range of wines. Finest from 6 ha GRAND CRU Furstentum (Ries, Gewurz, PINOT GR) and GRAND CRU SCHLOSSBERG (Ries). Also gd Pinot Bl.

Blanc de Noirs White (or slightly pink or "blush") wine from red grapes.

Blanquette de Limoux Midi w sp ★★ Gd-value creamy fizz from nr Carcassonne;

claims older history than CHAMPAGNE. Basic Mauzac improved by CHARD and Chenin Bl, esp in newer AC CRÉMANT DE LIMOUX. Large co-op with Sieur d'Arques label dominating AC. Also Rives-Blanques, Martinolles.

Blaye B'x r w ★→★★ **01 03 04 05'** (06) As of 2000, designation for top, concentrated reds (lower yields, longer ageing, etc) from PREMIÈRES CÔTES DE BLAYE. Also declining AC for simple dry whites. More change from 2007 vintage. See Côtes de Bordeaux box (p. 76).

Boillot Burg Interconnected Burgundy growers. Look for Jean-Marc (POMMARD) ★★★ for fine oaky reds and whites, Henri (VOLNAY) ★★★, Louis (CHAMBOLLE, married to GHISLAINE BARTHOD) ★★→★★★, and the late Pierre (MEURSAULT) ★★.

Boisset, Jean-Claude Burg The biggest Burgundy merchant, based in NUITS-ST-GEORGES. Owner of Bouchard-Aîné, Lionel Bruck, F Chauvenet, Delaunay, Jaffelin, Morin Père & Fils, de Marcilly, Pierre Ponnelle, Thomas-Bassot, Vienot, CELLIER DES SAMSONS (BEAUJOLAIS), Moreau (CHABLIS), and a share in MOMMESSIN. Involved in projects in Canada, California, Chile, Uruguay, and the Languedoc. Used to be fairly dire; Boisset label now resurrected. From 1999 own v'yds separated as DOM DE LA VOUGERAIE (★★★).

Boizel One of CHAMPAGNE's surest values: brilliant, aged BLANC DE BLANCS NV and prestige Joyau de France (95' **96 98**). Also Grand Vintage BRUT (**98 99 00** 02) and CUVÉE Sous Bois.

Bollinger Great individualistic CHAMPAGNE house, on a roll in recent vintages (viz. Grande Année 97, Grande Année Rosé 99). Luxury wines: RD (95'), VIEILLES VIGNES Françaises (96 02) from ungrafted Pinot N vines, La Côte aux Enfants, AŸ (**97 99** 02). See also LANGLOIS-CH.

Bonneau du Martray, Domaine Burg w r ★★★★ (w) ★★ (r) TWO GRANDS CRUS made to the highest standard – *exemplary, long-lived (10+ yrs) Corton-Charlemagne* and significantly improved if overpriced red CORTON.

Bonnes-Mares Burg r ★★★→★★★★ 78' **85' 88' 89** 90' 91 93 **95** 96' **97 98** 99' 00 02' 03 05' 06 GRANDS CRUS (15ha) between CHAMBOLLE-MUSIGNY and MOREY-ST-DENIS. Sturdy long-lived wines, less fragrant than MUSIGNY; to rival CHAMBERTIN. Best: DUJAC, Groffier, JADOT, ROUMIER, Dom des Varoilles, DE VOGÜÉ, VOUGERAIE.

Bonnezeaux Lo w SW ★★★→★★★★ **88 89' 90' 95' 96' 97'** 02 03' 04 05' (07) Magnificently rich, almost everlasting sweet Chenin Bl. QUARTS DE CHAUME top site in COTEAUX DU LAYON. Esp: Chx de Fesles, la Fresnaye, DOMS les Grandes Vignes, du Petit Val (Goizil), Ferme de la Sansonnière.

Bordeaux B'x r x (p) ★→★★ **01 03** 05' Catch-all AC for generic Bordeaux. Mixed quality, but can be great value when gd. Most brands are in this category.

Bordeaux Supérieur B'x r ★→★★ **00' 01 03** 04 **05'** Superior denomination to above. Higher minimum alcohol, lower yield, and longer ageing. 75% of production bottled at the property, the reverse of AC Bordeaux.

Borie-Manoux Admirable BORDEAUX shipper, ch-owner. Chx include Batailley, BEAU-SITE, Dom de L'EGLISE, HAUT-BAGES-MONPELOU, TROTTEVIEILLE.

Bouchard Père & Fils Burg Back among the top négociants since bought by HENRIOT in mid-1990s and development of new winery on edge of BEAUNE. Brilliant whites and exciting reds, esp BEAUNE, VOLNAY, POMMARD.

Bouches-du-Rhône Prov r p w ★ VDP from Marseille environs. Warming reds from southern varieties, plus Cab Sauv, Syrah, and Merlot.

Bourgeois, Henri Lo ★★→★★★★ **02 03** 04 05 06 07 Top-quality, leading SANCERRE grower/merchant in Chavignol. Also POUILLY-FUMÉ, MENETOU-SALON, QUINCY (CH), COTEAUX DU GIENNOIS (CH), and VDP. Top wines include MD de Bourgeois,

---

Words within entries marked like this *Alter Ego de Palmer* indicate wines especially enjoyed by Hugh Johnson over the past 12 months (mid '07–'08).

La Bourgeoise (r, w), Jadis, Sancerre d'Antan. See also Clos Henri (r, w) in Marlborough, New Zealand.

Bourgogne Burg r w (p) ★★ (r) 03 05 06 07 (w) 05 06 07 Catch-all AC, with higher standards than basic BORDEAUX. Light, often gd flavour, best at 2–4 yrs. Top growers make bargain beauties from fringes of CÔTE D'OR villages; do not despise. BEAUJOLAIS *crus* (except REGNIÉ) may be labelled Bourgogne.

Bourgogne Grand Ordinaire r (w) ★ DYA Ludicrous name for basic Burgundy, usually GAMAY for reds and CHARD for white.

Bourgogne Passe-Tout-Grains r (p) ★ Age 1–2 yrs, junior BURGUNDY: min 33% Pinot N, the balance Gamay, mixed in vat. Not as heady as BEAUJOLAIS.

Bourgueil Lo r (p) ★★→★★★(★) 96' 02 03 04 05' 06 07 Burly, full-flavoured TOURAINE reds and big, fragrant rosés based on Cab Fr. Best can easily age 10 yrs. Esp AMIRAULT, Audebert, Dom de la Butte, Dom de la Chevalerie, Delaunay, Druet, Dom des Ouches.See ST-NICOLAS-DE-BOURGUEIL.

Bouscassé, Domaine SW ★★★ 95' 00' 01' 04' (05') Alain Brumont's home base in MADIRAN making just as sturdy wines as his CH MONTUS.

Bouvet-Ladubay Lo ★→★★★ Major important sparkling SAUMUR house purchased by Indian beer company United Breweries in 2006. Best is the barrel-fermented Cuvée Trésor – both white and rosé. Also still wines mainly from ANJOU-SAUMUR.

Bouzereau Burg ★→★★ Family in MEURSAULT making gd whites at gd prices and reds. Jean-Baptiste, son of Michel B, and Vincent B are the 2 best producers.

Bouzeron Burg w ★ CÔTE CHALONNAISE AC specifically for ALIGOTÉ. Age 1–2 yrs. Top grower: de Villaine.

Bouzy Rouge Champ r ★★★ 90 95 96 97 99 02 Still red of famous Pinot N village. Like v. light Burgundy, but can last well in sunny vintages.

Brocard, J-M Burg ★★→★★★ One of the recent success stories of Chablis with a fine range of wines at all levels. Also on offer: a range of BOURGOGNE Blancs from different soil types (Kimmeridgian, Jurassic, Portlandian).

Brouilly Beauj r ★★ 05' 06 07 Biggest of the 10 *crus* of BEAUJOLAIS: fruity, round, refreshing wine, can age 3–4 yrs. Ch de la Chaize is largest estate. Top growers: Michaud, Dom de Combillaty, Dom des Grandes Vignes.

Brumont, Alain SW ★★★ Once, and some say still, the clear leader in MADIRAN. Specialist in highly extracted and oaked 100% Tannat wines – *eg* Le Tyre. Flagship wines: CH MONTUS, DOM BOUSCASSÉ, and gd-value Torus brand.

Brut Term for the dry classic wines of CHAMPAGNE.

Brut Ultra/Zéro Term for bone-dry wines in CHAMPAGNE.

Bugey Savoie r p w sp ★→★★ DYA VDQS for light sparkling, still, or half-sparkling wines from Roussette (or Altesse) and CHARD (gd). Best from Montagnieu; also Rosé de Cerdon, mainly Gamay.

Burguet, Alain Burg ★★→★★★ Superb GEVREY-CHAMBERTIN; esp Mes Favorites.

Buxy Burg w Village in AC MONTAGNY with gd co-op for CHARD and Pinot N.

Buzet SW r (w p) ★★ 04 05 06 New leadership at the co-op is breathing fresh life into this appellation, esp from its single properties (*eg* Chx de Gueyze, and improving, prize-winning Mazelières). Local character from (independent) ★★★ Dom du Pech, ★★ Chx du Frandat, Tournelles.

Cabardès Midi r (p w) ★→★★ 00 01 02 03 04 05 06 07 B'x Cab and Merlot meet MIDI Syrah and Grenache for original blends. Best is Dom de Cabrol; also Chx Pennautier and Ventenac.

Cabernet d'Anjou Lo p s/sw ★ Traditionally sweet but also demi-sec, often derided, rosé enjoying renaissance. Can be ageworthy. CH PIERRE-BISE; Doms de Bablut, CADY, Clau de Nell, les Grandes Vignes, Ogereau, de Sauveroy.

Cabrières Midi p (r) ★★ DYA COTEAUX DU LANGUEDOC. Traditional reputation based on rosé; also sound reds from village co-op.

Cady, Domaine Lo r p sw ★★→★★★ A reliable and excellent ANJOU grower of everything from dry whites to off-dry rosés, to lusciously sweet COTEAUX DU LAYON and CHAUME.

Cahors SW r ★→★★★ 85' 88 90' 95' 98 00 **01'** 02 04 (05') All-red AC based on Malbec (at least 70%). Nearly as many styles as growers (200); fruity, easy wines from ★★ Maison Vigoroux Pigmentum, Ch Latuc, Domaine Boliva; more traditional from ★★★ CLOS DE GAMOT (esp Cuvée Vignes Centenaires), ★★ Coutale, Chx du Cayrou, La Coustarelle, La Caminade, Gaudou, Les Ifs, Doms de la Bérengerai, de Cause, Paillas, Pineraie, Les Rigalets, Savarines (organic); more New World style from Ch Lagrézette, ★★★ Chx du Cèdre, Lamartine, Clos Triguedina, ★★ Ch Eugénie; better control of oak and gentler vinification from cult ★★★ Dom Cosse-Maisonneuve.

Cairanne S Rh r p w ★★→★★★ 98' 01' 03 04' 05' **06' 07** One of 2 best CÔTES DU RHÔNE-VILLAGES: classy fullness, prominent fruit, esp Doms D & D Alary, Ameillaud, Brusset, Escaravailles, Hautes Cances, l'Oratoire St-Martin, Présidente, Rabasse-Charavin, Richaud. Improving robust whites.

Canard-Duchêne CHAMPAGNE house. Inexpensive; improving with ALAIN THIÉNOT.

Canon-Fronsac B'x r ★★→★★★ 95 96 98 00' 01 03 05' 06 Full tannic reds of improved quality from west of POMEROL. Try Chx Barrabaque, Cassagne Haut-Canon, La Fleur Caillou, Gaby, Grand-Renouil, Haut-Mazeris, Lamarche Canon Candelaire, Pavillon, Moulin-Pey-Labrie, Vrai Canon Bouché.

Caramany Pyr r (w) ★ Theoretically superior AC for CÔTES DU ROUSSILLON-VILLAGES.

Carillon, Louis Burg ★★★ Sensibly priced and consistently fine PULIGNY producer; esp Combettes, Perrières, Referts.

Cassis Prov w (r p) ★★ DYA Fashionable sailing village east of Marseille with reputation for dry whites based on CLAIRETTE and Marsanne. Delicious with bouillabaisse (*eg* Dom de la Ferme Blanche, Clos Ste Magdeleine, Clos d'Albizzi). Growers fighting rearguard action with property developers. Do not confuse with cassis: blackcurrant liqueur from Dijon.

De Castellane BRUT NV; BLANC DE BLANCS; BRUT (**98 99 00** 02); Prestige Florens de Castellane (**98 99 02**). Traditional Epernay CHAMPAGNE house. Fair quality: better for vintage wines like cuvée Commodore Brut (98).

Cathiard Burg ★★★ Brilliant VOSNE-ROMANÉE producer on top form since late 1990s. Perfumed, sensual wines are charming young but will age.

Cave Cellar, or any wine establishment.

Cave coopérative Wine-growers' co-op winery; over half of all French production. Usually well run, well equipped, and wines gd value for money.

Cazes, Domaine Midi r p w sw Large family producer in ROUSSILLON. VDP pioneer, esp Le Credo, also CÔTES DU ROUSSILLON-VILLAGES and gd aged RIVESALTES.

Cellier des Samsons ★ BEAUJOLAIS/MÂCONNAIS co-op at Quincié which has 2,000 grower-members. Wines widely distributed; now owned by BOISSET.

Cérons B'x w dr sw ★★ 97' 98 99' 01' 02 03' **05'** Tiny neighbour of SAUTERNES with less intense wines, *eg* Chx de Cérons, Chantegrive, Grand Enclos.

Chablis Burg w ★★→★★★ 02' 05' 06' 07 At best magical mineral wine from N of Burgundy, but too much anonymous CHARD now made. Usually without oak.

Chablis Grand Cru Burg w ★★★→★★★★ 90' 95' 96' 97 98 99 00' 02' 03 06' 07 Small block of 7 v'yds on steep slope on right bank of Serein. Needs age for minerality and individual style to develop. V'yds: Blanchots, Bougros, Clos, Grenouilles, Preuses, Valmur, Vaudésir. Clos and Vaudésir best.

Chablis Premier Cru Burg w ★★★ 99 00 02 03 04 05 06 07 Technically second-rank but at best excellent; more typical of CHABLIS than its GRANDS CRUS. Can outclass more expensive MEURSAULT and other CÔTE DE BEAUNE. Best v'yds include Côte de Léchet, Fourchaume, Mont de Milieu, Montée de Tonnerre, Montmains, Vaillons.

Chambertin Burg r ★★★★ 78' **85' 88 89** 90' **91 93** 95 96' **97 98** 99' **00** 01 02' 03 05' 06 07 A 13-ha GRAND CRU; some of the meatiest, most enduring, best red burgundy. 20 growers inc BOUCHARD PÈRE & FILS, CHARLOPIN, Damoy, DROUHIN, LEROY, MORTET, PONSOT, Rossignol-Trapet, ROUSSEAU, TRAPET.

Chambertin-Clos de Bèze Burg r ★★★★ 78' **85' 88 89** 90' **91 93** 95 96' **97 98** 99' **00** 01 02' 03 05' 06 07 Neighbour of CHAMBERTIN (15 ha). Similarly splendid wines. May legally be sold as CHAMBERTIN. 15 growers, inc CLAIR, Damoy, DROUHIN, Drouhin-Laroze, FAIVELEY, Groffier, JADOT, ROUSSEAU.

Chambolle-Musigny Burg r ★★★ →★★★★ 90' **91 93** 95' **96' 97 98** 99' **00 01 02' 03** 04 05' 06 07 CÔTE DE NUITS village (170 ha): fragrant, complex, but never heavy wine. Best v'yds: Les Amoureuses, (BONNES-MARES), Les Charmes, MUSIGNY. Growers to note: Amiot-Servelle, BARTHOD, Digoia-Royer, DROUHIN, Groffier, HUDELOT-NOËLLAT, JADOT, MUGNIER, RION, ROUMIER, DE VOGÜÉ.

Champagne Sparkling wines of Pinots N and Meunier and/or CHARD, and its region (34,000 ha, 145 km/90 miles east of Paris); made by *méthode traditionnelle*. Bubbles from elsewhere, however gd, cannot be Champagne.

Champs-Fleuris, Domaine des Lo r w p sw ★★→★★★ Exciting 34-ha DOM. Top-notch SAUMUR Blanc; SAUMUR-CHAMPIGNY; fine CRÉMANT; pretty rosé; and, when vintage warrants, succulent COTEAUX DU SAUMUR called CUVÉE SARAH.

Champy Père & Cie Burg ★★→★★★ Oldest négociant in BEAUNE, rejuvenated by Meurgey family (also brokers DIVA). Range of v. well-chosen wines.

Chandon de Briailles, Domaine Burg ★★★ Small estate at SAVIGNY making light, fragrant PERNAND-VERGELESSES, Ile de Vergelesses, gd CORTON red and white.

Chanson Père & Fils Burg ★→★★★ Old grower-négociant at BEAUNE (45 ha). Esp BEAUNE Clos des Fèves, PERNAND-VERGELESSES Les Caradeux, SAVIGNY, CORTON. Fine quality now.

Chapelle-Chambertin Burg r ★★★ 90' **91 93** 95 **96' 97 98** 99' **00** 01 02' 03 04 05' 06 A 5.2-ha neighbour of CHAMBERTIN. Wine more "nervous", less meaty. V.gd in cooler yrs. Top producers: Damoy, JADOT, Rossignol-Trapet, Trapet.

Chapoutier N Rh ★★→★★★★ Old family grower, also merchant of big-bodied r and white Rhônes; biodynamic. Note special CUVÉES CHÂTEAUNEUF Barbe Rac, Croix de Bois (r), HERMITAGE: L'Ermite, Le Pavillon (r), L'Ermite, CUVÉE de l'Orée, Le Méal (w). Also CROZES red Les Varonniers, ST-JOSEPH, white Les Granits. Excellent Marsanne N Rhône whites, some reds extracted. Reliable, gd-value Meysonniers Crozes. New holdings in BANYULS, COLLIOURE, COTEAUX DU TRICASTIN, COTEAUX D'AIX-EN-PROVENCE, RIVESALTES promising. Also Australian joint ventures, esp Doms Tournon and Terlato & Chapoutier.

Chardonnay As well as a white wine grape, also the name of a MÂCON-VILLAGES commune. Hence Mâcon-Chardonnay.

Charlopin, Philippe Burg ★★★ Energetic GEVREY-CHAMBERTIN producer whose deep-coloured wines have been much imitated of late.

Charmes-Chambertin Burg r ★★★ 90'**93 95 96' 97 98** 99' **00 01 02'** 03 04 05' 06 07 30 ha inc neighbour MAZOYÈRES-CHAMBERTIN of mixed quality. Best has ntense, ripe, dark-cherry fruit and fragrant finish. Try Bachelet, DROUHIN, DUGAT, DUJAC, LEROY, Perrot-Minot, ROTY, ROUMIER, ROUSSEAU, VOUGERAIE.

Chassagne-Montrachet Burg w r ★★→★★★★ **99 00** 02' 04 05' 06' 07 Large village at south end of CÔTE DE BEAUNE. Soil more suited to reds but too often over-tough. Clos St Jean best red. More planted to white now, which can be brilliant in best spots: Caillerets, La Romanée, etc. Shares GRANDS CRUS MONTRACHET and BÂTARD-M with PULIGNY, plus all of CRIOTS-B-M. Best growers: COLIN, GAGNARD, MOREY families, Chx de la Maltroye, Pillot, Niellon, Ramonet.

Château Means an estate, big or small, gd or indifferent, particularly in Bordeaux (see Chx of Bordeaux). In France, château tends to mean, literally, castle or great house. In Burgundy, "DOMAINE" is the usual term.

FRANCE

Champagne growers to watch in 2009

Edmond Barnaut Bouzy. Complex, fine CHAMPAGNES mainly from Pinot N culminate in first-rate Sélection Ultra BRUT and delicious COTEAUX CHAMPENOIS Rosé.

Louise Brisson Ace Côte des Bar (Aube) DOM. Top CUVÉE Fût de Chêne (**99 00 02**).

Claude Cazals Exciting extra-BRUT BLANC DE BLANCS (**99**) and exceptional Clos Cazals (**96 ★★★★ 98**).

Richard Cheurlin One of best grower-winemakers of the Aube. Rich but balanced Carte d'Or and vintage-dated CUVÉE Jeanne (**96 98 00**).

Pierre Cheval-Gatinois Aÿ. Impeccable producer of mono-CRU CHAMPAGNES and excellent still Aÿ COTEAUX CHAMPENOIS (**99 02**).

Collard-Picard Rising Marne Valley and Côte des Blancs DOM. Impressive CUVÉE Prestige from all 3 CHAMPAGNE grapes, two gd vintages and part oak-fermented.

Pierre Gimonnet Leading Côte des Blancs grower at Cuis. V. dry CUVÉE Gastronome ideal with oysters, and complex Le Fleuron from old vines.

Henri Giraud Thoughtful grower-merchant making exceptional Pinot-led CHAMPAGNE. Excellent Prestige CUVÉE (**95 96 98**). Getting expensive.

Larmandier-Bernier Vertus; top BLANC DE BLANCS grower-maker, esp Terre de Vertus Non Dosé (03 04) and Cramant VIEILLES VIGNES (02).

David Léclapart Talented biodynamic grower in Trépail, known for feisty all-CHARDONNAY CHAMPAGNES (excellent CUVÉE Apôtre) and respectable COTEAUX CHAMPENOIS rouge.

Henri Mandois Classy Pinot Meunier/CHARDONNAY wines from 30-ha estate at Pierry. Cracking BLANC DE BLANCS 02.

José Michel Fresh yet mature Carte Blanche NV. Also excellent BLANC DE BLANCS (**98 99**) and vintage (**98 99**).

Château d'Arlay ★→★★ Major Jura estate; 65 ha in skilful hands. Wines include v.gd VIN JAUNE, VIN DE PAILLE, Pinot N, and MACVIN.

Château de Beaucastel S Rh r w ★★★★ 78' 79 81' 83 85 86' 88 89' 90' 94' **95'** 96' 97 98' 99' 00' 01' 03' 04 05' 06 Leading, high-profile CHÂTEAUNEUF estate. Deep, complex wines, drink first 2 yrs or from 7–8 yrs; unusual grape mix includes one-third Mourvèdre. Have softened in recent yrs. Small amount of wonderful old-vine Roussanne: keep 5–14 yrs. Top-grade CÔTES DU RHÔNE Coudoulet de Beaucastel red (lives 8+ yrs) and white Coudoulet de Beaucastel. Perrin RASTEAU, VINSOBRES v. solid quality. V.gd organic Perrin Nature CÔTES DU RHÔNE, GIGONDAS. (See also Tablas Creek, California.)

Château du Cèdre SW r ★★★ 01' 02 04 (**05'**) (06) Leading exponent of modern CAHORS. Also delicious white VDP from Viognier.

Château de la Chaize Beauj r ★★★ Best-known BROUILLY estate.

Château-Chalon Jura w ★★★ Not a CH but AC and village. Unique dry, yellow, sherry-like wine (Savagnin grape). Develops *flor* (see Port, Sherry & Madeira) while ageing in barrels for minimum 6 yrs. Ready to drink when bottled (62-cl clavelin bottle), but ages almost forever. A curiosity.

Château Fortia S Rh r (w) ★★ 78' 81' 88 90 95' 96' 97 98' 99 **00'** 01 03' 04' 05' 06' Traditional 30-ha CHÂTEAUNEUF property. Owner's father, Baron Le Roy, launched France's AC system in 1920s. Better form, better clarity recently, inc special, well-fruited Le Baron (lots of Syrah) and whites.

Château Fuissé Burg w ★★→★★★ Substantial producer with some of the best terroirs of POUILLY-FUISSÉ. Esp Les Clos, Combettes. Also négociant lines.

Châteaumeillant Lo r p ★→★★ DYA A small VDQ area (91 ha) S of Bourges in

Georges Sand country. Gamay and Pinot N for light reds, gris and rosés.

Château de Meursault Burg r w ★★ 61-ha estate owned by PATRIARCHE; gd v'yds and wines in BEAUNE, MEURSAULT, POMMARD, VOLNAY. Cellars open to public.

Château Mont-Redon S Rh r w ★★→★★★ 78' 85 88 89 90' 94' 95' 97' **98' 99' 00 01' 03'** 04' 05' 06' Gd 100-ha CHÂTEAUNEUF estate. Fine red, always best 6+ yrs, gains complexity; aromatic, early-drinking white. Also high-grade red LIRAC (mainly Grenache).

Château Montus SW r ★★★ 90' 95' 98' 01' 05' ALAIN BRUMONT's flagship MADIRAN property produces some of top wines in SW. Needs long ageing.

Château La Nerthe S Rh r w ★★★ 78' 81' 88 89' 90' 94 95' 96' 97 **98'** 99' 00 01 03' 04' 05' 06' Top-level 90-ha CHÂTEAUNEUF estate. Complete, smoothly composed modern-style wines, esp special CUVÉES Cadettes (red) and oaked Beauvenir (white). Takes 5 yrs to show. Also run v.gd Prieuré Montézargues Tavel, gd Dom de la Renjarde CÔTES DU RHÔNE, Ch Signac CHUSCLAN.

Châteauneuf-du-Pape S Rh r (w) ★★★ 78' 80 81' 83 85 86 88 89' 90' 94 **95' 96 98' 99' 00' 01' 03' 04'** 06' 07' 3,200 ha nr Avignon with core of 30 DOMS for v. fine wines (quality varies over remaining 90). Mix of up to 13 red, white varieties led by Grenache, Syrah, Mourvèdre, Counoise. Best are dark, strong, exceptionally long-lived, can be gd value. Growing number of expensive Prestige wines (old vines, new oak). Whites fruity, zesty or rather heavy: many now DYA. Top growers include: CHX DE BEAUCASTEL, FORTIA, Gardine, MONT-REDON, LA NERTHE, RAYAS, Vaudieu; Doms de Beaurenard, Bois de Boursan, Bosquet des Papes, Les Cailloux, Chante Cigale, Charvin, Font-de-Michelle, Grand Veneur, Marcoux, Millière, Pegaü, Roger Sabon, VIEUX TÉLÉGRAPHE, Vieille Julienne, Henri Bonneau, Clos du Mont-Olivet, CLOS DES PAPES, Clos St-Jean, Cuvée du Vatican, P Usseglio, Vieux Donjon.

Château Pierre-Bise Lo r p w ★★→★★★★ Terroir specialist COTEAUX DU LAYON, inc Chaume, QUARTS DE CHAUME, and SAVENNIÈRES, esp Clos de Grand Beaupreau and ROCHE-AUX-MOINES. V.gd Anjou-Gamay, ANJOU-VILLAGES, and ANJOU Blanc.

Château Rayas S Rh r (w) ★★★→★★★★ **78'** 79 81' 85 86 88' 89 90' 93 94 95' 96' 98' 99 00 01 03 **04' 05'** 06' Famous. v. traditional, one-off 12-ha estate in CHÂTEAUNEUF. Soft, subtle, red fruits, its Grenache ages superbly. Traditional-style white Rayas can be v.gd over 15+ yrs. Gd-value second wine: Pignan. V.gd Ch Fonsalette, CÔTES DU RHÔNE. All benefit from decanting. Also gd Ch des Tours VACQUEYRAS.

Château Simone Prov r p w ★★→★★★ Historic estate where Winston Churchill painted Mont St-Victoire. Virtually synonymous with AC PALETTE nr Aix-en Provence. Warming reds; white repays bottle ageing. Full-bodied rosé.

Château de Villeneuve Lo r w Top SAUMUR grower. Wonderful Saumur Blanc (esp Les Cormiers) and SAUMUR-CHAMPIGNY (esp VIEILLES VIGNES, Grand Clos). Superb Coteaux de Saumur in 2003.

Château-Grillet N Rh w ★★ 91' 95' 98' 00' **01' 04'** 05 06 07 Single 3.6-ha terraced granite amphitheatre of Viognier; one of France's smallest ACS. Overpriced, but recent revival. Takes 3+ yrs to open up. Decant.

Châtillon-en-Diois Rh r p w ★ DYA Small, ordinary AC east of middle Rhône in pre-Alps. Just adequate, mainly Gamay reds; white (some ALIGOTÉ) often made into sparkling CLAIRETTE DE DIE.

Chave, Gérard and Jean-Louis N Rh r w ★★★★ First-class HERMITAGE family DOM. Nine hillside sites. Rich, *gourmand*, long-lived wines, esp white, also gd occasional VIN DE PAILLE. Fruity J-L Chave brand ST-JOSEPH Offerus, also a select merchant HERMITAGE red and white.

Chavignol Picturesque SANCERRE village with famous steep v'yd, Les Monts Damnés. Clay-limestone soil gives full-bodied, mineral wines that age 5–7 yrs (or longer); esp from Boulay, BOURGEOIS, Cotat, and DAGUENEAU.

Chénas Beauj r ★★★ 05' 06 07 Smallest BEAUJOLAIS CRU, one of the weightiest; neighbour to MOULIN-À-VENT and JULIÉNAS. Growers inc Benon, Champagnon, Charvet, Ch Chèvres, DUBOEUF, Lapierre, Robin, Trichard, co-op.

Chevalier-Montrachet Burg w ★★★★ 89' 90 92 95 96 97 98 99' 00' 01 02' 04 05' 06' Neighbour of MONTRACHET (6.8 ha) making similarly luxurious wine, perhaps less powerful. Growers include: BOUCHARD PÈRE & FILS, Colin-Deleger, Jadot, Latour, LEFLAIVE, Niellon, PRIEUR, Ch de Puligny.

Cheverny Lo r p w ★→★★ 05' 06 07 Loire AC nr Chambord. Pungent dry white from Sauv Bl and CHARD. Also Gamay, Pinot N, or Cab Sauv. Richer, rarer, and more ageworthy Cour-Cheverny uses local Romorantin grape only. Sparkling use CRÉMANT de Loire and TOURAINE ACS. Esp Cazin, Clos Tue-Boeuf, Gendrier, Huards, Oisly & Thesée; Doms de la Desoucherie, du Moulin.

Chevillon, R Burg ★★★ Delicious, approachable NUITS-ST-GEORGES with v'yds in the best sites, esp Les St-Georges, Cailles, Vaucrains, Roncières.

Chidaine, François Lo dr sw w sp ★★★ Producer of ambitious, v. pure, v. precise Montlouis. In 2002 took over Clos Baudoin (formerly Prince Poniatowski), where he makes similarly styled VOUVRAY. Concentrates on dry and DEMI-SEC styles. Biodynamic principles followed in both DOMS.

Chignin Savoie w ★ DYA Light, soft white from Jacquère grapes for alpine summers. Chignin-Bergeron (with Roussanne grapes) is best and liveliest.

Chinon Lo r (p w) ★★→★★★ 89' 90' 95 96' 97 02 03 04 05' 06 07 Juicy, light to rich TOURAINE Cab Fr. Drink young; top vintages from top growers can age 10+ yrs. Increasing amount of taut dry Chenin Bl. Bestinc: ALLIET, BAUDRY, Baudry-Dutour; Chx de la Bonnelière, de Coulaine, Dom de la Noblaie.

Chiroubles Beauj r 05' 06 07 Gd but tiny BEAUJOLAIS CRU next to FLEURIE; fresh, fruity, silky wine for early drinking (1–3 yrs). Growers include Bouillard, Cheysson, DUBOEUF, Fourneau, Passot, Raousset, co-op.

Chorey-lès-Beaune Burg r (w) ★★ 99' 02' 03 05' 06 07 Minor AC north of BEAUNE. Three fine growers: Arnoux, Germain (Ch de Chorey), TOLLOT-BEAUT.

Chusclan S Rh r p w ★→★★ 04 05' 06' 07 CÔTES DU RHÔNE-VILLAGES with solid co-op. Soft textured reds, sound, lively rosés. Labels include CUVÉE de Marcoule, Seigneurie de Gicon. Also gd Ch Signac (more tannin, can age) and **special cuvées from André Roux**. Drink most young.

Clair, Bruno Burg ★★→★★★ Leading MARSANNAY estate. v.gd wines from there and GEVREY-CHAMBERTIN (esp CLOS DE BÈZE), FIXIN, MOREY-ST-DENIS, SAVIGNY.

Clairet V. light red wine. BORDEAUX Clairet is an AC. Try Chx Fontenille, Penin.

Clairette Traditional white grape of the MIDI. Its low-acid wine was a vermouth base. Improvements in winemaking produce easy-drinking glassfuls.

Clairette de Bellegarde Midi w ★ DYA Obscure AC nr Nîmes: fresh white.

Clairette de Die Rh w dr s/sw sp ★★ NV Locally popular dry or (better) semi-sweet, gd character. Traditional MUSCAT-flavoured sparkling wine from pre-Alps in east Rhône; or straight dry CLAIRETTE, can age 3–4 yrs. Worth trying on a Sunday morning. Achard-Vincent, A Poulet, J-C Raspail.

Clairette du Languedoc Midi w ★ DYA A rare white AC of the MIDI. Original identity soft and creamy; now some oak-ageing and even late-harvest wines. Much recent improvement.

Clape, La Midi r p w ★★→★★★ Cru of note in AC COTEAUX DU LANGUEDOC. In line for own AC. Warming spicy reds from sun-soaked hills between Narbonne and the Med. Tangy whites age surprisingly well. Gd: Chx l'Hospitalet, Mire l'Etang, Moyau, La Négly, Pech-Céléyran, Pech-Redon, Rouquette-sur-Mer.

Clape, Auguste and Pierre N Rh r (w) ★★★→★★★★ 97 98' 99' 00 01' 02 03' 04' 05' 06 07 Supreme 5+ ha Syrah v'yd at CORNAS, many old vines. Traditional reds, need 6+ yrs. Epitome of unspoilt, hands-off winemaking, always gd in lesser vintages. Gd CÔTES DU RHÔNE, ST-PÉRAY.

FRANCE

Climat Burgundian word for individually named v'yd, eg BEAUNE Grèves.

Clos A term carrying some prestige, reserved for distinct (walled) v'yds, often in one ownership (esp Burgundy and ALSACE).

Clos de Gamot SW ★★★ 85 89 90' 95 96 98' 00 01 02 05' 400-yr-old estate. Ultra-traditional, long-lived benchmark wines. Top ★★★★ CUVÉE Vignes Centenaires (made best yrs only) is outstanding.

Clos des Lambrays Burg r ★★★ 90' 95 99' 00 02 03 04 05' 06 07 GRAND CRU v'yd (6 ha) at MOREY-ST-DENIS. A virtual monopoly of the Dom du Clos des Lambrays, in recent yrs more severe in selecting only the best grapes.

Clos des Mouches Burg r w ★★★ Splendid PREMIER CRU BEAUNE v'yd, largely owned by DROUHIN. Whites and reds, spicy and memorable – and consistent. Little-known v'yds of the same name exist in SANTENAY and MEURSAULT too.

Clos des Papes S Rh r w ★★★★ V.gd, stylish 32-ha (18 plots) CHNEUF estate Avril-family-owned for centuries. Long-lived, complex red (mainly Grenache, Mourvèdre, drink from 6 yrs) and classy white (5–15 yrs).

Clos de la Roche r ★★★ 90' 91 93' 95 96' 97 98 99' 00 01 02' 03 05' 06 07 Arguably the finest GRAND CRU of MOREY-ST-DENIS, Arguably with as much grace as power. Best: Amiot, BOUCHARD, DUJAC, LEROY, H Lignier, PONSOT, ROUSSEAU.

Clos du Roi Burg r ★★★ The best v'yd in GRAND CRU CORTON and a PREMIER CRU v'yd in BEAUNE.

Clos Rougeard Lo r (sw) ★★★ Small, influential DOM – benchmark SAUMUR-CHAMPIGNY fine SAUMUR BL, and, when possible, luscious COTEAUX DE SAUMUR.

Clos St-Denis Burg r ★★★ 90' 91 93' 95 96' 97 98 99' 00 01 02' 03 05' 06 07 GRAND CRU at MOREY-ST-DENIS (6.4 ha). Splendid sturdy wine growing silky with age. Growers include: Bertagna, DUJAC, and PONSOT.

Clos Ste-Hune Al w ★★★★ Greatest Ries in ALSACE (**00' 02'**). V. fine, initially austere; needs 5–10+ yrs ageing. A Trimbach wine from GRAND CRU ROSACKE.

Clos St-Jacques Burg r ★★★ 90' 91 93 95' 96' 98 99' 00 01 02' 03 04 05' 06 07 6.7-ha hillside PREMIER CRU in GEVREY CHAMBERTIN with perfect southeast exposure. Five excellent producers: CLAIR, ESMONIN, Fourrier, JADOT, ROUSSEAU; powerful, velvety reds often ranked above many GRANDS CRUS.

Clos de Tart Burg r ★★★★ 90' 93 95 96' 97 99' 00 02' 03 04 05' 06 07 GRAND CRU at MOREY-ST-DENIS. Now first-rate and priced accordingly.

Clos de Vougeot Burg r ★★★ 78' 88 89' 90' 91 93' 95 96' 97 98 99' 00 01 02' 03' 04 05' 06 07 A 50-ha CÔTE DE NUITS GRAND CRU with many owners. Occasionally sublime. Maturity depends on grower's philosophy, technique, and position. Top growers include Ch de la Tour, DROUHIN, ENGEL, FAIVELEY, GRIVOT, GROS, HUDELOT-NOËLLAT, JADOT, LEROY, LIGER-BELAIR, MÉO-CAMUZÉT, MUGNERET, VOUGERAIE.

Coche-Dury Burg ★★★★ 8.4-ha MEURSAULT DOM (plus 0.5 ha of CORTON-CHARLEMAGNE) with the highest reputation for oak-perfumed wines. Even MEURSAULT-Villages is great (with age). Also v.gd ALIGOTÉ and reds.

Colin Burg ★★★ Leading CHASSAGNE-MONTRACHET and ST-AUBIN family, several members of the next generation succeeding either Marc Colin (Pierre-Yves) or Michel Colin-Deleger (Bruno, Philippe).

Collines Rhodaniennes N Rh r w ★→★★ Lively Rhône VDP, with character, gd value. Also young-vine CÔTE-RÔTIE. Mainly red, mainly Syrah (best), also Merlot, Gamay. Some Viognier (best), CHARD. Reds: Barou, Bonnefond, Chatagnier, J-M Gérin, Jamet, Jasmin, Monier, S Ogier. Whites: Barou, Cuilleron, Perret, G Vernay.

Collioure Pyr r r ★★ The table-wine twin of Banyuls with most producers making both. Warm, gutsy red wines from steep terraces overlooking the Med. Also rosé and, since 02, white, based on Grenache Blanc. Top growers: Le Clos des Paulilles, Doms du Mas Blanc, de la Rectorie, La Tour Vieille, Vial-Magnères.

FRANCE

Champagne – pre-empting prices in a bull market
Despite economic turbulence, CHAMPAGNE seems recession-proof. But, assuming that CHAMPAGNE sales continue to grow at the current rate, there will be a drought of fizz about 2013 as production reaches its limit. The only way to control growth is through price hikes, which are already apparent. It's not a bad idea to buy whatever vintage CHAMPAGNE you need now, esp 02; a great yr for Pinot Noir. Great buys for 02 Pinot-led CUVÉES: DRAPPIER Millésime d'Exception, Serge Mathieu Blanc de Noirs, Egly Ouriet Blanc de Noirs Vieilles Vignes, and POL ROGER Sir Winston Churchill as soon as it's released (early 2009?).

Comté Tolosan SW r p w ★ Mostly DYA VDP. Includes some nice surprises, a multitude of sins, and the whole of the southwest. ★★★ Ch de Cabidos for varietals from Petit Manseng grapes. ★★ DOM DE RIBONNET (Christian Gerber, south of Toulouse) for experimental use of non-indigenous grape varieties.

Condrieu N Rh w ★★★ 01' 02 03 04' 05 06 07 Full, fragrant, floral white of character and price from Viognier. Can be outstanding, but rapid growth of v'yd (now 125 ha; 75 growers) has made quality variable (except marvellous 04); more new oak also a doubtful move. Best: CHAPOUTIER, Y Cuilleron, DELAS, Dumazet, Gangloff, GUIGAL, JABOULET, F Merlin, Niéro, A Perret, C Pichon, G Vernay (esp supreme, long-lived Coteau de Vernon), F Villard. Regrettable move to over-opulent VENDANGE TARDIVE style by some growers.

Confuron, J-J Burg ★★★ Tiny NUITS-ST-GEORGES. Modern-style, full of fruit.

Corbières Midi r (p w) ★★→★★★ 98 99 00 **01 02 03** 04 05 06 The biggest AC of the LANGUEDOC, with *cru* of Boutenac. Wild scenery dominated by Mont d'Alaric and Cathar castles. Wines like the scenery: sun-soaked and rugged. Best estates include Chx Aiguilloux, la Baronne, de Cabriac, Lastours, des Ollieux, Les Palais, de la Voulte Gasparet, Doms du Grand Crès, de Fontsainte, du Vieux Parc, de Villemajou, Villerouge, la Crémad. Co-ops: Camplong, Embrès-et-Castelmaure, Tuchan.

Cornas N Rh r ★★→★★★ 78' 83' 85' 88' 89' 90' 91' 94' **95**' 96 97' **98**' 99' 00' 01' **02** 03' 04' 05' 06' Sturdy, mineral-edged, dark Syrah from 105-ha steep granite v'yds south of HERMITAGE. Needs to age 5–15 yrs but more can be drunk after 4 yrs now. Top: Allemand, Balthazar (traditional), CLAPE (benchmark), Colombo (new oak), Courbis (modern), DELAS, Dumien-Serrette (traditional), J & E Durand, JABOULET (esp St-Pierre CUVÉE), V Paris (v. promising), Tardieu-Laurent (modern, expensive), Voge (oak).

Corsica (Vin de Corse) r p w ACS Ajaccio, PATRIMONIO, better *crus* Coteaux du Cap Corse, Sartène, and Calvi. VDP: Ile de Beauté. Original light, spicy reds from Sciacarello and more structured wines from Nielluccio; gd rosés; herbal whites from Vermentino. Top growers: Abbatucci, Antoine Arena, Clos d'Alzeto, Clos Capitoro, Gentile, Yves Leccia, Montemagni, Peraldi, Vaccelli.

Corton Burg r (w) ★★★ 90' **91 93 95** 96' 97 **98** 99' 00 01 02' 03' 05' 06 07 160 ha classified as GRAND CRU, which only a few Corton v'yds such as CLOS DU ROI, Bressandes, Rognets actually deserve. These have weight and structure, others make appealing, softer reds. Look for d'Ardhuy, CHANDON DE BRIAILLES, Dubreuil-Fontaine, FAIVELEY, Camille Giroud, MÉO-CAMUZET, de Merode, TOLLOT-BEAUT. Occasional whites, *eg* HOSPICES DE BEAUNE.

Corton-Charlemagne Burg w ★★★★ **89' 90' 92'** 95 **96 98 99'** 00' 01 02' 03 04 05' 06 07 SW and W exposure of hill of Corton, plus a band round the top, all more suited to white wines. Intense minerality and great ageing potential, often insufficiently realized. Top growers: BONNEAU DU MARTRAY, COCHE-DURY, FAIVELEY, HOSPICES DE BEAUNE, JADOT, P Javillier, LATOUR, ROUMIER, VOUGERAIE.

Costières de Nîmes S Rh r p w ★→★★ 01' 03 **04'** 05' **06** W of CHÂTEAUNEUF red with strong fruit and body; best will age, are gd value. Look for Chx de Campuget, Grande Cassagne, Mas Neuf, Mourgues-du-Grès, Nages, d'Or et des Geules, Roubaud, de la Tuilerie; Mas des Bressades; Doms de la Patience, Tardieu-Laurent, du Vieux Relais. Best reds substantial: 6–8 yrs. Some stylish whites (inc oaked Roussanne).

Coteaux d'Aix-en-Provence Prov r p w ★→★★★ Sprawling AC from hills N of Aix and on plain around Etang de Berre. A fruit salad of grape varieties, both Bordelais and MIDI. Reds are best, esp from Chx Beaupré, Calissanne, Revelette, Vignelaure; Doms des Béates (CHAPOUTIER-owned), du Ch Bas. See also COTEAUX DES BAUX-EN-PROVENCE.

Coteaux d'Ancenis Lo r p w (sw) ★ Generally DYA VDQS – right bank of the Loire, east of Nantes. Chiefly for dry, demi-sec, and sweet Chenin Bl whites plus ageworthy Malvoisie; also light Gamay, Cab Fr, and Cab Sauv reds and rosés. Esp Guindon.

Coteaux de l'Aubance Lo w sw ★★→★★★★ 89' 90' **95' 96' 97'** 02 03 04 05' 06 (07) Small AC for sweet whites from Chenin Bl. Nervier less sumptuous than COTEAUX DU LAYON except when SÉLECTIONS DES GRAINS NOBLES. Often gd value. Esp Bablut, Haute-Perche, Montgilet, Richou, Rochelles.

Coteaux des Baronnies S Rh r p w ★ DYA Rhône VDP nr Nyons. Syrah, Cab Sauv, Merlot, CHARD, plus traditional grapes. Direct wines, from gd altitudes. DOMS du Rieu-Frais and Rosière worth a look.

Coteaux des Baux-en-Provence Prov r p ★→★★★ 98 99 00 **01 03** 04 05 From the dramatic bauxite outcrop of the Alpilles topped by tourist village of Les Baux. AC in own right for red and pink. White is COTEAUX D'AIX. Best estate is Trevallon, Cab Sauv/Syrah blend, but VDP, for lack of Grenache. Also Mas des Dames, Dom Hauvette.

Coteaux de Chalosse SW r p w ★ DYA, VDP from unusual local grapes. Co-op now merged with Tursan.

Coteaux Champenois Champ r w (p) ★★★ DYA (whites) AC for non-sparkling CHAMPAGNE. Vintages follow those for CHAMPAGNE. Not worth inflated prices.

Coteaux du Giennois Lo r p w ★ DYA Small appellation (196 ha) north of POUILLY. Scattered v'yds – Cosne to Gien. Light, potentially powerful red: blend of Gamay and Pinot N; Sauv Bl like a junior SANCERRE. Best: Emile Balland, BOURGEOIS, Paulat, Villargeau.

Coteaux de Glanes SW France r ★★ DYA Lively, gd-value VDP from upper Dordogne features the Ségalin grape. All from 8-grower CO-OP. Mostly drunk in local restaurants.

Coteaux du Languedoc Midi r p w ★★→★★★ 98 99 00 **01 02 03** 04 05 06 A sprawling AC from Narbonne to Nîmes, with various *crus* and sub-divisions. Newer names are GRÈS DE MONTPELLIER, TERRASSES DU LARZAC, and in 2007 PÉZENAS. Lots of new estates demonstrating exciting potential of the MIDI. Will disappear as larger AC LANGUEDOC, created 2007, becomes established.

Coteaux du Layon Lo w s/sw sw ★★→★★★★ **89 90 95 96 97** 02 03 04 05 06 07 Heart of ANJOU: sweet Chenin Bl; lush with admirable acidity, ages almost forever. New SÉLECTION DES GRAINS NOBLES Seven villages can add name to AC. Top ACS: BONNEZEAUX, QUARTS DE CHAUME, Chaume. Growers: Baudouin, BAUMARD, Delesvaux, des Forges, Dom Les Grands Vignes, Guegniard, Dom de Juchepie, Ogereau, Papin (CH PIERRE-BISE), Jo Pithon, Ch la Fresnaye.

Coteaux du Loir Lo r p w dr sw ★→★★★ **02 03 04 05'** (07) The Loir is a northern tributary of the Loire. Small region north of Tours, inc JASNIÈRES. Potentially fine, apple-scented Chenin Bl, Gamay, peppery Pineau d'Aunis that goes well with spicy foods and pungent cheeses. Top growers: DOM DE BELLIVIERE/ Nicolas, Chaussard/le Briseau, Fresneau, Gigou, Robinot de Rycke.

Coteaux du Lyonnais Beauj r p (w) ★ DYA Junior BEAUJOLAIS. Best EN PRIMEUR.

Coteaux de Pierrevert Prov r p w ★ Cool area producing easy-drinking co-op red, rosé, fresh white from high v'yds nr Manosque. Dom la Blaque, Ch Régusse, Ch Rousset. AC since 1998.

Coteaux du Quercy SW r ★→★★ 02 04 05' (06) S of CAHORS VDQS, queuing for AC. Cab Fr-based wines from ★★ Doms d'Aries, ★ de la Combarade, de Guyot, de Lafage, Lagarde, de Merchien. Worthy ★ co-op.

Coteaux de Saumur Lo w sw ★★→★★★ Sweet Chenin Bl. A tradition revived since 1989 – resembles COTEAUX DU LAYON but less rich. Esp DOM DES CHAMPS FLEURIS/Retiveau-Retif, CLOS ROUGEARD, Régis Neau, Vatan.

Coteaux et Terrasses de Montauban SW r p ★→★★ DYA ★★ Dom de Montels (who invented this appellation single-handed) and ★ Dom de Biarnès notably better than co-op at LAVILLEDIEU-DU-TEMPLE.

Coteaux du Tricastin S Rh r p w ★→★★ 04 05' 06 07 Fringe mid-Rhône AC of fair but irregular quality. Best include Doms de Bonetto-Fabrol, Grangeneuve (esp VIEILLES VIGNES), de Montine (gd white), St-Luc, and Ch La Décelle (inc white CÔTES DU RHÔNE).

Coteaux Varois-en-Provence Prov r p w ★→★★ 99 00 01 02 03 04 05 06 Sandwiched between COTEAUX D'AIX and CÔTES DE PROVENCE. Gd source of warming reds and deserves better reputation. Try Chx Routas, la Calisse, Dom les Alysses, du Deffends.

Coteaux du Vendômois Lo r p w ★→★★ DYA Marginal Loire AC W of Vendôme. The most characteristic wines are VINS GRIS from Pinot d'Aunis grape, which also gives peppery notes to red blends. Whites based on Chenin Bl. Producers incl Patrice Colin, Dom du Four à Chaux, Cave du Vendôme-Villiers.

Côte de Beaune Burg r w ★★→★★★★ Used geographically: the south half of the CÔTE D'OR. Applies as an AC only to parts of BEAUNE itself.

Côte de Beaune-Villages Burg r ★★ 99' 02' 03 05' 06 07 Regional appellation for lesser wines of classic area. Cannot be labelled "Côte de Beaune" without either "Villages" or village name added. Red wines only.

Côte de Brouilly Beauj r ★★ 05' 06 07 Fruity rich BEAUJOLAIS *cru*, one of the best. Try Ch Thivin.

Côte Chalonnaise Burg r w sp ★★ V'yd area between BEAUNE and MÂCON. See BOUZERON, GIVRY, MERCUREY, MONTAGNY, RULLY. Alias "Région de Mercurey".

Côte de Nuits Burg r (w) ★★→★★★★ Northern half of CÔTE D'OR. Mostly red wine.

Côte de Nuits-Villages Burg r (w) ★★ 99' 02' 03 05' 06 07 A junior AC for extreme N and S ends of CÔTE DE NUITS; well worth investigating for bargains.

Côte d'Or *Département* name applied to the central and principal Burgundy v'yd slopes: CÔTE DE BEAUNE and CÔTE DE NUITS. Not used on labels.

Côte Roannaise Central Fr r p ★→★★ 03 05' 06 07 Small AC (220 ha) on the high granite hills W of Roanne, NW of Lyon. Silky, focused Gamay. Doms du Fontenay, Lapandéry, des Millets, du Pavillon, Serol.

Côte-Rôtie N Rh r ★★★→★★★★ 78' 83' 85' 88' 89' 90' 91' 94' 95' 97 98' 99' 00 01' 03' 04' 05' 06 Finest, most Burgundian Rhône red, from S of Vienne, mainly Syrah, sprinkle of Viognier. Rich, complex softness and finesse with age (esp 5–10+ yrs). Top growers include: Barge, Bernard, Bonnefond (oak), Burgaud, CHAPOUTIER, Clusel-Roch, DELAS, Duclaux, Gaillard (oak), J-M Gérin (oak), GUIGAL, Jamet, Jasmin, Ogier (oak), ROSTAING, VIDAL-FLEURY.

Côtes d'Auvergne Central Fr r p (w) ★→★★ Generally DYA Small VDQS (412 ha). Mainly Gamay, though some Pinot N and CHARD. Best reds improve 2–3 yrs. Best villages: Boudes, Chanturgue, Châteaugay, Corent, Madargues. Producers: Cave St-Verny, Dom de Peyra (sells its wines as VDP).

Côtes de Bourg B'x r w ★→★★ 99 00' 01 02 03 04 05' (06) AC for earthy red and white from east of the Gironde. Steady quality. Top Chx: Brûlesécaille, Bujan,

Falfas, Fougas, Garreau, Guerry, Haut-Guiraud, Haut-Maco, Haut Mondésir, Macay, Mercier, Nodoz, Roc de Cambes, Rousset, Sociondo.

Côtes du Brulhois SW r p (w) ★→★★ **04** 05' 06 Nr Agen. Promising independents Le Bois de Simon, Ch la Bastide, Clos Pountet, Doms Coujétou-Peyret and des Thermes.

Côtes de Castillon B'x r ★→★★★ 98 **99** 00' 01 **02** 03 04 05' (06) Flourishing region east of ST-EMILION; similar wines. Ageing potential. Label changes from 07 vintage. Top chx: de l'A, d'Aiguilhe, Cap de Faugères, La Clarière-Laithwaite, Clos l'Eglise, Clos Les Lunelles, Clos Puy Arnaud, Poupille, Robin, Veyry, Vieux Ch Champs de Mars.

Côtes de Duras Dordogne r w p ★→★★★ **04** 05' 06 BORDEAUX satellite. Top include newcomers ★★★ DOMS Chator, Mouthes-les-Bihan, Petit Malromé, and Chx Condom Perceval, also more established ★★ des Allegrets, du Grand Mayne, Lafon and de Laulan. Co-op (Berticot) could do better.

Côtes du Forez Lo r p (sp) ★ DYA Loire AC (146 ha) nr St Etienne for easy-going Gamay reds and rosés. Main producer Les Vignerons Foréziens.

Côtes de Francs B'x r w ★★ **98** 00' 01 03 04 05' (06) Fringe BORDEAUX from east of ST-EMILION. Mainly red but some white: tasty and attractive. Reds can age a little. New AC from 07 vintage. Top CHX: Charmes-Godard, Francs, Laclaverie, Marsau, Pelan, La Prade, PUYGUERAUD.

Côtes de Gascogne SW w (r p) ★ DYA VDP. Huge production of v. popular wines led by Plaimont co-op and Grassa family (Ch de Tariquet). Sancet, de San Guilhem, Ch Monluc. Also from MADIRAN growers, notably BRUMONT.

Côtes du Jura r p w (sp) ★ DYA Many light tints/tastes. ARBOIS more substantial.

Côtes du Lubéron S Rh r p w ★→★★ **01** 03 04 05 06 Much improved country wines from far south of Rhône, often with modern methods. Many new producers . Star is Ch de la Canorgue. Also: Dom de la Citadelle, Ch Clapier, Fontvert, St-Estève de Neri, Tardieu-Laurent, Cellier de Marrenon, Val-Joanis.

Côtes du Marmandais Dordogne r p w ★→★★★ **01**' **02** 04 05' 06 Rapidly developing AC. ★★★ Cult wines from Elian da Ros (Clos Bacquey). V.gd: ★★ de Beaulieu (best are weighty, need ageing). Also ★ Dom Des Géais.

Côtes de Montravel Dordogne w dr sw ★★★ 97' 98 **00** 01' 03' 04 05' (06) Part of BERGERAC; traditionally medium-sweet, now less common. MONTRAVEL SEC is dry, HAUT-MONTRAVEL is sweet.

Côtes de Provence Prov r p w ★→★★★ r 01 03 04 05 06 07 (p w DYA) Large AC mainly known for rosé; enjoying big leap in quality, thanks to investment. Satisfying reds and herbal whites. STE-VICTOIRE a sub-zone, as well as Fréjus from 2007. Leaders: Castel Roubine, Commanderie de Peyrassol, Doms Bernarde, de la Courtade, Ott with Ch de Selle and Clos Mireille, des Planes, Rabiéga, Richeaume, Ch Routas, Ch Ste-Rosaline. See COTEAUX D'AIX, BANDOL.

Côtes du Rhône S Rh r p w ★→★★ **01**' 03 04 05 06' **07** Basic Rhône AC mainly Grenache, also Syrah. Best drunk young, even as primeur. Wide quality variations, Vaucluse area best: some heavy over-production.

Côtes du Rhône-Villages S Rh r p w ★→★★★ 98' 00' 01' 03 04' **05**' 06' **07** Wine from 7,700 ha, inc 18 best southern Rhône villages. Mainly reliable, sometimes delicious (and v.gd value). Red base is Grenache, with Syrah, Mourvèdre support. Improving whites, often with Viognier, Roussanne. See BEAUMES-DE-VENISE, CAIRANNE, CHUSCLAN, LAUDUN, RASTEAU, SABLET, SÉGURET, ST-GERVAIS. New villages from 2005: MASSIF D'UCHAUX, PLAN DE DIEU, PUYMÉRAS, PLATEAU DE SIGNARGUES. Gd value, eg, Chx Fontségune, Signac, Doms Cabotte, Deforge, Grand Moulas, Grand Veneur, Jérome, Montbayon, Rabasse-Charavin, Renjarde, Romarins, Rouge Garance, Ste-Anne, St Siffrein, Saladin, Valériane, Vieux Chêne, Mas Libian, Cave Estézargues, Cave Rasteau.

Côtes du Roussillon Pyr r r p w ★→★★ 01 02 **03** 04 05 06 07 East Pyrenees AC. AC

> **Top Côtes du Rhône producers:** Chx Courac, La Courançonne, l'Estagnol, Fonsalette, Grand Moulas, Haut-Musiel, Hugues, Montfaucon, St-Estève, Trignon (inc Viognier); Co-ops Chantecotes (Ste-Cécile-les-Vignes), Rasteau, Villedieu (esp white); Doms La Bouvade, Bramadou, Charvin, Combebelle, Coudoulet de Beaucastel (red, white), Cros de la Mûre, M Dumarcher, Espigouette, Ferrand, Gourget, Gramenon, Janasse, Jaume, Perrin, Réméjeanne, St-Siffrein, Soumade, Vieille Julienne, Vieux Chêne; DELAS, DUBOEUF, GUIGAL, JABOULET.

covers v'yds of Pyrénées-Orientales behind Perpignan. Dominated by co-ops, notably Vignerons Catalans. Red is best, predominantly from Carignan.

Côtes du Roussillon-Villages Pyr r ★★ 01 02 03 04 05 06 07 28 villages form best part of region. Dominated by Vignerons Catalans. Best labels: Cazes Frères, Doms des Chênes, la Cazenove, Gauby (also characterful white VDP), Piquemal, Seguela, Ch de Jau, Co-op Lesquerde.

Côtes du Roussillon des Aspres Pyr First vintage of newish AC 2003 for reds only. Similar to basic CÔTES DU ROUSSILLON. Rarely found outside area. Based on Grenache Noir, Carignan, Syrah, and Mourvèdre.

Côtes de St-Mont SW r w p ★★ (r) 05' 06 (p w) DYA Gers VDQS still patiently awaiting AC status. Created from nothing by Producteurs Plaimont, the most successful co-op in the southwest. Gd red from Dom des Maouries. Same grapes as MADIRAN and PACHERENC.

Côtes du Tarn SW r p w ★ DYA VDP overlaps GAILLAC; same growers but also Dom d'en Segur (does not produce GAILLAC AC).

Côtes de Thongue Midi r w ★ DYA Dynamic VDP from HÉRAULT. Intriguing blends in preference to single varietals. Reds will age. Doms Arjolle, les Chemins de Bassac, Coussergues, la Croix Belle, Magellan, Monplézy, Montmarin.

Côtes de Toul E France (Lorraine) p r w ★ DYA V. light wines; mainly VIN GRIS.

Côtes du Ventoux S Rh r p (w) ★★ 01' 03 04' 05' 06 07 6,000+ ha AC between Rhône and PROVENCE for tasty red (café-style to much deeper flavours), rosé, and gd white (though oak use growing). Cool flavours from altitude for some. Best: LA VIEILLE FERME (red) owned by BEAUCASTEL, co-op Bédoin, Goult, St-Didier, Doms Anges, Juliette Avril, Berane, Brusset, Cascavel, Fondrèche, Font-Sane, Grand Jacquet, Martinelle, Murmurium, Verrière, Pesquié, Pigeade, Terres de Solence, Valcombe, JABOULET, VIDAL-FLEURY.

Côtes du Vivarais S Rh r p w ★ 04 05' 06 07 DYA Over 580 ha across several Ardèche villages west of Montélimar; AC in 1999. Improving simple CUVÉES, strong Syrah fruit; mid-weight oak-aged reds. Note: Mas de Bagnols.

Coulée de Serrant Lo w dr sw (★★★★) 95 96 97 98 99 02 03 04 05 (07) A 6.4-ha Chenin Bl v'yd at SAVENNIÈRES. Evangelically biodynamic. Terroir-driven wine even when less than perfect. Decant 2 hrs before drinking – don't chill.

Courcel, Dom Burg ★★★ Leading POMMARD estate – top PREMIER CRU Rugiens.

Crémant In CHAMPAGNE meant "creaming" (half-sparkling). Since 1975, an AC for quality classic-method sparkling from ALSACE, Loire, BOURGOGNE, and most recently LIMOUX – often a bargain. Term no longer used in CHAMPAGNE.

Crépy Savoie w ★★ DYA Light, soft, Swiss-style white from south shore of Lake Geneva. Crépitant has been coined for its faint fizz.

Crozes-Hermitage N Rh r w ★★ 95' 98' 99' 00' 01' 03' 05 06 07 Nr Hermitage: larger, flatter Syrah v'yds (1,355 ha), mix hill/plain. Most fruity, early-drinking (2–5 yrs), some cask-aged (4–10 yrs). A minority are local; many are technical wines. Gd: Belle, Y Chave, Ch Curson, Darnaud, Doms Bruyères, du Colombier, Combier, des Entrefaux (oak), Hauts-Chassis, Mucyn, Murinais, du Pavillon-Mercurol, de Thalabert of JABOULET, CHAPOUTIER. Drink white early.

Cuve close Short-cut method of making sparkling wine in a tank. Sparkle dies away in glass much quicker than with *méthode traditionnelle* wine.

Cuvée Wine contained in a *cuve*, or vat. A word of many uses, inc synonym for "blend" and first-press wines (as in CHAMPAGNE); in Burg interchangeable with *cru*. Often just refers to a "lot" of wine.

DRC The wine geek's shorthand for DOM DE LA ROMANÉE-CONTI.

Dagueneau, Didier Lo ★★★→★★★★ Best producer of Pouilly-Fumé by far and a master of stunningly pure SAUV BL. Top CUVÉES: Pur Sang, Silex and ungrafted Asteroide. Also SANCERRE with small v'yd in Chavignol. See also JURANÇON for his Jardins de Babylone – beautifully balanced sweet Petit Manseng.

Degré alcoolique Degrees of alcohol, ie per cent by volume.

Deiss, Domaine Marcel ★★ High-profile grower at Bergheim, ALSACE. Favours blended wines from individual v'yd sites, more remarkable for range than for consistent top quality. Gewurz and Ries SCHOENENBOURG are his best wines. Now biodynamic.

Delamotte BRUT; Blanc de Blancs (**98 99** 00 02); CUVÉE Nicholas Delamotte. Fine small CHARD-dominated CHAMPAGNE house at Le Mesnil. Managed with SALON by LAURENT-PERRIER. Excellent vintage BLANC DE BLANCS (**85'** 99).

Delas Frères N Rh ★→★★★ Consistent, gd quality N Rhône house with CONDRIEU, CÔTE-RÔTIE, HERMITAGE v'yds. Top wines: CONDRIEU, CÔTE-RÔTIE Landonne, HERMITAGE M de la Tourette (red, white), Les Bessards. Owned by ROEDERER.

Demi-sec Half-dry: in practice more like half-sweet (eg of CHAMPAGNE).

Deutz Brut Classic NV; Rosé NV; Brut (**96 98** 00 02); BLANC DE BLANCS (**96 98** 00 02). One of top small CHAMPAGNE houses, ROEDERER-owned. V. dry, classic wines. **Superb cuvée William Deutz** (**96'** 98 02). See also New Zealand.

Domaine (Dom) Property, particularly in Burgundy and rural France. See under name, eg TEMPIER, DOMAINE.

Dom Pérignon CUVÉE **90' 95 96 98'** 99 00 02; Rosé **98** 99 02' Luxury CUVÉE of MOËT & CHANDON, named after legendary cellarmaster who first blended CHAMPAGNE. Astonishingly consistent quality and creamy character, esp with 10–15 yrs bottle-age. Late-disgorged oenothèque vintages back to 59.

Dopff & Irion ★→★★★ 17th-c ALSACE firm at Riquewihr now part of PFAFFENHEIM. MUSCAT Les Amandiers, Gewurz Les Sorcières. Also gd CRÉMANT D'ALSACE.

Dopff au Moulin ★★★ Ancient top-class family wine house at Riquewihr, ALSACE. Best: Gewurz GRANDS CRUS Brand, Sporen; Ries SCHOENENBOURG; Sylvaner de Riquewihr. Pioneers of ALSACE CRÉMANT; gd CUVÉES: Bartholdi, Julien.

Dourthe, Vins & Vignobles BORDEAUX merchant with wide range and quality emphasis: gd, notably CHX BELGRAVE, LE BOSCQ, LA GARDE. Beau-Mayne, Pey La Tour, and Dourthe No 1 are well-made generic BORDEAUX. Essence concentrated, modern.

Drappier, André Outstanding family-run AUBE CHAMPAGNE house. Pinot-led NV, BRUT Zéro, Rosé Saignée, Signature BLANC DE BLANCS (**99** 00 02), Millésime d'Exception (00 **02**), superb prestige CUVÉE Grande Sendrée (**98** 99 00 02).

Drouhin, J & Cie Burg ★★★→★★★★ Deservedly prestigious grower (61 ha). Cellars in BEAUNE; v'yds in Beaune, CHABLIS, CLOS DE VOUGEOT, MUSIGNY, etc, and Oregon, USA. Best include (white) ***Beaune-Clos des Mouches***, CHABLIS LES CLOS, CORTON-CHARLEMAGNE, PULIGNY-MONTRACHET, Les Folatières (red) GRIOTTE-CHAMBERTIN, MUSIGNY, GRANDS-ECHÉZEAUX.

Duboeuf, Georges ★★→★★★★ Most famous name of the BEAUJOLAIS, proponent of NOUVEAU. Huge range of CUVÉES and crus, but is the lustre fading?

Duclot BORDEAUX négociant; top-growth specialist. Linked with J-P MOUEIX.

Dugat Burg ★★★ Cousins Claude and Bernard (Dugat-Py) both make excellent, deep-coloured wines in GEVREY-CHAMBERTIN under their respective labels.

Dujac, Domaine ★★★→★★★★ Burgundy grower (Jacques Seysses) at MOREY-ST-

DENIS with v'yds in that village and BONNES-MARES, ECHÉZEAUX, GEVREY-CHAMBERTIN. Splendid long-lived wines incl white. Other top v'yds: VOSNE-ROMANÉE, Malconsorts, CLOS DE BÈZE purchased in 2005. Also négociant for village wines as Dujac Fils & Père. Also venture in COTEAUX VAROIS.

Dulong BORDEAUX merchant making unorthodox Rebelle blends. Also VDP.

Durup, Jean Burg ★★→★★★ One of the biggest CHABLIS growers with 152 ha, inc Dom de l'Eglantière and admirable Ch de Maligny.

Duval-Leroy Dynamic Côte des Blancs CHAMPAGNE house. 200 ha of family-owned v'yds source of gd Fleur de Champagne NV, fine Blanc de CHARD (**99 00** 02), and excellent prestige Femme de Champagne (96'). New single village/v'yd bottlings. Even half-litre bottles.

Echézeaux Burg r★★★ 90' **93** 95 96' **97 99**' 00 02' 03 05' 06 07 GRAND CRU (30 ha) between VOSNE-ROMANÉE and CLOS DE VOUGEOT. Can be superlative, fragrant. Of middling weight for GRAND CRU.

Ecu, Domaine de l' Lo dr w r ★★★ 89 90 **95** 96 97 02 03 04 05 06 07 Guy Bossard is a superb producer of biodynamic MUSCADET (esp mineral-rich CUVÉE Granite) and Gros Plant. Also excellent Cab Fr and sparkling Gros Plant.

Edelzwicker Al w ★ DYA Blended light white. Delicious Ch d'Ittenwiller (05).

d'Eguisheim, Cave Vinicole Al ★★ V.gd ALSACE co-op for excellent value: fine GRANDS CRUS Hatschbourg, HENGST, Ollwiller, Spiegel. Owns Willm. Top label: WOLFBERGER. Best: Grande Réserve, Sigillé, Armorié. Gd CRÉMANT and Pinot N.

Engel, R Burg ★★★ Top grower of CLOS DE VOUGEOT, ECHÉZEAUX, GRANDS-ECHÉZEAUX, and VOSNE-ROMANÉE until tragic early death of Philipp. Resurrected as Dom d'Eugénie by new owner François Pinault (owner of CH LATOUR) from 06 vintage.

Entraygues et du Fel SW r p w DYA ★ Fragrant VDQS. Diminutive appellation almost in Massif Central. Zinging white ★★ Dom Méjannassère and Laurent Mousset's red and rosé, esp red La Pauca (would keep).

Entre-Deux-Mers B'x w ★→★★ DYA Improved dry white BORDEAUX from between rivers Garonne and Dordogne (aka E-2-M). Blends of Sauv Bl, Sem and Muscadelle. Best Chx BONNET, Fontenille, Marjosse, Nardique-la-Gravière, Sainte-Marie, Tour de Mirambeau, Toutigeac.

Esmonin, Sylvie Burg ★★★ V. classy GEVREY-CHAMBERTIN, esp CLOS ST-JACQUES. Now darker and more concentrated.

L'Etoile Jura w dr sp (sw) ★★ Sub-region of the JURA known for stylish whites, inc VIN JAUNE, similar to CH-CHALON; gd sparkling.

Faiveley, J Burg ★★→★★★★ Family-owned growers and merchants at NUITS-ST-GEORGES. V'yds (109 ha) in CHAMBERTIN-CLOS DE BEZE, CHAMBOLLE-MUSIGNY, CORTON, MERCUREY, NUITS. Consistent high quality rather than charm.

Faller, Théo/Domaine Weinbach Al ★★→★★★★ Founded by Capuchin monks in 1612, now run by Colette Faller and 2 daughters. Outstanding wines now often drier, esp GRANDS CRUS SCHLOSSBERG (Ries), Furstentum (Gewurz). Wines of great character and elegance. Now biodynamic.

Faugères Midi r (p w) ★★ 01 02 **03 04** 05 06 07 Leading COTEAUX DU LANGUEDOC cru. Warming spicy reds from Syrah, Grenache, Carignan, plus Cinsault and Mourvèdre. AC in 1982 for red and 2004 for white, from Marsanne, Roussanne, and Rolle. Drink Doms Alquier, Estanilles, Ollier-Taillefer.

Fessy, Sylvain Beauj ★★ Dynamic BEAUJOLAIS merchant with wide range.

Fèvre, William Burg ★★★ CHABLIS grower with biggest GRAND CRU holding Dom de la Maladière (18 ha). Outstanding since bought by HENRIOT in 1998.

Fiefs Vendéens Lo r p w ★→★★★ Mainly DYA VDQS for easy-drinking wines from the Vendée close to Sables d'Orlonne. Range of varieties: CHARD, Chenin Bl, Sauv

FRANCE

Bl, Melon (whites), Grolleau (gris), Cab Fr, Cab Sauv, Gamay, Negrette, and Pinot N for reds and rosés. Top CUVÉES, esp from Michon/Dom St-Nicolas, are serious and ageworthy. Also Coirier, Ch Marie du Fou.

Fitou Midi r w ★★ 00 01 02 **03 04** 05 06 07 Powerful red, from hills south of Narbonne as well as coastal v'yds. THE MIDI'S oldest AC, for table wine, created in 1948, 11 months' barrel-ageing and benefits from bottle-age. Co-op at Tuchan a pacesetter among co-ops. Experiments with Mourvèdre. Gd estates include Ch de Nouvelles, Dom Bergé-Bertrand, Lérys, Rolland.

Fixin Burg r ★★★ 96' **98** 99' **01** 02' **03 04** 05' 06 07 Worthy and undervalued northern neighbour of GEVREY-CHAMBERTIN. Sometimes splendid reds. Best v'yds: Clos du Chapitre, Les Hervelets, Clos Napoléon. Growers include CLAIR, FAIVELEY, Gelin, Guyard.

Fleurie Beauj r ★★★ 05' **06 07** The best BEAUJOLAIS *cru* for immediate pleasure. Brilliantly perfumed, silky, racy strawberry fruit. Top sites include La Madone, Les Moriers. Look for Chapelle des Bois, Chignard, Depardon, Després, DUBOEUF, Ch de Fleurie, Métras, the co-op.

Floc de Gascogne SW r w Locally invented Gascon answer to PINEAU DES CHARENTES. Unfermented grape juice blended with ARMAGNAC.

Fronsac B'x r ★→★★★ 95 96 98 00' 01 03 05' 06 Hilly area west of ST-EMILION; one of the best-value reds in B'x. Top chx: DALEM, LA DAUPHINE, Fontenil, La Grave, Haut-Carles, Mayne-Vieil, Moulin-Haut-Laroque, Richelieu, LA RIVIÈRE, La Rousselle, Tour du Moulin, Les Trois Croix, La Vieille Cure, Villars. See also CANON-FRONSAC.

Frontignan Midi golden sw ★★ NV Small AC outside Sète for sweet fortified MUSCAT. Experiments with late-harvest unfortified wines. Quality steadily improving. Try Chx la Peyrade, de Stony.

Fronton SW r p ★★ 05' 06 (07) Red fruits, violets, liquorice earn the nickname "BEAUJOLAIS of Toulouse". Gd growers include Doms de Caze, Joliet, du Roc; Chx Baudare, Bellevue-la-Forêt, Boujac, Cahuzac, Cransac, Plaisance.

Gagnard, Jean-Noel Burg ★★★ At the top of the Gagnard clan. Beautifully expressive GRAND CRU, PREMIER CRU, and village wines in CHASSAGNE-MONTRACHET. Also cousins Blain-Gagnard, Fontaine-Gagnard.

Gaillac SW r p w dr sw sp ★→★★★ Mostly DYA except oaked reds **04 05 06**. Also sweet whites 01'**05 06** (07). ★★★ PLAGEOLES, Doms ★★ d'Arlus, Cailloutis, Causse-Marines, La Chanade, d'Escausses, Gineste, Larroque, Long Pech, Mayragues, de Ramaye, Rotier, Salmes, Sarrabelle, Ch Bourguet. Gd all-rounders ★★ Doms de Labarthe, Mas Pignou, La Vayssette.

Garage *Vins de garage* are (usually) BORDEAUX made on a v. small scale. Rigorous winemaking but a bottle costs much the same as a full service.

Gard, Vin de Pays du Languedoc ★ The Gard DÉPARTEMENT by mouth of the Rhône is important source of sound VDP production, inc Coteaux Flaviens, du Pont du Gard, SABLES DU GOLFE DU LION, Vaunage. Duché d'Uzès an aspiring AC.

Gauby, Domaine Gérard Midi r p w Pioneering ROUSSILLON producer. White VDP Côtes Catalanes Les Rocailles; La Coume Ginestre; red CÔTES DU ROUSSILLON-VILLAGES, Muntada, Les Calcinaires. First vintage 1985: "c'est moi, l'histoire" (of the estate). Also associated with VDP Le Soula.

Gers SW r w p ★ DYA VDP indistinguishable from nrby CÔTES DE GASCOGNE.

Gevrey-Chambertin Burg r ★★★ 90' 93 95 96' **98** 99' 00 01 02' **03** 04 05' 06 07 Village containing the great CHAMBERTIN, its GRAND CRU cousins and many other noble v'yds (*eg* PREMIERS CRUS Cazetiers, Combe aux Moines, Combottes, CLOS ST-JACQUES. Growers include Bachelet, L Boillot, BURGUET, Damoy, DROUHIN, DUGAT, ESMONIN, FAIVELEY, Geantet-Pansiot, Harmand-Geoffroy, JADOT, LEROY, MORTET, Rossignol-Trapet, ROTY, ROUSSEAU, SEÉRAFIN, TRAPET, Varoilles.

Gigondas S Rh r p ★★→★★★ 78' 89' 90' 95' 96 97 **98'** 99' 00' **01' 02 03'** 04' 05' **06'** 07 Robust neighbour to CHÂTEAUNEUF. Full-bodied, chewy, sometimes peppery, mostly Grenache. Genuine local punch. Try: Ch de Montmirail, St-Cosme, Clos du Joncuas, P Amadieu, Dom Bouïssière, Cassan, Cayron, Goubert, Gour de Chaulé, Grapillon d'Or, les Pallières, Piaugier, Raspail-Ay, Roubine, St-Gayan, Santa Duc, Tourelles, des Travers. Rosés often too heavy.

Ginestet Go-ahead BORDEAUX négociant. Quality controls for grape suppliers. Principal brands G de Ginestet, Marquis de Chasse, Mascaron.

Girardin, Vincent Burg r w ★★→★★★ Quality grower in SANTENAY, now dynamic merchant, specializing in CÔTE DE BEAUNE ACS. Inc Dom Henri Clerc in Puligny. Modern, oak and fruit style.

Givry Burg r (w) ★★ 03 **05'** 06 07 Underrated CÔTE CHALONNAISE village: light, tasty, typical Burgundy from eg, Joblot, LATOUR, Lumpp, Sarazin, THÉNARD.

Gorges et Côtes de Millau SW r p w ★ DYA Improving VDQS country wines: red best. Gd co-op at Aguessac. Intrepid private growers include ★★ Dom Du Vieux Noyer.

Gosset Old small CHAMPAGNE house at AŸ. Traditional full-bodied wine (esp Grand Millésime (**98 99** 00 02). Gosset Celebris (**98 99 00** 02) is finest CUVÉE.

Gouges, Henri Burg ★★★ Reinvigorated estate for rich, complex NUITS-ST-GEORGES with great ageing potential.

Grand Cru One of top Burgundy v'yds with its own AC. In ALSACE one of the 51 top v'yds covered by ALSACE GRAND CRU AC, but more vague elsewhere. In ST-EMILION, 60% of the production is covered by the ST-EMILION GRAND CRU AC.

Grande Champagne The AC of the best area of COGNAC. Nothing fizzy about it.

Grande Rue, La Burg r ★★★ 90' **93** 95 96' 97 99' 00 02' 03 04 05' 06 07 Narrow strip of VOSNE-ROMANÉE GRAND CRU (since 1991). MONOPOLE of Dom Lamarche now starting to make fine wines again.

Grands-Echézeaux Burg r ★★★★ 78' 88' 89' 90' **93** 95 96' 97 99' 00 02' 03 05' 06 07 Superlative 8.9-ha GRAND CRU next to CLOS DE VOUGEOT. Wines not weighty but aromatic. Viz: DRC, DROUHIN, ENGEL, GROS.

Grange des Pères, Domaine de la Midi r w VDP de l'HÉRAULT. Cult estate neighbouring MAS DE DAUMAS GASSAC, set up by Laurent Vaillé for first vintage 92. Red from Syrah, Mourvèdre, Cab Sauv; white Roussanne 80% plus Marsanne, Chard. Original wines; well worth seeking out.

Gratien, Alfred and **Gratien & Meyer** ★★→★★★ BRUT NV; BRUT 97' 98 00 02. Superb Prestige CUVÉE Paradis BRUT and Rosé (blend of fine yrs). Excellent quirky CHAMPAGNE house, now German owned. Fine, v. dry, lasting barrel-fermented wine incl The Wine Society's house CHAMPAGNE. Gratien & Meyer is counterpart at SAUMUR. (Gd CUVÉE Flamme.)

Graves B'x r w ★→★★ 00 01 04 05' Region south of BORDEAUX city with soft earthy red; dry minerally white more consistent. Top chx: ARCHAMBEAU, CHANTEGRIVE, CLOS FLORIDENE, Crabitey, l'Hospital, Léhoul, St-Robert CUVÉE Poncet Deville, Venus, Vieux Ch Gaubert, Villa Bel Air.

Graves de Vayres B'x r w ★ DYA Small AC within ENTRE-DEUX-MERS zone. Mostly consumed locally.

Grès de Montpellier Midi r p w Recently recognized sub-zone of AC COTEAUX DU LANGUEDOC covering v'yds in the hills behind Montpellier, inc St-Georges d'Orques, La Méjanelle, St-Christol, St-Drézery.

Griotte-Chambertin Burg r ★★★★ 88' 89' 90' **93** 95 96' 97 99' 00 02' 03 04 05' 06 07 Small GRAND CRU next to CHAMBERTIN. Less weight but brisk red fruit and ageing potential, at least from DUGAT, DROUHIN, PONSOT.

Grivot, Jean Burg ★★★→★★★★ Huge improvements at this VOSNE-ROMANÉE DOM in the past decade. Superb range topped by GRANDS CRUS CLOS DE VOUGET, ECHEZEAUX, RICHEBOURG.

Gros, Domaines Burg ★★★→★★★★ Excellent family of VIGNERONS in VOSNE-ROMANÉE comprising (at least) Doms Jean, Michel, Anne, Anne-François Gros, and Gros Frère & Soeur. Wines range from HAUTES CÔTES DE NUITS to RICHEBOURG.

Gros Plant du Pays Nantais Lo w ★ DYA Decidedly junior VDQS cousin of MUSCADET; sharper, lighter. From Gros Plant (Folle Blanche in COGNAC). Best great with oysters but v'yds diminishing rapidly. Try: Batard, Ch de la Preuille.

Guffens-Heynen Burg ★★★★ Belgian POUILLY-FUISSÉ grower. Tiny quantity, top quality. Heady Gamay. Also CÔTE D'OR wines (bought-in grapes) as VERGET.

Guigal, Ets E N Rh ★★→★★★★ High-profile grower: 31-ha CÔTE-RÔTIE, also CONDRIEU, HERMITAGE, ST-JOSEPH. Merchant: CONDRIEU, CÔTE-RÔTIE, HERMITAGE, South Rhône. Owns Dom de Bonserine, VIDAL-FLEURY. Top CÔTE-RÔTIE La Mouline, La Landonne, La Turque aged for 42 months in new oak, a break with local tradition to please (esp) American palates; all his reds are big volume. Standard wines: gd value, reliable, esp red, white CÔTES DU RHÔNE. Also full oaky CONDRIEU La Doriane, occasional sweet Luminescence.

Hautes-Côtes de Beaune/Nuits Burg r w ★★ r **03' 05' 06** 07 w **05' 06' 07** ACS for the villages in the hills behind the CÔTE DE BEAUNE. Attractive, lighter reds and whites for early drinking. Best: Cornu, Devevey, Duband, GROS, Jacob, Jayer-Gilles, Mazilly. Also large co-op nr BEAUNE.

Haut-Médoc B'x r ★★→★★★ **95 96** 98 00 01' **02** 03 04 05' Big AC. Source of gd-value, minerally, digestible wines. Some variation in soils and wines; sand and gravel in south, so finer; heavier clay and gravel farther north, so sturdier. Includes five classed growths (eg LA LAGUNE).

Haut-Montravel Dordogne w sw ★★★ **98' 00 01 03' 05'** 06 Locally much-appreciated sweet AC having a quiet revival. Best are Chx Moulin Caresse, Puy-Servain-Terrement, Roque-Peyre, Dom de Libarde.

Haut-Poitou Lo w r ★→★★ DYA VDQS Reds, whites, rosés, and sparkling from numerous grape varieties. Best are Sauv Bl and Gamay, esp from Cave du Haut Poitou (linked with DUBOEUF). Top individual producer: Ampelidae.

Heidsieck, Charles Brut Réserve NV; BRUT 96' **98** 02; Rosé **99'** Major Reims CHAMPAGNE house. *Excellent Mis en Cave Brut Reserve* (01 **03** 05) Outstanding Blanc des Millénaires (95' **96**) See also PIPER-HEIDSIECK.

Heidsieck Monopole Once illustrious CHAMPAGNE house. Fair quality.

Hengst Wintzenheim ALSACE GRAND CRU. Excels with top Gewurz from MANN; also Pinot-Auxerrois, Chasselas and Pinot N (not GRAND CRU).

Henriot BRUT Souverain NV; BLANCS DE BLANCS DE CHARD NV; Brut **95 96 98**; Brut Rosé **99** 02 Old family CHAMPAGNE house. Fine, fresh, creamy style. Outstanding prestige CUVÉE Les Enchanteleurs (88' 95). Also owns BOUCHARD PÈRE & FILS (since 1995) and FÈVRE.

Hérault Midi Biggest v'yd *département*: 94,800 ha and declining. Inc FAUGÈRES, St-Chinian, Pic St-Loup, GRÈS DE MONTPELLIER, PÉZENAS, TERRASSES DU LARZAC among AC COTEAUX DU LANGUEDOC. Source of VDPS de l'Hérault encompassing full quality spectrum, from pioneering to basic. Also VIN DE TABLE.

Hermitage N Rh r w ★★★→★★★★ 61' 66 **78'** 83' 85' 88 89' **90'** 91' 94 **95' 96** 97' **98' 99' 00 01'** 03' 04 05' 06' 07 Rich and profound, the truest example of Syrah from 133 ha on east bank of Rhône. Heady, abundant white (Marsanne, some Roussanne) best left for 6–7 yrs; top wines mature for 30 yrs. Best: Belle, CHAPOUTIER, CHAVE, Colombier, DELAS, Desmeure, Faurie, GUIGAL, Habrard (white), JABOULET, M Sorrel, Tardieu-Laurent. TAIN co-op gd (esp Gambert de Loche).

Hortus, Domaine de l' Midi r p w ★★ Pioneering producer of PIC ST-LOUP. Also VDP du Val de Montferrand. Elegant wines; reds Bergerie and oak-aged Grande Réserve.

Hospices de Beaune Burg Grand charity auction on third Sunday in Nov, recently revitalized by Christie's. Individuals can now buy as well as trade. Standards should be more consistent but excellent buys among BEAUNE CUVÉES or expensive GRANDS CRUS, *eg* CLOS DE LA ROCHE, CORTON (red), BATARD-M (white).

Hudelot-Noëllat, Alain Burg ★★★ Light but fine wines from VOUGEOT estate with bevy of GRANDS CRUS, inc CLOS DE VOUGEOT, ROMANÉE-ST-VIVANT, RICHEBOURG.

Huet Lo ★★★→★★★★ 88 89' 90' 95' 96' 97' 02' 03' 05' 06 (07) Biodynamic estate in VOUVRAY. Noël Pinguet, Gaston Huet's son-in-law, continues to run the estate. Three single v'yds: Le Haut Lieu, Le Mont, Clos du Bourg. All great agers: look for ancient vintages like 24, 47, and 59. Also PÉTILLANT.

Hugel & Fils ★★→★★★ Big ALSACE house, making superb late-harvest wines. 3 quality levels: Classic, Tradition, Jubilee. Opposed to GRAND CRU system.

Irancy Burg r (p) ★★ 05' 06 07 Formerly BOURGOGNE-Irancy. Light, tasty red made nr CHABLIS from Pinot N and local César. Best vintages mature well. Best: Colinot.

Irouléguy SW r p (w) ★★→★★★ 03 04 05' 06 Fashionable Basque wines made to go with rugby football and bull-fighting; less awesome than rival MADIRAN. Tannat-based reds now softened with Cab, to keep 5 yrs. Gd from Doms Abotia, Ameztia, Arretxea, Bordatho, Brana, Etchegaraya, Ilarria, Mouguy. Excellent co-op, esp white ★★★ Xuri d'Ansa.

Jaboulet Aîné, Paul N Rh Old family firm at TAIN, sold to Swiss investor early 2006. Once leading grower of HERMITAGE (esp La Chapelle ★★★), CORNAS St-Pierre, CROZES Thalabert (gd value), Roure; merchant of other Rhône wines, in particular CÔTES DU RHÔNE Parallèle 45, CÔTES DU VENTOUX, VACQUEYRAS. Modest whites, drink most young. Quality, prices and brand fever rising, and style more international.

Jacquart BRUT NV; BRUT Rosé NV (Carte Blanche and Cuvée Spéciale); BRUT 98 00 02 Co-op-based CHAMPAGNE marque; in quantity the sixth largest. Fair quality. Luxury brands: Cuvée Nominée Blanc 98 99 00 02 and Rosé 99 02. Fine Mosaïque BLANC DE BLANCS 00 02 and Rosé 99 02.

Jacquesson Bijou Dizy CHAMPAGNE house. Superb Avize GRAND CRU 96' 98; exquisite vintage wines: white (90 95 96'), new saignée rosé (00 02). Corne Bautray, Dizy 00 02, and *excellent NV cuvées* 728, 729, 730, 731, and 732.

Jadot, Louis Burg ★★→★★★★ High performance merchant house across the board with significant v'yd holdings in CÔTE D'OR and expanding fast in MÂCON and BEAUJOLAIS; esp MOULIN-À-VENT Ch des Jacques and Clos du Grand Carquelin. Mineral whites as gd as structured reds.

Jardin du Val de Loire Lo w r p DYA One of France's 4 regional VDP, formerly Jardin de la France. Wide range of single varietals inc CHARD, Cab Fr, Gamay, and Sauv Bl.

Jasnières Lo w dr (sw) ★★→★★★ 97 02 03 04 05 06 07 Singular, cellar-worthy VOUVRAY-like wine (Chenin Bl), both dry and off-dry from a tiny v'yd north of Tours. Esp Aubert la Chapelle, Chaussard/Le Briseau, Gigou, Nicolas/Dom de Belliviere, Robinot.

Jobard, François Burg ★★★ Small MEURSAULT DOM; classic, slow-evolving wines. Look out also for nephew Remi Jobard's more modern-style wines.

Joseph Perrier Cuvée Royale Brut NV; Cuvée Royale BLANC DE BLANCS NV; Cuvée Royale Rosé NV; Brut 96 98 99 Excellent smaller CHAMPAGNE house at Chalons with gd v'yds in Marne Valley. Supple fruity style; top prestige Cuvée Joséphine 95 96' 98.

Josmeyer ★★→★★★★ ALSACE house specializing in fine, elegant, long-lived organic wines in a dry style. Superb Ries GRAND CRU HENGST. Also v.gd wines from lesser varietals, esp Auxerrois.

Juliénas Beauj r ★★★ 05' 06 07 Leading *cru* of BEAUJOLAIS: vigorous, fruity wine to keep 2–3 yrs. Growers inc Chx du Bois de la Salle, des Capitans, de Juliénas, des Vignes; Doms Bottière, du Chapon, Monnet, Michel Tête, co-op.

Jurançon Pyr w sw dr ★→★★★ (sw) **95' 97' 00 01 02 03' 04' 05'** (dr) **03' 04' 05** 06 Success story from Pau in Pyrenean foothills. Production of dry and sweet wines increasing every yr. Growers: Doms Bellegarde, Bordenave, Capdevielle, Castéra, Cauhapé, Guirouilh, Jolys, Lapeyre, Larredya, Nigri, de Rousse, de Souch, Uroulat, Bellevue, Cabarrouy, Vignau-la-Juscle. Also ★★★★ DAGUENEAU's Les Jardins de Babylone, co-op esp gd for dry white.

Kaefferkopf Al w dr (sw) ★★★ Since 2006 the 51st GRAND CRU of ALSACE at Ammerschwihr. Permitted to make blends as well as varietal wines.

Kientzler, André ★★→★★★ Small, v. fine ALSACE grower at Ribeauvillé. V.gd Ries from GRANDS CRUS Osterberg and Geisberg and wonderfully aromatic Gewurz from GRAND CRU Kirchberg. Also v.gd Auxerrois and sweet wines.

Koehly, Christian ★★★ Front-rank ALSACE grower at Rodern. Top Ries from GRAND CRU Altenberg de Bergheim and v.gd PINOT GR GC Gloeckelberg. Exceptional late-picked wines esp in 02.

Kreydenweiss, Marc ★★→★★★ Fine ALSACE grower: 12 ha at Andlau, esp for PINOT GR (v.gd GRAND CRU Moenchberg), Pinot Bl, and Ries. Top wine: GRAND CRU Kastelberg (ages 20 yrs); also fine Auxerrois Kritt Klevner and gd VENDANGE TARDIVE. One of first in ALSACE to use new oak. Gd Ries/PINOT GR blend Clos du Val d'Eléon. Believer in terroir and biodynamic viticulture.

Krug Grande CUVÉE; Vintage **85 88 90 95 96**; Rosé; Clos du Mesnil (BLANC DE BLANCS) **81' 85 88 90 92 95 96**; Krug Collection **62 64 66 69 71 73 76 79 81** Small, supremely prestigious CHAMPAGNE house. Rich, nutty wines, oak fermented: long ageing, superlative quality. V. great vintage in 1996.

Kuentz-Bas ★→★★ Alsace Famous grower/merchant at Husseren-les Chx, esp PINOT GR, Gewurz. Gd VENDANGES TARDIVES. Owned by Caves J-B Adam.

Labouré-Roi Burg ★★→★★★ Reliable old-fashioned merchant with additional strings to its bow such as dynamic new-generation merchant Nicolas potel. Watch for further developments.

Ladoix Burg r (w) ★★ **99' 02' 03** 05' 06 Village at north end of CÔTE DE BEAUNE, inc some CORTON and CORTON-CHARLEMAGNE. Could deliver more. Best: Claude Chevalier, Michel Mallard.

Ladoucette, de L ★★→★★★ **02 03 04 05 06** (07) Largest individual producer of POUILLY-FUMÉ, based at Ch de Nozet. Luxury brand Baron de L can be wonderful. Also SANCERRE Comte Lafond, La Poussie; VOUVRAY Marc Brédif.

Lafarge, Michel Burg ★★★★ CÔTE DE BEAUNE 10-ha estate with excellent VOLNAYS, in particular Clos des Chênes and now Caillerets. New BEAUNE v'yds (red and white) on stream from 2005.

Lafon, Dom des Comtes Burg ★★★★ Top estate in MEURSAULT, LE MONTRACHET, VOLNAY. Glorious white; extraordinary dark red. Also in the Mâconnais.

Laguiche, Marquis de Burg ★★★★ Largest owner of LE MONTRACHET. Superb DROUHIN-made wines perhaps just below the summit.

Lalande de Pomerol B'x r ★★→★★★ **95 96 98 99 00' 01' 03** 04 05' Northerly neighbour of POMEROL. Wines similar, but less mellow. New investors and younger generation: improving quality. Top chx: des Annereaux, Bertineau-St-Vincent, La Croix-St-André, Les Cruzelles, La Fleur de Boüard, Garraud, Grand Ormeau, Les Hauts Conseillants, Jean de Gué, Perron (La Fleur), La Sergue, Siaurac, TOURNEFEUILLE.

Landron (Domaines) Lo dr w First-rate producer of organic MUSCADET DE SÈVRE-ET-MAINE with several CUVÉES, bottled by terroir, inc ultra-fresh, unfiltered Amphibolite and ageworthy Fief du Breil.

Langlois-Château Lo ★★→★★★ A top SAUMUR sparkling (CRÉMANT only) house – Bollinger owned. Also still wines, esp exceptional SAUMUR Bl VIEILLES VIGNES.

Languedoc Midi r p w General term for the MIDI and now AC enlarging COTEAUX DU LANGUEDOC to include MINERVOIS and CORBIÈRES, and also ROUSSILLON. Rules the same as for COTEAUX DU LANGUEDOC, with 5-yr transitional period for name-changing.

Lanson Père & Fils Black Label NV; Rosé NV; BRUT **98** 00 02 Important improving CHAMPAGNE house. Long-lived luxury brand: Noble CUVÉE BLANC DE BLANCS (**98 00** 02). Black Label improved by longer ageing.

Laroche ★★→★★★ Important grower and dynamic CHABLIS merchant, inc Doms La Jouchère, Laroche. Top wines: Blanchots (Réserve de l'Obédiencerie ★★★), CLOS VIEILLES VIGNES. Ambitious MIDI range, Dom La Chevalière.

Latour, Louis Burg ★★→★★★ Famous traditional family merchant making sound white wines from CÔTE D'OR v'yds, MÂCONNAIS and the ARDÈCHE (all CHARD) and less exciting reds (all Pinot) from CÔTE D'OR and Coteaux du Verdon. Merchant and grower with v'yds (49 ha) in BEAUNE, CORTON, etc. v.gd white: CHEVALIER-MONTRACHET Les Demoiselles, CORTON-CHARLEMAGNE, MONTRACHET. MONTAGNY and MÂCON-LUGNY gd value.

Latour de France Pyr r (w) ★→★★ 98 99 00 **01 02** 03 04 05 06 Theoretically superior village in CÔTES DE ROUSSILLON-VILLAGES. Esp Clos de l'Oum, Clos des Fées. Best wines often VDP des Côtes Catalanes.

Latricières-Chambertin Burg r ★★★ 88' 89' 90' 93 95 96' 97 99' 00 02' 03 05' 06 07 GRAND CRU neighbour of CHAMBERTIN (6.8 ha). Similar wine but lighter, *eg* from FAIVELEY, LEROY, Rossignol-Trapet, Trapet.

> **The French garden closes**
> VDP Jardin de la France has been renamed VDP du Val de Loire. Apparently very few people knew where the Jardin de la France was…

Laudun S Rh w r p ★→★★ 03 04 05' 06' 07 Village of CÔTES DU RHÔNE-VILLAGES (west bank). Mild reds, pretty rosés, stylish whites. Agreeable wines from Serre de Bernon co-op. Dom Pelaquié best, esp white. Also Ch Courac, Dom Duseigneur, Prieuré St-Pierre.

Laurent-Perrier BRUT NV; Rosé NV; BRUT **96** 98 99 00 02 Dynamic family-owned CHAMPAGNE house at Tours-sur-Marne. Fine minerally NV; excellent luxury brands: Grand Siècle La cuvée Lumière du Millésime (**90 96'**), CUVÉE Grand Siècle Alexandra BRUT Rosé (**96 99 02**). Also Ultra BRUT.

Lavilledieu-du-Temple SW r p w ★ DYA Face-lift at this lively co-op researching lost grape varieties of the southwest. Also independent Dom de Rouch.

Leflaive, Domaine Burg ★★★★ Among the best white Burgundy growers, at PULIGNY-MONTRACHET. Best v'yds: Bienvenues, CHEVALIER-MONTRACHET, Folatières, Pucelles, and (since 1991) Le Montrachet. Also MÂCON from 2004. Ever-finer wines on biodynamic principles.

Leflaive, Olivier Burg ★★→★★★ High-quality négociant at PULIGNY-MONTRACHET, cousin of the above. Reliable wines, mostly white, but drink them young.

Leroy, Domaine Burg ★★★★ DOM built around purchase of Noëllat in VOSNE-ROMANÉE in 1988 and Leroy family holdings (known as d'Auvenay). Extraordinary quality (and prices) from tiny biodynamic yields.

Leroy, Maison Burg ★★★★ Bugundy's ultimate négociant-éleveur at AUXEY-DURESSES. Sky-high standards and finest stocks of expensive old wine.

Liger-Belair Burg ★★★→★★★★ Two recently re-established DOMS of high quality. Vicomte Louis-Michel L-B makes brilliantly ethereal wines in VOSNE-ROMANÉE, while cousin Thibault makes plump red wines in NUITS-ST-GEORGES.

Limoux Pyr r w ★★ ac for sparkling BLANQUETTE DE LIMOUX or better CRÉMANT de Limoux, also unusual *Méthode Ancestrale*. Oak-aged CHARD for white Limoux AC. Red AC since 2003 based on Merlot, plus Syrah, Grenache, Cabernets,

Carignan. Pinot N in CRÉMANT and for VDP. Growers: Doms de Fourn, des Martinolles, Rives Blanques. Gd co-op: Sieur d'Arques.

Lirac S Rh r p w ★★ 98' 01' 03 04 05' 06' 07 Next to TAVEL. Approachable, sound-value red (can age 5+ yrs), recently firmer with raised use of Mourvèdre, more CHÂTEAUNEUF-DU-PAPE owners. More focus on red than rosé, esp Doms Devoy-Martine, Joncier, Lafond Roc-Epine, Lorentine, Maby (Fermade), André Méjan, de la Mordorée, Rocalière, R Sabon, F Zobel, Prieuré Sainte-Sixte, Chx d'Aquéria, de Bouchassy, Mont-Redon, St-Roch, Ségriès. Gd whites (5 yrs).

Listrac-Médoc B'x r ★★→★★★ 95 96 98 00' 01 03 04 05' Neighbour of MOULIS in the southern MÉDOC. Grown-up clarets with tannic grip. Now rounded out with more Merlot. Best chx: CLARKE, Ducluzeau, FONRÉAUD, FOURCAS-DUPRÉ, FOURCAS-HOSTEN, Mayne-Lalande.

Long-Depaquit Burg ★★★ BICHOT-owned CHABLIS DOM inc flagship GRAND CRU brand La Moutonne.

Lorentz, Gustave ★★ ALSACE grower and merchant at Bergheim. Esp Gewurz, Ries from GRAND CRUS Altenberg de Bergheim, Kanzlerberg. Also owns Jerome Lorentz. Equally gd for top estate and volume wines.

Loron & Fils ★→★★ Big-scale grower and merchant at Pontanevaux; specialist in BEAUJOLAIS and sound VINS DE TABLE.

Lot SW Increasingly important VDP often from CAHORS growers seeking wider market. Also from newly planted areas of surrounding countryside, *eg* ★★ Dom de Sully and Dom Belmon.

Loupiac B'x w sw ★★ 96 97' 98 99' 01' 02 03' 05' Across river Garonne from SAUTERNES. Lighter and fresher in style. Top Clos-Jean, LOUPIAC-GAUDIET, Mémoires, Noble, RICAUD, Les Roques.

Lussac-St-Emilion B'x r ★★ 95 98 00' 01 03 05' Lighter and more rustic than neighbouring ST-EMILION. Co-op the main producer. Top chx: Barbe Blanche, Bel Air, Bellevue, Courlat, la Grenière, Mayne-Blanc, Lussac, LYONNAT.

Macération carbonique Traditional fermentation technique: whole bunches of unbroken grapes in a closed vat. Fermentation induced inside each grape eventually bursts it, giving vivid, fruity, mild wine, not for ageing. Esp in BEAUJOLAIS; now much used in the MIDI and elsewhere, even CHÂTEAUNEUF.

Mâcon Burg r w (p) DYA Sound, usually unremarkable reds (Gamay best), tasty dry (CHARD) whites.

Mâcon-Lugny Burg (r) w sp ★★ 06' 07 Leading Mâconnais village. Try Les Charmes from excellent co-op or Genevrières from LATOUR.

Mâcon-Villages Burg w ★★→★★★ 05' 06' 07 Catch-all name for better Mâconnais wines, which may also use their own names, eg MÂCON-LUGNY, La Roche Vineuse, -Solutré, etc. More individual growers of quality emerging. Try Bonhomme, Guillot-Broux, LAFON, Maillet, Merlin, and co-ops at Lugny, Prissé, Viré.

Macvin Jura w sw ★★ AC for "traditional" MARC and grape-juice apéritif.

Madiran SW r ★★→★★★ 95' 98 00 01 02 03 04 05' (06) Tannat-based hearty red. New fruitier style from joint venture between Plaimont and Crouseilles co-ops;

Loire – Decision time for VDQS

With the Loire having a fair proportion of the remaining VDQS category, inc CHÂTEAUMEILLANT, COTEAUX D'ANCENIS, FIEFS VENDÉENS, GROS PLANT, HAUT-POITOU, and SAINT-POURÇAIN, decision time is fast arriving. The VDQS category will be phased out at the end of 2011. By the end of 2008 they will have to decide whether to apply for AC status or sell their wines as VDP. From 2009 to the end of 2011 only those that have applied either for AC or VDP status will be able to continue to sell their wines as VDQS.

but most need ageing. MONTUS and BOUSCASSÉ and best known, but Barrejat, Berthoumieu, Capmartin, Chapelle Lenclos, Clos Bastet, du Crampilh, Labranche-Laffont, Laffitte-Teston, Laplace, Fardet are worthy rivals.

Mähler-Besse B'x First-class Dutch négociant in BORDEAUX. Loads of old vintages. Has share in CH PALMER.

Mailly-Champagne Top CHAMPAGNE co-op. Luxury wine: CUVÉE des Echansons.

Maire, Henri ★→★★ The biggest grower/merchant of Jura wines, with half of the entire AC. Some top wines, many cheerfully commercial. Fun to visit.

Malepère Midi r ★ DYA Originally Côtes de la Malepère, now plain Malepère AC for reds that combine BORDEAUX and the MIDI. Fresh reds with a touch of rusticity provide original drinking.

Mann, Albert ★→★★★ Top growers of ALSACE at Wettolsheim: rich, elegant wines. v.gd Pinot Bl Auxerrois and Pinot N, and gd range of GRANDS CRUS wines from SCHLOSSBERG, HENGST, Furstentum, and Steingrubler.

Maranges Burg r (w) ★★ 99' 02' 03' 05' 06 07 CÔTE DE BEAUNE AC beyond SANTENAY (243 ha): one-third PREMIER CRU. Best from Contat-Grange, DROUHIN, GIRARDIN.

Marc Grape skins after pressing; also the strong-smelling brandy made from them (the equivalent of Italian grappa; see Italy).

Marcillac SW r p ★★ DYA Best 3 yrs or so after vintage. AC from 1990. Violet-hued with grassy red-fruit character. Doms du Cros, Costes, Mioula Vieux Porche and gd co-op.

Margaux B'x r ★★→★★★★ 89 90' 95 **96 98** 99 00' 01 02 **03** 04 05' 06 Largest communal AC in the southern MÉDOC, grouping v'yds from 5 villages, inc Margaux itself and Cantenac. Known for its elegant, fragrant style. Top chx: BRANE-CANTENAC, FERRIÈRE, MARGAUX, PALMER, RAUZAN-SÉGLA.

Marionnet, Henry Lo ★★→★★★ 04 05 06 07 Influential TOURAINE grower fascinated by grape varieties. Wines include Sauv Bls (top is Le M de Marionnet) and Gamay, esp the unsulphured Première Vendange, *Provignage (from ungrafted Romorantin vines planted 1850)*, and juicy Cot.

Marne & Champagne CHAMPAGNE house, and many smaller brands, inc BESSERAT DE BELLEFON. Alfred Rothschild brand v.gd CHARD-based wines.

Marque déposée Trademark.

Marsannay Burg p r (w) ★★ 02' 03 05' **06** 07 (rosé DYA) Easy-to-drink wines of all 3 colours, though little of note except reds from gifted producers such as Audoin, CHARLOPIN, CLAIR, Pataille and TRAPET.

Mas, Domaines Paul Midi r p w Big player in the MIDI; own estates and négociant wine, VDP and AC. Innovative marketing. Known for Arrogant Frog VDP range; also La Forge and Les Vignes de Nicole.

Mas de Daumas Gassac Midi r w p ★★★ 90 91 92 93 94 95 96 **97** 98 **99** 00 01 **02** 03 04 05 06 Pioneering VDP set an example of excellence in the MIDI, with Cab-based reds produced on apparently unique soil. Quality now rivalled by others, *eg* neighbouring GRANGE DES PÈRES. Wines include new super-CUVÉE Emile Peynaud, rosé Frizant, delicious, rich, fragrant white blend to drink at 2–3 yrs. VDP status. Intriguing sweet wine: Vin de Laurence (MUSCAT, Sercial).

Massif d'Uchaux S Rh r ★→★★ Southern Rhône Village since 2005, promising zone with gd growers, clear-cut, quite full wines. Note: Ch St Estève, Doms La Cabotte, Chapoton, Cros de la Mûre, de la Guicharde.

Maury Pyr r sw ★★ NV red VIN DOUX NATUREL from ROUSSILLON. From Grenache grown on island of schist amid limestone and clay. Recent improvement, esp at Mas Amiel. RANCIOS age beautifully. Also gd table wines.

Mazis- (or Mazy-) Chambertin Burg r ★★★ 88' 89' 90' **93** 95 96' 97 99' 00 02' 03 05' 06 07 GRAND CRU neighbour of CHAMBERTIN (12 ha); can be equally potent. Best from FAIVELEY, HOSPICES DE BEAUNE, LEROY, Maume, ROTY.

Mazoyères-Chambertin See CHARMES-CHAMBERTIN.

Médoc B'x r ★★ **98** 00' **02 03 04 05'** 06 AC for reds in the flatter, northern part of the MÉDOC peninsula. Gd if you're selective. Earthy, with Merlot adding flesh. Top chx: GREYSAC, LOUDENNE, Lousteauneuf, LES ORMES-SORBET, POTENSAC, Ramafort, Rollan-de-By (HAUT-CONDISSAS), LA TOUR-DE-BY, TOUR HAUT-CAUSSAN.

Meffre, Gabriel ★★ Biggest southern Rhône estate, based at GIGONDAS. Owns mid-range Dom Longue Toque. Recent progress, quality can vary. Also bottles, sells small CHÂTEAUNEUF DOMS. Decent northern Rhône Laurus (new oak) range, esp CROZES-HERMITAGE.

Mellot, Alphonse Lo r p w ★★→★★★ **02 03** 04 05 06 07 V. fine range of SANCERRE (white and esp reds) from leading grower: La Moussière (white and red), barrel-fermented CUVÉE Edmond, Génération XIX (red and white), Les Demoiselles and En Grands Champs (red). Since 2005 Les Penitents in Coteaux Charitois (VDP) CHARD and Pinot N.

Menetou-Salon Lo r p w ★★ **02 03 04 05 06 07** Revitalized AC (450 ha) just SW of SANCERRE – similar wines. Best producers: BOURGEOIS, Clement (Dom de Chatenoy), Jacolin, Henry Pellé, Jean-Max Roger, Teiller, Tour St-Martin.

Méo-Camuzet Burg ★★★★ V. fine DOM in CLOS DE VOUGEOT, NUITS-ST-GEORGES, RICHEBOURG, VOSNE-ROMANÉE. Jayer-inspired. Esp VOSNE-ROMANÉE Cros Parantoux. Now also some less expensive négociant CUVÉES.

Mercier & Cie, Champagne BRUT NV; BRUT Rosé NV; Demi-Sec BRUT One of biggest CHAMPAGNE houses at Epernay. Controlled by MOËT & CHANDON. Sold mainly in France. Full-bodied Pinot N-led CUVÉE Eugene Mercier.

Mercurey Burg (w) ★★→★★★ **99' 02' 03'** 05' 06 07 Leading red wine village of CÔTE CHALONNAISE. Gd middle-rank Burgundy, include improving whites. Try Ch de Chamirey, FAIVELEY, M Juillot, Lorenzon, Raquillet, de Suremain.

Mesnil-sur-Oger, Le Champ ★★★★ One of the top Côte des Blancs villages. Structured CHARD for v. long ageing.

Méthode champenoise Traditional method of putting bubbles into CHAMPAGNE by refermenting wine in its bottle. Makes outside CHAMPAGNE region must use terms "classic method" or "*méthode traditionnelle*" outside region.

Méthode traditionnelle See entry above.

Meursault Burg w (r) ★★★→★★★★ **99' 00' 01 02' 04** 05' 06' 07 CÔTE DE BEAUNE village with some of world's greatest whites: savoury, dry, nutty, mellow. Best v'yds: Charmes, Genevrières, Perrières. Also: Goutte d'Or, Meursault-Blagny, Poruzots, Narvaux, Tesson, Tillets. Producers include: AMPEAU, J-M BOILLOT, M BOUZEREAU, V BOUZEREAU, Boyer-Martenot, CH DE MEURSAULT, COCHE-DURY, Ente, Fichet, Grivault, *P Javillier*, JOBARD, LAFON, LATOUR, O LEFLAIVE, LEROY, Matrot, Mikulski, P MOREY, G ROULOT. See also BLAGNY.

Michel, Louis Burg ★★★ CHABLIS DOM noted for pure wines made exclusively in stainless steel. Perhaps not as dynamic as previously.

Microbullage Tiny quantities of oxygen are injected into wine to avoid racking, stimulate aeration, and accelerate maturity.

Midi Broad term covering Languedoc, Roussillon, and even Provence. A melting-pot; quality improves with every vintage. One of France's most exciting and challenging wine regions. ACS can be intriguing blends; VDP, esp D'OC, are often varietals. Brilliant promise, rewarding drinking.

Minervois Midi r (p w) br sw ★→★★ **00 01 02 03 04** 05' 06 07 Hilly AC region; gd; lively reds, esp Chx Bonhomme, Coupe-Roses, la Grave, Oupia, St Jacques d'Albas, La Tour Boisée, Villerembert-Julien, Clos Centeilles Ste Eulalie, Faiteau; co-ops La Livinière, de Peyriac, Pouzols. See ST-JEAN DE MINERVOIS.

Minervois-La Livinière Midi r (p w) ★→★★ Quality village (see last entry), only sub-appellation or cru in Minervois. Best growers: Abbaye de Tholomies, Borie de Maurel, Combe Blanche, Ch de Gourgazaud, Clos Centeilles, Laville-Bertrou, Doms Maris, Ste-Eulalie, Co-op La Livinière, Vipur.

Mis en bouteille au château/domaine Bottled at the CH, property or estate. NB *dans nos caves* (in our cellars) or *dans la région de production* (in the area of production) are often used but mean LITTLE.

Moët & Chandon By far the largest CHAMPAGNE house and enlightened leader of the community's v'yd research and development. Now owns 1,000 ha often in the best sites. Improved BRUT NV, recent fine run of BRUT Impérial vintages (**98 99 00 02** 04). Impressive CUVÉE DOM PERIGNON. Interesting GRANDS CRUS bottlings Aÿ, Chouilly, Sillery. Branches across Europe and New World.

Moillard Burg ★★→★★★ Big family firm in NUITS-ST-GEORGES, making full range, inc dark and v. tasty wines.

Mommessin, J ★→★★ BOISSET-owned BEAUJOLAIS and MÂCON merchant, better noted for reds than whites. Family still own CLOS DE TART in MOREY-ST-DENIS.

Monbazillac Dordogne w sw ★★→★★★★ 95' 97' 98' 00 01' 02 03' 05' (06) Rising standards today make this sweet BERGERAC a serious rival to SAUTERNES. Top producers: L'Ancienne Cure, Clos des Verdots, Chx de Belingard-Chayne, Le Fagé, Les Hauts de Caillavel, Poulvère, Theulet, Tirecul-la-Gravière, and La Grande Maison. Also the co-op's Ch de Monbazillac.

Mondeuse Savoie r ★★ DYA SAVOIE red grape. Potentially gd deep-coloured wine. Possibly same as Italy's Refosco. Don't miss a chance, *eg* G Berlioz.

Monopole A v'yd that is under single ownership.

Montagne-St-Emilion B'x r ★★ 95 98 00' 01 03 05' Largest and possibly best satellite of ST-EMILION. Similar style of wine. Top chx: Calon, Faizeau, Maison Blanche, Montaiguillon, Roudier, Teyssier, *Vieux Ch St-André*.

Montagny Burg w ★★ 05' 06' 07 CÔTE CHALONNAISE village. Between MÂCON and MEURSAULT, both geographically and gastronomically. Top producers: Aladame, J-M BOILLOT, Cave de Buxy, Michel, Ch de la Saule.

Monthélie Burg r (w) ★★→★★★ 99' 02' 03' 04 05' 06 Little-known VOLNAY neighbour, sometimes almost equal. Fragrant red, esp BOUCHARD PÈRE & FILS, COCHE-DURY, DROUHIN, Garaudet, LAFON, Ch de Monthelie (Suremain).

de Montille Burg ★★★ Hubert de M made long-lived VOLNAY, POMMARD. Son Etienne has expanded DOMAINE with purchases in BEAUNE, NUITS-ST-GEORGES, and potentially outstanding VOSNE-ROMANÉE Malconsorts. Etienne also runs Ch de Puligny and is involved with sister Alix in négociant venture Deux Montille (white wines).

Montlouis Lo w dr sw (sp) ★★→★★★ 89' 90' 95' 96' 97' 02 03' 05' 07 Directly across the river from VOUVRAY. Makes similar, though leaner, sweet or long-lived dry whites from Chenin Bl, also sparkling. Top growers include Alex-Mathur, Berger, Chatenay, CHIDAINE, Cossais, Damien Delecheneau/la Grange Tiphaine, Deletang, Moyer, Frantz Saumon, TAILLE-AUX-LOUPS.

Montrachet Burg w ★★★★ 1904 35 47 49 59 64 66 71 73 78 79 82 85' 86 89' 90 92' 93 95 96' 97 **99** 00' 01 02' 03 04 05' 06 07 8.01 ha GRAND CRU v'yd in both PULIGNY- and CHASSAGNE-MONTRACHET. Potentially the greatest white Burgundy: strong, perfumed, intense, dry yet luscious. Top wines: LAFON, LAGUICHE (DROUHIN), LEFLAIVE, Ramonet, ROMANÉE-CONTI. THÉNARD disappoints.

Montravel Dordogne ★★ p dr w DYA (r) 02' 04 05' (06) Now AC for all colours, adjoins and similar to BERGERAC. Gd examples from Doms De Bloy, de Krevel, chx Jonc Blanc, Laulerie, Masburel, Masmontet, Moulin-Caresse. Separate ACS for semi-sweet CÔTES DE MONTRAVEl, sweet HAUT-MONTRAVEL.

Morey, Domaines Burg ★★★ Various family members in CHASSAGNE-MONTRACHET, esp Bernard, inc BÂTARD-MONTRACHET. Also Pierre M in MEURSAULT.

Morey-St-Denis Burg r (w) ★★★ 90' 93 95 96' 97 98 99' 00 02' 03 05' 06 07 Small village with 4 GRANDS CRUS between GEVREY-CHAMBERTIN and CHAMBOLLE-MUSIGNY. Glorious wine often overlooked. Inc: Amiot, CLOS DES LAMBRAYS, DUJAC, H Lignier, Perrot-Minot, PONSOT, ROUMIER, ROUSSEAU, Taupenot-Merme.

Morgon Beauj r ★★★ **99'** 01 03 **05'** 06 07 Firm, tannic BEAUJOLAIS *cru*, esp from Côte de Py sub-district. Becomes meaty with age. Try, Desvignes, Foillard, Gaget, Lafont, Lapierre, Ch de Pizay.

Mortet, Denis ★★★ Ultra-perfectionist Denis made exceptionally powerful, deep-coloured wines in GEVREY-CHAMBERTIN until his untimely death in early 2006. Son Arnaud looks for more elegance. Try new, successful FIXIN.

Moueix, J-P et Cie B'x Legendary proprietor and merchant of ST-EMILION and POMEROL. Company now run by son Christian. Chx include LA FLEUR-PÉTRUS, HOSANNA, MAGDELAINE, PÉTRUS, TROTANOY. Also in California: see Dominus.

Moulin-à-Vent Beauj r ★★★ **96'** 99 00 01 03 **05'** 06 07 Biggest and potentially best wine of BEAUJOLAIS. Can be powerful, meaty, long-lived; can even taste like fine Rhône or Burgundy. Many gd growers, esp Ch du Moulin-à-Vent, Ch des Jacques, Dom des Hospices, JADOT, Janodet, Merlin.

Moulis B'x r ★★→★★★ 95 96 98 00' 01 02 03 04 05' 06 Tiny inland AC in the S MÉDOC, with many honest, gd-value wines. Top chx: Biston-Brillette, Branas Grand Poujeaux, BRILLETTE, CHASSE-SPLEEN, MAUCAILLOU, POUJEAUX.

Mouton Cadet Biggest-selling red BORDEAUX brand. Revamped and fruitier since 2004. Also white, rosé, GRAVES AC and MÉDOC AC.

Mugneret/Mugneret-Gibourg Burg ★★★ V.gd reds from top CÔTE DE NUITS sites.

Mugnier, J-F Burg ★★★→★★★★ Ch de Chambolle estate with first-class delicate CHAMBOLLE-MUSIGNY Les Amoureuses and MUSIGNY. Also BONNES-MARES. From 2004 has reclaimed family's NUITS-ST-GEORGES Clos de la Maréchale.

Mumm, G H & Cie Cordon Rouge NV; Mumm de Cramant NV; Cordon Rouge 98 00 02 04; Rosé NV Major CHAMPAGNE grower/merchant. Owned by Pernod-Ricard. Improved quality esp in US relaunched prestige Cuvée R Lalou 98'.

Muré, Clos St-Landelin ★★→★★★ One of ALSACE's great names with 16 ha of GRAND CRU Vorbourg, esp fine in full-bodied Ries and PINOT GR. The Pinot N Cuvée "V" (04 05), truly ripe and vinous, is the region's best.

Muscadet Lo w ★→★★★ DYA (but see below) Popular, gd-value, often delicious bone-dry wine from nr Nantes. Should never be sharp, but should always be refreshing. Perfect with fish and seafood. Best are from zonal ACS: MUSCADET-COTEAUX DE LA LOIRE, MUSCADET CÔTES DE GRAND LIEU, MUSCADET DE SÈVRE-ET-MAINE. Choose a SUR LIE.

Muscadet-Coteaux de la Loire Lo w ★→★★ **02 03** 04 05 06 07 Small MUSCADET zone E of Nantes (best SUR LIE). Esp Guindon, Les Vignerons de la Noëlle.

Muscadet Côtes de Grand Lieu ★→★★ **02 03** 04 05 06 07 Most recent (1995) of MUSCADET's zonal ACS and the closest to the Atlantic coast. Best are SUR LIE from, *eg* Bâtard,Choblet (Dom des Herbauges), Malidain.

Muscadet de Sèvre-et-Maine ★→★★★ **01 02 03** 04 05 06 07 Largest and best of MUSCADET's delimited zones. A safe bet. Top Guy Bossard (DOM DE L'ECU), Bernard Chereau, Bruno Cormerai, Michel Delhommeau, Douillard, Dom de la Haute Fevrie, Luneau-Papin, Louis Métaireau, Sauvion. Wines from these properties can age beautifully – try 86 or 89.

Muscat Distinctively perfumed and usually sweet wine from the grape of same name, often fortified as VIN DOUX NATUREL. Dry table wine in ALSACE.

Muscat de Lunel Midi golden sw ★★ NV Small AC based on MUSCAT, usually fortified, luscious, and sweet. Some experimental late-harvest wines. Look for Dom de Bellevue, Ch du Grès St Paul.

Muscat de Mireval Midi sw ★★ NV Tiny fortified MUSCAT AC nr Montpellier. Dom La Capelle the best.

Muscat de Rivesaltes Midi golden sw ★★ NV Sweet MUSCAT AC wine nr Perpignan. Popularity waning; best from Cazes Frères, Ch de Jau.

Musigny Burg r (w) ★★★★ 85' 88' 89' 90' 91 93 95 96' 97 98 99' 00 01 02' 03 04 05' 06 07 GRAND CRU in CHAMBOLLE-MUSIGNY (10 ha). Can be the most beautiful, if not the most powerful, of all red Burgundies. Best growers: DROUHIN, JADOT, LEROY, MUGNIER, PRIEUR, ROUMIER, DE VOGÜÉ, VOUGERAIE.

Napoléon Brand name of Prieur family's Vertus CHAMPAGNE house now owned by British wine merchant. Seek out mature vintages 95 96.

Nature "Natural" or "unprocessed" – esp of still CHAMPAGNE.

Négociant-éleveur Merchant who "brings up" (ie matures) the wine.

Nuits-St-Georges Burg r ★★→★★★★ 90' 91 93 95 96' 97 98 99' 00 01 02' 03 04 05' 06 Important wine town: wines of all qualities, typically sturdy, tannic, need time. Best v'yds: Les Cailles, Clos de la Maréchale, Clos des Corvées, Les Pruliers, Les St-Georges, Vaucrains. Many merchants and growers include: Ambroise, L'ARLOT, J Chauvenet, R CHEVILLON, CONFURON, FAIVELEY, GOUGES, GRIVOT, Lechéneaut, LEROY, LIGER-BELAIR, Machard de Gramont, Michelot, MUGNIER, RION.

d'Oc (Vin de Pays d'Oc) Midi r p w ★→★★ Vast regional VDP for LANGUEDOC and ROUSSILLON. Esp single-grape wines and VDP PRIMEURS. Tremendous recent technical advances. Main producers: Jeanjean, VAL D'ORBIEU, Doms Paul Mas, village co-ops, plus numerous small individual growers.

Orléans Lo r p w ★ DYA Recent (2006) AC for whites (chiefly CHARD), gris, rosé, and reds (Pinot N and particularly Meunier) from small area around Orléans.

Orléans-Clery Lo r ★ DYA Another AC for simple Cab Fr-based reds.

Pacherenc du Vic-Bilh SW Fr w dr sw ★★→★★★★ MADIRAN's answer to JURANÇON. Dry (DYA) and (better) sweet (age up to 5 yrs for oaked versions). For growers see MADIRAN.

Paillard, Bruno BRUT Première CUVÉE NV; Rosé Première CUVÉE; CHARD Réserve Privé, BRUT 96' 98. New Vintage BLANC DE BLANCS 98. Superb Nec Plus Ultra prestige CUVÉE (95 96). Youngest grand CHAMPAGNE house. Fine quality. Refined, v. dry style best expressed in BLANC DE BLANCS Réserve Privée and prestige Nec Plus Ultra (90') only now fully mature. Controls a CHAMPAGNE group and owns Ch de Sarrin, Prov.

Palette Prov r p w ★★ Tiny AC nr Aix-en-Provence. Full reds, fragrant rosés, and intriguing whites from CH SIMONE, the only producer of note.

Pasquier-Desvignes ★→★★ V. old firm of BEAUJOLAIS merchants nr BROUILLY.

Patriarche Burg ★→★★★ One of the bigger Burgundy merchants. Cellars in BEAUNE; also owns CH DE MEURSAULT (61 ha), sparkling Kriter, etc.

Patrimonio Corsica r w p ★★→★★★★ Wide range from limestone hills in north CORSICA. Some of island's best. Characterful reds from Nielluccio, intriguing whites from Vermentino. Top growers: Antoine Arena, Clos de Bernardi, Gentile, Yves Leccia, Pastricciola.

Pauillac B'x r ★★★→★★★★ 88' 89' 90' 94 95' 96' 98 99 00' 01 02 03' 04' 05' 06 Communal AC in the MÉDOC with three first-growths (LAFITE, LATOUR, MOUTON). Famous for its powerful, long-lived wines. Other fine chx include GRAND-PUY-LACOSTE, LYNCH-BAGES, PICHON-LONGUEVILLE, and PICHON-LALANDE.

Pécharmant Dordogne r ★★→★★★★ 01' 02 04 05' (06) Inner appellation of BERGERAC making sturdier wines from an iron-based terroir. Best: Dom du Haut-Pécharmant, Les Chemins d'Orient, Clos des Côtes, Ch d'Elle, Renaudie, Terre Vieille, de Tilleraie, *de Tiregand*. New World style from Dom des Costes. Also gd BERGERAC co-op at Le Feix.

Pernand-Vergelesses Burg r w ★★★ 99' 02' 03' 04 05' 06 07 Village next to ALOXE-CORTON containing part of the great CORTON-CHARLEMAGNE and CORTON v'yds. One other top v'yd: Ile des Vergelesses. Growers: CHANDON DE BRIAILLES, CHANSON, Delarche, Dubreuil-Fontaine, JADOT, LATOUR, Rapet, Rollin.

Perrier-Jouët BRUT NV; Blason de France NV; Blason de France Rosé NV; Brut 98 Excellent CHAMPAGNE house at Epernay, first to make dry CHAMPAGNE, and once the smartest name of all; now best for vintage wines. De luxe

FRANCE

Belle Epoque **95' 96** 98 02 (Rosé **95 97** 99 02) in a painted bottle.

Pessac-Léognan B'x r w ★★★→★★★★ 90' **95 96 98 00'** 01 **02** 04 05' 06 AC created in 1987 for the best part of N GRAVES, inc all the GRANDS CRUS, HAUT-BRION, LA MISSION-HAUT-BRION, PAPE-CLÉMENT, DOM DE CHEVALIER, etc. Plump minerally reds and B'x's finest dry whites. Some want Pessac to go it alone.

Petit Chablis Burg w ★ DYA Fresh and easy lighter CHABLIS from outlying v'yds. La Chablisienne co-op is gd.

Pézenas Midi r p w COTEAUX DU LANGUEDOC sub-region from v'yds around Molière's town. Prieuré de St-Jean-de-Bébian, Dom du Conte des Floris, des Aurelles, Stella Nova.

Pfaffenheim ★→★★ Respectable ALSACE co-op. Style can be a little rustic.

Pfersigberg Eguisheim ALSACE GRAND CRU with two parcels; v. aromatic wines. Gewurz does v. well. Ries, esp Paul Ginglinger, Bruno Sorg, and Léon Beyer Comtes d'Eguisheim. Top grower: KUENTZ-BAS.

Philipponnat NV; Rosé NV; Réserve Spéciale **98 99 00** 02; Clos des Goisses **96 98 99** 02 Small CHAMPAGNE house known for well-structured wines and now owned by BOIZEL Chanoine group. Remarkable single-v'yd Clos des Goisses and charming rosé. Also Le Reflet BRUT NV.

Picpoul de Pinet Midi w ★→★★ COTEAUX DU LANGUEDOC CRU and aspiring AC, exclusively from the old variety Picpoul. Best growers: AC St Martin de la Garrigue, Félines-Jourdan, co-ops Pomérols and Pinet. Perfect with an oyster.

Pic St-Loup Midi r (p) **96 97 98 99** 00 01 **02** 03 04 05 06 Notable COTEAUX DU LANGUEDOC *cru*, anticipating own AC. Growers: Cazeneuve, Clos Marie, de Lancyre, Lascaux, Mas Bruguière, Mas Mortiès, Dom de l'Hortus, Valflaunès.

Pineau des Charentes Strong, sweet apéritif: white grape juice and COGNAC.

Pinon, François Lo w sw sp ★★★ **89 90** 95 96 **97** 02 **03** 04 05 06 Eco-friendly producer of v. pure VOUVRAY in all its expressions, inc a v.gd PÉTILLANT.

Pinot Gris ALSACE grape formerly called Tokay d'Alsace: full, rich white, a subtler match for foie gras than usual MOELLEUX.

Piper-Heidsieck CHAMPAGNE-makers of old repute at Reims. Improved BRUT NV and fruit-driven BRUT Rosé Sauvage; BRUT **00** 02 04. Excellent CUVÉE. Sublime DEMI-SEC, rich yet balanced. Old Piper CUVÉE Rare (viz. **79'**) still lovely.

Pithon, Jo (Domaine) Lo w r sw ★★→★★★★ 95 **97** 02 **03** 04 05 06 Best known for v. fine mineral ANJOU Blanc, SAVENNIÈRES and concentrated COTEAUX DU LAYON. Also substantial reds.

Plageoles, Robert Though partially retired, still the arch-priest of GAILLAC and defender of the lost grape varieties of the Tarn. Amazingly eccentric wines include a rare, big, dry white from the Verdanel grape, a sherry-like VIN JAUNE, an ultra-sweet dessert wine (★★★★ Vin d'Autan) from Ondenc. Also a pure Mauzac sparkler called Mauzac Nature.

Plan de Dieu S Rh r ★→★★ New southern Rhône village since 2005, with robust wines from stony, windswept plain. Look for: Ch La Courançonne, Doms Durieu, Espigouette, Vieux-Chêne.

Pol Roger BRUT White Foil now renamed BRUT Réserve NV; BRUT **96' 98** 99; Rosé 99; Blanc de CHARD **98'** ★★★★. Supreme family-owned CHAMPAGNE house at Epernay, now with vines in AVIZE joining 85 ha of family v'yds. *V. fine floral NV*, new Pure BRUT (Zéro Dosage) and exquisite Blanc de CHARD (**98'**). Sumptuous CUVÉE: Sir Winston Churchill (**90 96 98** 02).

Pomerol B'x r ★★★→★★★★★ 88 89' 90' **94** 95 96 **98' 00'** 01 04 05' 06' Next village to ST-EMILION but no limestone; only clay, gravel, and sand. Famed for its Merlot-dominated, full, rich, unctuous style. Top chx: LA CONSEILLANTE, L'ÉGLISE-CLINET, L'ÉVANGILE, LAFLEUR, LA FLEUR-PÉTRUS, PÉTRUS, LE PIN, TROTANOY, VIEUX-CH-CERTAN.

Pommard Burg r ★★★ **88' 89' 90' 95** 96' **97 98** 99' 01 02' 03 04 05' 06 07 The biggest CÔTE D'OR village. Few superlative wines, but many potent, tannic ones to age 10+ yrs. Best v'yds: Epenots, HOSPICES DE BEAUNE CUVÉES, Rugiens. Growers include COMTE ARMAND, Billard-Gonnet, J-M BOILLOT, COURCEL, Gaunoux, LEROY, Machard de Gramont, DE MONTILLE, Ch de Pommard, Pothier-Rieusset.

Pommery BRUT NV; Rosé NV; BRUT **82' 98 00** 02 Historic CHAMPAGNE house; brand now owned by VRANKEN. Outstanding CUVÉE Louise (**89' 90'** 96).

Ponsot Burg ★★→★★★★ Controversial MOREY-ST-DENIS estate. Idiosyncratic high-quality GRANDS CRUS, inc CHAMBERTIN, CHAPELLE-CHAMBERTIN, CLOS DE LA ROCHE, CLOS ST-DENIS.

Portes de la Mediterranée New regional VDP from S Rhône/PROVENCE. Simple reds; whites more interesting, inc Viognier. Renamed VDP de Mediterranée.

Potel, Nicolas Burg ★★→★★★ Négociant for delicious, well-priced red wines from BOURGOGNE rouge to CHAMBERTIN and now a matching range of classy whites. His own DOM in BEAUNE will come on stream from 2007.

Pouilly-Fuissé Burg w ★★→★★★ 99' 00' 02' 03 04 05' **06'** 07 The best white of the MÂCON region, potent and dense. At its best (eg CH FUISSÉ VIEILLES VIGNES) outstanding, but usually overpriced compared with CHABLIS. Top growers: de Beauregard, Bret Bros, Ferret, Luquet, Merlin, Ch des Rontets, Saumaize, VERGET, Vincent.

Pouilly-Fumé Lo w ★→★★★★ **02' 03 04 05'** 06 07 Frequently disappointing white from upper Loire, nr SANCERRE. Best fruity and full flavoured. Must be Sauv Bl. Top CUVÉES can improve 5–6 yrs. Growers include BOURGEOIS, Cailbourdin, Chatelain, DAGUENEAU, Serge Dagueneau & Filles, Ch de Favray, Edmond and André Figeat, Masson-Blondelet, Redde, Ch de Tracy.

Pouilly-Loché Burg w ★★ 05' 06' 07 POUILLY-FUISSÉ's neighbour. Similar, cheaper; scarce. Can be sold as POUILLY-VINZELLES.

Pouilly-sur-Loire Lo w ★ DYA Neutral non-aromatic wine from the same v'yds as POUILLY-FUMÉ but different grape – Chasselas. Ever-diminishing – now less than 40 ha. Best from Serge Dagueneau & Filles, Landrat-Guyollot.

Pouilly-Vinzelles Burg w ★★ 02' 04 05' 06' 07 Superior neighbour to POUILLY-LOCHÉ. Best producers Bret Bros, Valette.

Premier Cru (1er Cru) First-growth in B'x; second rank of v'yds (after GRAND CRU) in Burgundy.

Premières Côtes de Blaye B'x r w ★→★★ 00' 01 03 04 05' (06) Mainly red AC east of the Gironde. Varied but improved quality. Top reds labelled BLAYE as of 2000. More changes from 07 vintage. See Côtes de Bordeaux box p.76. Best chx: Bel Air la Royère, Gigault CUVÉE Viva, Haut-Bertinerie, Haut-Colombier, Haut-Grelot, Haut-Sociando, Jonqueyres, Mondésir-Gazin, Montfollet, Roland la Garde, Segonzac, des Tourtes.

Premières Côtes de Bordeaux B'x r w (p) dr sw ★→★★ **98 00' 01 03** 05' (06) Long, narrow, hilly zone on the right bank of the Garonne opposite the GRAVES. Renamed Côtes de Bordeaux: Cadillac from 07 vintage. See box p. 76. Medium-bodied, fresh reds. Quality varied. Best chx: Carignan, Carsin, Chelivette, Grand-Mouëys, Lamothe de Haux, Lezongars, Mont-Pérat, Plaisance, Puy Bardens, Reynon, Suau all worth trying.

Prieur, Domaine Jacques Burg ★★★ MEURSAULT estate with amazing GRAND CRU holdings from MONTRACHET to CHAMBERTIN. Part owned by RODET, which has improved quality, but not yet to ★★★★ standard.

Primeur "Early" wine for refreshment and uplift; esp from BEAUJOLAIS; VDP too. Wine sold en primeur is still in barrel for delivery when bottled.

To decipher codes, please refer to "Key to symbols" on the front flap of jacket, or "How to use this book" on p.10.

Propriétaire récoltant Owner-manager.

Provence See CÔTES DE PROVENCE, CASSIS, BANDOL, PALETTE, COTEAUX DES BAUX-EN-PROVENCE, BOUCHES-DU-RHÔNE, COTEAUX D'AIX-EN-PROVENCE, COTEAUX VAROIS-EN-PROVENCE, PORTES DE LA MEDITERRANÉE.

Puisseguin St-Emilion B'x r ★★ **98 00' 01 03 05'** Satellite neighbour of ST-EMILION; wines firm and solid in style. Top chx: Bel Air, Branda, Durand-Laplagne, Fongaban, Laurets, Soleil. Also Roc de Puisseguin from co-op.

Puligny-Montrachet Burg w (r) ★★★→★★★★ **92' 95 00 01 02' 04** 05' 06' 07 Smaller neighbour of CHASSAGNE-MONTRACHET: potentially even finer, more vital and complex wine (apparent finesse can be result of over-production). V'yds: BÂTARD-MONTRACHET, Bienvenues-BÂTARD-MONTRACHET, Caillerets, CHEVALIER-MONTRACHET, Clavoillon, Les Combettes, MONTRACHET, Pucelles. Producers: AMPEAU, J-M BOILLOT, BOUCHARD PÈRE & FILS, CARILLON, Chavy, DROUHIN, JADOT, LATOUR, DOM LEFLAIVE, O LEFLAIVE, Pernot, SAUZET.

Puyméras S Rh r w ★ New, modest southern Rhône Village since 2005, based on sound co-operative, higher v'yds, and also decent whites. Look for: Cave La Comtadine, Puy de Maupas.

Pyrénées-Atlantiques SW DYA VDP for wines not qualifying for local ACS MADIRAN, PACHERENC DU VIC BILH, TURSAN, or JURANÇON.

Quarts de Chaume Lo w SW ★★★→★★★★ 89' 90' 95' 96' 97' 02 03 04 05' 06 07 Miniscule, celebrated hillside close to Layon devoted to Chenin Bl. Almost everlasting, potent, golden wine with strong mineral undertow. Esp BAUMARD, Branchereau, Yves Guegniard, CH PIERRE-BISE, PITHON.

Quatourze Midi r w (p) ★ 01 02 03 04 05 06 07 Tiny cru of COTEAUX DE LANGUEDOC by Narbonne. Reputation maintained almost single-handedly by Ch Notre Dame du Quatourze.

Quincy Lo w ★→★★ DYA Small area (224 ha) west of Bourges in Cher Valley. SANCERRE-style Sauv Bl. Worth trying. Growers: Mardon, Portier, Jacques Rouzé, Silice de Quincy, Tatin-Wilk (Doms Ballandors, Tremblay).

Rancio The most characteristic and delicious style of VIN DOUX NATUREL, reminiscent of tawny port, in BANYULS, MAURY, RIVESALTES, RASTEAU, wood-aged and exposed to oxygen and heat. Same flavour is a fault in table wine.

Rangen Most southerly GRAND CRU of ALSACE at Thann. 18.8 ha, extremely steep slopes, volcanic soils. Top wines: powerful Ries and PINOT GR from ZIND-HUMBRECHT and SCHOFFIT.

Rasteau S Rh r br sw (p w dr) ★★ 03 04' 05' 06 07 One of best two COTES DU RHÔNE villages – robust, quite feisty, esp Beaurenard, Cave des Vignerons, Ch du Trignon, Doms Didier Charavin, Girasols, Gourt de Mautens, Rabasse-Charavin, Soumade, St-Gayan, Perrin (gd white, too). Grenache dessert wine improving with more attention.

Ratafia de Champagne Sweet apéritif made in CHAMPAGNE of 67% grape juice and 33% brandy. Not unlike PINEAU DES CHARENTES.

Regnié Beauj r ★★ 05' 06 07 Former BEAUJOLAIS VILLAGES turned cru. Sandy soil makes for lighter wines than other crus. Try Aucoeur, Dom des Braves, DUBOEUF, Laforest, Pechard.

Reine Pédauque, La Burg ★ Long-established grower-merchant at ALOXE-CORTON. V'yds in ALOXE-CORTON, SAVIGNY, etc, and CÔTES DU RHÔNE. Owned by PIERRE ANDRÉ. Quality not impressive.

Reuilly Lo w (r p) ★→★★ 05' 06 07 Small AC (186 ha) west of Bourges for Sauv Bl whites plus rosés and VIN GRIS made from Pinot N and/or PINOT GR as well as reds from Pinot N. Best: Claude Lafond, Dom de Reuilly.

Ribonnet, Domaine de SW ★★ Just south of Toulouse, Christian Gerber makes pioneering range of VDP (red, rosé, white) from grapes often not seen in the southwest, eg Marsanne and Roussanne.

Riceys, Rosé des Champ p ★★★ DYA Minute AC in AUBE for a notable Pinot N rosé. Principal producers: A Bonnet, Jacques Defrance.

Richeaume, Domaine Prov r ★★ Gd Cab Sauv/Syrah. Organic; a model.

Richebourg Burg r ★★★★ 78' 85' 88' 89' 90' 91 93' 95 96' 97 98 99' 00 01 02' 03 05' 06 07 VOSNE-ROMANÉE GRAND CRU. Powerful, perfumed, expensive wine, among Burgundy's best. Growers: DRC, GRIVOT, GROS, LEROY, LIGER-BELAIR, MÉO-CAMUZET.

Rimage Modern trend for a vintage VIN DOUX NATUREL. For early drinking.

Rion, Patrice Burg ★★★ Premeaux-based DOMAINE with excellent NUITS-ST-GEORGES holdings, esp Clos des Argillières, Clos St Marc, and CHAMBOLLE. Also Doms Daniel R, Bernard & Armelle Raine.

Rivesaltes Midi r w br dr sw ★★ NV Fortified wine made nr Perpignan. A struggling but vibrant tradition. Top producers worth seeking out: Doms Cazes, Sarda-Malet, Vaquer, des Schistes, Ch de Jau. The best are delicious, esp old RANCIOS. See MUSCAT DE RIVESALTES.

Roche-aux-Moines, La Lo w sw ★★→★★★ 89' 90' 95' 96' 97' 99 02 03 04 05' 06 07 A 24-ha cru of SAVENNIÈRES, ANJOU. Potentially powerful, intensely mineral wine; age or drink "on the fruit". Growers include: COULÉE DE SERRANT, CH PIERRE-BISE.

Rodet, Antonin Burg ★★→★★★ Quality merchant based in MERCUREY with individual estates Chx de Chamirey, de Mercey, de Rully and Doms de la Ferté, Perdrix, and now Dufouleur. Part-owner of Dom PRIEUR in MEURSAULT. Also interests in LANGUEDOC and LIMOUX.

> **Burgundy négociants**
> The trend towards DOM bottling has caused the old-established merchant houses to raise their game, while those who cannot buy vineyards have to buy in grapes instead. Leading players in various categories include:
> **Classic Houses:** BOUCHARD PÈRE, DROUHIN, JADOT, LATOUR. Also CHAMPY, CHANSON. **Commercial success stories:** BICHOT, BOISSET, GIRARDIN, Picard.
> **White specialists:** Bret Bros, Deux Montille,
> O LEFLAIVE, Ricjkaert, VERGET. **Outsiders (talent from elsewhere):**
> Dominique Laurent, Lucien Lemoine, Alex Gambal. **Doms with négociant activities:** Ambroise, J-M BOILLOT, H BOILLOT, DUJAC, MEO-CAMUZET, Merlin.

Roederer, Louis BRUT Premier NV; Rich NV; Brut **97 99 00 02**; BLANC DE BLANCS **97 99 00** 02; BRUT Rosé **99** 02. Top-drawer family-owned CHAMPAGNE house with enviable 143 ha estate of top v'yds. Magnificent Cristal (can be greatest of all prestige CUVÉES) and Cristal Rosé (**90' 95 96** 99). Also owns DEUTZ, DELAS, CH DE PEZ, CH PICHON-LALANDE. See also California.

Rolland, Michel Ubiquitous and fashionable consultant winemaker and Merlot specialist working in B'x and worldwide, favouring super-ripe flavours.

Rolly Gassmann ★★ Distinguished ALSACE grower at Rorschwihr, esp for Auxerrois and MUSCAT from Moenchreben v'yds. Off-dry house style culminates in great rich Gewurz CUVÉE Yves (**00** 02').

Romanée, La Burg r ★★★★ 96' **97 98** 99' **00** 01 02' 03 05' 06 07 GRAND CRU in VOSNE-ROMANÉE (0.8 ha). MONOPOLE of LIGER-BELAIR. Now made with flair by Vicomte Louis-Michel L-B.

Romanée-Conti Burg r ★★★★ 57 59 62 64 66' 71 76 78' 80 85' 88' 89' 90' 93' 95 96' 97 98 99' 00 01 02' 03 04 05' 06 07 A 1.7-ha MONOPOLE GRAND CRU in VOSNE-ROMANÉE; 450 cases per annum. The most celebrated and expensive red wine in the world, with reserves of flavour beyond imagination.

NB Vintages in colour are those you should choose first for drinking in 2009.

FRANCE

Romanée-Conti, Domaine de la (DRC) ★★★★ Grandest estate in Burgundy. Includes the whole of ROMANÉE-CONTI and LA TÂCHE, major parts of ECHÉZEAUX, GRANDS-ECHÉZEAUX, RICHEBOURG, ROMANÉE-ST-VIVANT, and a tiny part of MONTRACHET. Crown-jewel prices (if you can buy them at all). Keep top vintages for decades.

Romanée-St-Vivant Burg r ★★★★ 78 88' 89' 90' 93 95 96' 97 99' 00 02' 03 04 05' 06 07 GRAND CRU in VOSNE-ROMANÉE (9.3 ha). Similar to ROMANÉE-CONTI but lighter and less sumptuous. Growers: CATHIARD, DRC, DROUHIN, HUDELOT-NOËLLAT, LEROY.

Rosacker ALSACE GRAND CRU of 26 ha at Hunawihr. Produces best Ries in ALSACE (see CLOS STE-HUNE, SIPP-MACK).

Rosé d'Anjou Lo p ★ DYA Pale, slightly sweet rosé enjoying a comeback in the hands of young *vignerons*; look for Mark Angeli, Clau de Nell, Doms de la Bergerie, les Grandes Vignes, des Sablonnettes.

Rosé de Loire Lo p ★→★★ DYA The driest of ANJOU's rosés. AC covers SAUMUR and TOURAINE too. Best: Bablut, Ogereau, CH PIERRE-BISE, Richou.

Rosette Dordogne w s/sw ★★ DYA Pocket-sized AC for charming off-dry apéritif wines, *eg* Clos Romain, Ch Puypezat-Rosette, Doms de la Cardinolle, de Coutancie.

Rostaing, René N Rh ★★★ CÔTE-RÔTIE 8-ha estate with top-grade plots, 3 wines esp refined Côte Blonde (5% Viognier) and La Landonne (darker fruits, 15–20 yrs). Accomplished style, turns on discreet finesse; some new oak. Also elegant CONDRIEU and LANGUEDOC.

Roty, Joseph Burg ★★★ Small grower of classic GEVREY-CHAMBERTIN, esp CHARMES-CHAMBERTIN and MAZIS-CHAMBERTIN. Long-lived wines.

Rouget, Emmanuel Burg ★★★★ Inheritor of the legendary estate of Henri Jayer in ECHÉZEAUX, NUITS-ST-GEORGES and VOSNE-ROMANÉE. Top wine: VOSNE-ROMANÉE-Cros Parantoux.

Roulot, Domaine G Burg ★★★ Outstanding MEURSAULT producer with a fine range of v'yd sites, esp Tessons Clos de Mon Plaisir and PREMIERS CRUS, *eg* Bouchères, Perrières.

Roumier, Georges Burg ★★★★ Reference DOM for BONNES-MARES and other brilliant CHAMBOLLE wines in capable hands of Christophe R. Long-lived wines but still attractive early.

Rousseau, Domaine Armand Burg ★★★★ Grower famous for CHAMBERTIN, etc, of highest quality. Wines are intense (not deep-coloured), long-lived, mostly GRAND CRU. Brilliant CLOS ST JACQUES.

Roussette de Savoie w ★★ DYA Tastiest fresh white from south of Lake Geneva.

Roussillon Midi Top region for VDNS (eg MAURY, RIVESALTES, BANYULS). Lighter MUSCATS and younger vintage wines are taking over from darker, heavier wines. See CÔTES DU ROUSSILLON (and CÔTES DU ROUSSILLON-VILLAGES), COLLIOURE, for table wines and VDP Côtes Catalanes. Now included in AC LANGUEDOC.

Ruchottes-Chambertin Burg r ★★★★ 88' 89' 90' 91 93' 95 96' 97 98 99' 00 01 02' 03 04 05' 06 07 GRAND CRU neighbour of CHAMBERTIN. Similar splendid, lasting wine of great finesse. Top growers: LEROY, MUGNERET, ROUMIER, ROUSSEAU.

Ruinart "R" de Ruinart BRUT NV; Ruinart Rosé NV; "R" de Ruinart BRUT (98 99). Oldest CHAMPAGNE house, owned by MOËT-Hennessy. Already high standards should go higher still with talented new cellar master (since 2007). Prestige Dom Ruinart is one of the 2 best vintage BLANC DE BLANCS in CHAMPAGNE (viz. 88' 95 96). DR Rosé also v. special (90').

Rully Burg r w (sp) ★★ (r) 05' 06 07 (w) 05' 06 07 CÔTE CHALONNAISE village. Still white and red are light but tasty. Gd value, esp white. Growers include Delorme, Devevey, FAIVELEY, Dom de la Folie, Jacqueson, A RODET.

Sables du Golfe du Lion Midi p r w ★ DYA vDP from Mediterranean sand-dunes: esp Gris de Gris from Carignan, Grenache, Cinsault. Small estates beginning to compete with giant Listel.

Sablet S Rh r w (p) ★★ **04' 05' 06' 07** Attractive, improving CÔTES DU RHÔNE village, often cleanly fruited reds, esp Doms de Boissan, Cabasse, Espiers, Les Goubert, Piaugier, de Verquière. Gd full whites – apéritif or food.

St-Amour Beauj r ★★ **06 07** Northernmost *cru* of BEAUJOLAIS: light, fruity, irresistible (esp on 14 Feb). Growers to try: Janin, Patissier, Revillon.

St-Aubin Burg w r ★★★ (w) **02' 04 05 06 07** (r) **02' 03 05' 06 07** Understated neighbour of CHASSAGNE-MONTRACHET. Several *Premiers Crus: light, firm, quite stylish wines; fair prices*. Top growers: J C Bachelet, JADOT, Lamy, Lamy-Pillot, H Prudhon, Ramonet, Thomas.

St-Bris Burg w ★ DYA Neighbour to CHABLIS. Unique AC for Sauv Bl in Burgundy. Fresh, lively, worth keeping from J-H Goisot.

St-Chinian Midi r ★→★★ **01 02 03 04** 05 06 07 Hilly area of growing reputation in COTEAUX DU LANGUEDOC. AC since 1982 for red, and for white since 2005, plus new *crus* Berlou and Roquebrun. Tasty southern reds, based on Syrah, Grenache, Carignan. Gd co-ops Berlou, Roquebrun; Ch de Viranel, Doms Canet Valette, Madura, Rimbaud, Navarre.

St-Emilion B'x r ★★→★★★★ 89' 90' **94** 95 96 **98' 00'** 01 03 04 05' Large, Merlot-dominated district on Bordeaux's Right Bank. ST-EMILION GRAND CRU CLASSÉ AC the top designation. Warm, full, rounded style; some firm and long-lived. Top chx: ANGÉLUS, AUSONE, CANON, CHEVAL BLANC, FIGEAC, MAGDELAINE, PAVIE. Also *garagistes* LA MONDOTTE and VALANDRAUD. Gd co-op.

St-Estèphe B'x r ★★→★★★★ 88' **89'** 90' **93 94** 95' **96' 98** 99 **00'** 01 02 03 04 05' 06 Most northerly communal AC in the MÉDOC. Solid, structured wines. Top chx: COS D'ESTOURNEL, MONTROSE, CALON-SÉGUR. Also many gd unclassified estates, *eg.* HAUT-MARBUZET, ORMES-DE-PEZ, DE PEZ, PHÉLAN-SÉGUR.

St-Gall BRUT NV; Extra BRUT NV; BRUT BLANC DE BLANCS NV; BRUT Rosé NV; BRUT BLANC DE BLANCS 99 **00** 02; Cuvée Orpale BLANC DE BLANCS **95 96' 98**. Brand name used by Union-Champagne: top CHAMPAGNE growers' co-op at AVIZE. Fine value Pierre Vaudon NV and excellent BLANCS DE BLANCS Orpale (**95'** 96).

St-Georges-St-Emilion B'x r ★★ **98 00'** 01 03 **05'** Tiny ST-EMILION satellite. Usually gd quality. Best chx: Calon, Macquin-St-G, Tour du Pas-St-Georges, Vieux Montaiguillon.

St-Gervais S Rh r (w, p) ★ **05' 06'** 07 west bank Rhône village. Sound co-op, star is excellent, long-lived Dom Ste-Anne red (marked Mourvèdre flavours); white includes Viognier. Also Dom Clavel.

St-Jean de Minervois Min w sw ★★ Fine sweet VDN MUSCAT. Much recent improvement, esp from Dom de Barroubio, Michel Sigé, village co-op.

St-Joseph N Rh r w ★★ 90' 98' **99'** 01' **03' 05' 06' 07** AC running length of N Rhône (65 km/40 miles). Delicious, red-fruited wines around Tournon in S; elsewhere quality mixed. More structure, better wines than CROZES-HERMITAGE, esp from CHAPOUTIER (Les Granits), Gonon, B Gripa, GUIGAL (Lieu-dit St-Joseph); also CHAVE, Chêne, Chèze, Courbis, Coursodon, Cuilleron, DELAS, B Faurie, P Faury, Gaillard, JABOULET, Monier, Paret, A Perret, Sept Lunes, F Villard. Gd, wholesome white (mainly Marsanne, drink with food), esp Chapoutier Granits, Cuilleron, Gonon, B Gripa, Faury, A Perret.

St-Julien B'x r ★★★→★★★★ 88' **89'** 90' 93 94 95 **96' 98** 99 **00'** 01 **02 03** 04 05' 06 Mid-MÉDOC communal AC with 11 classified (1855) estates, inc 3 LÉOVILLES, BEYCHEVELLE, DUCRU-BEAUCAILLOU, GRUAUD-LAROSE, etc. The epitome of harmonious, fragrant and savoury red wine.

St-Nicolas-de-Bourgueil Lo r p ★→★★★ 89' 90' 95 **96' 97** 02' **03** 04 05' 06 07 Companion appellation to BOURGUEIL producing identical wines from Cab Fr.

Ranges from easy drinking to ageworthy. More tannic and less supple than Chinon. Try: Yannick Amirault, Cognard, Lorieux, **Frédéric Mabileau**, Taluau-Foltzenlogel.

St-Péray N Rh w sp ★★ 01' 03' **04' 05' 06'** 07 White Rhône (mainly Marsanne) from hillside v'yds. Some sparkling – a curiosity worth trying. Still white gd flinty style, can age. Top names: S Chaboud, CHAPOUTIER, CLAPE, Colombo, B Gripa, J-L Thiers, TAIN co-op, du Tunnel, Voge. JABOULET now planting here.

St-Pourçain Central Fr r p w ★→★★ DYA VDQS Agreeable quaffers from the Allier. Light red and rosé from Gamay and/or Pinot N, white from Tressalier and/or CHARD (v. popular), or Sauv Bl. A strong candidate for AC status. Growers: *Barbara*, Dom de Bellevue, Pétillat, Ray, and gd co-op (Vignerons de St-Pourçain) with range of styles, inc drink-me-up CUVÉE Ficelle.

St-Romain Burg w r ★★ (w) 05' 06' 07 Overlooked village just behind CÔTE DE BEAUNE. Value, esp for firm, fresh whites. Reds have a clean cut. Top growers: De Chassorney, FÈVRE, Jean Germain, Gras, LEROY.

St-Sardos SW VDQS nr Montauban r p w DYA Worthy co-op has only one competitor, its founder Dom de la Tucayne.

St-Véran Burg w ★★ 05' 06' 07 AC loosely surrounding POUILLY-FUISSÉ with variable results depending on soil and producer. DUBOEUF, Deux Roches, Poncetys for value, Cordier, Corsin, Merlin for top quality.

Ste-Croix-du-Mont B'x w sw ★★ 97' 98' 99' 01' 02 03' 05' Sweet white AC facing SAUTERNES across the river Garonne. Well worth trying, esp Chx Crabitan-Bellevue, Loubens, du Mont, Pavillon, la Rame.

Ste-Victoire Prov r p New sub-zone of CÔTES DE PROVENCE from the southern slopes of the Montagne Ste-Victoire. Dramatic scenery as well as gd wine.

Salon ★★★★ The original BLANC DE BLANCS CHAMPAGNE, from Le Mesnil in the Côte des Blancs. Awesome reputation for long-lived wines – in truth sometimes inconsistent but on song recently, viz. **90 96'**.

Sancerre Lo w (r p) ★→★★★★ Still benchmark for Sauv Bl, often more aromatic and vibrant than POUILLY-FUMÉ, its neighbour across the Loire. Top wines can age 5+ yrs. Top growers now making remarkable reds (Pinot N). Sancerre rosé rarely worth the money. Occasional sweet VENDANGES TARDIVES (VDT). Best include: Gérard Boulay, BOURGEOIS, Cotat, François Crochet, Lucien Crochet, André Dezat, ALPHONSE MELLOT, Mollet, Vincent Pinard, Jean-Max Roger, Vacheron, André Vatan.

Santenay Burg r (w) ★★★ 99' 02' 03 05' **06** 07 Sturdy reds from village S of CHASSAGNE-MONTRACHET. Best v'yds: La Comme, Les Gravières, Clos de Tavannes. Top growers: GIRARDIN, Lequin-Roussot, Muzard. Watch Dom Jessiaume

Saumur Lo r w p sp ★→★★★ **02' 03** 04 05' 06 07 Umbrella AC for light whites plus more serious, particularly from SAUMUR-CHAMPIGNY zone; easy-drinking reds; pleasant rosés, pungent CRÉMANT and SAUMUR MOUSSEUX. Producers include: BOUVET-LADUBAY, Antoine Foucault, CLOS ROUGEARD, René-Hugues Gay, Guiberteau, Doms DES CHAMPS FLEURIS/Retiveau-Retif, Paleine, St-Just; CH DE VILLENEUVE Cave des Vignerons de Saumur.

Saumur-Champigny Lo r ★★→★★★ 95 96' 97 **02' 03** 04 05' **06 07** Popular 9-commune AC for quality Cab Fr, ageing nicely in gd vintages. Look for Chx de Targé, DE VILLENEUVE; Clos Cristal, CLOS ROUGEARD; Doms CHAMPS FLEURIS, de la Cune, Filliatreau, Legrand, Nerleux, Roches Neuves, St-Just, Val Brun; Cave des Vignerons de Saumur-St-Cyr-en-Bourg; Antoine Sanzay.

Saussignac Dordogne w sw ★★→★★★ 01' 03' 04 05 (06) Similar to but with a touch more acidity than MONBAZILLAC. Fully sweet since 2004.Best: Dom de Richard, Chx Le Chabrier, Court-les-Mûts, Lestevénie, La Maurigne, Les Miaudoux, Le Payral, Le Tap, Tourmentine, and Clos d'Yvigne.

Sauternes B'x w sw ★★→★★★★ 83' 86' 88' 89' 90' 95 96 97' 98 99' 01' 02 03' 05'
District of 5 villages (inc BARSAC) that make France's best sweet wine, strong
(14%+ alcohol), luscious and golden, demanding to be aged 10 yrs. Still
underpriced compared to red equivalents. Top CHX: D'YQUEM, GUIRAUD,
LAFAURIE-PEYRAGUEY, RIEUSSEC, SUDUIRAUT, LA TOUR BLANCHE, etc. Dry wines
cannot be sold as Sauternes. 05S are exceptional, must have.

Sauzet, Etienne Burg ★★★ Potentially outstanding PULIGNY grower and merchant.
Does not always age well. Look out for Combettes, BÂTARD-MONTRACHET.

Savennières Lo w dr sw ★★★→★★★★ 89' 90' 93 95 96' 97' 99 02' 03 04 05' 06
(07) Small ANJOU district for pungent, extremely mineral, long-lived whites.
BAUMARD, Closel, Ch de Coulaine (see CH PIERRE-BISE), Ch d'Epiré, Yves
Guigniard, Dom Laureau du Clos Frémur, Eric Morgat, Vincent Ogereau, Tijou.
Top sites: COULÉE DE SERRANT, ROCHE-AUX-MOINES, Clos du Papillon.

Savigny-lès-Beaune Burg r (w) ★★★ 96' 99' 02' 03 04 05' 06 07 Important village
next to BEAUNE; similar mid-weight wines, often deliciously lively, fruity. Top
v'yds: Dominode, Guettes, Lavières, Marconnets, Vergelesses; growers
include: BIZE, Camus, CHANDON DE BRIAILLES, CLAIR, Ecard, Girard, LEROY,
Pavelot, TOLLOT-BEAUT.

Savoie E France r w sp ★★ DYA Alpine area with light, dry wines like some Swiss
or minor Loires. APREMONT, CRÉPY, and SEYSSEL are best-known whites;
ROUSSETTE is more interesting. Also gd MONDEUSE red.

Schlossberg ALSACE GRAND CRU of 80 ha at Kientzheim famed since 15th century.
Glorious Ries from Faller/Dom Weinbach. Also v.gd Gewurz and PINOT GR.

Schlumberger, Domaines ★→★★★ Vast and top-quality ALSACE DOM at Guebwiller
owning approx 1% of all ALSACE v'yds. Holdings in GRANDS CRUS Kitterlé,
Kessler, Saering, and Spiegel. Range includes rare Ries, signature CUVÉE
Ernest, and, latest addition, PINOT GR GRAND CRU Kessler.

Schlumberger, Robert de Lo SAUMUR sparkling; by Austrian method. Delicate.

Schoenenbourg V. rich successful Riquewihr GRAND CRU (ALSACE): PINOT GR, Ries,
v. fine VENDANGE TARDIVE and SÉLECTION DES GRAINS NOBLES. Esp from DEISS and
DOPFF AU MOULIN. Also v.gd MUSCAT.

Schoffit, Domaine ★★→★★★ Colmar ALSACE house with GRAND CRU RANGEN PINOT
GR, Gewurz of top quality. Chasselas is unusual everyday delight.

Schröder & Schÿler Old BORDEAUX merchant, owner of CH KIRWAN.

Sciacarello Indigenous Corsican grape variety, for red and rosé.

Sec Literally means dry, though CHAMPAGNE so called is medium-sweet (and
better at breakfast, teatime, and weddings than BRUT).

Séguret S Rh r w ★★ 04 05' 07 Delightful picture-postcard hillside village nr
GIGONDAS. Peppery, quite full, direct reds; clear-fruited whites. Esp Ch La
Courançonne, Doms de Cabasse, Le Camassot, J David,Garancière,
Mourchon, Pourra, Soleil Romain.

Sélection des Grains Nobles Term coined by HUGEL for ALSACE equivalent to
German Beerenauslese, and since 1984 subject to v. strict regulations. GRAINS
NOBLES are individual grapes with "noble rot".

Sérafin Burg ★★★ Christian S has gained a cult following for his intense GEVREY-
CHAMBERTIN VIEILLES VIGNES and CHARMES-CHAMBERTIN GRAND CRU.

Seyssel Savoie w sp ★★ NV Delicate white, pleasant sparkling. *eg* Corbonod.

Sichel & Co One of BORDEAUX's most respected merchant houses, run by 5
brothers: interests in CH D'ANGLUDET and PALMER, in CORBIÈRES, and as
BORDEAUX merchants (Sirius a top brand).

Signargues, Plateau de ★→★★★ New CÔTES DU RHÔNE village in 4 areas between
Avignon and Nîmes. Light, fruity reds with some tannic kick. Note: Ch Haut-
Musiel, Dom Valériane.

Sipp, Jean & Louis ★★ ALSACE growers in Ribeauvillé (Louis also a négociant).

Both make v.gd Ries GRAND CRU Kirchberg. Jean's is youthful elegance; Louis's is firmer when mature. V.gd Gewurz from Louis, esp GRAND CRU Osterberg.

Sipp-Mack ★★→★★★ Excellent ALSACE dom of 20 ha at Hunnawihr. Great Ries from GRANDS CRUS ROSACKER and Osterberg; also v.gd PINOT GR.

Sorg, Bruno ★★ →★★★ First-class small ALSACE grower at Eguisheim for GRANDS CRUS Florimont (Ries) and PFERSIGBERG (MUSCAT). Also v.gd Auxerrois.

Sur Lie "On the lees". MUSCADET is often bottled straight from the vat, for maximum zest and character.

Tâche, La Burg r ★★★★ 64 66 71 78' **85' 88'** 89' **90'** 93' 95 96'97 98 99' 00 01 02' 03 04 05' 06 07 A 6-ha (1,500-case) GRAND CRU of VOSNE-ROMANÉE. One of best v'yds on earth: big perfumed, luxurious wine. See ROMANÉE-CONTI.

Taille-aux-Loups, Domaine de la Lo w sw sp ★★★ Jacky Blot, former wine broker, is now one of the Loire's leading producers – with CUVÉES of barrel-fermented MONTLOUIS and VOUVRAY, from dry to lusciously sweet; excellent Triple Zero Montlouis PÉTILLANT and fine reds from Domaine de la Butte in Bourgueil.

Tain, Cave Coopérative de 290 members in north Rhône ACS; owns one-quarter of HERMITAGE. Red Hermitage improved since 91 esp top Gambert de Loche; modern range, esp CROZES. Sound mainly Marsanne whites. Gd value.

Taittinger BRUT NV; Rosé NV; Brut 00 02; Collection Brut **90 95 96.** Once-fashionable Reims CHAMPAGNE grower and merchant sold to Crédit Agricole group 2006. Distinctive silky, flowery touch, though not always consistent, often noticeably dosed. Excellent luxury brand: Comtes de Champagne BLANC DE BLANCS (**96' 98**), Comtes de Champagne Rosé (**96** 02), also gd rich Pinot Prestige Rosé NV. New CUVÉES Nocturne and Prélude. (See also California: Dom Carneros.)

Tavel Rh p ★★ DYA France's most famous, though not best, rosé: strong, v. full, and dry – needs food. Best growers: Ch d'Aquéria, Dom Corne-Loup, GUIGAL, Lafond, Lafond Roc-Epine, Maby, Dom de la Mordorée, Prieuré de Montézargues, Ch de Trinquevedel.

Tempier, Domaine Prov r w p ★★★★ The pioneering grower of BANDOL. Wines of considerable longevity. Quality now challenged by several others.

Terrasses du Larzac Midi r w p Part of AC COTEAUX DU LANGUEDOC. Wild, hilly region inc Montpeyroux, St Saturnin, and villages nr the Lac du Salagou.

Terroirs Landais Gascony r p w ★ VDP, an extension in the *département* of Landes of the CÔTES DE GASCOGNE, a name that many growers prefer to use. Dom de Laballe is most-seen example.

Thénard, Domaine Burg Major grower of the GIVRY appellation, but best known for his substantial portion (1.6 ha) of LE MONTRACHET. Should be better.

Thevenet, Jean Burg ★★★ Mâconnais purveyor of rich, semi-botrytized wines, *eg* CUVÉE Levroutée at Dom de la Bongran. Also Dom Emilian Gillet.

Thézac-Perricard SW r p ★★ 05' 06 VDP Over the boundary of LOT from CAHORS. Same grapes but lighter style. Independent Domaine de Lancement even better than gd co-op.

Thiénot, Alain Broker-turned-merchant; dynamic force for gd in CHAMPAGNE. Ever-improving quality across the range. Impressive, fairly priced BRUT NV. Rosé NV BRUT **98 00** 02. Vintage Stanislas (**98 00** 02) and Voluminous Vigne aux Gamins BLANC DE BLANCS (98' 02). Top Grande CUVÉE 96' **98** 02. Also owns Marie Stuart and CANARD-DUCHÊNE in CHAMPAGNE, Ch Ricaud in LOUPIAC.

Thomas, André & fils ★★★ V. fine ALSACE grower at Ammerschwihr attached to rigorous biological methods. An artist-craftsman in the cellar: v.gd Ries Kaefferkopf and magnificent Gewurz Vieilles Vignes (both 05).

Thorin, J Beauj ★ Major BEAUJOLAIS négociant owned by BOISSET.

Thouarsais, Vin de Lo w r p ★ DYA Light Chenin Bl (with 20% CHARD permitted), Gamay, and Cab Fr from tiny (20-ha) VDQS south of SAUMUR. Esp Gigon.

Tollot-Beaut ★★★ Stylish, consistent Burgundy grower with 20 ha in CÔTE DE BEAUNE, inc v'yds at Beaune Grèves, CORTON, SAVIGNY (Les Champs Chevrey), and at its CHOREY-LÈS-BEAUNE base.

Touraine Lo r p w dr sw sp ★→★★★★ 02' 03 04 05' 06 07 Huge region with many ACS (eg VOUVRAY, CHINON, BOURGUEIL) as well as umbrella AC of variable quality – zesty reds (Cab Fr, Côt, Gamay, Pinot N), pungent whites (Sauv Bl, Chenin Bl), rosés, and MOUSSEUX. Many gd bistro wines, often gd value. Producers: Ch de Petit Thouars, Doms des Bois-Vaudons, Corbillières, Joël Delaunay, de la Garrelière (François Plouzeau), de la Presle; Clos Roche Blanche, Jacky Marteau, MARIONNET; Oisly & Thesée, Puzelat/Clos de Tue-Boeuf, Vincent Ricard, Sauvete.

Touraine-Amboise Lo r w p ★→★★ Touraine sub-appellation (220 ha). François Ier is tasty, food-friendly local blend (Gamay/Côt/Cab Fr). Chenin Bl for whites. Damien Delecheneau/la Grange Tiphaine, Dutertre, Xavier Frissant, de la Gabillière, .

Touraine-Azay-le-Rideau Lo ★→★★ Small TOURAINE sub-appellation (90 ha) for Chenin Bl-based dry, off-dry white and Grolleau-dominated rosé. Producers: Nicolas Paget and Pibaleau Père & Fils.

Touraine-Mesland Lo r w p ★→★★ TOURAINE sub-appellation (110 ha) best represented by its user-friendly red blends (Gamay/Côt/Cab Fr). Whites are mainly Chenin with a little CHARD. Ch Gaillard, Clos de la Briderie.

Touraine-Noble Joué Lo p ★→★★ DYA Ancient but recently revived rosé from 3 Pinots (N, Gr, Meunier) just south of Tours. Esp from ROUSSEAU and Sard. Became separate AC in 2001 and now from 24 ha.

Trapet Burg ★★→★★★ A long-established GEVREY-CHAMBERTIN DOM now enjoying new life and sensual wines with biodynamic farming. Ditto cousins Rossignol-Trapet – slightly more austere wines.

Trévallon, Domaine de Prov r w ★★★ 88' 89' 90' 91 92 93 94 95 96 97 98 99 00 01 03 04 05 06. 07 promises to be best vintage since 82. VDP Les Baux, fully deserving its huge reputation. Intense Cab Sauv/Syrah to age. White from Marsanne and Roussanne and a drop of CHARD. Worth seeking out.

Trimbach, F E ★★★ →★★★★ Growers of the greatest Ries in ALSACE (CLOS STE-HUNE) and its close contender (CUVÉE Frédéric-Emile). House style is dry but elegant with great ageing potential. Also v.gd PINOT GRIS and Gewurz. Based in Ribeauvillé; founded 1626.

Tursan SW France r p w ★★→★★★ (Most DYA) VDQS aspiring to AC. Easy-drinking holiday-style wines. Master chef Michel Guérard keeps much of his own ★★ wine (now red as well as white) for his famous restaurants at Eugénie-les-Bains, but more traditional ★★ Dom de Perchade is just as gd in its own way. Successful co-op the only other producer.

Vacqueyras S Rh r (w, p) ★★ 89' 90' 95' 96' 97 98 99' 00' 01' 03 04' 05' 06' 07 Full, peppery, pretty robust Grenache-based neighbour to GIGONDAS: more sinewed, should be cheaper. Lives 10+ yrs. Try Amouriers, Arnoux Vieux Clocher, JABOULET,Chx de Montmirail, des Tours; Clos des Cazaux, Doms Archimbaud-Vache, Charbonnière, Couroulu, Font de Papier, Fourmone, Garrigue, Grapillon d'Or, Monardière, Montirius, Montvac, Pascal Frères, Perrin, Sang des Cailloux.

Valençay Lo r p w ★ Recent AC (VDQS until 2004) in east TOURAINE; light, easy-drinking sometimes rustic and sharp wines from similar range of grapes as TOURAINE, esp Sauv Bl. Jacky Preys, Hubert & Olivier Sinson.

Val d'Orbieu, Vignerons du Association of some 200 top growers and co-ops in CORBIÈRES, COTEAUX DU LANGUEDOC, MINERVOIS, ROUSSILLON, etc, marketing a sound range of selected MIDI AC and VDP wines. Cuvée Mythique is flagship.

Valréas S Rh r (p w) ★★ 04 05' 06 07 CÔTES DU RHÔNE village with big co-op. Sound

FRANCE

mid-weight red (softer than CAIRANNE, RASTEAU) and improving white. Esp Emmanuel Bouchard, Dom des Grands Devers, Ch la Décelle.

Varichon & Clerc Principal makers and shippers of SAVOIE sparkling wines.

VDQS *vins délimite de qualité supérieure.*

Vendange Harvest. **Vendange Tardive** Late harvest. ALSACE equivalent to German Auslese but usually higher alcohol.

Verget Burg ★★→★★★ The négociant business of GUFFENS-HEYNEN with mixed range from MÂCON to MONTRACHET. Intense wines, often models, from bought-in grapes. New LUBÉRON venture: Verget du Sud. Follow closely.

Veuve Clicquot Yellow Label NV; White Label DEMI-SEC NV; Vintage Réserve **95 96 98' 99** 00 02; Rosé Reserve **95 96 98** 99' 02. Historic CHAMPAGNE house of highest standing, now owned by LVMH. Full-bodied, almost rich: one of CHAMPAGNE'S surest things. Cellars at Reims. Luxury brands: La Grande Dame (90' 96 **98**), Rich Réserve (**96** 99 02), La Grande Dame Rosé (**96** 98' **99** 02).

Veuve Devaux Premium CHAMPAGNE of powerful Union Auboise co-op. Excellent aged Grande Réserve NV, Oeil de Perdrix Rosé, Prestige Cuvée D.

Vidal-Fleury, J N Rh ★→★★★ Long-established GUIGAL-owned shipper of top Rhône wines and grower of CÔTE-RÔTIE, classy, v. elegant La Chatillonne (12% Viognier). Steady quality. Gd CÔTES DU VENTOUX, MUSCAT BEAUMES-DE-VENISE.

Vieille Ferme, La S Rh r w ★→★★★ V.gd brand of CÔTES DU VENTOUX (r) and CÔTES DU LUBÉRON (w) made by the Perrins, owners of CH DE BEAUCASTEL. Gd value.

Vieilles Vignes Old vines – therefore the best wine. Used by many, esp by BOLLINGER, DE VOGÜÉ, and CH FUISSÉ.

Vieux Télégraphe, Domaine du S Rh r w ★★★ 78' 81' 83 85 88 89' 90 94' **95'** 96' 97 **98' 99'** 00 01' 03' 04' 05' 06' 07 06 Top name, maker of well-fruited red CHÂTEAUNEUF, and tasty white (more *gourmand* since 1990s), which age well in lesser yrs. New gd-value second wine: Vieux Mas des Papes. Second DOM: de la Roquète, fruited, improving reds, fresh whites. Owns gd, understated GIGONDAS Dom Les Pallières with US importer Kermit Lynch.

Vigne or vignoble Vineyard (v'yd), vineyards (v'yds). **Vigneron** Vine-grower.

Vin Doux Naturel (VDN) Sweet wine fortified with wine alcohol, so the sweetness is natural, not the strength. The speciality of ROUSSILLON, based on Grenache or muscat. A staple in French bars, but the top wines, esp RANCIOS, can be remarkable.

Vin Gris "Grey" wine is v. pale pink, made of red grapes pressed before fermentation begins – unlike rosé, which ferments briefly before pressing. Oeil de Perdrix means much the same; so does "blush".

Vin Jaune Jura w ★★★ Speciality of ARBOIS: odd yellow wine like fino sherry. Normally ready when bottled (after at least 6 yrs). Best is CH-CHALON. See also PLAGEOLES. A halfway-house oxidized white is sold locally as *vin typé*.

Vin de Paille Wine from grapes dried on straw mats, so v. sweet, like Italian *passito*. Esp in the Jura. See also CHAVE and VIN PAILLÉ DE CORRÈZE.

Vin Paillé de Corrèze SW Revival of old-style VIN DE PAILLE nr Beaulieu-sur-Dordogne made today from Cab Fr, Cab Sauv, CHARD, Sauv Bl. 25 fanatical growers and small co-op.

Vin de Pays (VDP) Most dynamic category in France (with over 150 regions). The zonal VDP are best – *eg* CÔTES DE GASCOGNE, CÔTES DE THONGUE, Haute Vallée de l'Orb, Duché d'Uzès, among others. Enormous variety and sometimes wonderful surprises.

Vinsobres S Rh r (p w) ★→★★★ **04' 05' 06' 07** Village given full AC status 04 vintage on. Best are openly fruited, quite substantial reds, plenty of Syrah. Look for: Cave La Vinsobraise, Doms les Aussellons, Bicarelle, Chaume-Arnaud, Constant-Duquesnoy, Coriançon, Deurre, Jaume, Moulin, Peysson, Puy de Maupas, Ch Rouanne.

FRANCE

> **Twelve southwest growers to watch in 2009**
>
> **Dom Laurent Mousset (Entraygues-et-du-Fel):** working with Roussillon colleague to produce more serious wine.
>
> **Dom du Mioula (Marcillac):** Patrice Lescarret, enfant terrible from Gaillac, is consultant here.
>
> **Ch Bourguet (Gaillac):** best known for its sweet dessert wine.
>
> **Ch Cransac (Fronton):** accent on fruit; experimental vinification plant.
>
> **Dom Maison Neuve (Cahors):** traditional, but hell-bent on quality.
>
> **Dom Pountet (Côtes du Brulhois):** young oenologue with ambition and talent.
>
> **Ch Marnières (Bergerac):** rising star of this large appellation.
>
> **Ch Jonc Blanc (Montravel):** original winemaker working outside the appellation.
>
> **Dom Lauroux (Côtes de Gascogne):** recent arrival of new English owners.
>
> **Dom Pichard (Madiran):** famous estate in new hands.
>
> **Dom Mourguy (Irouléguy):** brother and sister winemakers have complementary talents.
>
> **Dom Larrédya (Jurançon):** better known by the experts than by consumers – so far.

Vin de Table Category of standard everyday table wine, not subject to particular regulations about grapes and origin. Can be source of unexpected delights if a talented winemaker uses this category to avoid bureaucratic hassle.

Viré-Clessé Burg w ★★ 05' 06' 07 AC based around 2 of the best white villages of MÂCON. Extrovert style, though residual sugar forbidden. Look for A Bonhomme, Bret Bros, Chaland, Clos du Chapitre, JADOT, Merlin, Ch de Viré, and co-op.

Visan S Rh r p w ★★ 04 05' 06' 07 Rhône village for medium-weight reds, fair whites. Young growers waking it up. Note: Doms Coste Chaude, Floriane, Fourmente, des Grands Devers, Roche-Audran.

Vogüé, Comte Georges de Burg ★★★★ Iconic CHAMBOLLE estate inc lion's share of MUSIGNY. Heralded vintages from 1990s taking time to come round.

Volnay Burg r ★★★→★★★★ 90' **91 93 95 96' 97 98** 99' **02' 03** 04 05' 06 07 Village between POMMARD and MEURSAULT: often the best reds of the CÔTE DE BEAUNE; structured and silky. Best v'yds: Caillerets, Champans, Clos des Chênes, Santenots, Taillepieds, etc. Best growers: D'ANGERVILLE, J-M BOILLOT, HOSPICES DE BEAUNE, *Lafarge*, LAFON, DE MONTILLE, Rossignol.

Volnay-Santenots Burg r ★★★ Excellent red wine from MEURSAULT is sold under this name. Indistinguishable from other PREMIER CRU VOLNAY. Best growers: AMPEAU, HOSPICES DE BEAUNE, LAFON, LEROY.

Vosne-Romanée Burg r ★★★→★★★★ **88' 89' 90' 91 93 95 96' 97 98** 99' **00** 01 02' 03 04 05' 06 07 Village with Burgundy's grandest *crus* (ROMANÉE-CONTI, LA TÂCHE, etc). There are (or should be) no common wines in Vosne. Many gd growers inc: Arnoux, CATHIARD, DRC, ENGEL, GRIVOT, GROS, Jayer, LATOUR, LEROY, LIGER-BELAIR, MÉO-CAMUZET, MUGNERET, RION.

Vougeot Burg r w ★★★ 90' **93 95**' 96' **97 98** 99' **00 01** 03 04 05' 06 07 Village and PREMIER CRU wines. See CLOS DE VOUGEOT. Exceptional Clos Blanc de Vougeot, white since 12th century. Bertagna and VOUGERAIE best.

Vougeraie, Domaine de la Burg r ★★→★★★ DOM uniting all BOISSET's v'yd holdings. Gd-value BOURGOGNE rouge up to fine MUSIGNY GRAND CRU.

Vouvray Lo w dr sw sp ★★→★★★★ For sweet Vouvray: **89' 90' 95' 96' 97' 03'** 05'.

NB Vintages in colour are those you should choose first for drinking in 2009.

For dry Vouvray: **89 90 96' 97 02' 03 05'** 06 07. Important AC east of Tours: increasingly gd and reliable. DEMI-SEC is classic style, but in gd yrs MOELLEUX can be intensely sweet, almost immortal. Gd, dry sparkling: look out for PÉTILLANT. Best producers: Allias, Vincent Careme, Champalou, Clos Baudoin (CHIDAINE), Dhoye-Deruet (Dom de la Fontanerie), Foreau, Fouquet (Dom des Aubuisière), Ch Gaudrelle, Dom de la Haute Borne, HUET, DOM DE LA TAILLE-AUX-LOUPS, Vigneau-Chevreau. If you find ancient vintages – like 47 or 59 – don't hesitate.

Vranken Ever more powerful CHAMPAGNE group created in 1976 by Belgian marketing man. Sound quality. Leading brand: Demoiselle. Owns HEIDSIECK MONOPOLE, POMMERY, and Bricout.

Wolfberger Al ★★ Principal label of Eguisheim co-op. Exceptional quality for such a large-scale producer. V. important for CRÉMANT.

"Y" (pronounced "ygrec") B'x **79' 80' 85 86 88 94 96** 00 02 **04 05** Intense dry white wine produced at CH D'YQUEM, lately with more regularity. Most interesting with age. Now changing style and modernizing.

Zind Humbrecht, Domaine ★★★★ ALSACE growers since 1620. Current DOM established in 1959, now vying with FALLER/DOM WEINBACH as the greatest in ALSACE: rich, powerful yet balanced wines, using v. low yields. Top wines from single v'yds Clos St-Urbain, Jebsal (superb PINOT GRIS **02'**) and Windsbuhl, and GRANDS CRUS RANGEN, HENGST, Brand, Goldert.

To decipher codes, please refer to "Key to symbols" on the front flap of jacket, or "How to use this book" on p.10.

Châteaux of Bordeaux

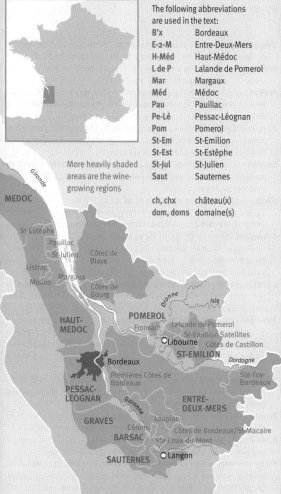

The following abbreviations
are used in the text:

B'x	Bordeaux
E-2-M	Entre-Deux-Mers
H-Méd	Haut-Médoc
L de P	Lalande de Pomerol
Mar	Margaux
Méd	Médoc
Pau	Pauillac
Pe-Lé	Pessac-Léognan
Pom	Pomerol
St-Em	St-Emilion
St-Est	St-Estèphe
St-Jul	St-Julien
Saut	Sauternes
ch, chx	château(x)
dom, doms	domaine(s)

BORDEAUX

More heavily shaded
areas are the wine-
growing regions

Gironde

MEDOC

St-Estèphe
Pauillac
St-Julien Côtes de
Listrac   Blaye
Moulis Margaux
              Côtes de
              Bourg

HAUT-
MEDOC

Dronne   Isle

POMEROL
Fronsac Lalande de Pomerol
              St-Emilion Satellites
○Libourne Côtes de Castillon
Bordeaux   ST-EMILION Dordogne

Premières Côtes de
Bordeaux   Ste-Foy-
                            Bordeaux
PESSAC-
LEOGNAN   ENTRE-
              DEUX-MERS
GRAVES   Loupiac
      Cérons   Côtes de Bordeaux/St-Macaire
BARSAC   Ste-Croix-du-Mont

SAUTERNES ○Langon

We might as well get used to it; top-class Bordeaux is now a luxury item. *En primeur* prices for 2006 classed growths did come down from the incredibly expensive 2005s, but only by an average 8.6%, so once more châteaux owners have set a new benchmark. Despite misgivings about its quality 2007 is not settling at old-fashioned prices either.

But these represent only 5% of Bordeaux's annual 800-million-bottle production, so take a look elsewhere in the region. The best of what used to be called the "Crus Bourgeois" of the Médoc (see box p. 85) as well as the pick of the likes of Fronsac, Côtes de Castillon, Lalande-de-Pomerol, and sometimes generic Bordeaux offer the unique Bordeaux flavour at fair prices. And even the 2005s are affordable here. The other good news is Sauternes: prices may rise with the excellent quality of the 2007s, but they'll still be underpriced compared with reds of equivalent standing. And don't you just love a bargain?

d'Agassac H-Méd r ★★ 98 99 00' 02 03 **04 05** 06 "Sleeping Beauty" 14th-century moated fort. 42 ha v. nr BORDEAUX suburbs. Modern, accessible Médoc.

Andron-Blanquet St-Est r ★★ **95 96** 98 00' 03 **04** 05' 06 16-ha sister CH to COS-LABORY. Smoother and riper in latter yrs.

Angélus St-Em r ★★★★ 89' 90' 92' **95 96** 98' 99 00' **01 02** 03' 04 05 06 Leading PREMIER GRAND CRU CLASSÉ on ST-ÉMILION CÔTES. Pioneer of the modern style; dark, rich, sumptuous. Second wine: Le Carillon de L'Angélus.

d'Angludet Cantenac-Mar r ★★★ 90 **94** 95 **96'** 98' **00 02** 03 04 05 06 32-ha estate owned and run by NÉGOCIANT Sichel; classed-growth quality. Lively long-living MARGAUX of great style popular in UK. Gd value.

Archambeau Graves r w d (sw) ★★★ (r) 98 00 02 04 **05** 06 (w) **00 01 02** 04 05 04 05 06 Up-to-date 27-ha property at Illats. Gd fruity dry white; fragrant barrel-aged reds (two-thirds of v'yd).

d'Arche Saut w sw ★★ 96 97' 98 99 00 **01' 02 03'** 05 Much improved 27-ha classed growth. Top vintages are creamy. Ch d'Arche-Lafaurie is a richer selection. Also bed-and-breakfast in 17th-century *chartreuse*.

d'Armailhac Pau r ★★★ 88' 89 90' **93 94** 95' **96'** 98 99 00 **01** 02 **03** 04 05' 06 Formerly Ch Mouton Baronne Philippe. Substantial Fifth Growth under Rothschild ownership. 51 ha: top-quality PAUILLAC with more finesse than sister CLERC MILON but less punch. MOUTON ROTHSCHILD is big brother of both.

L'Arrosée St-Em r ★★★ **95 96** 98' 00 **01 02 03** 04 05' 06' A 9.7-ha CÔTES estate with new owner and investment from 2002. Structured wines with plenty of Cab Fr and Cab Sauv (60%).

Ausone St-Em r ★★★★ 85 **86'** 88 **89'** 90 93 94 95 **96'** 97 98' **99** 00' 01' 02 03' 04 05' 06 Illustrious First Growth with 6.8 ha (about 2,500 cases); best position on the CÔTES with famous rock-hewn cellars. On superb form since 1996. Long-lived wines with volume, texture and finesse. Second wine: La Chapelle d'Ausone also excellent.

Bahans-Haut-Brion Pe-Lé r ★★★ 89' 90 **93 94** 95 **96'** 98 99 00 01 02 03 04 05' 06 The second wine of CH HAUT-BRION. Gd value if you can find it. Blend changes considerably with each vintage.

Balestard-la-Tonnelle St-Em r ★★ **95 96** 98' **00'** 01 **03** 04 05 06 Historic 11-ha classed growth on limestone plateau. More concentration since 2003.

Barde-Haut St-Em r ★★ 98 99 00 01 02 **03** 04 05' 06 The 17-ha sister property of CLOS L'ÉGLISE and HAUT-BERGEY. Rich, modern, and opulent in style.

Bastor-Lamontagne Saut w sw ★★ 95 96' 97' 98 99 01' **02 03'** 05 Large (56 ha) Preignac sister to BEAUREGARD. Consistent quality; excellent rich wines. Second label: Les Remparts de Bastor. Fruity Caprice (from 2004) for early drinking. Also Ch St-Robert at Pujols: red and white GRAVES.

Vintages shown in light type should be opened now only out of curiosity to gauge their future. Vintages in bold are deemed (usually by their makers) ready for drinking. Remember, though: the French tend to enjoy the vigour of young wines, and many 89s, 90s, 95s, and 96s have at least 10 more years of development before them. Vintages marked ' are regarded as particularly successful for property in question. Vintages in colour are first choice for 2009.

Batailley Pau r ★★★ **94** 95 96 98 **00** 02 03 04 05' 06 Fifth Growth property (55 ha) bordering PAUILLAC and ST-JULIEN. Fine, firm, strong-flavoured. Gd-value PAUILLAC. Even better since 2000. Home of Castéja family of BORIE-MANOUX.

Beaumont Cussac, H-Méd r ★★ **95** 96 98 00' **02 04** 05' 06 Over 80 ha MÉDOC estate; easily enjoyable wines. Second label: Ch Moulin d'Arvigny. 40,000 cases. In the same hands as BEYCHEVELLE.

Beauregard Pom r ★★★ **89' 90' 94'** 95' 96' 98' 00' **01 02 03** 04 05' 06 A 17-ha v'yd; fine 17th-century CH nr LA CONSEILLANTE. Top-rank rich wines. Consultant Michel ROLLAND. Second label: Benjamin de Beauregard.

Beau-Séjour-Bécot St-Em r ★★★ **89' 90'** 94 95' 96 **98'** 99 00' **01 02 03** 04 05' 06 18-ha estate owned by the Bécots since 1969. Controversially demoted in class in 1985 but properly re-promoted to PREMIER GRAND CRU CLASSÉ in 1996 (and endorsed in 2006). More finesse from 2001. GRAND-PONTET and LA GOMERIE in same family hands.

Beauséjour-Duffau St-Em r ★★★ **89' 90' 93' 94** 95 96 98 99 00 **02 03** 04 05' 06 7-ha PREMIER GRAND CRU CLASSÉ estate on west slope of the CÔTES owned by Duffau-Lagarrosse family; only 2,000+ cases of firm-structured, concentrated, even hedonistic wine.

Beau-Site St-Est r ★★ **95** 96 98 00 **03** 04 05 (06) Property in same hands as BATAILLEY etc. Usually solid and firm, if unexceptional.

Belair St-Em r ★★★ **88'** 89' 90' 94 95' **96** 98 99 00' **01 02 03** 04 05' 06 Classed-growth neighbour of AUSONE. Long-time winemaker Pascal Delbeck now the owner, with négociant J-P MOUEIX having share. Fine, fragrant, elegant style; deceptively long-lived. Second wine: Ch Haut Roc Blanquant.

Belgrave St-Laurent, H-Méd r ★★ **95** 96' 98' **00'** 02' **03** 04' 05' 06 60-ha Fifth Growth well managed by CVBG-Dourthe (SEE LA GARDE, REYSSON). Progress and investment since 1998. Second label: Diane de Belgrave.

Bellefont-Belcier St-Em r ★★ **98** 99 00 **01 02 03** 04 05' 06 13.5 ha GRAND CRU CLASSÉ (2006) on the CÔTES at St-Laurent-des-Combes. Neighbour of LARCIS-DUCASSE. Taken in hand from 1994. Ripe, modern but minerally.

Bel-Orme-Tronquoy-de-Lalande St-Seurin-de-Cadourne, H-Méd r ★★ **95** 96 98' 00 02 03 04 05 (06) 24-ha estate north of ST-ESTÈPHE. Known for tannic wines; more tempting since 1997. Same owner as CROIZET-BAGES, RAUZAN-GASSIES.

Berliquet St-Em r ★★ 95 96 98' 99 **00'** 01 02 03 04 05' 06 A 9.3-ha GRAND CRU CLASSÉ well located on the CÔTES. Moved into top gear from 1997 onwards.

Bernadotte H-Méd r ★★ 98 99 00' **01 02 03** 04 05' 06 30-ha estate managed by PICHON-LALANDE team since 1997. CHAMPAGNE ROEDERER owner since 2006. Fine, structured wines.

Bertineau St-Vincent L de P r ★★ 98 99 00' 01 03 **04** 05 06 Top oenologist MICHEL ROLLAND owns this 4-ha estate. Consistent quality. (See also LE BON PASTEUR.)

Beychevelle St-Jul r ★★★ 95 96 **98** 99 00' **01 02 03** 04 05 06 Fourth Growth (90 ha) with historic mansion. Greater consistency since 1995. Wines of elegance rather than power. Second wine: Amiral de Beychevelle.

Biston-Brillette Moulis r ★★ **98** 00 01 02 **03** 04 05' 06 Attractive, fruit-bound, gd-value MOULIS. 24 ha in production.

Bonalgue Pom r ★★ **95 96'** 98' 99 00 01 03 **04** 05 06 Dark, rich, meaty POMEROL. As gd value as it gets. Michel ROLLAND consults.

Bonnet E-2-M r w ★★ (r) 00 01 03 **04 05** (w) DYA Owned by André Lurton. Big producer (270 ha!) of some of the best ENTRE-DEUX-MERS and red BORDEAUX. New CUVÉE Prestige, Divinus, from 2000.

Le Bon Pasteur Pom r ★★★ 89' 90' **93' 94'** 95 96' 98' 99 00 01 **02 03** 04 05' 06 Excellent property on ST-ÉMILION border, owned by MICHEL ROLLAND. Concentrated, even creamy wines virtually guaranteed. (See also BERTINEAU ST-VINCENT.)

> **Why Bordeaux?**
> People ask whether Bordeaux still justifies its separate 22-page section of this international guide. The answer: it remains the motor of the fine wine world, by far its biggest producer, stimulating debate, investment and collectors worldwide.

Le Boscq St-Est r ★★ **95' 96'** 98 00 01 **03 04** 05' 06 Quality-driven 18-ha estate owned by CVBG-Dourthe, giving excellent value in tasty ST-ESTÈPHE.

Bourgneuf-Vayron Pom r ★★ **95' 96'** 98' 99 00 01' **03** 04 05' 06 Rich, warm, firm-edged POMEROL from this 9-ha estate on sandy-gravel soils.

Bouscaut Pe-Lé r w ★★ (r) **89 90 94 95** 98 00 01 02 04 05' 06 (w) **96 98** 00 01 02 03 04 **05'** 06 Steadily improving classed growth owned by daughter of BRANE-CANTENAC's Lucien Lurton. Hitting its stride since 2004.

Boyd-Cantenac Mar r ★★★ 90 94' **95** 96' 98' 00 02 03 04 05' 06 Little-known 18-ha Third Growth in better form since 2000. Cab Sauv-dominated with a little peppery Petit Verdot. Second wine: Jacques Boyd. See also POUGET.

Branaire-Ducru St-Jul r ★★★ 89' 90' **93' 94** 95 96 **98 99** 00 01 **02** 03 04 05' 06 Fourth Growth ST-JULIEN of 51 ha. Has set the bar of quality and consistency high. Dense, linear, cassis style. Second label: Duluc.

Brane-Cantenac Cantenac-Mar r ★★★ 89' **95 96** 98 99 **00'** 01 **02 03** 04 05' 06 Big (85-ha) Second Growth. Dense, fragrant MARGAUX. Second label: Baron de Brane.

Brillette Moulis r ★★ **95 96** 98 99 00 **02 03 04** 05 06 A 40-ha MOULIS estate making wines of gd depth and fruit. Reliable and attractive. Second label: Berthault Brillette.

Cabanne, La Pom r **95 96** 98' 00 **04** 05 06' Well-regarded 10-ha property. More rustic POMEROL in style but finer and fleshier in 06. Second wine: Dom de Compostelle.

Cadet-Piola St-Em r ★★ 94' **95** 98 **00 01 03** 04 05 (06) Distinguished small property (7 ha) on ST-ÉM's limestone plateau. Fresh, firm, long-lived wines.

Caillou Saut w sw ★★ 88' 89' 90' 95 96 97 98 99 **01'** 02 03' 05 Well-run second-rank 13-ha BARSAC v'yd for firm fruity wine. CUVÉE Reine (**97 99 01'** 03') is a top selection.

Calon-Ségur St-Est r ★★★ 89' 90' **94** 95 96' **98** 99 00' 01 **02** 03 04 05' 06 Big (60-ha) Third Growth with great historic reputation. Greater consistency since 1995. Second label: Marquis de Calon.

Cambon La Pelouse H-Méd r ★★ **96' 98' 99** 00 01 02 03 **04** 05' 06 Big, accessible southern HAUT-MÉDOC *cru*. A sure bet for supple MÉDOC.

de Camelote E2M r w ★ Touted property with many consultants.

Camensac St-Laurent, H-Méd r ★★ 95 96' 98 **00** 01 **03** 05 06 75-ha Fifth Growth. Quite lively if not exactly classic wines. New owner (2005) has CHASSE-SPLEEN connection; expect change. Second label: La Closerie de Camensac.

Canon St-Em r ★★★ **96** 98' 99 00 01 02 **03** 04 05' 06 Famous first-classed growth with 22 walled-in hectares on plateau west of the town, bought in 1996 by (Chanel) owners of RAUZAN-SÉGLA. Investment and restructuring of the v'yd has paid. Elegant, long-lived wines. Second label: Clos Canon.

Canon-de-Brem Canon-Fronsac r ★★ 98 99 00 01 03 **04** 05' RIP from 2006. Bought by Jean Halley of Carrefour supermarkets in 2000, the wine has now been absorbed into CH DE LA DAUPHINE. Massive recent investment. Firm, pure expression.

Canon La Gaffelière St-Em r ★★★ 89' 90' 94' 95 96 **98'** 99 00' 01 02 **03** 04 05' 06 Leading 19-ha GRAND CRU CLASSÉ on the lower slopes of the CÔTES. Same ownership as CLOS DE L'ORATOIRE, LA MONDOTTE, and Aiguilhe in Castillon.

Stéphane Derenoncourt consults. Stylish, upfront, impressive wines.

Cantegril Graves r Saut w sw ★★ (r) 00 02 04 **05** 06 (w) **01** 02 03 04 05' Supple, digestible red and fine, aromatic BARSAC-SAUTERNES from DOISY-DAËNE and CLOS FLORIDÈNE connection.

Cantemerle Macau, H-Méd r ★★★ 89' 90 **95** 96' 98 00 01 02 03 04 05' 06 Large 90-ha property in south MÉDOC. Now merits its Fifth Growth status. Sandy-gravel soils give finer style. Second label: Les Allées de Cantemerle.

Cantenac-Brown Cantenac-Mar r ★★→★★★ 90' 94 95 **96** 98 99 00 01 02 03 04 05' 06 42-ha Third Growth sold in 2006 to private investor Simon Halabi (big price asked for this vintage!); owned since late 80s by AXA Millésimes. Powerful, but more elegance since 2000. Second label: Brio du Ch Cantenac Brown.

Capbern-Gasqueton St-Est r ★★ **95** 96 98 00 02 03 04 05 (06) 34-ha property offering solid fare; same owner as CALON-SÉGUR.

Cap de Mourlin St-Em r ★★ **95** 96 98' 99 00 01 03 04 05 06 Well-known 15-ha property of the Capdemoulin family, also owners of CH BALESTARD and Ch Roudier, MONTAGNE-ST-EMILION. A vigorous but tasty ST-EMILION.

Carbonnieux Pe-Lé r w ★★ 90' **95** 96 **98** 99 00 02 04 05' 06 Large (90-ha), historic estate at LÉOGNAN for sterling red and white. The whites, 65% Sauv Bl (eg **96 97** 98 99 00 01 02 03 04 **05** 06), can age up to 10 yrs. Chx Le Pape and Le Sartre are also in the family. Second label: La Tour-Léognan.

de Carles Fronsac r ★★ **98** 99 00 01 02 03 04 05' 06 Haut Carles is the top selection here with its own modern, gravity-fed cellars. Iron fist in a velvet glove. de Carles now the juicy second wine.

Les Carmes Haut-Brion Pe-Lé r ★★★ 89' 90' **94** 95 96 98 99 00 01 02 03 04 05' 06 Small (4-ha) neighbour of HAUT-BRION with classed-growth standards. Old vintages show its potential.

Caronne-Ste-Gemme St-Laurent, H-Méd r ★★→★★★ **98** 99 00 01 02 **03** 04 05 06 40-ha MÉDOC estate. Steady, stylish quality repays patience.

Carteau Côtes-Daugay St-Em r ★★ **95** 96' 98' 99 00 01 02 03 04 05 (06) Consistent 13-ha GRAND CRU; full-flavoured wines maturing fairly early.

Certan-de-May Pom r ★★ 90' **94 95** 96 98 00' 01' 04 05' 06 Tiny property (1,800 cases) on the POMEROL plateau. Has been inconsistent but 2005 shows the true potential. Opulent with firm, fine tannic frame.

Chantegrive Graves r w ★★ →★★★ 98' 99' 00 01 **02** 03 04 05' 06 With 87 ha, the largest estate in the AC; modern GRAVES of v.gd quality. Reds rich and finely oaked. CUVÉE Caroline is top white (98' 99 00 01 02 03 04 **05'** 06).

Chasse-Spleen Moulis r ★★★ **95** 96 98 99 00 01 02 03 04 05' 06 A 80-ha estate at classed-growth level. Consistently gd, often outstanding (eg **90' 00'** 05'), long-maturing wine. Second label: Ermitage de Chasse Spleen. One of the surest things in Bordeaux. Makes a little white too. See also CAMENSAC and GRESSIER-GRAND-POUJEAUX.

Chauvin St-Em r ★★ **95** 96 98' 99 00 01 03 04 05 06 Steady performer; increasingly serious stuff. New v'yds purhased in 1998.

Cheval Blanc St-Em r ★★★★ 85' **86 88** 89 90' **93 94** 95 96' 97 98' 99 00' 01' 02 03 04 05' 06 40-ha PREMIER GRAND CRU class (a) of ST-ÉMILION. High percentage of Cabernet Franc (60%). Rich, fragrant, vigorous wines with some of the voluptuousness of neighbouring POMEROL. Delicious young; lasts a generation. For many, the first choice in Bordeaux. Second wine: Le Petit Cheval. Like all all First Growths prices are super high.

Chevalier, Domaine de Pe-Lé r w ★★★ 89 90' 95 **96' 98'** 99' **00' 01'** 02 03 04' 05' 06 Superb estate of 38 ha at LÉOGNAN. Impressive since 1998, the red has gained in finesse, fruit. texture. Complex white matures slowly and develops

BORDEAUX

> **Four appellations in one**
> 2007 will see the first vintage of the new appellation of Côtes de
> Bordeaux. The label is set to embrace and eventually replace CÔTES DE
> CASTILLON, CÔTES DE FRANCS, PREMIÈRES CÔTES DE BLAYE, and PREMIÈRES
> CÔTES DE BORDEAUX. Cross-blending of wines from these regions will be
> allowed. For those wanting to maintain the identity of a single terroir,
> stiffer controls will permit AC Côtes de Bordeaux with the suffixes Blaye,
> Castillon, Francs, and Cadillac (for the Premières Côtes de Bordeaux). The
> CÔTES DE BOURG is not part of the new designation.

rich flavours (**89 90' 93 94 95 96' 97 98' 99 00 01 02 03 04 05'** 06). Second
wine: Esprit de Chevalier. Look out for Dom de la Solitude, PESSAC-LÉOGNAN.

Cissac Cissac-Méd r ★★ **90 94' 95 96' 98 00 02 03** 04 05 (06) Pillar of the
bourgeoisie. 50-ha MÉDOC *cru*. Steady record for tasty, long-lived wine.
Second wine: Les Reflets du Ch Cissac.

Citran Avensan, H-Méd r ★★ **90' 95 96 98 99 00 02 03 04** 05' 06 90-ha estate
owned by Villars-Merlaut family since 1996 (see CHASSE-SPLEEN, GRUAUD-
LAROSE). Now ripe; supple; accessible early. Second label: Moulins de Citran.

Clarke Listrac r (p w) ★★ **98' 99 00 01 02 03** 04 05' 06 Large (54-ha) Listrac estate.
Massive Rothschild investment. Now v.gd Merlot-based red. Also a dry white
Le Merle Blanc du Ch Clarke. Ch Malmaison in MOULIS same connection.

Clerc Milon Pau r ★★★ **89' 90' 94 95 96' 98'** 99 00 01 02 03 04 05 06 Once-
forgotten Fifth Growth owned by (Mouton) Rothschilds. Now 30 ha and a top
performer; weightier than sister ARMAILHAC.

Climens Saut w sw ★★★★ 76 78 83' 85' 86' 88' 89 90' 95 96 97' 98 99' 00 01' 02
03' 04 05' 06 A 30-ha BARSAC classed growth making some of the world's most
stylish wine (but not the sweetest) for a gd 10 yrs' maturing. (Occasional)
second label: Les Cyprès. Owned by Berenice Lurton. Pricier than in the past.

Clinet Pom r ★★★★ 95 96 **98'** 99 00 01 02 **03** 04 05' Made a name for intense,
sumptuous wines in the 1980s. New owner (1998) continues the style. MICHEL
ROLLAND consults. New winery 2004. Second label: Fleur de Clinet.

Clos de l'Oratoire St-Em r ★★ 95 96 98 99 **00'** 01 **03** 04 05' 06 Serious performer
on the northeastern slopes of ST-ÉMILION. Same stable as CANON-LA-GAFFELIÈRE
and LA MONDOTTE, but lighter than both.

Clos l'Eglise Pom r ★★★ 95 96 98 99 **00' 01** 02 03 04 05' 06 A 6-ha v'yd on one of
the best sites in POMEROL. Fine wine with more depth since 1998. Same family
owns HAUT-BERGEY and BARDE-HAUT.

Clos Floridène Graves r w ★★ (r) 99 00 01 02 03 04 05 06 (w) 98 99 00 01' 02 03
04' **05'** 06 A sure thing from one of Bordeaux's most famous white-
winemakers, Denis Dubourdieu. Oak-fermented Sauv Bl/Sem to keep 5+ yrs;
fruity red. See also Chx CANTEGRIL, DOISY-DAËNE and REYNON.

Clos Fourtet St-Em r ★★★ 89 90 94 95 **96 98** 99 00 01 02 03 04 05' 06 Well-placed
First Growth on the plateau, cellars almost in town. New owner and
investment from 2001. Now on stellar form. Also owns POUJEAUX. Second
label: Dom de Martialis.

Clos Haut-Peyraguey Saut w sw ★★ 86' 88' 89 90' 95' 96 **97'** 98 99 00 01' 02 03'
04 05' 06 Tiny production (12 ha) of excellent medium-rich wine. Haut-
Bommes is the second label.

Clos des Jacobins St-Em r ★★ 95 96 98 00 01 02 03 04 05' 06 Classed growth with
greater stature since 2000. New ownership from 2004; new creamy style.
ANGÉLUS owner consults. Same family owns Ch La Commanderie.

Clos du Marquis St-Jul r ★★→★★★ 98 99 00 01 02 03 04 05 06 The outstanding
second wine of LÉOVILLE-LAS-CASES, cut from the same durable and powerful

cloth and is regularly a match for many well-rated classed growths.

Clos Puy Arnaud Castillon r ★★ **00** 01' **02** 03 04 05' 06 Biodynamic estate at the top of this revived AC. 8.5 ha producing wines of depth and distinction. Owner formerly connected to PAVIE.

Clos René Pom r ★★ 95 96 98' **00' 01** 04 05' (06) Merlot-dominated wine with a little spicy Malbec. Less sensuous than top POMEROL but gd value. Alias Ch Moulinet-Lasserre.

La Clotte St-Em r ★★ 95' 96 98' 99 00' **01 02 03** 04 05 Tiny CÔTES GRAND CRU CLASSÉ: pungent, supple wine. Drink at owners' ST-EMILION restaurant, Logis de la Cadène. Second label: Clos Bergat Bosson.

Colombier-Monpelou Pau r ★★ 98 99 **00' 02** 03 **04** 05 06 24-ha PAUILLAC estate; fairly supple, early drinking style of wine.

La Conseillante Pom r ★★★★ 88 89 90' 94 95' 96' **98'** 99 00' 01 02 **03** 04 05' 06' Historic 12-ha property on plateau between PÉTRUS and CHEVAL BLANC. Some of the noblest and most fragrant POMEROL; drinks well young or old.

Corbin St-Em r ★★ 96 98 99 **00' 01 02** 04 05 Much improved 12-ha GRAND CRU CLASSÉ. New management and investment since 1999. Round and supple with soft red fruit.

Corbin-Michotte St-Em r ★★ 95 96 98' 99 **00 01 02 04** 05 06 Well-run, modernized, 7.6-ha classed growth; generous POMEROL-like wine. In same hands as Chx Calon and Cantelauze.

Cordeillan-Bages Pau r ★★ A mere 1,000 cases of savoury PAUILLAC. Rarely seen outside Bordeaux. Better known for its luxury restaurant and hotel.

Cos d'Estournel St-Est r ★★★★ 88' 89' 90' 94 95 **96' 98'** 00 01 02 03 04 05' 06 A 67-ha Second Growth with eccentric pagoda CHAI. Most refined ST-ESTÈPHE and regularly one of the best wines of the MÉDOC. New cellars in 2008. Pricey white from 2005. Second label: Les Pagodes de Cos. Same owner as CH MARBUZET and super-modern Goulée (Médoc).

Cos-Labory St-Est r ★★ 89' 90' 94 95 **96' 98'** 99 00 02 03 04 05' 06 Little-known Fifth Growth neighbour of COS D'ESTOURNEL with 15 ha. Recent vintages have more depth and structure. Gd value. ANDRON-BLANQUET is sister CH.

Coufran St-Seurin-de-Cadourne, H-Méd r ★★ 95 96 **98** 99 00 01 **02 03 04** 05 06 76 ha Coufran and VERDIGNAN, in extreme north of the HAUT-MÉDOC, are co-owned. Coufran is mainly Merlot for supple wine. SOUDARS is another, smaller sister.

Couhins-Lurton Pe-Lé w r ★★→★★★ (w) 98' 99 00 01 02 **03 04 05** 06 (r) 02 03 04 05 Fine, minerally, long-lived classed-growth white produced from Sauv Bl. Now a little red from 2002. Same family as LA LOUVIÈRE.

La Couspaude St Em r ★★ 95 96 98 99 **00' 01 02 03** 04 05 06 Classed growth well located on the ST-EMILION plateau. Modern style; rich and creamy with lashings of spicy oak.

Coutet Saut w sw ★★★ 83' 85 86' 88' 89' 90' 95 96 97' **98' 99** 01' **02** 03' 04 05 Traditional rival to CLIMENS; 37 ha in BARSAC. Slightly less rich; at its best equally fine. CUVÉE Madame is a v. rich selection in certain yrs (90 95 01).

Couvent des Jacobins St-Em r ★★ 95 96 **98' 99** 00' 01 03 04 05 06 Well-known 10.5-ha v'yd on eastern edge of ST-EMILION. Splendid cellars. Lighter, easy style. Denis Dubourdieu consults. Second label: Ch Beau-Mayne.

Le Crock St-Est r ★★ 95 96 98 99 **00' 01 02** 03 04 05 06 Outstanding property of 30 ha in the same family as LÉOVILLE-POYFERRÉ. Classic, robust ST-ESTÈPHE.

La Croix Pom r ★★ 95 96 98 99 **00 01** 04 05 06 Well-reputed 10-ha property. Appealing plummy POMEROL. Also La Croix-St-Georges, La Croix-Toulifaut, Castelot, and HAUT-SARPE (ST-EMILION).

La Croix du Casse Pom r ★★ 95 96 98 99 **00' 01'** 04 05 06 A 9-ha property on sandy-gravel soils in the south of POMEROL. Usually lighter in style. Since 2005 owned by BORIE-MANOUX.

La Croix-de-Gay Pom r ★★★ 89 90 94' 95 96 98 99 00' 01' 02 04 05 06 12 ha in the best part of the commune. Recently on fine form. LA FLEUR-DE-GAY is the best selection. Same family as Quinault L'Enclos and Faizeau.

Croizet-Bages Pau r ★★ 89 90' 95 96' 98 00' 03 04 05 06 A 26-ha Fifth Growth. Same owners as RAUZAN-GASSIES. A new regime in the cellar is producing richer, more serious wines, but could still be better.

Croque-Michotte St-Em r ★★ 95 96 98 00 01 03 04 05 A 14-ha estate on the POMEROL border. Gd steady wines but not grand enough to be *classé*.

Cru Bourgeois, Cru Bourgeois Supérieur, Cru Bourgeois Exceptionnel See Médoc classification box, p.oo.

de Cruzeau Pe-Lé sw r w ★★ (r) 95 96 98 00 01 02 04 05 06 (w) 00 01 02 03 04 05 06 Large 97-ha (two-thirds red) PESSAC-LÉOGNAN v'yd developed by André Lurton of LA LOUVIÈRE. Gd value wines. Sauv Bl-dominated white.

Dalem Fronsac r ★★ 95 96' 98' 99 00 01 02 03 04 05' 06 Used to be a full-blooded FRONSAC. Now a feminine touch has added more charm. 15 ha: 85% Merlot.

Dassault St-Em r ★★ 95 96 98' 99 00 01 02 03 04 05' 06 Consistent, solid, modern, juicy, oak-lined 23-ha GRAND CRU CLASSÉ.

de la Dauphine Fronsac r ★★ 98' 99 00 01 03 04 05 06' Total makeover since purchased by new owner in 2000. Renovation of CH and v'yds plus new, modern winery in 2002. Stablemate CANON-DE-BREM integrated in 2006 so look out for a more structured style.

Dauzac Labarde-Mar r ★★→★★★ 89' 90' 94 95 96 98' 99 00' 01 02 03 04 05 A 49-ha Fifth Growth south of MARGAUX; underachiever for many yrs but evolution since the 1990s. Owned by an insurance company; managed by André Lurton of LA LOUVIÈRE. Second wine: La Bastide Dauzac.

Desmirail Mar r ★★→★★★ 95 96 98 00' 01 02 03 04 05 06 Third Growth (30 ha) owned by Denis Lurton, brother of Henri BRANE CANTENAC. Fine, delicate style.

Destieux St-Em r ★★ 98 99 00' 01 02 03' 04 05' 06 Promoted to GRAND CRU CLASSÉ in 2006. 8 ha estate to the east of ST-EMILION at St-Hippolyte. New CHAI and investment since 1996. MICHEL ROLLAND consults. Firm, bold, powerful style.

Doisy-Daëne Barsac w (r) sw dr ★★★ 88' 89' 90' 95 96 97' 98' 99 01' 02 03 04 05 06 Forward-looking 15-ha estate producing a crisp, oaky, dry white and CH CANTEGRIL, but above all renowned for its notably fine (and long-lived) sweet BARSAC. L'Extravagant (90 96 97 01 02 03 04 05 06) is a super-CUVÉE.

Doisy-Dubroca Barsac w sw ★★ 88' 89 90' 95 96 97' 99 01 03' 04 05 Tiny (3.4-ha) BARSAC classed growth allied to CH CLIMENS.

Doisy-Védrines Saut w sw ★★★ 88' 89' 90 95 96 97' 98 99 01' 03' 04 05 A 20-ha classed growth at BARSAC, nr CLIMENS and COUTET. Delicious, sturdy, rich: for keeping almost indefinitely. A sure thing for many yrs.

Le Dôme St-Em r ★★★ Micro-wine that used to be super-oaky (200%) but is now aimed at elegance and terroir expression. (Though the 200%-new-oak 1998 has turned out v. well.) Owned by Jonathan Maltus, who has a string of other St-Emilions (eg Ch Teyssier) and Australia's Barossa Valley (Colonial Estate).

La Dominique St-Em r ★★★ 89' 90' 94 95 96 98 99 00' 01 03 04 05' 06 Classed growth adjacent to CHEVAL BLANC with potential for rich, aromatic wines. Owner of VALANDRAUD has managed since 2006. To watch. Second label: St Paul de Dominique.

Ducluzeau Listrac r ★★ 94 95 96 00 01 03 04 05 06 Tiny sister property of DUCRU-BEAUCAILLOU. 4 ha, unusually 90% Merlot.

Ducru-Beaucaillou St-Jul r ★★★★ 82' 83' 85' 94 95' 96' 98 99 00' 01 02 03 04 05' 06 Outstanding Second Growth, excellent form except for a patch in the late 1980s; 49 ha overlooking the river. Classic cedar-scented claret suited to long ageing. See also LALANDE-BORIE. Second wine: Croix de Beaucaillou.

Duhart-Milon Rothschild Pau r ★★★ 90 94 95 96' 98 00' 01 02 03 04' 05' 06

Fourth Growth neighbour of LAFITE, under same management. Greater precision from 2002; increasingly fine quality and reputation. Second label: Moulin de Duhart.

Durfort-Vivens Mar r ★★★ 89' 90 94 95 96 98 99 00 02 03 04 05' 06 Relatively small (32-ha) Second Growth owned and being improved by Gonzague Lurton, brother of Henri (BRANE-CANTENAC) and Denis (DESMIRAIL). Recent wines have structure (lots of Cab Sauv) and finesse.

de l'Eglise, Domaine Pom r ★★ 89 90 95 96 98 99 00 01 02 03 04 05' 06 Small property on the clay-gravel plateau: stylish, resonant wine distributed by BORIE-MANOUX. Denis Dubourdieu consults.

L'Eglise-Clinet Pom r ★★★ 89 90' 93' 94 95 96 98' 99 00' 01' 02 03 04 05' 06 A 6-ha estate. Top-flight POMEROL with great consistency; full, concentrated, fleshy wine. Expensive and limited quantity. Second label: La Petite Eglise.

L'Evangile Pom r ★★★★ 88' 89' 90 95 96 98' 99 00' 01 02 03 04' 05' 06 13 ha between PÉTRUS and CHEVAL BLANC. Deep-veined elegant style in a POMEROL classic. Investment by owners (LAFITE) Rothschild has greatly improved quality. New cellars in 2004. Second wine: Blason de l'Evangile.

de Fargues Saut w sw ★★★ 85' 86 88 89 90 95 96 97 98 99' 00 01 02 03' 04 05' 06 A 15-ha v'yd by ruined castle owned by Lur-Saluces, previous owner of YQUEM. Rich, unctuous wines, but balanced – maturing earlier than YQUEM.

Faurie-de-Souchard St-Em r ★★ 95 96 98' 00 03 04 05 06 Underperforming CH on the CÔTES. Lost classified status in 2006 but recent investment and greater effort from new generation. Stéphane Derenoncourt consults.

de Ferrand St-Em r ★★ 90' 94 95 96 98 00 01 03 04 05 Big (30-ha) St-Hippolyte estate. Rich, oaky wines, with plenty of tannin to age.

Ferrande Graves r (w) ★★ 00 01 02 04 05 Major estate at Castres owned by NÉGOCIANT Castel: over 40 ha. Easy, enjoyable red and gd white wine; at their best at 1–4 yrs.

Ferrière Mar r ★★→★★★ 95 96' 98 99 00' 02 03 04 05 06 Tiny third growth restored by same capable hands as LA GURGUE and HAUT-BAGES-LIBÉRAL. Dark, firm, perfumed wines need time.

Feytit-Clinet Pom r ★★ 90' 94 95 96 98 99 00 01 03 04 05' 06 Tiny 6.5-ha property. Once managed by J-P MOUEIX; back with owning Chasseuil family since 2000. Improvements since. Rich, full POMEROL with ageing potential.

Fieuzal Pe-Lé r (w) ★★★ (r) 98' 00 01 05 06 (w) 98' 99 01 02 03 05 06 Classed growth at LÉOGNAN. Recent form has dipped from the heights of the mid-1980s but improvements from 2005. ANGÉLUS owner now consults for reds. New technical director from 2006. So back to winning ways?

Figeac St-Em r ★★★★ 95' 96 98' 99 00' 01 02 03 04 05' 06 First growth, 40-ha gravelly v'yd with unusual 70% Cab Fr and Cab Sauv. Rich but elegant wines; deceptively long ageing. Second wine: Grange Neuve de Figeac.

Filhot Saut w sw dr ★★ 90 95 96' 97' 98 99 01' 02 03' 04 05 Second-rank classed growth with splendid CH, 60-ha v'yd. Difficult young, more complex with age. Light and fine in style.

Fleur Cardinale St-Em r ★★ 98 99 00 01 02 03 04 05' 06 18 ha property east of ST-EMILION. Gd from the 1980s but into overdrive since 2001 with new owner and chai. GRAND CRU CLASSÉ in 2006. Ripe, unctuous, modern style.

La Fleur-de-Gay Pom r ★★★ 1,000-case super-CUVÉE of CH LA CROIX DE GAY.

La Fleur-Pétrus Pom r ★★★★ 89' 90' 94 95 96 98' 99 00' 01 02 03 04 05' 06 A 13-ha v'yd flanking PÉTRUS; same J-P MOUEIX management. Concentration, richness, finesse. This is POMEROL at its most stylish (and expensive).

Words within entries marked like this *Alter Ego de Palmer* indicate wines especially enjoyed by Hugh Johnson over the past 12 months (mid '07–'08).

Fombrauge St-Em r ★★→★★★ 95 96 98 99 00' 01 02 03 04 05 06 A Bernard Magrez wine (see PAPE CLÉMENT), so don't expect restraint. Big estate: 52 ha east of ST-EMILION. Since 1999 rich, dark, chocolatey, full-bodied wines. Magrez-Fombrauge is its GARAGE wine.

Fonbadet Pau r ★★ 95 96' 98' 00' 01 02 03 04 05 06 20-ha PAUILLAC estate. Reliable, gd value and typical of AC style.

Fonplégade St-Em r ★★ 95 96 98 00' 01 03 04 05 06' A 19-ha grand cru classé New owner and investment from 2004. Michel ROLLAND consults. Watch for riper, modern, fruit-driven style.

Fonréaud Listrac r ★★ 95 96 98 00' 02 03 04 05 06 One of the bigger (39 ha) and better LISTRACS producing savoury, mouthfilling wines. Investment since 1998. 2 ha of white: Le Cygne, barrel-fermented. See LESTAGE.

Fonroque St-Em r ★★★ 88 89' 90' 94 95 96 98 01 03 04 05 06 19 ha on the plateau north of ST-EMILION. Biodynamic culture being introduced. Big, deep, dark wine: firm, tannic edge. Managed by Alain Moueix (see MAZEYRES).

Fontenil Fronsac r ★★ 94 95 96 98' 99' 00' 01' 02 03 04 05 06 Leading FRONSAC started by MICHEL ROLLAND in 1986. Dense, oaky, new-style. Défi de Fontenil is its GARAGE wine.

Les Forts de Latour Pau r ★★★ 86 88 89' 90' 93 94 95' 96' 97 98 99 00' 01 02 03 04' 05' 06 The (worthy) second wine of CH LATOUR; the authentic flavour in slightly lighter format at a(relatively) modest price. Until 1990 unique in being bottle-aged at least 3 yrs before release; now offered EN PRIMEUR.

Fourcas-Dupré Listrac r ★★ 89' 90 95 96' 98' 99 00' 01 02 03 04 05 06 Top-class 46-ha estate making consistent wine in tight LISTRAC style. Second label: Ch Bellevue-Laffont. Complete renovation in 2000.

Fourcas-Hosten Listrac r ★★→★★★ 89' 90' 95' 96' 98' 00 01 02 03 04 05 A 48-ha estate with new owners (Hermès fashion connection) from 2006. Firm wine with a long life. Less consistent than FOURCAS-DUPRÉ.

de France Pe-Lé r w ★★ (r) 90' 95' 96' 98 99 00 02 03 04 05 06 (w) 96 98 99 01' 02 03 04 05 06 Well-known northern GRAVES property (the name helps) making consistent wines in a ripe, modern style. MICHEL ROLLAND consults.

Franc-Mayne St-Em r ★★ 90' 94 95 96 98' 99 00' 01 03 04 05 06 A 7.2-ha GRAND CRU CLASSÉ. Ambitious new owners in 1996 and again in 2004. Investment and renovation. Round but firmly constituted wines. To watch.

du Gaby Canon-Fronsac r ★★ 00' 01' 03 04 05 06 Perhaps the finest situation in Bordeaux. New owners in 1999 and again in 2006. Serious wines.

La Gaffelière St-Em r ★★★ 88' 89' 90' 94 95 96 98' 99 00' 01 03 04 05' 06 A 22-ha First Growth at foot of the CÔTES. Elegant, long-ageing wines. More precision and purity from 2000. Stéphane Derenoncourt consulting from 2004.

Galius St-Em r ★★ 00 01 03 04 05 Oak-aged selection from ST-EMILION co-op, to a high standard. Formerly called Haut Quercus.

La Garde Pe-Lé r w ★★ (r) 96' 98' 99 00 01' 02 04 05 06 (w) 01 02 04 05 06 Substantial property of 58 ha owned by négociant CVBG-Dourthe; reliable red and improving. More Merlot planted 2000.

Le Gay Pom r ★★★ 89' 90' 95 96 98 99 00 01 03 04 05' 06 Fine 5.6-ha v'yd on northern edge of POMEROL. Major investment, with MICHEL ROLLAND consulting. Now v. ripe and plummy in style. Ch Montviel same stable and AC.

Gazin Pom r ★★★ 89' 90' 94' 95 96 98' 99 00' 01 02 03 04 05' 06 Large (for POMEROL): 23 ha, family-owned neighbour of PÉTRUS. Recently on gd form. Second label: L'Hospitalet de Gazin.

Gilette Saut w sw ★★★ 49 53 55 59 61 67 70 75 76 78 79 81 82 83 85 86 Extraordinary small Preignac CH stores its sumptuous wines in concrete vats to a great age. Only about 5,000 bottles of each. Ch Les Justices is its sister (96 97 99 01 02 03' 05).

Giscours Labarde-Mar r ★★★ **88** 89' 90 **94 95 96' 98** 99 00' 01 02 03 04 05' 06 Splendid Third Growth south of Cantenac. Excellent vigorous wine in 1970s; 1980s v. wobbly; new ownership from 1995 and revival since 1999. Second label: La Sirène de Giscours. Ch La Houringue is its baby sister.

du Glana St-Jul r ★★ 95 96 98 99 00 00 02 **03** 04 05 06 Large, 44-ha St-Julien estate. Expansion through the acquisition of parcels of land from CH LAGRANGE. Undemanding; undramatic; value. Second wine: Pavillon du Glana.

Gloria St-Jul r ★★→★★★ 95' 96 98 99 **00' 01 02 03** 04 05' 06 A 45-ha ST-JULIEN estate. Same ownership as ST-PIERRE. Wines of vigour, with a recent return to long-maturing style. Second label: Peymartin.

La Gomerie St-Em 1,000 cases, 100% Merlot, *garagiste*. See BEAU-SÉJOUR-BÉCOT.

Grand-Corbin-Despagne St-Em r ★★→★★★ 90' 94 95 96 98 99 00' 01 03 04 05 06 Demoted from GRAND CRU CLASSÉ in 1996 but reinstated in 2006. In between: investment and hard graft. Aromatic wines now with a riper, fuller edge. Also Ch Maison Blanche, MONTAGNE ST-EMILION.

Grand Cru Classé see St-Emilion classification box, p.89.

Grand-Mayne St-Em r ★★★ 89' 90' **94** 95 96 98 99 00' 01' 02 03 04 05' Leading 16-ha GRAND CRU CLASSÉ on western CÔTES. Noble old CH with wonderfully rich, tasty wines. New generation in control.

Grand-Pontet St-Em r ★★★ 95' **96** 98' 99 **00'** 01 02 03 04 05 06 A 14-ha estate revitalized since 1985. Quality much improved. See BEAU-SÉJOUR-BÉCOT.

Grand-Puy-Ducasse Pau r ★★★ 89' 90 **94** 95 96' 98' 99 00 01 02 **03** 04 05' 06 Fifth Growth enlarged to 40 ha under expert management; improvements in the 1990s, but lacks vigour of next entry. Second label: Ch Artigues-Arnaud.

Grand-Puy-Lacoste Pau r ★★★ **82** 85' **86' 88 89'** 90' 94 95' **96' 98** 99 00' 01 02 03 04 05' 06 Leading 50-ha Fifth Growth famous for excellent full-bodied, vigorous examples of PAUILLAC. Same ownership as HAUT-BATAILLEY. Second label: Lacoste-Borie.

La Grave à Pomerol Pom r ★★★ **89' 90 94** 95 96 98' 00 01 **02 03** 04 05 06 Verdant CH with small but first-class v'yd owned by Christian MOUEIX. Beautifully structured POMEROL of medium richness.

Gressier-Grand-Poujeaux Moulis r ★★→★★★ **89 90 94** 95 96 **98** 00 01 03 04 05 (06) 20-ha MOULIS property. Fine firm wine with gd track record. Repays patient cellaring. Since 2003, same owners as CHASSE-SPLEEN.

Greysac Méd r ★★ **95 96** 98 00' **02 03** 04 05 06 Elegant 70-ha MÉDOC estate. Same management as CANTEMERLE. Fine, consistent style.

Gruaud-Larose St-Jul r ★★★★ **86' 88 89'** 90' 94 95' **96' 98** 99 00' 01 02 04 05' 06 One of the biggest, best-loved Second Growths. 82 ha. Smooth, rich, stylish claret; ages 20+ yrs. Second wine: *Sarget de Gruaud-Larose*.

Guadet-St-Julien St-Em ★★ **89** 90' **95 96'** 98 00 01 04 05 06 Firm, classic style. Poor track record resulted in contested demotion from GRAND CRU CLASSÉ in 2006. Now a Stéphane Derenoncourt consultancy.

Guiraud Saut w (r) sw (dr) ★★★ **88' 89'** 90' 95 96' 97' 98 **99 01'** 02 03 04 05' 06 Top quality classed growth. Over 100 ha. New owning consortium from 2006 includes existing manager, Xavier Planty, and CANON-LA-GAFFELIERE and DOM DE CHEVALIER connections.

La Gurgue Mar r ★★ 98 00' 01 **02 03** 04 05' 06 Well-placed 10-ha property, for fine MARGAUX. Same management as HAUT-BAGES-LIBÉRAL.

Hanteillan Cissac r ★★ **96 98** 00' 02 **03** 04 05' Huge 82-ha HAUT-MÉDOC v'yd: v. fair wines, conscientiously made. 50% Merlot. Second wine: Ch Laborde.

Haut-Bages Averous Pau r ★★ **95 96** 98 99 00 **01 02 03** 04 05 The second wine of

To decipher codes, please refer to "Key to symbols" on the front flap of jacket, or "How to use this book" on p.10.

LYNCH-BAGES. Tasty drinking and fairly consistent.

Haut-Bages-Libéral Pau r ★★★ **96' 98 99 00 01 02** 03 04 05' 06 Lesser-known Fifth Growth of 28 ha (next to LATOUR) in same stable as LA GURGUE. Results are excellent, full of PAUILLAC vitality. Usually gd value.

Haut-Bages-Monpelou Pau r ★★ **95 96 98 99 00 03** 04 05 06 A 15-ha stablemate of CH BATAILLEY on former DUHART-MILON land. Gd minor PAUILLAC.

Haut-Bailly Graves r ★★★ 89' 90' 95 96 **98' 99 00' 01 02 03** 04 05' 06 Over 28 ha at LÉOGNAN. Since 1979 some of the best savoury, round, intelligently made red GRAVES. New ownership and investment from 1998 (but same manager) have taken it to greater heights. Second label La Parde de Haut-Bailly.

Haut-Batailley Pau r ★★★ **89' 90'** 95 96' 98 99 00 02 03 04 05' 06 Smaller part of divided Fifth Growth BATAILLEY: 20 ha. Gentler than sister CH GRAND-PUY-LACOSTE. New cellar in 2005;more precision. Second wine: La Tour-d'Aspic.

Haut-Beauséjour St-Est r ★★ **95 98 99 00 01 03** 04 05 18-ha property revitalised since 1992 by owner CHAMPAGNE house ROEDERER. See also DE PEZ.

Haut-Bergey Pessac-L r (w) ★★ (r) 98 99 00 01 02 01 05 06 (w) **02 03 04 05** 06 A 26-ha estate now producing a denser, more modern GRAVES with oak overlay. Also a little dry white. Completely renovated in the 1990s. Same ownership as BARDE-HAUT and CLOS L'ÉGLISE. Sister Ch Branon.

Haut-Brion Pessac, Graves r ★★★★ (r) **78' 79' 81 82' 83'** 85' 86' 88' 89' 90' 93 **94 95' 96'** 97 **98' 99** 00' 01 02 03 04 05' 06 Oldest great CH of Bordeaux and only non-MÉDOC First Growth of 1855. 48 ha. Deeply harmonious, never-aggressive wine with endless, honeyed, earthy complexity. Consistently great since 1975. A little dry, sumptuous white: **90 93 94** 95 96 **98 99 00'** 01 02 03 **04'** 05' 06. See BAHANS-HAUT-BRION, LA MISSION-HAUT-BRION, LAVILLE-HAUT-BRION.

Haut Condissas Méd r ★★ **99 00 01 02 03** 04 05 06 Aspiring new *cru* at Bégadan. Old-vine selection from Ch Rollan-de-By. Same ownership as Chx La Clare, La Tour Séran.

Haut-Marbuzet St-Est r ★★·→★★★ 89' 90' 95 96' 98 99 **00' 01** 02 03 04 05' 06 Leading non-classified ST-ESTÈPHE estate. Rich, unctuous wines that age well. M Dubosq has reassembled ancient Dom de Marbuzet, in total 71 ha. Also owns Chambert-Marbuzet, MacCarthy, Tour de Marbuzet. Haut-Marbuzet is 60% Merlot, seductive and remarkably consistent.

Haut-Pontet St-Em r ★★ **98 00 01 03 04** 05 Reliable 4.8-ha Merlot v'yd of the CÔTES. New owner (Janoueix – see next entry) from 2007.

Haut-Sarpe St-Em r ★★ 89 90' **94 95 96 98 00'** 01 03 04 05 06 21-ha GRAND CRU CLASSÉ with elegant CH and park, 70% Merlot. Same owner (Janoueix) as CH LA CROIX, POMEROL. Modern style.

Hortevie St-Jul r ★★ **90** 95 96 98 00 02 03 04 05 (06) One of the few non-classified ST-JULIENS. This tiny v'yd and its bigger sister TERREY-GROS-CAILLOU are gd value.

Hosanna Pom r ★★★★ **99 00 01 02 03** 04 05' 06 Formerly Certan-Guiraud until purchased and renamed by J-P MOUEIX. Only the best 4.5 ha retained. First vintages confirm its class. New cellar in 2007. Worthy stablemate of PÉTRUS and TROTANOY.

d'Issan Cantenac-Mar r ★★★ 95 96' **98 99 00' 01 02** 03 04' 05 06 Beautifully restored moated CH nr Gironde with 30-ha Third Growth v'yd. Fragrant wines; more substance since late 90s. Second label: Blason d'Issan.

Kirwan Cantenac-Mar r ★★★ 88 89' 90' **94 95 96 98 99 00' 01** 02 **03** 04 05' 06 A 35-ha Third Growth; from 1997 majority owned by SCHRÖDER & SCHŸLER. Mature v'yds now giving classy wines. Rich style: MICHEL ROLLAND influenced until 2007. Second label: Les Charmes de Kirwan.

Labégorce Mar r ★★ 95 96 98 99 00 01 02 03 04 05' Substantial 41-ha estate north of MARGAUX revamped since 1989; meaty, long-lived MARGAUX. See also next entry and MARQUIS D'ALESME-BECKER.

Labégorce-Zédé Mar r ★★–★★★ 89' 90' 95 96' 98 99 00' 01 02 03 04 05' 06 28 ha north of MARGAUX with same ownership as LABEGORCE. Typically delicate, fragrant, classic. Second label: Dom Zédé. One to watch.

Lafaurie-Peyraguey Saut w sw ★★★ 82 83' 85 86' 88' 89' 90' 95 96' 97 98 99 00 01' 02 03'04 05' 06 Fine 40-ha classed growth at Bommes; owners Groupe Banque Suez. One of best buys in SAUTERNES. Second wine: La Chapelle de Lafaurie.

Lafite-Rothschild Pau r ★★★★ 82' 83 85 86' 88' 89' 90' 93 94 95 96' 97 98' 99 00' 01' 02 03' 04' 05' 06 First Growth of famous elusive perfume and style, but never huge weight, although more density and sleeker texture from 1996. Great vintages keep for decades; recent vintages well up to form. Amazing circular cellars. Joint ventures in Chile (1988), California (1989), Portugal (1992), Argentina (1999), and now the Midi and Italy. Second wine: Carruades de Lafite. 91 ha. Also owns CHX DUHART-MILON, L'ÉVANGILE, RIEUSSEC.

Lafleur Pom r ★★★★ 83 85' 86 88' 89' 90' 93 94 95 96 98' 99' 00' 01' 02 03 04' 05' 06 Superb 4.8-ha property. Resounding wine of the elegant, intense, less fleshy kind for long maturing and investment. 50% Cab Fr. Second wine: Pensées de Lafleur.

Lafleur-Gazin Pom r ★★ 89 90 94 95 96 98 00 01 04 05 06 Distinguished small J-P MOUEIX estate on the northeastern border of POMEROL.

Lafon-Rochet St-Est r ★★★ 88' 89' 90' 94 95 96' 98 99 00' 01 02 03' 04 05' 06 Fourth Growth neighbour of COS D'ESTOURNEL, 45 ha with distinctive yellow cellars (and label). Investment, selection, and a higher percentage of Merlot have made this ST-ESTÈPHE more opulent since 1998. Second label: Les Pèlerins de Lafon-Rochet.

Lagrange Pom r ★★ 89' 90' 94 95 96 98 00 01 04 05 06 An 8-ha v'yd in the centre of POMEROL run by the ubiquitous house of J-P MOUEIX. Gd value but not in the same league as HOSANNA, LA FLEUR-PÉTRUS, LATOUR-À-POMEROL, etc.

Lagrange St-Jul r ★★★ 88' 89' 90' 94 95 96 98 99 00' 01 02 03 04 05' 06 Formerly neglected Third Growth owned since 1983 by Suntory. 113 ha now in tip-top condition with wines to match. Marcel Ducasse oversaw the resurrection until retirement in 2007. Second wine: Les Fiefs de Lagrange.

La Lagune Ludon, H-Méd r ★★★ 90'95 96' 98 00' 02 03 04 05' 80-ha Third Growth in southern MÉDOC with sandy-gravel soils. Dipped in the 1990s but on form from 2000. Fine-edged, now with added structure and depth. New CHAI 2004. Owned by Jean-Jacques Frey, who recently acquired JABOULET AÎNÉ (Rhône).

Lalande-Borie St-Jul r ★★ 96 98 00 01 02 03 04 05 06 A baby brother of the great DUCRU-BEAUCAILLOU created from part of the former v'yd of CH LAGRANGE. Gracious, easy-drinking wine.

de Lamarque Lamarque, H-Méd r ★★ 90' 94 95 96 98 99 00' 02 03 04 05 06 Splendid medieval fortress in central MÉDOC with 35-ha v'yd; competent, mid-term wines. Second wine: Donjon de L.

Lamothe Bergeron H-Méd r ★★ 89 90 95 96' 98' 00 02 03 04 05 (06) Large 67-ha estate in Cussac Fort Médoc making reliable claret.

Lanessan Cussac, H-Méd r ★★ 89' 90' 94 95 96' 98 00' 02 03 04 05 (06) Distinguished 44-ha property just south of ST-JULIEN. Fine rather than burly, but ages well. Horse museum and tours.

Langoa-Barton St-Jul r ★★ 90' 94 95' 96' 98 99 00' 01 02 03 04' 05' 06 20-ha Third Growth sister CH to LÉOVILLE-BARTON. V. old (1821) Barton-family estate; impeccable standards, great value. Second wine: Réserve de Léoville-Barton.

Larcis-Ducasse St-Em r ★★ 88' 89' 90' 94 95 96 98' 00 02 03 04 05' 06 Top classed-growth property of St-Laurent, eastern neighbour of ST-EMILION, on the CÔTES. 12 ha in a fine situation; wines on an upward swing since new management in 2002 (PAVIE-MACQUIN and PUYGUERAUD).

Larmande St-Em r ★★★ **89' 90' 94 95' 96** 98' 00' 01 03 04 05 Substantial 24-ha property owned by Le Mondiale insurance (as is SOUTARD). Replanted, re-equipped, and now making rich, strikingly scented wine, silky in time. Second label: Ch des Templiers.

Laroque St-Em r ★★→★★★ **88 89** 90 **94** 95 **96** 98 **99** 00' 01 02 03 04 05 06 Important GRAND CRU CLASSÉ in St-Christophe: 58-ha v'yd on the ST-EMILION CÔTES with 17th-century CH. Well-structured wines for ageing. More progress from 2000.

Larose-Trintaudon St-Laurent, H-Méd r ★★ **98 00 01 02 03 04 05** The biggest v'yd in the MÉDOC: 172 ha. Modern methods make reliable, fruity and charming wine to drink young. Second label: Larose St-Laurent. Special CUVÉE (from 1996): Larose Perganson; from 33-ha parcel.

Laroze St-Em r ★★ **90' 95 96' 98' 99** 00 01 **02** 05 06 Large v'yd (30 ha) on western CÔTES. Lighter-framed wines from sandy soils, more depth from 1998; approachable when young. New "tribaie" grape-sorting machine (v. ingenious, sorts according to specific gravity, and thus ripeness) in use.

Larrivet-Haut-Brion Pe-Lé r w ★★ (r) **90 94 95 96' 98' 00 01 02 03 04' 05' 06** Substantial 56-ha LÉOGNAN property with classed-growth aspirations; MICHEL ROLLAND consulting. Rich, modern red. Also 4,500 cases of fine, barrel-fermented white (**96' 98' 99 00 01 02 04' 05** 06). New barrel cellar and tasting room in 2007. Second wine: Les Demoiselles de Larrivet-Haut-Brion.

Lascombes Mar r (p) ★★★ **89' 90'** 95 **96' 98' 99 00** 01 **02** 03 04 05' 06 A 97-ha Second Growth. Wines have been wobbly, but real improvements from 2001. MICHEL ROLLAND consults. Second label: Chevalier de Lascombes.

Latour Pau r ★★★★ **78' 81 82' 85 86' 88' 89' 90'** 91 93 **94 95' 96' 97 98 99** 00' 01 02 03' 04' 05' 06 First Growth considered the grandest statement of the MÉDOC. Profound, intense, almost immortal wines in great yrs; even weaker vintages have the characteristic note of terroir and run for many yrs. 60 ha sloping to river Gironde. Latour always needs 10 yrs to show its hand. New state-of-the-art CHAI (2003) allows more precise vinification. Second wine: LES FORTS DE LATOUR; third wine: PAUILLAC.

Latour-Martillac Pe-Lé r w ★★ (r) **98 00 01** 01 02 03 04 05' 06 A 42-ha classed-growth property in Martillac. Regular quality (red and white); gd value at this level. The white can age admirably (**98' 99 00 01 02 03 04 05** 06).

Latour-à-Pomerol Pom r ★★★ **86 88' 89' 90' 94 95 96 98' 99 00' 01 02** 04 05' 06 Top growth of 7.6 ha under J.P. MOUEIX management. POMEROL of great power and perfume, yet also ravishing finesse.

des Laurets St-Em r ★★ **03 04 05** Major property in PUISSEGUIN-ST-EMILION and MONTAGNE-ST-EMILION (to the east), with 72 ha of v'yd evenly split on the CÔTES (40,000 cases). Owned by Benjamin de Rothschild (2003).

Laville-Haut-Brion Pe-Lé w ★★★★ **89' 90 92 93' 94 95' 96' 98 99 00'** 01 02 03 04' 05' 06 Only 6,000 bottles/yr of v. best white GRAVES for long, succulent maturing, made at La Mission-Haut-Brion. Great consistency. Mainly Sem.

Léoville-Barton St-Jul r ★★★★ **86' 88' 89' 90' 93' 94' 95' 96' 98** 99 00' 01 02 03' 04 05' 06 A 45-ha portion of the great Second Growth LÉOVILLE v'yd in Anglo-Irish hands of the Barton family for over 150 yrs. Powerful, classic claret; traditional methods, v. fair prices. Major investment raised already high standards to Super Second. See also LANGOA-BARTON.

Léoville-Las-Cases St-Jul r ★★★★ **82' 83' 85' 86' 88 89' 90' 93 94 95' 96' 97 98 99** 00' 01 02 03' 04' 05' 06 The largest LÉOVILLE; 97 ha with daunting reputation. Elegant, complex, powerful, austere wines, for immortality. Second label CLOS DU MARQUIS is also outstanding.

Léoville-Poyferré St-Jul r ★★★ **86' 88 89' 90' 94 95 96 98 99** 00' 01 02 03' 04 05' 06 For yrs the least outstanding of LÉOVILLES. but a renaissance in the 1980s and 1990s. Now at Super Second level with dark, rich, spicy, long-ageing wines. ROLLAND consults at the 80-ha estate. Second label: Ch Moulin-Riche.

Lestage Listrac r ★★ 90' 95 96 98 00 02 03 04 05 06 A 42-ha LISTRAC estate in same hands as CH FONREAUD. Firm, slightly austere claret. Second wine: La Dame du Coeur de Ch Lestage.

Lilian Ladouys St-Est r ★★ 95 96 98 00 02 03 04 05 06 Created in the 1980s, the v'yd now covers 45 ha with 100 parcels of vines. Firm, sometimes robust wines; recent vintages more finesse. Georges Pauli (GRUAUD-LAROSE connections) winemaker.

Liot Barsac w sw ★★ 88 89' 90' 95 96 97' 98 99 01' 02 03 05 Consistent, fairly light, golden wines from 20 ha. Gd to drink early, but they last.

Liversan St-Sauveur, H-Méd r ★★ 90' 94 95 96 98 00 02 03 04 05 (06) A 47-ha estate inland from PAUILLAC. Same owner – Jean-Michel Lapalu – as PATACHE D'AUX. Quality oriented. Second wine: Les Charmes de Liversan.

Loudenne St-Yzans, Méd r ★★ 90 94 95 96' 98 00 01 02 03 04 05 (06) Beautiful riverside CH owned for a century (until 2000) by Gilbeys. MICHEL ROLLAND consults, so wines are getting bigger, denser. Well-made red from 63 ha. Also an oak-scented Sauv Bl white best at 2–4 yrs (99' 00 01 02 04 05 06).

Loupiac-Gaudiet Loupiac w sw ★★ 96 97 98 99 01 02 03' 05 A reliable source of gd-value "almost-SAUTERNES", just across river Garonne.

La Louvière Pe-Lé r w ★★★ (r) 95 96' 98' 99 00' 01 02 04 05 06 (w) 98' 99 00 01 02 03 04' 05' 06 A 55-ha LÉOGNAN estate with classical mansion restored by André Lurton. Excellent white and red of classed-growth standard. See also BONNET, DE CRUZEAU, COUHINS-LURTON, and DE ROCHEMORIN.

de Lussac St-Em r ★★ 99 00 03 04 05 06 One of the best estates in LUSSAC-ST-EMILION. New owners and technical methods since 2000.

Lynch-Bages Pau r (w) ★★★★ 82' 85' 86' 88' 89' 90' 94 95' 96' 98 99 00' 01 02 03 04' 05' 06 Always popular, now a regular star. 90 ha. Rich, robust wine: deliciously dense, brambly; aspiring to greatness. See also HAUT-BAGES-AVEROUS. From 1990, gd intense oaky white – Blanc de Lynch-Bages. Same owners (Cazes family) as LES ORMES-DE-PEZ and Villa Bel-Air.

Lynch-Moussas Pau r ★★ 90' 95' 96' 98 00' 01 02 03 04 05' Fifth Growth restored by the director of CH BATAILLEY. On the up since 2000 but still relatively simple.

du Lyonnat Lussac-St-Em r ★★ 98 00' 01 03 04 05 A 49-ha estate; well-distributed, reliable wine.

Macquin-St-Georges St-Em r ★★ 95 96 98 99 00 01 03 04 05 Steady producer of delicious, not weighty, satellite ST-EMILION at ST-GEORGES.

Magdelaine St-Em r ★★★ 86 88 89' 90' 94 95 96 98' 99 00 01 03 04 05 06 Leading CÔTES First Growth: 11 ha owned by J-P MOUEIX. Top-notch, Merlot-led wine; complex, fine and deceptively long-lived.

Malartic-Lagravière Pe-Lé r (w) ★★★ (r) 90' 95 96 98 99 00' 01 02 03 04' 05' 06 (w) 98 99 00 01' 02 03 04' 05' 06 LÉOGNAN classed growth of 53 ha (majority

BORDEAUX

Au revoir Crus Bourgeois

The 2003 reclassification of the Crus Bourgeois of the Médoc has been officially annulled and the words banned from labels. It's a complete inanity as the inscription was clearly a reference for consumers. To be uncharacteristically PC, we've taken out all mentions of CB from this edition, but the designation is likely to be used for vintages up to and including 2006. Behind the scenes the winemakers' associations, l'Alliance des Crus Bourgeois du Médoc is working on a new certificate, "Qualification Cru Bourgeois", to be awarded on a yearly basis according to a set of rules. So watch this space.

red). Rich, modern red wine since late 1990s; a little long-ageing Sauv Bl white. Belgian owner (since 96) has revolutionized the property. ROLLAND advises. Ch Gazin Rocquencourt (PESSAC-LÉOGNAN) new acquisition in 2006.

Malescasse Lamarque, H-Méd r ★★ **96 98 00 01 02 03 04** 05 06 Renovated property with 40 well-situated ha between MARGAUX and ST-JULIEN. Second label: La Closerie de Malescasse. Supple wines, accessible early.

Malescot-St-Exupéry Mar r ★★★ 90' **94 95 96 98 99 00'** 01 **02 03** 04 05' 06 Third Growth of 24 ha returned to fine form in the 1990s. Now ripe, fragrant, and finely structured. MICHEL ROLLAND advises.

de Malle Saut w r sw dr ★★★ (w sw) **89' 90' 94 95 96' 97' 98 99 00' 02** 03' 05 06 Beautiful Preignac CH of 50 ha. V. fine, medium-bodied SAUTERNES; also M de Malle dry white and GRAVES Ch du Cardaillan.

Marbuzet St-Est r ★★ 90 **94 95' 96' 98** 99 00' 01 **02** 03 04 05' 06 Second label of COS-D'ESTOURNEL until 1994. Same owners. Now a separate estate of 7 ha. Firm but generous ST-ESTÈPHE style.

Margaux, Château Mar r (w) ★★★★ **83' 85' 86' 88' 89' 90' 91 93 94 95' 96' 97 98' 99** 00' 01' 02 03' 04' 05' 06 First Growth (85 ha); the most seductive and fabulously perfumed of all in its frequent top vintages. Pavillon Rouge (**96' 98 99 00' 01 02 03** 04' 05') is second wine. Pavillon Blanc is best white (Sauv Bl) of MÉDOC, but expensive (**99 00' 01' 02** 03 04' **05** 06).

Marojallia Mar r ★★★ 99 **00' 01 02 03** 04 05' 06 Micro-CH with 2.5 ha, looking for big prices for big, rich, beefy, un-MARGAUX-like wines. Upmarket bed-and-breakfast as well. Second wine: Clos Margalaine.

Marquis-d'Alesme-Becker Mar r ★★ **89 90** 95 98 00 **01 04** 05 06 17-ha Third Growth. Disappointing in recent yrs. Purchased by CH LABÉGORCE in 2006, so keep an eye out for change.

Marquis-de-Terme Mar r ★★→★★★ **89' 90'** 95 96 98 99 00' **01 02 03** 04 05' 06 Renovated Fourth Growth of 40 ha. Wobbled in the 1990s but looks better since 2000. Solid rather than elegant MARGAUX.

Martinens Mar r ★★ **96** 98 99 00 **02 03** 04 05 (06) Worthy 30-ha in Cantenac.

Maucaillou Moulis r ★★ **96 98' 00' 01 02 03 04** 05 06 An 80-ha property in MOULIS with gd standards. Clean, fresh, value wines. Cap de Haut-Maucaillou is second wine.

Mazeyres Pom r ★★ 95 **96' 98' 99** 00 **01 04** 05' 06 Consistent, if not exciting lesser POMEROL. 20 ha. Better since 1996. Alain Moueix, cousin of Christian of J-P MOUEIX, manages here. See FONROQUE.

Meyney St-Est r ★★→★★★ **89' 89'** 90' **94** 95 96 98 00 **01 02** 03 04 05' 06 Big (50-ha) riverside property in a superb situation next to MONTROSE. Rich, robust, well-structured wines. Second label: Prieur de Meyney.

La Mission-Haut-Brion Pe-Lé r ★★★★ **83 85' 86 88 89' 90' 93 94** 95 **96' 98' 99** 00' **01** 02 03 04' 05' 06 Neighbour and long-time rival to HAUT-BRION; since 1983 in same hands. Consistently grand-scale, full-blooded, long-maturing wine; more flamboyant than HAUT-BRION and sometimes more impressive. 20 ha. Second label: La Chapelle de la Mission. White: LAVILLE-HAUT-BRION.

Monbousquet St-Em r (w) ★★★ **95 96** 98 99 **00'** 01 **02** 03 04 05' 06 Substantial property on St-Emilion's gravel plain revolutionized by new owner. Now super-rich, concentrated and voluptuous wines. Elevated to GRAND CRU CLASSÉ in 2006. Rare white (AC BORDEAUX) from 1998. New owners also acquired PAVIE and PAVIE-DECESSE in 1998.

Monbrison Arsac-Mar r ★★→★★★ **88' 89'** 90 95 **96'** 98 99 00 **01 02** 04 05 06 MARGAUX of a v. fine, elegant, lacy style. Sometimes too light. 13 ha.

La Mondotte St-Em r ★★★→★★★★ **96'** 97 98' 99 **00' 01 02** 03 04' 05' 06 Intense, always firm, virile *garagiste* wines from micro-property owned by Comte Stephan von Neipperg (CANON-LA-GAFFELIÈRE, CLOS DE L'ORATOIRE).

Montrose St-Est r ★★★→★★★★ 88 89' 90' 93 94 95 96' 98 99 00' 01 02 03'04' 05' 06 64-ha Second Growth famed for deep-coloured, forceful claret. Known as the LATOUR of ST-ESTÈPHE. Vintages 79–85 (except 82) were lighter. After 110 yrs in same family hands, change of ownership in 2006. Ex-HAUT-BRION director, Jean-Bernard Delmas, now managing. New investment. Second wine: La Dame de Montrose.

Moulin du Cadet St-Em r p ★★ 95 96 98 00 01 03 05 Little 5-ha GRAND CRU CLASSÉ v'yd on the limestone plateau, now managed by Alain Moueix (see also MAZEYRES). Biodynamics practised. Fragrant, medium-bodied wine.

Moulinet Pom r ★★ 95 96 98 00 01 04 05 06 One of POMEROL's bigger CHX; 18 ha on lightish soil. Denis Durantou of l'ÉGLISE-CLINET consults.

Moulin Pey-Labrie Canon-Fronsac r ★★ 90 94 95 96 98' 99 00' 01 02 03 04 05' 06 Leading property in FRONSAC. Stylish wines with elegance and structure.

Moulin de la Rose St-Jul r ★★ 95 96 98 00' 01' 02 03 04 05 06 Tiny 4-ha in ST-JULIEN; high standards.

Moulin-St-Georges St-Em r ★★ 95 96 98 99 00' 01 02 03 04 05 06 Stylish and rich wine. Classed-growth level. Same ownership as AUSONE.

Moulin-à-Vent Moulis r ★★ 95 96' 98 00' 02 03 04 05' 06 A 25-ha MOULIS estate; usually regular quality. Lively, forceful wine.

Mouton Rothschild Pau r (w) ★★★★ 82' 83' 85' 86' 88' 89' 90' 93' 94 95' 96 97 98' 99 00' 01' 02 03 04' 05' 06' Officially a First Growth since 1973, though in reality far longer. 71 ha (87% Cab Sauv) can make majestic, rich wine, often MÉDOC's most opulent (also, from 1991, white Aile d'Argent). Artists' labels and unique private museum of art relating to wine. Second wine: Le Petit Mouton from 1997. See also Opus One (California) and Almaviva (Chile).

Nairac Saut w sw ★★ 86' 88 89 90' 95' 96 97' 98 99 01' 02 03' 04 05' Perfectionist BARSAC classed growth. Rich, intense, botrytized wines from 16 ha.

Nenin Pom r ★★★ 89 90 94' 95 96 98 99 00' 01 02 03 04 05 06 LÉOVILLE-LAS-CASES ownership since 1997. Massive investment. New cellars. 4 ha of former Certan-Giraud acquired in 1999. Now a total of 34 ha. On an upward swing. Gd-value second wine: Fugue de Nenin.

Olivier Graves r w ★★★ (r) 95 96 00 01 02 04' 05' 06 (w) 96 97 98' 00 01 02 03 04' 05' 06 A 55-ha classed growth, surrounding a moated castle at LÉOGNAN. A sleeper finally being turned around. Greater purity, expression, and quality from 2002 onwards.

Les Ormes-de-Pez St-Est r ★★→★★★ 90' 94 95 96 98 99 00' 01 02 03 04 05 06 Outstanding 29-ha property owned by LYNCH-BAGES. Consistently one of the most delicious ST-ESTÈPHES. Crus Bourgeoise (until the term was suspended.)

Les Ormes-Sorbet Méd r ★★ 95 96 98' 99 00' 01 02 03' 04 05 06 Long-time leader in northern MÉDOC. 21 ha at Couquèques. Elegant, gently oaked wines that age. Second label: Ch de Conques.

Palmer Cantenac-Mar r ★★★★ 70' 78' 81 82 83' 85 86' 88' 89 90 93 94 95 96' 98' 99 00 01' 02 03 04' 05' 06 The star of Cantenac: a Third Growth on a par with the Super Seconds. Wine of power, flesh, delicacy, and much Merlot. 52 ha with Dutch, British (the SICHEL family), and French owners. Second wine: Alter Ego de Palmer (a steal for early drinking).

Pape-Clément Pe-Lé r (w) ★★★→★★★★ (r) 90' 94 95 96 98' 99 00' 01 02 03 04 05 06 (w) 01 02 03 04 05' Ancient PESSAC v'yd owned by wine tycoon Bernard Magrez; record of seductive, scented, not ponderous reds. 2.5 ha of elegant, barrel-fermented white. Ambitious new-wave direction, oak and potency from 2000. Also Ch Poumey at Gradignan.

de Parenchère r (w) ★★ 00 01 02 03 04 05 Steady supply of useful AC Ste-Foy BORDEAUX and AC BORDEAUX SUPÉRIEUR from handsome CH with 65 ha. CUVÉE Raphael best.

Patache d'Aux Bégadan, Méd r ★★ **98 99** 00 **02** 03 **04** 05' 06 A 43-ha property in the northern MÉDOC. Fragrant, largely Cab Sauv wine with the earthy quality of its area. See also LIVERSAN.

Pavie St-Em r ★★★ 90' **94 95 96 98' 99** 00' 01 **02** 03' 04 05' 06 Splendidly sited First Growth; 37 ha mid-slope on the CÔTES. Great track record. Bought by owners of MONBOUSQUET, along with adjacent PAVIE-DECESSE. This is new-wave ST-EMILION: thick, intense, sweet, mid-Atlantic, and subject of heated debate.

Pavie-Decesse St-Em r ★★ 90 95 **96 98' 99 00'** 01' **02** 03 04 05' 06 Small 3.6-ha classed growth. Brother to the above and on form since 1998.

Pavie-Macquin St-Em r ★★★ 89' 90' **94** 95 96' **98' 99 00' 01 02** 03 04 05' 06 Surprise elevation to PREMIER GRAND CRU CLASSÉ in 2006. 15-ha v'yd on the limestone plateau east of ST-EMILION. Astute management and winemaking by Nicolas Thienpont of PUYGUERAUD and consultant Stéphane Derenoncourt. Powerful, structured wines that need time in bottle.

Pedesclaux Pau r ★★ 98' 99 **00 02** 03 04 05 06 Underachieving Fifth Growth being steadily revived. New management and investment from 1996. Supple wines with up to 50% Merlot.

Petit-Village Pom r ★★★ 90' **94** 95 **96 98' 99 00'** 01 **03** 04 05 06 Top property aiming for greater heights. Stéphane Derenoncourt now consulting. New cellar in 2007. 11 ha; same owner (AXA Insurance) as PICHON-LONGUEVILLE since 1989. Powerful, plummy wine. Second wine: Le Jardin de Petit-Village.

Pétrus Pom r ★★★★ 71' 75' 76 78 79' 81 82' 83 85' 86 88' **89'** 90 93' 94 **95'** 96 97 **98'** 99 00' 01 02 03 04' 05' 06 The (unofficial) First Growth of POMEROL: Merlot solo *in excelsis*. 11 ha of gravelly clay giving 5,000 cases of massively rich and concentrated wine, on allocation to the world's millionaires. Each vintage adds lustre. Long-time winemaker Jean-Claude Berrouet (44 vintages) retired in 2007. Son Olivier now at helm. Christian Moueix remains incharge.

Peyrabon St-Sauveur, H-Méd r ★★ **98 99** 00' 01 **02 03 04** 05 (06) Serious 53-ha HAUT-MÉDOC estate owned by négociant. Also La Fleur-Peyrabon in PAUILLAC.

de Pez St-Est r ★★·→★★ **89 90' 94 95' 96 98' 99** 00 01 **02** 03 04 05' 06 Outstanding ST-ESTÈPHE *cru* of 24 ha. As reliable as any of the village's classed growths, if not quite so fine. Bought in 1995 by ROEDERER.

Phélan-Ségur St-Est r ★★·→★★★ 88' 89' 90' 95 **96' 98** 99 00' 01 **02** 03 04 05' 06 Big and important estate (89 ha); rivals the last as one of ST-ESTÈPHE's best. From 1988 has built up a strong reputation.

Pibran Pau r ★★ 88 **89'** 90' **94** 95 96 99 00 **01** 03 04 05' 06 Small 17-ha property allied to PICHON-LONGUEVILLE. Classy wine with PAUILLAC drive.

Pichon-Longueville (formerly **Baron de Pichon-Longueville**) Pau r ★★★★ 83 85 86' 88' 89' 90' 93 94' **95 96 98 99** 00' 01 02 03' 04 05' 06 Second Growth (70 ha) with revitalized powerful PAUILLAC wine on a par with the following entry. Owners AXA Insurance. Second label: Les Tourelles de Longueville.

Pichon-Longueville Comtesse de Lalande (Pichon Lalande) Pau r ★★★★ 76 78' 79' 81 82' 83 85' 86' 88' 89' 90' **94** 95 96 **98** 99 00 **01** 02 03' 04 05' 06 Super-Second Growth neighbour to LATOUR (75 ha). Always among the v. top performers; a long-lived, Merlot-marked wine of fabulous breed, even in lesser yrs. ROEDERER now owner; same management. Second wine: Réserve de la Comtesse. Other property: CH BERNADOTTE.

Le Pin Pom r ★★★★ 82 83 85 86 88 89 90' **94 95 96** 97 **98' 99 00 01** 02 04' 05' 06 The original of the BORDEAUX cult mini-*crus*. A mere 500 cases of Merlot, with same family behind it as VIEUX-CH-CERTAN (a much better buy). Almost as rich as its drinkers, but prices well beyond PÉTRUS are ridiculous.

de Pitray Castillon r ★★ 95 **96' 98'** 00' 03 **04** 05 Large (31-ha) v'yd on CÔTES DE CASTILLON. Flavoursome wines, once the best-known of the AC.

Plince Pom r ★★ 89' **90 94** 95 **96 98'** 99 00' 01 **04** 05 06 Reliable 8-ha property nr

Libourne. Vines planted in a single parcel on sandy soil. Lightish wine.

La Pointe Pom r ★★→★★★ 89' 90' 95 96 98' 99 00' 01 04 05' 06 Prominent 25-ha estate; wines recently plumper and more pleasing. New (insurance co) owner.

Pontac-Monplaisir Pe-Lé r (w) ★★ 96 98 99 00 02 04 05' 06 16-ha property nearly lost to B'x sprawl. Useful white and red of surprising quality.

Pontet-Canet Pau r ★★★ 86' 88 89' 90 94' 95 96' 98 99 00' 01 02' 03 04' 05' 06 An 81-ha neighbour to MOUTON-ROTHSCHILD. Dragged its feet for many yrs. Old hard tannins were a turn-off. Since mid-1990s v. fine results. V. PAUILLAC in style. Biodynamic aspirations. Second wine: Les Hauts de Pontet-Canet.

Potensac Méd r ★★ 90' 94 95 96 98 99 00' 01 02 03 04' 05' Well-known 70-ha property of northern MÉDOC. Owned and run by Delon family of LEOVILLE-LAS-CASES. Class shows, in the form of rich, silky, balanced wines for ageing.

Pouget Mar r ★★ 89 90 94 95 96 98' 00' 02 03 04 05' 06 An 11-ha Fourth Growth attached to BOYD-CANTENAC. MARGAUX style. New *chai* in 2000.

Poujeaux Moulis r ★★ 89' 90' 94' 95' 96' 98 99 00' 01 01 03 03 04 05 06 Recently purchased (2007) by CLOS FOURTET owner; 57 ha. With CHASSE-SPLEEN and MAUCAILLOU the high point of Moulis. 20,000-odd cases of characterful tannic wine for a long life. Second label: La Salle de Poujeaux.

Premier Grand Cru Classé See ST-EMILION classification box below.

Prieuré-Lichine Cantenac-Mar r ★★★ 89' 90' 94' 95 96 98' 99 00' 01 02 03 04 05 06 A 70-ha Fourth Growth brought to the fore by the late Alexis Lichine. New owners 1999; now advised by Stéphane Derenoncourt (see CANON LA GAFFELIÈRE, PAVIE-MACQUIN). Fragrant MARGAUX currently on gd form. Second wine: Ch de Clairefont. A gd white B'x, too.

Puygueraud Côtes de Francs r ★★ 95' 96 98 99 00' 01' 02 03 04 05' (06) Leading CH of this tiny AC. Wood-aged wines of surprising class. Chx Laclaverie and Les Charmes-Godard follow the same lines. Special CUVÉE George from 2000 with Malbec in blend. Same winemaker as PAVIE-MACQUIN.

Rabaud-Promis Saut w sw ★★→★★★ 88' 89' 90 95 96 97' 98 99 01' 02 03' 05' 06 A 30-ha classed growth at Bommes. Nr top rank since 86. Rich stuff.

Rahoul Graves r w ★★ (r) 95 96 98' 00' 01 02 04 05 30-ha v'yd at Portets; still a sleeper despite long record of gd red (60%) and white (00 01 02 04' 05).

Ramage-la-Batisse H-Méd r ★★ 95 96' 98 99 00' 02 03 04 05' Consistent and widely distributed HAUT-MÉDOC; 65 ha at St-Sauveur, N of PAUILLAC. Ch Tourteran is second wine.

Rauzan-Gassies Mar r ★★ 90' 95 96' 98 99 00 01' 02 03 04 05' The 30-ha Second Growth neighbour of RAUZAN-SÉGLA that has long lagged behind it. New generation making evident strides since 2000 but still has a long way to go.

Rauzan-Ségla Mar r ★★★★ 86' 88 89' 90' 94' 95 96 98 99 00' 01 02 03 04' 05 A Second Growth (51 ha) long famous for its fragrance; owned by owners of Chanel (see CANON). A great MÉDOC name right at the top, with rebuilt CH and *chais*. second wine: *Ségla*.

Raymond-Lafon Saut w sw ★★★ 85 86' 88 89' 90' 95 96' 97 98 99' 01' 02 03' 04 05 06 Serious SAUTERNES estate (18 ha) acquired by YQUEM ex-manager and now run by his children. Rich, complex wines that age. Classed-growth quality.

Rayne Vigneau Saut w sw ★★★ 88' 89 90' 95 96 97 98 99 01' 02 03 05' Large 80-

---

2006 St-Emilion classification stands

France's highest administrative court has validated the 2006 ST-EMILION classification, so at the time of writing it officially stands, although there's further legal action pending. The latest of the ten-yearly reclassifications comprises 15 PREMIERS GRANDS CRUS CLASSÉS and 46 GRANDS CRUS CLASSÉS. There's no point in us arguing.

BORDEAUX

ha classed growth at Bommes. Gd but less power and intensity than the top growths. Sweet wine and dry Rayne sec.

Respide Médeville Graves r w ★★ (r) **99** 00' 01 **02** 04 05' 06 (w) **96' 99** 00 01 02 04' **05'** One of the better unclassified properties for both red and white. Drink the reds at 4–6 yrs; longer for the better vintages.

Reynon Premières Côtes r w ★★ 40 ha for fragrant white from Sauv Bl **01' 02 03** 04' 05' 06; also serious red (**98 99 00** 01 **02 03** 04' **05'** 06), too. See also CLOS FLORIDÈNE. Second wine (red): Ch Reynon-Peyrat. From 1996 v.gd Ch Reynon Cadillac liquoreux, too.

Reysson Vertheuil, H-Méd r ★★ **95 96** 00 **02 03 04** 05 06 Recently replanted 49-ha HAUT-MÉDOC estate; managed by négociant CVBG-Dourthe (see BELGRAVE, LA GARDE). Rich, modern style.

Ricaud Loupiac w sw (r dr) ★★ **96 97 99** 01' **02** 03' 05 Substantial grower of SAUTERNES-like ageworthy wine just across the river.

Rieussec Saut w sw ★★★★ **82 83' 85 86' 88' 89' 90' 95** 96' **97' 98 99** 01' 02 03' 04 05' 06 Worthy neighbour of YQUEM with 90 ha in Fargues, bought in 1984 by the (LAFITE) Rothschilds. Vinified in oak since 96. Fabulously opulent wine. Also dry "R", now made in modern style – with less character. Second wine: Carmes de Rieussec.

Ripeau St-Em r ★★ **95 98 00'** 01 **04** 05' 06 Lesser 16-ha GRAND CRU CLASSÉ on sandy soils nr CHEVAL BLANC. Lower yields and improvement from 2000.

de la Rivière Fronsac r ★★ **95 96' 98' 99** 00' 01 **02** 03 **04** 05' 06 The biggest and most impressive FRONSAC property, with a Wagnerian castle and cellars. Formerly big, tannic wines are now more refined. New winery in 1999. MICHEL ROLLAND consults. Special CUVÉE: Aria.

de Rochemorin Pe-Lé r w ★★→★★★ (r) **95 96 98' 99** 00' 01 **02 04** 05 (06) (w) **00 01 02 03** 04 05 06 An important restoration at Martillac by the Lurtons of LA LOUVIÈRE: 105 ha (three-quarters red) of maturing vines. New state-of-the-art winery in 2004. Fairly consistent quality and widely distributed.

Rol Valentin St-Em r ★★★ **95 96 98 99** 00' 01' 02 03 04 05' 06 New (1994) 7.5-ha estate going for modestly massive style (and price). Owned by former footballer. 1,900 cases. Stéphane Derenoncourt consults.

Rouget Pom r ★★ **89' 90 95 96 98' 99** 00' 01' 03 04 05' 06 Attractive old estate on the northern edge of POMEROL. 17 ha. New owners in 1992 and plenty of investment since (new cellars). Now excellent; rich, unctuous wines.

Royal St-Emilion Brand name of important, dynamic growers' CO-OP. See GALIUS.

St-André-Corbin St-Em r ★★ **98' 99 00'** 01 03 **04** 05 A 22-ha estate in MONTAGNE- and ST-GEORGES-ST-EMILION. Above-average wines.

St-Georges St-Georges-St-Em r ★★ **89' 90' 95' 96 98'** 00' 01 03 **04** 05' Noble 18th-century CH overlooking the ST-EMILION plateau from the hill to the north. 51 ha (25% of St-George AC). Gd wine sold direct to the public.

St-Pierre St-Jul r ★★★ **82' 85** 89 90' **94** 95' **96' 98 99** 00' 01' 02 03 04 05' 06 Fourth Growth (17 ha). Stylish and consistent classic ST-JULIEN. See GLORIA.

de Sales Pom r ★★ **89' 90' 95 96 98'** 00' 01' **04** 05 06 Biggest v'yd of POMEROL (47 ha) on sandy-gravel soils, attached to grandest CH. Lightish wine; never poetry. Try top vintages. Second label: Ch Chantalouette.

Sansonnet St-Em r ★★ **99 00'** 01 **02** 03 04 05' 06 A small 6.8-ha estate ambitiously run in the new ST-EMILION style (rich, fat) since 1999. Stéphane Derenoncourt consulting from 2006.

Saransot-Dupré Listrac r (w) ★★ **90 95 96 98' 99 00'** 01 02 03 04 05 (06) Small 12-ha property with delicious, appetizing wines. Lots of Merlot. Also one of LISTRAC's little band of whites.

Sénéjac H-Méd r (w) ★★ **90' 94 95 96 98 99** 00 01 **02 03 04** 05' 06 37-has in southern MÉDOC owned since 1999 by the same family as TALBOT. Tannic reds to age and unusual all-Sem white, also to age. Special CUVÉE: Karolus.

La Serre St-Em r ★★ **90 94 95 96 98' 99 00' 01 02 03** 04 05 06 Small (6.5-ha) GRAND CRU CLASSÉ, on the limestone plateau. Pleasant, stylish wines; more flesh and purity of fruit since 2000.

Sigalas-Rabaud Saut w sw ★★★ **83 85 86 88 89' 90' 95' 96' 97' 98 99 01' 02** 03' 04 05' The smaller part of the former Rabaud estate: 14 ha in Bommes; same winemaking team as LAFAURIE-PEYRAGUEY. V. fragrant and lovely. Top-ranking now. Second wine: Le Cadet de Sigalas Rabaud.

Siran Labarde-Mar r ★★→★★★ **86 88 89' 90' 95 96 98** 99 00' **01** 02 03 04 05 06 A 40-ha property of passionate owner who resents lack of classé rank. The wines age well and have masses of flavour. MICHEL ROLLAND consults.

Smith-Haut-Lafitte Pe-Lé r (w p) ★★★ (r) 90' 94 95 **96 98** 99 **00' 01** 02 **03** 04' 05' 06 (w) **96 97 98 99' 00' 01** 02 03 04 05 06 Classed growth at Martillac: 56 ha (11 ha make oak-fermented white). Ambitious owners (since 1990) continue to spend hugely to spectacular effect, inc a luxurious wine therapy (external!) spa and hotel-restaurant. White is riper, less oaky than before. Second label: Les Hauts de Smith. Also look out for their Ch Cantelys, PESSAC-LÉOGNAN.

Sociando-Mallet H-Méd r ★★★ **88' 89' 90'** 94 95 **96' 98' 99 00' 01'** 02 03 04 05' 06 Splendid, widely followed estate at St-Seurin. Classed-growth quality; 75 ha. Conservative big-boned wines to lay down for yrs. Second wine: Demoiselles de Sociando.

Soudars H-Méd r ★★ **94 95 96' 98 99 00' 01** 03 04 05 06 Sister to COUFRAN and VERDIGNAN; 22 ha. Relatively traditional and regular quality.

Soutard St-Em r ★★★ **88' 89' 90' 94 95 96 98' 99 00' 01** 02 03 04 05 06 Potentially excellent 19-ha classed growth on the limestone plateau; 70% Merlot. Potent wines can be long-lived. Now owned by same insurance group as LARMANDE (2006). Changes in store. Second label: Clos de la Tonnelle.

Suduiraut Saut w sw ★★★★ 81 82' 83 **85 86 88' 89' 90' 95 96 97' 98 99' 01' 02** 03' 04 05' 06 One of the best classed-growth SAUTERNES: 90 ha with renovated CH and gardens by Le Nôtre. New owner, AXA Insurance, has achieved greater consistency and luscious quality. See PICHON-LONGUEVILLE. Second wine: Castelnau de Suduiraut. New dry wine, S, v. promising.

du Tailhas Pom r ★★ **90 94 95 96' 98' 99** 00 01 **04** 05 10-ha property nr FIGEAC. POMEROL of the lighter kind.

Taillefer Pom r ★★ **89 90 94** 95' **96 98' 00' 01** 02 **03** 04 05' 11-ha v'yd on the edge of POMEROL. Astutely managed by Catherine Moueix. Less power than top estates but gently harmonious. Gd value.

Talbot St-Jul r (w) ★★★ **88' 89' 90 94 95 96' 98' 99 00' 01** 02 03 04 05' 06 Important 102-ha Fourth Growth, for many yrs younger sister to GRUAUD-LAROSE. Wine similarly attractive: rich, consummately charming, reliable. Second label: Connétable de Talbot. White: Caillou Blanc matures as well as a gd Graves, but drinks well young. SÉNÉJAC in same family ownership.

Terrey-Gros-Caillou St-Jul r ★★ **90 94 95 96 98 99 00 02 03** 04 05 (06) Sister CH to HORTEVIE; 15 ha; at best, equally noteworthy and stylish.

du Tertre Arsac-Mar r ★★★ **89' 90' 94 95 96' 98' 99 00' 01** 03 04' 05' 06 Fifth Growth (50 ha) isolated south of MARGAUX. History of undervalued fragrant and fruity wines. Since 1997, same owner as CH GISCOURS. New techniques and massive investment have produced a really concentrated, structured wine, really humming from 2003.

Tertre Daugay St-Em r ★★★ **89' 90' 94 95 96 98 99 00' 01** 03 04 05 06 Small, well sited estate, sister toLA GAFFELIÈRE. Declassified from GRAND CRU CLASSÉ in 2006 but improvement in progress. Derenoncourt consulting from 2004.

Tertre-Rôteboeuf St-Em r ★★★★ **86 88 89' 90' 93 94 95 96 98' 99 00' 01 02 03'** 04 05' 06 A cult star making concentrated, dramatic, largely Merlot wine since

1983. Frightening prices. Also CÔTES DE BOURG property, Roc de Cambes.

Thieuley E-D-M r p w ★★ Supplier of consistent quality red and white AC Bordeaux; fruity CLAIRET; oak-aged red and white CUVÉE Francis Courselle. Also owns Clos Ste-Anne in PREMIÈRES CÔTES DE BORDEAUX.

La Tour-Blanche Saut w (r) sw ★★★ 83' 85 86 88' 89' 90' 95 **96 97' 98 99 01' 02** 03 04 05' 06 Historic leader of SAUTERNES, now a government wine college. Coasted in 1970s; since 1988 a top player again.

La Tour-de-By Bégadan, Méd r ★★ **89' 90' 94 95 96' 98** 00 01 **02 03 04** 05' 06 V. well-run 74-ha family estate in northern MÉDOC with a name for sturdy but reliable wines with a leafy note.

La Tour-Carnet St-Laurent, H-Méd r ★★ **85 86** 89' 90 **94'** 95 96 **98 99** 00' **01 02** 03 04' 05' 06 Fourth Growth (65 ha) with medieval moated fortress, long neglected. New ownership (SEE FOMBRAUGE, PAPE-CLÉMENT) and investment from 2000 have produced richer wines in a more modern style. Second wine: Les Douves de Ch La Tour Carnet.

La Tour Figeac St-Em r ★★ **89' 90' 94'** 95 96' **98'** 99 00' 01' **02** 04 05 06 A 15-ha GRAND CRU CLASSÉ between FIGEAC and POMEROL. California-style ideas since 1994. Biodynamic methods. Opulent at its best.

La Tour Haut Brion Graves r ★★★ **89** 90 **94** 95 **96' 98'** 99 00' 01 02 03 04' 05' 2005 the last vintage of this classed growth. The 4.8 ha v'yd has now been integrated into that of LA MISSION-HAUT-BRION. Same owner.

Tour Haut-Caussan Méd r ★★ **96 98** 00' 01 **02 03 04** 05' (06) Well-run 16-ha property at Blaignan to watch for full, firm wines. Same ownership as Ch Cascadais in CORBIÈRES.

Tour-du-Haut-Moulin Cussac, H-Méd r ★★ **88' 89'** 90' **94** 95 **96 98** 00' **02** 03 04 05' 06 Conservative grower in Cussac Fort Médoc: intense, consistent, no-nonsense wines to mature.

La Tour de Mons Soussans-Mar r ★★ **89** 90' **94 95 96'** 98' 99 00 01 **02** 04 05' (06) Famous MARGAUX *cru* of 44 ha, in the same family for 3 centuries. A long dull patch but new (1995) TALBOT influence is returning to the old fragrant, vigorous, ageworthy style.

Tournefeuille Lalande de Pom r ★★ **95'** 98' 99 00' **01' 02 03** 04 05 06 Well-known Néac CH. 17 ha. On the upswing since 1998 with new owners.

Tour-du-Pas-St-Georges St-Em r ★★ **95** 96 **98** 99 00' 01 03 04 05 Wine from 16 ha of ST-GEORGES-ST-EMILION made by BELAIR owner.

La Tour du Pin St-Em r ★★ **89' 90' 95 96 98** 00' **01 04** 05 06 8 ha, formerly La Tour du Pin Figeac-Moueix but bought and renamed by CHEVAL BLANC in 2006. Unimpressive form resulted in demotion from GRAND CRU CLASSÉ in 2006 but new team turning things around. To watch.

Tour-St-Bonnet Méd r ★★ **95 96 98 99** 00' **02 03 04** 05 06 Consistently well-made potent northern MÉDOC from St-Christoly; 40 ha.

Tronquoy-Lalande St-Est r ★★ **89** 90' **94 95 96 98** 99 00' **02 03** 04 05 06 Same owners as MONTROSE from 2006. Lots of Merlot and Petit Verdot; 25 ha. High-coloured wines to age.

Troplong-Mondot St-Em r ★★★ **88'** 89' 90' **94' 95 96' 98'** 99 00' 01' 02 03 04 05' 06 Recently promoted PREMIER GRAND CRU CLASSÉ (2006). Well-sited 30 ha on a high point of the limestone plateau. Wines of power and depth with increasing elegance. MICHEL ROLLAND consults. Second wine: Mondot.

Trotanoy Pom r ★★★★ 85' **88** 89' 90' 93 94 95 **96** 98' 99 00' 01 **02** 03 04' 05' 06 Potentially the second POMEROL, after PÉTRUS, from the same stable. Only 7 ha; at best (eg **98**) a glorious, fleshy, structured, perfumed wine. Wobbled a bit in the 1980s, but back on top form since 1989.

Trottevieille St-Em r ★★★ 89' 90 **94** 95 **96 98** 99 00' 01 02 03' 04 05' 06 First Growth on the limestone plateau. Dragged its feet for yrs. Same owners as

BATAILLEY have raised its game since 2000. Denis Dubourdieu consults.

Valandraud St-Em r ★★★★ 93 94 95' **96 98** 99 **00' 01'** 02 03 04 05' 06 Leader among *garagiste* micro-wines fulfilling aspirations to glory. But silly prices for the sort of thick, vanilla-scented wine California can make. V'yds now expanded to 20 ha; better terroir and more balance. Second and third wines: Virginie and Axelle.

Valrose St-Est r ★★ **02 03** 04 05' (06) A newcomer since 1999, co-owned with CLINET. Special CUVÉE: Aliénor. To watch.

Verdignan Méd r ★★ 95' **96** 98 99 **00'** 01 **02 03** 04 05 06 Substantial 60-ha HAUT-MÉDOC estate; sister to COUFRAN and SOUDARS. More Cab Sauv than COUFRAN. Gd value and ageing potential.

La Vieille Cure Fronsac r ★★ **95 96 98 99** 00' 01' **02** 03 04 05 06 A 20-ha property, US-owned, leading the commune. Accessible from 4 yrs. Reliable value.

Vieux-Ch-Certan Pom r ★★★★ **82' 83'** 85 **86' 88'** 89 90' **94 95' 96' 98'** 99 00' 01 02 04' 05' 06 Traditionally rated close to PÉTRUS in quality, but totally different in style; almost HAUT-BRION build with plenty of finesse. 14 ha. Same (Belgian) family owns tiny LE PIN.

Vieux Ch St-André St-Em r ★★ **00'** 01 **02 03 04** 05 06 Small 6-ha v'yd in MONTAGNE-ST-EMILION owned by former winemaker of PÉTRUS. Regular quality.

Villegeorge Avensan, H-Méd r ★★ **89 90 94** 95 **96' 98'** 99 **00'** 02 03 04 05 06 A 15-ha HAUT-MÉDOC north of MARGAUX. Fine, traditional MÉDOC style. Sister Chx Duplessis in MOULIS and La Tour de Bessan in MARGAUX.

Vray Croix de Gay Pom r ★★ **88 89** 90 95 96 98' **00'** 04 05 06 V. small (4 ha) but ideally situated; in the best part of POMEROL. Greater efforts from 2004. Sister to Ch Siaurac in LALANDE DE POMEROL and Le Prieuré in ST-EMILION.

Yon-Figeac St-Em r ★★ **90 95 96** 98 99 00' **02 03** 04 05 06 24-ha estate. V'yd restructured between 1985 and 1995. Improvements from 2000 but too late to prevent declassification from GRAND CRU CLASSÉ in 2006.

d'Yquem Saut w sw (dr) ★★★★ 76' **79 80' 81'** 83' 85 **86' 88' 89'** 90' 93 **94 95'** 96 **97' 98 99'** 00 01' **02** 03' 04 05' The world's most famous sweet wine estate. 101 ha; only 200 bottles per hectare of v. strong, intense, luscious wine, kept 4 yrs in barrel. Most vintages improve for 15+ yrs; some live 100+ yrs in transcendent splendour. After centuries in the Lur-Saluces family, in 1998 control was surrendered to Bernard Arnault of LVMH. The new management is forward-thinking, and pushing prices sky-high. Also makes dry "Y" (ygrec).

Italy

More heavily shaded areas are the wine-growing regions

The following abbreviations are used in the text:

Ab	Abruzzo	Sar	Sardinia
Ap	Apulia	Si	Sicily
Bas	Basilicata	T-AA	Trentino-Alto Adige
Cal	Calabria		
Cam	Campania	Tus	Tuscany
E-R	Emilia-Romagna	Umb	Umbria
F-VG	Friuli-Venezia Giulia	VdA	Valle d'Aosta
		Ven	Veneto
Lat	Latium		
Lig	Liguria		
Lom	Lombardy	cs	Cantine Sociale
Mar	Marches	fz	*frizzante*
Pie	Piedmont	pa	*passito*

VALLE D'AOSTA
L Como
L Maggiore
Milan
LOMBARDY
Turin O PIEDMONT
Genoa O
LIGURIA
Ligurian Sea

Wine lovers often complain that Italian wines are difficult to understand. Understandably. There are over 350 DOC wines, 35+ DOCGs and more than 120 IGTs. There are in excess of 100 grape varieties in regular use and hundreds more in limited use or capable of being brought into wider use. In fact, Italian ampelographers (vine-type researchers) are in quite a ferment these days about all the undiscovered treasures – the "biodiversity", they like to call it – that lurk in historic vineyards up and down this ancient "Enotria" or "land of wine". On top of that, the cult of individualism pushes each red-blooded Italian to try and distinguish himself from his neighbour, so instead of emphasizing a grape variety such as Chardonnay or Sangiovese on the label, instead even of highlighting a DOC like Chianti or Soave, he will give each of his wines an individual fantasy or *cru* name. How on earth do you keep track of such a plethora of permutations?

Well, you don't. You can't. You simply have to adopt one of three ploys. You could plump for a familiar producer's name, like Antinori, or seek out a recognizable denomination like Barolo or Salice Salentino. Dependable, but slightly boring, considering the vastness of the potential you are discarding by demanding the recognizable. Or you could throw caution to the winds and experiment freely among all the unknown quantities, but that can be dodgy. There is a third way: seek help.

Ask a good wine merchant or someone you trust to steer you safely through the shoals to the shores of vinous golden sand. There is, too, an increasing store of information on the internet – in a word, Google it. Then there are the guides, like this one. See below for grapes, regions, styles, and recommended producers. Check vintages. And try not to drown in names.

ITALY

Recent Vintages

Tuscany

2007 A rainy May followed a mild, dry winter and summery Apr. Summer itself was very hot and arid. Late Aug rains came to the rescue. Ideal vintage-conditions made for a smaller than average cropbut high quality crop.

2006 A year of balance, no temperature extremes, measured rainfall. Cool Aug but good weather at vintage time apart from two days' downpour late Sept. A top oenologist in Chianti Classico dubbed it "the greatest of the last 20 vintages".

2005 Much rain and generally irregular results, most successful along the coast and for those who picked early. Sangiovese at every quality level imaginable, from first-rate to diluted.

2004 Exceptionally promising along the coast, in Montepulciano, and in Montalcino, even if 5* (Brunello) is exaggerated. Despite cool temperatures some truly elegant wines throughout.

2003 Considerable vine stress from searing heat and three months of drought. High sugar content meant uppish alcohol with green tannins for early-picked grapes, or low-acid jamminess for later-picked.

2002 Cool Aug, frequent rains in Sept/Oct. Dilution and rot widespread. Generally poor with some notable exceptions.

2001 A scorching Aug, unusually cool in early Sept, then humid when warm weather returned. Some irregularity, wines outstanding to just good.

Older fine vintages: 99 97 95 90

Piedmont

2007 Very short but good to excellent quality for Barolo/Barbaresco. Early and mid-term ripeners like Dolcetto and Barbera fared well too, again at a cost in volume. Very high alcohol levels and lowish acidity could be a problem.

2006 Excellent Dolcetto, very fine Nebbiolo and Barbera; along with 2001 and 2004 the finest vintage of the new millennium.

2005 Pleasurable Dolcetto; spotty for Barbera, with some rot from persistent rains; Nebbiolo rather uneven, though promising wines are not lacking.

2004 Very long growing season, high level of quality for all major red grapes (Dolcetto, Barbera, Nebbiolo), the first since 1999.

2003 Sweltering summer, but nonetheless very positive for Barbera, Dolcetto, and Moscato. Nebbiolo more irregular, with late pickers more successful.

2002 Cool, damp growing season and serious hail damage in Barolo.

2001 Classy and firm Nebbiolo and Barbera, other grapes less successful.

Older fine vintages: 00 99 98 97 96 95 90 89 88

Amarone, Veneto

2007 High hopes were dashed for some by vicious hailstorms at the end of Aug. Those not wiped out made some excellent wines, but very short crop, steeply rising prices.

2006 Outstanding, with new record established for the grape tonnage reserved for drying, 30% higher than any previous vintage.

2005 A difficult harvest due to damp weather, but grape-drying technology saved Amarone and Recioto. Less successful vintage for Soave and whites.

2004 A damp Nov caused some concern, but a return of drier weather helped avoid rot. Classic, less concentrated and rich than 2003.

2003 The hottest and driest vintage of the post-war period. Very concentrated and sugar-rich grapes; can be outstanding.

2002 Heavy rains throughout the ripening season. Best wines were downgraded top *crus*.

2001 Very balanced weather in the growing season. Promising and classic.

Marches & Abruzzo reds

2007 Spectacularly low crop due to heat and water shortage, pointing way to worryingly high price increases across the board. But some excellent quality.

2006 Irregular. Generally positive where hail did not fall; better than 2004 and 2005, but not as good as 2003.

2005 A year of heavy rainfall, saved by a dry second half of October. Wines of good ripeness and structure for those who waited to pick.

2004 Considerable Oct rains; irregular results. Better in Rosso Conero than Rosso Piceno in the Marches; best in Colline Teramane DOCG, Abruzzo.

2003 One of the most successful areas in Italy in 2003, as the Montepulciano grape stood up to the heat and drought, giving first-rate results.

2002 Cool, damp year; only fair results.

2001 Ideal weather, fine balance of power and elegance in the wines, which are fragrant with much complexity and depth.

Campania & Basilicata

2007 V low yields due to heat/drought aggravated by failure of some to bother picking due to peronospera (downy mildew) devastation. Good quality for those who sprayed and waited for balanced grapes.

2006 Rain and problems of rot in lower-lying zones, much sun and a very long growing season in higher vineyards, with predictably superior results.

2005 Traditionally the last grapes to be picked, Aglianico had weight, complexity, and character – perhaps the finest wines of all Italy in 2005.

2004 Slow and uncertain ripening for Aglianico, and only a warm second half of Oct enabled growers to salvage the grapes.Has pleased beyond original expectations.

2003 Scorching and drought-stressed growing conditions, but the altitude of the v'yds worked in late-picked Aglianico's favour. Generally a success.

2002 Heavy rains during vintage ; part salvaged, but generally disastrous.

2001 Hot, dry and very regular from July to the end of Oct; textbook weather. Intense, perfumed, and ageworthy wines.

Abboccato Semi-sweet.

Aglianico del Vulture Bas DOC r dr (s/sw sp) ★★★ 97' 98 99' 00' 01' 03' 04' 05' 06 07' VECCHIA after 3 yrs, RISERVA after 5 yrs. Top: Allegretti, Alovini, d'Angelo, Basilium, Bisceglia, Francesco Bonifacio, Cantina del Notaio, Cantina di Venosa, Consiglio, Elena Fucci, Lelusi, Lucania, Macarico, Di Palma, PATERNOSTER, Le Querce, Tenuta del Portale, Torre degli Svevi, Sasso, and Viticoltori Associati del Vulture.

Alba Major wine city of PIEDMONT, on river Tanaro, southeast of Turin. Centre of various DOC/GS inc BAROLO, BARBARESCO, NEBBIOLO d'Alba, ROERO, BARBERA d'Alba and DOLCETTO d'Alba. Recently proposed as DOC in own right.

Albana di Romagna E-R DOCG w dr s/sw (sp) ★★→★★★ DYA Varietal white, Italy's first white DOCG, justifiably for the sweet PASSITO version, not for the undistinguished dry styles. ZERBINA, Fattoria Paradiso and Giovanna Madonia make excellent versions, Fattoria Paradiso and Tremonti's are v.gd.

Alcamo Si DOC w ★ Racy if somewhat one-dimensional whites from prolific Catarratto grape. Rapitala is best of an uninspired lot.

Aleatico Red Muscat-flavoured grape for sweet, aromatic, often fortified wines, chiefly in south Aleatico di Puglia DOC (best: Candido and Santa Lucia) is better and more famous than Aleatico di Gradoli (Latium) DOC, best example Occhipinti's Monte Maggiore. Other gd examples come from Jacopo Banti and Brancatelli in VAL DI CORNIA and Sapereta, Acquabona on ELBA.

Alessandria, Gianfranco ★★★ Small, new-wave producer of high-level ALBA wines at Monforte d'Alba, esp BAROLO San Giovanni, BARBERA D'ALBA Vittoria.

Alezio Ap DOC p (r) ★★ One of many quasi-superfluous DOCS in Puglia's Salento peninsula all sharing similar regulations based on NEGROAMARO, making perfumed but sturdy rosés and juicy reds. Best producers Rosa del Golfo/Calò with Rosa del Golfo (p) and Michele Calò with NEGROAMARO IGT Spano (r).

Allegrini Ven ★★★ Top-quality Veronese producer; outstanding single-v'yd IGT wines (Palazzo della Torre, Grola, and Poja), AMARONE, and RECIOTO.

Altare, Elio Pie ★★★ Pioneering, influential small producer of v.gd modern BAROLO. Look for BAROLO Arborina, BAROLO Brunate, LANGHE Gd Arborina (Nebbiolo), Larigi (BARBERA), La Villa, VDT L'Insieme and DOLCETTO D'ALBA.

Alto Adige T-AA DOC r p w dr sw sp ★→★★★ Alto Adige or SÜDTIROL DOC inc almost 50 types of wine, the best being white and varietal. Sub-denominations include VALLE ISARCO/Eisacktal, TERLANO/Terlaner, Val Venosta/Vinschgau, AA SANTA MADDALENA/ST MAGDALENER, Bozner Leiten, MERANESE DI COLLINA/Meraner).

Ama, Castello di ★★★ One of the best and most consistent modern CHIANTI CLASSICO estates, near Gaiole. La Casuccia and Bellavista are top single-v'yd wines. Gd IGTS, CHARD, and MERLOT (L'Apparita).

Amabile Means semi-sweet, but usually sweeter than ABBOCCATO.

Amaro Bitter. When prominent on label, contents are not wine but "bitters".

Amarone della Valpolicella (formerly Recioto della Valpolicella Amarone) Ven DOC r ★★★ **90' 93 95 97'** 98 00' 01' 03 05' 06 07' *Relatively dry version of Recioto della Valpolicella*: from air-dried VALPOLICELLA grapes; concentrated, fairly long-lived. Best: Accordini, Serego Alighieri, ALLEGRINI, Begali, BERTANI, BOLLA, Boscaini, BRUNELLI, Buglioni, BUSSOLA, Ca' La Bianca, Campagnola, Castellani, Cesari, Corteforte, Corte Sant Alda, CS Valpantena, CS VALPOLICELLA, DAL FORNO, Farina, Aleardo Ferrari, Guerrieri-Rizzardi, La Costa di Romagnano, LE RAGOSE, LE SALETTE, MASI, Mazzi, Nicolis, Novaia, PASQUA, QUINTARELLI, Roccolo Grassi, Sant'Antonio, Speri, TEDESCHI, Tommasi, Trabucchi, Valentina Cubi, Vaona, Venturini, Villa Monteleone, VIVIANI, ZENATO, Zeni. Older vintages are hard to come by and tend to show their age.

Anselmi, Roberto ★★★ A leader in SOAVE with his single-v'yd Capitel Foscarino and exceptional sweet dessert RECIOTO i Capitelli. Having renounced the DOC(G), this rebel's wines are now IGT.

Antinori, Marchesi L & P ★★→★★★★ V. influential, long-established Florentine house of highest repute (mostly justified), owned by Piero A, sharing management with his 3 daughters and oenologist Renzo Cotarella. Famous for CHIANTI CLASSICO (Tenute Marchese Antinori and Badia a Passignano), Umbrian (CASTELLO DELLA SALA), and PIEDMONT (PRUNOTTO) wines. Pioneer of new IGT, eg TIGNANELLO, SOLAIA (TUSCANY), *white Cervaro della Sala (Umbria)*. Expanding into south Tuscan MAREMMA, MONTEPULCIANO (La Braccesca), MONTALCINO, in ASTI (for BARBERA), in FRANCIACORTA for sparkling (Lombardy), and in APULIA ("Vigneti del Sud"). V.gd DOC BOLGHERI Guardo al Tasso.

Apulia Puglia. Italy's heel, producing almost a sixth of Italy's wine, most blended in northern Italy/France. Region to follow in increasing quality/value. Best DOC: BRINDISI, CASTEL DEL MONTE, MANDURIA (PRIMITIVO DI), SALICE SALENTINO. Producers: ANTINORI, Botromagno, Candido, Cantine Paradiso, Casale Bevagna, Castel di Selva, Giancarlo Ceci, Tenuta Cocevola, Co-op Copertino, Co-op Due Palme, Conti Zecca, Coppadoro, La Corte, Li Veli, D'Alfonso del Sordo, Fatalone, Felline, Gianfranco Fino, Masseria Monaci, Masseria Pepe, Michele Calò, Mille Una, Ognissole, Resta, RIVERA, Rubino, Rosa del Golfo, Santa Lucia, Sinfarosa, TAURINO, Valle dell'Asso, VALLONE.

Aquileia F-VG DOC r w ★→★★ (r) **01 03** 04 05 06, 07 A group of 12 moderately interesting single-varietal wines from around the town of Aquileia. Gd REFOSCO, Sauv Bl. Ca' Bolani and Denis Montanar are not bad.

Argiano Top BRUNELLO estate. Castello di Argiano is another.

Argiolas, Antonio ★★→★★★ Important SARDINIAN producer. High-level CANNONAU, NURAGUS, VERMENTINO, Bovale. *Red IGTS Turriga* (★★★) and Korem are among the best the island has to offer.

Arneis Pie DOCG w ★★ DYA Potentially excellent peachy/appley white from around ALBA, revived from nr extinction in 1970s. Fragrant, fruity, intense. DOC: ROERO Arneis, northwest of ALBA, normally better than LANGHE Arneis. Try: Almondo, Bric Cencurio, Ca' du Russ, Cascina Chicco, Correggia, BRUNO GIACOSA, Malvirà, Monchiero-Carbone, Morra, Angelo Negro, PRUNOTTO, Sorilaria, VIETTI.

Assisi Umb IGT r (w) ★→★★ DYA IGT ROSSO and BIANCO di Assisi, a town more notable for tourism than wine. Sportoletti is acceptable.

Asti Pie DOCG w sw sp ★→★★ NV Sweet Muscat fizz, which rarely rises above the industrial. The big Asti houses are not interested in improving quality of 80 million bottles. Despite unique potential, Asti is a cheap supermarket product. A few producers care: Alasia, Walter BERA, CASCINA FONDA, CONTRATTO, Dogliotti-Caudrina, Vignaioli di Santo Stefano (see also MOSCATO D'ASTI).

Avignonesi ★★★ Noble MONTEPULCIANO house; highly ambitious and adventurous, with a v. fine range: VINO NOBILE, Desiderio, 50:50 – a SANGIOVESE/MERLOT joint venture with CAPANNELLE. Best known for long-aged, super low-production VIN SANTO (★★★★).

Azienda agricola/agraria Estates (large and small) making wine from own grapes.

Azienda/casa vinicola Négociants making wine from bought-in and own grapes.

Azienda vitivinicola A (specialized) wine estate.

Badia a Coltibuono Historic CHIANTI CLASSICO producer famous for RISERVAS, run by Stucchi Prinetti family.

Banfi (Castello or Villa) ★★→★★★ Space-age MONTALCINO CANTINA of biggest US importer of Italian wine. Huge plantings at Montalcino, mostly SANGIOVESE of recently developed or own experimental clones; also SYRAH, PINOT N, CAB SAUV, CHARD, SAUV BL, etc.: part of a drive for quality plus quantity. *Poggio all'Oro* and Poggio alle Mura are ★★★ BRUNELLOS. Summus and Excelsus are top SANT'ANTIMO reds. In PIEDMONT, also gd Banfi Brut, BRACCHETTO D'ACQUI, GAVI, PINOT GR.

Barbaresco Pie DOCG r ★★→★★★★ 89' 90' 93 95 96' 97' 98' 99' 00 01' 03 04' 05 06' 07' Classic Italian red, 100% NEBBIOLO. Like its neighbour BAROLO, comines depth of complex flavour with bright clean tannins. At 4 yrs becomes RISERVA. Producers include Marziano Abbona, Antichi PODERI di Gallina, Bera, Piero Busso, Ca' del Baio, Cascina Luisin, CERETTO, CIGLIUTI, Fontanabianca, FONTANAFREDDA, Fratelli Giacosa, GAJA, BRUNO GIACOSA, GRESY, La Ca' Bianca, La Contea, Cortese, Lano, MOCCAGATTA, Montaribaldi, Morassino, Fiorenzo Nada, Paitin, Giorgio Pelissero, PIO CESARE, PRODUTTORI DEL BARBARESCO, PRUNOTTO, Punset, Ressia, Massimo Rivetti, Roagna, Albino Rocca, BRUNO ROCCA, GIORGIO RIVETTI, Ronchi, Serragilli, Sottimano, Vano, Varaldo.

Barbatella, Cascina La ★★★ Top producer of BARBERA D'ASTI: excellent VIGNA dell'Angelo and MONFERRATO Rosso Sonvico (BARBERA/CAB SAUV).

Barbera Prolific red variety, dominant in PIEDMONT, also varietally in Lombardy and (for blends) throughout Italy, indeed the world. High acidity, low tannin and distinctive cherry fruit are defining characteristics. Capable of diverse wine-styles from BARRIQUED and serious to semi-sweet and frothy.

Barbera d'Alba Pie DOC r ★★→★★★ 00' 01' 03, 04' 05, 06' 07' Potentially acidic red here generally smoothed by BARRIQUE ageing, but all too often playing second fiddle to NEBBIOLO. Best age up to 7 yrs. Some excellent wines, often from producers of BAROLO, BARBARESCO and ROERO. Top houses: Marziano Abbona, ALESSANDRIA, Almondo, Baudana, Bric Cencurio, BOGLIETTI, Boroli, Bovio, BRICCO Maiolica, I Calici, Cascina Chicco, Cascina Cucco, Cascina Luisin, Caviola, CLERICO, ALDO CONTERNO, Giovanni Conterno, Paolo Conterno, Conterno-Fantino, Cordero di Montezemolo, Corino, Correggia, Damilano, De Stefanis, Gagliaso, Germano, Ghisolfi, ELIO GRASSO, Silvio Grasso, Hilberg, GIOVANNI MANZONE, Mauro Mascarello, Massolino, Molino, Monchiero-

Carbone, Montaribaldi, Paolo Monti, Morra, OBERTO, Paitin, Pelissero, Luigi Pira, Principiano, PRUNOTTO, Revello, Giuseppe Rinaldi, Giorgio Rivetti, Massimo Rivetti, Albino Rocca, Tenuta Rocca, Rocche Costamagna, Ruggieri Corsini, SANDRONE, SCAVINO, Seghesio, Edoardo Sobrino, Sottimano, VAJRA, Varaldo, Veglio, Vietti, ROBERTO VOERZIO.

Barbera d'Asti Pie DOC r ★★→★★★ **00' 01'** 03 04' 05 06' 07' The real thing, some say, from lands where BARBERA comes first. Two styles, fresh, fruity and somewhat sharp, or rounded by wood ageing. Top growers: Olim Bauda, BAVA, BERA, Bersano, Bertelli, Alfiero Boffa, BRAIDA, Brema, Ca' del Fer, Ca' del Prete, Cascina Castlèt, Cascina Ferro, Cascina Tavijn, Castino, CHIARLO, Contratto, COPPO, CS Nizza, CS Vinchio e Vaglio, Dezzani, Domanda, Il Falchetto, Ferraris, Fidanza, Garetto, La Giribaldina, Mauro Grasso, HASTAE, Hohler, La Barbatella, La Lune del Rospo, La Meridiana, La Morandina, L'Arbiola, L'Armangia, La Tenaglia, Malgrà, Marchesi Alfieri, Marengo, Beppe Marino, Martinetti, Mongetto, Oddero, Agostino Pavia, Pico Maccario, *Prunotto*, GIORGIO RIVETTI, Bruno Rocca, Scrimaglio, Scagliola, Tenute dei Vallarino, Terre da Vino, *Vietti*.

Barbera del Monferrato Pie DOC r ★★→★★ DYA Easy-drinking BARBERA from ALESSANDRIA and ASTI. Pleasant, slightly fizzy, sometimes sweetish. Delimited area is almost identical to BARBERA D'ASTI but style simpler although serious and more important wines now appearing from Accornero, Valpane, Vicara.

Barco Reale Tus DOC r ★★ 03 04' 05 06' 07' DOC for junior wine of CARMIGNANO, using the same grapes.

Bardolino Ven DOC r (p) ★→★★ DYA Pale, summery, slightly bitter red from Lake Garda. Bardolino CHIARETTO: paler and lighter. Best include Buglioni, Cavalchina, Giovanna Tantini, Guerrieri Rizzardi, MONTRESOR, Pantini, ZENATO, Zeni.

Barolo Pie DOCG r ★★★→★★★★ 88' **89' 90' 93' 95** 96' 97' 98' 99' 00 01' 03 04' 05 06' 07' Compact but v'yd-covered area south of ALBA with one of Italy's supreme reds: rich, tannic, alcoholic (min 13%), dry but wonderfully deep and fragrant (also crisp and clean) in the mouth. From NEBBIOLO grapes. Ages for up to 20–25 yrs (minimum 3 yrs, RISERVA after 5 yrs).

Barolo Chinato A dessert wine made from BAROLO DOCG, alcohol, sugar, herbs, spices, and Peruvian bark. Producers: Cappellano, CERETTO, Giulio Cocchi.

Barrique This 225-litre French oak container has been the major weapon of the internationalists in Italy and the *bête noire* of the traditionalists, who reject its smoky, vanilla tones in favour of the greater neutrality of the Slavonian oak BOTTE. The battle is inclining towards the trads.

Basciano ★★ Producer of gd DOCG CHIANTI RUFINA and IGT wines.

Bava ★★ Producer of BARBERA D'ASTI Piano Alto and Stradivarius, MONFERRATO BIANCO, BAROLO CHINATO; the Bava family controls the old firm Giulio Cocchi in ASTI, where it produces gd sparkling METODO CLASSICO.

Bellavista ★★★ FRANCIACORTA estate with expensive but convincing Champagne-style wines (Gran Cuvée Franciacorta is top). Also Satèn (a crémant-style sparkling). TERRE DI FRANCIACORTA DOC and Sebino IGT Solesine (both CAB SAUV/MERLOT blends). Owner Vittorio Moretti also expanding into Tuscan MAREMMA, Val di Cornia, and Monteregio.

Bera, Walter ★★→★★★ Small estate nr BARBARESCO. V.gd MOSCATO D'ASTI, ASTI, BARBERA D'ASTI, BARBARESCO, and LANGHE NEBBIOLO.

Berlucchi, Guido ★★ Italy's biggest producer of sparkling METODO CLASSICO.

Bersano Historic wine house in Nizza Monferrato, with BARBERA D'ASTI Generala, and BAROLO Badarina, most PIEDMONT DOC wines inc BARBARESCO, MOSCATO D'ASTI, ASTI SPUMANTE.

Bertani ★★→★★★★ Well-known quality wines from Verona, esp traditional AMARONE.

Bianco White.

Bianco di Custoza Ven DOC w (sp) ★→★★ DYA Fresh white from Lake Garda, made

> **The Barolo role of honour**
> **The traditionalists:** Anselma, Ascheri, Barale, Bergadano, Giacomo Borgogno, Brezza, Brovia, Burlotto, Cappellano, Cavallotto, Ciabot Berton, ALDO CONTERNO, GIACOMO CONTERNO, Paolo Conterno, Dosio, FONTANAFREDDA, BRUNO GIACOSA, Marcarini, BARTOLO MASCARELLO, GIUSEPPE MASCARELLO, Massolino, Monchiero, PIO CESARE (BAROLO), Poderi Colla, Renato Ratti, Francesco Rinaldi, Giuseppe Rinaldi, Schiavenza, VIETTI.
> **The modernists:** Abbona, ALESSANDRIA, ALTARE, BOGLIETTI, Bongiovanni, Boroli, Bric Cenciurio, Bruna Grimaldi, Cabutto, Camerano, Cascina Ballarin, Cascina Luisin, CHIARLO, CLERICO, CONTERNO-FANTINO, CORDERO DI MONTEZEMOLO, Corino, Ruggieri Crosini, Damilano, Gagliasso, Ettore Germano, Ghisolfi, ELIO GRASSO, Silvio Grasso, Paolo Manzone, GIOVANNI MANZONE, Giacomo Marengo, MOLINO, OBERTO, PARUSSO, Luigi Pira, Porro, Principiano, PRUNOTTO, Revello, Giorgio Rivetti, Rocche Costamagna, ROCCHE DEI MANZONI, Giovanni Rosso, SANDRONE, Saffirio, SCAVINO, Fratelli Seghesio, Tenuta Rocca, VAJRA, Veglio, Viberti, Gianni Voerzio, ROBERTO VOERZIO, and many others.

from an eclectic mix of grapes inc SOAVE'S GARGANEGA. Gd Corte Sant'Arcadio, Le Tende, Le VIGNE di San Pietro, MONTRESOR, Zeni.

Bibi Graetz Important reds from hills of Fiesole nr Florence, old-vine SANGIOVESE, Canaiolo, and Colorino of character and depth.

Biondi-Santi ★★★★ Founding family, on Il Greppo estate, in 19th century of BRUNELLO DI MONTALCINO. Tannic/acidic but genuinely long-lasting wines capable of great finesse.

Bisol Top brand of PROSECCO.

Boca Pie DOC r ★★ 96' 97' 98' **99' 00 01'** 03 04' 05 06' 07 Obscure, NEBBIOLO-based red from northern PIEDMONT. Look for Le Piane and Poderi ai Valloni (Vigneto Cristiana ★★★).

Boccadigabbia ★★★ Top Marches producer of IGT wines: SANGIOVESE, CAB SAUV, PINOT N, CHARD. Proprietor Elvidio Alessandri also owns fine Villamagna estate in ROSSO PICENO DOC.

Boglietti, Enzo ★★★ Dynamic young producer of La Morra in BAROLO zone. Top modern-style Barolos and outstanding BARBERA d'Alba.

Bolgheri Tus DOC r p w (sw) ★★→★★★★ Ultra-modish region on the coast south of Livorno. Inc 7 types of wine: BIANCO, VERMENTINO, Sauv Bl, ROSSO, ROSATO, VIN SANTO, and Occhio di Pernice, plus top IGTS. Newish DOC Bolgheri ROSSO: CAB SAUV/MERLOT/SANGIOVESE blend. Top producers: Argentiera, CA' MARCANDA, Caccia al Piano, Giorgio Meletti Cavallari, Campo alla Sughera, Campo al Mare, Casa di Terra, Ceralti, Chiappini, Cipriani, ORNELLAIA, Poggio al Tesoro, San Guido/SASSICAIA, Enrico Santini, Sapaio, Serni, Terre del Marchesato, Tringali, VIGNA al Cavaliere (SANGIOVESE).

Bolla ★★ Famous Verona firm for VALPOLICELLA, AMARONE, SOAVE, etc. Also RECIOTO. Top wines: Castellaro, Creso (red and white), Jago. Wines, particularly AMARONE and SOAVE selections, are once again on the upswing.

Bonarda 04 05 06 07 Minor and confusing red grape or grapes (name often erroneously used for Croatina) widely grown in PIEDMONT, Lombardy, Emilia-Romagna, and blended with BARBERA.

Bonarda Lom DOC r ★★ **04 05** 06 07 Soft, fresh FRIZZANTE and still wines from OLTREPÒ PAVESE, actually made from Croatina grapes; impressive new wines now appearing from CS Casteggio, Cigognola.

Borgo del Tiglio ★★★→★★★★ FRIULI estate for one of northeast Italy's top MERLOTS, ROSSO della Centa; also superior COLLIO CHARD, TOCAI, and BIANCO.

Now expanding into Marches with Sangiovese and Montepulciano.

Boscarelli, Poderi ★★★ Small estate with v.gd VINO NOBILE DI MONTEPULCIANO and barrel-aged IGT Boscarelli.

Botte Large barrel, anything from 6 to 250 hectolitres, traditionally of Slavonian but increasingly of French oak. To traditionalists the ideal vessel for wines in which an excess of oak aromas is undesirable.

Brachetto d'Acqui Pie DOCG r sw (sp) ★★ DYA Sweet, sparkling red with enticing Muscat scent.

Braida ★★★ The late Giacomo Bologna's estate; for top BARBERA D'ASTI (BRICCO dell'Uccellone, BRICCO della Bigotta, Ai Suma).

Bramaterra Pie DOC r ★★ 97' 98' 99' 00 01' 03 04 Neighbour to GATTINARA. NEBBIOLO grapes predominate in a blend. Gd producer: Sella.

Breganze Ven DOC r w ★→★★★ (r) 97' 98 99 00 01 Catch-all for many varieties nr Vicenza. Best: CAB SAUV, CHARD, PINOT GR. Top producers: MACULAN, Miotti.

Bricco Term for a hilltop (and by implication v.gd) v'yd in PIEDMONT.

Brindisi Ap DOC r p ★★ 00 01 03' 04 05 06 07 Strong NEGROAMARO, esp from VALLONE, Due Palme, Rubino, and forthcoming wines from ZONIN.

Brolio, Castello di ★★→★★★ Historic, once trend-setting estate now thriving in the hands, once again, of the Ricasoli family after a period of foreign-managed decline. V.gd CHIANTI CLASSICO and IGT Casalferro.

Brunelli ★★→★★★ V.gd quality producer of AMARONE and RECIOTO.

Brunelli, Gianni ★★★ Small-scale producer of elegant, refined BRUNELLO DI MONTALCINO and owner of Siena's excellent restaurant, Le Logge. Not to be confused with others called Brunelli.

Brunello di Montalcino Tus DOCG r ★★★→★★★★ 85' 87 88 90' 93 95' 97' 99 00 01 03 04 05 06 07 With BAROLO, Italy's most celebrated red: strong, full-bodied, high-flavoured, tannic, long-lived. Four yrs' ageing; after 5 yrs becomes RISERVA. Quality is ever improving. MONTALCINO is 25 miles south of Siena. See below for "Best buys".

Bussola, Tommaso ★★★ Leading producer of AMARONE and RECIOTO in VALPOLICELLA.

Cabernet Franc Increasingly preferred to CAB SAUV by Italy's internationalists.

Cabernet Sauvignon The great B'x grape has played a key role in the renaissance of Italian red wine (eg see SASSICAIA). Particularly influential in Tuscany as a lesser partner for SANGIOVESE. Now losing ground to indigenous blenders.

Ca' del Bosco ★★★★ FRANCIACORTA estate; some of Italy's best sparklers (*outstanding DOCG Annamaria Clementi* ★★★★) and Zero, v.gd CHARD and CAB SAUV blend (Maurizio Zanella), PINOT N (Pinèro). Intriguing Carmenère.

Ca' dei Frati ★★★★ The best producer of DOC LUGANA, also v.gd dry white blend IGT Pratto, sweet Tre Filer and red IGT Ronchedone.

Best Brunello di Montalcino to buy

Altesino, ARGIANO, BANFI, Barbi, Baricci, BIONDI-SANTI, GIANNI BRUNELLI, La Campana, Campogiovanni, Canalicchio di Sopra, Caparzo, CASANOVA DI NERI, Casanova delle Cerbaie, Casato Prime Donne, Camigliano, CASE BASSE, CASTELGIOCONDO, Cerbaiona, Cerrino, COL D'ORCIA, Il Colle, Collelceto, Collemattoni, Collosorbo, La Colombina, Corte Pavone, Costanti, EREDI FULIGNI, Fanti-San Filippo, Ferrero, La Fiorita, La Fuga, La Gerla, Gorelli, Lambardi, LISINI, La Magia, La Mannella, Marroneto, Oliveto, SIRO PACENTI, Franco Pacenti, Palazzo, Pertimali, Ciacci Piccolomini, PIEVE DI SANTA RESTITUTA, Podere Brizio, La Poderina, POGGIO ANTICO, POGGIONE, La Rasina, Salvioni-Cerbaiola, San Filippo, Scopetone, La Serena, Sesta, Sesti, Talenti, La Torre, Uccelliera, Val di Suga, Valdicava, Vasco Sassetti, Ventolaio, Verbena, Villa Le Prata, Vitanza.

Cafaggio, Villa ★★★ V. reliable CHIANTI CLASSICO estate with excellent IGTS San Martino (SANGIOVESE) and Cortaccio (CAB SAUV).

Calatrasi Si ★★→★★★ Gd red/white IGT producer, esp D'Istinto range.

Caldaro (Lago di Caldaro) T-AA DOC r ★ DYA German name Kalterersee. Light, soft, bitter-almond SCHIAVA. From a huge area. CLASSICO – smaller area – is better.

Ca' Marcanda BOLGHERI estate created by GAJA since 1996. Focus on international varieties: CAB SAUV, MERLOT, CAB FR, SYRAH.

Campania Historic centre of Italy's southern mainland with capital in Naples. Excellent grape varieties (Aglianico, Falanghina, FIANO, GRECO, Piedirosso), volcanic soils, and high, cool v'yds all add up to great potential. Best DOCS are FALERNO DEL MASSICO, FIANO D'AVELLINO, GRECO DI TUFO, ISCHIA, TAURASI, but many newer areas now coming to the fore. Established producers include Caggiano, Caputo, Colli di Lapio, D' Ambra, De Angelis, Benito Ferrara, FEUDI DI SAN GREGORIO, GALARDI, MASTROBERARDINO, MONTEVETRANO, Mustilli, and VILLA MATILDE. Many new faces are worthy of note: Alois, Cantina del Taburno, Casavecchia, Marisa Cuomo, Felicia, Grotta del Sole, Macchialupa, Molettieri, Amore Perrotta, Poderi Foglia, Quintodecimo, Selvanova, Spada, Torre Gaia, Trabucco, Vesevo, Vestini Campagnano, Villa Raiano, Vinosia, Vuolo.

Cannonau di Sardegna Sar DOC r (p) dr s/sw ★★ 00 01 02 **03** 04 05 06 Cannonau (Grenache) is the basic red grape of the south. From v. potent to fine and mellow. Look for: ARGIOLAS, CONTINI, Giuseppe Gabbas, Jerzu, Loi, Sedilesu.

Cantalupo, Antichi Vigneti di ★★→★★★ Top GHEMME wines, esp single-v'yd Breclemae and Carellae.

Cantina Cellar or winery. See CS.

Capannelle ★★★ V.gd producer of IGT and CHIANTI CLASSICO, plus 50:50 SANGIOVESE/MERLOT joint venture with AVIGNONESI nr Gaiole.

Capezzana, Tenuta di (or Villa) ★★★ Tuscan estate of the Contini Bonacossi family. Gd Barco Reale, excellent CARMIGNANO (esp Villa Capezzana, Villa Trefiano). Also v.gd B'x-style red, Ghiaie Della Furba.

Capichera ★★★ Proclaimed, high-price producer of VERMENTINO DI GALLURA, esp VENDEMMIA Tardiva. Excellent red Mantènghja from Carignano grapes.

Caprai ★★★→★★★★ Widely copied, superb DOCG SAGRANTINO, esp 25 Anni, v.gd DOC ROSSO DI MONTEFALCO. Highly rated.

Capri Cam DOC r p w ★→★★ Legendary island with widely abused name. Only interesting wines are from La Caprense.

Carema Pie DOC r ★★→★★★ 89' 90' 93 95 96' 97' 98 99' 00 **01** 03 04 06 07 Elegant NEBBIOLO red from steep slopes on Aosta border. Best: Luigi Ferrando.

Carignano del Sulcis Sar DOC r p ★★→★★★ Ageworthy red. Best: TERRE BRUNE and Rocca Rubia from CS DI SANTADI.

Carmignano Tus DOCG r ★★★ 90' 93 94 95 97' 98 99' 00 01' 03 04 05 06 07 Region west of Florence. CHIANTI grapes plus CAB FRANC, MERLOT make distinctive, potentially excellent red. Best: Ambra, CAPEZZANA, Farnete, PIAGGIA, Le Poggiarelle, Pratesi.

Carpenè-Malvolti Leading producer of classic PROSECCO and other sparkling wines at Conegliano, Veneto. Seen everywhere in Venice.

Carso F-VG DOC r w ★★→★★★ (r) 99' 00 01 02 03 04 05 06 07 V. obscure DOC nr Trieste includes gd MALVASIA. Terrano del Carso is a REFOSCO red. Top growers: EDI KANTE, Zidanich.

Cartizze Famous, frequently too expensive, and too sweet DOC PROSECCO of supposedly best sub-zone of Valdobbiadene.

Casanova di Neri ★★★ BRUNELLO DI MONTALCINO, Pietradonice (SANGIOVESE/CAB SAUV) and v.gd ROSSO DI MONTALCINO from Neri family.

Cascina Fonda ★★★ Brothers Marco and Massimo Barbero have risen to the top in MOSCATO D'ASTI DOC. VENDEMMIA Tardiva and METODO CLASSICO ASTI SPUMANTE.

ITALY

> **Who makes really good Chianti Classico?**
> AMA, Antica Fornace di Ridolfo, ANTINORI, BADIA A COLTIBUONO, Bibbiano,
> Bossi, BROLIO, Cacchiano, CAFAGGIO, Candialle, Canonica a Cerreto,
> Capaccia, La Cappella, CAPANNELLE, Capraia, Carobbio, Casa Emma,
> Casafrassi, Casale dello Sparviero, Casaloste, Casa Sola, Castello di San
> Sano, Castel Ruggero, CASTELLARE, Castell'in Villa, Collelungo, Colombaio
> di Cencio, Le Corti, Mannucci Droandi, FELSINA-BERARDENGA, Le Filigare,
> FONTERUTOLI, FONTODI, ISOLE E OLENA, Ispoli, LE CINCIOLE, Lilliano, Lornano,
> Lucignano, LA MASSA, MONSANTO, MONTE BERNARDI, NITTARDI, PALAZZINO,
> PANERETTA, Panzanello, Petroio-Lenzi, Poggerino, Poggiolino,
> Poggiopiano, Poggio Amorelli, Poggio al Sole, Poggio Bonelli, Querceto,
> QUERCIABELLA, RAMPOLLA, RIECINE, Rocca di Castagnoli, Rocca di
> Montegrossi, RUFFINO, San Fabiano Calcinaia, SAN FELICE, SAN GIUSTO A
> RENTENNANO, Savignola Paolina, Selvole, Solatione, Vecchie Terre di
> Montefili, VERRAZZANO, Villa Mangiacane, Villa La Rosa, Viticcio, VOLPAIA.

Case Basse ★★★★ Eco-geek Gianfranco Soldera claims to make the definitive BRUNELLO, and maddeningly he is right. V. expensive and rare.

Castelgiocondo ★★★ FRESCOBALDI estate in MONTALCINO: v.gd BRUNELLO and IGT MERLOT Lamaïone.

Castellare ★★→★★★ Small but admired CHIANTI CLASSICO producer. First-rate SANGIOVESE IGT I Sodi di San Niccoló and sprightly GOVERNO di Castellare: old-style CHIANTI updated. Also Poggio ai Merli (MERLOT) and Coniale (CAB SAUV).

Castello Castle. (See under name – eg SALA, CASTELLO DELLA.)

Castell' in Villa ★★★ V. gd CHIANTI CLASSICO estate in Castelnuovo Berardenga.

Castel del Monte Ap DOC r p w ★★→★★★ (r) Dry, fresh, well-balanced wines. Rosé best known. Gd Pietrabianca and excellent Bocca di Lupo from Vigneti del Sud (ANTINORI). V.gd Il Falcone, Puer Apuliae, and Cappellaccio from RIVERA, Le More from Santa Lucia. Interesting new reds from Cocevola, Giancarlo Ceci.

Castelluccio ★★→★★★ Pioneering producer of quality SANGIOVESE di Romagna, today owned by family of oenologist Vittorio Fiore. IGT RONCO dei Ciliegi and RONCO delle Ginestre. Massicone is an excellent SANGIOVESE/CAB SAUV blend.

Cataratto Sicilian white grape of high (generally unexplored) promise.

Caudrina-Dogliotti Romano ★★★ Top MOSCATO D'ASTI: La Galeisa and Caudrina.

Cavalleri ★★→★★★ V.gd reliable FRANCIACORTA producer, esp sparkling.

Cavicchioli E-R ★→★★ Large producer of LAMBRUSCO and other sparkling wines: Lambrusco di Sorbara VIGNA del Cristo is best. Also TERRE di FRANCIACORTA.

Ca' Viola PIEDMONT home base of influential consultant Bepe Caviola. Classy DOLCETTO and BARBERA-based wines.

Ca' Vit (Cantina Viticoltori) Group of co-ops nr Trento. Top wines: Brune di Monte (red and white) and sparkling Graal.

Cecchi Tus ★→★★ Bottler, producer; La Gavina, Spargolo, CHIANTI CLASSICO RISERVA.

Cerasuolo Ab DOC p ★ The ROSATO version of MONTEPULCIANO D'ABRUZZO.

Cerasuolo di Vittoria Si DOCG r ★★ 01 03 04 05 06 07 Garnet, medium-bodied, aromatic red from Frappato and NERO D'AVOLA grapes; try PLANETA, Valle dell'Acate, and Cos.

Ceretto ★★→★★★ Much hyped grower of BARBARESCO (BRICCO Asili), BAROLO (BRICCO Rocche, Brunate, Prapò), LANGHE ROSSO Monsordo, and ARNEIS. Also v.gd METODO CLASSICO SPUMANTE La Bernardina.

Chardonnay The Burgundian white variety has a vast and important presence in Italy, from ALTO ADIGE to SICILY and from PIEDMONT to FRIULI.

Chianti Tus DOCG r ★→★★★★ Local wine of Florence, Siena. At best fresh, fruity, tangy. Of the sub-districts, RUFINA (★★→★★★★), COLLI Fiorentini (★→★★★),

CHIANTI Montespertoli can make CLASSICO-style RISERVAS. Montalbano, COLLI Senesi, Aretini, Pisani: lighter wines.

Chianti Classico Tus DOCG r ★★→★★★★ 97' 99' 00 01' 03 04' 05 06' 07' (single-v'yd and RISERVA) **90' 95** 97' 99 01 03 04' 06' 07' The historic CHIANTI from the Chianti hills of central Tuscany. Currently the fight is on between modernists who are allowed 20% of Bordeaux (and other) grapes with 80% SANGIOVESE, and purists who see this as a travesty. Battle leaning toward latter. The Gallo Nero (black rooster) CONSORZIO now controls DOCG registration, so all producers are obliged to cooperate.

Chiaretto Rosé (the word means "claret") produced esp around Lake Garda. See BARDOLINO, RIVIERA DEL GARDA BRESCIANO.

Chiarlo, Michele ★★→★★★ Gd PIEDMONT producer (BAROLOS Cerequio and *Cannubi*, BARBERA D'ASTI, LANGHE, and MONFERRATO ROSSO). Also BARBARESCO.

Chionetti ★★→★★★ Makes top DOLCETTO di Dogliani (look for Briccolero).

Cigliuti, Renato ★★★ Small quality estate for BARBARESCO and BARBERA D'ALBA.

Le Cinciole ★★→★★★ DOCG CHIANTI CLASSICO, the best is RISERVA Petresco.

Cinqueterre Lig DOC w dr sw ★★ Fragrant, fruity white from precipitous coast nr La Spezia. PASSITO is known as SCIACCHETRÀ (★★→★★★). Gd from Co-op Agricola di Cinqueterre and Forlini Cappellini.

Cirò Cal DOC r (p w) ★→★★★ Strong red from Gaglioppo grapes; light, fruity white (DYA). Best: Caparra, Ippolito, LIBRANDI (Duca San Felice ★★★), San Francesco (Donna Madda), RONCO dei Quattroventi), Santa Venere, Siciliani.

Classico Term for wines from a restricted area within the limits of a DOC. By implication, and often in practice, the best of the district. When applied to sparkling wines, it denotes the classic method (as for Champagne).

Clerico, Domenico ★★★ Established modernist BAROLO producer, esp *crus* Percristina and Ciabot Mentin Ginestra. Also NEBBIOLO/BARBERA blend Arte.

Coffele ★★★ Grower with some of the finest v'yds in SOAVE CLASSICO, making steely, minerally wines of classic concept.

Colle Santa Mustiola High-level SANGIOVESE from small estate just outside VINO NOBILE DI MONTEPULCIANO zone.

Colli Hills (from sing. Colle). Occurs in many wine names.

Colli Berici Ven DOC r p w ★★ 99 00 01 03 04 05 06 07 Hills south of Vicenza. Best wine is CAB SAUV. Top producer: Villa Dal Ferro.

Colli Bolognesi E-R DOC r w ★★ Southwest of Bologna, 8 wines, 5 varieties. TERRE ROSSE, the pioneer, now joined by Bonzara (★★→★★★) and others.

Colli Euganei Ven DOC r w dr s/sw (sp) ★→★★★ DYA DOC southwest of Padua for 7 wines. Adequate red; white and sparkling are pleasant. Best producers: Ca' Lustra, La Montecchia, Speaia, VIGNALTA.

Colline Novaresi Pie DOC r w ★→★★ DYA New DOC for old region in Novara province. Seven different wines: BIANCO, ROSSO, NEBBIOLO, BONARDA, Vespolina, Croatina, BARBERA. Includes declassified BOCA, FARA, GHEMME, SIZZANO.

Collio F-VG DOC r w ★★→★★★★ (r) Makes 19 wines, 17 named after their grapes. V.gd whites from: Attems, BORGO DEL TIGLIO, Il Carpino, Casa Zuliani, La Castellada, CASTELLO di Spessa, Damijan, MARCO FELLUGA, Fiegl, GRAVNER, Renato Keber, LIVON, Aldo Polencic, Primosic, Princic, RONCO dei Tassi, Russiz Superiore, SCHIOPETTO, Tercic, Terpin, Toros, Venica & Venica, VILLA RUSSIZ.

Colli Orientali del Friuli F-VG DOC r w dr sw ★★→★★★★ Hills E of Udine. 20 wines (18 named after their grapes). Both white and red can be v.gd: Best: Angoris, Bastianich, Rosa Bosco, Castello di Buttrio, Centa Sant'Anna, Dorigo, Dri, LE DUE TERRE, LIVIO FELLUGA, Meroi, Miani, Moschioni, Perusini, Petrussa, Rocca Bernarda, Ronchi di Cialla, Ronchi di Manzano, RONCO delle Betulle, RONCO DEL GNEMIZ, RONCO di Vico, SCHIOPETTO, Scubla, Specogna, Torre di Rosazzo, La Viarte, VIGNA Traverso, Le Vigne di Zamò, Volpe Pasini.

Colli Piacentini E-R DOC r p w ★→★★ DYA DOC inc traditional GUTTURNIO and Monterosso Val d'Arda among 11 types grown south of Piacenza. Gd fizzy MALVASIA. Most wines FRIZZANTE. New French and local reds: Montesissa, Mossi, Romagnoli, Solenghi, La Stoppa, Torre Fornello, La Tosa.

Colli del Trasimeno Um DOC r w ★→★★★ (r) **99' 00** 01' 03 04' 05 06' 07' Lively white wines from nr Perugia, but now more important reds as well. Best: Duca della Corgna, La Fiorita, Pieve del Vescovo, Poggio Bertaio.

Colterenzio CS (or Schreckbichl) T-AA ★★→★★★ Pioneering quality leader among ALTO ADIGE co-ops. Look for: Cornell line of selections; Lafoa CAB SAUV and SAUV BL; Cornelius red and white blends.

Col d'Orcia ★★★ Top MONTALCINO estate. Best wine: BRUNELLO.

Colpo e mancanza Ap r ★ Frequent source of two typical reds.

Consorzio In Italy there are 2 types of association recognized by wine law. One is dedicated to the observance of DOC regulations (eg Consorzio Tutela del CHIANTI CLASSICO). The second promotes the wines of its members (eg Consorzio del Marchio Storico of CHIANTI CLASSICO, previously Gallo Nero).

Conterno, Aldo ★★★★ Legendary grower of BAROLO at Monforte d'Alba. V. gd CHARD Bussiadoro, BARBERA D'ALBA Conca Tre Pile. Best BAROLOS: Gran Bussia, Cicala, Colonello. Langhe Nebbiolo Favot and Langhe Rosso Quartetto v.gd.

Conterno, Giacomo ★★★★ Iconic grower of BAROLO at Monforte d'Alba, now in hands of Giacomo's grandson Roberto. Two Barolos: Cascina Francia and legendary Monfortino, long-macerated to age for yrs.

Conterno-Fantino ★★★ Two families joined to produce excellent BAROLO Sori Ginestra and Vigna del Gris at Monforte d'Alba. Also NEBBIOLO/BARBERA blend.

Contini, Attilio ★→★★★ Famous SARDINIAN producer of VERNACCIA DI ORISTANO; best is vintage blend Antico Gregori. Also gd Cannonau.

Contratto ★★ At Canelli (owned by GRAPPA-producing family Bocchino); produces v.gd BARBERA D'ASTI, BAROLO, SPUMANTE, ASTI (De Miranda), MOSCATO D'ASTI.

Copertino Ap DOC r (p) ★★ 99 00 01 04 Savoury, ageworthy, strong red of NEGROAMARO from the heel of Italy. Look for the CS's RISERVA and Masseria Monaci, esp new barrel-aged Le Braci.

Coppo ★★→★★★ Ambitious producers of BARBERA D'ASTI (Pomorosso), CHARD.

Cordero di Montezemolo-Monfalletto ★★→★★★ Historic maker of gd BAROLO, now with fine BARBERA D'ALBA and CHARD.

Corini New house in remote area of Umbria. Produces intriguing, innovative blend of SANGIOVESE/MONTEPULCIANO/MERLOT.

Cortese di Gavi See GAVI. (Cortese is the grape.)

Cortona Tuscan DOC contiguous to Montepulciano's Vino Nobile. Various red and white grapes, best results so far from AVIGNONESI's Desiderio, a B'x blend, and first-rate SYRAH from Luigi d'Alessandro, Il Castagno, La Braccesca.

Corzano & Paterno, Fattoria di ★★★ Dynamic CHIANTI COLLI Fiorentini estate. V.gd RISERVA, red IGT Corzano, and outstanding VIN SANTO.

CS, Cantina Sociale Cooperative winery.

Dal Forno, Romano ★★★★ V. high-quality VALPOLICELLA, AMARONE, and RECIOTO grower whose perfectionism is the more remarkable for the fact that his v'yds are outside the Classico zone.

Del Cerro, Fattoria ★★★ Estate with v.gd DOCG VINO NOBILE DI MONTEPULCIANO (esp

> **DOC, Denominazione di Origine Controllata**
> Means much the same as *appellation d'origine contrôlée* (see France).
>
> **DOCG, Denominazione di Origine Controllata e Garantita**
> Like DOC but with an official "guarantee" of quality.

RISERVA), red IGTS Manero (SANGIOVESE), and Poggio Golo (MERLOT). Controlled by insurance company. Also owns La Poderina (BRUNELLO DI MONTALCINO) and Colpetrone (MONTEFALCO SAGRANTINO).

Di Majo Norante ★★ →★★★ Lone star of Molise, south of Abruzzo, with v.gd Biferno ROSSO, Molise MONTEPULCIANO, Ramitello Don Luigi, and AGLIANICO Contado, white blend Falanghina-Greco and Moscato Passito Apianae.

Dolce Sweet.

Dolcetto ★→★★★ PIEDMONT's earliest-ripening red grape, for v. attractive everyday wines: dry, youthful, fruity, fresh, with deep purple colour. Gives its name to several DOCs: d'Acqui; d'Asti; di Diano d'Alba (also Diano DOC, esp Alari, BRICCO Maiolica, Cascina Flino, FONTANAFREDDA, and Marco; di Dogliani (esp from M & E Abbona, Francesco Boschis, CHIONETTI, Gillardi, Pecchenino, Poderi Luigi Einaudi, San Fereolo, San Romano); delle Langhe Monregalesi (look for Barone Ricatti); and di Ovada (best from La Gioia, La Guardia, Villa Sparina). Most familiar is Dolcetto d'Alba: ALESSANDRIA, ALTARE, Azelia, Baudana, BOGLIETTI, Brovia, Cabutto, Cavallotto, CA' VIOLA, CLERICO, ALDO CONTERNO, CONTERNO-FANTINO, Corino, De Stefanis, Gagliasso, Gastaldi, Germano, BRUNO GIACOSA, GRESY, MANZONE, G. mascarello, Massolino, Mauro Molino, Mossio, Fiorenzo Nada, OBERTO, Pelissero, Gianmatteo Pira, Luigi Pira, PRUNOTTO, Rocche Costamanga, SANDRONE, SCAVINO, Schiavenza, Fratelli Seghesio, Sottimano, VAJRA, Gianni VOERZIO, Roberto VOERZIO.

Donnafugata Si w r ★★→★★★ Well-crafted Sicilian whites (best from Chiaranda and VIGNA di Gabri) and reds, esp Mille e Una Notte and Tancredi, fine Moscato Passito di Pantelleria Ben Rye. Wines in DOC Contessa Entellina.

Duca di Salaparuta Si ★★ Vini Corvo. Popular SICILIAN wines. Sound dry reds; pleasant soft whites. Duca Enrico (★★→★★★) was one of SICILY's pioneeering ambitious reds. Valguarnera is premium oak-aged white.

Le Due Terre Small producer in COLLI ORIENTALI DEL FRIULI for choice MERLOT, PINOT N, Sacrisassi ROSSO (Refosco/Schioppettino), and white Sacrisassi BIANCO.

Elba Tus r w (sp) ★→★★ DYA The island's white is v. drinkable with fish. In exile here, Napoleon loved the sweet red ALEATICO. Promising new wines from Sapereta, both reds and dessert. Try Acquabona, Accuacalda, Cecilia.

Enoteca Wine library; also wine shop or restaurant with extensive wine list. The impressive original is the state-financed Enoteca Italiana of Siena.

Eredi Fuligni ★★★ V.gd producer of BRUNELLO and ROSSO DI MONTALCINO.

Est! Est!! Est!!! Lat DOC w dr s/sw ★ DYA Unextraordinary white from Montefiascone, north of Rome. Trades on the improbable origin of its name.

Etna Si DOC r p w ★★ (r) **95 97 98 99 00 01 04 05 06 07** Wine from volcanic slopes and often considerable altitude. New investment from Andrea Franchetti (TRINORO) and broker Marc De Grazia. Gd producers: Benanti, Cambria, Bonaccorsi. Newest wines show potential for Nerello Mascalese grape.

Falchini ★★ Producer of gd DOCG VERNACCIA DI SAN GIMIGNANO (esp Castel Selva and VIGNA a Solatio). Some of the area's best reds, eg IGT Campora (★★).

Falerno del Massico ★★→★★★ Cam DOC r w ★★ (r) **97' 98 99 00' 01'** 03 04 06 07 Falernum (or Falernian) was the best-known wine of ancient times, probably white and sweet. Today elegant red from AGLIANICO, fruity white from Falanghina. V.gd producer: VILLA MATILDE. Other producers: Amore Perrotta, Felicia, Moio, Trabucco.

Falesco ★★→★★★ Latium estate of Cotarella brothers, v.gd MERLOT Montiano and CAB SAUV Marciliano (both ★★★). Gd red IGT Vitiano and DOC EST! EST!! EST!!!

Fara Pie DOC r ★★ **90 95' 96' 97 98 99 00' 01** 03 04 05 06' 07' Gd NEBBIOLO from

Novara, north PIEDMONT; worth ageing; esp from Dessilani'.

Farnese Ap ★★ Good quality supplier of the Abruzzi's favourites. To follow.

Farnetella, Castello di ★★ Estate nr MONTEPULCIANO where Giuseppe Mazzocolin of FELSINA makes gd SAUV BL and CHIANTI COLLI Senesi. Also v.gd PINOT N Nero di Nubi and red blend Poggio Granoni.

Faro Si DOC r ★★ **97 98 99** 00 01' 04' 05 06' 07' Full-bodied red from a recently virtually extinct DOC at Messina. Palari administered the kiss of life; splendid wines from the hitherto scorned Nerello Mascalese grape.

Fattoria Central Italian term for an agricultural property, normally wine-producing, of a certain size. (See under name – eg MONTELLORI, FATTORIA DI.)

Fazi-Battaglia ★★ Well-known producer of VERDICCHIO, best selections: Massaccio, Le Moie, San Sisto. Owns Fassati (VINO NOBILE DI MONTEPULCIANO).

Felluga, Livio ★★★ Substantial estate, consistently fine COLLI ORIENTALI DEL FRIULI wines, esp PINOT GR, Sauv Bl, TOCAI, PICOLIT, and MERLOT/REFOSCO blend.

Felluga, Marco ★★ →★★★ The brother of Livio owns a négociant house bearing his name plus Russiz Superiore in COLLIO DOC, Castello di Buttrio in COLLI ORIENTALI DOC. Marco's daughter Patrizia is now owner of Zuani estate in COLLIO.

Felsina-Berardenga ★★★ CHIANTI CLASSICO estate; famous for BARRIQUE-aged RISERVA Rancia, IGT Fontalloro, both 100% SANGIOVESE. Regular CHIANTI CLASSICO and RISERVA, less fashionable and less expensive, are more traditional. Also gd IGT CHARD and CAB SAUV.

Ferrari T-AA ★★ →★★★ Cellars making cheery sparkling nr Trento. Giulio Ferrari RISERVA is best. New reds from TUSCANY and Umbria as well.

Feudi di San Gregorio ★★ →★★★ Top Campania producer, with DOCG TAURASI, DOCG FIANO, Falanghina, Greco di Tufo. Red IGT Serpico and Patrimo (MERLOT), white IGT Campanaro. Now active in Basilicata and APULIA as well.

Fiano di Avellino Cam DOCG w ★★ →★★★ DYA Fiano is rapidly becoming seen as the best native white grape of southern Italy, planted successfully in Molise, Puglia, Calabria and Sicily as well as in Campania, its birthplace. Fiano di Avellino can be intense, slightly honeyed, memorable. Best producers: Caggiano, Caputo, COLLI di Lapio, Benito Ferrara, FEUDI DI SAN GREGORIO, Grotta del Sole, MASTROBERARDINO, San Paolo, Vesevo, Villa Raiano.

Florio Historic quality producer of MARSALA. Best wine: Donna Franca.

Folonari Ambrogio Folonari and son Giovanni have split off from RUFFINO to create their own house. Will continue to make Cabreo (a CHARD and a SANGIOVESE/CAB SAUV), wines of NOZZOLE (inc CAB SAUV Pareto), BRUNELLO DI MONTALCINO La Fuga, VINO NOBILE DI MONTEPULCIANO Gracciano Svetoni, with new offerings from BOLGHERI, MONTECUCCO, and COLLI ORIENTALI DEL FRIULI.

Fontana Candida ★★ One of the biggest producers of FRASCATI. Single-v'yd Santa Teresa stands out. See also GRUPPO ITALIANO VINI.

Fontanafredda ★★ →★★★ Producer of PIEDMONT wines on former royal estates, inc single-v'yd BAROLOS and ALBA DOCS. V.gd SPUMANTE Brut (esp ★★★ Gattinera).

Fonterutoli ★★★ Historic CHIANTI CLASSICO estate of the Mazzei family at Castellina. Notable are CASTELLO di Fonterutoli (dark, oaky, fashionable CHIANTI), IGT Siepi (SANGIOVESE/MERLOT). Mazzei also owns Tenuta di Belguardo in MAREMMA, gd MORELLINO DI SCANSANO and IGT wines.

Le Fonti ★★ →★★★ V.gd CHIANTI CLASSICO house in Poggibonsi; look for RISERVA and IGT Vito Arturo (SANGIOVESE).

Fontodi ★★★ Top Panzano CHIANTI CLASSICO estate for CHIANTI and RISERVA, esp RISERVA del Sorbo. Top SUPER TUSCAN 100% SANGIOVESE IGT Flaccianello, Case Via PINOT N, Case Via SYRAH.

Foradori ★★★ Elizabetta F makes *best Teroldego*. Also oak-aged TEROLDEGO Granato, white IGT Myrto. Wines from new Ampeleia estate in Tuscan MAREMMA already first class.

Forte, Podere Pasquale Forte's Val d'Orcia estate, just south of MONTALCINO, puts cutting-edge technology at the service of ambitious SANGIOVESE and CAB SAUV/MERLOT/Petit Verdot wines.

Forteto della Luja ★★★ Pioneer in LOAZZOLO; v.gd BARBERA/PINOT N Le Grive.

Fossi, Enrico ★★★ High-level small estate in Signa, west of Florence, v.gd SANGIOVESE, CAB SAUV, SYRAH, Malbec, Gamay, and CHARD.

Franciacorta Lom DOCG w (p) sp ★★→★★★★ Small Champagne-style sparkling-wine centre growing in quality and renown. Wines exclusively bottle-fermented. Top producers: Barone Pizzini, BELLAVISTA, CA' DEL BOSCO, Castellino, CAVALLERI, Gatti, UBERTI, villa; also v.gd: Contadi Gastaldi, Cornaleto, Majolini, Monte Rossa, La Montina, Il Mosnel, Ricci Curbastri, Ronco Calino, Vezzoli. For white and red, see TERRE DI FRANCIACORTA.

Frascati Lat DOC w dr s/sw sw (sp) ★→★★ DYA Best-known wine of Roman hills: should be limpid, golden, tasting of whole grapes. Most is disappointingly neutral today: look for Castel de Paolis, Conte Zandotti, Villa Simone, or Santa Teresa from FONTANA CANDIDA. The sweet version is known as Cannellino.

Freisa Pie DOC r dr s/sw sw (sp) ★★ DYA Usually v. dry (except nr Turin), often FRIZZANTE red, said to taste of raspberries and roses. With enough acidity it can be highly appetizing, esp with salami. Gd wines from Brezza, CIGLIUTI, CLERICO, ALDO CONTERNO, COPPO, Franco Martinetti, GIUSEPPE MASCARELLO, Parusso, Pecchenino, Pelissero, Sebaste, Trinchero, VAJRA, Vigneti Massa, and VOERZIO.

Frescobaldi ★★→★★★★ Ancient noble family, leading CHIANTI RUFINA pioneer at CASTELGIOCONDO (★★★). Outright owner of joint venture with Mondavi nr MONTALCINO, LUCE, Lucente, and ORNELLAIA. New v'yds in COLLIO DOC and MAREMMA. Important new v'yds nr Montespertoli, SE of Florence .

Friuli-Venezia Giulia The northeast region on the Slovenian border. Many wines; the DOCS ISONZO, COLLIO, and COLLI ORIENTALI include most of the best.

Frizzante (fz) Semi-sparkling. Used to describe wines such as LAMBRUSCO.

Gaja ★★★★ Old family firm at BARBARESCO under direction of Angelo Gaja. Top-quality – and price – wines, esp BARBARESCO, the only Piedmontese DOCGS remaining after Gaja downclassed Barbaresco *crus* SORÌ Tildin, SORÌ San Lorenzo and Costa Russi as well as Barolo Sperss to LANGHE DOC so that he could blend small proportions of BARBERA in with NEBBIOLO. CHARD (Gaia e Rey), CAB SAUV Darmagi. Acquisitions elsewhere in Italy: Marengo-Marenda estate (BAROLO), commercial Gromis label; PIEVE DI SANTA RESTITUTA (BRUNELLO) CA' MARCANDA in BOLGHERI.

Galardi ★★★→★★★★ Producer of Terra di Lavoro, a mind-boggling blend of AGLIANICO and Piedirosso, in north Campania nr FALERNO DEL MASSICO DOC.

Gambellara Ven DOC w dr s/sw (sp) ★ DYA Neighbour of SOAVE. Dry wine similar. Sweet (RECIOTO DI GAMBELLARA), nicely fruity. Top producer: La Biancara.

Gancia Famous ASTI house also producing dry sparkling.

Garda Ven DOC w p r ★→★★ DYA (w p) **01 03 04** 05 06 07 (r) Catch-all DOC for generally early-drinking wines of various colours from provinces of Verona in Veneto, Brescia and Mantua in Lombardy. Gd are Cavalchina, Zeni.

Garganega Principal white grape of SOAVE and GAMBELLARA.

Garofoli ★★→★★★★ One of quality leaders in the Marches (nr Ancona). Notable style in VERDICCHIO Podium, Macrina, and Serra Fiorese. ROSSO CONERO Piancarda and v.gd Grosso Agontano.

Gattinara Pie DOCG r ★★★ **89' 90' 95 96' 97' 98 99'** 00 01' 03 04' 05 06 07' Very tasty NEBBIOLO-based red, historically finest from north PIEDMONT. Best: Travaglini (RISERVA), Antoniolo (single-v'yd wines). Others: Bianchi, Nervi, Torraccia del Piantavigna.

Gavi Pie DOCG w ★→★★★ DYA At (rare) best, subtle dry white of Cortese grapes. LA

SCOLCA is best-known, gd from BANFI (esp VIGNA Regale), Castellari Bergaglio, Franco Martinetti, Toledana, Villa Sparina . Broglia, Cascina degli Ulivi, CASTELLO di Tassarolo, CHIARLO, La Giustiniana, PODERE Saulino are also fair.

Ghemme Pie DOCG r ★★ **89' 90' 93 95 96'** 97' 98 99' 00 01' 03 04 05 Neighbour of GATTINARA not considered as gd but sometimes better. Stars: Antichi Vigneti di Cantalupo, Ioppa, Rovellotti and Torraccia del Piantavigna.

Giacosa, Bruno ★★ →★★★★ Considered Italy's greatest winemaker by some, this brooding genius recently suffered a major stroke but continues at the helm, crafting outstanding traditional-style BARBARESCOS (Asili, Santo Stefano) and BAROLOS (Falletto, Rocche di Falletto). Plus a range of fine reds (DOLCETTO, NEBBIOLO, BARBERA), whites (ARNEIS) and an amazing Brut METODO CLASSICO.

Governo Old TUSCAN custom, enjoying mild revival. Dried grapes or must are added to young wine to induce second fermentation and increase body and alcohol, sometimes instead of adding must concentrate

Gradi Degrees (of alcohol), ie per cent by volume.

Grappa Pungent and potent spirit made from grape pomace (skins, etc, after pressing), can be anything from disgusting to inspirational.

Grasso, Elio ★★★ V.gd BAROLO (look for Runcot, Gavarini, Casa Maté), full, barrel-aged BARBERA D'ALBA VIGNA Martina, DOLCETTO D'ALBA, and CHARD Educato.

Grave del Friuli F-VG DOC r w ★→★★ (r) **01 03** 04 05 06 07 DOC covering 15 different wines, 14 named after their grapes, from central part of region. Gd REFOSCO, MERLOT, and CAB SAUV. Best producers: Borgo Magredo, Le Fredis, Di Lenardo, Le Monde, Plozner, Vicentini-Orgnani, Villa Chiopris.

Gravner, Josko ★★★Controversial COLLIO producer, believing in maceration on skins and long wood ageing for whites. People tend to either love his wines for their complexity or hate them for being oxidized, though they're expensive and difficult to obtain.

Grechetto White grape; more flavour than TREBBIANO, increasingly used in blends or solo in ORVIETO and other parts of Umbria. Look for Bigi, Busti, Caprai, Cardeto, Colli Amerini, FALESCO, Palazzone, Le Poggetto.

Greco Various "Grecos" (of Greek origin?) exist in southern Italy, not necessarily related, eg GRECO DI TUFO is different from Greco di CIRO.

Greco di Tufò Cam DOCG w (sp) ★★→★★★★ DYA One of the best whites from the south: fruity, slightly wild in flavour, and ageworthy. V.gd examples from Caggiano, Caputo, Benito Ferrara, FEUDI DI SAN GREGORIO, Macchialupa, MASTROBERARDINO (Nova Serra and Vignadangelo), Vesevo, Villa Raiano.

Gresy, Marchesi di (Cisa Asinari) ★★★ Consistent, sometimes inspired producer of traditional-style BARBARESCO (*crus* Gaiun and Camp Gros). Also v.gd SAUV BL, CHARD, MOSCATO D'ASTI, BARBERA D'ASTI.

Grevepesa CHIANTI CLASSICO co-op – quality now rising.

Grignolino d'Asti Pie DOC r ★ DYA lively light red of PIEDMONT. Look for: BRAIDA, Castino, Due Pini, La Luna del Rospo, Marchesi Incisa della Rocchetta.

Grignolino del Monferrato Casalese Much like GRIGNOLINO D'ASTI but firmer. Try: Accornero, BRICCO Mondalino, Colonna, Mongetto, La Scamuzza, La Tenaglia.

Gruppo Italiano Vini (GIV) Complex of co-ops and wineries, biggest v'yd holders in Italy; estates include Bigi, Ca`Bianca, Conti Serristori, FOLONARI, FONTANA CANDIDA, LAMBERTI, Macchiavelli, MELINI, Negri, Santi, Vignaioli di San Floriano. Has also expanded into south : Sicily and Basilicata.

Guerrieri-Gonzaga ★★★ Top TRENTINO estate; esp San Leonardo blend.

Gutturnio dei Colli Piacentini E-R DOC r dr ★→★★ DYA BARBERA/BONARDA blend from the hills of Piacenza, often FRIZZANTE. Producers: Cardinali, Castelli del Duca, La Stoppa, La Tosa, Torre Fornello.

Haas, Franz ★★★ ALTO ADIGE producer; v.gd PINOT N, LAGREIN, and IGT blends.

Hastae ★★★ New super-BARBERA from ASTI from group of producers: BRAIDA,

> **IGT, Indicazione Geografica Tipica**
> 1990s category for quality wines unable to fit into DOC zones or
> regulations; replaced anomaly of glamorous VDTS.

CHIARLO, COPPO, PRUNOTTO, VIETTI.

Hofstätter ★★★ ALTO ADIGE producer of top PINOT N. Look for Barthenau Vigna Sant'Urbano, LAGREIN, CAB SAUV/Petit Verdot, Gewurz.

Ischia Cam DOC w (r) ★ →★★ DYA Island off Naples. Top producer D'Ambra: DOC red Dedicato a Mario D'Ambra, IGT red Tenuta Montecorvo, IGT white Tenuta Frassitelli, and Piellero. Also gd: Il Giardino Mediterraneo, Pietratorcia.

Insolia Southern and Sicilian white grape with untapped potential.

Isole e Olena ★★★ →★★★★ Top CHIANTI CLASSICO estate run by astute Paolo de Marchi, with fine red IGT Cepparello. V.gd VIN SANTO, CAB SAUV, CHARD, and *L'Eremo syrah*. See also LESSONA.

Isonzo F-VG DOC r w ★★★ (r) DOC covering 19 wines (17 varietals) in northeast. Best white and MERLOT compare to COLLIO wines. Esp from Borgo Conventi, Borgo San Daniele, La Bellanotte, LIS NERIS, Masut da Rive, Pierpaolo Pecorari, RONCO del Gelso, Sant'Elena, VIE DI ROMANS, Villanova.

Jermann, Silvio ★★ →★★★ Family estate with v'yds in COLLIO and ISONZO: top white VDT, inc blend Vintage Tunina, oak-aged Capo Martino, and "Were dreams, now is just wine" (yes, really). Also excellent red Pignacolusse from the Pignolo grape.

Kalterersee German (and local) name for LAGO DI CALDARO.

Kante, Edi ★★ →★★★ Leading light of CARSO; fine DOC CHARD, Sauv Bl, MALVASIA; gd red Terrano.

Lacrima di Morro d'Alba DYA Curiously named Muscatty light red from a small commune in the Marches, no connection with ALBA or La Morra in PIEDMONT. Gd producer: Mancinelli.

Lacryma (or Lacrima) Christi del Vesuvio Cam r p w dr (sw fz) ★ →★★ DYA Famous but disappointing wines from Vesuvius (DOC Vesuvio). Caputo, De Angelis, Grotta del Sole and MASTROBERARDINO are producers.

La Fiorita Lamborghini family property nr Lake Trasimeno in Umbria, with touchstone SANGIOVESE/MERLOT blend Campoleone.

Lageder, Alois ★★ →★★★ Top ALTO ADIGE producer. Exciting wines include oak-aged Löwengang CHARD and Römigberg CAB SAUV. Single-v'yd Lehenhof Sauv Bl, PINOT GR Benefizium Porer, PINOT N Krafuss, LAGREIN Lindenberg, TERLANO Tannhammer. Also owns Cason Hirschprunn for v.gd IGT blends.

Lago di Caldaro See CALDARO.

Lagrein T-AA DOC r p ★★ →★★★ 99 00' 01 03 04' 05 06' 07' Highly coloured grape with a bitter twist. Gd, fruity wine – at best, full, minerally, and v. appealing. The rosé: Kretzer; the dark: Dunkel. Best growing zone: commune of Gries. Best producers: Colterenzio co-op, Gojer, Gries co-op, HAAS, HOFSTÄTTER, LAGEDER, Laimburg, Josephus Mayr, Thomas Mayr, Muri Gries, NIEDERMAYR, NIEDRIST, St-Magdalena, TERLANO co-op.

Lamberti ★★ Large producer of SOAVE, VALPOLICELLA, BARDOLINO, etc., at Lazise on the eastern shore of Lake Garda. Owned by GIV.

Lambrusco E-R DOC (or not) r p dr s/sw ★ →★★ DYA Once extremely popular fizzy red in industrial, semi-sweet, non-DOC version. Best is secco, traditional with second fermentation in bottle (with sediment). DOCS: L Grasparossa di Castelvetro, L Salamino di Santa Croce, L di Sorbara. Best: Bellei, Caprari,

Casali, CAVICCHIOLI, Graziano, Lini Oreste, Medici Ermete (esp Concerto), Rinaldo Rinaldini, Venturini Baldini. *Forget your prejudices – try it.*

Langhe The hills of central PIEDMONT, home of BAROLO, BARBARESCO, etc. Has become name for recent DOC (r w ★★→★★★) for eight different wines: ROSSO, BIANCO, NEBBIOLO, DOLCETTO, FREISA, ARNEIS, Favorita, and CHARD. BAROLO and BARBARESCO can now be declassified, as by GAJA, to DOC Langhe Nebbiolo which allows for 15% of other grapes in the blend.

Latisana F-VG DOC r w ★→★★ (r) DOC for 13 varietal wines from 80 km (50 miles) northeast of Venice. Best wine is TOCAI Friulano. Try wines of Grandi e Gabana.

Lessona Pie DOC r ★★ **96' 97' 98** 99' 00 01' 03 04 05 06' 07' Soft, dry, claret-like wine from Vercelli province. NEBBIOLO, Vespolina, BONARDA grapes. Best producer: Sella, plus new estate of Paolo de Marchi of ISOLE E OLENA.

Librandi ★★★ Top Calabria producer. V.gd red CIRÒ (RISERVA Duca San Felice is ★★★), IGT Gravello (CAB SAUV/Gaglioppo blend), Magno Megonio (r) from Magliocco grape and Efeso IGT (w) from Mantonico grape.

Liquoroso Means strong; usually sweet and always fortified.

Lisini ★★★→★★★★ Historic small estate for some of the finest BRUNELLO.

Lis Neris ★★★ Top ISONZO estate known for high-quality white wines, esp PINOT GR (Gris), CHARD (Jurosa), SAUV BL (Picol), plus blends Confini and Lis. Also v.gd Lis Neris Rosso (MERLOT/CAB SAUV) and sweet white Tal Luc (VERDUZZO/RIES).

Livon ★★→★★★ Substantial COLLIO producer, also some COLLI ORIENTALI wines like VERDUZZO. Expanded into the CHIANTI CLASSICO and MONTEFALCO DOCGS.

Loazzolo Pie DOC w SW ★★★ 00 01' 03 04 05 06 07 DOC for MOSCATO dessert wine from botrytized, air-dried grapes: expensive and sweet. Gd from Borgo Isolabella, Forteto della Luja, and Pianbello.

Locorotondo Ap DOC w (sp) ★ DYA Pleasantly fresh southern white.

Luce ★★★ Ambitious joint Mondavi/FRESCOBALDI venture launched in 1998, now solely FRESCOBALDI. SANGIOVESE/MERLOT blend. Sometimes accused of being overpriced and overhyped.

Lugana Lom and Ven DOC w (sp) ★→★★ DYA whites of southern Lake Garda: can be fragrant, smooth, full of body and flavour.Best: CA' DEI FRATI, ZENATO, Zeni.

Lungarotti ★★→★★★ Leading producer of TORGIANO, with cellars, hotel, and museum nr Perugia. Star wine Rubesco RISERVA DOCG. Gd IGT Sangiorgio (SANGIOVESE/CAB SAUV), Aurente (CHARD), and Giubilante. Now operating in Montefalco as well. See TORGIANO.

Le Macchiole ★★★→★★★★ Outstanding red DOC BOLGHERI Paleo (100% CAB FR), gd DOC ROSSO (SANGIOVESE/CAB FR etc), world-class Messorio IGT (MERLOT), and v.gd Scrio IGT (SYRAH).

Maculan Ven ★★★ Excellent CAB SAUV (Fratta, Ferrata), CHARD (Ferrata), MERLOT (Marchesante), and Torcolato (esp RISERVA Acininobili).

Malvasia Ancient grape of Greek origin planted so widely for so long that various sub-varieties can bear little resemblance to one another: can be white or red, sparkling or still, strong or mild, sweet or dry, aromatic or neutral; often IGT.

Manduria (Primitivo di) Ap DOC r s/sw ★★→★★★ Dark red, naturally strong, rarely sweet from nr Taranto. Gd: Accademia dei Racemi (inc Dunico, Felline, Masseria Pepe, Pervini, Sinfarosa), also Casale Bevagna, Feudi di San Marzano, Ginafranco Fino, Pozzopalo.

Manzone, Giovanni ★★★ V.gd ALBA wines from estate nr Monforte d'Alba. Single-v'yd BAROLO, BARBERA D'ALBA, DOLCETTO.

Marchesi di Barolo ★★ Important ALBA house: BAROLO (esp Cannubi and Sarmassa), BARBARESCO, DOLCETTO D'ALBA, BARBERA, FREISA D'ASTI, and GAVI.

Maremma Southern coastal area of TUSCANY in provinces of Livorno and Grosseto. DOCS include BOLGHERI and VAL DI CORNIA (Livorno), MONTECUCCO, MONTEREGIO, MORELLINO DI SCANSANO, PARRINA, Pitigliano, SOVANA (Grosseto).

Attracting much interest and investment for high-quality potential demonstrated by wines. Maremma IGT, limited to province of Grosseto, now used by many top producers, inc new investors, for major wines. Look for: Ampeleia, Belguardo, La Carletta, Casina, Col di Bacche, Fattoria di Magliano, Lhosa, Marsiliana, Monteti, MORIS FARMS, Montebello, Podere 141, La Parrina, Poderi di Ghiaccioforte, Poggio Argentiera, Poggio Foco, Poggio al Lupo, Poggio Paoli, Poggio Verrano, Rascioni e Cecconello, Rocca di Frasinello, San Matteo, Sassotondo, La Selva, Solomaremma, Suveraia.

Marino Lat DOC w dr s/sw (sp) ★→★★ DYA A neighbour of FRASCATI with similar wine; often a better buy. Look for Di Mauro.

Marsala DOC w sw Sicily's once famous fortified wine (★→★★★), invented by Woodhouse Bros from Liverpool in 1773. An excellent apéritif or for dessert, but sadly came to be used mostly in the kitchen in inferior versions for desserts such as zabaglione. Dry ("virgin"), sometimes made by the solera system, must be 5 yrs old. Top producers: FLORIO, Pellegrino, Rallo. See also VECCHIO SAMPERI. V. special old vintages ★★★★.

Martini & Rossi Vermouth and sparkling-wine house now controlled by Bacardi group. (Has a fine wine-history museum in Pessione, nr Turin.)

Marzemino Trentino T-AA DOC r ★→★★ 00 01 03 04 05 06 07 Pleasant local red. Fruity and slightly bitter. Esp from Bossi Fedrigotti, CA' VIT, De Tarczal, Gaierhof, Letrari, Longariva, Simoncelli, E Spagnolli, Vallarom.

Mascarello The name of 2 top producers of BAROLO, etc: Bartolo M and Giuseppe M & Figli. Look for the latter's supreme BAROLO Monprivato.

Masi ★★→★★★ Fanatical exponent and researcher of VALPOLICELLA, AMARONE, RECIOTO, SOAVE, etc, inc fine red Campo Fiorin. V.gd barrel-aged red IGT Toar.

La Massa ★★★ Highly rated producer of v.gd CHIANTI CLASSICO; Giorgio Primo.

Mastroberardino ★★→★★★ Historic producer of mountainous Avellino province in Campania, quality torch-bearer for Italy's south during dark yrs of mid-20th century. Top TAURASI (look for Historia Naturalis and Radici).

Melini ★★ Long-established producers of CHIANTI CLASSICO at Poggibonsi. Gd quality/price; look for single-v'yd CHIANTI CLASSICO Selvanella and RISERVAS La Selvanella and Masovecchio. See GRUPPO ITALIANO VINI.

Meranese di Collina T-AA DOC r ★ DYA Light red of Merano.

Merlot Red grape today grown throughout Italy, used varietally and increasingly to blend with Sangiovese et al. Merlot DOCS are many esp in the northeast, where the grape is traditional. Best producers: BORGO DEL TIGLIO, Livio FELLUGA (Sossò), Renato Keber, LE DUE TERRE, Miani, Radikon, VILLA RUSSIZ (De la Tour) in FRIULI-VENEZIA GIULIA; BOCCADIGABBIA in the Marches; FALESCO (Montiano) in Latium; PLANETA in Sicily; FEUDI DI SAN GREGORIO (Patrimo) in Campania; and TUSCAN Super-IGTS AMA (L'Apparita), Cantine Leonardo da Vinci (Artisti), La Cappella (Cantico), Castello di Bossi (Girolamo), Fattoria del Cerro (Poggio Golo), FRESCOBALDI (Laimaione), Macchiole (Messorio), ORNELLAIA (Masseto), Pagani De Marchi (Casa Nocera), Petrolo (Galatrona), SAN GIUSTO A RENTENNANO (La Ricolma), TUA RITA (Redigaffi).

Metodo classico or tradizionale Mandatory terms to identify classic method sparkling wines. "Metodo Champenois" banned since 1994 and now illegal.

Mezzacorona ★★ TRENTINO CO-OP with gd DOC TEROLDEGO, METODO CLASSICO Rotari.

Moccagatta ★★→★★★ Specialist in impressive single-v'yd BARBARESCO: Basarin, Bric Balin (★★★), and VIGNA Cole. Also BARBERA D'ALBA and LANGHE.

Molino ★★★ Talented producer of elegant ALBA wines at La Morra; look for BAROLOS Gancia and Conca, BARBERA Gattere, and DOLCETTO.

La Monacesca ★★→★★★ Fine producer of VERDICCHIO DI MATELICA. Top wine: Mirus.

Monferrato Pie DOC r p w sw ★★ Hills between river Po and Apennines. A recent DOC; inc ROSSO, BIANCO, DOLCETTO, Casalese, FREISA, and Cortese.

Monica di Sardegna Sar DOC r ★→★★ DYA The mainstay of Sardinian light dry red.

Monsanto ★★★ Esteemed CHIANTI CLASSICO estate, esp for Il Poggio v'yd and IGTS Fabrizio Bianchi (SANGIOVESE) and Nemo (CAB SAUV).

Montalcino Small town in province of Siena (TUSCANY), famous for concentrated, expensive BRUNELLO and more approachable, better-value ROSSO DI MONTALCINO.

Montecarlo Tus DOC w r ★★ DYA (w) White, and increasingly red, wine area nr Lucca in northern TUSCANY. Whites are smooth, neutral blend of TREBBIANO with range of better grapes; basic reds are CHIANTI-style. Gd producers: Buonamico (red IGTS Cercatoja Rosso and Fortino), Carmignani (v.gd red IGT For Duke), red IGTS of La Torre, Montechiari, Fattoria del Teso.

Montecucco Recent TUSCAN DOC between MONTALCINO and MORELLINO DI SCANSANO. Try: Basile, Begnardi, Castello di Vicarello, Ciacci Piccolomini, Colli Massari, Fattoria di Montecucco, Montesalario, Poggio Leone, Poggio Mandorlo, Poggio Saccone, Villa Patrizia. Much new investment: FOLONARI, MASI, Pertimali, RIECINE, Talenti.

Montefalco Sagrantino Umb DOCG r dr (sw) ★★★→★★★★ Powerful, super-tannic, long-lasting SECCO wines, plus limited production of sweet PASSITO red from Sagrantino grapes. Gd from Alzatura, Antigniano, Antonelli San Marco, Benincasa, *Caprai*, Castelbuono, Colpetrone, Madonna Alta, Martinelli, Le Mura Saracene, Novelli, Pardi, Perticaia, Scacciadiavoli, Spoleto Ducale, Tabarrini, Terre della Custodia, Terre de' Trinci, Tiburzi, Tudernum.

Montellori, Fattoria di ★★ →★★★ TUSCAN producer making CHIANTI, all-SANGIOVESE IGT Dicatum, CAB SAUV/MERLOT blend Salamartano, white IGT Sant'Amato (SAUV BL), and METODO CLASSICO SPUMANTE.

Montepulciano An important red grape of east central Italy as well as the famous TUSCAN town (see below).

Montepulciano, Vino Nobile di See VINO NOBILE DI MONTEPULCIANO.

Montepulciano d'Abruzzo Ab DOC r p ★→★★★ 00' 01' 03' 04' **05 06 07'** Highly popular, deep-coloured, full-flavoured red and zesty, savoury pink (CERASUOLO) of generally excellent value for money from Adriatic coast. Best: Barba, Barone Cornacchia, Nestore Bosco, Caldora, Cataldi-Madonna, Ciccio Zaccagnini, Contesa, Feuduccio, Filomusi-Guelfi, Illuminati, Marammiero, Masciarelli, Monti, Montori, Nicodemi, Orlandi Contucci Ponno, Roxan, Terre d'Aligi, Tollo, Torre dei Beati, La Valentina, VALENTINI, Valle Reale, Valori, Villa Bizzarri, Villa Medoro, Ciccio Zaccagnini.

Monteregio Emerging DOC nr Massa Marittima in MAREMMA, high-level SANGIOVESE and CAB SAUV wines from Campo Bargello, MORIS FARMS, Massa Vecchia, Montebelli, La Pierotta, Suveraia, Tenuta del Fontino. Big-name investors (ANTINORI, BELLAVISTA, Eric de Rothschild, ZONIN) have flocked in.

Monte Schiavo ★★→★★★ Medium-large producer of gd to outstanding VERDICCHIO and MONTEPULCIANO-based reds in the Marches.

Montescudaio Tus DOC r w ★★ DOC between Pisa and Livorno; best are SANGIOVESE or SANGIOVESE/CAB SAUV blends. Try Aione, Fontemorsi, Marchesi Ginori Lisci, Merlini, Poggio Gagliardo, La Regola, Sorbaiano.

Montevertine ★★★ Radda estate. IGT Le Pergole Torte a pioneering and still splendid example of small barrel-aged SANGIOVESE.

Montevetrano ★★★ Small Campania producer; superb IGT Montevetrano.

Montresor ★★ Verona wine house: gd LUGANA, BIANCO DI CUSTOZA, VALPOLICELLA.

La Morandina ★★★ Small family estate with top MOSCATO and BARBERA D'ASTI.

Morellino di Scansano Tus DOC r ★★→★★★ 00' 01' 03' 04' 05 06' 07' Local SANGIOVESE of the MAREMMA, the south TUSCAN coast. Cherry-red, *should be lively and tasty, young or matured; many have been over-oaked.* Producers to try: Belguardo, La Carletta, Casina, Col di Bacche, Compagnia del Vino, Fattoria di Magliano, Fattorie LE PUPILLE, Mantellasi, MORIS FARMS, Podere 414,

Poderi di Ghiaccioforte, Poggio Argentiera, Poggio al Lupo, Poggio Paoli, San Matteo, La Selva, Cantina di Scansano, Terre di Talamo, and Villa Patrizia.

Moris Farms ★★★ V.gd producer in MONTEREGIO and MORELLINO DI SCANSANO, respectively to north and south of Grosseto; look for RISERVA and IGT Avvoltore, a rich SANGIOVESE/CAB SAUV/SYRAH blend.

Moscadello di Montalcino Tus DOC w sw (sp) ★★ DYA Revived traditional wine of MONTALCINO, once better known than BRUNELLO. Sweet fizz and sweet to high-octane MOSCATO PASSITO. Best: BANFI, COL D'ORCIA, La Poderina.

Moscato Family of fragrant fruity grapes which include Moscato Bianco/di Canelli (used in ASTI), Moscato Giallo (TRENTINO-ALTO-ADIGE, Ven, etc) and Moscato d'Alessandria (Sicily, Pantelleria), making a diverse range of wines: sparkling or still, light or full-bodied, but always sweet.

Moscato d'Asti Pie DOCG w sp sw ★★→★★★ DYA Similar to DOCG ASTI, but usually better grapes; lower alcohol, sweeter, fruitier, often from small producers. Best DOCG MOSCATO: L Armangia, BERA, BRAIDA, Ca'd'Gal, CASCINA FONDA, Cascina Pian d'Oro, Caudrina, Il Falchetto, FONTANAFREDDA, Forteto della Luja, DI GRESY, Icardi, Isolabella, Marino, LA MORANDINA, Marco Negri, Elio Perrone, Rivetti, Saracco, Scagliola, VAJRA, Vietti, Vignaioli di Sante Stefano, Viticoltori Acquese.

Müller-Thurgau Variety of some interest in TRENTINO-ALTO ADIGE and FRIULI. Leading producers: LAGEDER, Lavis, POJER & SANDRI, Zeni. Tiefenbrunner's Feldmarschall from 1,000-metre high v'yd in ALTO ADIGE is possibly the best dry M-T in the world.

Murana, Salvatore Si ★★★ V.gd MOSCATO and PASSITO DI PANTELLERIA.

Muri Gries ★★ V.gd producer of ALTO ADIGE DOC, specialists in LAGREIN.

Nada, Fiorenzo ★★★ Fine producer of smooth, elegant DOCG BARBARESCO.

Nebbiolo The best red grape of PIEDMONT, possibly of Italy, used in BAROLO, BARBARESCO and other wines of the northwest (eg Lombardy's VALTELLINA), though unsuccessful elsewhere in the wine world.

Nebbiolo d'Alba Pie DOC r dr (s/sw sp) ★★ 97' 98 99 00 01' 03 04' 05 06' 07' From Alba but 2 styles: full and complex, similar to BAROLO/BARBARESCO; and light, fruity and fragrant. Top examples of former from PIO CESARE, GIACOSA, MASCARELLO. Other gd ones from Marziano Abbona, Alario, BRICCO Maiolica, Cascina Chicco, La Contea, Paolo Conterno, Correggia, Damilano, De Marie, FONTANAFREDDA, Bruna Grimaldi, Hilberg, Mario Marengo, Gianmatteo Pira, Paitin, PRUNOTTO, Rizieri, SANDRONE, Tenuta Rocca, Val di Prete. See also ROERO.

Negri See GRUPPO ITALIANO VINI.

Negroamaro Literally "black bitter"; APULIAN red grape with high-quality potential. See ALEZIO, BRINDISI, COPERTINO, and SALICE SALENTINO.

Nerello Mascalese Medium-coloured, characterful Sicilian red grape which seemed to have lost its spark till rediscovered by the excellent Palari on the upper slopes of ETNA.

Nero d'Avola Dark red grape (Avola is south of Siracusa) with great promise, alone or in blends.

Niedermayr ★★★ V.gd DOC ALTO ADIGE, esp LAGREIN, PINOT N, Gewurz, SAUV BL, and IGT Euforius (LAGREIN/CAB SAUV) and Aureus (sweet white blend).

Niedrist, Ignaz ★★★ Small, gifted producer of white and red ALTO ADIGE wines (esp LAGREIN, PINOT N, PINOT BL, RIES).

Nipozzano, Castello di ★★★ FRESCOBALDI estate in RUFINA east of Florence making Montesodi CHIANTI.

Nittardi ★★ ·★★★ Reliable source of high-quality CHIANTI CLASSICO.

Nosiola (Trentino) T-AA DOC w dr sw ★ DYA Light, fruity white from Nosiola grapes. Also gd VIN SANTO. Best from Castel Noarna, POJER & SANDRI, Giovanni Poli, Pravis, Zeni.

Nozzole ★★ ·★★★ Famous estate now owned by Ambrogio FOLONARI, in heart of

CHIANTI CLASSICO, north of Greve. Also v.gd CAB SAUV Pareto.

Nuragus di Cagliari Sar DOC W ★★ DYA Lively Sardinian white.

Oasi degli Angeli Benchmark all-MONTEPULCIANO wines from small producer in southern Marches; lush and mouth-filling.

Oberto, Andrea ★★→★★★ Small La Morra producer: top BAROLO, BARBERA D'ALBA.

Oddero ★★→★★★ Well-known La Morra estate for excellent BAROLO (look for Mondocco di Bussia, Rocche di Castiglione, and VIGNA Rionda).

Oltrepò Pavese Lom DOC r w dr sw sp ★→★★★ 14 wines from Pavia province, most named after grapes. Sometimes v.gd PINOT N and SPUMANTE. Top growers: Anteo, Barbacarlo, Casa Re, Castello di Cigognola, CS Casteggio, Le Fracce, Frecciarossa, Monsupello, Mazzolino, Ruiz de Cardenas, Travaglino, Vercesi del Castellazzo, La Versa co-op.

Ornellaia Tus ★★★★ 95 97 98' 99 00 01 03 04' 05 06' 07' Lodovico ANTINORI-founded estate nr BOLGHERI on the TUSCAN coast. FRESCOBALDI bought out former joint-venture partner Mondavi. Estate has many prestigious wines: excellent BOLGHERI DOC Ornellaia, superb IGT Masseto (MERLOT), v.gd BOLGHERI DOC Le Serre Nuove and IGT Le Volte.

Orvieto Umb DOC w dr s/sw sw ★→★★★ DYA The classic Umbrian white, from the ancient spiritual centre of the Etruscans. Wines comparable to Vouvray from tufaceous soil. SECCO version is most popular today, AMABILE is more traditional. Sweet versions from noble rot (*muffa nobile*) grapes can be superb, eg BARBERANI's Calcaia. Other gd producers Co.Vi.O, Decugnano del Barbi, La Carraia, Palazzone, Vi.C.Or. See CASTELLO DELLA SALA.

Pacenti, Siro ★★★ V. international-style BRUNELLO and ROSSO DI MONTALCINO.

Pagani De Marchi New face north of BOLGHERI. Impressive IGT varietal wines from CAB SAUV, SANGIOVESE and, in particular, MERLOT.

Palazzino, Podere Il ★★★ Small estate with admirable CHIANTI CLASSICO.

Pancrazi, Marchese ★★→★★★ Estate nr Florence: highly touted but v. untypical PINOT N.

Paneretta, Castello della ★★→★★★ To follow for v. fine CHIANTI CLASSICO, IGTS Quatrocentenario, Terrine.

Pantelleria Island off the Sicilian coast noted for MOSCATO, particularly intense brown PASSITO. Watch for Abraxas, Colosi, DONNAFUGATA, MURANA.

Parrina Tus DOC r w ★★ Grand estate nr classy resorts of Argentario. Gd white Ansonica, improving reds (SANGIOVESE/CAB SAUV and MERLOT) from MAREMMA.

Pasqua, Fratelli ★★ Massive producer and bottler of Verona wines: VALPOLICELLA, AMARONE, SOAVE. Also BARDOLINO and RECIOTO.

Passito (pa) Strong, mostly sweet wine from grapes dried on the vine, on trays under the sun, or indoors on trays or hanging vertically.

Paternoster ★★★ Top AGLIANICO DEL VULTURE, esp Don Anselmo, Villa Rotondo.

Patriglione Ap IGT r ★★★ Dense, strong red IGT (NEGROAMARO/MALVASIA Nera). See TAURINO.

Pecorino Ab IGT Colli Pescaresi w ★★→★★★ Not a cheese but alluring dry white from a recently nr-extinct variety. Gd producers Contesa, Franco Pasetti.

Petit Verdot This lesser Bordelais vine has begun to catch on in Italy, esp (obviously) among internationalists. Casale del Giglio in Latium makes an interesting varietal.

Piaggia Outstanding producer of Carmignano Riserva, IGT Il Sasso and superb new CAB FR Poggio dei Colli.

Piave Ven DOC r w ★→★★★ (r) 03 04 05 06 07 (w) DYA Flourishing DOC northwest of Venice for 4 red and 4 white wines named after their grapes. CAB SAUV, MERLOT, and RABOSO reds can all age. Gd examples from Duca di Castelanza, Loredan Gasparini, Molon, Villa Sandi.

Picolit F-VG DOC w s/sw sw ★★→★★★ 01 03 04 05 06 07 Delicate sweet wine from

COLLI ORIENTALI DEL FRIULI, but with an exaggerated reputation. A little like France's Jurançon. Ages up to 6 yrs, but v. overpriced. Best, and v.gd, from LIVIO FELUGA, Meroi, Perusini, Specogna, VILLA RUSSIZ, Vinae dell'Abbazia.

Piedmont (Piemonte) With TUSCANY, the most important Italian region for top-quality wine. Turin is the capital, ASTI and ALBA the wine centres. See BARBARESCO, BARBERA, BAROLO, DOLCETTO, GRIGNOLINO, MOSCATO, etc.

Piemonte Pie DOC r w p (sp) ★→★★ All-PIEDMONT blanket DOC inc BARBERA, BONARDA, BRACHETTO, Cortese, GRIGNOLINO, CHARD, SPUMANTE, MOSCATO.

Pieropan ★★★ Outstanding SOAVE and RECIOTO: deserving its fame, esp Soave La Rocca and Calvarino, sweet PASSITO DELLA ROCCA.

Pieve di Santa Restituta ★★★ GAJA estate for admirable BRUNELLO DI MONTALCINO.

Pigato Lig DOC w ★★ Often outclasses VERMENTINO as Liguria's finest white, with rich texture and structure. Gd from Bruna, Colle dei Bardellini, Durin, Feipu, Foresti, Lupi, Poggio dei Gorlieri, TERRE ROSSE, Vio.

Pinot Bianco (Pinot Bl) Potentially excellent grape making many DOC wines in the northeast, esp from high sites in ALTO ADIGE ★★★. Best AA growers include Colterenzio, HOFSTÄTTER, LAGEDER, Nals Margreid, NIEDRIST, TERLANO, Termeno. Gd COLLIO ★★→★★★ producers include Renato Keber, Aldo Polencic, RUSSIZ SUPERIORE, SCHIOPETTO, VILLA RUSSIZ. Best from COLLI ORIENTALI ★★→★★★ La Viarte, Zamò & Zamò. From ISONZO try Masut da Rive.

Pinot Grigio World-popular varietal white of medium-low acidity and broadly appealing fruit, in such demand it has given birth to countless copycat, not to say fraudulent versions. *Caveat emptor.* The real thing can be excellent, usually dry (unlike Alsace's residual-sugar Pinot Gr), full-bodied and velvety; and not cheap. Best from DOCS ALTO ADIGE (SAN MICHELE APPIANO, CALDARO, LAGEDER, Nals Margreid, Termeno), COLLIO (Renato Keber, LIVON, Aldo Polencic, RUSSIZ SUPERIORE, SCHIOPETTO, Tercic, Terpin, Venica, VILLA RUSSIZ), COLLI ORIENTALI (Livio FELUGA), and ISONZO (Borgo San Daniele, LIS NERIS, Masut da Rive, Pierpaolo Pecorari, Ronco del Gelso, VIE DI ROMANS).

Pinot Nero (Pinot Noir) Planted in much of northeast Italy. DOC status and some surprisingly high quality in ALTO ADIGE (the co-ops of Caldaro, Colterenzio, Cortaccia, and Nals Margreid, HAAS, Haderburg, HOFSTÄTTER, LAGEDER, Laimburg, NIEDERMAYR, NIEDRIST, SAN MICHELE APPIANO, Termeno) and in OLTREPÒ PAVESE (Frecciarossa, Ruiz de Cardenas). Promising trials elsewhere, eg FRIULI (LE DUE TERRE, Masut da Riva), TUSCANY (Ama, FARNETELLA, FONTODI, Pancrazi), and on Mount Etna in SICILY. Also fine from several regions: TRENTINO (Lunelli, POJER & SANDRI), Lombardy (CA' DEL BOSCO, Ronco Calino), Umbria (ANTINORI), Marches (BOCCADIGABBIA).

Pio Cesare ★★→★★★ Long-established ALBA producer, offers BAROLO and BARBARESCO in both modern (BARRIQUE) and traditional (large cask- aged) versions. Probably the best NEBBIOLO D'ALBA.

Planeta ★★→★★★ Top SICILIAN estate: Segreta BIANCO blend, Segreta ROSSO; *outstanding Chard*, CAB SAUV, Fiano, MERLOT, NERO D'AVOLA (Santa Cecilia).

Podere Small TUSCAN farm, once part of a big estate. (See under name eg BOSCARELLI, PODERI.)

Poggio Means "hill" in Tuscan dialect. "POGGIONE" means "big hill".

Poggio Antico ★★★ Admirably consistent, top-level BRUNELLO DI MONTALCINO.

Poggione, Tenuta Il ★★★ V. reliable estate for BRUNELLO, ROSSO DI MONTALCINO.

Pojer & Sandri ★★→★★★ GdTRENTINO producers red and white wines, SPUMANTE.

Poliziano ★★★ MONTEPULCIANO estate. Federico Carletti makes superior VINO NOBILE (esp Asinone) and gd IGT Le Stanze (CAB SAUV/MERLOT).

Pomino Tus DOC w r ★★★ r **01 03** 04 06 07 Fine red and white blends (esp Il Benefizio). Virtually a FRESCOBALDI exclusivity.

Pra ★★★ Excellent SOAVE CLASSICO producer, esp *cru* Monte Grande and new

ITALY

Staforte, 6 months in steel tanks on lees with *bâtonnage*.

Produttori del Barbaresco ★★→★★★ Co-op and one of DOCG's most reliable producers. Often outstanding single-v'yd wines (Asili, Montefico, Montestefano, Rabajà).

Prosecco di Conegliano-Valdobbiadene Ven DOC w s/sw fz sp (dr) ★★ DYA Fashionable light sparkling consumed as apéritif in all bars in Venice and throughout Italy. Off-dry is normal, truly dry (brut) is rare. Sweetest are called Superiore di Cartizze. CARPENÈ-MALVOLTI best known; also Adami, BISOL, Bortolin, Canevel, Case Bianche, Col Salice, Le Colture, Col Vetoraz, Nino Franco, Gregoletto, La Riva dei Frati, Ruggeri, Zardetto.

Prunotto, Alfredo ★★★→★★★★ Traditional ALBA company modernized by ANTINORI in 1990s. V.gd BARBARESCO, BAROLO, NEBBIOLO, BARBERA D'ALBA, DOLCETTO, etc. Also BARBERA D'ASTI (look for Costamiole) and MONFERRATO ROSSO Mompertone, BARBERA/SYRAH blend.

Puglia See APULIA.

Le Pupille ★★★ Top producer of MORELLINO DI SCANSANO (look for Poggio Valente), excellent IGT blend Saffredi (CAB SAUV/MERLOT/ALICANTE).

Querciabella ★★★ Top CHIANTI CLASSICO estate with RISERVA, IGT Camartina (SANGIOVESE/CAB SAUV), barrel-fermented white Batàr, and Palafreno, a SANGIOVESE/MERLOT.

Quintarelli, Giuseppe ★★★★ No spitting allowed at the winery of this arch-traditionalist, artisanal producer of VALPOLICELLA, RECIOTO, and AMARONE. No wonder, considering the v. high prices.

Raboso del Piave (now DOC) Ven r ★★ **01 03** 04 05 06 07 Powerful, sharp, interesting country red; at best, needs age. Look for Molon.

Le Ragose ★★→★★★ Family estate, one of VALPOLICELLA's best. AMARONE and RECIOTO top quality; CAB SAUV and VALPOLICELLA v.gd, too.

Rampolla, Castello dei ★★★→★★★★ Fine estate in Panzano in CHIANTI CLASSICO, notable CAB SAUV-based IGT wines Sammarco and Alceo.

Recioto di Soave Ven DOCG w sw (sp) ★★★→★★★★ **00 01 03** 04 05 06 07 SOAVE made from selected half-dried grapes: sweet, fruity, slightly almondy; high acidity masked by sweetness as sweetness is cut by acidity. Outstanding from ANSELMI, COFFELE, Gini, PIEROPAN, Tamellini, often v.gd from Ca' Rugate, Pasqua, Suavia, Trabuchi.

Recioto della Valpolicella Ven DOC r s/sw (sp) ★★★→★★★★ Potentially stunning, rich cherry-chocolaty red from grapes dried on trays up to 6 months. Ages for many yrs. Best: ALLEGRINI, BUSSOLA, DAL FORNO, QUINTARELLI, TEDESCHI, VIVIANI. Also gd from Stefano Accordini, Serègo Alighieri, Baltieri, BOLLA, BRUNELLI, Campagnola, Ca' Rugate, Castellani, Aleardo Ferrari, LE RAGOSE, LE SALETTE, Sant'Alda, Speri, Trabucchi, CS VALPOLICELLA, Villa Bellini, Villa Monteleone.

Refosco (dal Peduncolo Rosso) r ★★→★★★ **99' 00** 01 03 04 05 06 07 Interesting, full, dark, gutsy red sometimes gd for ageing. Best from COLLI ORIENTALI DOC, Moschioni, Le Vigne di Zamo, Volpi Pasini: also gd from LIVIO FELLUGA and Miani and from Dorigo, Ronchi di Manzano, Venica, Ca' Bolani, and Denis Montanara in AQUILEIA DOC.

Regaleali See TASCA D'ALMERITA.

Ribolla Colli Orientali del Friuli and Collio, F-VG DOC w ★→★★ DYA Acidic but characterful northeastern white. The best comes from COLLIO. Top estates: Il Carpino, La Castellada, Damijan, Fliegl, GRAVNER, Primosic, Radikon, Tercic.

Ricasoli Historic TUSCAN family, 19th-century proposers of CHIANTI blend, whose CHIANTI CLASSICO is named after the medieval castle of BROLIO. Related Ricasolis own Castello di Cacchiano and Rocca di Montegrossi.

Riecine Tus r ★★★ First-class CHIANTI CLASSICO estate at Gaiole, created by its late English owner, John Dunkley. Also fine IGT La Gioia SANGIOVESE.

Riesling Today refers only to Rheinriesling, used mainly in blends of northeast. Best from DOC ALTO ADIGE ★★ (esp HOFSTÄTTER, Kuenhof, Laimburg, NIEDRIST, La Vis co-op, Unterortl); DOC OLTREPÒ PAVESE (Lom) ★★ (Brega, Frecciarossa, Le Fracce); DOC ISONZO RONCO del Gelso and VIE DI ROMANS. Also gd from Le Vigne di San Pietro (Ven), JERMANN, VAJRA (Pie).

Ripasso VALPOLICELLA re-fermented on RECIOTO or AMARONE grape skins to make a more complex, longer-lived, fuller wine. V.gd from BUSSOLA, Castellani, DAL FORNO, QUINTARELLI, ZENATO. MASI's Campo Fiorin IGT claimed to be first and therefore entitled to exclusivity of the title, others say it's traditional and the name is generic. Others have won.

Riserva Wine aged for a statutory period, usually in casks or barrels.

Riunite One of the world's largest co-op cellars, nr Reggio Emilia, v. powerful at height of LAMBRUSCO craze, now long past.

Rivera ★★ Reliable winemakers at Andria in APULIA. ★★★ CASTEL DEL MONTE Il Falcone RISERVA; v.gd Cappellaccio; VIGNA al Monte; Puer Apuliae.

Rivetti, Giorgio (La Spinetta) ★★★ Fine MOSCATO d'Asti, excellent BARBERA, interesting IGT Pin, series of super-concentrated Parker-style BARBARESCOS. Now owner of v'yds both in the BAROLO and the CHIANTI Colli Pisane DOCGS. Early vintages of BAROLO along lines of BARBARESCO.

Riviera del Garda Bresciano Lom DOC w p r (sp) ★→★★ 01 03 04 05 06 07 (r) Superfluous DOC (post introduction of GARDA DOC) in southwest corner of Lake Garda. Producers include Ca' dei Frati, Comincioli, Costaripa, Monte Cigogna.

Rocca, Bruno ★★★ Young producer with admirable BARBARESCO (Rabajà) and other ALBA wines, also v. fine BARBERA D'ASTI.

Rocche dei Manzoni ★★★ Modernist estate at Monforte d'Alba. Oaky BAROLO (esp VIGNA d'la Roul, Cappella di Stefano, Pianpolvere), BRICCO Manzoni (pioneer BARBERA/NEBBIOLO blend), Quatr Nas (LANGHE).

Roero Pie DOCG r ★★ 96 97' 98' 99' 00 01' 03 04' 05 06' 07' Potentially serious, occasionally BAROLO-level NEBBIOLOS from the LANGHE hills across the Tanaro from ALBA. Best: Almondo, Buganza, Ca' Rossa, Cascina Chicco, Correggia, Funtanin, Malvirà, Monchiero-Carbone, Morra, Pace, Pioiero, Taliano, Val di Prete. See also ARNEIS.

Ronco Term for a hillside v'yd in northeast Italy, esp FRIULI-VENEZIA GIULIA.

Ronco del Gnemiz ★★★ Small estate, v. fine COLLI ORIENTALI DEL FRIULI.

Rosato Rosé; also CHIARETTO, esp around Lake Garda; and CERASUOLO, from Ab.

Rosato del Salento Ap p ★★ DYA From near BRINDISI. Sturdy, juicy wine from a zone that has long specialized in rosé. See COPERTINO, SALICE SALENTO.

Rosso Red.

Rosso Conero Mar DOCG r ★★→★★★ 00 01' 03' 04 05 06' 07' Some of Italy's best MONTEPULCIANO (the grape, that is): GAROFOLI's Grosso Agontano, Moroder's RC Dorico, MONTE SCHIAVO's Adeodato, TERRE CORTESI MONCARO's Nerone and Vigneti del Parco, Le Terrazze's Sassi Neri and Visions of J. Also gd: Casato, FAZI-BATTAGLIA, Lanari, Leopardi Dittajuti, Malacari, Marchetti, Piantate Lunghe, Poggio Morelli, UMANI RONCHI.

Rosso di Montalcino Tus DOC r ★★ →★★★ 97' 98 99' 00' 01' 03 04' 05 06' 07' DOC for younger wines from BRUNELLO grapes. See BRUNELLO DI MONTALCINO.

Rosso di Montefalco Umb DOC r ★★ →★★★ 97' 98 99' 00' 01' 03 04' 05 06' 07' SANGIOVESE/Sagrantino blend. For producers, see MONTEFALCO SAGRANTINO.

Rosso di Montepulciano Tus DOC r ★★ 03 04 05 06 07 Junior version of VINO NOBILE DI MONTEPULCIANO, growers similar. While ROSSO DI MONTALCINO is increasingly expensive, ROSSO DI MONTEPULCIANO offers value.

Rosso Piceno Mar DOC r 01' 03 04 05 06 07 Gluggable MONTEPULCIANO /SANGIOVESE blend from southern half of Mar, SUPERIORE from restricted classic zone nr Ascoli, much improved in recent yrs. Best include: Aurora,

BOCCADIGABBIA, Bucci, Le Caniette, Ciù Ciù, COLLI Ripani, Damiani, De Angelis, Fonte della Luna, Forano, Laila, Laurentina, Montecappone, MONTE SCHIAVO, Saladini Pilastri, San Giovanni, San Savino, TERRE CORTESI MONCARO, Velenosi Ercole, Villamagna, Villa Ragnola.

Ruchè (also Rouchè/Rouchet) Rare old grape of French origin; fruity, fresh, rich-scented red wine (sweet/semi-sweet). Ruchè di Castagnole MONFERRATO is recent DOC. Look for Biletta, Borgoggnone, Dezzani, Garetto. SCARPA's Rouchet Briccorosa: dry (★★★).

Ruffino ★→★★★ Famous CHIANTI merchant at Pontassieve, east of Florence. Best are RISERVA Ducale and Santedame. V.gd IGT CHARD Solatia, SANGIOVESE/CAB SAUV Modus. Owns Lodola Nuova in MONTEPULCIANO for VINO NOBILE DI MONTEPULCIANO, and Greppone Mazzi in MONTALCINO for BRUNELLO DI MONTEPULCIANO. Excellent MERLOT/Colorino blend Romitorio from Santedame estate. Also owns Borgo Conventi estate in FRIULI-VENEZIA GIULIA.

Rufina ★★★ Important sub-region of CHIANTI in hills east of Florence. Best wines from Basciano, CASTELLO DI NIPOZZANO (FRESCOBALDI), CASTELLO del Trebbio, Colognole, Frascole, Lavacchio, SELVAPIANA, Tenuta Bossi, Travignoli.

Sagrantino di Montefalco See MONTEFALCO.

Sala, Castello della ★★→★★★ ANTINORI estate at ORVIETO. Campogrande is the regular white. Top wine is Cervaro della Sala, oak-aged CHARD/GRECHETTO. Muffato della Sala was a pioneering example of an Italian botrytis-influenced dessert wine. PINOT N also gd.

Le Salette ★★→★★★ Small VALPOLICELLA producer: look for v.gd AMARONE Pergole Vece and RECIOTO Le Traversagne.

Salice Salentino Ap DOC r ★★→★★★ 00 01' 03 04 06 07 Smooth red from the flatlands of Puglia's southern tip, made from NEGROAMARO and MALVASIA NERA grapes and redolent of plums and prunes. RISERVA after 2 yrs. Top makers: Apollonio, Candido, Castello Monaci, Due Palme, Resya, Tornavento, TAURINO, Valle dell'Asso, VALLONE.

Sandrone, Luciano ★★★ 95 97' 99' 00 01' 03 04' 05 06 07' Exponent of modern-style ALBA with deep, concentrated BAROLO Cannubi Boschi and Le Vigne, DOLCETTO, BARBERA D'ALBA, and NEBBIOLO D'ALBA.

San Felice ★★ Large CHIANTI CLASSICO resort/estate. Fine RISERVA Poggio ROSSO. Also red IGT Vigorello and BRUNELLO DI MONTALCINO Campogiovanni.

San Gimignano TUSCAN town famous for its towers and dry white VERNACCIA, mysteriously a DOCG despite generally mediocre level. Some gd red wines. Producers include Le Calcinaie, Cesani, Cusona, FALCHINI, Fontaleoni, Mormoraia, Palagetto, Palagione, PARADISO, La Rampa di Fugnano, Le Tre Stelle.

Sangiovese (Sangioveto) Principal red grape of west central Italy. Dominant in CHIANTI, VINO NOBILE, BRUNELLO DI MONTALCINO, MORELLINO DI SCANSANO and various fine IGT offerings. Also in Umbria generally (eg MONTEFALCO ROSSO and TORGIANO RISERVA, and across the Apennines in ROMAGNA and the Marches (BOCCADIGABBIA, Ciù Ciù). Not so clever in the warmer, lower-altitude v'yds of the Tuscan coast, indeed quite moody wherever it's planted, though new clones are beginning to yield more reliable fruit.

Sangiovese di Romagna Mar DOC r ★★→★★★ Often well made and v.gd value from Balia di Zola, La Berta, Berti, Calonga, Ca' Lunga, Campo del Sole, Cesari, Drei Donà, Madonia, Pandolfa, Paradiso, Poderi dal Nespoli, San Patrignano, Santini, San Valentino, Tenuta Diavoletto, Tenuta Valli, Terragens, Tre Monti, Trere (E-R doc), Uva delle Mura, La Viola, Zerbina, IGT RONCO dell Ginestre, RONCO dei Ciliegi from CASTELLUCCIO.

San Giusto a Rentennano ★★★→★★★★ One of the best CHIANTI CLASSICO producers (★★★). Delicious but v. rare VIN SANTO. Superb SANGIOVESE IGT Percarlo (★★★★).

San Guido, Tenuta See SASSICAIA.

San Leonardo ★★★ Top estate in TRENTINO, with *outstanding San Leonardo (Cab Sauv)* and promising Villa Gresti MERLOT.

San Michele Appiano Top ALTO ADIGE co-op, esp for whites. Look for PINOT BIANCO Schulthauser and Sanct Valentin (★★★) selections: CHARD, PINOT GR, SAUV BL, CAB SAUV, PINOT N, Gewurz.

Santadi ★★★ Consistently fine wines from SARDINIAN co-op, esp DOC CARIGNANO DEL SULCIS Grotta Rossa, TERRE BRUNE, Rocca Rubia, and IGT Baie Rosse (Carignano), VERMENTINO Villa Solais, Villa di Chiesa (VERMENTINO/CHARD).

Santa Maddalena (or St-Magdalener) T-AA DOC r ★→★★ DYA Superior SCHIAVA ALTO ADIGE red, usually blended with LAGREIN for added body. CS St-Magdalena (Huck am Bach), Gojer, Josephus Mayr, Georg Ramoser, Hans Rottensteiner (Premstallerhof), Heinrich Rottensteiner.

Santa Margherita Large Veneto (Portogruaro) merchants, famous for decent but overpriced PINOT GR which has swept America. Also owns: Veneto (Torresella), ALTO ADIGE (Kettmeir), TUSCANY (Lamole di Lamole and Vistarenni), and Lombardy (CA' DEL BOSCO).

Sant'Antimo Tus DOC r w sw ★★→★★★ Catch-all DOC for (almost) everything in Montalcino zone that isn't BRUNELLO DOCG or ROSSO DOC.

Santi See GRUPPO ITALIANO VINI.

Saracco, Paolo ★★★ Small estate with top MOSCATO D'ASTI.

Sardinia (Sardegna) The Mediterranean's 2nd-biggest island produces much decent and some excellent wines, eg, Turriga from ARGIOLAS, Arbeskia and Dule from Gabbas, VERMENTINO of CAPICHERA, CANNONAU RISERVAS of Jerzu and Loi, VERMENTINO and CANNONAU selections from Dettori and the amazing sherry-like VERNACCIA of CONTINI. Best DOCS: VERMENTINO di Gallura (eg Canayli from Cantina Gallura) and CARIGNANO DEL SULCIS (TERRE BRUNE and Rocca Rubia from SANTADI).

Sartarelli ★★★ One of top VERDICCHIO DEI CASTELLI DI JESI producers (Tralivio); outstanding, rare Verdicchio VENDEMMIA Tardiva (Contrada Balciana).

Sassicaia Tus r ★★★★ 85' 88' 90' 95' 97 98' 99 01' 03 04' 05 06 07' First Italian CAB SAUV to take on the world, considered Italy's best wine in 1970s and 1980s, no longer since indigenous varieties took centre stage. Made by Marchese Incisa della Rocchetta at Tenuta San Guido BOLGHERI. Promoted early 1990s from SUPER TUSCAN VDT to special sub-zone status in BOLGHERI DOC. Conservative style, real finesse.

Satta, Michele ★★★ Virtually the only BOLGHERI grower to succeed with 100% SANGIOVESE (Cavaliere). Also BOLGHERI DOC red blends Piastraia and SUPERIORE I Castagni.

Sauvignon Blanc The Loire's great white grape is vinified varietally throughout the northeast and elsewhere in Italy, generally for blending. Particularly successful in AA and F-VG.

Scarpa ★★→★★★ Old-fashioned Piedmontese house with BARBERA D'ASTI (La Bogliona), rare Rouchet (RUCHÈ), v.gd DOLCETTO, BAROLO, BARBARESCO.

Scavino, Paolo ★★★ Successful modern-style BAROLO producer. Sought-after single-v'yd wines: Rocche dell'Annunziata, Bric del Fiasc, Cannubi, and Carobric. Also oak-aged BARBERA and Langhe Corale.

Schiava High-yielding red grape of ALTO ADIGE, used for light reds such as LAGO DI CALDARO, SANTA MADDALENA, etc. Known locally as Vernatsch.

Schiopetto, Mario ★★★→★★★★ Legendary late COLLIO pioneer with spacious modern winery. V.gd DOC SAUV BL, PINOT BL, TOCAI, IGT blend Blanc de Rosis, etc. Recent offerings include wines from COLLI ORIENTALI v'yds.

Sciacchetrà See CINQUETERRE.

La Scolca ★★ Famous GAVI estate for gd GAVI and SPUMANTE.

ITALY

Secco Dry.

Sella & Mosca ★★ Major SARDINIAN grower and merchant with v. pleasant white Torbato and light, fruity VERMENTINO Cala Viola (DYA). Gd Alghero DOC Marchese di Villamarina (CAB SAUV) and Tanca Farrà (CANNONAU/CAB SAUV). Also interesting port-like Anghelu Ruju.

Selvapiana ★★★ Top CHIANTI RUFINA estate. Best wines are RISERVA Bucerchiale and IGT Fornace. Also, under the Petrognano label, some fine red DOC POMINO, the DOC's only significant producer apart from FRESCOBALDI.

Sforzato See VALTELLINA.

Sicily The Med's largest island has been dubbed the "new California" for its creative approach to winemaking, using both native grapes (NERO D'AVOLA, Frappato, Inzolia, Grecanico) and international varieties. To watch: Abraxas, Agareno, Benanti, Bonaccorsi, Capocroce, Ceusi, Colosi, Cos, Cottanera, CS Corbera, Cusumano, De Bartoli, Di Giovanna, DONNAFUGATA, DUCA DI SALAPARUTA, Fatasci, Fazio, Feudo Maccari, Feudo Montoni, Feudo Santa Teresa, Firriato, Fondo Antico, Fornaci, Grottarossa, Gulfi-Ramada, Miceli, Morgante, MURANA, Passopisciano, Pellegrino, PLANETA, Principe di Butera (ZONIN), Rapitalà, Rudini, Sallier de la Tour, Santa Anastasia, SIV, Spadafora, TASCA D'ALMERITA, Tenuta dell'Abate, Terre Nere, VECCHIO SAMPERI, Zemmer, Zisoli.

Sizzano Pie DOC r ★★ 97' 99 00 01' 03 04 06 07 Full-bodied red from Sizzano, (Novara); mostly NEBBIOLO. Ages up to 10 yrs. Esp: Bianchi, Dessilani.

Soave Ven DOC w (sw) ★→★★★ DYA Famous, still underrated Veronese. From the CLASSICO zone can be intense, mineral, v. fine and quite long-lived. When labelled SUPERIORE is DOCG, but best CLASSICO producers shun the "honour", stick to DOC. Sweet RECIOTO can be superb. Best: Cantina del Castello, La Cappuccina, Ca' Rugate, Cecilia Beretta, COFFELE, Dama del Rovere, Fattori, Gini, Guerrieri-Rizzardi, Inama, Montedonto, PIEROPAN, Portinari, Pra, Sartori, Suavia, Tamellini, TEDESCHI.

Solaia Tus r ★★★★ 85' 90' 95' 97' 99' 01' 04 06 07' V. fine B'x-style IGT of CAB SAUV and a little SANGIOVESE from ANTINORI; first made in 1978. Italy's best CAB SAUV in the 1990s, and a great wine by any standards.

Sorì Term for a high south-, southeast-, or southwest-oriented site in PIEDMONT.

Sovana MAREMMA DOC; inland nr Pitigliano. Look for SANGIOVESE, Ciliegiolo from Tenuta Roccaccia, Pitigliano, Ripa, Sassotondo, CAB SAUV from ANTINORI.

Spanna Local name for NEBBIOLO in a variety of north PIEDMONT zones (BOCA, BRAMATERRA, FARA, GATTINARA, GHEMME, LESSONA, SIZZANO).

Sportoletti ★★★ V.gd wines from Spello, nr ASSISI, esp Villa Fidelia.

Spumante Sparkling, inc both METODO CLASSICO (best from TRENTINO, ALTO ADIGE, FRANCIACORTA, PIEDMONT, OLTREPÒ PAVESE; occasionally gd from FRIULI and Veneto) and tank-made cheapos of higher pressure (as distinct from lower-pressure FRIZZANTE. What used to be called ASTI Spumante is now just ASTI.

Südtirol The local name of German-speaking ALTO ADIGE.

Superiore Wine with more ageing than normal DOC and 0.5–1% more alcohol.

Super Tuscan Term coined in 1980s for innovative wines from TUSCANY, often involving pure SANGIOVESE or international varieties, BARRIQUES, heavy bottles, and elevated prices.

Syrah The Rhône's great grape has taken Italy, esp TUSCANY and SICILY, by storm, mainly as a blender. For gd varietals try TUSCANY's Il Bosco from d'Alessandro or l'Eremo from ISOLE E OLENA.

Tasca d'Almerita ★★★ Historic SICILIAN producer owned by noble family (between Palermo and Caltanissetta to the southeast). Gd IGT red, white, and ROSATO Regaleali; ***v.gd Rosso del Conte***; impressive CHARD and CAB SAUV.

Taurasi Cam DOCG r ★★★ 95 97' 98 99 00 01' 03' 04' 05 06 07' CAMPANIA's historic and most celebrated red, one of Italy's outstanding wines, though not easy to appreciate. RISERVA after 4 yrs. V.gd from Caggiano, Caputo, FEUDI DI SAN GREGORIO, MASTROBERARDINO, Molettieri, Vesevo, and Villa Raiano.

Taurino, Cosimo ★★★ Best-known producer of Salento-APULIA when Cosimo was alive, v.gd SALICE SALENTINO, VDT Notarpanoro, and IGT PATRIGLIONE ROSSO.

Tedeschi, Fratelli ★★→★★★ Well-known producer of VALPOLICELLA, AMARONE, RECIOTO. Gd Capitel San Rocco red IGT.

Tenuta Farm or estate. (See under name – eg SAN GUIDO, TENUTA.)

Terlano T-AA w ★★ →★★★ DYA Terlano DOC incorporated into ALTO ADIGE. ALTO ADIGE Terlano DOC is applicable to one white blend and 8 white varietals, esp PINOT BIANCO and SAUV BL. Top producer CS Terlano (Pinot Bianco Vorberg, capable of remarkable ageing), also LAGEDER, NIEDERMAYR, NIEDRIST.

Teroldego Rotaliano T-AA DOC r p ★★ →★★★ Attractive blackberry-scented red; slightly bitter aftertaste; can age v. well. Esp FORADORI's. Also gd from CA' VIT, Dorigati, Endrizzi, MEZZACORONA'S RISERVA, Zeni.

Terre Brune Sard r ★★★ Splendid earthy Carignano/Boveladda blend from SANTADI, a flag-carrier for SARDINIA.

Terre Cortesi Moncaro Mar ★★★ Marches co-op, now making wines that compete with the best of the region at remarkably low prices: gd VERDICCHIO DEI CASTELLI DI JESI, ROSSO CONERO, and ROSSO PICENO.

Terre di Franciacorta Lom DOC r w ★★ **01 03 04** 06 07 Usually pleasant reds (blends of CAB SAUV, BARBERA, NEBBIOLO, MERLOT); quite fruity and balanced whites (CHARD, PINOT GR). Best producers: see FRANCIACORTA.

Terre Rosse ★★ Pioneering small estate nr Bologna. Its CAB SAUV, CHARD, PINOT BL, RIES, even Viognier, were trail-blazing wines for the region.

Terre da Vino ★→★★★ Association of 27 PIEDMONT co-ops and private estates inc most local DOCs. Best: BARBARESCO La Casa in Collina, BAROLO PODERE Parussi, BARBERA D'ASTI La Luna e I Falò.

Terriccio, Castello di ★★★ Large estate south of Livorno: excellent, v. expensive IGT Lupicaia, v.gd IGT Tassinaia, both CAB SAUV/MERLOT blends. Impressive new IGT Terriccio, an unusual blend of mainly Rhône grapes.

Tignanello Tus r ★★★ **95 96 97' 98** 99' 00 01' 03 04' 05 06' 07' SANGIOVESE/SAUV blend, BARRIQUE-aged, perhaps the first SUPER TUSCAN, created by ANTINORI in the early 1970s. No longer out front.

Tocai ★→★★ Controversial white grape bearing no resemblance to Hungarian Tokaji but banned by the EU from using its historic name. Best is what used to be called Tocai Friulano, now Friulano (the issue is not resolved), from FRIULI-VENEZIA GIULIA (esp COLLIO and COLLI ORIENTALI) ★★→★★★. Best producers: Borgo San Daniele, BORGO DEL TIGLIO, Livio FELLUGA, Renato Keber, Masut da Rive, Meroi, Mirani, Aldo Polencic, RONCO del Gelso, RONCO DEL GNEMIZ, Russiz Superiore, SCHIOPETTO, Venica & Venica, LE VIGNE DI ZAMÒ, VILLA RUSSIZ.

Torgiano Umb DOC r w p (sp) ★★ and **Torgiano, Rosso Riserva** Umb DOCG r ★★→★★★ **95 97** 99 00' 01' 03 04 06 07' Gd to excellent red from Umbria, resembles CHIANTI CLASSICO in style. Rubesco: standard. LUNGAROTTI'S RISERVA VIGNA Montecchi outstanding in vintages such as 75, 79, 85; keeps for many yrs. Antignano's Torgiano offers interesting contrast.

Traminer Aromatico T-AA DOC w ★★→★★★ DYA (German: Gewürztraminer) Pungent white with, these days, all the aromatics of the Alsatian versions with no residual sugar. Best from its birthplace Tramin (Italian: Termeno), notably CS Termeno and HOFSTÄTTER. Other gd producers include co-ops Caldaro, Colterenzio, Prima & Nuova, SAN MICHELE APPIANO, TERLANO plus Abbazia di Novacella, HAAS, Kuenhof, LAGEDER, Laimberg, Nals Margreid, NIEDERMAYR.

Trebbiano Principal white grape of TUSCANY, found all over Italy. Sadly, a waste of gd v'yd space, with v. rare exceptions, inc mainly VIN SANTO.

Trebbiano d'Abruzzo Ab DOC w ★→★★ DYA Gentle, neutral white grape of gd acidity from Pescara. That of VALENTINI is considered excellent but no one else gets close. Try Contesa, Masciarelli. Nicodemi, La Valentina, and Valori.

Trentino T-AA DOC r w dr sw ★→★★★ DOC for 20 wines, most named after grapes. Best: CHARD, PINOT BL, MARZEMINO, TEROLDEGO. Provincial capital is Trento.

Triacca ★★→★★★ V.gd producer of VALTELLINA; also owns estates in TUSCANY (CHIANTI CLASSICO: La Madonnina; MONTEPULCIANO: Santavenere).

Trinoro, Tenuta di ★★★ Isolated and exceptional TUSCAN red wine estate (B'x varieties) in DOC Val d'Orcia between MONTEPULCIANO and MONTALCINO. Early vintages of CAB SAUV/PETIT VERDOT Trinoro are jaw-dropping in the modern manner. Andrea Franchetti also makes wine at Passopisciano estate on Mt Etna.

Tua Rita ★★→★★★★ Recently arrived producer in Suvereto (Tuscan Maremma), possibly Italy's greatest MERLOT in Redigaffi, also B'x blend Giusto di Notri.

Tuscany (Toscana) Italy's central wine region, includes DOCS CHIANTI, MONTALCINO, MONTEPULCIANO, etc, regional IGT Toscana, and – of course – SUPER TUSCAN.

Uberti ★★→★★★ Producer of DOCG FRANCIACORTA. V.gd TERRE DI FRANCIACORTA.

Umani Ronchi ★★→★★★ Leading Marches merchant and grower, esp for VERDICCHIO (Casal di Serra, Plenio), ROSSO CONERO Cumaro white IGT Le Busche, red IGT Pelago.

Vajra, G D ★★★ V.gd consistent BAROLO producer, esp for BARBERA, BAROLO, DOLCETTO, LANGHE, etc. Also a serious still FREISA.

Valcalepio Lom DOC r w ★→★★ From nr Bergamo. Pleasant red from B'x varieties; lightly scented fresh white from Burgundy grapes. Gd from Brugherata, CASTELLO di Grumello, Monzio.

Val di Cornia Tus DOC r p w ★★→★★★ 97 98 99' 00 01' 03 04' 05 06' 07' DOC near Livorno, competing in quality with BOLGHERI. SANGIOVESE, CAB SAUV, MERLOT, and MONTEPULCIANO. Look for: Ambrosini, Jacopo Banti, Brancatelli, Il Bruscello, Bulichella, Gualdo del Re, Incontri, Montepeloso (Gabbro, Nardo), Petra, Le Pianacce, Russo, San Giusto, San Luigi, San Michele, Sant'Agnese, Suveraia, Tenuta Casadei Casa Dei,Terricciola, Tua Rita (Redigaffi).

Valdadige T-AA DOC r w dr s/sw ★ Name for the simple wines of the valley of the ALTO ADIGE – in German, Etschtaler.

Valentini, Edoardo ★★★ Eccentric, long-macerating, non-filtering, non-fining, hand-bottling producer of MONTEPULCIANO and TREBBIANO D'ABRUZZO. Now deceased, but his son continues the tradition.

Valle d'Aosta (VdA) DOC r w p ★★ Regional DOC for some 25 Alpine wines, geographically or varietally named, inc Premetta, Fumin, Blanc de Morgex et de La Salle, Chambave, Nus Malvoisie, Arnad Montjovet, Torrette, Donnas, and Enfer d'Arvier. Tiny production, wines rarely seen abroad.

Valle Isarco Eisacktal, T-AA DOC w ★★ DYA ALTE ADIGE Valle Isarco DOC is applicable to 7 varietal wines made northeast of Bolzano. Gd Gewurz, MÜLLER-THURGAU, RIES, and Silvaner. Top producers: Abbazia di Novacella, Eisacktaler, Kuenhof.

Vallone, Agricole ★★→★★★ Large scale private v'yd-holder in APULIA's Salento peninsula, best known for its AMARONE-like semi-dried-grape wine Graticciaia.

Valpolicella Ven DOC r ★→★★★ 97 98 00 01 03 04 05 06 07 (SUPERIORE) Complex denomination inc everything from light quaffers through stronger SUPERIORES to AMARONES and RECIOTOS of ancient lineage. Bitter cherry the common flavour characteristic. Best tend, but not necessarily, to come from CLASSICO sub-zone. Gd to superb: Stefano Accordini, Bertani, BOLLA, BRUNELLI, Buglioni, BUSSOLA, Campagnola, Ca' Rugate, Michele Castellani, CS Negrar, CS VALPOLICELLA, DAL FORNO, Guerrieri-Rizzardi, MASI, Mazzi, PASQUA, LE RAGOSE, LE SALETTE, I Saltari, Sant'Alda, Sant'Antonio, Sartori, Speri, TARRELLI, TEDESCHI, Tommasi, Trabuchi, Vaona, Venturini, Villa Monteleone, VIVIANI, ZENATO. Interesting IGTS: BUSSOLA's L'Errante, MASI's Toar and Osar, ALLEGRINI's La Grola, La Poja, Palazzo della Torre (★★★), Zyme's Harlequin, OZ.

Valtellina Lom DOC r ★★ →★★★ DOC for tannic but elegant wines: mainly from Chiavennasca (NEBBIOLO) in northern Alpine Sondrio province. V.gd SUPERIORE DOCG from Grumello, Inferno, Sassella, Valgella v'yds. Best: Caven Camuna, Conti Sertoli-Salis, Fay, Nera, **Nino Negri**, Plozza, Rainoldi, TRIACCA. *Sforzato is the most concentrated type of Valtellina; similar to Amarone.*

VDT, Vino da Tavola "Table wine": the humblest class of Italian wine. No specific geographical or other claim to fame, but occasionally some excellent wines that do not fit into official categories despite prohibition, since 1990s, of mention of place or grape name, or vintage, on label. See IGT.

Vecchio Old.

Vecchio Samperi Si ★★★ MARSALA-like VDT from outstanding estate. Best is barrel-aged 30 yrs. Owner Marco De Bartoli also makes top DOC MARSALAS.

Vendemmia Harvest or vintage.

Verdicchio dei Castelli di Jesi Mar DOC w (sp) ★★ →★★★ DYA Versatile white from nr Ancona, can be light and quaffable, or sparkling, or structured, complex and long-lived (esp RISERVA, minimum 2 yrs old). Also CLASSICO. Best from: Accadia, Bonci-Vallerosa, Brunori, Bucci, Casalfarneto, Cimarelli, Colonnara, Coroncino, FAZI-BATTAGLIA, Fonte della Luna, GAROFOLI, Laila, Lucangeli Aymerich di Laconi, Mancinelli, Montecappone, Monte Shiavo, Santa Barbara, SARTARELLI, TERRE CORTESI MONCARO, UMANI RONCHI.

Verdicchio di Matelica Mar DOC w (sp) ★★ →★★★ DYA Similar to above, smaller, less known, longer lasting. Esp Barone Pizzini, Belisario, Bisci, La Monacesca, Pagliano Tre, San Biagio.

Verduno Pie DOC r ★★ DYA Pale red with spicy perfume, from Pelaverga grape. Gd producers: Alessandria and Castello di Verduno.

Verduzzo Colli Orientali del Friuli, F-VG DOC w dr s/sw sw ★★ →★★★ Full-bodied white from native grapes. Ramandolo is highly regarded sub-zone. Top: Dario Coos, Dorigo, Giovanni Dri, Meroi. Superb sweet VDT from LIS NERIS.

Vermentino Lig w ★★ DYA Best seafood white of Riviera, esp from Pietra Ligure and San Remo. DOC is Riviera Ligure di Ponente. See PIGATO. Esp gd: Colle dei Bardellini, Durin, Lambruschi, Lunae Bosoni, Lupi, Picedi Benettini, Poggio dei Gorlieri, La Rocca di San Niccolao. Also Tuscan coast: ANTINORI, SAN GIUSTO A RENTENNANO, SATTA, Tenuta Vignale, Terre di Talamo.

Vermentino di Gallura Sar DOCG w ★★ →★★★ DYA Best dry white of SARDINIA, stronger and more intensely flavoured than DOC Vermentino di Sardegna. Esp from CAPICHERA,, CS di Gallura, CS del Vermentino, Depperu.

Vernaccia di Oristano Sar DOC w dr (sw fz) ★ →★★★ **90' 93' 97'** 00 01 04 06 Sardinian speciality, like light sherry, a touch bitter, full-bodied. SUPERIORE 15.5% alcohol, 3 yrs of age. Top: CONTINI.

Vernaccia di San Gimignano Tus DOCG w ★ →★★★ DYA Generally dull tourist wine. Since granting of DOCG with tougher production laws, some improvement. Best: Le Calcinaie, Cesani, Cusona, FALCHINI, Fontaleoni, Mormoraia, Palagetto, Palagione, Il Paradiso, Rampa di Fugnano,Le Rote, TERUZZI E PUTHOD.

Verrazzano, Castello di ★★ Gd CHIANTI CLASSICO estate near Greve.

Vestini Campagnano Small producer north of Naples specializing in forgotten local grapes. Excellent results from Casavecchia, Pallagrello BIANCO, and Pallagrello Nero.

Vicchiomaggio ★★ →★★★ CHIANTI CLASSICO estate nr Greve, owned by Brit John Matta.

Vie di Romans ★★★ →★★★★ Gianfranco Gallo has built up his father's ISONZO estate to top FRIULI status. Excellent ISONZO CHARD, PINOT GR, SAUV BL, MALVASIA, RIES, and white blend called Flors di Uis.

Vietti ★★★ Exemplary producer of characterful PIEDMONT wines, inc BAROLO, BARBARESCO, BARBERA D'ALBA, and D'ASTI at Castiglione Falletto in BAROLO region.

Vigna (or vigneto) A single v'yd, generally indicating superior quality.

Vignalta ★★ Top producer in COLLI EUGANEI near Padova (Veneto); v.gd COLLI Euganei CAB SAUV RISERVA and MERLOT/CAB SAUV blend Gemola.

Vignamaggio ★★→★★★ Historic, beautiful, and v.gd CHIANTI CLASSICO estate nr Greve. Leonardo is said to have painted the Mona Lisa here.

Le Vigne di Zamò ★★★ First-class FRIULI estate. PINOT BIANCO, TOCAI, Pignolo, CAB SAUV, MERLOT, and Picolit from v'yds in 3 areas of COLLI ORIENTALI DEL FRIULI DOC.

Villa ★★→★★★ Worthy producer of DOCG FRANCIACORTA.

Villa Matilde ★★★ Top Campania producer of Falerno ROSSO (Vigna Camararato) and BIANCO (Vigna Caracci), Eleusi PASSITO.

Villa Russiz ★★★ Impressive w DOC COLLIO Goriziano: v.gd SAUV BL and MERLOT (esp "de la Tour" selections), PINOT BL, PINOT GR, TOCAI, CHARD.

Vino da arrosto "Wine for roast meat" – ie gd, robust, dry red.

Vino Nobile di Montepulciano Tus DOCG r ★★→★★★ 95' 97' 98 99' 00 01' 03 04' 05 06' 07' Historic SANGIOVESE from the town (as distinct from the grape) MONTEPULCIANO, often tough with drying tannins, but complex and long-lasting from best producers, who include AVIGNONESI, Le Berne, Bindella, BOSCARELLI, La Braccesca, La Calonica, Canneto, Le Casalte, Casanova, La Ciarliana, I Cipressi, Contucci, Dei, Il Faggeto, Fassati, Fattoria del Cerro, Gavioli, Gracciano della Seta, Gracciano Svetoni, Icario, Lunadoro, Macchione, Nottola, Palazzo Bandino, Palazzo Vecchio, Paterno, POLIZIANO, Romeo, Salcheto, Tre Berte, Trerose, Valdipiatta, Vecchia Cantina, Villa Sant'Anna. RISERVA after 3 yrs. Relative to rival BRUNELLO, reasonably priced.

Vino novello Italy's equivalent of France's *primeurs* and just as bad if not worse.

Vin Santo or Vinsanto, Vin(o) Santo Term for certain strong, sweet wines made from PASSITO grapes, usually TREBBIANO, MALVASIA and/or SANGIOVESE in TUSCANY ("Vin Santo"), Nosiola in TRENTINO ("Vino Santo").

Vin Santo Toscano Tus w s/sw ★→★★★★ Extremely variable wine which can be anything from quasi-dry and sherry-like to sweet and incredibly rich. May spend 3–10 unracked yrs in small barrels called *caratelli*. AVIGNONESI's is mythic. Also excellent are CAPEZZANA, CORZANO & PATERNO, Fattoria del Cerro, FELSINA, Frascole, ISOLE E OLENA, Rocca di Montegrossi, San Gervasio, SAN GIUSTO A RENTENNANO, SELVAPIANA, Villa Sant'Anna, Villa di Vetrice.

Vivaldi-Arunda ★★→★★★ Winemaker Josef Reiterer makes top ALTO ADIGE sparkling wines. Best: Extra Brut RISERVA, Cuvée Marianna.

Viviani ★★★ Claudio Viviani is among the best of the new-wave producers who are transforming VALPOLICELLA. Outstanding AMARONE Tulipano Nero.

Voerzio, Roberto ★★★→★★★★ BAROLO modernist. Top single-v'yd BAROLOS: Brunate, Cerequio, Rocche dell'Annunziata-Torriglione, Sarmassa, Serra; impressive BARBERA D'ALBA.

Volpaia, Castello di ★★→★★★ First-class CHIANTI CLASSICO estate at Radda.

VQPRD Vini di Qualità Prodotti in Regione Delimitata, on DOC labels.

Zenato Ven ★★ V. reliable estate for VALPOLICELLA, SOAVE, AMARONE, LUGANA.

Zerbina, Fattoria ★★★ Leader in Romagna; best sweet ALBANA DOCG (Scacco Matto), v.gd SANGIOVESE (Pietramora); BARRIQUE-aged IGT Marzieno.

Zibibbo Si ★★ Local PANTELLERIA name for Muscat of Alexandria. Best from: MURANA, De Bartoli.

Zonin ★→★★ One of Italy's biggest private estates, based at GAMBELLARA, with DOC and DOCG VALPOLICELLA. Also in ASTI, APULIA, CHIANTI CLASSICO, SAN GIMIGNANO, FRIULI, SICILY and Virginia (US). Quality rising under winemaker Franco Giacosa.

Germany

The following abbreviations of
regional names are used in the text:

Bad	Baden
Frank	Franken
M-M	Mittelmosel
M-S-R	Mosel-Saar-Ruwer
Na	Nahe
Pfz	Pfalz
Rhg	Rheingau
Rhh	Rheinhessen
Würt	Württemberg

More heavily shaded
areas are the wine-
growing regions

GERMANY

Any overview of German wines usually begins, or concludes, with a
lament that the wines are under-appreciated, that the wine laws and
labelling regulations are hopelessly complicated and offputting to new
consumers, and that even well-intentioned schemes such as the VDP's
v'yd classification create more confusion than clarity.

But there are clear signs that consumers beyond the country's borders
have been ignoring those who wail and gnash their teeth, and are
purchasing ever-larger quantities of German wine. Riesling in particular is
subject to growing demand worldwide, and exports have soared. Perhaps
this is a reward for Germany's tireless wine marketing after decades of
public indifference; or perhaps wine drinkers everywhere are finally

paying heed to writers (like me) and importers who have for so long been imploring them to take notice of and enjoy Germany's unique white wines. Whatever has prompted the growing consumption of German wines, it is certainly a welcome trend.

If Britain still consumes rather more mediocre German wine than a proud wine-drinking nation should, Americans have woken up to the virtues of great Riesling, which is being exported there in significantly increased quantities. Nor is the boom limited to Rieslings and other whites. German red wine, especially Spätburgunder, is also increasingly seen and drunk outside Germany.

Riesling remains supreme, for sure. But there is a growing recognition that Germany has more cards to play. Along with Alsace, there is no area in the world more successful with Pinot Blanc (Weissburgunder). The bracing, mineral Silvaners of Franken have their own marked personality. Moreover, both of these wines are inexpensive. Would that were equally true of German reds. There is no shortage of well-priced German reds from varieties such as Schwarzriesling (Pinot Meunier), Trollinger, and Lemberger, but there is a shortage of clients outside the regions of production who actually want to buy and drink these wines. The more serious examples from Württemberg or Baden are also seriously expensive, which diminishes their appeal to a world market with no lack of structured red wines to choose from.

Nevertheless Germany is no longer perceived as a one-trick pony. Nothing will ever displace Riesling from its throne, but canny consumers know that Germany can now offer a wide range of wine styles, mostly at the lighter end of the spectrum and thus occupying an area where more fashionable areas such as California or Australia simply can't compete.

Recent vintages

Mosel-Saar-Ruwer

Mosels (including Saar and Ruwer wines) are so attractive young that their keeping qualities are not often enough explored. But well-made Riesling wines of Kabinett class gain from at least five years in bottle and often much more, Spätlese from five to 20, and Auslese and Beerenauslese anything from 10 to 30 years. As a rule, in poor years the Saar and Ruwer make sharp, lean wines, but in good years, which are becoming increasingly common, they can surpass the whole world for elegance and thrilling, steely "breed".

2007 A warm, cloudy summer and rainy Aug did not bode well, but a fine Sept ripened the grapes fully and in time for an early Oct harvest. Very early flowering meant that the growing season was exceptionally long, giving the wines great extract. Good quality and good quantity too, and some botrytis at the end of harvest. Close to 2005 in quality.

2006 A cool, wet Aug and more poor weather during the autumn dampened expectations; rot was widespread, persuading growers to pick early and fast. There will be some mediocre wines, but the best growers achieved very high ripeness and vibrant acidity. But ruthless selection means that quantities are very low.

2005 Superb warm autumn weather from late Sept through to Nov brought grapes to very high ripeness levels, but with far better acidity than, say, 2003. An exceptional year, especially in the Saar.

2004 A humid summer led growers to fear the worst, but the vintage was saved by a glorious autumn. At harvest, grapes were healthy and very ripe. A fine year to start drinking.

2003 Hot weather brought high ripeness levels but rather low acidity. Ironically, some great sites suffered from drought, while less esteemed cooler sites often fared better. So there is considerable variation in quality, with the best, including some powerful dry wines, superb. Some sensational Trockenbeerenauslesen too.

2002 It is a small miracle how the Riesling grapes survived one of the wettest harvests on record to give ripe, succulent, lively wines (mostly Kabinett and Spätlese), attractive drunk young or mature.

2001 Golden Oct resulted in the best Mosel Riesling since 1990. Saar and Ruwer less exciting but still perfect balance. Lots of Spätlesen and Auslesen.

2000 Riesling stood up to harvest rain here better than most other places. Dominated by good QbA and Kabinett. Auslesen rarer, but exciting.

1999 Excellent in Saar and Ruwer, lots of Auslesen; generally only good in the Mosel due to high yields. Best drank well young and will age.

1998 Riesling grapes came through a rainy autumn to give astonishingly good results in the Middle Mosel; the Saar and Ruwer were less lucky, with mostly QbA. Plenty of Eiswein.

1997 A generous vintage of consistently fruity, elegant wines from the entire region. Marvellous Auslesen in the Saar and Ruwer.

1996 Variable, with fine Spätlesen and Auslesen, but only from top sites. Many excellent Eisweins.

1995 Excellent vintage, mainly of Spätlesen and Auslesen of firm structure and long ageing potential.

1994 Another good vintage, with unexceptional QbA and Kabinett, but many Auslesen and botrytis wines.

1993 Small, excellent vintage: lots of Auslesen/botrytis; near perfect harmony. Ready to drink except top Auslesen.

1992 A very large crop, with only 30% QmP. To drink soon.

1991 A mixed vintage. Drink up.

1990 Superb vintage, though small.

Fine older vintages: 89 88 76 71 69 64 59 53 49 45 37 34 21.

Rheinhessen, Nahe, Pfalz, Rheingau

Even the best wines can be drunk with pleasure when young, but Kabinett, Spätlese, and Auslese Riesling gain enormously in character by keeping for longer. Rheingau wines tend to be longest-lived, improving for 15 years or more, but best wines from the Nahe and Pfalz can last as long. Rheinhessen wines usually mature sooner, and dry Franken and Baden wines are generally best at three to six years.

2007 Those who waited to pick until Oct, and sunny autumn conditions allowed this, had very ripe grapes with cool nights conserving good acidity levels. Should be excellent for Spätburgunder (Pinot Noir) and other reds as well as Riesling. As in the Mosel, an exceptionally long growing season should result in wines of structure and extract. Yields were high, however, and there may be some dilution.

2006 Warm, rainy weather in Sept and early Oct forced growers to pick early before rot took too firm a hold. Top estates in the Pfalz and Rheinhessen were obliged to leave rotting fruit unpicked. Grauburgunder (Pinot Gris) worst affected, also Pfalz Riesling. Much of what was picked turned out well, so not a disastrous vintage, though quantities low.

2005 The summer was warm, but rain kept drought at bay. A very fine autumn led to high ripeness levels, accompanied by excellent acidity and extract. A superb year.

2004 After an indifferent summer, a fine autumn delivered ripe, healthy grapes throughout the Rhein lands. A larger than average crop, so there could be some dilution, though not at top estates.

2003 Very hot weather led to rich wines in the Rheingau; many lack acidity. The Pfalz produced superb Rieslings. Red wines fared well everywhere.

2002 Few challenge the best from 01, but very good for both classic-style Kabinett/Spätlese and for dry. Excellent Pinot Noir.

2001 Though more erratic than in the Mosel, here, too, this was often an exciting vintage for both dry and classic styles; excellent balance.

2000 The farther south, the more difficult was the harvest, the Pfalz catching worst of harvest rain. However, all regions have islands of excellence.

1999 Quality was average where yields were high, but for top growers an excellent vintage of rich, aromatic wines with lots of charm.

1998 Excellent: rich, balanced wines, many good Spätlesen and Auslesen with excellent ageing potential. Rain affected much of Baden and Franken. But a great Eiswein year.

1997 Very clean, ripe grapes gave excellent QbA, Kabinett, Spätlese in dry and classic styles. Little botrytis, so Auslesen and higher are rare.

1996 An excellent vintage, particularly in the Pfalz and the Rheingau, with many fine Spätlesen. Great Eiswein.

1995 Rather variable, but some excellent Spätlesen and Auslesen maturing well – like the 90s. Weak in the Pfalz due to harvest rain.

1994 Good vintage, mostly QmP, with abundant fruit and firm structure. Some superb sweet wines.

1993 A small vintage of very good to excellent quality. Spätlesen and Auslesen now at their peak.

1992 Very large vintage; would have been great but for Oct cold and rain. Drink soon.

1990 Small and exceptionally fine. Drink now, but will keep for years.

Fine older vintages: 83 76 71 69 64 59 53 49 45 37 34 21.

Achkarren Bad w (r) ★★ Village on the KAISERSTUHL, known esp for GRAUBURGUNDER. First Class v'yd: Schlossberg. Wines generally best drunk during first 5 yrs. Gd wines: Engist, DR. HEGER, Michel, and co-op.

Adelmann, Weingut Graf ★★→★★★ Estate based at the idyllic Schaubeck castle in WÜRTTEMBERG. The specialities are subtle red blends (notably Vignette), RIES, and the rare Muskattrollinger.

German vintage notation

The vintage notes after entries in the German section are given in a different form from those elsewhere in the book. Two styles of vintage are indicated:

Bold type (eg **99**) indicates classic, ripe vintages with a high proportion of SPÄTLESEN and AUSLESEN; or, in the case of red wines, gd phenolic ripeness and must weights.

Normal type (eg 98) indicates a successful but not outstanding vintage.

German white wines, esp RIESLING, have high acidity and keep well, and they display pure fruit qualities because they are unoaked. Thus they can be drunk young for their intense fruitiness, or kept for a decade or two to develop more aromatic subtlety and finesse. This means there is no one ideal moment to drink them, so no vintages are specifically recommended for drinking now.

Ahr Ahr r ★→★★ **95 97** 98 **99 01 03 04** 05 06 **07** South of Bonn. Light, elegant SPÄTBURGUNDER and FRÜHBURGUNDER, esp from Adeneuer, DEUTZERHOF, Kreuzberg, MEYER-NÄKEL, Nelles, STODDEN.

Aldinger, Weingut Gerhard ★★★ WÜRTTEMBERG'S leading red wine estate: LEMBERGER SPÄTBURGUNDER, and B'x varieties are the specialities. Gd RIES too.

Amtliche Prüfungsnummer See PRÜFUNGSNUMMER.

APNr Abbreviation of AMTLICHE PRÜFUNGSNUMMER.

Assmannshausen Rhg r ★→★★★ **93 95 96** 97 98 **99 01** 02 **03 04 05** 06 **07** Craggy RHEINGAU village known specifically for its SPÄTBURGUNDERS. First Class v'yd: Höllenberg. Growers include KESSELER, Robert König, Hotel KRONE, and the STATE DOMAIN.

Auslese Wines from selective harvest of super-ripe bunches, in many yrs affected by noble rot (*Edelfäule*) and correspondingly unctuous in flavour. Dry Auslesen are usually too alcoholic and clumsy for me.

Ayl M-S-R (Saar) r ★★★ **90 93 95** 96 **97 99** 00 **01 02 03 04 05** 06 **07** All Ayl v'yds since 1971 are known by the name of its historically best site: Kupp. Growers inc BISCHÖFLICHE WEINGÜTER, LAUER.

Bacchus Modern, often kitsch grape found mostly in RHEINHESSEN and FRANKEN. Often flabby wines. Deservedly in decline.

The Pinot Noir bandwagon

It is natural to think of Germany as primarily a white wine producer. Indeed Riesling remains its trump card. But Germans themselves have always had a thirst for red wines, hitherto slaked by mostly indifferent Spätburgunder (Pinot Noir) or fruity if bland Dornfelder. Demand has increased, and quality has been rising too – perhaps thanks to climatic change which is resulting in ever riper red grapes. Still, few would have imagined that by 2007 Germany would have become the world's third largest Pinot Noir grower, with almost 12,000 ha under vine. Over the last 20 yrs the surface planted has almost doubled, and Germany's Pinot Noir v'yds are now greater in extent than those of Australia, New Zealand, and Chile combined. Only France and the United States have more Pinot Noir planted than Germany.

Bacharach w (r) ★→★★★ **93 96** 97 98 **01 02** 03 **04 05** 06 **07** Main wine town of MITTELRHEIN. Racy, austere RIES, some v. fine. First Class v'yds: Hahn, Posten, Wolfshöhle. Growers include BASTIAN, JOST, RATZENBERGER.

Bad Dürkheim Pfz w (r) ★★→★★★ **93** 94 **96 97 98 99 01** 02 **03 04 05** 06 **07** Main town of MITTELHAARDT, with the world's biggest barrel and an ancient September wine festival. First Class v'yds: Michelsberg, Spielberg. Growers: Darting, Fitz-Ritter, Hensel, Schmitt, Schäfer.

Baden Bad Huge southwest area of scattered v'yds best known for the Pinots, and pockets of RIES, usually dry. Best areas: KAISERSTUHL, ORTENAU.

Badische Bergstrasse/Kraichgau (Bereich) Widespread district of north BADEN. WEISSBURGUNDER and GRAUBURGUNDER make best wines.

Badischer Winzerkeller Germany's (and Europe's) biggest co-op, absorbing the entire crop of 38 other co-ops to produce almost half of BADEN'S wine: dependably unambitious.

Bad Kreuznach Nahe w ★★ **85 89 90** 92 **93** 94 95 96 97 98 **99** 00 **01 02 03 04 05** 06 **07** Spa town with fine v'yds. First Class: Brückes, Kahlenberg, Krötenpfuhl. Growers include Emrich-Montigny, Korrell.

Bassermann-Jordan ★★★ **90 96 97 98 99 01** 02 **03 04 05** 06 **07** MITTELHAARDT estate, under new ownership since 2003, with 45 ha of outstanding v'yds in DEIDESHEIM, FORST, RUPPERTSBERG, etc. Winemaker Ulrich Mell excels at

GERMANY

producing majestic dry RIES and lavish sweet wines too.

Bastian, Weingut Friedrich ★★ 6 ha BACHARACH estate. Racy, austere RIES with MOSEL-like delicacy, esp from the First Class Posten v'yd.

Becker, J B ★★→★★★ The best estate at WALLUF specializing in powerful dry RIES and SPÄTBURGUNDER.

Beerenauslese, BA Luscious sweet wine from exceptionally ripe, individually selected berries concentrated by noble rot. Rare, expensive.

Bercher ★★★ KAISERSTUHL estate; 24 ha at Burkheim, yielding consistently excellent WEISSBURGUNDER, RIES, and SPÄTBURGUNDER.

Bergdolt, Weingut ★★ Just south of NEUSTADT in the PFALZ, this 23-ha estate produces outstanding WEISSBURGUNDER (Pinot Bl), as well as gd RIES.

Bernkastel M-M w ★→★★★★ 83 88 89 90 93 94 95 97 98 **99** 00 **01 02** 03 **04 05 06 07** Top wine town of the MITTELMOSEL; the epitome of RIES. Great First Class (if overpriced) v'yd: Doctor, 3.2 ha; First Class v'yds: Graben, Lay. Top growers include KERPEN, LOOSEN, PAULY-BERGWEILER, PRÜM, Studert-Prüm, THANISCH (both estates), WEGELER.

Bernkastel (Bereich) Inc all the MITTELMOSEL. Wide area of deplorably dim quality and superficial flowery character. Mostly MÜLLER-THURGAU. Avoid.

Beulwitz, Weingut von ★★→★★★ Reliable 6-ha RUWER estate with wines from Kaseler Nies'chen.

Biffar, Josef ★★★ Important 12-ha estate in DEIDESHEIM and WACHENHEIM. Frequent changes of winemaker have led to inconsistent quality.

Bingen Rhh w ★→★★ **90 93** 94 **96 97 98** 99 **01 02** 03 **04 05** 06 **07** Town where rivers Nahe and Rhine meet. Best v'yd is First Class Scharlachberg.

Bischöfliche Weingüter M-S-R ★★ Famous estate located at TRIER, uniting cathedral's v'yds with those of two other charities, the Bischöfliches Priesterseminar and the Bischöfliches Konvikt. Owns 106 ha of top v'yds, esp in SAAR and RUWER. But middling quality.

Bocksbeutel Squat, inconvenient, flask-shaped bottle used in FRANKEN and north BADEN.

Bodensee (Bereich) Idyllic district of south BADEN, on Lake Constance. Dry wines are best drunk young. RIES-like MÜLLER-T a speciality.

Boppard ★→★★★ **90 93** 95 **97 98 01 02** 03 **04 05** 06 **07** Important wine town of MITTELRHEIN with best sites all in amphitheatre of vines called Bopparder Hamm. Growers: Toni Lorenz, Matthias Müller, August Perll, WEINGART. Unbeatable value for money.

Brauneberg M-M w ★★★★ 88 89 **90 93** 94 95 96 **97 98 99** 00 **01 02** 03 **04 05** 06 **07** Top M-S-R village nr BERNKASTEL (304 ha): excellent full-flavoured RIES – *grand cru* if anything on the Mosel is. Great First Class v'yd: Juffer-SONNENUHR. First Class v'yd: Juffer. Growers: F HAAG, W HAAG, PAULINSHOF, RICHTER, SCHLOSS LIESER, THANISCH.

Breuer, Weingut Georg ★★★→★★★★ Family estate of 24 ha in RÜDESHEIM and 7.2 ha in RAUENTHAL, giving superb, full-bodied dry RIES. Superb SEKT too. Pioneering winemaker Bernhard Breuer died suddenly in 2004, quality is undiminished.

Buhl, Reichsrat von ★★★ Historic PFALZ estate, returning to historic form as of 1994. 55 ha (DEIDESHEIM, FORST, RUPPERTSBERG). Bought in 2005 by businessman Achim Niederberger, who also owns BASSERMANN-JORDAN. 80% dry wines.

Bürgerspital zum Heiligen Geist ★★→★★★ Ancient charitable WÜRZBURG estate.

Remember that vintage information for German wines is given in a different form from the ready/not ready distinction applying to other countries.
See the explanation at the bottom of p. 130.

> **Beware of Bereich**
> District within an *Anbaugebiet* (region). "BEREICH" on a label should be treated as a flashing red light. Do not buy. See under BEREICH names – eg BERNKASTEL (BEREICH).

111 ha. Rich, dry wines, esp SILVANER, RIES, and in some yrs, such as 2005, great TBA.

Bürklin-Wolf, Dr. ★★★→★★★★ Dynamic PFALZ family estate. 85 ha in FORST, DEIDESHEIM, RUPPERTSBERG, and WACHENHEIM, inc many First Class sites. The full-bodied dry wines from these are often spectacular. Now biodynamic. Family bust-up in 2006 leaves quality unaffected.

Busch, Weingut Clemens M-S-R ★★→★★★ Since 1985 Busch has demonstrated the excellence of steep but obscure Pündericher Marienburg in lower MOSEL. Both dry and notably sweet RIES. Organic.

Castell'sches Fürstlich Domänenamt ★→★★★ Historic 65-ha estate in FRANKEN. SILVANER, RIESLANER, dry and sweet, and a growing reputation for red wines.

Chardonnay Now grown throughout Germany; with over 1,020 ha. Quality now more sure-footed. Best: BERCHER, BERGDOLT, HUBER, JOHNER, REBHOLZ, DR. WEHRHEIM, WITTMANN.

Christmann ★★★ 15-ha estate in Gimmeldingen (PFALZ) making rich, dry RIES and SPÄTBURGUNDER from First Class v'yds, notably Königsbacher Idig. Young Stefan Christmann is new president of the VDP.

Christoffel, J J ★★★ Tiny domain in URZIG. Classic, elegant RIES. Since 2001 leased to Robert Eymael of MÖNCHHOF.

Clüsserath-Weiler, Weingut ★★★ Classic RIES from top TRITTENHEIMER Apotheke and the rare Fährfels v'yd. Steadily improving quality.

Crusius ★★→★★★ 17-ha family estate at TRAISEN, NAHE. Vivid and ageworthy RIES from Bastei and Rotenfels of TRAISEN and SCHLOSSBÖCKELHEIM.

Dautel, Weingut Ernst ★★★ One of WÜRTTEMBERG'S, and indeed Germany's, few masters of serious red wines, esp SPÄTBURGUNDER and LEMBERGER. Reliable whites too.

Deidesheim Pfz w (r) ★★→★★★★ **89 90 92 94** 95 **96** 97 **98 99** 01 02 03 **04 05** 06 **07** Largest top-quality village of the PFALZ (405 ha). Richly flavoured, lively wines. First Class v'yds: Grainhübel, Hohenmorgen, Kalkofen, Kieselberg, Langenmorgen, Leinhöhle. Top growers: BASSERMANN-JORDAN, BIFFAR, BUHL, BÜRKLIN-WOLF, CHRISTMANN, DEINHARD, MOSBACHER.

Deinhard In 1997 the WEGELER family sold the 200-yr-old merchant house and SEKT producer Deinhard to sparkling-wine giant Henkell-Söhnlein. But the splendid Deinhard estates remain in family ownership (see WEGELER).

Deinhard, Dr. ★★★ Fine 35-ha estate: some top sites in DEIDESHEIM and FORST.

Deutscher Tafelwein Officially the term for v. humble German wines. Now, confusingly, the flag of convenience for some costly novelties as well, often barrique-aged.

Deutzerhof, Weingut ★★→★★★ 9-ha AHR estate producing concentrated, barrique-aged SPÄTBURGUNDER. Fine quality, alarming prices.

Diel, Schlossgut ★★★ Fashionable 17-ha NAHE estate; pioneered ageing GRAUBURGUNDER and WEISSBURGUNDER in barriques. Its traditional RIES is often exquisite. Also serious SEKT.

Domäne German for "domaine" or "estate".

Dönnhoff, Weingut Hermann ★★★★ 90 94 95 96 97 98 99 00 00 01 02 03 04 05 06 07 16-ha leading NAHE estate with magnificent RIES at all quality levels from NIEDERHAUSEN, Oberhausen, SCHLOSSBÖCKELHEIM. Dazzling EISWEIN.

Dornfelder Red grape making deep-coloured, usually rustic wines. Plantings

GERMANY

have doubled since 2000 to an astonishing 8,250 ha.

Durbach Baden w (r) ★★→★★★ 96 97 **98** 99 00 **01** 02 **04** 05 06 07 Village with 314 ha of v'yds, of which Plauelrain is First Class. Top growers: LAIBLE, H. Männle, Schloss Staufenberg. KLINGELBERGER (RIES) is the outstanding variety.

Edel Means "noble". *Edelfäule* means "noble rot".

Egon Müller zu Scharzhof ★★★★ 76 79 83 85 **88 89** 90 92 **93 94** 95 96 **97** 98 **99** 00 **01** 02 03 **04** 05 06 07 Top SAAR estate of 8 ha at WILTINGEN, the v'yds rising steeply behind the Müllers' manor house. Its rich and racy SCHARZHOFBERGER RIES in AUSLESEN vintages is among the world's greatest wines, sublime, honeyed, immortal; best are given gold capsules. ***Kabinetts are feather-light.*** Le Gallais is a second 4-ha estate in WILTINGER Braune Kupp; gd quality, but the site is less exceptional.

Eiswein Made from frozen grapes with the ice (i.e. water content) discarded, producing v. concentrated wine in flavour, acidity, and sugar – of BEERENAUSLESE ripeness or more. Alcohol content can be as low as 5.5%. V. expensive. Outstanding Eiswein vintages were 98, 02, and 04.

Eitelsbach M-S-R (Ruwer) w ★★→★★★★ 89 90 93 94 95 96 **97 98** 99 00 01 02 **03 04** 05 06 07 RUWER village bordering TRIER, inc superb Great First Class KARTHAUSERHOFBERG v'yd site.

Elbling Grape introduced by the Romans, widely grown on upper MOSEL. Can be sharp and tasteless, but capable of real freshness and vitality (e.g. at Nittel or SCHLOSS THORN in the OBERMOSEL).

Ellwanger, Weingut ★★→★★★ Jürgen Ellwanger pioneered oak-aged red wines in WÜRTTEMBERG. Today aided by his sons, who continue to turn out sappy but structured LEMBERGER and SPÄTBURGUNDER.

Eltville Rhg w ★★→★★★ 90 93 94 **95** 96 97 98 **99** 00 01 02 **03 04** 05 06 07 Major wine town with cellars of RHEINGAU STAATSWEINGÜTER and LANGWERTH VON SIMMERN estates. First Class v'yd: Sonnenberg.

Emrich-Schönleber ★★★ Located in NAHE village of Monzingen. Since the late 1980s winemaker Werner Schönleber has produced RIES that is now among Germany's finest, esp his sumptuous EISWEIN.

Enkirch M-M w ★★ 90 94 96 97 98 **99** 01 02 03 **04** 05 06 07 Little-known MITTELMOSEL village, but with lovely light, tasty wine. The best grower is IMMICH-BATTERIEBERG.

Erbach Rhg w ★★★ 89 90 93 95 96 **98** 99 00 01 02 **03 04** 05 06 07 RHEINGAU area: big, perfumed, ageworthy wines, inc First Class v'yds: Hohenrain, MARCOBRUNN, Siegelsberg, Steinmorgen, Schlossberg. Leading producers: KNYPHAUSEN, LANGWERTH VON SIMMERN, SCHLOSS REINHARTSHAUSEN, SCHLOSS SCHÖNBORN. Also BECKER, Jakob Jung, etc.

Erben Word meaning "heirs", often used on old-established estate labels.

Erden M-M w ★★★ 88 89 90 93 95 96 **97 98** 99 00 01 02 03 **04** 05 06 07 Village adjoining ÜRZIG: noble, full-flavoured, vigorous wine (more herbal and mineral than the wines of nearby BERNKASTEL and WEHLEN but equally long-living). Great First Class v'yds: Prälat, Treppchen. Growers include J J CHRISTOFFEL, Erbes, LOOSEN, Lotz, Meulenhof, MÖNCHHOF, Peter Nicolay, Weins-Prüm.

Erstes Gewächs Literally translates as "first growth". Applies only to RHEINGAU v'yds.

Erzeugerabfüllung Bottled by producer. Being replaced by GUTSABFÜLLUNG, but only by estates. Co-ops will continue with *Erzeugerabfüllung*.

Escherndorf Frank w ★★→★★★ 93 97 98 99 **00** 01 02 03 04 **05** 06 07 Important wine town nr WÜRZBURG. Similar tasty, dry wine from RIES and SILVANER. First Class v'yd: Lump. Growers include Michael Fröhlich, JULIUSSPITAL, H SAUER, Rainer Sauer, Egon Schäffer.

Feinherb Imprecisely defined term for wines with around 10–20 g of sugar per litre. Favoured by some as a more flexible alternative to HALBTROCKEN. Used on label by, among others, KERPEN, VON KESSELSTATT, MOLITOR.

Forst Pfz w ★★→★★★★ 90 94 96 97 **98** 99 01 02 03 04 05 06 07 MITTELHAARDT village with over 200 ha of Germany's best v'yds. Ripe, richly fragrant, full-bodied but subtle wines. First Class v'yds: Jesuitengarten, Kirchenstück, Freundstück, Pechstein, Ungeheuer. Top growers incl: BASSERMANN-JORDAN, BÜRKLIN-WOLF, DEINHARD, MOSBACHER, Eugen Müller, H Spindler, Werlé, WOLF.

Franken Franconia region of distinctive dry wines, esp SILVANER, always bottled in round-bellied flasks (BOCKSBEUTEL). The centre is WÜRZBURG. Bereich names: MAINDREIECK, Steigerwald. Top producers: BÜRGERSPITAL, CASTELL, FÜRST, JULIUSSPITAL, LÖWENSTEIN, RUCK, H SAUER, STAATLICHER HOFKELLER, STÖRRLEIN, WIRSCHING, etc.

Franzen, Weingut Reinhold ★→★★★ From Europe's steepest v'yd, Bremmer Calmont, Franzen makes dependable, sometimes exciting dry RIES and EISWEIN.

Friedrich-Wilhelm Gymnasium ★ Once important charitable estate with v'yds throughout M-S-R. In 2003 it was leased by the BISCHÖFLICHE WEINGÜTER, but some v'yds have been sold off.

Germany's quality levels

The official range of qualities and styles in ascending order is:

1 Deutscher Tafelwein: sweetish light wine of no specified character. (From certain producers, can be atypical but excellent.)

2 Landwein: dryish Tafelwein with some regional style.

3 Qualitätswein: dry or sweetish wine with sugar added before fermentation to increase its strength, but tested for quality and with distinct local and grape character. Don't despair.

4 Kabinett: dry or dryish natural (unsugared) wine of distinct personality and distinguishing lightness. Can occasionally be sublime.

5 Spätlese: stronger, often sweeter than Kabinett. Full-bodied. Today many top SPÄTLESEN are *trocken* or completely dry.

6 Auslese: sweeter, sometimes stronger than SPÄTLESE, often with honey-like flavours, intense and long-lived. Occasionally dry and weighty.

7 Beerenauslese: v. sweet, sometimes strong, intense. Can be superb.

8 Eiswein: from naturally frozen grapes of BEEREN- or TROCKENBEERENAUSLESE quality: concentrated, sharpish, and v. sweet. Some examples are extreme, unharmonious.

9 Trockenbeerenauslese (TBA): intensely sweet and aromatic; alcohol slight. Extraordinary and everlasting.

Frühburgunder An ancient mutation of Pinot N, found mostly in the AHR but also in PFALZ and WÜRTTEMBERG, where it is confusingly known as Clevner. Lower acidity and thus more approachable than Pinot N.

Fuhrmann See PFEFFINGEN.

Fürst ★★★→★★★★ 18-ha estate in Bürgstadt making some of the best wines in FRANKEN, particularly Burgundian SPÄTBURGUNDER (arguably Germany's finest), full-flavoured RIES, and oak-aged WEISSBURGUNDER.

Gallais, Le See EGON MÜLLER ZU SCHARZHOF.

Geisenheim Rhg w ★★→★★★★ 90 93 95 96 **98** 99 00 **01** 02 03 **04** 05 06 07 Home

GERMANY

to Germany's best-known wine school. The v'yds produce v.gd aromatic wines. First Class v'yds: Kläuserweg, Rothenberg. Top growers: JOHANNISHOF, WEGELER. See also HESSISCHE FORSCHUNGSANSTALT.

Gewürztraminer (or Traminer) Highly aromatic grape, speciality of Alsace, also impressive in Germany, esp in PFALZ, BADEN, SACHSEN, WÜRTTEMBERG.

Gimmeldingen Pfz w ★★ **94 96** 97 **98** 99 01 02 03 **04 05** 06 **07** Village just south of MITTELHAARDT. At best, rich, succulent wines. First-class v'yd: Mandelgarten. Growers include CHRISTMANN, MÜLLER-CATOIR, Weegmüller.

Graach M-M w ★★★ **88 89 90 93 94 95** 96 **97** 98 **99** 00 01 02 **03 04 05** 06 **07** Small village between BERNKASTEL and WEHLEN. First Class v'yds: Domprobst, Himmelreich, Josephshof. Many top growers, inc: Kees-Kieren, von KESSELSTATT, LOOSEN, M MOLITOR, J J PRÜM, S A PRÜM, SCHAEFER, SELBACH-OSTER, WEINS-PRÜM.

Grans-Fassian ★★★ Fine mosel estate at Leiwen. V'yds there and in TRITTENHEIM and PIESPORTER. EISWEIN a speciality. Consistently high quality since 1995.

Grauburgunder (or Grauer Burgunder) Both synonyms of RULÄNDER or Pinot Gris: grape giving soft full-bodied wine. Best in BADEN and south PFALZ. 4,400 ha planted.

Grosser Ring Group of top (VDP) MOSEL-SAAR-RUWER estates, whose annual September auction often sets world-record prices.

Grosses Gewächs Translates as "great/top growth". This is the top tier in the v'yd classification launched in 2002 by the growers' association VDP, except in the RHEINGAU, which has its own ERSTES GEWÄCHS classification. Wines released as *Grosses Gewächs* must meet strict quality criteria.

Grosslage A collection of individual sites with seemingly similar character but no indication of quality.

Gunderloch ★★★→★★★★ **93 96 97 98** 99 00 **01** 02 03 **04 05** 06 **07** At this NACKENHEIM estate Fritz Hasselbach makes some of the finest RIES on the entire Rhine, esp at AUSLESE level and above. Also owns Balbach estate in NIERSTEIN.

Guntrum, Louis 11-ha family estate in top sites of NIERSTEIN, OPPENHEIM, etc, aiming high with new ideas.

Gutedel German name for the ancient Chasselas grape, grown in south BADEN. Fresh, but neutral, white wines.

Gutsabfüllung Estate-bottled. Term for genuinely estate-bottled wines.

Haag, Weingut Fritz M-S-R ★★★★ **88 89 90 94 95** 96 97 98 **99** 00 **01 02 03 04 05** 06 **07** BRAUNEBERG's top estate, run for decades by MITTELMOSEL veteran Wilhelm Haag and now by his son Oliver. *Mosel Ries of crystalline purity* for long ageing. Haag's other son, Thomas, runs SCHLOSS LIESER estate.

Haag, Weingut Willi M-S-R ★★ 6-ha BRAUNEBERG estate. Full, old-style RIES. Some fine AUSLESEN.

Haart, Reinhold ★★★★ The best estate in PIESPORT and WINTRICH. Refined, aromatic wines capable of long ageing. Mineral and racy, these are copybook MOSEL RIES.

Hain, Weingut Kurt ★★→★★★ Small but focused PIESPORT estate of steadily increasing quality.

Halbtrocken Medium-dry (literally "semi-dry"), with 9–18 g of unfermented sugar per litre. Popular category, often better balanced than TROCKEN. See also FEINHERB.

Hallgarten Rhg w ★→★★★ **90 95** 96 **97** 98 **99** 00 **01** 02 03 **04 05** 06 **07** Village

Remember that vintage information for German wines is given in a different form from the ready/not ready distinction applying to other countries. See the explanation at the bottom of p. 130.

perched just inland from HATTENHEIM. Renowned a century ago, less so today. First class v'yds: Jungfer, Schönhell. Top growers: LÖWENSTEIN, PRINZ.

Hattenheim Rhg w ★★–★★★★ 90 93 95 96 **97** 98 **99** 00 **01** 02 **03** 04 05 06 07 Superlative 202-ha wine town, though not all producers achieve full potential. The First Class v'yds are Mannberg, Nussbrunnen, Pfaffenberg, Wisselbrunnen, and, most famously, STEINBERG (ORTSTEIL). Estates include Barth, KNYPHAUSEN, LANG, LANGWERTH VON SIMMERN, RESS, SCHLOSS SCHÖNBORN, STAATSWEINGUT.

Heger, Dr. ★★★ Leading estate of KAISERSTUHL in BADEN with excellent dry WEISSBURGUNDER, GRAUBURGUNDER, and powerful oak-aged SPÄTBURGUNDER reds. Less emphasis on RIES and Muscat, which can also be v.gd. Wines from rented v'yds released under Weinhaus Joachim Heger label.

Heilbronn Würt w r ★–★★★ 96 97 99 01 02 **03** 04 05 06 07 Wine town with many small growers. Top v'yd: Stiftberg. Best wines are RIES and LEMBERGER. Top growers include Amalienhof, Drautz-Able, Heinrich.

Henkell See DEINHARD.

Hessen, Prinz von ★★★ Famous 42-ha estate in JOHANNISBERG, KIEDRICH, and WINKEL. Improving quality since the late 1990s but yet to show full potential.

Hessische Bergstrasse w (r) ★★–★★★ 93 **96** 97 98 **99** 01 02 03 04 **05** 06 07 Small wine region (436 ha), north of Heidelberg. Pleasant RIES from STAATSWEINGÜTER, Simon-Bürkle, and Stadt Bensheim.

Hessische Forschungsanstalt für Wein-Obst & Gartenbau Famous wine school and research establishment at GEISENHEIM, RHEINGAU.

Heyl zu Herrnsheim ★★ Leading NIERSTEIN estate, 80% RIES. Inconsistent in recent vintages; bought in 2006 by Detlev Meyer. Occasional dry RIES and sweet wines of exceptional quality.

Heymann-Löwenstein ★★★ Estate in Lower Mosel nr Koblenz with most consistent dry RIES in MOSEL-SAAR-RUWER and some remarkable AUSLESEN and TROCKENBEERENAUSLESEN. Löwenstein has inspired other WINNINGEN growers to adopt his style. Spectacular wines in 05.

Hochgewächs Supposedly superior level of QBA RIES, esp in MOSEL-SAAR-RUWER. Rarely encountered.

Hochheim Rhg w ★★–★★★★★ 90 93 95 96 **97** 98 **99** 00 **01** 02 **03** 04 05 06 07 242-ha wine town 24 km (15 miles) east of main RHEINGAU area, once thought of as best on Rhine. The region's most full-bodied wines, whether dry or sweet; can be earthy. First Class v'yds: Domdechaney, Hölle, Kirchenstück, Königin Viktoria Berg (5-ha monopoly of Hupfeld family). Growers include Königin-Victoriaberg, KÜNSTLER, W J Schaefer, SCHLOSS SCHÖNBORN, STAATSWEINGUT, WERNER.

Hock Traditional English term for Rhine wine, derived from HOCHHEIM.

Hoensbroech, Weingut Reichsgraf zu ★★ Top KRAICHGAU estate. Dry WEISSBURGUNDER from Michelfelder Himmelberg is the best wine.

Hohenlohe-Oehringen, Weingut Fürst zu ★★ Noble 17-ha estate in Oehringen, WÜRTTEMBERG. Earthy, bone-dry RIES and powerful, structured reds from LEMBERGER, Merlot, and other grapes.

Hövel, Weingut von ★★★ Fine SAAR estate at OBEREMMEL (Hütte is 4.8-ha monopoly) and in SCHARZHOFBERG. Erratic quality, but 05s best in many yrs.

Huber, Bernhard ★★★ Leading estate of Breisgau area of BADEN, with powerful long-lived SPÄTBURGUNDER, MUSKATELLER, and Burgundian-style WEISSBURGUNDER, CHARD.

Ihringen Bad r w ★–★★★ 93 **96** 97 99 00 **01** 02 03 04 05 06 07 Justly celebrated village of the KAISERSTUHL, BADEN. Proud of its SPÄTBURGUNDER red, WEISSHERBST, and GRAUBURGUNDER. Top growers: Dr. HEGER, Konstanzer, Pix, Stigler.

Immich-Batterieberg, Weingut ★★ This ENKIRCH estate, grown on 7.5 ha of dynamite-blasted slate slopes, produces gd, sometimes excellent, RIES in varying styles.

Ingelheim Rhh r w ★→★★ **93 97** 98 **99 01** 02 **03 04 05** 06 **07** Town opposite RHEINGAU historically known for its SPÄTBURGUNDER. Few wines today live up to reputation.

Iphofen Frank w ★★→★★★ **93 97** 98 99 **00 01** 02 03 **04 05** 06 **07** Village nr WÜRZBURG renowned for RIES, SILVANER, RIESLANER. First Class v'yds: Julius-Echter-Berg, Kalb. Growers: JULIUSSPITAL, RUCK, WIRSCHING, Zehntkeller.

Jahrgang Year – as in "vintage".

Johannisberg Rhg w ★★→★★★★ **89 90 93 95** 96 **97** 98 **99** 00 01 02 03 **04 05** 06 **07** A classic RHEINGAU village with superlative long-lived RIES. First Class v'yds: Hölle, Klaus, SCHLOSS JOHANNISBERG. GROSSLAGE: Erntebringer. Top growers: JOHANNISHOF, SCHLOSS JOHANNISBERG, HESSEN, Trenz.

Johannishof ★★★ JOHANNISBERG family estate RIES that are often the best from the great Johannisberg v'yds. Excellent RÜDESHEIM wines too.

Johner, Karl-Heinz ★★★ 17-ha BADEN estate at Bischoffingen, long specializing in New World-style SPÄTBURGUNDER and oak-aged WEISSBURGUNDER, CHARD, GRAUBURGUNDER.

Josephshof First Class v'yd at GRAACH, the sole property of KESSELSTATT.

Jost, Toni ★★★ Leading estate of the MITTELRHEIN: 9 ha, mainly RIES, in BACHARACH (sharply mineral wines), and also at WALLUF in the RHEINGAU.

Juliusspital ★★★ Ancient WÜRZBURG religious charity with 170 ha of top FRANKEN v'yds. Consistently gd quality. *Look for its dry Silvaners* and RIES and its top white blend called BT.

Kabinett See "Germany's quality levels" box on p.135.

Kaiserstuhl Outstanding BADEN district, with notably warm climate and volcanic soil. Villages include ACHKARREN, Burkheim, IHRINGEN. Renowned for Pinot varieties, white and red, and some surprising RIES and Muscat.

Kallstadt Pfz w (r) ★★→★★★ **93** 94 **96 97 98 99** 00 **01** 02 **03 04 05** 06 07 Some of the best dry RIES of the north MITTELHAARDT comes from superb Saumagen v'yd. Fine AUSLESE too. Growers include Henninger and KOEHLER-RUPRECHT.

Kanzem M-S-R (Saar) w ★★★ **93** 94 **95** 96 **97 99** 01 02 **03 04 05** 06 **07** Small neighbour of WILTINGEN. First Class v'yd: Altenberg. Growers include BISCHÖFLICHE, WEINGÜTER, OTHEGRAVEN, J P Reinert, VEREINIGTE HOSPITIEN.

Karlsmühle ★★★ Small estate with two Lorenzhöfer monopoly sites making classic RUWER RIES; also wines from First Class KASEL v'yds sold under Patheiger label. Consistently excellent quality.

Karthäuserhofberg ★★★★ Outstanding RUWER estate of 19 ha at Eitelsbach. Easily recognized by bottles with only a neck label. Admired if austere TROCKEN wines (made less austere by a run of warm yrs), but magnificent AUSLESEN.

Kasel M-S-R (Ruwer) w ★★→★★★ **90 93** 94 **95 97** 98 **99** 01 02 **03 04 05** 06 07 Stunning flowery RIES. First Class v'yds: Kehrnagel, Nies'chen. Top growers: BEULWITZ, BISCHÖFLICHE, WEINGÜTER, KARLSMÜHLE, KESSELSTATT.

Keller Wine cellar.

Keller, Weingut ★★★★ Deep in unfashionable southern RHEINHESSEN, the Kellers show what can be achieved with scrupulous site selection. Superlative, crystalline GROSSES GEWÄCHS RIES from Dalsheimer Hubacker and 2 other v'yds. Also astonishing TBA.

Kellerei Winery (i.e. a big commercial bottler).

Kerner Modern aromatic grape variety, earlier ripening than RIES. 4,000 ha planted. Acceptable wines that lack the inbuilt grace and harmony of RIES. Best in SACHSEN.

Kerpen, Weingut Heribert ★★ Small gd estate in BERNKASTEL, GRAACH, WEHLEN, specializing in elegant sweeter styles.

Kesseler, Weingut August Rhg ★★★ 21-ha estate making the best SPÄTBURGUNDER reds in ASSMANNSHAUSEN and RUDESHEIM. Also v.gd classic-style RIES.

Kesselstatt, von ★★★ The largest private MOSEL estate, 650 yrs old. Run for two decades by the quality-obsessed Annegret Reh-Gartner. Some 38 ha through MOSEL-SAAR-RUWER producing aromatic, generously fruity MOSELS. *Consistently high quality wines from Josephshof* monopoly v'yd, PIESPORTER Goldtröpfchen, KASEL, and SCHARZHOFBERG.

Kesten M-M w ★→★★★ **93** 94 **95** 96 **97** 98 **99 01** 02 **03 04 05** 06 **07** Neighbour of BRAUNEBERG. Best wines (from Paulinshofberg v'yd) similar. Top growers: Bastgen, Kees-Kieren, PAULINSHOF.

Kiedrich Rhg w ★★→★★★★ **93 95** 96 **97** 98 **99** 00 **01** 02 **03 04 05** 06 **07** Neighbour of RAUENTHAL; equally splendid and high-flavoured. First Class v'yds: Gräfenberg, Wasseros. Growers include HESSEN, KNYPHAUSEN, Speicher-Schuth. WEIL NOW RHEINGAU's top estate for sweet RIES.

Klingelberger ORTENAU (BADEN) term for RIES, esp at DURBACH.

Kloster Eberbach Rhg Glorious 12th-century Cistercian abbey in HATTENHEIM forest. Monks planted STEINBERG, Germany's Clos de Vougeot. Now the label of the STAATSWEINGÜTER with a string of great v'yds in ASSMANNSHAUSEN, RÜDESHEIM, RAUENTHAL, etc. Director Dieter Greiner has injected new life into a previously moribund organization. New winery under construction.

Klüsserath M-M w ★→★★★ **93** 95 **97** 98 **99** 00 **01** 02 03 **04 05** 06 **07** Little-known MOSEL village whose wine-growers joined forces to classify its top site, Brüderschaft. Growers: Kirsten, Regnery.

Knebel, Weingut ★★★ WINNINGEN is the top wine village of the Lower MOSEL and Knebel showed how its sites could produce remarkable RIES in all styles. The founder died tragically in 2004; the estate continues to maintain high quality.

Knipser, Weingut ★★★ Brothers Werner and Volker specialize in barrique-aged SPÄTBURGUNDER and other red from the PFALZ; dry RIES can be exceptional.

Knyphausen, Weingut Freiherr zu Rhg ★→★★★ Noble 22-ha estate on former Cistercian land in ERBACH, HATTENHEIM, and KIEDRICH. Classic RHEINGAU wines yet lacklustre in recent yrs.

Koehler-Ruprecht ★★★★ **93** 94 **96 97** 98 **99** 00 **01** 02 **03 04 05** 06 **07** Outstanding KALLSTADT grower. Bernd Philippi's winemaking is entirely traditional, delivering v. long-lived dry RIES from Kallstadter Saumagen. Outstanding SPÄTBURGUNDER and striking barrique-aged Pinot varieties under the Philippi label.

Kraichgau Small BADEN region south of Heidelberg. Top growers: Burg Ravensburg, HOENSBROECH.

Krone, Weingut Rhg ★★ The Hotel Krone in ASSMANNSHAUSEN has its own 4-ha estate, producing full-bodied SPÄTBURGUNDER in ev. conceivable style. Best sampled at its own restaurant.

Kröv M-M w ★→★★★ **93 98 99 01** 02 03 04 **05** 06 **07** Popular tourist resort famous for its GROSSLAGE name: Nacktarsch, or "bare bottom". Be v. careful. Best growers: Martin Müllen, Staffelter Hof.

Kruger-Rumpf, Weingut ★★→★★★ Most important estate of MÜNSTER, NAHE, with

---

Remember that vintage information for German wines is given in a different form from the ready/not ready distinction applying to other countries. See the explanation at the bottom of p. 130.

GERMANY

charming RIES and well-crafted SPÄTBURGUNDER. Best enjoyed at the family's inn in MÜNSTER.

Kühn, Weingut Peter Jakob ★★★ Excellent RHEINGAU estate in OESTRICH. Kühn's obsessive v'yd management pays dividends in a full range of classic wines.

Künstler, Franz Rhg ★★★ 25-ha estate in HOCHHEIM run by the uncompromising Gunter Künstler. Produces **superb dry Ries**, esp from First Class Domdechaney, Hölle, and Kirchenstück v'yds; also excellent AUSLESE.

Kuntz, Sybille M-S-R ★★ Successful protagonist of untypical dry MOSEL RIES of AUSLESE strength from LIESER.

Laible, Weingut Andreas ★★★ 7-ha DURBACH estate. Limpid, often crystalline dry RIES from Plauelrain v'yd as well as SCHEUREBE and GEWÜRZ. Consistently rewarding quality.

Landwein See "Germany's quality levels" box on p.135.

Lang, Weingut Hans Rhg ★★ Reliable RIES, both dry and sweet, and other varieties from one of HATTENHEIM'S most versatile growers.

Langwerth von Simmern, Weingut ★★→★★★ Famous ELTVILLE family estate. Top v'yds: Baiken, Mannberg, MARCOBRUNN. After disappointing quality during the 1990s back on form since 01.

Lauer, Weingut Peter ★★ The SAAR village of AYL lacked conscientious growers, until in the early 2000s Florian Lauer began exploring its subtleties with a range of v.gd parcel selections. NB Lauer's hotel.

Leitz, J ★★★ Fine RÜDESHEIM family estate for rich but elegant dry and sweet RIES. Since 1999 Johannes Leitz has gone from strength to strength.

Leiwen M-M W ★★→★★★ **93** 94 95 96 **97** 98 **99** 00 01 02 03 **04 05** 06 07 First Class v'yd: Laurentiuslay. Village between TRITTENHEIM and TRIER. GRANS-FASSIAN, Carl LOEWEN, Rosch, SANKT URBANS-HOF have put these once overlooked v'yds firmly on the map.

Lemberger Red grape variety imported to Germany and Austria in the 18th century, from Hungary, where it is known as Kékfrankos. Blaufränkisch in Austria. Deep-coloured, moderately tannic wines; best from WÜRTTEMBERG.

Liebfrauenstift A 10.5-ha v'yd in city of Worms; origin of Liebfraumilch.

Lieser M-M W ★★ **93 95** 96 **97** 98 **99** 00 **01 02** 03 **04 05** 06 07 Once neglected v'yds between BERNKASTEL and BRAUNEBERG. First Class v'yd: Niederberg-Helden. Top grower: SCHLOSS LIESER.

Lingenfelder, Weingut ★→★★ Commercially astute Grosskarlbach (PFALZ) estate: gd dry and sweet SCHEUREBE, full-bodied RIES, hit-and-miss SPÄTBURGUNDER.

Loewen, Carl ★★→★★★ Enterprising grower of LEIWEN on MOSEL making ravishing AUSLESE from town's First Class Laurentiuslay site, and from Thörnicher Ritsch, a v'yd Loewen rescued from obscurity.

Loosen, Weingut Dr. M-M ★★★★ **93 94 95** 96 **97** 98 **99** 00 **01 02 03 04 05** 06 07 Dynamic 15-ha estate in BERNKASTEL, ERDEN, GRAACH, ÜRZIG, WEHLEN. Deep, intense classic RIES from old vines in some of the MITTELMOSEL'S greatest v'yds. Reliable Dr. L RIES, from bought-in grapes. Also leases WOLF in the PFALZ since 1996. Joint-venture RIES from 1999 Washington State with Château Ste Michelle: TBA style usually more convincing than Eroica (dry).

Lorch Rhg w (r) ★→★★ **90 94** 95 96 97 98 99 00 **01 02** 03 **04 05** 06 07 Extreme west of RHEINGAU. Some fine MITTELRHEIN-like RIES. Best growers: von Kanitz, Kesseler, Ottes.

Löwenstein, Fürst ★★★ Top 30-ha FRANKEN estate. Tangy, savoury SILVANER from historic Homberger Kallmuth, v. dramatic slope. Also owns a large RHEINGAU estate in HALLGARTEN.

Lützkendorf, Weingut ★→★★ Leading SAALE-UNSTRUT estate, producing a wide range of varietals.

Maindreieck (Bereich) District name for central FRANKEN, inc WÜRZBURG.

Marcobrunn Historic RHEINGAU v'yd; one of Germany's v. best. See ERBACH.

Markgräflerland (Bereich) District south of Freiburg, BADEN. Typical GUTEDEL wine can be refreshing when drunk v. young, but best wines are the BURGUNDERS: red and white. Also SEKT.

Maximin Grünhaus M-S-R (Ruwer) w ★★★★ **88 89 90 93** 94 **95** 96 **97** 98 99 **01** 02 **03 04 05** 06 07 Supreme RUWER estate of 31 ha at Mertesdorf. Wines, dry and sweet, that are miracles of delicacy, subtlety and longevity. Greatest wines come from Abtsberg v'yd, but Herrenberg can be almost as fine, and if warmer summers continue, might end up as gd or better.

Meyer-Näkel, Weingut ★★★★ AHR estate; 15 ha. Fine SPÄTBURGUNDERS in Dernau, Walporzheim, and Bad Neuenahr exemplify modern oak-aged German reds. Werner Näkel is also making wine at joint ventures in Portugal and S Africa.

Crossings

Ever since MÜLLER-THURGAU was created in 1883 by crossing RIESLING with Gutedel (Chasselas), German growers have been besotted by grape crossings. In a climate where ripening is tricky and disease often rampant, this is understandable. Indeed, 14,000 ha of MÜLLER-THURGAU remain in production.

The quest for new crossings has switched to red varieties, and over the past decade the research institute at Weinsberg in WÜRTTEMBERG has released a whole range. By crossing FRÜHBURGUNDER with TROLLINGER, it created Helfensteiner, by crossing that with Heroldrebe, it created the successful DORNFELDER. Crossing LEMBERGER and Cabernet Sauvignon has given both Cabernet Cubin and Cabernet Mitos, and there are at least three other Cabernet crossings in the Weinsberg portfolio. Perhaps a couple of hundred ha of these disease-resistant new varieties are in production. Given the brief vogue for and then rapid decline of white crossings such as Ortega, Albalonga, and Sieggerrebe, one wonders why so much time and money are being invested in proliferating red-grape crossings rather than adapting sites to appropriate existing varieties.

Mittelhaardt The north central and best part of the PFALZ, inc DEIDESHEIM, FORST, RUPPERTSBERG, WACHENHEIM, largely planted with RIES.

Mittelmosel M-M The central and best part of the MOSEL, inc BERNKASTEL, PIESPORT, WEHLEN, etc. Its top sites are (or should be) entirely RIES.

Mittelrhein Northern and dramatically scenic Rhine area popular with tourists. BACHARACH and BOPPARD are the most important villages of this 465-ha region. Delicate yet steely RIES, underrated and underpriced.

Molitor, Markus M-M ★★★ With 38 ha of outstanding v'yds throughout the MOSEL and SAAR, Molitor has since 1995 become a major player in the region. Magisterial sweet RIES, and acclaimed if earthy SPÄTBURGUNDER.

Mönchhof, Weingut M-M ★★ From an exquisite manor house in ÜRZIG, Robert Eymael makes fruity, stylish RIES from ÜRZIG and ERDEN. ERDENER Prälat usually the best wine. Also leases J.J. CHRISTOFFEL estate.

Morio-Muskat Stridently aromatic grape variety now on the decline. 600 ha remain.

Mosbacher, Weingut Pfz ★★★ Fine 15-ha estate for some of best GROSSES GEWÄCHS RIES of FORST. A property going from strength to strength. Decent Sauv Bl.

Moselland, Winzergenossenschaft Huge MOSEL-SAAR-RUWER co-op, at BERNKASTEL, inc Saar-Winzerverein at WILTINGEN, and, since 2000, a major NAHE co-op too. Its 3,290 members, with a collective 2,400 ha, produce 25% of MOSEL-SAAR-RUWER wines (inc classic-method SEKT). Little is above average.

Mosel-Saar-Ruwer M-S-R 9,080-ha region between TRIER and Koblenz; includes MITTELMOSEL, RUWER, and SAAR. 58% RIES. From 2007 wines from the three regions can be labelled only as Mosel.

Müller-Catoir, Weingut Pfz ★★★→★★★★ 90 93 94 96 97 98 99 01 02 03 04 05 06 07 Since the 70s, this outstanding NEUSTADT estate has bucked conventional wisdom, focusing on non-interventionist winemaking. Resulting wines are v. aromatic and powerful (GEWURZ, GRAUBURGUNDER, MUSKATELLER, RIES, RIESLANER, SCHEUREBE, WEISSBURGUNDER), with impressive dry and sweet.

Müller-Thurgau Fruity, early ripening, usually low-acid grape; most common in PFALZ, RHEINHESSEN, NAHE, BADEN, and FRANKEN; was 21% of German v'yds in 1998, but 14% today. Should have been banned from all top v'yds.

Münster Nahe w ★→★★★ 93 94 96 97 98 99 00 01 02 03 04 05 06 07 Best north NAHE village; fine, delicate wines. First Class v'yds: Pittersberg, Dautenpflänzer, Rheinberg. Top growers: GÖTTELMANN, KRUGER-RUMPF.

Muskateller Ancient aromatic white grape with crisp acidity. A rarity in the PFALZ, BADEN, and WÜRTTEMBERG, where it is mostly made dry.

Nackenheim Rhh w ★→★★★★ 93 96 97 98 99 01 02 03 04 05 06 07 NIERSTEIN neighbour also with top Rhine terroir; similar best wines (esp First Class Rothenberg). Top grower: GUNDERLOCH, Kühling-Gillot.

Nahe Na Tributary of the Rhine and a high-quality wine region with 4,120 ha. Balanced, fresh, clean, but full-bodied, even minerally wines; RIES best. EISWEIN a growing speciality.

Neckar The river with many of WÜRTTEMBERG'S finest v'yds, mainly between Stuttgart and HEILBRONN.

Neipperg, Graf von ★★→★★★ Noble estate in Schwaigern, WÜRTTEMBERG: elegant dry RIES and robust LEMBERGER. MUSKATELLER up to BEERENAUSLESE quality a speciality. A scion of the family, Count Stephan von Neipperg, makes wine at Ch Canon La Gaffelière in St Emilion.

Neumagen-Dhron M-M w ★★ Fine neighbour of PIESPORT. Top growers: Adam, Eifel, Heinz Schmitt.

Neustadt Central town of PFALZ with a famous wine school. Top growers: MÜLLER-CATOIR, Weegmüller.

Niederhausen Nahe w ★★→★★★★ 93 95 96 97 98 99 00 01 02 03 04 05 06 07 Neighbour of SCHLOSSBÖCKELHEIM. Graceful, powerful RIES. First Class v'yds include Hermannsberg, Hermannshöhle. Growers: CRUSIUS, DÖNNHOFF, Gutsverwaltung Niederhausen-Schlossböckelheim, Mathern, J Schneider.

Nierstein Rhh w ★→★★★★ 93 96 97 98 99 01 02 03 04 05 06 07 526 ha. Famous but treacherous village name. Beware GROSSLAGE Gutes Domtal: a supermarket deception now less frequently encountered. Superb First-Class v'yds: Brüdersberg, Glöck, Hipping, Oelberg, Orbel, Pettenthal. Ripe, aromatic, elegant wines, dry and sweet. Try Gehring, Guntrum, HEYL ZU HERRNSHEIM, Kühling-Gillot, ST-ANTONY, SCHNEIDER, Strub.

Nobling White crossing created in 1939: light fresh wine, still and sparkling, in BADEN, esp MARKGRÄFLERLAND. In decline.

Norheim Nahe w ★★→★★★ 93 95 96 97 98 99 00 01 02 03 04 05 06 07 Neighbour of NIEDERHAUSEN. Primarily RIES. First Class v'yds: Dellchen, Kafels, Kirschheck. Growers: CRUSIUS, DÖNNHOFF, Mathern.

Oberemmel M-S-R (Saar) w ★★→★★★ 90 93 94 95 96 97 98 99 00 01 02 03 04 05 06 07 Next village to WILTINGEN. V. fine from First Class v'yd Hütte, etc. Growers: von HÖVEL, Willems-Willems.

Remember that vintage information for German wines is given in a different form from the ready/not ready distinction applying to other countries. See the explanation at the bottom of p. 130.

Obermosel (Bereich) District name for the upper MOSEL above TRIER. Wines from the ELBLING grape, generally uninspiring unless v. young.

Ockfen M-S-R (Saar) w ★★→★★★★ 90 93 94 **95** 96 **97** 98 **99** 00 01 02 **03** 04 05 06 **07** Superb fragrant wines from First Class v'yd: Bockstein. Growers: Dr. Fischer, Weinhof Herrenberg, SANKT URBANS-HOF, WAGNER, ZILLIKEN.

Oechsle Scale for sugar content of grape juice.

Oestrich Rhg w ★★→★★★ **90** 93 **95** 96 **97** 98 **99** 00 01 02 **03** 04 05 06 07 Big village; variable, but some splendid RIES. First Class v'yds: Doosberg, Lenchen. Top growers: August Eser, Peter Jakob KÜHN, Querbach, SPREITZER, WEGELER.

Offene weine "Wines by the glass", the way to order it in wine villages.

Oppenheim Rhh w ★→★★★★ **93** 96 97 98 99 01 02 03 04 **05** 06 07 Town south of NIERSTEIN; spectacular 13th-century church. First Class Kreuz and Sackträger. Growers include: Heyden, Kühling-Gillot. None of these, though, is realizing the full potential of these sites.

Ortenau (Bereich) District just south of Baden-Baden. Gd KLINGELBERGER (RIES), SPÄTBURGUNDER, and RULÄNDER. Top village: DURBACH.

Ortsteil Independent part of a community allowed to use its estate v'yd name without the village name – e.g. SCHLOSS JOHANNISBERG, STEINBERG.

Othegraven, Weingut von ★★→★★★ Until the late 90s, this KANZEM, SAAR estate was mediocre. In 1999 Dr Heidi Kegel inherited the estate, with its superb Altenberg v'yds, and has restored its reputation.

Palatinate English for PFALZ.

Paulinshof, Weingut M-M ★★ 8-ha estate, once monastic, in KESTEN and BRAUNEBERG. Unusually for the MITTELMOSEL, the Jüngling family specializes in TROCKEN and HALBTROCKEN wines, as well as fine AUSLESEN.

Pauly-Bergweiler, Dr. ★★★ Fine BERNKASTEL estate. V'yds there and in WEHLEN, but wines sold under the Peter Nicolay label from ÜRZIG and ERDEN are usually best. EISWEIN and TBA can be sensational.

Perlwein Semi-sparkling wine.

Pfalz Pfz Usually balmy 23,400-ha v'yd region south of RHEINHESSEN. The MITTELHAARDT area is the source of full-bodied, often dry RIES. The more southerly SÜDLICHE WEINSTRASSE is better suited to the Pinot varieties, white and red. Biggest RIES area after MOSEL-SAAR-RUWER. Formerly known as the Rheinpfalz.

Pfeffingen, Weingut ★★★ Doris and Jan Eymael make v.gd RIES and sometimes remarkable SCHEUREBE at UNGSTEIN.

Piesport M-M w ★→★★★★★ 90 **93** 94 95 96 **97** 98 **99** 00 01 **02** 03 **04 05** 06 07 Tiny village with famous vine amphitheatre: at best glorious rich, aromatic RIES. Great First Class v'yds: Goldtröpfchen, Domherr. Treppchen far inferior. GROSSLAGE: Michelsberg (mainly MÜLLER-THURGAU; avoid). Esp gd are GRANS-FASSIAN, Joh. Haart, R HAART, KURT HAIN, KESSELSTATT, SANKT URBANS-HOF, Weller-Lehnert.

Portugieser Second-rate red wine grape, mostly grown in RHEINHESSEN and PFALZ, now often used for WEISSHERBST. Almost 5,000 ha in production.

Prädikat Special attributes or qualities. See QMP.

Prinz, Fred Rhg w ★★ 6 ha of some of the best RIES in village of HALLGARTEN.

Prüfungsnummer Official identifying test-number of a quality wine, the AP number (see APNR).

Prüm, J J ★★★★ 75 79 83 85 **86 88 89** 90 94 **95** 96 **97** 98 **99** 00 01 **02 03** 04 05 06 **07** Superlative and legendary 19-ha MOSEL estate in BERNKASTEL, GRAACH, WEHLEN. Delicate but long-lived wines with astonishing finesse, esp in WEHLENER SONNENUHR. Long lees ageing makes the wines hard to taste when young but they reward patience. Gd vintages keep 30 yrs.

Prüm, S A ★★→★★★ **89 90** 94 **95** 96 **97** 98 **99 01 02 03** 04 **05** 06 **07** If WEHLEN neighbour JJ PRÜM is resolutely traditional, Raimond Prüm has dipped his toe into the late 20th century. Sound, if sometimes inconsistent, wines from WEHLEN and GRAACH.

QbA, Qualitätswein bestimmter Anbaugebiete The middle quality of German wine, with sugar added before fermentation (as in French chaptalization), but controlled as to areas, grapes, etc.

QmP, Qualitätswein mit Prädikat Top category, for all wines ripe enough not to need sugaring (KABINETT to TBA).

Randersacker Frank w ★★→★★★ **93 94 97** 98 99 **00 01** 02 03 04 **05** 06 **07** Leading village just south of WÜRZBURG known for distinctive dry wine. First Class v'yds include Pfülben, Sonnenstuhl. Top growers inc: BURGERSPITAL, JULIUSSPITAL, STAATLICHER HOFKELLER, Robert Schmitt, STÖRRLEIN, Trockene Schmitts.

Ratzenberger ★★ Estate making racy dry and off-dry RIES in BACHARACH; best from First Class Posten and Steeger St-Jost v'yds. Gd SEKT, too.

Rauenthal Rhg w ★★★→★★★★★ **93** 94 95 **97 98 99** 00 **01** 02 **03 04 05** 06 **07** Supreme village on inland slopes: spicy, complex wine. First Class v'yds: Baiken, Gehrn, Nonnenberg, Rothenberg, Wülfen. Top growers: BREUER, KLOSTER EBERBACH, LANGWERTH VON SIMMERN.

Rebholz Pfz ★★★→★★★★★ Top SÜDLICHE WEINSTRASSE estate for decades, maintaining extraordinary consistency. Makes some of the best dry MUSKATELLER, GEWÜRZ, CHARD (Burgundian style), and SPÄTBURGUNDER in PFALZ. Outstanding GROSSES GEWÄCHS RIES.

Regent New dark red grape enjoying considerable success in southern wine regions. 2,160 ha are now planted.

Ress, Balthasar ★★ 35-ha RHEINGAU estate based in HATTENHEIM. Also runs SCHLOSS REICHARTSHAUSEN. Commercially astute, with original artists' labels. Quality more reliable now. Gd estate Ries, and basic "Von Unserm" label, red and white, can offer gd value.

Restsüsse Unfermented grape sugar remaining in (or in cheap wines added to) wine to give it sweetness. Can range from 3 grams/litre in a TROCKEN wine to 300 in a TBA.

Loosen opts for miniatures

With the 2006 vintage, Mosel star Ernst Loosen decided to bottle some of his BEERENAUSLESE, of which he had atypically large quantities, in quarter bottles of 187ml. This pioneering move will allow wine-lovers who cannot usually afford to buy this high-priced speciality to sample its exotic glories at a modest price. The only drawback is that the wine is unlikely to age as well as the same wine in larger formats. So drink up.

Rheingau Rhg Best v'yd region of Rhine, west of Wiesbaden. 3,137 ha. Classic, substantial but subtle RIES, yet on the whole recently eclipsed by brilliance elsewhere and hampered by some underperfoming if grand estates. Controversially, one-third of the region is classified since 2000 as ERSTES GEWÄCHS (First Growth), subject to regulations that differ from those created by the VDP for GROSSES GEWÄCHS.

Rheinhessen Vast region (26,230 ha) between Mainz and Worms, bordered by river NAHE to west. Much dross, but includes top RIES from NACKENHEIM, NIERSTEIN, OPPENHEIM, etc. Remarkable spurt in quality in south of region from growers such as KELLER.

To decipher codes, please refer to "Key to symbols" on front flap of jacket, or "How to use this book" on p. 10.

Rheinpfalz See PFALZ.

Richter, Weingut Max Ferd ★★→★★★ Top MITTELMOSEL estate, at Mülheim. *Fine Ries made from First Class v'yds*: BRAUNEBERGER Juffer-SONNENUHR, GRAACHER Domprobst, Mülheim (Helenenkloster), WEHLENER SONNENUHR. Produces superb EISWEIN from Helenenkloster almost every yr. Wines from purchased grapes carry a slightly different label.

Rieslaner Cross between SILVANER and RIES; makes fine AUSLESEN in FRANKEN, where most is grown. Also superb from MÜLLER-CATOIR and KELLER.

Riesling The best German grape: fragrant, fruity, racy, long-lived. Only CHARD can compete as the world's best white grape.

Ruck, Weingut Johann ★★ Reliable and spicy SILVANER and RIESLANER from IPHOFEN in FRANKEN.

Rüdesheim Rhg w ★★→★★★★ 89 90 92 93 95 96 97 98 99 00 01 02 03 04 05 06 07 Rhine resort with First Class v'yds; the 3 best are called Rüdesheimer Berg. Full-bodied wines, fine-flavoured, often remarkable in off yrs. Many of the top RHEINGAU estates own some Rüdesheim v'yds. Best growers: BREUER, JOHANNISHOF, KESSELER, LEITZ, RESS, SCHLOSS SCHÖNBORN, STAATSWEINGÜTER.

Ruländer (Pinot Gris) Now more commonly known as GRAUBURGUNDER.

Ruppertsberg Pfz w ★★→★★★ 94 96 97 98 99 01 02 03 04 05 06 07 Southern village of MITTELHAARDT. Patchy quality but First Class v'yds inc Gaisböhl, Linsenbusch, Nussbein, Reiterpfad. Growers include: BASSERMANN-JORDAN, BIFFAR, BUHL, BÜRKLIN-WOLF, CHRISTMANN, DR DEINHARD.

Ruwer 89 90 94 95 97 98 99 01 02 03 04 05 06 07 Tributary of MOSEL nr TRIER. V. fine, delicate but highly aromatic and remarkably long-lived RIES both sweet and dry. A string of warm summers has helped ripeness. Villages include EITELSBACH, KASEL, Mertesdorf.

Saale-Unstrut 95 97 00 01 02 03 04 05 06 07 Climatically challenging region of 660 ha around confluence of these two rivers at Naumburg, nr Leipzig. The terraced v'yds of WEISSBURGUNDER, SILVANER, GEWÜRZ, RIES, and SPÄTBURGUNDER have Cistercian origins. Quality leaders: Böhme, Gussek, Kloster Pforta, LÜTZKENDORF, Pawis, Thüringer Weingut.

Saar 89 90 93 94 95 96 97 98 99 01 02 03 04 05 06 07 Hill-lined tributary of the MOSEL south of RUWER. Most v'yds located in chilly side valleys. The most brilliant, austere, steely RIES of all. Villages include AYL, KANZEM, OCKFEN, Saarburg, SERRIG, WILTINGEN (SCHARZHOFBERG). Many fine estates here, often at the top of their game.

Sachsen 95 97 98 99 00 01 02 03 04 05 06 07 A region of 411 ha in the Elbe Valley around Dresden and Meissen. MÜLLER-THURGAU still dominates, but WEISSBURGUNDER, GRAUBURGUNDER, TRAMINER, and RIES give dry wines with real character. Best growers: Vincenz Richter, SCHLOSS PROSCHWITZ, Schloss Wackerbarth, Martin Schwarz, Zimmerling.

St-Antony, Weingut ★★ Once excellent Rheinhessen estate, now faltering. But new owner (same as HEYL ZU HERRNSHEIM) seems to be turning things around. At best, rich GROSSES GEWÄCHS RIES from First Class v'yds of NIERSTEIN.

Salm, Prinz zu Owner of SCHLOSS WALLHAUSEN in NAHE and Villa Sachsen in RHEINHESSEN. Until 2006 president of VDP, which implemented the v'yd classification system against some stern opposition.

Salwey, Weingut ★★★ Leading BADEN estate at Oberrotweil, esp for RIES, WEISSBURGUNDER, and RULÄNDER. SPÄTBURGUNDER can be v.gd too, and fruit schnapps are an intriguing sideline.

Samtrot Red WÜRTTEMBERG grape, a mutation of Pinot Meunier. Makes Germany's closest shot at Beaujolais. Gd examples from ALDINGER and DAUTEL.

Sankt Urbans-Hof ★★★ New star based in LEIWEN, PIESPORT, and OCKFEN. Limpid RIES of impeccable purity and raciness from 38 ha.

Sauer, Horst ★★★ ESCHERNDORFER Lump is one of FRANKEN'S top sites, and Sauer is the finest exponent of its SILVANER and RIES. Notable dry wines, and sensational TROCKENBEERENAUSLESEN.

Schaefer, Willi ★★★ The finest grower of GRAACH (but only 3 ha). Classic pure MOSEL RIES.

Schäfer-Fröhlich, Weingut ★★★ Increasingly brilliant RIES, dry and nobly sweet, from this 12-ha estate in Bockenau, NAHE.

Scharzhofberg M-S-R (Saar) w ★★★★ 83 88 89 90 93 94 95 96 97 98 **99** 00 01 02 **03 04 05** 06 07 Superlative SAAR v'yd: austerely beautiful wines, the perfection of RIES, best in AUSLESE. Top estates: BISCHÖFLICHE WEINGÜTER, EGON MÜLLER, VON HÖVEL, VON KESSELSTATT, VAN VOLXEM.

Schaumwein Sparkling wine.

Scheurebe Grapefruit-scented grape of high quality (and RIES parentage), esp used in PFALZ. Excellent for botrytis wine (BEERENAUSLESEN, TROCKENBEERENAUSLESEN). Try LINGENFELDER and PFEFFINGEN.

Schillerwein Light red or rosé QBA; speciality of WÜRTTEMBERG (only).

Schlossböckelheim Nahe w ★★→★★★★ 90 93 95 96 97 **98** 99 00 01 02 03 04 05 06 07 Village with top NAHE v'yds, inc First Class Felsenberg, In den Felsen, Königsfels, Kupfergrube. Firm yet delicate wine that ages well. Top growers: CRUSIUS, DÖNNHOFF, Gutsverwaltung NIEDERHAUSEN-SCHLOSSBÖCKELHEIM, SCHÄFER-FRÖHLICH.

Schloss Johannisberg Rhg w ★★→★★★ 90 94 95 96 97 98 **99** 00 01 02 **03 04 05** 06 07 Famous RHEINGAU estate of 35 ha, 100% RIES, owned by HENKELL. Deservedly popular tourist destination, but more importantly the original Rhine "first growth". Since 1996 there has been a return to form, though there still seems to be an element of complacency. Could still be better. High prices reflect reputation more than quality.

Schloss Lieser ★★★ 9-ha estate owned by Thomas Haag, from Fritz HAAG estate, making pure racy RIES from underrated Niederberg Helden v'yd in LIESER.

Schloss Neuweier ★★★ Leading producer of dry RIES in BADEN, from Mauerberg and Schlossberg v'yds nr Baden-Baden.

Schloss Proschwitz ★★ A resurrected princely estate at Meissen in SACHSEN, which leads former East Germany in quality, *esp with dry Weissburgunder and Grauburgunder*.

Schloss Reichartshausen Rhg 4-ha HATTENHEIM v'yd run by RESS.

Schloss Reinhartshausen Rhg ★★★ Fine estate in ERBACH, HATTENHEIM, KIEDRICH, etc. Originally property of Prussian royal family, now in private hands. Model RHEINGAU RIES. The mansion beside the Rhine is now a luxury hotel. Under new management since 2003, the estate is back on form with excellent 05s.

Schloss Saarstein, Weingut ★→★★★ 90 93 95 97 99 01 02 03 04 05 06 07 Steep but chilly v'yds in SERRIG need warm yrs to succeed but can deliver steely minerally, and long-lived AUSLESE and EISWEIN.

Schloss Schönborn ★★★ Widespread 50-ha RHEINGAU estate with superb sites, based at HATTENHEIM. Full-flavoured wines, variable, but excellent when at their best. The Schönborn family also own a large wine estate in FRANKEN.

Schloss Sommerhausen, Weingut ★★ Ancient FRANKEN estate producing gd dry whites and a dependable range of SEKT.

Schloss Thorn Ancient OBERMOSEL estate; remarkable ELBLING, RIES, and castle.

Schloss Vollrads Rhg w ★★→★★★ 90 94 98 **99** 00 01 02 **03 04 05** 06 07 One of the greatest historic RHEINGAU estates, owned by a bank since the sudden death of owner Erwein Count Matuschka in 1997. Since 1998, quality, under Rowald

Words within entries marked like this *Alter Ego de Palmer* indicate wines especially enjoyed by Hugh Johnson over the past 12 months (mid '07–'08).

Hepp, is much improved, but the estate's full potential has yet to be defined.

Schloss Wallhausen ★→★★ The 12-ha NAHE estate, among Germany's oldest, of Prince SALM. 60% RIES. The prince's duties as president of the VDP growers' association led to some neglect of quality here, but son Constantin aims to change that.

Schnaitmann, Weingut ★★→★★★ Although this new WÜRTTEMBERG star makes gd RIES and Sauv Bl, its reputation rests on a complex range of full-bodied red wines from a range of varieties.

Schneider, Weingut Georg Albrecht ★★ An impeccably run 14-ha estate. Classic off-dry and sweet RIES in NIERSTEIN, the best from Hipping v'yd.

Schoppenwein Café (or bar) wine, i.e. wine by the glass.

Schwarzer Adler, Weingut ★★→★★★ Fritz Keller makes top BADEN dry GRAU-, WEISS-, and SPÄTBURGUNDER on 51 ha at Oberbergen, KAISERSTUHL. Selection "A" signifies the top wines.

Schwarzriesling "Black Riesling" is a contradiction in terms, and this grape, with 2,460 ha, is none other than the Pinot Meunier of northern France. Often grown for SEKT production but, in WÜRTTEMBERG and BADEN, also a light-bodied still red.

Schweigen Pfz w r ★★ **97 98 99 01** 02 **03 04 05** 06 **07** Southern PFALZ village. Best growers: Friedrich Becker, esp for SPÄTBURGUNDER, Bernhart, Julg.

Sekt German sparkling wine, best when the label specifies RIES, WEISSBURGUNDER, or SPÄTBURGUNDER.

Selbach-Oster ★★★ Scrupulous 17-ha ZELTINGEN estate among MITTELMOSEL leaders. Also makes wine from purchased grapes: estate bottlings are best.

Serrig M-S-R (Saar) w ★★→★★★ **90 93 95 97** 99 **01** 02 **03** 04 **05** 06 **07** Village giving steely wines, excellent in sunny yrs. First Class v'yds: Herrenberg, Schloss Saarstein, Würtzberg. Top growers: SCHLOSS SAARSTEIN, Herrenberg (Siemens).

Silvaner Third-most-planted German white grape variety with 5,380 ha and thus 5% of the surface. Best examples in FRANKEN: the closest thing to Chablis in Germany. Worth looking for in RHEINHESSEN and KAISERSTUHL.

Sonnenuhr Sundial. Name of several v'yds, esp First Class sites at WEHLEN and ZELTINGEN.

Spätburgunder (Pinot Noir) The best red wine grape in Germany – especially in BADEN and WÜRTTEMBERG, and increasingly PFALZ – steadily improving quality, but most still underflavoured or over-oaked. The best are convincing (e.g. CHRISTMANN, KLOSTER EBERBACH, STODDEN, etc). KLOSTER EBERBACH claims to have had the grape planted for longer than anyone else in the world: 20 years longer than Burgundy's Domaine de la Romanée-Conti. Cistercians planted both.

Spätlese Late harvest. One better (riper, with more alcohol, more substance and usually more sweetness) than KABINETT. Gd examples age at least 7 yrs, often longer. TROCKEN Spätlesen, often similar in style to GROSSES GEWÄCHS, can be v. fine with food.

Spreitzer, Weingut ★★★ Since 1997, brothers Andreas and Bernd Spreitzer in OESTRICH, RHEINGAU, have been making deliciously racy and consistent RIES.

Staatlicher Hofkeller ★★ The Bavarian STATE DOMAIN. 140 ha of the finest FRANKEN v'yds with spectacular cellars under the great baroque Residenz at WÜRZBURG. Quality sound but rarely exciting.

Staatsweingut (or Staatliche Weinbaudomäne) The state wine estates or domains; the best in the RHEINGAU at KLOSTER EBERBACH. Some have been privatized in recent yrs.

State Domain See STAATSWEINGUT.

Stein, Weingut Am ★★ Although this FRANKEN winery is located within the famous

WÜRZBURGER Stein, most vines lie to the north, in Stetten. Improving RIES, SILVANER, and RIESLANER.

Steinberg Rhg w ★★→★★★ **90 95 96** 97 **99** 00 **01** 02 **03 04 05** 06 07 Famous 32-ha HATTENHEIM walled v'yd, planted by Cistercian monks 700 yrs ago. A monopoly of KLOSTER EBERBACH. Disappointing for years but now one to watch.

Steinwein Wine from WÜRZBURG'S best v'yd, Stein.

Stodden, Weingut Jean ★★★ A new star in the AHR. Burgundy enthusiast Gerhard Stodden crafts richly oaky SPÄTBURGUNDER. First rate since 1999, but v. pricey.

Störrlein, Weingut ★★ Sterling dry SILVANER and RIES from RANDERSACKER in FRANKEN; fine GROSSES GEWÄCHS from Sonnenstuhl v'yd.

Südliche Weinstrasse (Bereich) District name for south PFALZ. Quality has improved tremendously in past 25 yrs. See BERGDOLT, REBHOLZ, SCHWEIGEN, DR. WEHRHEIM.

Tafelwein See "Germany's quality levels" box on p. 135.

Tauberfranken (Bereich) Minor Badisches Frankenland BEREICH of north BADEN: FRANKEN-style wines.

TBA See Trockenbeerenauslese.

Tesch, Weingut ★★ Once an unremarkable estate in Langenlonsheim, NAHE, this has become a fine source of rich, rounded, dry RIES.

Red Riesling

Rote RIESLING is believed to be the forerunner of the white RIESLING we are familiar with today. It has been conserved at viticultural institutes for research purposes, and was recently planted in the HESSISCHE BERGSTRASSE where it produced a crop for the first time in 2007. Further plantings in the more prestigious WINKELER Hasensprung by the Allendorf estate in the RHEINGAU will produce an initial crop in 2008.

Thanisch, Weingut Dr. ★★→★★★ BERNKASTEL estate, inc part of the Doctor v'yd. This famous estate was divided in the 80s, but the two confusingly share the same name: Erben Müller-Burggraef identifies one; Erben Thanisch the other. Similar in quality but the latter sometimes has the edge.

Traben-Trarbach M-M w ★→★★ **93 96** 97 **98 99** 01 02 **03 04 05** 06 07 Substantial but underperforming wine town of 324 ha, 87% of it RIES. Top v'yds: Ungsberg, Würzgarten. Top growers: Martin Müllen, VOLLENWEIDER.

Traisen Nahe w ★★★ **90 93 95 96** 97 **98** 99 00 **01 02 03 04 05** 06 07 Small village inc First Class Bastei and Rotenfels v'yds, capable of making RIES of concentration and class. Top grower: CRUSIUS.

Traminer See GEWÜRZTRAMINER.

Trier M-S-R w ★★→★★★ Great wine city of Roman origin, on MOSEL, between RUWER and SAAR. Big Mosel charitable estates have cellars here among imposing Roman ruins. Growers include Deutschherren-Hof, Terges.

Trittenheim M-M w ★★★ **90 93 95** 96 97 **98 99** 00 **01** 02 **03 04 05** 06 07 Attractive south MITTELMOSEL light wines, much improved in quality over past decade. Top v'yds were Altärchen, Apotheke, but now include second-rate flat land; First Class v'yds are Felsenkopf, Leiterchen. Growers include Ernst Clüsserath, Clüsserath-Weiler, GRANS-FASSIAN, Milz.

Trocken Dry. *Trocken* wines have a maximum 9 g of unfermented sugar per litre. Some wines are austere, others (better) have more body and alcohol. Quality has increased dramatically since the 1980s, when most were tart, even sour. Most dependable in PFALZ and all points south. Mosel Kabinett Trocken is a risk.

Trockenbeerenauslese (TBA) Sweetest, most expensive category of German wine, extremely rare, with concentrated honey flavour. Made from selected shrivelled grapes affected by noble rot (botrytis). See also EDEL.

Trollinger Pale red grape variety of WÜRTTEMBERG; over-cropped but locally v. popular.

Ungstein Pfz w ★★→★★★ **90 93 95 96** 97 **98 99** 00 **01** 02 03 **04 05** 06 **07** MITTELHAARDT village with fine harmonious wines. First Class v'yds include Herrenberg, Weilberg. Top growers include: Darting, Fitz-Ritter, PFEFFINGEN, Karl Schäfer, Egon Schmitt.

Urzig M-M w ★★★★ **90 92 93** 94 95 96 **97** 98 **99** 00 **01** 02 **03 04 05** 06 **07** Village on red sandstone and red slate, famous for firm, full, spicy wine unlike other MOSELS. First Class v'yd: Würzgarten. Growers include Berres, CHRISTOFFEL, LOOSEN, MÖNCHHOF, PAULY-BERGWEILER (Peter Nicolay), WEINS-PRÜM.

Van Volxem, Weingut ★★→★★★ Lacklustre SAAR estate revived by brewery heir Roman Niewodniczanski since 1999. V. low yields from top sites result in ultra-ripe dry RIES. Atypical but impressive.

VdP, Verband Deutscher Prädikats und Qualitätsweingüter The pace-making association of premium growers. Look for its eagle insignia on wine labels. President: Steffen CHRISTMANN.

Vereinigte Hospitien ★★ "United Hospices". Ancient charity at TRIER with large holdings in PIESPORT, SERRIG, TRIER, WILTINGEN, etc. Wines below their wonderful potential, although signs of improvement in 05.

Vollenweider, Weingut ★★★ Daniel Vollenweider from Switzerland has since 2000 revived the Wolfer Goldgrube v'yd nr TRABEN-TRARBACH. Excellent RIES, but v. small quantities.

Wachenheim Pfz w ★★★→★★★★ **94 96** 97 **98 99** 01 02 03 04 05 06 **07** 340 ha, inc exceptional RIES. First Class v'yds: Belz, Gerümpel, Goldbächel, Rechbächel, etc. Top growers: BIFFAR, BÜRKLIN-WOLF, Karl Schäfer, WOLF.

Wagner, Dr. ★★ 9-ha estate with v'yds in Saarburg and OCKFEN. Many fine wines, inc TROCKEN.

Wagner-Stempel, Weingut ★★★ 13-ha estate, 50% RIES, in RHEINHESSEN nr NAHE border in obscure Siefersheim. Recent yrs have provided excellent wines, great in 2005, both GROSSES GEWÄCHS and nobly sweet.

Walluf Rhg w ★★★ **90 92** 96 **97** 98 **99** 00 **01** 02 03 **04 05** 06 **07** Neighbour of ELTVILLE. Underrated wines. First Class v'yd: Walkenberg. Growers include BECKER, JOST.

Wegeler ★★→★★★★ Important family estates in OESTRICH, MITTELHARDT, and BERNKASTEL. The Wegelers owned the merchant house of DEINHARD until 1997. Estate wines remain of high quality.

Wehlen M-M w ★★★→★★★★ **89 90 93 94 95** 96 **97 98 99** 00 **01 02** 03 **04 05** 06 **07** BERNKASTEL neighbour with equally fine, somewhat richer wine. Location of First Class v'yd: SONNENUHR. Top growers are: KERPEN, LOOSEN, M MOLITOR, J J PRÜM, S A PRÜM, RICHTER, Studert-Prüm, SELBACH-OSTER, WEGELER, WEINS-PRÜM.

Wehrheim, Weingut Dr. ★★★ In warm SÜDLICHE WEINSTRASSE Pinot varieties and CHAR as well as RIES ripen fully. Both whites and reds are v. successful here.

Weil, Weingut Robert ★★★ **90 94 96** 97 **98 99** 00 **01 02** 03 **04 05** 06 **07** Outstanding estate in KIEDRICH; owned since 1988 by Suntory of Japan. Superb EISWEIN, TROCKENBEERENAUSLESEN, BEERENAUSLESEN; standard wines also v.gd. Generally accepted to be RHEINGAU's No 1 in sweet wines, with prices to match.

Weingart, Weingut ★★→★★★ Outstanding MITTELRHEIN estate, with 11 ha in BOPPARD. Superb value.

Remember that vintage information for German wines is given in a different form from the ready/not ready distinction applying to other countries. See the explanation at the bottom of p. 130.

Weingut Wine estate.

Weins-Prüm, Dr. ★★★ Classic MITTELMOSEL estate; 4 ha based at WEHLEN. WEHLENER SONNENUHR is usually top wine. Scrupulous winemaking from owner Bert Selbach, who favours a taut, minerally style.

Weinstrasse Wine road: a scenic route through areas of v'yd. Germany has several.

Weissburgunder (Pinot Blanc) Most reliable grape for TROCKEN wines: low acidity, high extract. Also much used for SEKT.

Weissherbst Usually a pale pink wine, QBA or above and occasionally BEERENAUSLESE, made from a single variety, often SPÄTBURGUNDER. Speciality of BADEN, PFALZ, and WÜRTTEMBERG.

Werner, Domdechant ★★ 12-ha family estate on best HOCHHEIM slopes: top wines usually ERSTES GEWÄCHS and AUSLESEN.

Wiltingen M-S-R (Saar) w ★★→★★★★ **90 93 95** 96 **97** 98 **99** 00 01 02 **03 04 05** 06 **07** Heartland of the SAAR. 320 ha. Beautifully subtle, austere wine. Great First Class v'yd is SCHARZHOFBERG (ORTSTEIL); and First Class are Braune Kupp, Gottesfuss, Hölle. Top growers: BISCHÖFLICHE WEINGÜTER, EGON MÜLLER, KESSELSTATT, VAN VOLXEM, etc.

Winkel Rhg w ★★★ **93 94 95** 96 97 98 **99** 00 **01** 02 **03 04 05** 06 07 Village famous for full, fragrant wine. First Class v'yds include Hasensprung, Jesuitengarten, SCHLOSS VOLLRADS, Schlossberg. Growers include Dahn, Hamm, VON HESSEN, SCHLOSS SCHÖNBORN, WEGELER.

Winningen M-S-R w ★★→★★★ Lower MOSEL town nr Koblenz: excellent dry RIES and TBA. First Class v'yds: Röttgen, Uhlen. Top growers: HEYMANN-LÖWENSTEIN, KNEBEL, Richard Richter.

Wintrich M-M w ★★→★★★ **92 93 95 97 98 99** 00 **01** 02 03 **04 05** 06 **07** Smaller neighbour of PIESPORT; similar wines. First Class v'yd: Ohligsberg. Top grower: HAART.

Winzergenossenschaft (WG) A wine-growers' cooperative, often making sound and reasonably priced wine. Referred to in this text as "co-op". V. important in BADEN and WÜRTTEMBERG.

Winzerverein The same as above.

Wirsching, Hans ★★★ Estate in IPHOFEN, FRANKEN. Dry RIES and *Silvaner* have improved greatly in recent vintages. 72 ha in First Class v'yds: Julius-Echter-Berg, Kalb, etc.

Wittmann, Weingut ★★★ Philipp Wittmann since 1999 has propelled this 25-ha organic estate to the top ranks in RHEINHESSEN. Powerful, dry GROSSES GEWÄCHS RIES and magnificent TROCKENBEERENAUSLESEN.

Wöhrwag, Weingut ★★→★★★ Just outside Stuttgart, this 20-ha WÜRTTEMBERG estate produces succulent reds and often brilliant RIES, esp EISWEIN.

Wolf J L ★★→★★★ Estate in WACHENHEIM leased long-term by Ernst LOOSEN of BERNKASTEL. Dry PFALZ RIES with a MOSEL-like finesse. Sound and consistent rather than dazzling.

Wonnegau (Bereich) District name for south RHEINHESSEN.

Württemberg Wurt **93 96 97 99** 00 **01** 02 **03** 04 **05 06** 07 Vast area in the south, little known outside Germany despite some v.gd RIES (esp NECKAR Valley) and steadily improving reds: LEMBERGER, SAMTROT, SPÄTBURGUNDER, TROLLINGER.

Würzburg Frank ★★→★★★★ **93 94 97** 98 99 **00 01** 02 03 **04 05** 06 **07** Great baroque city on the Main, centre of FRANKEN wine: fine, full-bodied, dry RIES and esp SILVANER. First Class v'yds: Abtsleite, Innere Leiste, Stein, Stein-Harfe. See MAINDREIECK. Growers: BÜRGERSPITAL, JULIUSSPITAL, STAATLICHER HOFKELLER, AM STEIN.

Zehnthof, Weingut ★★ Wide-ranging wines, notably SILVANER and Pinot varieties, from Luckert family's 12-ha estate in Sulzfeld, FRANKEN.

Zell M-S-R w ★→★★★ **93 95 97** 98 99 **01** 02 **03 04 05** 06 **07** Best-known lower MOSEL village, esp for awful GROSSLAGE: Schwarze Katz (Black Cat). RIES on steep slate gives aromatic wines. Top growers:S. Fischer, Kallfelz.

Zeltingen M-M w ★★→★★★★ **90 93 95** 96 **97 98 99** 00 **01** 02 **03 04 05** 06 **07** Top but sometimes underrated MOSEL village nr WEHLEN. Lively crisp RIES. First Class v'yd: SONNENUHR. Top growers: Gessinger, Markus MOLITOR, J J PRÜM, Schömann, SELBACH-OSTER.

Ziereisen, Weingut ★★ A full palette from BADEN: dry Pinot whites, lively SPÄTBURGUNDER, and Syrah, and intense TBA. An estate to watch.

Zilliken, Forstmeister Geltz ★★★→★★★★ Former estate of Prussian royal forester with 10 ha at Saarburg and OCKFEN, SAAR. Produces *intensely minerally Ries from Saarburger Rausch*, inc superb AUSLESE and EISWEIN with excellent ageing potential.

Luxembourg

Luxembourg has 1,250 ha of v'yds on limestone soils on the Moselle's left bank. High-yielding Elbling and Rivaner (Müller-Thurgau) have been the dominant varieties, but are in gradual decline; Chardonnay is growing, though primarily for sparkling wine. There are also Riesling, Gewürztraminer, and (usually best) Auxerrois, Pinot Blanc, and Pinot Gris. These give light to medium-bodied (10.5–11.5% alcohol), dry, Alsace-like wines. Perhaps as a result of climatic change, there has been a growth in more full-bodied, richer wines, inc some late-harvested Vendanges Tardives and *vins de paille*. Pinot Noir now accounts for 7% of plantings. The most important producer by far is Les Doms des Vinsmoselle, a grouping of six co-ops. The Domaine et Tradition association, founded in 88, groups seven estates that impose stricter rules on themselves than the regulations demand. The following vintages were all **gd**: 89 90 92 95 97; **outstanding** 97; **average** 98; similar but **softer** 99; **poor** 00 and 06; much **better** 01 and 02; **average** 04; while 03 and 05 are gd for red as well as white wines. Best from: Bastian, Bentz, Cep d'Or, Abi Duhr, Gales, Alice Hartmann, Krier Frères, Krier-WelbesBernard Massard (gd classic method sparkling), Château Pauqué, Schumacher-Knepper, and Sunnen-Hoffmann.

To decipher codes, please refer to "Key to symbols" on the front flap of jacket, or "How to use this book" on p.10.

Spain & Portugal

More heavily shaded areas are the wine-growing regions

The following abbreviations are used in the text:

Alen	Alentejo
Bair	Bairrada
Bul	Bullas
Cos del S	Costers del Segre
El B	El Bierzo
Emp	Empordà-Costa Brava/Ampurdán
Est	Estremadura
La M	La Mancha
Mont-M	Montilla-Moriles
Nav	Navarra
Pen	Penedès
Pri	Priorato/Priorat
Rib del D	Ribera del Duero
Rib del G	Ribera del Guadiana
R Ala	Rioja Alavesa
R Alt	Rioja Alta
RB	Rioja Baja
Set	Setúbal
Som	Somontano
U-R	Utiel-Requena
res	*reserva*

Spain makes life easy for wine-drinkers: it has a national flavour. The range of grape varieties is relatively small, compared to Portugal, and Tempranillo and/or Garnacha find their way into the vast majority of reds. This is good news for consumers seeking rich, velvety wines with plenty of juiciness; but problems can arise when producers in less well-known regions try to make their mark by pumping up the muscle of their wines. Over-oaking can be a problem in Spain; but it's a phase that many up-and-coming regions of the world go through, and it will pass.

Spain may have hogged the limelight for Iberian wines but it should not be complacent. Its much smaller neighbour, Portugal, is winning plenty of plaudits for wines from an increasingly diverse roll call of producers, regions, and grape varieties. Food-friendly and individual, with a freshness to balance their fruit, Portuguese wines have a closer affinity with Italian wines than Spanish. Reds, especially Douro and Alentejo, have the highest profile, but a new wave of whites is revolutionary, offering concentration and depth, in stark contrast to the bite and lightness of the best-known white, Vinho Verde.

Port, sherry and madeira have a separate chapter on p 174.

Spain

Recent vintages of the Spanish classics

Rioja

2007 A long, selective harvest following spring hail and summer mildew. Considered very satisfactory and of good ageing potential.

2006 Biggish harvest of lowest yields since 2001 with a generally favourable weather cycle. Results considered generally positive and expectations good. Wines are lightish but extremely fragrant.

2005 A large, healthy, and plentiful harvest, with exceptionally favourable weather. Rated as exceptional and unprecedented. Wines are full, immediate, and without much complexity.

2004 A large harvest with magnificent quality expectations for those who were selective enough given the tricky weather. Wines are dark, structured and tannic, and many ready to drink.

2003 Biggish harvest of fair quality. The top *cuvées* are sublime; but most have proved short-lived and are already past their prime.

2002 Small harvest of doubtful quality, like a cross between 1999 and 2000. The best are still delicious; the run-of-the-mill have already peaked.

2001 Medium-sized harvest of excellent quality; the best are at their peak or just over.

2000 Huge harvest; wines distinctly bland, with little real flavour or definition.

1999 A difficult harvest; its light but very graceful wines have mainly peaked.

1998 A huge vintage of high quality; its wines are now largely over-mature.

Ribera del Duero

2007 The DO is happy with second best vintage ever (up 20% on 06) which is at odds with the opinions of quality producers, who consider it the most disastrous vintage since 97. All appeared fine until a very damp spring followed by a summer lacking in both heat and sunshine; Sept saw not only frost, but rain and fog, the so grapes had no opportunity to ripen properly. In Oct, locals were predicting a 70% shortfall in harvest and the greatest quality challenge in the region's history; if volume is up, it is purely because of so many new hectares coming on stream.

2006 A dry, mild winter followed by a hot spring; midsummer storms with flash downpours caused widespread oidium; then intense heat in early Sept followed by copious rain and the threat of botrytis. Some picked a whole month early, but the true professionals picked super-selectively and finished a month later. Results will be as polarized as 05.

2005 A bitterly cold winter, followed by sparse rainfall yet high temperatures in May, June, and the run-up to an early harvest (with one major frost in mid-Sept). 30% below expectations, with musts of tremendous aromas and extract, but alcohol levels often too high. Those who picked too early have green, unbalanced wines. Very good only for the true professionals.

2004 A better year than in most regions. Despite extremes of temperature in Sept, good-quality wines and a plentiful harvest.

2003 A cold winter, mild spring, scorching summer, and Oct rains resulted in a tricky harvest. The best wines are of good colour, glycerine, and alcohol, but low in acidity.

2002 Hot weather followed by heavy rain in late summer led to a large harvest. Quality generally very good.

2001 Medium-sized harvest of excellent quality; wines fulfilling their promise.

2000 Very large harvest but ripening was uneven. Some bodegas made spectacular wines; but in general good.

1999 Almost perfect weather and bumper harvest, but rainfall around harvest time resulted in lack of acidity. Very good, but fading.

Navarra

2007 Following a damp spring, mild summer of lowish temperatures and little sunshine, but a dry autumn. Exceptional for early-ripening, high-altitude Merlot and Tempranillo and sheltered sandy and gravel vineyards with good exposure to the sun. At best fantastically aromatic, impeccably balanced fruit which will produce exceptional wines that will age well.

2006 Complicated, given a wet spring, hot summer, mild, damp autumn. V'yds on poor soils, pronounced slopes and good drainage did best resulting in good fruit, but moderate alcohol and concentration. Good for young wines. Only true professionals will produce wines of any ageing potential.

2005 Possibly best ever vintage, with perfect climatic conditions, resulting in wines of immense colour, full flavours, and sweet, powerful tannins.

2004 Low spring and summer temperatures with much rain. Good, intense wines for those who picked late and selectively.

2003 The hot, dry summer was followed by extended torrential rain and outbreaks of botrytis and mildew. As in 02, only the best and most professional producers obtained decent results, so quality is patchy and the best are already mature.

2002 Torrential Aug rains affected the quality of wines from the south of the region; others are excellent but drinking now.

2001 An excellent year, with big, ripe, balanced wines that are still developing.

2000 Very dry year of prolific yields, calling for rigorous selection. Best wines are big and fleshy, and drinking nicely.

1999 Most frost-afflicted vintage of the decade, with soaring grape prices. Wines are well structured and long-ageing. Excellent but now hard to find.

Penedès

2007 A textbook year of optimum weather has led to the vintage being qualified as excellent and considered one of the best in the last 50 years. Down between 5 and 20% after many consecutive dry years.

2006 An average-sized vintage. Gd climatic conditions, despite a burst of heavy mid-Sept rain, healthy and properly developed fruit resulted in very good acidity and alcohol levels. The vintage is officially excellent on all levels.

2005 The hardest drought of the last 50 years reduced yields by 30–40%, but thanks to cold summer nights quality was excellent for reds and whites.

2004 A cold spring and late summer rains delayed the harvest, but sunny days and cold nights in autumn resulted in a memorable year for red wines.

2003 A very dry and long summer, refreshed with rains in Aug, then cool nights and sunny days in Sept, resulted in a great vintage.

2002 A splendid Sept gave wines of good quality.

2001 Apr frosts reduced the yield but warm summer produced very good wines.

2000 Perfect ripening of the grapes gave well-balanced wines. Very good.

1999 Dry summer but abundant harvest. Very good.

Aalto, Bodegas y Viñedos Rib del D r ★★→★★★ 99 00 01 02 03 04 Newish estate with 2 spectacular, lavishly concentrated traditional reds with dense, plummy black fruit, big tannins, liquorice, and oodles of spicy, toasty vanilla oak. Top *cuvée* PS is more than twice the price.

Abadía Retuerta Castilla y León r ★★★ 04 05 06 Famous non-DO/VDT winery on the fringes of RIBERA DEL DUERO making a range of pricey, savoury reds from Tempranillo, Cab Sauv, Merlot, and Syrah. Round, fruity Rivola (04 05); spicier, more austere Selección Especial (04 05); loftier, chocolatey Pure Tempranillo PAGO Negralada (03 04); and elegant, mineral Syrah PAGO la Garduña (04).

Albariño High-quality aromatic white grape of GALICIA, erroneously associated with Ries thanks to monastic influences, and the best-regarded Spanish white variety. See GERARDO MÉNDEZ, PALACIO DE FEFIÑANES, PAZÓ DE BARRANTES, PAZO DE SEÑORANS, RÍAS BAIXAS.

Albet i Noya Pen r w p ★★→★★★ 01 03 04 05 Spain's most famous organic producer continues to make a wide, old-fashioned selection at big prices. Best is Cab/Syrah/Tempranillo/Merlot La Milana (05).

Alella r w (p) dr sw ★★ DYA Small demarcated region north of Barcelona with just 6 wineries; best for fresh, lively whites made from indigenous Pansa Blanca. Best producers PARXET, Alta Alella, Marfil Alella.

Alicante r (w) ★ 01 02 03 04 05 06 DO. Improvements here with more wineries (currently 53). Most wines still excessively Mediterranean so avoid whites in favour of big-flavoured reds made from Monastrell, Syrah, Cab, Garnacha and

Merlot. Petit Verdot and Pinot N also grown. All best DYA as do not age well; sweet Moscatels recommended. Best producers: GUTIÉRREZ DE LA VEGA Enrique Mendoza, Bernabé Navarro, El Sequé, Sierra Salinas.

Alión Rib del D r ★★→★★★★ 99 00 01 02 03 04 VEGA SICILIA'S second BODEGA makes rich, elegant, damson/blackberry 100% Tempranillo aged in Nevers.

Allende, Finca R Ala r ★★★→★★★★★ 04 BRIONES-based Miguel Angel de Gregorio personifies RIOJA'S supposed new wave (big colour, pronounced primary fruits and balance) making since 1995 a series of flavoursome reds which signalled the region might move forward and emulate the success of PRIORATO and RIBERO DEL DUERO. Best-known Allende is still the benchmark but the wild, dark, exuberantly fruity Calvario really excites. The massively priced Aurus is a showy, Parkeresque affair.

Artadi Bodegas y Viñedos R Ala r (w p) ★★★→★★★★★ 02 04 05 Quality-orientated former co-op excellent at serious, pricey levels with a series of pure Tempranillos: layered, oaky, VIÑAS del Gaín; taut, dry, powerful VIÑA El Pisón; spicy, elegant PAGOS Viejos.

Astrales, Bodegas Los Rib del D r ★★★→★★★★ 01 02 03 04 Small exciting estate in Anguix with old-vine Tempranillo vinified 18 months in new oak; first vintage 01. Came into its own with lush, vibrant yet feminine 03, with 04 promising, but significantly lighter.

Bai Gorri, Bodegas R Ala r (w p) ★★★→★★★★ 03 04 Spectacular newish winery producing pricey new-wave RIOJA reds with dark colours, primary black fruits, manageable tannins, and upbeat oak. Best: buzzy CRIANZA (04), lush RESERVA (03), more strident Garage (03), which benefits from major aeration.

Berberana, Bodegas Once a great winery with marvellous old vintages. Now just a brand belonging to BODEGAS UNIDAS.

Bierzo r w ★→★★ 03 04 05 06 Fashionable DO north of Léon finally making something of the indigenous black Mencía and sometimes aromatic white Godello. Top wineries: Bodegas Peique, Bodegas Pittacum, DOMINIO DE TARES. One firm, Descendientes de J Palacios, recently hit headlines with fiercely coloured, French-oaked Mencías – Moncerbal 03, Pétalos del Bierzo 03 and Villa de Corullón 04 – beneath which interesting things may lie.

Binissalem r w ★★ 04 05 Fifteen producers in this tiny but best-known MALLORCA DO. Best: Macía Batle.

Bodega Spanish term for (i) a wineshop; (ii) a concern occupied in the making, blending, and/or shipping of wine; and (iii) a cellar.

Briones Small Riojan hilltop town nr Haro, peppered with underground cellars. Home to FINCA ALLENDE and one of the most comprehensive wine museums in the world, El Museo de la Cultura de Vino.

Bullas ★→★★ 03 04 05 06 Small, high (400-800 m), dry Murcia DO trying hard in an excessively Mediterranean climate. Best current offering Chaveo Monastrell (05).

Calatayud ★→★★ 04 05 06 High, mountainous Aragón DO (one of 4) specializing in dark, broody Garnacha often from old vines, sometimes blended with Syrah. Best producer: Bodegas y Viñedos el Jalón.

Campo de Borja ★→★★★ 04 05 06 07 Aragón DO making excellent DYA modern, juicy Garnachas and Tempranillos. Best for these appealing fruit-driven styles is Bodegas Aragonesas, which also makes an excellent, gd-value old-vine Garnacha Centenaria (06 07). For more complexity, try Tres Picos Garnacha (05) from Bodegas Borsao.

Canary Islands (Islas Canarias) r w p ★→★★ Best known for occasionally stunning dessert Malvasías and Moscatels. Despite many native varieties (white Listán and Marmajuelo, black Negramoll and Vijariego), given climate and shallow volcanic soils it is worth keeping an eye on. Quality still wines are hard to come by. A case of over-zealous handing out of DOS: there are 9!

Cariñena ★→★★★ **01 02 03 04 05 06** Aragón DO that's never quite made it, due perhaps to the lack of either a regional microclimate or significantly varied soil types. Only 2 producers count, albeit with distinctly mixed offerings: San Valero and Grandes Vinos y Viñedos.

Castillo, Casa Jumilla r (w p) ★★→★★★★ **03 05 06** One of the best wineries in JUMILLA, producing immediate, brambly, Parkeresque styles such as spicy Syrah Valtosca (**06**), pre-phylloxera Monastrell Pie Franco (**05**) and Las Gravas (**03**). Enjoy but don't keep.

Casta Diva See GUTIÉRREZ DE LA VEGA.

Castell del Remei Cos del S r w p ★★→★★★ **01 03 05** Picturesque restored 18th-century estate. Best wines: vanilla-tinged, sour-red-cherry-flavoured Gotim Bru (**05**) and marvellous, minerally, long-lasting 1780 (**01 03 04**).

Castilla-La Mancha, Vino de la Tierra In 1999 some 600,000 ha of this vast region were granted VDT status by the EU. Since then dozens of large firms have moved into the area to make wine.

Castillo de Ygay R Alt r w ★★★★ (r) **54 64 70 89 91 94 96 97 98 99 01** Legendary, long-lived top wines from MARQUÉS DE MURRIETA.

Catalunya 03 04 05 06 DO since 2004 covering the whole Catalan area. Confusion arises as this now includes wines from over 200 well-known producers using grapes from outside their own strictly local DO. Constituent wineries include: ALBET I NOYA, Mas Gil, JEAN LÉON, and TORRES. PENEDÈS DO claims that 20% of its production "escapes" into this alternative.

Cava "Mobile" DO (since 1986) covering traditional-method fizz from over 270 producers up and down Spain. Most is produced in or around San Sadurní de Noya in PENEDÈS. The industry is dominated by FREIXENET and CODORNÍU – each with a number of satellite wineries. Quality is often higher, with a price tag to match, from smaller producers such as Castell Sant Antoni, CASTILLO DE PERELADA, GRAMONA, Jané Ventura, JUVÉ & CAMPS, MARQUÉS DE MONISTROL, Mestres, PARXET, Raimat, Recaredo, Signat, and Sumarroca. Cava is best drunk young; local taste often favour those with major bottle age.

Castilla de Perelada, Vinos y Caves del Emp r w p res sp ★★→★★★ **01 03 04** Large range of still wines and CAVA, inc fresh spritzy lemony DYA VDT Blanc Pescador and 3 opulent, old-style, top reds: lush Gran Claustro (**03**), finer, mineral Finca Garbet (**04**), the Ex Ex (Experiencias Excepcionales) series (**04**).

Cérvoles, Celler Cos del S r w ★★→★★★ **03 04 05** High mountainous estate just north of PRIORATO making exuberantly concentrated blackcurranty reds (**04 05**) and powerful, creamy, lemon-tinged barrel-fermented Blanc (**06 07**).

Chacolí País Vasco w (r) ★★ DYA Now split into 3 separate DOS: Alava, Guetaria (the heartland), and Vizcaya. All produce fragrant DYA but often unduly sharp, *pétillant* whites often poured into tumblers from a height in the manner of cider. Only one, the historic Chueca-family-owned Txomin Etxaniz impresses by rounding off the aggression of the primary Hondarrabi Zuri (white) with 15% of low-alcohol Hondarribi Beltza.

Chivite, Bodegas Julián Nav r w (p) dr sw res ★★→★★★★ **03 04 05** Biggest, most historic and best-known NAVARRA BODEGA. Excellent popular, benchmark Gran Feudo range (v.gd Chard; Garnacha; attractive multiblend **04** CRIANZA; and fresh, delicious DYA sweet Moscatel). High spot of pricier Colección 125 is the lush Tempranillo/Merlot **03**.

Cigales r p (w) ★→★★★ Small, high DO north of Valladolid. Once known primarily for dry, forthright rosé, is more interesting for its old Tempranillo v'yds. Two outstanding producers each make a single wine: the lush, voluptuous César Príncipe (**03 04**); and more restrained, old-school Translanzas (**02 03**).

Clos d'Agón See MAS GIL.

SPAIN

Clos Mogador Pri r ★★★→★★★★ 98 00 01 02 03 04 05 René Barbier continues to rank as one of PRIORATO's tops. Simpler, second wine Manyetes (04) is good but Clos Mogador is breathtaking and usually gd for a decade. Also unusual, spicy, fragrant, honeyed, floral Garnacha Blanca/Viognier/Marsanne/ Macabeo/Pinot N Clos Nelin white (05).

Codorníu Pen w sp ★★→★★★ One of the two largest CAVA firms owned by the Raventós family. It has always been at odds with arch-rival FREIXENET for favouring the use of non-indigenous varieties, esp Chard. Best offerings: Jaume de Codorníu, *Anna de Codorníu*, the very dry Non Plus Ultra, and pale, smoky Pinot N. Also owns the formerly dynamic but now lacklustre Raïmat in COSTERS DEL SEGRE, as well as the once great but now slumbering Bilbainas.

Compañía Vinícola del Norte de España (CVNE) R Alt r w dr (p) ★→★★★ Famous RIOJA BODEGA; benchmark 20 yrs ago. Seek out its pre-1970 GRS of light, elegant, high-acid Imperial or fleshier VIÑA Real. See also CONTINO.

Conca de Barberà w (r p) 02 04 05 Small Catalan DO once purely a feeder of quality fruit to large enterprises such as TORRES now has 18 wineries, inc the biodynamic ESCODA-SANAHUJA.

Condado de Haza Rib del D r ★★→★★★ 03 04 Pure, oak-aged Tinto Fino from PESQUERA, Alejandro Fernández's 1988-founded second winery. The almost too easy 03 was followed by a slightly formulaic and voluptuous 04.

Consejo Regulador Organization for the control, promotion, and defence of a DO.

Contino, Viñedos del R Ala r res ★★★ 00 01 03 First single-v'yd of RIOJA (1973) and a subsidiary of CVNE, makes fine long-lasting reds. Gd, balsamic Graciano (04 05), straight RESERVA (02 03) and premium VIÑA del Olivo (04 05).

Costers del Segre S r w p sp ★★→★★★ 94 95 96 01 02 03 04 05 Smallish area around city of Lleida (Lérida) recently strangely subdued. Initially known purely for the modern, fruity wines and vivacious CAVA of CODORNÍU-owned Raimat. With CASTELL DEL REMEI has almost 5,000 ha and 29 producers, inc CÉRVOLES, TOMÁS CUSINÉ and VINYA L'HEREU DE SERÓ.

Criado y embotellado por... Spanish for "Grown and bottled by..."

Crianza Literally "nursing"; the ageing of wine. New or unaged wine is *sin crianza* or JOVEN. Reds labelled *crianza* must be at least 2 yrs old (with 1 yr in oak, in some areas 6 months), and must not be released before the third yr.

Cusiné, Tomás Cos del S r ★★★ 03 04 05 The former motor of CASTELL DEL REMEI and CELLER CÉRVOLES on his own since 2003. Two wines: modern, upbeat Vilosell 05 (Tempranillo/Cab/Merlot/Grenache/Syrah) and oakier, intense Geol (04 05).

DO, Denominación de Origen Official wine region.

DOCa, Denominación de Origen Calificada Classification for wines of the highest quality; so far only RIOJA (since 1991) and PRIORATO (DOQ – the Catalan equivalent – since 2002) benefit.

Empordà-Ampurdán r w p ★→★★ 03 04 05 06 Fashionable demarcated region abutting Pyrenees in northeast Catalonia. Now with 39 wineries. Best are CASTILLO DE PERELADA, Oliver Conti, and Pere Guardiola; though most playful and experimental is Espelt, though with variable results. Stick to reds.

Escoda-Sanahuja Conca de Barbera r ★★★ 03 04 05 Unique, worthwhile producers of biodynamic wines. Uncompromising and hard to find, the 03s and 04s need extensive decanting, the 05s are totally user-friendly. Coll de Sabater (04) is hillside Merlot and Cab Fr; La Llopetera (05) is pure Pinot; and Les Paradetes (04/05) is Sumoll with a little Garnacha and Cariñena.

Enate DO r w p res ★★★ 01 02 03 04 05 06 Best producer in SOMONTANO with excellent DYA Gewurz, splendid barrel-fermented Chard (03), gd if somewhat overpowering Syrah (05), but round, satisfyingly balanced, mature *Cab/Merlot reserva Especial (01)*.

Espumoso Sparkling (but see CAVA).

Finca Farm (See under name – eg ALLENDE, FINCA.)

Freixenet, Cavas Pen w sp ★★→★★★ Huge CAVA firm owned by the Ferrer family. Arch-rival of similarly enormous CODORNÍU; considerably more dynamic albeit less interesting. Best known for frosted black-bottled Cordón Negro and standard Carta Nevada. Fortunes spent on advertising. Dull still wines – Ash Tree Estate – seek to emulate Californian and Australian brand leaders. Also controls Castellblanch, Conde de Caralt, and Segura Viudas.

Galicia Rainy northwest corner of Spain producing some of Spain's best whites (see RÍAS BAIXAS, VALDEORRAS, MONTERREI, and RIBEIRO). Reds also proliferate, often made of the Mencía (and a host of other predominantly local varieties). Can be astringent and are best drunk locally and chilled, or avoided.

Generoso Apéritif or dessert wine rich in alcohol.

Gramona Pen r w dr sw res ★★→★★★ Sizeable family firm making wide range of varietals. Gd DYA Gewurz, savoury Pinot N (06), and quirky sweet Chard/Sauv Gra a Gra Blanco Dulce. Gd CAVA, esp spicy Xarel-lo dominated Celler Batlle.

Gran Reserva (GR) See RESERVA.

Guelbenzu, Bodegas r res ★★→★★★ 01 03 04 05 Historic, ex-NAVARRA DO family enterprise now VDT Ribera del Queiles with estates in Navarra (Cascante) and Aragón (La Lombana) specializing in stylish reds: upfront fruits-of-the-forest Garnacha multiblend Vierlas (06), Tempranillo/Cab/Merlot French-oaked Azul (04 05), intense Graciano-predominant La Lombana (05 06), deep cedary Cab/Merlot Evo (04), and fine elegant super-*cuvée* Lautus (01). Also in Chile.

Gutiérrez de la Vega, Bodegas Alicante r (w) res ★★→★★★ 02 05 06 Small estate founded by opera-loving former general in 1978. Expanding range all branded CASTA DIVA with excellent, fragrant sweet whites made from Moscatel. Best are Cosecha Miel and Monte Diva (05). Other wines less successful.

Hacienda Monasterio, Bodegas Rib del D res ★★→★★★ 03 04 05 Peter Sisseck's involvement since 1990 has resulted in excellent Tinto Fino/ Cab/Merlot blends. Currently a delicious, expressively fruity Tinto 04, approachable CRIANZA 05, and elegantly round, complex RESERVA 03.

Haro Spiritual and historic centre of the RIOJA Alta. Though growing, still infinitely more charming and intimate than commercial capital Logroño; and home to LÓPEZ DE HEREDIA, MUGA, BODEGAS LA RIOJA ALTA, among others.

Inurrieta, Bodega Nav r p w res ★★→★★★ 03 04 05 Hi-tech estate nr Falces. Gd French-oaked Norte Cab/Merlot and attractive US-oaked Sur Garnacha/Syrah as well as lively DYA Mediodía Rosado. Top wine: Altos de Inurrieta (04). Also DYA aromatic Orchídea white and blackcurranty 400 CRIANZA (04).

Jaro, Bodegas y Viñedos del Rib del D r res ★→★★★ 03 04 05 Founded in 2000 by a member of the Osborne (sherry) family. Best: intense, mineral Chafandín (05), seriously expensive, opulent, black-fruit-scented Sed de Caná (04).

Joven (vino) Young unoaked wine. Also see CRIANZA.

Jumilla r (w p) ★→★★★ 02 03 04 05 06 Arid DO in mountains north of Murcia, best known for dark, fragrant Monastrell, often blended. Also gd Tempranillo, Merlot, Cab, Syrah and now Petit Verdot. Wines don't generally age gracefully so drink within 2 or 3 yrs. Many gd producers: Agapito Rico, CASA CASTILLO, Casa de la Ermita, Juan Gil, Luzón, and Valle del Carche.

Juvé & Camps Pen w sp ★★★ 02 03 04 Family firm making top-quality CAVA from free-run juice. RESERVA de la Familia is the stalwart, with top-end GR (03) and Milesimé Chard GR (02).

León, Jean Pen r w res ★★★ 99 02 03 04 Small firm; TORRES-owned since 1995. Gd oaky Chards; expressive Merlot (04); and complex, high-priced super-*cuvée* Zemis (03). Also refreshing v. gd DYA CATALUNYA Terrasola Muscat and big, spicy Terrasola Tempranillo/Monastrell (04).

López de Heredia R Alt r w (p) dr sw res ★★→★★★★ 81 85 87 88 89 95 96 98 99 01 02 Picturesque, old-established family BODEGA in HARO that still ferments everything in wood and oak-ages in old casks; these traditional wines are not for beginners. Graceful, plummy Cubillo (01 02), medium-intense Bosconia (RESERVA 99 and GR 81), and lighter, ripe Tondonia (GR 85) currently best.

Málaga Once-famous DO now all but vanished as producers, obliged to bottle within city limits, were forced out by rocketing real-estate values. One large, super-commercial firm remains – with wide range of styles: Málaga Virgen. TELMO RODRÍGUEZ also has a joint venture here, making clear, subtle, sweet white *Molino Real Moscatel*, mostly sold in the US.

Mallorca Small, pricey producers continue to flourish here. Best: Anima Negra, tiny Sa Vinya de Can Servera, Hereus de Ribas and Son Bordils (both surprisingly VDT). Stick to reds, usually a blend of traditional varieties (Mantonegro, Callet and Fogoneu) plus Cab, Syrah and Merlot. Whites (usually native Prensal plus Chard or Malvasía) less successful.

La Mancha r w ★→★★ 98 99 00 01 02 03 04 05 06 Vast demarcated region north and northeast of VALDEPEÑAS. The area has long been striving to improve its reds, which are mainly Cencibel-based (Tempranillo). Best producers are the relatively small Centro Españolas (with an excellent Tempranillo/Merlot), giant Vinícola de CASTILLA and Vinícola de Tomelloso. Don't expect too much.

Marqués de Cáceres, Bodegas R Alt r p w res ★★★ 00 01 05 Gd, reliable, commercial RIOJAS made by modern French methods.

Marqués de Griñón Dominio de Valdepusa r w ★★★ 02 03 Enterprising nobleman Carlos Falcó, a graduate of Davis in California, is one of Spain's pioneering wine personalities. The first Spaniard to cultivate Syrah and Petit Verdot, introduce drip irrigation and a scientific approach to v'yd management on his estate nr Toledo. His varietals, which also include Cab, are savoury, worthwhile and v. concentrated – try the v. approachable Summa blend first, designed to be enjoyed immediately. Top *cuvée* Emeritus is excellent but v. pricey. Confusingly, the Griñón name also appears on a cheap Rioja from BERBERANA – a leftover from an old distribution deal. See BODEGAS UNIDAS.

> **Old and new Spain**
> Spanish wines inside Spain and Spanish wines outside Spain can be very different. Not necessarily better or worse, just different. Spaniards drink their own wines first and foremost; it has been estimated that less than 0.33 % of all wine consumed nationally was from beyond the border. Spaniards don't particularly like the big, fruit-forward, New World style. While exporters may make these wines for foreign drinkers, many people at home, the older generation, at least, stick to what they're used to: paler, frailer wines of elegance and maturity. New players in Spain tend to aim abroad, or for a small, young market at home.

Marqués de Monistrol, Bodegas Pen p r sp dr sw res ★→★★ Old BODEGA now owned by BODEGAS UNIDAS. Gd reliable CAVA; but once lively modern PENEDÈS reds no longer so lively.

Marqués de Murrieta R Alt r p w res ★★★→★★★★ 98 02 03 Historic BODEGA at Ygay nr Logroño, growing all its own grapes and making intense RESERVA reds. Most famous for its magnificent CASTILLO DE YGAY. Best value is the dense, flavoursome RESERVA with excellent acid balance (01 02); most striking is the intense, modernist premium red Dalmau (03). See also PAZO DE BARRANTES.

Marqués de Riscal R Ala & Rueda r (p) w dr ★★★→★★★★ 01 02 03 Best-known BODEGA in Rioja Alavesa, with striking new hotel and restaurant designed by Frank Gehry of Guggenheim Bilbao fame. Gd light but stylish reds and a splendid, powerful black Barón de Chirel RESERVA (**01 02**) made with some Cab Sauv. Also mature, ripe, pure Tempranillo Selección Gehry (**01**). Also pioneer in RUEDA (since 1972) where makes gd fragrant DYA Sauv Bl and lively Verdejo/Viura blend. Gd VDT 1860 Tempranillo (**05**) too.

Marqués de Vargas, Bodegas R Ala ★★★ **01 02** Relative newcomer (1989) making outstanding, well-balanced old-style wines: a RESERVA (**02**), RESERVA Privada (**01**), and limited-production Hacienda Pradolagar RESERVA Especial.

Mas d'en Gil Pri r ★★★→★★★★ **03 04 05 06** Small estate in Calonge, Gerona, making fresh, spicy, herbal Viognier/Roussanne/Marsanne Clos d'Agón Blanc (**05 06**) and delicious modern, deeply flavoured Cab /Syrah /Merlot /Cab Fr Clos d'Agón Negre (**03** 04 05) as well as lesser seen Clos Valmaña duo.

Mas Martinet Pri r ★★★ →★★★★ 99 00 01 02 03 04 05 Boutique PRIORATO pioneer, producer of excellent Clos Martinet. Second wine Martinet Bru.

Mauro, Bodegas r 01 02 03 04 05 Young BODEGA in Tudela del Duero making gd, round, reliable non-DO/VDT reds. Straight Mauro (**04 05**) now with a touch of Syrah; best is pricey Old-World-meets-New, complex, layered VENDIMIA Seleccionada (**03**) though "top *cuvée*" is actually the awesomely Parkeresque Terreus (03). Sister winery Maurodos, in TORO.

Méndez, Gerardo Rías Baixas ★★★ Tiny family estate making exuberant new-style, minerally, high-acid ALBARIÑO plus a single tank of sought-after Cepas Vellas from 1 ha of old vines with touch of botrytis. Brand name Do Ferreiro.

Miguel Merino, Bodegas R Alt r Enthusiasts' tiny Briones BODEGA with tasty traditional wines, eg, GR 2000.

Monterrei w ★→★★★ DYA Small but growing DO in Ourense, south central GALICIA, making interesting, full-flavoured aromatic whites from Treixadura, Godello, and Doña Blanca. Best is Gargalo.

Montilla-Moriles w sw ★→★★★ Medium sized DO in southern Córdoba once best known for unfortified fino styles but now concentrating on dark, unctuous, often bittersweet dessert wines made from PX (Pedro Ximénez). Until recently TORO ALBALÁ was virtually the only player, but Alvear and Pérez Barquero are now also seriously in the frame.

Montsant r ★→★★★ **03 04 05 06** Small newish DO (since 2001) in an enclave of PRIORATO. Its best wines are big, dense, minerally, and made from the same varieties – but often have an astringent edge, hold their alcohol and age less gracefully because of quite different soils. Pioneering Celler de Capçanes makes the most approachable wines; also try Agrícola Falset-Marçà, Cellers Capafons-Ossó, Celler Masroig and Joan D'Aguera.

Muga, Bodegas R Alt r (w sp) res ★★★→★★★★ 98 00 01 03 04 Family firm in HARO, known for some of RIOJA's most spectacular and balanced reds. Gd barrel-fermented DYA Viura slightly reminiscent of Burgundy; reds finely crafted and highly aromatic. ***Best are wonderfully fragrant GR Prado Enea (98 00)***; warm, full and long-lasting Torre Muga (**00 01 03 04**); expressive and complex Aro (**04**); and dense, rich, structured, full-flavoured Seleccíon Especial (**01 03**).

Navajas, Bodegas R Alt r w res ★★→★★★ 01 03 04 05 Unpretentious family firm in picturesque Navarrete making young, fruity reds and decent, balanced CRIANZAS – in Tinto, Blanco (both **04 05**) and even Rosé (**03 05**).

Navarra r p (w) ★★→★★★ 00 01 02 03 04 05 06 Extensive DO east of RIOJA. Once known for rosé, most of its 122 BODEGAS produce v.gd mid-priced Tempranillo /Cab Sauv blends that are often more lively than those of its more illustrious neighbour RIOJA – despite often higher yields. Unlike RIOJA, no outstanding estates, with possible exception of CHIVITE; much of the region's success is due to the v.gd value of its young, fruity, modern reds. Once primarily made of Garnacha, these are increasingly Merlot but more usually Tempranillo. Best producers: CHIVITE, INURRIETA, Nekeas, Otazu, PAGO de Cirsus, Sarría.

Pago A v'yd or area of limited size giving rise to exceptional wines. The term now has legal status, eg DO Dominio de Valdepusa (see MARQUÉS DE GRIÑÓN).

Pago de Carraovejas Rib del D r res ★★★ 99 01 03 04 05 Founded in 1988, quality still excellent and still unable to satisfy demand. Newest releases: big, round, immediate CRIANZA 05 and stolid 04 RESERVA, unfortunately following sublime, perhaps best ever, 03. Top *cuvée* v.gd Cuesta de las Liebres (03).

Palacio de Fefiñanes Rías Baixas w dr ★★★ DYA Oldest BODEGA of RÍAS BAIXAS – first bottled wines in 1927. Standard *cuvée* remains one of the finest, most delicate pure ALBARIÑOS. Two superior styles: creamy but light-of-touch barrel-fermented version (06) 1583 (the year the winery was founded); and a super-fragrant, pricey, lees-aged, mandarin-orange scented III (04).

Palacios, Alvaro Pri r ★★★★ 01 02 03 04 05 Best known for excessively priced and short-lived L'Ermita, the outstanding Finca Dofí is the one to cellar and Les Terrasses the one to drink. See also PALACIOS REMONDO.

Palacios, Rafael Vald w ★★→★★★ Small estate with old Godello vines in Bibei Valley making 2 distinct styles, both DYA: As Sortes is intense, toasty, with striking citric and white peach elements as well as high acidity; and Louro do Bolo is easier, fresher and peachier. Rafael is ÁLVARO PALACIOS' kid brother.

Palacios Remondo, Bodegas RB w r ★★→★★★ 04 05 Following his phenomenal success in PRIORATO, ÁLVARO PALACIOS has turned his attention to his family winery (founded 1945). Interesting DYA oaked white Plácet with citric, peach and fennel characters; and in red, super-fruity, unoaked La Vendimia (05); organic, smoky, red-fruit-flavoured La Montesa; and big, mulberry-flavoured, Garnacha-dominated Propiedad (both 04 05).

Parxet Alella w p sp ★★→★★★ DYA Small CAVA producer valiantly competing with realtors from Barcelona. Zesty CAVA styles include *cuvée* 21, excellent Brut Nature, fragrant Titiana Pinot N and expensive dessert version *Cuvée* Dessert; best known for refreshing, off-dry Pansa Blanca and still white Marqués de Alella. Concentrated Tionio (03 04) is from outpost in RIBERA DEL DUERO.

Pazo de Barrantes Rías Baixas w ★★★ DYA ALBARIÑO RÍAS BAIXAS; estate owned by MARQUÉS DE MURRIETA. Firm, delicate, exotic, but vintages variable.

Pazo de Señorans Rías Baixas w dr ★★★ DYA Exceptionally fragrant wines from a BODEGA considered a benchmark of the DO by virtue of its finesse.

Penedès r w sp ★→★★★ 98 99 00 01 02 03 04 05 Demarcated region west of Barcelona best known for CAVA and TORRES, has had trouble establishing an identity – light, short-life citric whites and highly oaked reds. Other gd producers include: ALBET I NOYA, Can Ràfols dels Caus, GRAMONA, JEAN LEÓN.

Pérez Pascuas Hermanos Rib del D r res ★★★ 00 01 05 Immaculate family BODEGA founded 1980 and run by 3 brothers. Opulent, approachable VIÑA Pedrosa CRIANZA 05, tighter, more intense Cepa Gavilán 05 and mature but balanced VIÑA Pedrosa GR 00.

Pesquera Rib del D r ★★★ 94 95 04 05 Alejandro Fernández was the creative force behind modern RIBERA DEL DUERO and is still a benchmark. Satisfying CRIANZA 05, tougher 04, and excellent, mature, well-seasoned Janus 05 for those who can afford the price tag. See also CONDADO DE HAZA.

Pingus, Dominio de Rib del D r ★★★ 01 03 04 05 Danish Peter Sisseck's 5-ha estate has since 1995 wowed the few who can afford its tiny productions. Pingus is intense, fresh and opulent with minerally black fruits, fresh herbal overtones, subtle interlaced oak and tannins; second label Flor de Pingus is more floral fruit. Drink earlier.

Plá i Llevant de Mallorca r w dr ★→★★★ 03 04 05 06 11 wineries comprise this tiny DO in MALLORCA. Aromatic but not particularly modern whites and intense, spicy reds. Best: Toni Gelabert, Jaime Mesquida, and Vins Can Majoral.

Priorato/Priorat br r ★★★ 01 03 04 05 DO enclave of Tarragona, once known for

RANCIO and rustic co-op-produced tarry Garnacha/Cariñena reds. The early new wave – CLOS MOGADOR, MAS MARTINET and ÁLVARO PALACIOS – are still the best, producing balanced, minerally reds; with over 70 wineries now, results are often uneven and prices stellar. Other gd producers: Celler Val-Llach, Cims de Porrera, Clos Erasmus, Clos de l'Obac, Mas Perinet, Viñedos de Íthaca.

Remírez de Ganuza, Bodegas Fernando R Ala w dr r res ★★→★★★ 02 03 04 Respected boutique winery making somewhat austere, old-fashioned Tempranillo-based wines.

Remelluri, La Granja R Ala w dr r res ★★★ 99 03 Small mountainous estate making pedigree RIOJA reds from its own 105 ha. Best is the delicate, graceful RESERVA (03), other wines increasingly old-fashioned; though DYA white made from 6 different varieties remains intriguing.

Reserva Gd-quality wine matured for long periods. Red *reservas* must spend at least 1 yr in cask and 2 yrs in bottle; *gran reservas*, 2 yrs in cask and 3 yrs in bottle. Thereafter, many continue to mature for years.

> **Rancio**
> Once Catalan farmers would put their high-alcohol Garnacha Blanca in loosely stoppered barrels, draw off the tasty, slightly oxidized results and top up annually with new wine. One firm – De Muller, from Tarragona – exercised this informal solera system formally, often with spectacular results.

Rías Baixas w ★★→★★★ DYA Best GALICIAN DO originally founded on the ALBARIÑO variety, now embracing 5 sub-zones – the original Val do Salnés, O Rosal, Condado do Tea, Soutomaior and Ribera do Ulla. Four million bottles now exported annually to over 60 markets. Problem: 07 harvest down 40–50%. Current best wineries: Adegas Galegas, As Laxas, Castro Baroña, Coto de Xiabre, Marqués de Vizhoja, GERARDO MÉNDEZ, PALACIO DE FEFIÑANES, PAZO DE BARRANTES, Quinta do Lobelle, Santiago Ruiz, Terras Gauda, La Val, Valdamor and recently nationally acclaimed VIÑA Nora.

Ribeiro w r ★→★★★ DYA GALICIAN DO in western Ourense. Has struggled to cast off its low, co-op-based reputation, now has over 100 wineries and is, after RIOJA, Spain's favourite tipple. Whites are low in alcohol and acidity, fresh and not too modern. Its white varieties – Treixadura, Torrontés, Godello, Loureiro, Lado – have character. It is hoped standards will continue to rise.

Ribera del Duero Rib del D 99 00 01 02 03 04 05 06 Fashionable, still-expanding DO east of Valladolid with almost 250 wineries. Tinto Fino (Tempranillo) holds sway, Some Cab and Merlot also used. A handful of outstanding wineries; also indifferent coat-tailers; a healthy middle ground is emerging. In 2006, the fourth most popular DO in terms of domestic wine sales. Big worry is plans for new motorway right across the middle. Best producers: AALTO, ALIÓN, ASTRALES, CONDADO DE HAZA, HACIENDA MONASTERIO, Jaro, Pago de los Capellanes, PAGO DE CARRAOVEJAS, PÉREZ PASCUAS HERMANOS, PESQUERA, PINGUS, VALBUENA, VEGA SICILIA. See also VDT ABADÍA RETUERTA and MAURO. Others to look for: Balbás, Bohórquez, Dehesa de los Canónigos, O. Fournier, Hermanos Sastre, Tinio (see PARXET), and Vallebueno.

Rioja Alta, Bodegas La R Alt r w (p) dr (sw) res ★★★ 94 95 97 98 99 00 01 Excellent traditional RIOJAS from a historic house definitely not moving with the times. Delicate, mature drinking through a range of styles. Alberdi (00 01) is light and cedary with overtones of tobacco and redcurrants; Arana (98) is similar but with rather more body and depth; Ardanza (99 00) riper, a touch spicier but still v. elegant; the magnificent, tangy, vanilla-edged GR 904 (95 97) and the exceptionally fine, multilayered GR 890 (94 95).

Roda, Bodegas R Alt r ★★★★ **98 99 00 01 02 03 04 05** Newish (1994) BODEGA making much sought-after, fine, intense and long-lasting RESERVA reds from low-yield Tempranillo. On an upward scale of intensity and price: Roda (**03 04**), Roda I (**03 04**) and Cirsión (**05**).

Rueda br w ★★→★★★ DYA Small but ever-growing DO south of Valladolid with Spain's most modern DYA whites, made from indigenous Verdejo, Sauv Bl, Viura and blends thereof. Has been invaded by the big companies, boasts nearly 50 wineries. Prices continue to rise as Verdejo is now fashionable in Spain and barrel-fermented versions are all the rage. Best: Belondrade, MARQUÉS DE RISCAL, Martinsancho, Naia, Ossian, and SITIOS DE BODEGA.

Sandoval, Finca Manchuela ★★★ **02 03 05** Victor de la Serna is back on form with his 05s: his Finca Sandoval (Syrah/Monastrell/Bobal) a wine of impressive balance, dark fruits, soft tannins, herbal notes and gd acid; second wine Salia (Syrah/Garnacha/Bobal) altogether simpler and half the price.

Sitios de Bodega ★★→★★★ Fifth-generation winemaker Ricardo Sanz and siblings left father Antonio Sanz's Palacio de Bornos to set up their own winery in 2005. Excellent DYA RUEDA whites (Con Class and Palacio de Menade). Associated Bodegas Terna, from its base in La Seca, produces interesting, high-quality reds from other regions, inc Spain's first sweet Tempranillo – La Dolce Tita (**04**) VDT.

Somontano ★★→★★★ **02 03 04 05 06** Fashionable cool-climate DO in Pyrenean foothills east of Zaragoza still fails to fulfil expectations. Whites should be more expressive and reds are often over-extracted, over-oaked, without sufficient maturity of fruit or any binding regional character. Opt for Merlot, Gewurz or Chard. Best producers: ENATE, VIÑAS DEL VERO; interesting newcomers include the space-age Bodegas Irius and Bodegas Laus.

Tares, Dominio de El B r w ★★★ **03 04 05** Up-and-coming producer whose dark, spicy purple-scented Bembibre (**04**) and Cepas Viejas (**04**) prove what can be done with Mencía. Sister winery VDT Dominio dos Tares makes a range of wines from the interesting black Prieto Picudo variety: the simple Estay (**05**), more muscular Leione (**05**) and big, spicy Cumal (**04**).

Telmo Rodríguez, Compañía de Vinos r w ★★→★★★ Gifted oenologist Telmo Rodríguez, formerly of REMELLURI, makes and sources a wide range of excellent

---

Rioja

r p w sp ★★→★★★★ **64 70 75 78 81 82 85 89 91 92 94 95 96 98 99 00 01 02 03 04**

Situated in the Ebro Valley, Spain's best-known wine region now consists of 1,200 wineries. Once known for its graceful, long-lived reds, today it is hard to say what is typical. A few, notably LA RIOJA ALTA and LÓPEZ DE HEREDIA, continue to make exceptional, old-fashioned styles; there are the pedigree traditionalists such as CONTINO, MARQUÉS DE MURRIETA, MARQUÉS DE RISCAL, MARQUÉS DE VARGAS, PALACIOS REMONDO, REMELLURI, RODA, and San Vicente; others, like FINCA ALLENDE, ARTADI, MUGA, and the v. new BAI GORRI, are producing more energetic styles. There are also many brands: the vigorous but basic VIÑA Pomal of formerly revered Bilbaínas; dark, often jarring Campo Viejo, the once spectacular CVNE, the smooth reds of Faustino, the eminently quaffable Bordón from Franco Españolas, the ever-reliable MARQUÉS DE CÁCERES; and VALDEMAR. There are lots of small, workmanlike producers who simply make gd wine, such as the very drinkable, sometimes modern Luis Cañas, NAVAJAS, Sierra Cantabria, and Tobía. With sales of Rioja whites decreasing, in 2007 the DO authorized Chard, Sauv Bl and Verdejo.

DO wines from all over Spain inc MÁLAGA (Molina Real Moscatels **03** and **05**), RIOJA (Lanzaga and Matallana), RUEDA (Basa), TORO (Dehesa Gago, Gago, and Pago la Jara), and VALDEORRAS (DYA Gaba do Xil Godello).

Toro r ★→★★★ **03 04 05 06** Increasingly fashionable DO in Zamora province, west of Valladolid. Forty wineries now do their best with the local Tinta de Toro (acclimatized Tempranillo). Most continue to be clumsy, rustic, and over-alcoholic. Two exceptions are Maurodos – with fresh, black-fruit-scented Prima (**06**) and glorious old-vine San Román (**03 04**) as well as VEGA SICILIA-owned Pintia (**05**). Also recommended: Dom Magrez Espagne, PAGO la Jara (**04**) from TELMO RODRÍGUEZ, Quinta de la Quietud, and Sobreño.

Toro Albalá Mont-M ★★→★★★★ Antonio Sánchez is known for his eccentric wine museum and his remarkable old PXs. Labelled Don PX and made from sun-dried grapes, barrique-aged for a minimum of 25 yrs. Black, replete with flavours of molasses, treacle, figs, they age indefinitely. Current vintage is 1979, yet the 1910 released only last yr. Look out for young, unaged amber-coloured DYA Dulce de Pasas (**05 06**), tasting of liquid raisins and apricots.

Torres, Miguel Pen r w p dr s/sw res ★★→★★★★ **01 02 03 04 05** Spain's best-known family firm with historic bases in Chile and California, continues to make some of the best: ever-reliable DYA CATALUNYA Viña Sol and grapey VIÑA Esmeralda and exceptional PENEDÈS Sauv/**Parellada Fransola** (**06**). Best reds include: rich CATALUNYA GranSangre de Toro (**03**), fine PENEDÈS **Cabernet Mas la Plana** (**03**) balanced, old-style RESERVA Real (**02**). Its CONCA de BARBERÀ duo (Milmanda **05** – one of Spain's finest Chards – and **Grans Muralles 02** multiblend) are stunning, and JEAN LEÓN has v.gd offerings too. The range continues to expand with a workmanlike offering from RIBERA DEL DUERO (Celeste **04**), gd PRIORATO (Salmos **05**) and wines now on horizon from RIOJA. Monumental new BODEGA for estate wines 2008.

Unidas, Bodegas Umbrella organization controlling MARQUÉS DE MONISTROL, and the BERBERANA brand, as well as workmanlike RIOJA Marqués de la Concordia and Durius from RIBERA DEL DUERO. Has developed working *haciendas* where wine tourists can stay, eg the Hohenloe estate in Ronda. Controls MARQUÉS DE GRIÑÓN Rioja brand – totally unrelated to Carlos Falcó for some time.

Utiel-Requena U-R r p (w) ★→★★★ Satellite region of VALENCIA attempting to forge its own identity by virtue of excellent Bobal variety but hampered by its size (over 40,000 ha), which has made it primarily a feeder for the industrial requirements of nearby VALENCIA.

Valbuena Rib del D r ★★★★ **99 00 01 02** Made with the same grapes (Tinto Fino, Cab, Merlot, Malbec and a touch of Albillo) as VEGA SICILIA but sold when just 5 yrs old. Best at about 10 yrs; some prefer it to its elder brother. For a more modern take see ALIÓN.

Valdemar, Bodegas R Ala r p w res ★→★★★ **85 99 01 02 03 06** The Martínez-Bujanda family, from their base in Oyón, have been making wines since 1890 and continue to offer a wide choice of reliable RIOJA styles on all levels.

Valdeorras w r ★→★★★ DYA GALICIAN DO in northwestern Ourense fighting off its co-op-inspired image by virtue of its DYA Godello: a highly aromatic and nationally fashionable variety, also grown in nearby BIERZO. Best producers: Adegas A Coroa, RAFAEL PALACIOS, A Tapada and TELMO RODRÍGUEZ.

Valdepeñas La M r (w) ★→★★ **98 99 01 02 04 05** Biggish DO nr Andalucían border. V.gd-value lookalike RIOJA reds, made primarily from Cencibel grape. Young reds often over-extracted and its old RESERVAS just old. One producer shines, Félix Solís: VIÑA Albali brand offers full-flavoured reds at bargain prices.

Valencia r w ★ **00 01 03 04 05** Biggish DO of some 18,000 ha exporting vast quantities (71% of production) of clean and drinkable table wine. Also primary source of sweet, budget, Spanish Moscatel.

SPAIN

Vega Sicilia Rib del D r res ★★★★ 60 62 68 70 81 87 89 90 91 94 95 96 Spain's most famous and historic BODEGA, whose costly, sought-after wines are still matured v. slowly in oak and best at 12–15 yrs. Wines are deep in colour, with aromatic cedarwood nose, intense and complex in flavour, finishing long. Dense, un-vintaged RESERVA Especial can be spectacular but commands mega prices. See also VALBUENA, ALION, Pintia in TORO, and Oremus Tokaji (Hungary).

Vendimia Vintage.

Viña Literally, a v'yd. But wines such as Tondonia (LÓPEZ DE HEREDIA) are not necessarily made only with grapes from the v'yd named.

Viña Meín Ribeiro ★★★ Small estate, in a gradually emerging DO, making two DYA exceptional whites of same name: one in steel and one barrel-fermented; both from some seven local varieties.

Viñas del Vero Som w p r res ★★→★★★ 03 04 05 06 SOMONTANO estate. Gd commercial varietals and best is DYA Gewurz, though Chards improving. mature, toasty Cab/Merlot/Gran Vos Reserva (03) is also worth a look.

Vino común/corriente Ordinary wine.

Vino de la Tierra (VDT) Table wine of superior quality made in a demarcated region without DO. Covering immense geographical possibilities, this category incl many prestigious producers who are non-DO by choice in order to be freer from often inflexible regulation and produce the varieties they want.

Vinos de Pago This category, introduced in 2002, confers special DO status to 4 individualistic estates striving for major quality in the CASTILLA-LA MANCHA region: Dehesa del Carrizal, the admirable Dominio de Valdepusa (see MARQUÉS DE GRIÑÓN), Manuel Manzeneque's Finca Elez, and the Sánchez Militerno family's Pago Guijoso. Only one, Carlos Falcó, really delivers.

Vinya L'Hereu de Seró Cos del S r ★★★ 03 04 05 14-ha estate since 2002 making 2 intensely flavoured wines from Syrah, Cab and Merlot. Richest and most complex with extra maturity is Flor de Grealó (03 04) whereas younger brother Petit Grealó (03 04 05) is considerably tighter.

Vivanco, Dinasti R Alt Major family-run commerical BODEGA at BRIONES with simple juicy wines and an astonishing wine museum. *Vaut le détour*.

Portugal

Recent vintages

2007 Low yields, a cool summer and dry autumn produced aromatic whites and well-balanced reds with round tannins.

2006 Another very warm, dry summer. Expect forward reds with soft, ripe fruit and whites with less acidity than usual.

2005 An extraordinarily dry summer, especially in the south, produced powerful reds; the Douro's finely balanced reds shine.

2004 A cool, wet summer but a glorious Sept and Oct. Well-balanced reds.

2003 Hot summer produced soft, ripe, early-maturing wines, especially in the south. Best Bairrada for a decade.

2002 Challenging vintage with heavy rain during picking. Better in the south.

2001 Large vintage throughout. Those producers who undertook careful selection made very good wines.

Adega A cellar or winery.

Alenquer Est r w ★★→★★★ 02 03' 04 05 06 Sheltered DOC making gd reds just north of Lisbon. Estate wines from PANCAS, QUINTA da Setencostas (see CASA SANTOS LIMA) and MONTE D'OIRO.

Alentejo r (w) ★→★★★ 00' 01 02 03 04' 05 06 07 Expansive, southerly DOC divided into sub-regions with own DOCS: BORBA, REDONDO, REGUENGOS, PORTALEGRE, Evora, Granja-Amareleja, Vidigueira, and Moura. A reliably dry climate makes rich, ripe reds: key international varieties include Syrah and Alicante Bouschet. Antâo Vaz, blended with ARINTO and Roupeiro makes best whites. Established players CARMO, CARTUXA, CORTES DE CIMA, ESPORÃO, Herdade de MOUCHÃO, MOURO, JOÃO RAMOS and Zambujeiro have potency and style. Uber-consultant Luis Duarte impresses despite young vines at Herdades de MALHADINHA and Grous. Best co-ops are at BORBA, REDONDO, and REGUENGOS.

Algarve r w ★→★★ Southern coast DOCS include Lagos, Tavira, Lagoa, and Portimão. Mostly summer quaffers but getting serious with crooner Cliff Richard's Vida Nova and QUINTA do Morgado.

Aliança, Caves Bair r w sp res ★★ →★★★ Large firm with 4 estates in BAIRRADA, inc QUINTA das Bacelada making gd reds and classic-method sparkling. Also interests in BEIRAS (Figueira de Castelo Rodrigo), ALENTEJO (QUINTA da Terrugem), DÃO (QUINTA da Garrida), and the DOURO (QUATRO VENTOS).

Alorna, Quinta de Ribatejo r w ★→★★ DYA Appealingly zippy, ARINTO-driven whites, creamy rosé and gd reds from indigenous and international varieties.

Altano Douro DYA Well-made red from Symington family. Look out for Reserva.

Alvarinho With LOUREIRO, best white grape in VINHO VERDE, making fragrant, attractive wines. Known as ALBARIÑO in neighbouring Galicia.

Ameal, Quinta do w ★★★ DYA One of best VINHOS VERDES. 100% LOUREIRO.

Aragonez Successful red grape (Spain's Tempranillo) in ALENTEJO for varietal wines. See TINTA RORIZ.

Arinto White grape. Best from central and south Portugal have Ries-like citrus acidity – adds zip to blends and produces fragrant, crisp, dry white wines.

Arruda r w ★ DOC in ESTREMADURA with large co-op.

Aveleda, Quinta da w ★→★★ DYA Reliable estate-grown VINHO VERDE made by the Guedes family whose portfolio includes acclaimed brands CASAL GARCÍA (VINHO VERDE), Charamba (DOURO) and smart new Follies (VINHO VERDE and BAIRRADA) with national and international varieties.

Azevedo, Quinta do w ★★ DYA Superior VINHO VERDE from SOGRAPE. 100% LOUREIRO grapes.

Bacalhoa, Quinta da Set r res ★★★ 01 02 03 04 Estate nr SETÚBAL. Its fruity, reliable, mid-weight Cab Sauv/Merlot blend is made by BACALHOA VINHOS. Palácio de Bacalhoa has more Merlot in the blend.

Bacalhoa Vinhos Set Est Alen ★★→★★★ Formerly JP Vinhos. Wide range of modern reds BACALHOA, JP, Serra de Azeitão, TINTO DA ANFORA (ALENTEJO), Só Syrah, JP GARRAFEIRA plus Catarina FERNÃO PIRES/Chard, Cova da Ursa Chard and traditional SETÚBAL Moscatel.

Bairrada r w sp ★→★★★ 97' 98 99 00 01 03' 04 05' 06 DOC in central Portugal. Reputation for astringent reds from challenging Baga grape being laid to rest now law permits different grape varieties. New DOC Bairrada Classico stipulates min 50% Baga. Best Baga wines reward keeping: eg CASA DE SAIMA, LUÍS PATO, Caves SÃO JOÃO will keep for yrs. Most white sparkling; see LUIS PATO.

Barca Velha Douro r res ★★★★ 52 54 58 64 65 66' 78 81 82 85 91' 95' 99 Portugal's most famous red, made in v. limited quantities in the Upper DOURO. Intense, complex red with deep bouquet made by FERREIRA which forged the DOURO's reputation for stellar wines. Now stiff competition from other modern DOURO reds. Second wine known as Reserva Ferreirinha.

Beira Interior ★ Isolated DOC nr Spain's border. Huge potential from old v'yds.

Beiras ★→★★ VINHO REGIONAL covering DÃO, BAIRRADA, and granite mountain ranges of central Portugal.

Borba Alen r ★→★★ ALENTEJO sub-region small DOC; also well-managed co-op making fruity reds inc varietal range.

Branco White.

Brejoeira, Palácio de w ★★ DYA Best-known ALVARINHO from Portugal; facing increasing competition from VINHO VERDE estates around Moncão.

Bright Brothers ★★ DYA Go-ahead Australian-owned label in Portugal; latest innovation Bright Pink aluminium-bottled rosé. Well-made wines from DOURO, RIBATEJO, ESTREMADURA, and BEIRAS. See also FIUZA & BRIGHT.

Buçaco Beiras r w (p) res ★★★★ (r) 53 59 62 63 70 78 82 85 89 92 Legendary speciality of the Palace Hotel at Buçaco, north of Coimbra, not seen elsewhere. *An experience worth the journey.*

Bucelas Est w ★★ DYA Tiny demarcated region north of Lisbon with 3 main producers. QUINTAS da Romeira and da Murta make racy wines (known as "Lisbon Hock" in 19th-century England) from the ARINTO grape.

Cabriz, Quinta de r w ★★→★★★ 03 04 05 Owned by DÃO SUL; fruity and fresh well-priced reds and whites.

Cadaval, Casa Ribatejo r w ★★ 01' 02 03 05' Gd varietal reds esp TRINCADEIRA, Pinot N, Cab Sauv, and Merlot. Great-value Padre Pedro and stunning red Reserva, Marquês de Cadaval.

Campolargo Bair r w 03 04 05 Large estate, until 2004 sold grapes to ALIANÇA. Interesting reds from Baga, Cab Sauv, Petit Verdot, and Pinot N. Early days but B'x varietals promising, esp Diga Petit Verdot.

Carmo, Quinta do Alen r w res ★★→★★★ 99 00' 01 03 04 50-ha ADEGA, part-owned by Rothschilds (Lafite). Fresh white and *polished reds with Cab Sauv* have Bordeaux restraint. Second wine: Dom Martinho.

Cartuxa, Herdade de Alen r w ★★→★★★ (r) 00 01 03 04 05 (w) DYA 200-ha estate nr Evora, rather disappointing in recent vintages. Pera Manca (94 95 97 98 01) big but pricey red. Also Foral de Evora, Cerca Nova, EA.

Carvalhais, Quinta dos Dão r w ★★★ (r) 99 00 01 03 04 05 (w) DYA Excellent single-estate SOGRAPE wine. Gd red varietals (TOURIGA NACIONAL, Alfrocheiro Preto) and white Encruzado.

Casal Branco, Quinta de Ribatejo r w ★★ Large family estate. Gd entry-level Cork Grove blends local CASTELÃO and FERNÃO PIRES with others. Old-vine, local fruit struts pedigree in Falcoaria range, esp Reserva red (01 03 04' 05').

Casal García w ★★ DYA Big-selling off-dry VINHO VERDE, made at AVELEDA.

Casal Mendes w ★ DYA The VINHO VERDE from ALIANÇA.

Castelão Planted throughout south Portugal, esp in TERRAS DO SADO. Nicknamed PERIQUITA. Firm-flavoured, raspberryish reds develop a figgish, tar-like quality.

Chocapalha, Quinta de Est r w ★★→★★★ (r) 03 04 05 (w) DYA Fine modern estate. TOURIGA NACIONAL and TINTA RORIZ underpin rich reds, Cab Sauv is sinewy. New ARINTO-driven unoaked white joins fine oaked Chard/native white blend.

Chryseia Douro r ★★★→★★★★ 01' 03' 04 05' V. successful partnership of Bordeaux's Bruno Prats and the Symington family; dense yet elegant wine from port varieties now sourced from dedicated v'yd, QUINTA de Perdiz. V.gd second wine Post Scriptum (02 04 05').

Churchill Estates Douro r 03 04 05 Gd reds from port shipper Churchill, esp single-estate QUINTA da Gricha.

Colares r w ★★ Small DOC on the sandy coast west of Lisbon. Unique heritage of ungrafted Ramisco vines saved from developers by Fundação Oriente and Stanley Ho charities. Traditional, tannic reds; decent Malvaseía-based whites.

Consumo (vinho) Ordinary (wine).

Cortes de Cima Alen r w ★★★ (r) 01 02 03 04 05 (w) DYA Southerly estate nr Vidigueira owned by Danish family. produces heady, fruit-driven reds from ARAGONEZ, TRINCADEIRA, TOURIGA NACIONAL, Syrah (inc flagship Incognito) and PERIQUITA. Chaminé: second label.

Côtto, Quinta do Douro r w res ★★→★★★★ r **99 00 01** 03 w DYA Pioneer of unfortified wines from port country and now screwcaps; traditional red Grande Escolha (95 00 01).

Crasto, Quinta do Douro r dr sw ★★→★★★★ **00 01 02** 03' 04 05' Excellent lush varietal wines (TOURIGA NACIONAL, TINTA RORIZ) and blends; res and **2 superb single-v'yd wines made only in top vintages** from low-yielding old vines: Vinha da Ponte (98 00' 01 03 04) and María Theresa (00' 03' **05'**) Also Port. Xisto is joint-venture red with Jean-Michel Cazes from Bordeaux.

Dão r w ★★→★★★ 00' 01 02 03' 04 05 Established DOC in central Portugal. Once dominated by co-ops, investment by quality-focused producers large and small has improved consistency and calibre. Established names: SOGRAPE (CARVALHAIS, DUQUE DE VISEU, GRÃO VASCO) and Quintas MAIAS, PELLADA, ROQUES and SAES. Rising stars: DÃO SUL, Casa da Insua and Casa da Mouraz (organic). Structured, elegant reds and substantial, dry whites come into own with food.

Dão Sul Dão r w ★★→★★★★ Dynamic DÃO-based venture. Impressive range with international appeal inc QUINTAS CABRIZ, SANTAR and dos Grilos (DÃO), Sá de Baixo and das Tecedeiras (DOURO), do Encontro (BAIRRADA), do Gradil (ESTREMADURA) and Herdade Monte da Cal (ALENTEJO). Innovative multi-regional Portuguese and cross-border blends: Homenagen (with LUÍS PATO); Four Cs; Dourat (DOURO TOURIGA NACIONAL/Spanish Garnacha) and Pião (DÃO TOURIGA NACIONAL/Italian Nebbiolo).

DFJ Vinhos r w ★→★★ DYA Huge, gd-value range, mostly from RIBATEJO and ESTREMADURA. Premium label Grand'Arte also sourced from the DOURO, Dão and ALENTEJO. Gd fruity, entry-level brands inc Pink Elephant rosé, Segada (r w) Manta Preta (r) and Bela Fonte.

DOC, Denominacão de Origem Controlada Demarcated wine region controlled by a Regional Commission. See also IPR, VINHO REGIONAL.

Doce (vinho) Sweet (wine).

Douro r w ★★→★★★★ 97 00' 01 02 03' 04' 05'06 Famous for port and increasingly sumptuous powerfully built red wines, the best with sinewy, mineral core. Port shipper QUINTA do Noval latest to join trend. New development is surprisingly fine whites with Burgundian depth and complexity. Look for BARCA VELHA, CHRYSEIA, CRASTO, NIEPOORT, VALE DONA MARIA, VALE MEÃO, and young guns, WINE & SOUL and POIERA.

Duas Quintas Douro ★★★ r 01 02 03' 04 05 DYA Gd red from port shipper Ramos Pinto. V.gd Reserva and outstanding but expensive Reserva Especial.

Duque de Viseu Dão ★★ r w (r) 03 04 05 (w) DYA V.gd value red DÃO from SOGRAPE.

Esporão, Herdade do Alen w r ★★→★★★ 01 02 03 04 05 Quality-driven big estate (600 ha). Top brand Monte Velho, Alandra and Vinha da Defesa showcase ALENTEJO's ripe fruit. Quatro Castas, single-varietal range, Esporão Reservas (r w), GARRAFEIRA and new flagship Torre do Esporão offer depth and complexity.

Espumante Sparkling.

Esteva Douro r ★ DYA V. drinkable DOURO red from port firm FERREIRA.

Estremadura ★→★★★ VINHO REGIONAL on west coast. Gd, inexpensive wines from local estates and co-ops; handful of ambitious premium wines: CHOCAPALHA, MONTE D'OIRO. DOCS: ALENQUER, ARRUDA, BUCELAS, CARCAVELOS, COLARES, Encostas d'Aire, Obidos, TORRES VEDRAS.

Falua Rib r w p DYA JOÃO PORTUGAL RAMOS' state-of-the-art venture. Gd entry-level Tagus Creek range of indigenous and international blends, plus more upmarket Tâmara and Conde de Vimioso.

Fernão Pires White grape making aromatic, ripe-flavoured, slightly spicy whites in RIBATEJO. (Known as María Gomes in BAIRRADA.)

Ferreira Douro r ★→★★★★ SOGRAPE-owned port shipper making gd to v.gd DOURO wines under Casa Ferreirinha labels: ESTEVA, Vinha Grande, QUINTA de Leda, Reserva Ferreirinha, and BARCA VELHA.

Fiuza & Bright Ribatejo r w ★★ DYA Joint venture between Peter Bright (BRIGHT BROTHERS) and the Fiuza family. Gd inexpensive Chard, Merlot, Cab Sauv and Portuguese varietals.

Fonseca, José María da Est r w dr sw sp res ★★→★★★ Historic family-owned estate. Oldest producer of SETÚBAL fortified Moscatel, but also ahead-of-their-time brands LANCERS and PERIQUITA. Dynamic sixth generation remains at vanguard: no expense spared winery home to new brands inc Montado, Terras Altas (DÃO), QUINTA de Camarate, Pasmados, Privada Domingos Soares Franco and flagships: FSF, Domini (DOURO) and Hexagon.

Gaivosa, Quinta de Douro r w ★★★→★★★★ 01 03 04 05' Leading estate nr Régua. Characterful, concentrated reds from port grapes inc flagship Abandonado (80+ yr-old vines), QUINTA das Caldas and Vale da Raposa; new white: Alves de Sousa Reserva Pessoal.

Garrafeira Label term: merchant's "private reserve", aged for minimum of 2 yrs in cask and one in bottle, often much longer.

Gatão w ★ DYA Standard Borges & Irmão VINHO VERDE.

Gazela w ★★ DYA Reliable VINHO VERDE made at Barcelos by SOGRAPE.

Generoso Apéritif or dessert wine rich in alcohol.

Grão Vasco Dão r w ★★ DYA Leading DÃO brand from SOGRAPE. *Fine red Garrafeira* fresh young white.

IPR (Indicação de Proveniência Regulamentada) Portugal's second tier of wine regions: Lafões, Biscoitos, Pico, Graciosa. See also DOC.

Lagoalva, Quinta da Ribatejo r w ★★ 02 03 05' Go-ahead RIBATEJO estate; judicious use of Portuguese and international varieties. Second label: Monte da Casta.

Lancers p w sp ★ Semi-sweet (semi-sparkling) rosé, extensively shipped to the US by JOSÉ MARÍA DA FONSECA. Also Lancers ESPUMANTE Brut, a decent sparkler made by a continuous process of Russian invention.

Lavadores de Feitoria Douro r w 15 small quality-conscious estates blending fruit from across the 3 Douro regions. Principal labels: Meruge, Três Bagos.

Loureiro Best VINHO VERDE grape variety after ALVARINHO: crisp, fragrant whites.

Madeira br dr sw ★★→★★★★ Portugal's Atlantic island: makes unfortified reds and whites (Terras Madeirenses VINHO REGIONAL and Madeirense DOC), mostly for the local market; whites from Verdelho on the up. See Madeira section for famous fortified dessert and apéritif wines.

Maias, Quinta das Dão ★★ r 01 03 04 05' w DYA Sister QUINTA of ROQUES. Benchmark Jaen (possibly Spain's Tinta Mencia) and DÃO's only Verdelho.

Malhadinha Nova, Herdade de Alen r w p ★★★ 03' 04 05 Young vines but mature, quality-focused approach: v.gd big spicy reds and rich, oak-aged white from ALENTEJO's deep south.

Mateus Rosé Bair p (w) ★ World's best-selling, medium-dry, lightly carbonated rosé, from SOGRAPE made in BAIRRADA, also now in south of France (Shiraz) and Spain (Tempranillo).

Messias r w ★→★★★ Large BAIRRADA-based firm; interests in DOURO (inc port). Old-school reds best.

Minho River between north Portugal and Spain. Gives name to a VINHO REGIONAL.

Monte d'Oiro, Quinta do Est r w ★★★→★★★★ 01 03 04' José Bento dos Santos' flagships are outstanding Rhône-style Syrah/Viognier reds and Madrigal, Viognier. Gd second wine: Vinha da Nora. Chapoutier (see France) consults on winemaking and biodynamics and is new joint-venture partner for exciting Bento & Chapoutier Ex Aequo Syrah/TOURIGA NACIONAL.

Mouchão, Herdade de Alen r res ★★★ 99 00 01 03' Intense, fragrant wines from this leading traditional estate realize the full potential of the Alicante Bouschet grape. Flagship Tonel 3–4, exceptional yrs only, has fabulous complexity and persistence. Second wine Dom Rafael gd value but variable.

Mouro, Quinta do Alen r ★★★→★★★★ 98 99 00 04' Fabulous old-style reds, mostly ALENTEJO grapes. Dry farmed, low yields, concentrated, supple wines.

Murganheira, Caves ★ Largest producer of ESPUMANTE. Now owns RAPOSEIRA.

Niepoort Douro r w ★★★→★★★★ Family port shipper making exceptional ageworthy DOURO wines in new dedicated gravity-fed winery, inc aromatic Tiara (w), vibrant Vertente (r), elegant Redoma (r w p) 01 03 04 05'; sinewy Batuta (r) 01' 03 04 05' and sumptuous Charme (r) 02 04 05'. Dado is DOURO/DÃO joint venture with Alvaro Castro of PELLADA.

Palmela Terras do Sado r w ★→★★★ Promising DOC: CASTELÃO can be long-lived. Best producers: BACALHOA VINHOS, Cooperativa de Pegões and Casa Ermelinda Freitas (QUINTA da Mimosa and Leo d'Honor).

Pancas, Quinta das Est r w res ★★→★★★★ (r) 00' 01 03 (w) DYA Prestigious estate nr ALENQUER joined ambitious Companhia das Quintas portfolio in 2006. Outstanding red Premium (00' 03) and varietals from ARAGONEZ, TOURIGA NACIONAL, Syrah, Cab Sauv, and CASTELÃO.

Passadouro, Quinta do Douro r V.gd red joined by layered, concentrated Reserve in 2003 (03 04' 05') from single parcel of older vines. Also Port.

Pato, Filipa Bair r w sp sw Daughter of LUÍS PATO; finely-honed wines under eponymous label from BAIRRADA and DÃO. Inc Ensaio, FLP (innovative dessert wine made with father), "3b" fizz and terroir-driven "Lokal" reds.

Pato, Luís Bair r w sp sw ★★→★★★★ 95' 97 99 00 01' 03' 04 05' BAIRRADA'S most skilful exponent of tannic Baga grape: Vinhas Barrio, Pan Barrosa and flagship QUINTA do Ribeirinho Pé Franco (ungrafted vines) are superb single-v'yd Baga. QUINTA do Ribeirinho 1st Choice is a Baga/TOURIGA NACIONAL blend. João Pato is 100% TOURIGA NACIONAL. Shows equal flair with whites (Vinhas Formal and Velhas). Uses BEIRAS classification.

Pegos Claros r 99 00 01 03 Benchmark PALMELA CASTELÃO, foot-trodden and bottle-aged minimum3 yrs before release.

Pellada, Quinta de Dão r w 04 05' Owned with SAES by leading DÃO light Alvaro de Castro. Intense not dense reds. Primus is old-vine, well textured white.

Periquita The nickname for the CASTELÃO grape and successful brand name for JOSÉ MARÍA DA FONSECA CASTELÃO. Periquita Clássico esp gd value (01 04).

Poeira Douro r ★★★★ (02 03' 04' 05) Elegant red from north-facing slopes from Jorge Moreira, QUINTA de la ROSA'S winemaker. New second wine "J".

Ponte de Lima, Cooperativa de r w sp ★ Impressive top tier "Seleccionado" VINHO VERDE inc bone-dry red.

Portal, Quinta do Douro r w p ★→★★★ 01 03 04 05' New plantings and winery reaping dividends at former Sandeman estate; satisfying red wines and port.

Portalegre Alen r w ★→★★★ Northernmost ALENTEJO DOC producing ageworthy, balanced reds at Monte de Penha and go-ahead local co-op.

Quatro Ventos, Quinta dos Douro r 03 04 05 Well-made reds from estate belonging to Caves ALIANÇA; Bordeaux oenologist Pascal Chatonnet consults.

Quinta Estate (see under name, eg PORTAL, QUINTA DO).

Ramos, João Portugal Alen r w DYA Well-made range from Loios and Vila Santa to premium single-varietal range and blends: QUINTA da Viçosa and v.gd flagship Marqués de Borba. Reserva (01 03).

Raposeira Douro w sp ★★ Well-known fizz with native varieties and Chard made by classic method at Lamego.

Real Companhia Velha Douro r w p sw ★★→★★★★ r 00' 01' 02 03 Historic port company with extensive premium table wine v'yds across the DOURO inc Chard, Sauv Bl, Semillon, Cab Sauv. Brands: Evel, Porca de Murça, QUINTA dos Aciprestes, QUINTA de Cidro, Grantom and sweet Granjó from botrytis-affected Sem.

Redondo Alen r w ★ DOC in heart of ALENTEJO with well-managed co-op.

Reguengos Alen r (w) res ★→★★★ Important DOC nr Spanish border. Includes JOSÉ DE SOUSA and ESPORÃO estates, plus large co-op for gd reds.

Ribatejo Rib r w Engine room of gd-value wines from CASTELÃO, TRINCADEIRA and FERNÃO PIRES raising its game with switch to poorer soils and introduction of Portugal's best red varieties, TOURIGA NACIONAL, TINTA RORIZ and international grapes: Cab Sauv, Syrah, Pinot N, Chard, and Sauv Bl. Gd results already at, eg Pinhal da Torre and FALUA. Sub-regions: Almeirim, Cartaxo, Coruche, Chamusca, Tomar, Santarem. Also VINHO REGIONAL Ribatejano.

Roques, Quinta dos Dão r w ★★→★★★ (r) oo o1 o3' o4 V.gd estate for big, solid, oaked reds and white Encruzado. Varietal wines from TOURIGA NATIONAL, TINTA RORIZ, Tinta Cão, and Alfrocheiro Preto. Gd value entry-level Correio label.

Roriz, Quinta de Douro r ★★★ **02 03'** o4 o5' One of the great QUINTAS of the DOURO, now making fine reds (and vintage port). Second wine: Prazo de Roriz.

Rosa, Quinta de la Douro r w p ★★★ oo o3' o4 o5' Firm, rich reds, esp Reserva. QUINTA da Bandeira dedicated to table wine. Douro Tinto v.gd value for money.

Rosado Rosé.

Saes, Quinta de Dão r w ★★★→★★★★ o1 o2 o3 Alvaro Castro's other v'yd (see PELLADA), producing polished reds Pape, Carousel (100% TOURIGA NACIONAL) and Dado – see NIEPOORT.

Saima, Casa de Bair r (w DYA) sp p ★★★ oo o1 **02 03'** o4 o5' Small, traditional estate; big tannic reds (esp GARRAFEIRAS 90' **91** 95' 97' o1) and fresh whites.

Santar, Casa de Dão r ★★★ oo o1 o2 o3 o4 Well-established estate now linked to DÃO SUL making welcome comeback. Structured reds; Burgundian approach paying dividends with Reserva and Condessa whites.

Santos Lima, Casa Est r w p ★★ DYA New-wave family-owned ALENQUER company. Diverse, well-made range reflects extensive v'yds at QUINTAS da Boavista/das Setencostas, de Bons-Ventos, da Espiga, das Amoras, do Vale Perdido, do Espírito Santo and do Figo.

São João, Caves Bair ★★→★★★ r **95** 97 oo o1 o3 w DYA Small, traditional firm for v.gd old-fashioned wines. Reds can age for decades. BAIRRADA: Frei João. DÃO: Porta dos Cavaleiros. Poço do Lobo: well-structured Cab Sauv.

Seco Dry.

Serradayres r ★ DYA Everyday red enjoying something of a comeback, having been taken over by CAVES DOM TEODÓSIO.

Setúbal Set br (r w) sw (dr) ★★★ Tiny demarcated region south of the River Tagus. Fortified dessert wines made predominantly from the Moscatel (Muscat) grape inc rare red Moscatel Roxo. Main producers: José Maria da FONSECA and BACALHOA VINHOS.

Sezim, Casa de w ★★ DYA Beautiful estate making v.gd VINHO VERDE.

Sogrape ★→★★★★ Portugal's largest wine concern, making VINHO VERDE, DÃO, BAIRRADA, ALENTEJO, MATEUS ROSÉ, and owner of FERREIRA, Sandeman Offley port and BARCA VELHA in the DOURO. Brands Pena de Pato and Callabriga offer approachable wines from leading DOCS VINHO VERDE, DOURO, DÃO, ALENTEJO.

Sousa, José de Alen r res ★★→★★★ o1 **03** o4 Small ALENTEJO firm acquired by José María da FONSECA; wines now slightly lighter in style but flagshipMayor is solid, foot-trodden red fermented in clay amphoras and aged in oak.

Teodósio, Caves Dom Ribatejo r w ★→★★ Large producer in the RIBATEJO now making a welcome comeback. Everyday wines under the SERRADAYRES label.

Terras do Sado VINHO REGIONAL covering sandy plains around Sado Estuary.

Tinta Roriz Major port grape (alias Tempranillo) making v.gd DOURO wines. Known as ARAGONEZ in ALENTEJO.

Tinto Red.

Tinto da Anfora Alen r ★★→★★★ 03 **04** 05' Reliable red from BACALHOA VINHOS. Impressively rich Grande Escolha.

Torres Vedras Est r w ★ DOC north of Lisbon, famous for the Duke of Wellington's "lines". Major supplier of bulk wine.

Touriga Nacional Top red grape used for port and DOURO table wines; now increasingly elsewhere, esp DÃO, ALENTEJO, and ESTREMADURA.

Trás-os-Montes DOC with sub-regions Chaves, Valpaços and Planalto Mirandês. Reds and whites from international grape varieties grown in the DOURO. VINHO REGIONAL Transmontano.

Trincadeira V.gd red grape in ALENTEJO for spicy varietal wines.

Tuella Douro r w ★★ DYA Gd-value DOURO red from Cockburn (see Port chapter).

Vale Dona Maria, Quinta do Douro ★★★ r w 01 **02** 03' 04' 05' Cristiano van Zeller's highly regarded QUINTA. *V.gd trio of plush yet elegant reds* inc CV, Casa Casal de Loivos and new VZ. Also gd port.

Vale Meão, Quinta do Douro r ★★★★ **00 01'** 03 04 05' Once the source of BARCA VELHA. Impressively structured wines typified by high percentage of TOURIGA NACIONAL and warm easterly location. V.gd second wine: Meandro.

Vallado ★★★ r w (r) 01 **02 03'** 04 05' (w) DYA Family-owned DOURO estate; v.gd-value sweet fruited varietals and blends, esp Reserve; new, old-vine red raises bar.

Verde Green (see VINHO VERDE).

Vidigueira Alen w r ★→★★★ DOC for traditionally made, unmatured whites and plummy reds from the hottest part of Portugal. Best producer: CORTES DE CIMA. On the up, respected consultant Paulo Laureano's eponymous wines.

Vinho Regional Larger provincial wine region, with same status as French Vin de Pays. They are: ACORES, ALENTEJANO, ALGARVE, BEIRAS, Duriense, ESTREMADURA, MINHO, RIBATEJANO, Terras Madeirenses, TERRAS DO SADO, Transmontano. See also DOC, IPR.

Vinho Verde w r ★→★★★ (w) ★ (r) DOC between river DOURO and north frontier, for "green wines": made from high-acidity grapes. Large brands usually blend with added carbon dioxide. Ready for drinking in spring after harvest. Best have natural spritz and are single QUINTA, single-varietal wines. Look out for wines from Monção made from ALVARINHO (eg QUINTA Soalheiro) and LOUREIRO (eg AMEAL).

Wine & Soul Douro r w (r Pintas) **02** 03' 04' 05' (w Guru) **05** 06' Rich, imposing wines (and port) from husband and wife team Sandra Tavares and Jorge Serôdio Borges, at Quinta do VALE D. MARIA and Quinta do PASSADOURO respectively.

To decipher codes, please refer to "Key to symbols" on the front flap of jacket, or "How to use this book" on p.10.

Port, Sherry, & Madeira

S ome fortified wines are on a roll. Good port, for example. True, the quality of basic ruby and tawny suffers from deep discounting, but late bottled, vintage and age-dated tawnies have never been better, thanks to an artful blend of tradition and science. The Douro is positively upbeat.

It has also never been more accessible. The Douro is a UNESCO World Heritage Site, and home to an increasing number of luxury boutique hotels; after centuries of remoteness it is almost a resort.

In comparison madeira is struggling. Perhaps the answer lies with a talented generation of younger winemakers keen to seduce their peers with wines fresher in style and substance.

Sherry, one has to accept, is in long-term decline. Too many boring medium sherry was made for too long. Nevertheless fine sherries are unique, and there are signs – in restaurants especially – that it is coming back into fashion. Consider their virtues: no wine stimulates the jaded appetite like a cold fino or manzanilla; amontillados and olorosos have a restrained intensity from ageing which few wines can approach; traditional palo cortado has become a cult in the mystery of its origin, halfway between amontillado and oloroso; the sweet wines – from PX and Moscatel grapes – carry an astonishing weight of sweetness from raisined grapes with surprising ease. And sherries are the cheapest fine wines in the world. The only problem is finding them. But be persistent. And make fino a change from champagne.

Recent port vintages

2005 Not an allowed vintage but a single-quinta year. Stars: Niepoort, Taylor de Vargellas, Dow da Senhora da Ribeira – iron fist in velvet glove.

2004 Also a single-quinta year. Stars: Pintas, Taylor Vinha Velha, Quinta de la Rosa – balanced, elegant wines.

2003 Classic vintage year. Hot, dry summer. Powerfully ripe, concentrated wines, universally declared. Drink from 2015/2020.

2001 Another single-quinta year. Stars: Noval Nacional, Fonseca do Panascal, do Vale Meão – wet year; relatively forward wines.

2000 Classic year. A very fine vintage, universally declared. Rich, well-balanced wines for the long term. Drink from 2015.

1999 Single-quinta year. Stars: Vesuvio, Taylor de Terra Feita, do Infantado – smallest vintage for decades; powerful.

1998 Single-quinta year. Stars: Dow da Senhora da Ribeira, Graham dos Malvedos, Cockburn dos Canais – bullish, firm wines.

1997 Classic year. Fine, potentially long-lasting wines with tannic backbone. Most shippers declared. Drink 2012 onwards.

1996 Single-quinta year. Stars: Graham dos Malvedos, Warre da Cavadinha, Taylor de Vargellas – power and finesse.

1994 Classic year. Outstanding vintage with ripe, fleshy fruit disguising underlying structure at the outset. Universal declaration. Drink 2010–2030.

1992 Classic year. Favoured by a few (especially Taylor and Fonseca) over 91. Richer, more concentrated, a better year than 91. Drink 2008–2025.

1991 Classic year. Favoured by most shippers (especially Symingtons with Dow, Graham, and Warre) over 92; classic, firm but a little lean in style. Drink now–2020.

1987 Classic year. Dense wines for drinking over the medium term, but only a handful of shippers declared. Drink now–2015.

1985 Classic year. Universal declaration which looked good at the outset but has thrown up some disappointments in bottle. Now–2020 for the best wines.

1983 Classic year. Powerful wines with sinewy tannins. Most shippers declared. Now–2020.

1982 Classic year. Rather simple, early-maturing wines declared by a few shippers. Drink up.

1980 Classic year. Lovely fruit-driven wines, perfect to drink now and over the next 15 years. Most shippers declared.

1977 Classic year. Big, ripe wines declared by all the major shippers except Cockburn, Martinez, and Noval. Many evolved wines, drink soon.

1975 Classic year. Soft and early maturing. Drink up.

1970 Classic year. Structured, tight-knit wines – the best just reaching their peak. Now–2020+.

1966 Classic year. Wines combine power and elegance. The best rival 1963. Now–2020+.

1963 Classic year. Superb, structured wines, some past their best but others will go on.

Almacenista Stockholder; owner of relatively small bodega who sells sherries to shippers. A few left in JEREZ and EL PUERTO; still important to MANZANILLA production. Wines are often superb quality. LUSTAU started commercial range in 80s and names almacenista suppliers on label.

Alvaro Domecq ★★→★★★ Members of 5 branches of the DOMECQ sherry family purchased the SOLERAS of Pilar Aranda – said to be the oldest bodega in JEREZ – thus re-establishing Domecq as an independent name in sherry. Fine FINO La Janda. V.gd 1730 label wines, inc PALO CORTADO, OLOROSO. Best sherry vinegar to be found.

Alvear Largest producer of v.gd sherry-like apéritif and sweet wines in MONTILLA.

Andresen Family-owned port house *making gd Colheita* (68 82); first to register a white port with an age indication (10-yr-old white).

Barbadillo, Antonio ★★→★★★★ The largest SANLÚCAR firm with a wide range of MANZANILLAS and sherries, inc Muy Fina FINO, Solear MANZANILLA austere Príncipe AMONTILLADO, Obispo Gascon PALO CORTADO, Cuco dry OLOROSO, Eva Cream, and excellent Reliquía line of AMONTILLADO, PALO CORTADO, OLOROSO SECO, and PX. Largest producer of table wines with Castillo de San Diego.

Barbeito Dynamic producer of intense, finely honed madeiras with no added caramel. Pioneers of robotic LAGARE for madeira, Fortnum & Mason Christmas Pudding Madeira, single-cask COLHEITAS and VERDELHO/BUAL blend ("vb"). New classic releases: Boal (78 82 99) and Malvasia 30-yr-old.

Barros Almeida Large port house with several brands (inc Feist, Feuerheerd, KOPKE) owned by Sogevinus: excellent 20-yr-old TAWNY and COLHEITAS (78' 96').

Barros e Sousa Family-owned v. traditional madeira producer. Tiny output of 100% CANTEIRO-aged wines includes rare vintages, gd 10-yr-old and unusual 5-yr-old Listrao blend.

Blandy The best-known name of the MADEIRA WINE COMPANY thanks to popular entry-level 3-yr-old "Duke" range; Duke of Clarence sports sharp new livery. Impressive inventory of aged wines consistently yields fine old vintages (eg BUAL 1920, 1964, and SERCIAL 1966). Recent innovations include COLHEITAS (MALMSEY 1999) Alvada, a moreish blend of BUAL and MALVASIA.

Borges, H M Family company; full range. V.gd 10-yr-olds, stylish COLHEITAS

(VERDELHO & SERCIAL 1995, MALVASIA 1998) and vintages, esp SERCIAL.

Bual (or Boal) One of Madeira's traditional grapes, making tangy, smoky, sweet wines; not as rich as MALMSEY.

Burdon English-founded sherry bodega owned by Caballero. Puerto FINO, Don Luís AMONTILLADO, and raisiny Heavenly CREAM are top lines.

Burmester Small port house owned by Sogevinus. Vintage and single-QUINTA vintage Nova de Nossa Senhora do Carmo. Fine, soft, sweet 20-yr-old TAWNY and COLHEITAS (1963, 1990).

Cálem Established port house. Velhotes is the main brand; gd LBV. Fine reputation for COLHEITAS (90) and v.gd VINTAGE PORTS in 66' and 70'; returning to form (03') . Gd value single-QUINTA wines from Quinta de Foz.

Canteiro Method of naturally cask-ageing the finest madeira in warehouses known as lodges. Creates subtler, more complex wines than ESTUFAGEM.

Churchill 82 85 91 94 97 00 03 Independent, family-owned port shipper founded in 1981. V.gd traditional LBV. Quinta da Gricha is the single-QUINTA port (01 04 05'). Benchmark aged white port.

Cockburn Owned since 2005 by the US Fortune brands, which sold its assets to the SYMINGTON family (see DOW) in 2006. Popular Special Reserve RUBY. Dry house style for VINTAGE PORTS. Vintages: **63** 70 75 83' **91 94** 97 00 03'. Gd single-QUINTA wines from Quinta dos Canais (98 01' 05').

Colheita Vintage-dated port or madeira of a single yr, cask-aged at least 7 yrs for port and 5 yrs for madeira. Bottling date shown on the label.

> **Shhh...**
> Port is one of the most futuristic wines in the world. You want laser-guided bulldozers for cutting vineyard terraces? You want infra-red photography and GPS satellite technology to monitor vineyard vigour and evaluate ripeness? You want robotic "feet" for treading grapes? Just don't tell anyone.

Cossart Gordon Top-quality label of the MADEIRA WINE COMPANY; drier style than BLANDY. Best known for the Good Company brand. Also 5-yr-old reserves, COLHEITAS (SERCIAL 1988, BUAL 1995, MALVASIA 1995), old vintages (1977 Terrantez, 1908, 1958 BUAL).

Crasto, Quinta do Gd single-QUINTA port and LBV; increasingly known for v.gd modern table wines; see Portugal.

Croft One of the oldest firms, shipping VINTAGE PORT since 1678. Now part of the Fladgate Partnership, who reintroduced foot-treading for the much-improved 03 VINTAGE PORT. Vintages: **63' 66 67** 70 75 77 **82 85 91 94** 00 03'. Lighter QUINTA da Roêda. Triple Crown and Distinction: most popular brands. New rosé port (yes, really) should ruffle feathers.

Croft Jerez Founded in 1970; now owned and revjved by GONZÁLEZ-BYASS. Best known for sweet Original Pale CREAM and drier Particular.

Crusted Style of port favoured by the British houses, usually blended from several vintages. Bottled young and then aged so it throws a deposit, or "crust", and needs decanting like VINTAGE PORT.

Delaforce Port shipper, part of the Fladgate. 20-yr-old TAWNY: Curious and Ancient and COLHEITAS (64 **79 88**) are jewels VINTAGE PORTS are improving: 63 66 70' 75 77 **82 85 92' 94** 00 03. Single-QUINTA wines from Quinta da Corte.

Delgado, Zuleta ★★→★★★ Old SANLÚCAR firm, best known for marvellous aged La Goya MANZANILLA PASADA.

Dios Baco ★→★★ Family-owned JEREZ bodega. v.gd Imperial PALO CORTADO and PX.

Domecq ★★→★★★★ Giant sherry bodega in JEREZ owned by international conglomerate Beam Brands but still advised by the supremely knowledgeable

Sherry styles

Manzanilla A pale, dry sherry with characteristics unique enough for its own Denomination of Origin; usually more delicate than a FINO. Matured in the more humid, maritime conditions of SANLÚCAR DE BARRAMEDA (as opposed to the other towns of the "Sherry Triangle" (EL PUERTO DE SANTA MARÍA and JEREZ). Should be drunk cold and fresh. Deteriorates rapidly once opened (always refrigerate and use half bottles if possible). Eg HEREDEROS DE ARGÜESO San León.

Manzanilla Pasada MANZANILLA aged longer than most, v. dry, complex and fascinating. Eg Hidalgo's Manzanilla Pasada Pastrana.

Fino Along with MANZANILLA, the lightest and finest of sherries; both have minimum age of 3 yrs. Delicate dry and pungent. Eg GONZÁLEZ-BYASS Tío Pepe. Drink cold and fresh.

Amontillado A FINO in which the layer of protective yeast, FLOR, which grows on the wine in barrel, has died, allowing the wine to oxidize and create darker, more powerful characteristics, still with a sense of FLOR. Naturally dry. Eg VALDESPINO'S Tío Diego.

Oloroso Not aged under FLOR. Heavier, less brilliant than FINO when young, but matures to richness and pungency. Naturally dry. Also sweetened with PEDRO XIMÉNEZ and sold as an oloroso dulce/sweet oloroso. Eg DOMECQ Río Viejo (dry), LUSTAU Old East India (sweet).

Palo Cortado A less common style falling somewhere between AMONTILLADO and OLOROSO in character. Dry, rich, complex – worth looking for. Eg BARBADILLO Obispo Gascon and GUTIÉRREZ COLOSÍA.

Cream A blended sherry sweetened with grape must, PX, and/or MOSCATEL for an inexpensive, medium-sweet style. Unashamedly commercial. Eg HARVEY'S Bristol Cream, CROFT Pale Cream.

Pedro Ximénez (or PX) Raisined sweet, dark sherry from partly sun-dried Pedro Ximénez grapes. Concentrated, unctuous, decadent, and a bargain. The perfect thing to drink with ice cream. Overall, the world's sweetest wine. Eg REY FERNANDO DE CASTILLA'S Antique.

Moscatel As with Pedro Ximenez grape, though it rarely reaches PX's level of concentration or richness. Eg LUSTAU Centenary Selection Las Cruces.

Age-dated sherries Relatively new category of vintage-dated wines (in contrast to SOLERA-aged wines). Applies only to AMONTILLADO, OLOROSO, PALO CORTADO, and PX styles. Exceptional quality at relatively low prices makes these among the fine-wine world's best bargains. 20-yr-old is called VOS (Very Old Sherry/Vinum Optimum Signatum); 30-yr-old is VORS (Very Old Rare Sherry/Vinum Optimum Rare Signatum). Also 12-yr-old and 15-yr old. E.g. VOS WILLIAMS & HUMBERT Don Guido Solera Especial Oloroso (sweet); VORS GONZÁLEZ-BYASS AMONTILLADO del Duque.

Beltran Domecq. La Ina FINO is excellent. Recently: a range of wonderful v. old SOLERA sherries. Also in Rioja and Mexico.

Douro Rising in Spain as the Duero, the river Douro flows through port country, lending its name to the region, which is divided into the Cima (Upper) Corgo and Douro Superior, home of the best ports, and the Baixo Corgo.

Dow Brand name of port house Silva & Cosens. Belongs to the SYMINGTON family; drier style than other producers in group (GOULD CAMPBELL, GRAHAM, QUARLES HARRIS, RORIZ, SMITH WOODHOUSE, VESÚVIO, WARRE). V.gd range, inc CRUSTED, 20- and 30-yr-old TAWNIES, single-QUINTAS Bomfim and, since 1998, v.g da Senhora da Ribeira; vintage: **63 66** 70 72 75 77 **80 83 85' 91 94** 97 00' 03.

> **Shhh 2...**
> Do you ever eat smoked salmon? Smoked eel? Oysters? Forget Sauvignon Blanc, even skip Chardonnay. Open a cold bottle of Manzanilla – and polish it off.

Duff Gordon Sherry shipper best-known for El Cid AMONTILLADO. Gd FINO Feria; Niña Medium OLOROSO. OSBORNE-owned; name also second label for Osborne's ports.

Emilio Hildago ★★→★★★★ Small JEREZ bodega making exquisite Privilegio 1860 PALO CORTADO and v.gd Santa Ana PX. FINO Panesa is gd value.

Estufagem Bulk process of slowly heating, then cooling, cheaper madeiras to attain characteristic scorched-earth tang; less subtle than CANTEIRO process.

Ferreira Leading Portuguese-owned shipper belonging to Sogrape. Bestselling brand in Portugal. Fine 10- and 20-yr-old TAWNIES, Quinta do Porto and Duque de Bragança. Early-maturing vintages : **63 66 70 75 77 78 80 82 85 87 91** 94 95 97 00 03.

Fladgate See Taylors.

Flor Spanish word for "flower": refers to the layer of saccharomyces yeasts that grow atop FINO/MANZANILLA sherry in barrel, keeping oxidation at bay and changing the wine's flavour, making it aromatic and pungent. When the *flor* dies, the wines are aged further without it, becoming AMONTILLADO.

Fonseca Guimaraens Port shipper; belongs to the Fladgate Partnership. Renowned Bin 27 reserve RUBY joined by organic Terra Prima in 2006. Sumptuous yet structured vintages among best: Fonseca **63' 66' 70 75 77' 80 83 85'** 92 94' 97 00' 03'. Impressive, earlier-maturing Fonseca Guimaraens made if no classic declaration. Occasional single-QUINTA do Panascal.

Forrester See OFFLEY.

Frasqueira The official name for "vintage" madeira from a single yr. Exceptionally intense wines bottled after at least 20 yrs in wood. Date of bottling compulsory; the longer in cask, the more concentrated and complex .

Garvey ★→★★★★ Famous old sherry shipper in JEREZ. Classic San Patricio FINO, Tío Guillermo AMONTILLADO, and Ochavico OLOROSO. Also age-dated 1780 line.

González-Byass ★→★★★★ Large family bodega with the most famous and one of the best FINOS: Tío Pepe. Other brands include La Concha AMONTILLADO, Elegante FINO, El Rocío MANZANILLA, 1847 sweet OLOROSO. Age-dated line includes Del Duque AMONTILLADO, Matúsalem OLOROSO, Apóstoles PALO CORTADO and the outstanding ultra-rich Noé PX. One of the few JEREZ bodegas to sell vintage sherries. Growing business in quality table wines from JEREZ region, as well as large interests in brandy.

Gould Campbell Port shipper belonging to the SYMINGTON family. Gd-value, full-bodied VINTAGE PORTS 70 **77' 80 83 85' 91 94** 97 00 03'.

Gracia Hermanos Mont-M Firm within the same group as PÉREZ BARQUERO and Compañía Vinícola del Sur making good-quality MONTILLAS. Its labels include María del Valle FINO, Montearruit AMONTILLADO, OLOROSO CREAM, and Dulce Viejo PX.

Graham One of port's greatest names, belonging to the SYMINGTON family. v.gd range from Six Grapes RESERVE RUBY, LBV and TAWNY (reserve) to excellent yr-aged TAWNIES and some of richest, sweetest VINTAGE PORTS **63 66 70 75 77 80 83' 85'** 91' 94 97 00' 03'. V.gd single-QUINTA vintage: Quinta dos Malvedos.

Gran Cruz The single biggest port brand. Mostly light, inexpensive tawnies.

Guita, La ★→★★★ Especially fine MANZANILLA PASADA made by Pérez Marín in SANLÚCAR. Also owns Gil Luque label for other sherries.

Gutiérrez Colosía ★★★ Family-owned and ran former ALMACENISTA on the

Guadalete R. in EL PUERTO with a consistent range. Excellent old PALO CORTADO.

Hartley & Gibson See VALDESPINO.

Harvey's ★→★★ Major producer, owned by Beam Brands, along with Domecq. Famed for Bristol CREAM (medium-sweet) in blue bottles and Club AMONTILLADO. Recent attempts to revive reputation, relaunch includes FINO.

Henriques, Justino The largest madeira shipper belonging, along with GRAN CRUZ ports, to Martiniquaise. Gd 10-yr-old, sweet/fine rich COLHEITA (1995, 1996) and vintage – eg 1934 VERDELHO.

Henriques & Henriques Independent madeira shipper. Rich, well-structured wines. Outstanding 10- and 15-yr-olds; v. fine reserves, vintage and solera wines, inc SERCIAL 1964, Terrantez 1976, MALVASIA 1954, BUAL 1954 and 1980, Century Malmsey-Solera 1900. Innovative extra-dry apéritif Monte Seco and Tinta Negra Mole COLHEITA Single Harvest Fine Rich Madeira 1995. John Cossart, chairman and industry spokesman, died in 2008.

Herederos de Argüeso ★★→★★★ MANZANILLA specialist in SANLÚCAR with v.gd San León and Las Medallas; and the desirable VOS AMONTILLADO Viejo. Under new ownership.

Hidalgo, La Gitana ★★★→★★★★ Old family sherry firm in SANLÚCAR fronted by the indefatigable Javier Hidalgo. Flagship is the excellent pale *manzanilla La Gitana*; also fine OLOROSO, lovely PALO CORTADOS, and single vyd, v. fine Pastrana MANZANILLA PASADA, and AMONTILLADO.

Jerez de la Frontera Centre of sherry industry, between Cádiz and Seville. "Sherry" is a corruption of the name, pronounced "hereth". In French, Xérès.

Jordões, Casal dos Organic port producers: decent LBV and vintage wines.

Kopke The oldest port house, founded in 1638. Now belongs to BARROS ALMEIDA. Mostly early-maturing, fair-quality vintage wines, but some excellent (83 85 87 89 91 94 97 00 03); excellent COLHEITAS (**80'**).

Krohn Port shipper; gd 20-yr-old TAWNY and excellent COLHEITAS (**64 66 82**), some dating back to 1800s.

Lagare Shallow granite "paddling pool" in which port is trodden by foot – or, these days, increasingly by robot.

LBV (Late Bottled Vintage) Port from a single yr kept in wood for twice as long as VINTAGE PORT (about 5 yrs) so ready to drink on release; much larger volumes, robustly fruity but much less powerful and complex than vintage. No need to decant unless unfiltered wine which can age for 10 yrs or more (CHURCHILL, FERREIRA, NIEPOORT, NOVAL, SMITH WOODHOUSE, WARRE).

Leacock Volume label of the MADEIRA WINE COMPANY. Main brand is St John, popular in Scandinavia. Older vintages include 1963 SERCIAL, 1914 BUAL, and SOLERA 1860.

Lustau ★★→★★★★ Sherry house based in JEREZ, owned by the Caballero group. Extensive range of wines. Best-known as pioneer shipper of excellent ALMACENISTA sherries inc MANZANILLA AMONTILLADO Jurado, PALO CORTADO Vides. Other v.gd sherries include East India Solera, Emilín MOSCATEL.

Madeira Wine Company Formed in 1913 by 2 firms as the Madeira Wine Association, subsequently to include all 26 British madeira firms; today it produces over 100 different labels. Though cellared together, wines preserve individual house styles; BLANDY and COSSART GORDON lead the pack. Now controlled by the SYMINGTON family (see DOW); improved production facilities. All wines 5-yrs old plus CANTEIRO-aged traditional grape varieties with exception of Tinta Negra Mole COLHEITA.

Malmsey (or Malvasia) The sweetest and richest of traditional madeira grape varieties; dark amber and honeyed, yet with madeira's unique sharp tang.

Martinez Gassiot Port firm now owned by the SYMINGTON family, known esp for excellent rich, and pungent Directors 20-yr-old TAWNY. Gd-value, ageworthy vintages in drier, traditional style: **63 67 70 75 82 85 87 91** 94 97 00 03. V.gd single-QUINTA wines from Quinta da Eira Velha.

Medina, José Major sherry exporter, esp to the Low Countries. Owns WILLIAMS & HUMBERT, also Pérez Megia and Luis Paez.

Miles Madeira shipper, part of the MADEIRA WINE COMPANY. Basic wines only.

Montecristo Mont-M Brand of popular MONTILLAS by Compañía Vinícola del Sur.

Montilla-Moriles Mont-M DO nr Córdoba. Not sherry, but close, with soft FINO and AMONTILLADO, and luscious PX. At best, singularly toothsome apéritifs. Important source for PX for use in DO JEREZ, to make up for shortfall.

Niepoort Small family-run port house of Dutch origin; sensational table wines. Consistently fine vintages (63 66 70' **75 77 78 80 82 83 87** 91 92 94 97 00' 03 05); Garrafeira is aged in glass 18th-century demijohns. Second vintage label: Secundum. Exceptional TAWNIES and COLHEITAS.

Noval, Quinta do Historic port house now French (AXA) owned. Intensely fruity, structured, elegant vintage port; around 2.5 ha of ungrafted vines make small quantity of Nacional – extraordinarily dark, full, velvety, slow-maturing. Also v.gd age-dated TAWNY and gd COLHEITAS. Vintages: 62 63 66 **67 70 75 78 82 85 87** 91 **94'** 95 97' 00' 03' 04. Second vintage label: Silval. Also v.gd LBV.

Offley Brand name belonging to port shipper Forrester. Duke of Oporto is main brand and a big seller in Portugal. Baron de Forrester is gd TAWNY. Owns Quinta da Boa Vista. Gd early-maturing vintages: **63 66 67 70 72 75 77 80 82 83 85 87 89** 94 95 97 00' 03.

Osborne ★→★★★★ Huge Spanish firm producing sherry, a wide range of Spanish wines, and quality port. Its instantly recognizable bull logo dots the Spanish countryside. Sherries include FINO Quinta, Coquinero, FINO AMONTILLADO. Declared VINTAGE PORTS (now made by TAYLOR'S) in 95 97 00' 03'.

Top tawny/colheita selection for 2009

10-Year-Old Tawny: WARRE Otima, FONSECA, QUINTA DE VENTOZELO.

20-Year-Old Tawny: DELAFORCE Curious & Ancient, COCKBURNS, QUINTA DO NOVAL.

30-Year-Old Tawny: RAMOS PINTO, NIEPOORT, SANDEMANS.

40-Year-Old Tawny: FONSECA, TAYLOR'S, Dow.

Colheita: BARROS 1978, DELAFORCE 1979, KOPKE 1980.

Paternina, Federico ★★→★★★★ Marcos Eguizabal from Rioja acquired the sherry firm Diez-Merito, retaining 3 VORS wines for his Paternina label, the excellent and unique FINO Imperial, OLOROSO Victoria Regina, and PX Vieja SOLERA.

Pedro Romero ★→★★★ Expanding SANLÚCAR family operation in an array of bodegas, recently acquired Gaspar Florido. V. wide range; inconsistent.

Pereira d'Oliveira Vinhos Family-owned madeira company since 1850. Gd basic range, COLHEITAS and fine old vintages back to 1850 labelled as Reserve (1937 SERCIAL, 1966 VERDELHO, 1968 BUAL).

Pérez Barquero Mont-M Excellent MONTILLAS include Gran Barquero FINO, AMONTILLADO, and OLOROSO.

Pilar Plá/El Maestro Sierra ★→★★★★ Owned by JEREZ's grandest dame Pilar Plá. Wines inconsistent, but some great value at medium ages esp AMONTILLADO.

Poças Portuguese family port firm; v.gd tawnies and COLHEITAS. gd LBV and recent vintages (97 00' 03). Single-QUINTA wines from Quinta Sta Barbera.

Puerto de Santa María, El The former port of sherry, one of the 3 towns forming the "Sherry Triangle". Production now in serious decline; remaining bodegas include former ALMACENISTA GUTIÉRREZ COLOSÍA.

PX Pedro Ximénez grape, partly sun-dried, either bottled alone as top-class sweet wine or used for sweetening other sherries.

Quarles Harris One of the oldest port houses, since 1680 , now owned by the SYMINGTON family (see DOW). Mellow, well-balanced vintages, often v.gd value: **63 66** 70 75 **77 80 83 85** 91 94 97 00' 03.

Quinta Portuguese for "estate", traditionally denotes VINTAGE PORTS from shipper's single v'yds; declared in gd but not exceptional yrs. An increasing number of independent *quintas* (growers) make wines from top vintages. Exciting newcomers include Passadouro, Portal, Whytingham's Vale Meão, and Wine & Soul's Pintas.

Ramos Pinto Dynamic port house owned by Champagne house Louis Roederer. Outstanding single-QUINTA de Ervamoira and TAWNIES (de Ervamoira and do Bom Retiro). Rich, sweet, generally early maturing vintages.

Reserve/Reserva Premium ports, mostly Reserve RUBY but some Reserve TAWNY, bottled without a vintage date or indication of age but better than the basic style.

Rey Fernando de Castilla ★★→★★★★ JEREZ veteran Norwegian Jan Pettersen has made a small sherry revolution with his excellent wines, which, although he chooses not to label them Age-Dated, could easily be so. Top Antique line of AMONTILLADO, OLOROSO, and PX; FINOS less so.

Roriz, Quinta de Historic estate now working with Cristiano van Zeller of VALE D MARIA. V.gd single-QUINTA DOURO wines and ports: 99 00' 01 02 03' 04 05.

Rosa, Quinta de la V.gd single-QUINTA port from the Bergqvist family. Traditional methods and stone LAGARES. Look for **94 95** 00 03' 04 05' vintages and wines from a small plot of old vines called Vale do Inferno.

Royal Oporto Main port brand within Real Companhia Velha, now focusing on unfortified Douro wines. Some gd TAWNIES, COLHEITAS and recent vintages.

Rozès Port shipper owned by Champagne house Vranken alongside São Pedro das Aguias. V. popular in France.

Ruby Youngest and cheapest port style: simple, sweet, red. Best are vigorous, full of flavour; others merely strong, thin, spirity. See also RESERVE.

Sanchez Romate ★★→★★★ Family firm in JEREZ since 1781. Best known in Spanish-speaking world, esp for brandy Cardenal Mendoza. Gd sherry: OLOROSO La Sacristía de Romate, PX Duquesa, AMONTILLADO NPU.

Sandeman ★→★★★ Large firm, now part of Sogrape group. Founder George Sandeman set up twin establishments in Oporto and JEREZ in 1790. Gd sherries include an aged Don FINO, dry and sweet Imperial Corregidor and Royal Ambrosante OLOROSOS. Port: gd aged TAWNIES, esp 20-yr-old. Vintage patchy but new winery at Quinta do Seixo bodes well (**63 66** 70 75 **77 94** 97 00 03). Second label: approachable Vau Vintage. How will Sandeman compete with stablemate FERREIRA now they're under the same ownership? Ferreira might be the one allowed to shine.

Sanlúcar de Barrameda One of the 3 towns of the "Sherry Triangle" at the mouth of the Guadalquivir. Strong maritime influence affects the MANZANILLA.

Santa Eufemia, Quinta de Family port estate with v.gd old TAWNIES.

Sercial Madeira grape for the driest of the island's wines – supreme apéritif.

Silva, C da Port shipper. Mostly inexpensive RUBIES and TAWNIES, but gd aged TAWNIES and COLHEITAS under Dalva label.

Smith Woodhouse Port firm founded in 1784. Mostly a supplier of own-label but v.gd unfiltered LBV and some v. fine vintages: **63 66** 70 75 77' **80 83 85** 91 94 97 00' 03. Occasional single-estate wines from Quinta da Madelena.

Solera System used in ageing sherry. Consists of topping up progressively more mature barrels with slightly younger wine of same sort from next stage or criadera, the object being continuity in final wine and maintaining vigour of *flor* in FINO and MANZANILLA soleras. Used to be applied to madeiras; old solera wines in bottle fetch high prices.

Symington See DOW and MADEIRA WINE COMPANY.

Tawny Style of port that implies ageing in wood (hence tawny in colour), though many basic tawnies are little more than attenuated RUBIES. Look for wines with an indication of age: 10-, 20-, 30-, 40-yr-old or RESERVE.

Taylor, Fladgate & Yeatman (Taylor's) One of the best known port shippers, highly rated for its rich, long-lived VINTAGE PORTS (**63 66 70 75 77'** 80 83 85 92' 94 97 00' 03'). Member of the Fladgate Partnership alongside CROFT, DELAFORCE and FONSECA GUIMARAENS. V.gd range inc RESERVE, LBV and aged TAWNIES. QUINTAS Vargellas and Terra Feita produce impressive single-QUINTA vintage, esp rare ***Vargellas "Vinha Velha"*** (95, 97, 00, 04) from 70 +-yr-old vines. Recently acquired A-rated QUINTA da Eira Velha.

Terry, S A ★→★★ Sherry bodega at EL PUERTO; part of Beam Brands.

Tío Pepe The most famous of FINO sherries (see GONZÁLEZ-BYASS).

Toro Albalá, Bodegas Mont-M Family firm located in a 1920s power station and aptly making Eléctrico FINOS, AMONTILLADOS, and a PX that is among the best in MONTILLA and Spain.

Tradición ★★★→★★★★ One of the new wave of sherry bodegas focusing exclusively upon small quantities of VOS PX and VORS AMONTILLADO, PALO CORTADO, and OLOROSO, from anart-filled cellar in back streets of JEREZ.

Valdespino ★→★★★★ Famous JEREZ bodega producing Inocente FINO from the esteemed Macharnudo v'yd. Notably Inocente is fermented in American oak not stainless steel, and SOLERA has 10 stages or *criaderas*. ***Tío Diego*** is terrific dry AMONTILLADO; also SOLERA 1842 OLOROSO; remarkable, aged Toneles MOSCATEL. In the US its sherries are sold as Hartley & Gibson.

Valdivia ★★ New producer of sherry, part of JEREZ revival. Project also includes restaurant and hotel within bodega. V.gd 15-yr-old Sacromonte AMONTILLADO and OLOROSO.

Vale D Maria, Quinta do Gd value, beautifully elegant, forward single-QUINTA VINTAGE PORT (**00** 01 02 03 05).

Ventozelo, Quinta de Huge, beautifully situated estate recently acquired and renovated by a Spanish family. Gd value single-QUINTA VINTAGE PORTS.

Verdelho Traditional madeira grape for medium-dry wines; pungent but without the searing austerity of SERCIAL. Increasing in popularity for table wines.

Vesúvio, Quinta do 19th-century estate restored to former glory by SYMINGTON family, who have doubled vyd area. Only VINTAGE PORT: **91 92 94 95' 96'** 97 00' 01 03' 04 05'.

Vila Nova de Gaia City on the south side of the river DOURO from Oporto, where major port shippers traditionally mature their wines in lodges.

Vintage port Classic vintages are the best wines declared in exceptional yrs by shippers between 1 Jan and 30 Sept in the 2nd yr after vintage. Bottled without filtration after 2 yrs in wood, the wine matures v. slowly in bottle throwing a CRUST or deposit – always decant. Modern vintages broachable earlier but best will last over 50 yrs. Single-QUINTA vintage ports also drinking earlier.

Warre Oldest of British port shippers (since 1670); owned by the SYMINGTON family (see DOW) since 1905. Fine, elegant, long-maturing vintage wines, gd RESERVE, vintage character (Warrior), excellent unfiltered, bottle-matured LBV; 10- and 20-yr-old Otima TAWNY. Single-QUINTA vintage from Quinta da Cavadinha. Vintages: **63 66 70' 75 77' 80 83 85 91** 94 97 00' 03.

White port Port made with white grapes, occasionally sweet (*lagrima*) but mostly off-dry apéritif styles (driest labelled "Dry"), perfect with tonic and fresh mint. Look for wines with cask age: BARROS, CHURCHILL, NIEPOORT. Since 2006, the designations 10-, 20-, 30-, or 40-yr-old can be used.

Williams & Humbert ★★→★★★★ First-class sherry bodega. Dry Sack (medium AMONTILLADO) is bestseller; SOLERA Especial is its famous old PALO CORTADO.

Switzerland

More heavily shaded areas are the wine-growing regions

Switzerland produces an average of 1.1 million hectolitres of wine from its 15,000 ha of vineyards each year, of which a small majority is white. Average consumption is around 38 litres per head, and imports are going strong, mostly from Italy, France and Spain. New World wines are doing well, but European wines are the favourites.

Swiss wine has two faces these days. On one hand there are traditional styles, with lots of Pinot Noir (Blauburgunder), Chasselas and Müller-Thurgau. On the other hand, newly created or newly discovered varieties, such as Cabernet Dorsa, Vidal or Johanniter, are booming. And, curiously, more and more warm-climate varieties are being planted.

Recent vintages

2007 Reds are less opulent than 2006. Whites are superb.

2006 Very promising and being compared to 2005.

2005 Low in quantity but high in quality.

2004 Less complex than 2003 but very promising. Drink now.

2003 Some will already be over the top. Drink up.

Aargau 05' 06 07 Eastern canton for fragrant Müller-THURGAU, rich BLAU-BURGUNDER. Best producer: Weingut zum Sternen.

Aigle Vaud r w ★★→★★★ Well known for elegant whites and supple reds.

Amigne Traditional VALAIS white grape, esp of VÉTROZ. Full-bodied, tasty, often sweet. Best producer: André Fontannaz ★★ 05 06 07'. Quality rating based on residual sugar: one bee – yes, as in the insect – means 0–8 grams per litre RS, 2 bees mean 9–25g/l RS, 3 bees mean over 25 g/l RS.

AC Compulsory from Jan 1, 2008 for all wine regions.

Agroscope Federal research station in Changins and Wädensweil.

Arte Vitis Group of the best wine producers of VAUD.

Arvine Old VALAIS white grape (also Petite Arvine): dry and sweet, elegant, long-lasting wines with salty finish. Best in SIERRE, SION, Granges, FULLY. Producers: Marie-Thérèse Chappaz, Benoît Dorsaz, Simon Maye & Fils, Rouvinez.

Auvernier Neuchâtel r p w ★★→★★★ Old wine village on Lake NEUCHÂTEL and biggest wine-growing commune of the canton.

Basel Second-largest Swiss town and canton. Best wines: Müller-THURGAU, PINOT N (104 ha) and Bacchus.

Bern Capital and canton. V'yds in west (BIELERSEE: CHASSELAS, PINOT N, white SPÉCIALITÉS) and east (Thunersee: BLAUBURGUNDER, Müller-THURGAU); 262 ha.

Bielersee r p w ★→★★ 05' 06 07' Wine region on northern shore of the Bielersee lake (dry, light CHASSELAS, PINOT N and specialities such as Viognier, Sauv Bl and Malbec). Best producers: Dom Grillette, Charles Steiner.

Blauburgunder German name for PINOT N; aka Clevner. Wide range of wines, from rosé to heavily oaked reds. Switzerland's main red variety (4,490 ha).

Blauburgunderland Successful promotion body for the wines of SCHAFFHAUSEN.

Bündner Herrschaft Grisons r p w ★★→★★★ Best German-Swiss region includes top villages: Fläsch, Jenins, Maienfeld, Malans. BLAUBURGUNDER ripens esp well due to warm Föhn wind, cask-aged v.gd. Also Chard, Müller-THURGAU, COMPLETER. Best: Gantenbein ★★★, Davaz ★★, Fromm ★★★ 03' 04 05' 06 07'. Switzerland's best BLAUBURGUNDER is from here.

Chablais Vaud r w ★★→★★★ Wine region on right bank of Rhône and upper end of Lake GENEVA, includes villages AIGLE, Bex, Ollon, Villeneuve, YVORNE.

Champagne Wine-growers from Vaudois village of Champagne have lost their objection at the European Court of Justice in Luxembourg. Since June 1, 2004, they have not been allowed to use the name "Champagne" on the label.

Chasselas (Gutedel in Germany) French cantons, white grape; neutral flavour, takes on local character: elegant (GENEVA); refined, full (VAUD); exotic, racy (VALAIS); pétillant (lakes Bienne, NEUCHÂTEL, Murtensee). Only east of BASEL. Called FENDANT in VALAIS. Accounts for almost a third of Swiss wines but increasingly replaced. Best: Dom Blaise Duboux, Philippe Gex, Raymont Paccot. More and more producers avoid the malolactic fermentation thus conserving acidity in wines, and have started to use oak barrels.

Completer Native white grape, mostly used in GRISONS, making aromatic wines with high acidity. ("Complet" was a monk's final daily prayer, or "nightcap".) Related to the VALAIS grape Lafnetscha. Best: Adolf Boner, Malans ★★, Volg Weinkellereien.

Cornalin ★★→★★★ 03' 04 05 06 Local VALAIS speciality that has become more popular since production increased; dark, spicy, v. strong red. Best: Jean-René Germanier (★★), Denis Mercier, Provins. Oldest living vine in Switzerland is a Cornalin plant in Leuk, Valais, from 1798 (www.vitisantiqua1798.ch).

La Côte Vaud r p w ★→★★★ Largest VAUD wine area between LAUSANNE and GENEVA. Traditional whites with elegant finesse; fruity, harmonious reds. Esp from MONT-SUR-ROLLE, Vinzel, Luins, FÉCHY, MORGES, etc.

Dézaley Vaud w (r) ★★→★★★ Celebrated LAVAUX v'yd on slopes above Lake GENEVA, once tended by Cistercian monks. Potent CHASSELAS, develops esp after ageing. Red Dézaley is a GAMAY/PINOT N/MERLOT/Syrah rarity.

Dôle Valais r ★★→★★★ Appellation for PINOT N, often blended with GAMAY and other reds from the VALAIS: full, supple, often v.gd. Lightly pink Dôle Blanche is pressed straight after harvest.

D-Vino Discounter Denner's new Zurich wine bars. Cheap, gd wines by the glass.

Epesses Vaud w (r) ★→★★★ 06 07' LAVAUX AC: supple, full-bodied whites.

Ermitage Alias Marsanne; a VALAIS SPÉCIALITÉ. Concentrated, full-bodied dry white, sometimes with residual sugar. Best: Dom Cornulus, Philippoz Frères.

Féchy Vaud ★→★★ Famous appellation of LA CÔTE, esp elegant whites.

Federweisser German-Swiss name for white wine from BLAUBURGUNDER.

Fendant Valais w ★→★★★ VALAIS appellation for CHASSELAS. The ideal wine for Swiss cheese dishes such as fondue or raclette.

Flétri/Mi-flétri Late-harvested grapes for sweet/slightly sweet wine .

Fribourg Smallest French-Swiss wine canton (115 ha, nr Jura). Esp for PINOT N, CHASSELAS, GAMAY, SPÉCIALITÉS from VULLY, Lake Murten, south Lake NEUCHÂTEL.

Fully Valais r w ★★→★★★ Village nr Martigny: excellent ERMITAGE and GAMAY. Best producer: Marie-Thérèse Chappaz sw ★★→★★★ 05' 06 07.

Gamay Beaujolais grape; abounds in French cantons. Mainly thin wine used in blends (SALVAGNIN, DÔLE) and also more and more as a single variety. Gamay accounts for 14% of grapes in Switzerland.

Gantenbein, Daniel & Martha Most famous growers in Grisons. 04 05' 06 07.

Geneva Capital, and French-Swiss wine canton; third largest (1,425 ha). Key areas: Mandement, Entre Arve et Rhône, Entre Arve et Lac. Mostly CHASSELAS, GAMAY. Also Gamaret, Chard, PINOT N, Muscat, and gd Aligoté. Best: Jean-Michel Novelle ★★★; interesting: Jacques Tatasciere, Dom de la Rochette ★★.

Germanier, Jean-René VÉTROZ winemaker; Cayas (100% Syrah) ★★★ 01 02 03' 04 05' 06; Mitis (sweet) ★★★ 01' 02 03 04 05' . New release: a pure Cornalin 05' 06 and the PINOT N Clos du Four ★★★.

Glacier, Vin du (Gletscherwein) Fabled oxidized, wooded white from rare Rèze grape of Val d'Anniviers. Almost impossible to find on sale.

Grisons (Graubünden) Mountain canton, mainly in German Switzerland (BÜNDNER HERRSCHAFT, Churer Rheintal; esp BLAUBURGUNDER) and partly south of Alps (Misox, esp MERLOT). 416 ha, primarily PINOT N, also Müller-THURGAU and SPÉCIALITÉS.

Heida (Païen) Old VALAIS white grape (Jura's Savagnin) for country wine of upper Valais (VISPERTERMINEN v'yds at 1,000+ m). Full-bodied wine with high acidity. Best: Josef-Marie Chanton ★★ 04 05' 06 07'. Try Heida from PROVINS.

Humagne Strong native white grape (VALAIS SPÉCIALITÉ), older than CHASSELAS. Also Humagne rouge. Esp from Chamoson, Leytron, Martigny.

Johannisberg Synonym for SYLVANER in the VALAIS.

Lausanne Capital of VAUD. No longer with v'yds in town area, but long-time owner of classics: Abbaye de Mont, Ch Rochefort (LA CÔTE); Clos des Moines, Clos des Abbayes, Dom de Burignon (LAVAUX). Pricey.

Lavaux Vaud w (r) ★→★★★ DYA Scenic region on north shore of Lake GENEVA between Montreux and LAUSANNE. Since 2007 a UNESCO World Heritage Site. Delicate, refined whites, gd reds. Best: Calamin, Chardonne, DÉZALEY, EPESSES, Lutry, ST-SAPHORIN, VEVEY-MONTREUX, Villette.

MDVS Mémoires des Vins Suisses – a collection of the most important Swiss wines; also older vintages, to protect the country's heritage (www.mdvs.ch).

Merlot Brought to the TICINO in 1907 by the scientist Alderige Fantuzzi (after phylloxera destroyed local varieties): soft to v. powerful wines. Also used with Cab Sauv. Best: Castello Luigi, Conte di Luna,Stucky Zanini.

Mont-sur-Rolle Vaud w (r) ★★ DYA Important appellation within LA CÔTE.

Morges Vaud r p w ★→★★ DYA Largest LA CÔTE/VAUD AC: CHASSELAS, fruity reds.

Neuchâtel City and canton; 600 ha from Lake Neuchâtel to BIELERSEE. CHASSELAS: fragrant, lively (sur lie, sparkling). Gd OEIL DE PERDRIX, PINOT GRIS, Chard.

Nostrano Word meaning "ours", applied to red wine of TICINO, made from native and Italian grapes (Bondola, Freisa, Bonarda, etc).

Oeil de Perdrix PINOT N rosé. DYA esp NEUCHÂTEL'S; name can be used anywhere.

Pinot Blanc (Weissburgunder) Booming variety producing full-bodied, elegant wines. Best: Bad Osterfingen 06 07'.

SWITZERLAND

Pinot Gris (Malvoisie) Widely planted white grape for dry and residually sweet wines. Makes v. fine late-harvest wines in VALAIS (called Malvoisie).

Pinot Noir (Blauburgunder) Top red grape (33% of v'yds). Esp BÜNDNER HERRSCHAFT, NEUCHÂTEL, THURGAU, VALAIS, ZÜRICH. Try: Gantenbein; Davaz (Fläsch); Kesselring (Ottoberg); Pircher (Eglisau); Baumann (Oberhallau); Meier (Kloster Sion); Christian Obrecht (Jenins) ★★★ 03' 04 05' 06 07.

Provins Biggest cooperative in the VALAIS with a large range.

Rauschling Old white ZÜRICH grape; discreet fruit and elegant acidity.

Riesling Petit Rhin Mainly in the VALAIS. Try Kesseling (Ottoberg) 06 07.

Riesling-Sylvaner Old name for Müller-THURGAU, a vine celebrating its 125th birthday. Typically elegant wines with flowery aroma and some acidity. Best producers: Daniel Marugg, Baumann (Oberhallau) ★★ 06' 07'.

St-Gallen Eastern wine canton (218 ha). Esp for BLAUBURGUNDER, Müller-THURGAU, SPÉCIALITÉS. Includes Rhine Valley, Oberland, upper Lake ZÜRICH.

St-Saphorin Vaud w (r) ★★→★★★ 06' 07' Famous LAVAUX AC for fine, light whites.

Salvagnin Vaud r ★→★★★ 03 GAMAY and/or PINOT N appellation. (See also DÔLE.)

Schaffhausen German-Swiss canton/wine town on the Rhine. BLAUBURGUNDER; also Müller-THURGAU and SPÉCIALITÉS. Best: Baumann, Bad Osterfingen ★★. The latest trend is reds and whites with plenty of residual sugar.

Schenk Europe-wide wine giant, founded and based in Rolle (VAUD). Owns firms in France (Burgundy and Bordeaux), Germany, Italy, and Spain.

Sierre Valais r w ★★→★★★ Sunny resort and famous wine town. Known for FENDANT, PINOT N, ERMITAGE, MALVOISIE. V.gd DÔLE.

Sion Valais r w ★★→★★★ Capital/wine centre of VALAIS. Esp FENDANT de Sion.

Spécialités (Spezialitäten) Wines of unusual grapes: vanishing local Gwäss, Himbertscha, Roter Eyholzer, Bondola, etc, ARVINE and AMIGNE, or modish Chenin Bl, Sauv Bl, Cab Sauv, Syrah. Of 47 VALAIS varieties, 43 are SPÉCIALITÉS.

Swisswine Wine promotion body, mainly government financed. Organizes the Grand Prix du Vin Suisse every 2 yrs. 2007 winner: Adrian Mathier, Salgesch.

Sylvaner (Johannisberg, Gros Rhin) White grape esp in warm VALAIS v'yds.

Thurgau German-Swiss canton beside Bodensee Lake (265 ha). Wines from Thur Valley: south shore of the Untersee. Typical: BLAUBURGUNDER, also gd Müller-Thurgau. SPÉCIALITÉS include Kerner, PINOT GR, Regent. Best producer: Hans Ulrich Kesselring ★★★ 04 05' 06' 07.

Ticino Italian-speaking southern Switzerland (with Misox), growing mainly MERLOT (gd from mountainous Sopraceneri region) and SPÉCIALITÉS. Try Cab Sauv (oaked B'x style), Sauv Bl, Sem, Chard, Merlot white, and rosé (1,020 ha). Best producers: Guido Brivio, Daniel Huber, Adriano Kaufmann, Werner Stucky, Luigi Zanini, Christian Zündel. All ★★★ 03' 04 05' 06 07'.

Valais (Wallis) Rhône Valley from German-speaking upper-Valais to French lower-Valais. Largest and most varied and exciting wine canton in Switzerland (5,198 ha; source of 30% of Swiss wine). Wide range: 47 grape varieties, plus many SPÉCIALITÉS; FLÉTRI/MI-FLÉTRI wines.

Vaud (Waadt) French Switzerland's second largest wine canton; stronghold of CHABLAIS, LA CÔTE, LAVAUX, Bonvillars, Côtes de l'Orbe, VULLY. CHASSELAS.

Vétroz Valais w r ★★→★★★ Top village nr SION, esp famous for AMIGNE.

Vevey-Montreux Vaud r w ★★ Up-and-coming appellation of LAVAUX. Famous wine festival held about every 30 yrs.

Visperterminen Valais w (r) ★→★★★ Upper VALAIS v'yds, esp for SPÉCIALITÉS. The highest v'yds in Europe (at 1,000+ m).

Vully Vaud w (r) ★→★★ Refreshing white from Lake Murten/FRIBOURG area.

Yvorne Vaud w (r) ★★ 04 05 Top CHABLAIS AC for strong, fragrant wines.

Zürich Capital of largest canton. BLAUBURGUNDER mostly; esp Müller-THURGAU, RAUSCHLING, Kerner (623 ha). Try Ladolt, Schwarzenbach, Zweifel Weine.

Austria

More heavily shaded areas are the wine-growing regions

Austria has the knack of producing wines which are exciting without being flashy, serious without being austere, utterly drinkable without being obvious. And that's quite a knack. Look out for mineral Riesling and profound Grüner Veltliner, delicate Gelber Muskateller, and fine Sauvignon Blanc and Chardonnay among the dry whites, the indigenous Blaufränkisch, Zweigelt, St Laurent and increasingly fascinating Pinot Noir among the reds. Botrytis sweet wines and Icewines are among the world's greatest and mainly produced around Lake Neusiedl.

Recent vintages

2007 A year of two halves. Up to the swelteringly hot Aug, wine growers thought that harvest would be one of the earliest on record. Then came a cool, rainy autumn, and in Lower Austria harvests extended far into Nov. In Styria, the cool autumn brought gd qualities. Spring hail in the Middle and Southern Burgenland reduced quantities, but overall the Burgenland shows fine fruit and about average yields with good results for Blaufränkisch, Zweigelt and Pinot Noir. In Lower Austria, selection was tough and the harvest stretched far into Nov for higher qualities. Excellent yields in Vienna. Overall, wines with good acidity but no extreme sugar graduations, better for Grüner Veltliner than for Riesling.

2006 A great year. A cold winter was followed by a wet spring and one of the hottest late summers on record. Healthy and perfectly ripe grapes produced wonderfully well-rounded and complex wines with great ageing potential. Very good for reds and outstanding for whites.

2005 A cool year yielding exceptionally elegant wines to those practising rigorous grape selection, particularly in Lower Austria, but with great discrepancies in quality. Not outstanding for reds. Sensational botrytis conditions for Burgenland dessert wines.

2004 A cooler year. Grüner Veltliner and Riesling fared well after meticulous vineyard care, especially in Wachau. A mild Oct in Burgenland helped reds ripen nicely, while bringing plentiful botrytis for dessert wines.

2003 A hot dry summer, a powerful year. Very good for Grüner Veltliner whites and Burgenland reds, esp Blaufränkisch and Zweigelt. Little botrytis.

2002 Much maligned, but the best producers created wonderfully elegant and balanced wines. Difficult for reds but excellent dessert wines. Drink now.

2001 Great for dry whites; very good late-harvest wines. Reds more erratic.

2000 Hailed as the vintage of the century, but many wines were too alcoholic and too unbalanced to live long. Only the v. best are still intact.

Achs, Paul r (w) ★★→★★★ Exceptional GOLS estate, esp reds: Pannobile blends, Ungerberg, BLAUFRÄNKISCH and Pinot N. BIODYNAMIC producer (see below).

Alzinger w ★★★★ 93 94 95 97 98 **99** 00 01 02 03 04 05 06 07 Outstanding WACHAU estate: deep, mineral RIES and GRÜNER VELTLINER.

Angerer, Kurt ★ Maverick KAMPTAL winemaker producing highly original and powerful GRÜNER VELTLINER and RIES.

Aumann, Leopold THERMENREGION producer with gd Merlot and opulent CHARD.

Ausbruch PRÄDIKAT wine with sweetness levels between Beerenauslese and Trockenbeerenauslese. Traditionally produced in RUST.

Ausg'steckt ("hung out") HEURIGEN are not open all yr; when they are, a green bush is hung above their doors, also to show wine is being served.

Bayer r w ★★★ Well-made reds from bought-in grapes in international styles, often v. elegant: In Signo Leonis, In Signo Sagittarii, In Signo Tauri.

Beck, Judith r w ★★ BIODYNAMIC Neusiedlersee estate . Gd Pinot N.

Blauburger Austrian red grape variety. A cross between BLAUER PORTUGIESER and BLAUFRÄNKISCH. Dark-coloured but produces light-bodied, simple wines.

Biodynamism

An organic growing method eschewing all chemical treatments and practising agriculture in harmony with natural rhythms. Despite some strange-looking practices some great wines have been produced in this way around the world. The best Austrian biodynamic producers are P ACHS, J BECK, Fritsch, Geyerhof, GRAF HARDEGG, HIRSCH, LOIMER, Sepp Muster, NIKOLAIHOF, OTT, J NITTNAUS, Pittnauer, WENINGER.

Blauer Burgunder (Pinot Noir) Undergoing a renaissance and stylistic evolution among top winemakers. Best in BURGENLAND, KAMPTAL, THERMENREGION (from growers ACHS, BECK, BRÜNDLMAYER, LOIMER, PÖCKL, Preisinger, PRIELER, SCHLOSS GOBELSBURG, SCHLOSS HALBTURN, WENINGER, WIENINGER).

Blauer Portugieser Light, fruity wines to drink slightly chilled when young. Also a gd blending variety.

Blauer Zweigelt BLAUFRÄNKISCH/ST LAURENT cross. High-yielding grape, rich in colour. Lower yields and improved methods can produce appealing, velvety reds. Top producers: Grassl, HEINRICH, Markowitsch, J NITTNAUS, Pitnauer, PÖCKL, Scheibelhofer, UMATHUM, WINKLER-HERMADEN.

Blaufränkisch Lemberger in Germany, Kékfrankos in Hungary. Austria's top-potential red grape variety, widely planted in MITTELBURGENLAND: gd body and structure, peppery acidity, a characteristic salty note, berry aromas and eucalyptus. Often blended with Cab Sauv or ZWEIGELT. Best from P ACHS, Gesellmann, HEINRICH, Igler, KOLLWENTZ, KRUTZLER, MORIC, J NITTNAUS, PRIELER, Schiefer, ERNST TRIEBAUMER, WENINGER.

Bouvier Indigenous aromatic grape, generally producing light, low-acidity wines, esp gd for Beeren- and Trockenbeerenauslesen.

Brandl, Günter w ★ Small but outstanding KAMPTAL estate known esp for his fine RIES and GRÜNER VELTLINER Novemberlese.

Bründlmayer, Willi r w sw sp ★★★★ **99 00 01 02** 03 04 05 06 07 Outstanding Langenlois-KAMPTAL estate. Passionate innovator making excellent RIES, GRÜNER VELTLINER; top international styles, inc CHARD. Also Austria's best Sekt made by *méthode champenoise*.

Burgenland Province and wine region (14,564 ha) in the east bordering Hungary. Warm climate. Ideal conditions for red wines and esp botrytis wines nr NEUSIEDLERSEE. Four areas: MITTELBURGENLAND, NEUSIEDLERSEE, NEUSIEDLERSEE-HÜGELLAND, SÜDBURGENLAND.

Buschenschank A wine tavern, often a HEURIGE country cousin.

Carnuntum r w Up-and-coming region southeast of VIENNA now showing gd reds. Best: Glatzer, Grassl, G Markowitsch, Netzl, Pitnauer, Weingut Marko.

Chardonnay Both oaked and unoaked, often international in style, particularly in STYRIA and BURGENLAND. Known in STYRIA as MORILLON: strong fruit, lively acidity. Esp BRÜNDLMAYER, GROSS, KOLLWENTZ, LOIMER, Malat, POLZ, SATTLER, STIEGELMAR, TEMENT, VELICH, WIENINGER.

Deutschkreutz r (w) MITTELBURGENLAND red wine area, esp for BLAUFRÄNKISCH.

Districtus Austriae Controllatus (DAC) Austria's first appellation system, introduced in 2003. Similar to France's AC and Italy's DOC. Currently 5 DACs: WEINVIERTEL, CARNUNTUM, MITTELBURGENLAND, KREMSTAL, and TRAISENTAL.

Donabaum, Johann w ★★ Young and v. talented WACHAU grower with fine RIES and GRÜNER VELTLINER.

Federspiel Medium quality level of the VINEA WACHAU categories, roughly corresponding to Kabinett. Fruity, elegant, dry wines.

Feiler-Artinger Burgenland r w sw ★★★→★★★★ **95 96 97 98 99** 00 01 02 03 04 05 06 Outstanding RUST estate with top AUSBRUCH dessert wines. Also gd dry whites and exciting red blends. Beautiful baroque house, too.

Freie Weingärtner Wachau w (r) ★★→★★★ **96 97 98 99 00** 00 01 02 03 06 07 Important growers' co-op in Dürnstein. Back from the wilderness and on song once more. v.gd GRÜNER VELTLINER and RIES. Dom WACHAU range.

Gemischter Satz A blend of grapes (mostly white) grown, harvested, and vinified together, particularly in VIENNA. Traditional wine, currently undergoing a renaissance with v. interesting results.

Gols r w dr sw Wine commune on north shore of NEUSIEDLERSEE in BURGENLAND. Top producers: P ACHS, J BECK, GSELLMANN & HANS, G HEINRICH, A & H Nittnaus, Pitnauer, Preisinger, Renner, STIEGELMAR.

Graf Hardegg r w ★★→★★★ Top WEINVIERTEL estate steered by Peter Veyder-Malberg, who introduced Austria's first Viognier and port-style Forticus. V.gd Syrah, Pinot N, and RIES. Changes are afoot as Veyder-Malberg is leaving Hardegg to work on his own.

Gross w ★★★→★★★★ **97 98 99 00** 01 02 03 04 05 06 07 Outstanding and perfectionist South Styrian producer. Esp CHARD, Sauv Bl, and Pinot Bl, which he regards as his finest varietal.

Grüner Veltliner Austria's flagship white grape covering 37% of v'yds. Remarkably diverse: from lively spiced fruitiness in youth, to concentrated elegance with age. Best: ALZINGER, BRÜNDLMAYER, HIRTZBERGER, Högl, M Huber, KNOLL, Laurenz V, LOIMER, MANTLERHOF, NEUMAYER, NIGL, NIKOLAIHOF, OTT, PFAFFL, FX PICHLER, PRAGER, Schmelz, Sommer.

Gsellmann & Hans r w sw ★★→★★★★ Formerly Gsellmann & Gsellmann, in GOLS.

G'spritzer Popular, refreshing summer drink, usually of white wine mixed with soda or mineral water. Esp in HEURIGEN.

Gumpoldskirchen w r dr sw Famous HEURIGE village south of VIENNA, centre of THERMENREGION. Distinctive, tasty, often sweet wines from ZIERFANDLER and

ROTGIPFLER grapes. Best producers: Biegler, Spaetrot, Zierer.

Heinrich, Gernot r w dr sw ★★★→★★★★ 96 97 98 99 00 01 02 03 04 05 06 07 Top GOLS estate, a leading member of the Pannobile group now successfully focusing on balance rather than power.

Heinrich, Johann r w dr sw ★★★ 97 98 99 00 01 02 03 04 05 06 Leading MITTELBURGENLAND producer. v.gd BLAUFRÄNKISCH Goldberg Reserve. Ever more balanced and stylish wines, esp excellent *cuvée* Cupido.

Heurige Wine of the most recent harvest, called "new wine" for one yr. Heurigen are wine taverns in which growers-cum-patrons serve their own wine with simple local food – a Viennese institution.

Hiedler w sw ★★★ Leading KAMPTAL producer. V.gd RIES Maximum.

Hirsch w ★★★ Innovative KAMPTAL producer. Esp Heiligenstein, Lamm, and Gaisberg v'yds. Also Austria's screwcap pioneer.

Hirtzberger, Franz w ★★★★ 95 97 98 99 00 01 02 03 04 05 06 07 Top WACHAU producer with 20 ha at SPITZ AN DER DONAU. Great dry RIES and GRÜNER VELTLINER, esp from the Honivogl and Singerriedel v'yds.

Horitschon MITTELBURGENLAND region for reds: Anton Iby, WENINGER.

Huber, Markus (r) w ★★ TRAISENTAL producer with varying styles of GRÜNER VELTLINER. Also gd Sauv Bl and CHARD.

Illmitz w (r) dr sw SEEWINKEL region famous for Beeren- and Trockenbeeren-auslesen. Best from Angerhof, Martin Haider, KRACHER, Helmut Lang,OPITZ.

Jamek, Josef w ★★ 97 98 99 00 01 02 03 04 05 06 07 Well-known WACHAU estate with restaurant. Not typical WACHAU style: often some residual sugar.

Jurtschitsch/Sonnhof w (r) dr (sw) ★★★ 97 98 99 00 01 02 03 04 05 06 07 Large KAMPTAL estate run by 3 brothers: v.gd whites (RIES, GRÜNER VELTLINER, CHARD).

Kamptal r w Wine region, along river Kamp N of WACHAU. Top v'yds: Langenlois, Strass, Zöbing. Best growers: Angerer, Brandl, BRÜNDLMAYER, Dolle, Ehn, Hiedler, Hirsch, JURTSCHITSCH, LOIMER, Rabl, Sax, SCHLOSS GOBELSBURG, Topf.

Kattus ★ Producer of traditional Sekt in VIENNA.

Kerschbaum r ★★★ MITTELBURGENLAND BLAUFRÄNKISCH specialist, individualist and often fascinating.

Klosterneuburg r w Main wine town of Donauland. Rich in tradition, with a famous Benedictine monastery and a wine college founded in 1860. Best producers: Stift Klosterneuburg, Zimmermann.

KMW Abbreviation for Klosterneuburger Mostwaage ("must level"), the unit used in Austria to measure the sugar content in grape juice.

Knoll, Emmerich w ★★★★ 97 98 99 00 01 02 03 04 05 06 07 Traditional, highly regarded estate in Loiben, WACHAU. Showpiece GRÜNER VELTLINER and RIES.

Kollwentz-Römerhof w r dr (sw) ★★★★ 93 94 95 96 97 98 99 00 01 02 03 04 05 06 07 Pioneering producer nr Eisenstadt: Sauv Bl, CHARD, Eiswein, v.gd reds.

Kracher w (r) dr (sw) ★★★★ 91 93 94 95 96 97 98 99 00 01 02 03 04 05 06 Top-class ILLMITZ producer specializing in botryized PRÄDIKATS (dessert); barrique-aged (Nouvelle Vague), others in steel (Zwischen den Seen); gd reds since 97. After Alois Kracher's death in 2007 the estate is now led by his son Gerhard.

Kremstal w (r) Wine region esp for GRÜNER VELTLINER and RIES. Top growers: Malat, S MOSER, NIGL, SALOMON, WEINGUT STADT KREMS.

Krutzler r ★★★ SouthBURGENLAND producer of v.gd Blaufränkisch, esp Perwolff.

Leithaberg V'yd hill on the northern shore of Lake Neusiedl, also a lively group of producers seeking to refine regional styles.

Loimer, Fred (r) w ★★→★★★★ Highly innovative KAMPTAL producer with BIODYNAMIC 31-ha estate, 50% GRÜNER VELTLINER; also RIES, CHARD, Pinot Gr, v.gd Pinot N. One of the leading exponents of BIODYNAMIC winemaking.

NB Vintages in colour are those you should choose first for drinking in 2009.

Mantlerhof ★★★ Fine KREMSTAL producer with a well-considered, traditional approach. Gd Roter Veltliner. BIODYNAMIC producer.

Mayer am Pfarrplatz w Traditional Viennese producer and Heurigen now in new ownership, with marked improvement in the wines.

Mittelburgenland r (w) dr (sw) Wine region on Hungarian border protected by 3 hill ranges. Makes large quantities of red (esp BLAUFRÄNKISCH). Producers: GSELLMANN & HANS, J HEINRICH, Iby, Igler, P Kerschbaum, WENINGER.

Moric ★★★Outstanding red, terroir-oriented BLAUFRÄNKISCH wine made by Roland Velich from old vines in the MITTELBURGENLAND. Stylistically a beacon.

Morillon Name given in STYRIA to CHARD.

Moser, Lenz Large commercial producer nr Krems. LM III invented Hochkultur high-vine training system. Also includes wines from Schlossweingut Malteser Ritterorden (wine estate of Knights of Malta) and Klosterkeller Siegendorf (BURGENLAND). Perfectly all right, but could be a lot better.

Moser, Sepp ★★ KREMSTAL grower of elegant , aromatic RIES, GRÜNER VELTLINER.

Müller, Domaine Individualist West Styrian producer with international outlook, esp Sauv Bl and CHARD.

Müller-Thurgau See RIES-SYLVANER.

Muskateller Rare, aromatic grape for dry whites. Best from STYRIA and WACHAU. Top growers: Gross, HIRTZBERGER, Lackner-Tinnacher, FX PICHLER, POLZ, SATTLER.

Muskat-Ottonel Grape for fragrant, often dry whites, interesting PRÄDIKATS.

Neuburger Indigenous white grape that has long been neglected but has its stubborn advocates; mainly in the WACHAU (elegant, flowery), THERMENREGION (mellow and ample-bodied), and north BURGENLAND (strong, full). Best from BECK, FREIE WEINGÄRTNER, HIRTZBERGER.

Neumayer w ★★★ 96 97 98 99 00 01 02 03 04 05 06 Top TRAISENTAL estate making powerful, focused, dry GRÜNER VELTLINER and RIES.

Neumeister w ★★★ V.gd innovative SE Styrian producer, esp Sauv Bl and CHARD.

Neusiedlersee (Lake Neusiedl) V. shallow BURGENLAND lake on Hungarian border. Warmth and autumn mists encourage botrytis. See next entry.

Neusiedlersee r w dr sw Wine region N and E of Lake Neusiedl. Best: ACHS,BECK, HEINRICH, KRACHER, J NITTNAUS, PÖCKL, STIEGELMAR, UMATHUM, VELICH.

Neusiedlersee-Hügelland r w dr sw Wine region west of Neusiedlersee based around Oggau, RUST, and Mörbisch on the lake shores, and Eisenstadt in the Leitha Mts foothills. Best producers: FEILER-ARTINGER, KOLLWENTZ, Prieler, Schandl, SCHRÖCK, Sommer, ERNST TRIEBAUMER, WENZEL.

Niederösterreich (Lower Austria) Northern region with 58% of Austria's v'yds: CARNUNTUM, Donauland, KAMPTAL, KREMSTAL, THERMENREGION, TRAISENTAL, WACHAU, WEINVIERTEL.

Nigl w ★★★★ 94 95 96 97 98 99 00 01 02 03 04 05 06 07 The best in KREMSTAL, making sophisticated dry ageworthy RIES and GRÜNER VELTLINER with remarkable mineral character from Senftenberg v'yd.

Nikolaihof w ★★★★ 92 94 95 97 98 99 00 01 02 03 04 05 06 07 Built on Roman foundations, this impeccable WACHAU estate has pioneered BIODYNAMISM in Austria and produces focused RIES from the Steiner Hund site.

Nittnaus, John w r sw ★★★ Searching, organic NEUSIEDLERSEE winemaker. Esp elegant and ageworthy reds.

Opitz, Willi ★★ Tiny, impressively promoted ILLMITZ estate for late-harvest wines.

Ott, Bernhard w ★★–★★★ GRÜNER VELTLINER specialist from Donauland; Austria's freshest. Fass 4; also Der Ott and Rosenberg. Part of BIODYNAMIC movement.

Pfaffl w r ★★★ 97 98 99 00 01 02 03 04 05 06 07 WEINVIERTEL estate nr VIENNA, in Stetten. Known for wonderful dry GRÜNER VELTLINER (Goldjoch) and RIES (Terrassen Sonnleiten), he also makes surprisingly gd reds. Also runs nearby Schlossweingut Bockfliess estate.

Pichler, Franz Xavier w ★★★★ 93 94 95 96 97 98 99 00 01 02 03 04 05 06 07 Top WACHAU producer and one of Austria's best. V. intense, concentrated RIES and GRÜNER VELTLINER (esp Kellerberg).

Pichler, Rudi w ★★★→★★★★ Fine WACHAU producer of powerful, expressive RIES and GRÜNER VELTLINER.

Pöckl, Josef & René r (sw) ★★ Father-and-son team in NEUSIEDLERSEE (Mönchhof). Well-made reds, esp Admiral, Rêve de Jeunesse, and Rosso e Nero. Also gd Pinot N and ZWEIGELT.

Polz, Erich & Walter w ★★★ 97 98 99 00 01 02 03 04 05 06 07 V.gd large south STYRIAN (Weinstrasse) growers; esp Hochgrassnitzberg: Sauv Bl, CHARD, Grauburgunder, WEISSBURGUNDER.

Prädikat, Prädikatswein Quality-graded wines from Spätlese upwards (Spätlese, Auslese, Eiswein, Strohwein, Beerenauslese, AUSBRUCH, and Trockenbeerenauslese). See Germany.

Prager, Franz w ★★★★ 92 93 94 95 96 97 98 99 00 01 02 03 04 05 06 07 Pioneer, together with JOSEF JAMEK, of top-quality WACHAU dry whites. RIES and GRÜNER VELTLINER of impeccable elegance and mineral structure.

Prieler w r ★★★ V.gd NEUSIEDLERSEE-HÜGELLAND producer. Esp gd: BLAUFRÄNKISCH Goldberg.

Proidl, Erwin ★★ Fine and highly individual KREMSTAL grower making interesting, ageworthy RIES and GRÜNER VELTLINER.

Rabl, Günter ★→★★ Fine KAMPTAL grower long overshadowed by more famous colleagues. V.gd GRÜNER VELTLINER.

Riesling On its own, this always means Rhine RIES. WELSCHRIESLING is unrelated. In Austria this is one of the greatest varieties, particularly in KAMPTAL, KREMSTAL, and WACHAU. Top growers: ALZINGER, BRÜNDLMAYER, HIRTZBERGER, Högl, KNOLL, NIGL, NIKOLAIHOF, PFAFFL, FX PICHLER, PRAGER, SALOMON.

Matters of style

After Austria's overwhelming successes in recent years leading producers want to conquer new shores by refining styles and emphasizing terroir. Most interesting in this respect is the boom in good and very good Pinot N, a grape variety that thrives on delicacy and transparency, not power. There are now some fine Austrian Pinots, and similar trends are visible for indigenous red varietals such as St Laurent and Blaufränkisch.

Riesling-Sylvaner Name used for Müller-Thurgau (about 7% of Austria's grapes). Best producers: HIRTZBERGER, JURTSCHITSCH.

Rotgipfler Fragrant, indigenous grape of THERMENREGION. With ZIERFANDLER, makes lively interesting wine. Esp Biegler, Spaetrot, Stadlmann, Zierer.

Rust w r dr sw BURGENLAND region, famous since 17th century for dessert AUSBRUCH; now also for red and dry white. Esp from FEILER-ARTINGER, Schandl, HEIDI SCHRÖCK, ERNST TRIEBAUMER, Paul Triebaumer, WENZEL.

St Laurent Indigenous red variety with brambly aromas and gd tannic structure. Esp from BECK, Fischer, Johanneshof, Pitnauer, Hannes Schuster, UMATHUM.

Salomon-Undhof w ★★★ V.gd Krems producer: RIES, WEISSBURGUNDER, Traminer. V.gd quality for more than a decade. Since Erich Salomon's death his brother Berthold, who produces wine in Australia, is in charge of v'yds and cellar.

Sattler, Willi w ★★★★ 97 98 99 00 01 02 03 04 05 06 07 Top south STYRIA grower. Esp for Sauv Bl, MORILLON, often grown on v. steep v'yds. Recentl his style has become more classical.

Words within entries marked like this *Alter Ego de Palmer* indicate wines especially enjoyed by Hugh Johnson over the past 12 months (mid '07–'08).

Schilcher Rosé wine from indigenous Blauer Wildbacher grapes (sharp, dry: high acidity). A local taste, or at least an acquired one. Speciality of west STYRIA. Try: Klug, Lukas, Reiterer, Strohmeier.

Schloss Gobelsburg ★★★→★★★★ **01 02 03** 04 05 06 07 Renowned KAMPTAL estate run by Michael Moosbrugger. Excellent dry RIES and GRÜNER VELTLINER of discreet opulence. Also outstanding RIES and GRÜNER VELTLINER Tradition, vinified as it would have been 100 yrs ago, and fine Pinot N.

Schloss Halbturn w r sw ★★→★★★ Recently revitalized estate creating ever-better wines with German and French winemakers. Esp *cuvée* Imperial, also outstanding Pinot N. With new v'yds coming into production a lot may be expected here.

Schlumberger Largest sparkling winemaker in Austria (VIENNA); wine is bottle-fermented by unique "Méthode Schlumberger". Also on the Loire.

Schmelz w ★★→★★★ Rising WACHAU producer, esp outstanding Ries. Dürnsteiner Freiheit.

Schröck, Heidi w sw r ★★★→★★★★ Wines of great purity and focus from a thoughtful grower. V.gd AUSBRUCH. Also v.gd Furmint. See Hungary.

Seewinkel ("lake corner") Name given to the part of NEUSIEDLERSEE inc Apetlon, ILLMITZ, and Podersdorf. Ideal conditions for botrytis.

Smaragd Highest-quality category of VINEA WACHAU, similar to dry Spätlese.

Spätrot-Rotgipfler Typical, 2-grape blend of THERMENREGION. Aromatic and weighty wines.

Spitz an der Donau w Cool WACHAU microclimate, esp from Singerriedel v'yd. Top growers are: DONAUBAUM, HIRTZBERGER, Högl, Lagler.

Steinfeder VINEA WACHAU quality category for light fragrant dry wines.

Stiegelmar (Juris-Stiegelmar) w r dr sw ★★ Important GOLS grower. CHARD, Sauv Bl. Reds: ST LAURENT.

Styria (Steiermark) Southernmost wine region of Austria. Some gd dry whites, esp Sauv Bl and CHARD, called MORILLON in Styria. Also cool fragrant MUSKATELLER. Inc SÜDSTEIERMARK, SÜD-OSTSTEIERMARK, WESTSTEIERMARK (South, Southeast, West Styria).

Südburgenland r w Small BURGENLAND wine region. V.gd BLAUFRÄNKISCH wines. Best producers: Krutzler, Wachter-Wiesler, Schiefer.

Süd-Oststeiermark SE Styria w (r) STYRIAN region with islands of excellent v'yds. Best producers: Neumeister, Winkler-Hermaden.

Südsteiermark S Styria w Best STYRIA region; popular whites (MORILLON, MUSKATELLER, WELSCHRIESLING, and Sauv Bl). Best: Gross, Jaunegg, Lackner-Tinnacher, POLZ, Potzinger Sabathi, SATTLER, Skoff, TEMENT, Wohlmuth.

Tement, Manfred w ★★★★ **97 98 99 00** 01 02 03 04 05 06 07 Renowned south STYRIA estate with well-made Steirische Klassik and gently oaked Sauv Bl and MORILLON from Zieregg site. International-style wines, modern reds.

Thermenregion r w dr sw Wine/hot-springs region, south of VIENNA. Indigenous grapes (eg ZIERFANDLER, ROTGIPFLER), historically one of the most important regions for reds (esp ST LAURENT) from Baden, GUMPOLDSKIRCHEN, Tattendorf, Traiskirchen areas. Producers: Alphart, Biegler, Fischer, Johanneshof, Schafler, Stadelmann, Zierer.

Traisental 700 ha just south of Krems on Danube. Dry whites can be similar to WACHAU in style, not usually in quality. Top producers: Huber, NEUMAYER.

Triebaumer, Ernst r (w) dr sw ★★★★ **93 94 95 97 98 99** 00 01 02 03 04 05 06 07 RUST producer; some of Austria's best reds: BLAUFRÄNKISCH (inc the legendary Mariental), Cab Sauv/Merlot blend. v.gd AUSBRUCH. One of several Triebaumers – known as ET.

Umathum, Josef w r dr sw ★★★ **97 98 99** 00 01 02 03 04 05 v.gd and thoughtful NEUSIEDLERSEE producer. v.gd reds inc Pinot N, ST LAURENT; gd whites.

Velich Neusiedlersee w sw ★★★★ A searching, intellectual producer. Excellent Burgundian-style Tiglat CHARD (**99 00 01** 02 03) with fine barrel-ageing. Some of top PRÄDIKATS in the SEEWINKEL.

Vienna w (r) ("Wien" in German and on labels) Wine region in suburbs. Generally simple, lively wines, served to busloads of tourists in HEURIGEN, but quality producers on the rise: Christ, WIENINGER, Zahel.

Vinea Wachau WACHAU appellation started by winemakers in 1983 with 3 categories of dry wine: STEINFEDER, FEDERSPIEL, and the powerful SMARAGD.

Wachau w World-renowned Danube region, home to some of Austria's best wines. Top producers: Alzinger, J DONABAUM, FREIE WEINGÄRTNER WACHAU, HIRTZBERGER, Högl, JAMEK, KNOLL, Lagler, NIKOLAIHOF, FX PICHLER, R Pichler, PRAGER, Schmelz, Wess.

Wagram w (r) Wine region just west of VIENNA, inc KLOSTERNEUBURG. Mainly whites, esp GRÜNER VELTLINER. Best producers include: Ehmoser, Fritsch, Stift Klosterneuburg, Leth, BERNHARD OTT, Wimmer-Czerny, R Zimmermann.

Weingut Stadt Krems ★★ Co-op now steered by former FREIE WEINGÄRTNER WACHAU guru Fritz Miesbauer, who has transformed the quality of the whites. Miesbauer now also vinifies for Stift Göttweig.

Weinviertel ("Wine Quarter") w (r) Largest Austrian wine region, between Danube and Czech border. First to adopt DAC appellation status. Looking for increasing quality and regional character. Mostly refreshing whites, esp from Poysdorf, Retz. Best: Bauer, J Diem, GRAF HARDEGG, Gruber, PFAFFL, Schwarzböck, Weinrieder, Zull.

Weissburgunder (Pinot Blanc) Ubiquitous: gd dry wines and PRÄDIKATS. Esp BECK, Fischer, Gross, HEINRICH, HIRTZBERGER, Lackner-Tinnacher, POLZ, TEMENT.

Welschriesling White grape, not related to RIES, grown in all wine regions: simple, fragrant dry wines for everyday drinking.

Weninger, Franz r (w) ★★★ Top MITTELBURGENLAND (Horitschon) estate, with fine reds, esp BLAUFRÄNKISCH, Dürrau, and Merlot. Formerly an exponent of "red power", Weninger has switched to BIODYNAMIC production, more finely structured wines. Son runs Hungarian estate.

Wenzel w r sw ★★★ V.gd AUSBRUCH. Junior Michael is interested in reds. Father Robert pioneered the Furmint revival in RUST.

Weststeiermark W Styria p Small wine region specializing in SCHILCHER. Best: Klug, Lukas, DOM MÜLLER, Reiterer, Strohmeier.

Wien See VIENNA.

Wieninger, Fritz w r ★★→★★★ **97 98 99 00 01 02 03** 04 05 06 07 V.gd VIENNA-Stammersdorf grower with HEURIGE: CHARD, BLAUER BURGUNDER, esp gd GRÜNER VELTLINER and RIES. Wines of great balance and depth.

Winkler-Hermaden r w sw ★★★ Outstanding and individual southeast STYRIAN producer, excellent Traminer and MORILLON, also one of the region's few v.gd reds, the ZWEIGELT-based Olivin.

Winzer Krems Important KREMSTAL co-op with 1,300 growers. Esp GRÜNER VELTLINER.

Zierfandler (Spätrot) White variety almost exclusive to THERMENREGION. Often blended with ROTGIPFLER. Best: Biegler, Spaetrot, Stadelmann, Zierer.

Zweigelt See BLAUER ZWEIGELT.

To decipher codes, please refer to "Key to symbols" on the front flap of jacket, or "How to use this book" on p.10.

Central & Southeast Europe

More heavily shaded
areas are the wine-
growing regions

Hungary

Over the past 17 years Hungary's wine culture has started to recover from its
Communist past. Quality has improved considerably, with many dedicated
family-owned wineries appearing. The luscious sweet wines of Tokaji are still
Hungary's crowning glory, the best great by any standard. There are currently 22
wine districts, within six regions: North Pannonia, Balaton, South Pannonia,
Great Plain, North Hungary and Tokaj-Hegyalja.

Alföld Hungary's Great Plain makes everyday wine. Incorporates 3 districts:
 Hajós-Baja (Brillant Holding, Sümegi), Csongrád (Somodi), Kunság
 (Frittmann).

Árvay & Co w dr sw ★★→★★★★ 99 00 TOKAJ cellar established in 2000 and
 headed by former DISZNÓKŐ winemaker János Árvay. Hétfürtös is the brand
 name. V. gd ASZÚ (5/6 PUTTONYOS) and superb *cuvée* Edés Élet (**01'**).

Ászár-Neszmély Wine region in northwest Hungary nr the Danube. International
 and native grapes, predominantly white. Hilltop is leading winery (Kamocsay).

Aszú Botrytis-shrivelled grapes and the sweet wine made from them in TOKAJ, similar to Sauternes. The wine is graded in sweetness, from 3 PUTTONYOS up.

Aszú Eszencia Tokaj SW ★★★★ 93 96' **99' 00'** 02 03 (05) (06) Second sweetest TOKAJI quality (see ESZENCIA). 7 PUTTONYOS+; should be superb amber elixir.

Badacsony w dr sw ★★→★★★ Wine district on north shore of Lake BALATON, on slopes of extinct volcano, home to native variety KÉKNYELÜ. The basalt soil can give rich, highly flavoured white wines; esp well-made Ries and SZÜRKEBARÁT; Pinot N also promising. The leader is SZEREMLEY's Szent Orbán winery.

Balaton Europe's largest freshwater lake. Wines from BADASCONY and BALATONFURED-CSOPAK on north shore. Wines from BALATONBOGLÁR on south.

Balatonboglár r w dr sw ★★→★★★ Name of wine district and also a progressive winery owned by Henkell & Söhnlein on south shore of Lake BALATON. Decent whites (Chard, Sem, Muscat). Also *cuve close* sparkling. Top producers: GARAMVÁRI, KONYÁRI, Léglí.

Balatonfured-Csopak r w dr ★★ District on north shore of Lake BALATON. Mainly whites, esp Olaszrizling, Chard. Best producers Jasdi, Figula.

Balaton-Melleke (S Pannonia) w dr Small region in Zala Hills. Mainly whites, esp Tramini, Pinot Gr, OLASZRIZLING. Wines of Dr Bussay impress.

Beres w dr sw ★★★ New and immaculate TOKAJ producer.

Bikavér r ★→★★★ **02 03** 04 05 (06) Literally "Bull's Blood" with past reputation for ordinary quality. Now being revived as potential flagship blended red. Can be produced by law only in SZEKSZÁRD and EGER. Egri Bikavér gained protected origin status from 04 vintage. Must be blend of at least 3 varieties; best producers include a local grape, usually KÉKFRANKOS, and in SZEKSZÁRD sometimes KADARKA. Reserve level requires minimum of 4 varieties, obligatory tasting, and restricted yield. Best producers for Egri Bikavér: Grof Buttler, TIBOR GÁL, St Andrea, Thummerer.

Bock, József r dr ★→★★★ Family winemaker in VILLÁNY. Hearty reds, varietal and blends. Best wines are Cab Fr-based Capella Cuvée **99 00** 03 and Syrah **03'**.

Bodrogkeresztúr Village in TOKAJ region with several up-and-coming estates inc DERESZLA, Füleky, Tokajbor Bene, TIMON.

Bor "Wine": *vörös* is red; *fehér* is white; *asztali* is table; *táj* is country.

Csányi r ★→★★ Major investment in VILLÁNY with substantial v'yds. Ch Teleki range is best.

Dégenfeld, Grof w dr sw ★★→★★★ Large TOKAJ estate. Produces dry FURMINT, classic ASZÚ, v. attractive late-harvest Andante and EDES SZAMORODNI Also a luxury hotel at TARCAL.

Dereszla w dr sw 50-ha TOKAJ estate owned by French D'Aulan family from Champagne. V.gd ASZÚ, inc ASZÚ ESZENCIA and flor-matured dry SZAMORODNI.

Disznókő w dr sw ★★→★★★★ **96' 97 99'** 00 02(03) Important TOKAJ estate, owned by French company AXA. Sauternes-style wines of the early yrs have given way to more typically Hungarian note, imparted by a Hungarian, instead of Sauternais, winemaker. Single-v'yd Kapi 6 PUTTONYOS ASZÚ 99' is notable.

Dobogó ★★★ **99' 00'** (03) (05) (06) Fine small TOKAJ estate for ASZÚ. Also excellent late-harvest Mylitta and *v.gd dry Furmint 05 (06)*.

Edes Sweet wine (but not as luscious as ASZÚ).

Eger r w dr sw ★→★★★ Best-known red wine centre of N Hungary with attractive baroque city of cellars. BIKAVÉR most famous wine, but increasingly recognized for Cab Fr, Pinot N, and Syrah. Whites inc fresh LEÁNYKA, OLASZRIZLING, Chard, Pinot Bl. Top producers: Grof Buttler, Demeter, Tibor Gál's GIA, Gundel Cellar, Ostoros, Pók-Polonyi, St Andrea, Vilmos Thummerer (consistent BIKAVÉR), Béla Vincze, and the huge Egervin.

Eszencia ★★★★ 93 96 99 (03)The fabulous quintessence of TOKAJI: intensely sweet and aromatic from grapes wizened by botrytis. Properly grape juice of v. low, if any, alcoholic strength, reputed to have miraculous properties: incl raising the dead. Its sugar content can be over 850g per litre.

Etyek-Buda (Észak-Dunántúl) Wine region nr Budapest. Some gd crisp varietal whites, esp Chard and Sauv Bl, Pinot Gr, and IRSAI OLIVÉR. Leading producers: Etyeki Kúria, Nyakas (Budai label), György Villa (owned by TÖRLEY).

Ezerjó Literally "thousand blessings". Widespread traditional grape variety: one-dimensional wines with little aroma and sharp acids. Best from MÓR.

Furmint The classic grape of TOKAJ, with great flavour, acidity, and fire, also grown for table wine in TOKAJ and in SOMLÓ.

Gál, Tibor r w dr ★★→★★★ Winery in EGER founded by charismatic Tibor Gál, who made his name as winemaker at Ornellaia. Tragically died in 2005; his family continues his work, esp single-v'yd bottlings of Pinot N and v.gd dry Viognier.

Garamvári r w d sp ★→★★ Family-owned v'yd and St Donatus winery at Balatonlelle. Also owns Ch Vincent, Hungary's top bottle-fermented sparkling wine, plus négociant Vinarium.

Gere, Attila r ★★→★★★ Family winemaker in VILLÁNY with gd, forward-looking reds, esp rich Solus Merlot (03), intense Kopar Cuvée (03 04), plus oak-aged Cab Sauv (00 03 04) and Cuvée Phoenix 04.

Gundel TOKAJ venture at MÁD, making wines for famous Gundel's restaurant in Budapest. Also v'yds and cellar at EGER.

Hárslevelü "Linden-leaved" grape variety widely grown. Gd in SOMLÓ and important as second grape of TOKAJ. Gentle, mellow wine; peach aroma.

Hétszölö w dr sw ★★→★★★ Noble first-growth 55-ha TOKAJ estate owned by French group Grands Millésimes de France. Wines sadly uneven. Winemaker is highly regarded Tibor Kóvacs.

Hilltop Neszmély w r dr sw ★ Winery in ÁSZÁR-NESZMÉLY makes international-style wines, inc Riverview and Woodcutters White from Cserszegi Füszeres. Premier Vintage range best.

Irsai Olivér Local white cross of 2 table varieties making aromatic Muscat-like wine for drinking young.

Kadarka Traditional red grape in south largely fallen out of production, but can produce ample flavour when fully mature. Considered by some an essential element of BIKAVÉR, esp in SZEKSZÁRD. Known as Gamza in Bulgaria.

Kékfrankos Hungarian for Blaufränkisch. Most widely planted red variety. Gd light or full-bodied reds.

Kéknyelü "Blue stalk". High-flavoured, low-yielding white grape needing a cross pollinator and making the best and most structured wine of BADACSONY. Best is complex with mineral undertones from SZEREMLEY.

Királyudvar w dr sw ★★→★★★★ TOKAJ winery in old royal cellars at Tarcal, owned by Anthony Hwang. Wines include dry and late-harvest FURMINT, Cuvée Ilona (early-bottled ASZÚ), and exciting 6 PUTTONYOS Lapis Aszú (99 02).

Konyári r w dr ★★→★★★ Father-and-son team making high-quality red and white from own estate, esp Loliense and Sessio Merlot.

Leányka "Little girl". White grape from Transylvania known as Fetească Albă in Romania. Attractive, aromatic, light dry wine. Királyleányka ("Royal") or Fetească Regală is a cross of Fetească Albă with Grasă of Cotnari.

Mád Old commercial centre of the TOKAJ region with top v'yds. Growers inc Vince Gergely, GUNDEL, József Monyok, ROYAL TOKAJI, SZEPSY, Tokaj Classic.

Malatinszky r w dr ★★★ Owner/winemaker was previously sommelier at GUNDEL. Immaculate winery making top-quality unfiltered Kuria Cab Fr 03' 04 (06) Cab Sauv 03' 04 (06). Gd KÉKFRANKOS rosé **06**, Pinot Bleu 06, Siklosi Chard **05** 06.

Mátra w (r) ★→★★★ District in foothills of Mátra range. Promising dry SZÜRKEBARÁT (Pinot Gr), Chard, MUSKOTÁLY, Sauv Bl. Producers worth a mention are family-owned Szöke Mátyás and former state farm turned co-operative Szölöskert (selling under Nagyrede and Spice Trail labels).

Megyer, Château w dr sw ★★→★★★ TOKAJ estate bought by Jean-Louis Laborde of Ch Clinet in Pomerol. Also owns CH PAJZOS. Megyer is lighter wine from cooler N of region. Quality improving, esp dry FURMINT (06), ASZÚ 6 PUTTONYOS (99). Appealing dry Muscat.

Mézes Mály In TARCAL. This and SZARVAS are historically the best v'yds of TOKAJ.

Minőségi Bor Quality wine. Hungary's appellation contrôlée (see France).

Mór N Hungary w ★→★★ Region famous for fresh, dry EZERJÓ. Now also Ries and Sauv Bl. Wines mostly exported. István Bozóky is most respected winery.

Muskotály Muscat; usually Ottonel, except TOKAJ where Sárga Muskotály is yellow Muscat or Muscat Lunel. Makes light but long-lived wine in TOKAJ and EGER. A little goes into the TOKAJI blend. V. occasionally makes a wonderful ASZÚ wine solo.

Olaszrizling Hungarian name for the Italian Ries or Welschriesling. Better examples can have a burnt-almond aroma.

Oremus w dr sw ★★→★★★★ Ancient TOKAJ v'yd of founding Rakóczi family, owned by Spain's Vega Sicilia with HQ at Tolcsva. First-rate ASZÚ and recently v. gd dry FURMINT Mandolás. Also a lesser TOKAJ grape, renamed Zeta.

Patricius w dr sw ★★→★★★ New quality TOKAJ estate, first vintage in 2000. V.gd dry FURMINT and ASZÚ wines. 4 PUTTONYOS is unusual but has lovely balance.

Pajzos, Château w dr sw ★★→★★★ Bordeaux-owned TOKAJ estate with some fine ASZÚ. See MEGYER.

Pannonhalma w r dr ★★ Region toward north with mostly small growers. Recent joint venture has revived historic Pannonhalma Abbey winery and v'yds dating back to 996. Soil and climate Alsace-like: TRAMINI Ries do well and v.gd value. Also attractive white blend Tricollis Cuvée and young Pinot N.

Pécs (S Pannonia) formerly Mecsek w (r) ★→★★ Newly renamed wine district in southern Hungary, based around the city of Pécs. Known for whites, inc OLASZRIZLING, local Cirfandl, and Sauv Bl. Pinot N reported to be promising. Ebner Borhaz most respected producer.

Pendits Winery w sw ★★★ TOKAJ estate in conversion to organic production run by Márta Wille-Baumkauff. Luscious ASZÚ ESZENCIA (00), Botrytis Selection (01).

Puttonyos Measure of sweetness in TOKAJI ASZÚ. A "puttony" is a 25-kg measure, traditionally a hod of grapes. The number of "putts" per barrel (136 litres) of dry base wine or must determines the final richness of the wine, from 3 putts to 6 (3 putts = 60g of sugar per litre, 4 = 90g, 5 = 120g, 6 =150g, 7 = 180g). See also ASZÚ ESZENCIA and ESZENCIA.

Royal Tokaji Wine Co Pioneer foreign joint venture at MÁD in 1989. 81 ha, mainly first- or second-growth. First wines 90 91 and (esp) 93 led renaissance of TOKAJ. 99 00 03 to follow. (I am a co-founder.) Also well-made dry FURMINT and v.gd Late Harvest Áts Cuvée. New investment and building in 2008.

Siklós (S Pannonia) City in southern Hungary; part of VILLÁNY-SIKLÓS district. Mainly small producers, known for whites: esp HÁRSLEVELŰ. Ripe, fruity Chard promising; also TRAMINI, OLASZRIZLING.

Somló N Hungary w ★★ Isolated small district N of BALATON: whites (formerly of high repute) from FURMINT and Juhfark ("sheep's tail") in both traditional barrel-fermented and fresh, fruity styles. Top producers include Fekete, Györgykovács, Inhauser, Tornai.

Sopron W Hungary r ★★→★★★ Historic enclave south of Neusiedlersee (see Austria). Traditionally known for lighter reds from KÉKFRANKOS but showing promise for more full-bodied reds, plus Cab Sauv, Syrah, Pinot N. Top producer WENINGER, promising Jandl, Lövér, Luka, Pfneiszl, Taschner.

Szamorodni Literally "as it was born"; describes TOKAJI not sorted in the v'yd. Dry or (fairly) sweet, depending on proportion of ASZÚ grapes present. In vintage TOKAJ ASZÚ yrs, sweet style can offer ASZÚ character at less cost. Recent trend for late-harvest wines that are similar but bottled younger in more fruity style.

Száraz Dry, esp of TOKAJI SZAMORODNI.

Szarvas Tokaj v'yd at Tarcal; a top site. Solely owned by TOKAJ TRADING HOUSE and state-run Research Institute for Vine and Wine.

Szekszárd (Pannon) r ★★–★★★★ District in south Hungary; some of country's top reds from KÉKFRANKOS, Cab Sauv, Cab Fr, and Merlot. Also KADARKA being revived. Look for: Dúzsi, Heimann, Mészáros, Sárosdi, Sebestyén, Szent Gaál Pincészet, Takler, Vesztergombi, Vida, Dom Gróf Zichy. Aranyfurt coop makes decent, value-for-money wines sold through Vinarium.

Szepsy, István w dr sw ★★★★ Legendary name and impeccable small production of long-ageing TOKAJI ASZÚ from own winery in MÁD. Recent releases of excellent dry single-v'yd wines from FURMINT and HÁRSLEVELÜ, and new sweet Szamorodni from 03. Same family name as the man who created the ASZÚ method in 17th century, though not related.

Szeremley, Huba r w dr sw ★★–★★★ Leader in BADACSONY. Ries, SZÜRKEBARÁT, KÉKNYELÜ, sweet Zeus are modern models. Promising Pinot N since 03. Szent Orbán is another label.

Szürkebarát Literally "Grey Monk": Pinot Gr. Widely planted and produces high-quality dry wines and inexpensive Italian lookalikes, esp around BALATON.

Tarcal TOKAJ commune with 2 great first growths and several gd producers: GRÓF DEGENFELD, KIRÁLYUDVAR, Andrássy Kúria.

Tiffán, Ede ★★ VILLÁNY grower: full-bodied, oaked reds.

Tinon, Samuel French ASZU specialist at BODROGKERESZTÚR. Also fine SZAMORODNI.

Tokaj/Tokaji w dr sw ★★–★★★★★ Tokaj is the town; Tokaji is the wine, Tokay the old French and English name. Appellation covers 5,967 ha. See ESZENCIA, FURMINT, PUTTONYOS, SZAMORODNI. Also dry table wine of character.

Tokaj Trading House State-owned TOKAJ company, buying grapes from over 2,000 small growers plus 55 ha own vines inc the fine SZARVAS v'yd. Also called Kereskedöház or Crown Estates. Castle Island is the brand for dry wines.

Tolcsva-Bor Kft (Tokaj) Gd late-harvest wines. Consider 5 PUTTONYOS ASZÚ.

Tolna Declared separate region from SZEKSZÁRD in 1997. Largest single estate is Antinori-owned Bátaapáti with 155ha. Good TRAMINI, Chard, blended reds. German-owned Danubiana based here though most of its v'yds are at MÁTRA.

Törley Large company (previously Hungarovin): international varietals (Chard, Cab Sauv, Merlot), also *cuve close*, transfer, and classic sparkling (the one to try). Owned by German Sekt specialist Henkell & Söhnlein.

Tramini Gewurz, esp in SIKLÓS.

Villány-Siklós (S Pannonia) Southern wine region with 2 main towns. Villány makes mostly red, often good-quality B'x styles. Siklós makes mostly white. High-quality producers: BOCK, CSÁNYI, ATTILA GERE, Gere Tamas, Günzer, Jekl, MALATINSZKY, Mayer, Polgár, TIFFÁN, Wunderlich, VYLAN.

Vylyan r w dr ★★–★★★★ Significant investment by late Pal Debreczeni, now run by his wife Monika. 130 ha planted with local and international varieties. Influence of Burgundian consultant shows in increasingly stylish Pinot N. *Duennium Cuvée* (Cab Fr, Cab Sauv, Merlot, and Zweigelt) is flagship red.

Weninger r ★★★ Standard-setting winery in Balf, SOPRON, run by Austrian Franz Weninger Jr. Biodynamic since 2006. Single-v'yd Spern Steiner KÉKFRANKOS one of best in country. Syrah, Pinot N, and red blends also impressive.

Weninger & Gere r ★★★ Austro-Hungarian joint venture since 1992 between Franz Weninger Sr and attila gere. Cab Fr Selection excellent (02 03 04).

Zéta A cross of Bouvier and FURMINT used by some in ASZÚ production.

HUNGARY

Bulgaria

Good-quality wines are now being produced by boutique wineries, but with a buoyant domestic market not much is exported. Specialist wine merchants rather than supermarkets have a good selection. The 07 vintage was, with 03, the best for a decade.

Assenovgrad r ★→★★ Ageworthy MAVRUD and RUBIN specialists. MAVRUD 03.

Belvedere Group Group owning Menada, Katarzyna, Oriachovitza, and Vinimpex brands.

Bessa Valley r ★★★ Exciting winery nr Pazardjik. Started by B'x specialist Stephan von Neipperg and K-H Hauptmann. Enira and Enira Reserve **04**.

Blueridge r w ★→★★ Major DOM BOYAR winery, label.

Chateau de Val r ★★ New small producer of distinctive top-end wines. Grand Claret **03** recommended.

Controliran Like France's AC. Wine law published in 2000, updated in 2004.

Damianitsa r ★★→★★★ Quality-soaring winery specializing in MELNIK grape. V.gd ReDark Merlot **03**; Uniqato and No Man's Land labels consistent quality.

DGO "Quality wines with declared geographical origin".

Dimiat Native white grape. Gd examples from BLUERIDGE and POMORIE.

Domaine Boyar Exporter to UK, own v'yds and wineries.

Gamza Red grape (Kadarka of Hungary) with potential, mainly from Danube region. NOVO SELO is specialist.

Katarzyna ★★ Promising quality from new cellar.

Khan Krum ★→★★ Gd whites, esp Chard and TRAMINER.

Korten ★→★★ Boutique cellar of DOMAINE BOYAR. Traditional styles.

Leventa ★★ Small new winery in Russe with particularly gd whites, esp TRAMINER. 06 Chard and Merlot Grand Selections also recommended.

Logodaj ★→★★ New winery at Blagoevgrad. Soetto Cab Fr **05**. Gd value.

Mavrud Considered the best indigenous red variety, v. popular at home. Can make highly ageworthy, dark, plummy wines only grown in the south.

Maxxima r (w) Full-bodied reds esp Cab Sauv, Merlot, and Mavrud. First producer of Premium |Reserve oak-aged reds. Private Reserve is top wine.

Melnik Southwest village and highly prized grape variety grown throughout Struma Valley. Dense reds that can age up to 20 yrs.

Menada Stara Zagora r ★★ Thracian Plain winery, owned by Belvedere group. Menada Trinity Mavrud **04**.

Eduardo Miroglio r w ★★ Italian investor with own v'yds. Improving quality, still pricey. Newly launched sparkling wine, Sauv Bl, and Pinot N recommended.

Misket Indigenous grape, mildly aromatic. The basis for most country whites. Sungurlare and Karlovo in the Valley of the Roses are specialists.

Novo Selo Gd red GAMZA from the northwest.

Oriachovitza r ★★ Winery owned by Belvedere. Also Thracian Plain area for CONTROLIRAN Cab Sauv and Merlot. Also winery with gd Reserve Cab Sauv **04**. Richly fruity reds at their best after 4–5 yrs.

Pamid Light, soft, everyday red in southeast and northwest.

Pomorie w (r) ★ Black Sea winery. Esp gd Chard and MISKAT.

Rubin Bulgarian cross (Nebbiolo x Syrah); gd in blends, but gaining favour in single-varietal niche wines.

Sakar Southeast area with some of Bulgaria's best Merlot.

Santa Sarah r w ★★ Premium wine brand for fine Cab Sauv, Merlot. Privat **04 05** outstanding. MAVRUD 03. Also gd whites.

Shumen w r ★ New World-style reds and esp whites from Black Sea-region winery. Good TRAMINER, popular on home market.

Slaviantsi ★ Gd varietal whites.

Sliven, Vini r (w) ★→★★ Thracian Valley winery for Merlot, MISKET, and Chard. Promising barrique-aged Cab Sauv.

Targovishte w ★ Winery in east. Quality Chard, Sauv Bl, and TRAMINER.

Telish r Innovative winery in north. Quality Cab Sauv and Merlot. Gd value.

Terra Tangra r w ★★→★★★ New winery in southeast nr Harmanli, own v'yds in a gd area. Really impressive wines, widely recommended. Try the Cab Sauv and Merlot Gran Reserves **05**. The winery to watch.

Todoroff r (w) ★→★★ Thracian-region high-profile winery (25 ha): Cab Sauv, MAVRUD, Merlot.

Traminer Fine whites with hints of spice. Most popular white in Bulgaria.

Valley Vintners ★★ Bulgaria's first terroir wine Sensum **03** is excellent. Also Le Cubiste label.

Villa Lyubimets ★→★★ V'yds in southeast nr Greek-Turkish borders. Mainly reds. Villa Hissar is sister white label.

Vinimpex A major exporter of Bulgarian wines. Formerly state owned.

Yambol r w ★ Winery in Thracian Plain, specializing in Cab Sauv and Merlot.

Slovenia

Rapidly established itself as the class act of the Balkans with many strings to its bow. Although reds are more highly regarded by Slovenians and fetch higher prices, it helps to think white when in Slovenia. Recently more skin contact has boosted flavours. The vintage of 06 is considered very good to excellent, and 07 is not far behind.

Batič ★★ Organic v'yd in VIPAVA. Try Bonissimus and Zarja 06'.

Bjana ★★→★★★ Top BRDA sparkling producer. Intense, full-bodied wines.

Brda (Goriška) district in PRIMORJE. Centre of quality with many v.gd producers, among them BJANA, Blažič, Četrtič, EDI SIMČIČ, Erzetič, JAKONČIČ, Kabaj, Klinec, KTISTANČIČ, MOVIA, Prinčič, SIMČIČ, ŠČUREK, VINSKA KLET GORIŠKA BRDA.

Čotar ★★→★★★ Leading producer from KRAS. Hazy white blend Dražna and Vitovska are made with long skin contact. Also Teran and Terra Rossa.

Čurin Legendary pioneer of private wine-growing from early 1970s onward. PREDIKATS is world-class ★★★★ and ★★ dry/medium varietal line. Also brand PRA-Vino.

Cviček Locally popular trad pink blend of POSAVJE. Low alcohol, high acid.

Dveri-Pax ★★★Excellent winery nr Maribor. Basic line offers crisp, good value whites. Premium line, inc renowned Renski Rizling "M" 06 07, is mostly from single v'yds. Modri Pinot **06'** 07' and Modra Frankinja **06'** 07' are excellent.

Istenič ★★→★★★ NV Barbara and Miha are gd value, while Gourmet vintage range is often Slovenia's best. Brut Nature Prestige 03' is brut zero fizz.

Jakončič ★★★ V.gd BRDA producer with elegant whites and reds. Top wines: white **04' 05'** and red **04'** blend Carolina. Also try lighter varietals.

Jeruzalem Top v'yd village in LJUTOMER ORMOŽ.

Jeruzalem Ormož ★★ **06' 07'** Well-known co-op producing crisp whites, esp Šipon (Furmint), Sauv Bl, RENSKI RIZLING (Ries), and blend Terase.

Joannes ★★ Winery nr Maribor, esp Ries **04'** 05' 06' and Chard.

Kogl ★★★ Hilltop winery nr Ormož, dating back to 16th century. Replanted 1984. Whites among Slovenia's best, either varietal (Mea Culpa) or Duo, Trio, and Quartet blends. Premium blends (red and white) Magna Domenica. Exceptionally delicate PREDIKATS. Repays ageing.

Koper Coastal district in PRIMORJE, known for REFOŠK and constantly improving MALAVAZIJA. SANTOMAS and VINAKOPER excel.

Kras Small, famous district in PRIMORJE. Best known for TERAN but trend is toward whites, esp MALVAZIJA. Look for ČOTAR, Jazbec, Lisjak Boris, RENČEL.

Kristančič (Dušan) ★★ Important quality producer from BRDA. Consistent varietal line and oak-aged Pavo ("peacock") line.

Kupljen ★★→★★★ Dry wine pioneer nr JERUZALEM known for RENSKI RIZLING, Sauv Bl, SIVI PINOT, Chard, Pinot N, 2 blends: red and white Star of Stiria blends.

Laški Rizling Welschriesling. Most-planted variety, but rarely made as a varietal.

Ledeno vino Icewine. Only in exceptional yrs and can be sublime.

Ljutomer Ormož ★★→★★★ Traditionally top wine sub-district in PODRAVJE, known for white varietals and top botrytis, has still more to deliver. See: ČURIN, JERUZALEM ORMOŽ, KOGL, Krainz, Krajnc, KUPLJEN.

Macerated whites Recently v. popular. Whites produced with several days' long maceration at higher temperatures. There is hardly an important producer in PRIMORSKA not using this technique at least in part.

Malvazija Slightly bitter yet generous flavour, which goes v. well with seafood. M by VINAKOPER is incredible value. Also v. gd from Pucer, Rojac. In recent yrs successfully grown in BRDA and KRAS.

Mlečnik ★★★ Disciple of Italy's Joško Gravner from VIPAVA. The closest anyone in Slovenia comes to organics.

Modra Frankinja Austria's Blaufränkisch. Traditionally best in POSAVJE, but DVERI-PAX and PTUJSKA KLET are giving a challenge.

Movia ★★★★ Best-known Slovenian winery. Releases only mature vintages of top wines: Veliko Rdeče **96' 00'** 01' (red) and Belo (white) **03'** 04. Varietals usually v.gd. Lunar (REBULA) 05 **06'** 07 and sparkling Puro are unusual.

Penina Quality sparkling wine made by either charmat or traditional method. Lots of styles available. Look for RADGONSKE GORICE (biggest), ISTENIČ (biggest private), BJANA (most fashionable).

Podravje Most respected Slovenian region in the northeast. Recent comeback with aromatic whites and increasingly fine reds, mostly Modri Pinot.

Posavje Conservative wine region in the southeast. Notable producers are ISTENIČ, PRUS, ŠTURM.

Predikat Wines made from botrytis-affected grapes with high sugar content. Only in PODRAVJE and POSAVJE regions. Pozna Trgatev is Spätlese, Izbor is Auslese, Jagodni Izbor is Beerenauslese, Suhi Jagodni Izbor is Trockenbeerenauslese, while LEDENO VINO is Icewine.

Primorje Region in the southwest from the Adriatic to BRDA. The most forward-looking Slovenian wine region for both reds and whites.

Prus Small producer from the Bela Krajina district in POSAVJE. His delicate and complex PREDIKATS are ★★★★.

Ptujska Klet ★★→★★★ Winery in Ptuj with a collection of vintages from 1917. Improvements since 03. Brand Pullus since 07. Sauv Bl is regularly v.gd.

Radgonske Gorice ★★ Well-known co-op producing best-selling Slovenian sparkler Srebrna ("silver") PENINA, classic-method Zlata ("golden") PENINA, and legendary demi-sec Traminec with black label.

Rebula Traditional white variety of BRDA. Can be exceptional. Top blends are v. often made from Rebula and Chard.

Refošk Refosco. Ruby, light, and green version is v. popular in local bars and restaurants. SANTOMAS and VINAKOPER show the results can be different.

Renčel ★★★ Remarkable producer from KRAS (tiny quantities, experiments).

Renski Rizling Ries. Best: DVERI-PAX, JERUZALEM-ORMOŽ, JOANNES, Krajnc, KUPLJEN.

Santomas ★★★ KOPER. Gd mature, international-style REFOŠK Cab Sauv.

Sauvignonasse Aka Tocai Friulano, mostly in BRDA. V. popular locally and in Italy.

Ščurek ★★→★★★ V. reliable BRDA producer (Chard, REBULA, Tokaji, Sauv Bl, Cab Fr). V. particular red and white blends, Stara Brajda and classy white Dugo.

Since 02 excellent premium red blend Up.

Simčič, Edi ★★★★ Highly reputed BRDA producer. Look for Chard, REBULA, SIVI PINOT. Outstanding red blend Duet Lex **02** 03' and v. expensive Kolos 03.

Simčič, Marjan ★★★★ Excellent BRDA producer (Chard, SIVI PINOT). REBULA-based blend Teodor is outstanding. Sauv Bl is oak-aged, while muscular Modri Pinot gets more and more elegant. In selected yrs great sweet Leonardo.

Sivi Pinot Italy's Pinot Gr. Increasingly fine, fruity, with much more character and body than in neighbouring Fruili Venezia-Giulia.

Štajerska Slovenija New and important wine district since 2006 which encompasses practically whole PODRAVJE region.

Steyer ★★ Top name from RADGONSKE GORICE. Best known for TRAMINEC in all possible forms and styles.

Šturm ★★ Long-established, yet lone star of the Bela Krajina district in POSAVJE. Many PREDIKATS are outstanding.

Sutor ★★★ Excellent producers from VIPAVA. Excellent Modri Pinot 06 and Chard 04 **05'**, white blend Burja **04' 05' 06'**, and Merlot **03'** 04.

Teran ★ REFOŠK from KRAS. Dark, high-acidity red, v. popular locally.

Valdhuber ★★★ Dry wine pioneers in PODRAVJE. Top wine is (dry) Traminec.

Verus Vinogradi ★★→★★★ 07' Young team with distinctive white varietals in JERUZALEM.

Vinakoper ★★→★★★ Large company with own v'yds in KOPER. Many rewarding varietals inc MALVAZIJA, Cab Sauv, and REFOŠK; gd-value Capris line and Premium Capo d'Istria Cab Sauv **99'** 02 **03'**.

Vinska Klet Goriška Brda **★★→★★★** Immensely improved big winery from BRDA. Big range, mostly varietals, often excellent value, esp Quercus line.

Vipava District in PRIMORJE. Fine producers: BATIČ, Guerila Lisjak Radivoj, MLEČNIK, SUTOR, Tilia. Vipava co-op ★ has premium brand Lanthieri ★★.

Croatia

With the Croatian coast fashionable with tourists few wines are exported, so visiting the country is the best way of finding them. The 06 vintage is considered excellent, and 07 is close to it.

Agrolaguna ★→★★ Co-op at Poreč, ISTRIA. Solidly gd value, esp reds.

Babić Dark, long-lived, native red from Primošten (north DALMATIA). Can be of high quality. Unique v'yd site. Try Gracin, VINOPLOD.

Badel 1862 ★→★★★ Biggest wine producer in the country with wineries from all over. Usually best: IVAN DOLAC (PZ Svirče), DINGAČ (PZ i Vinarija Dingač).

Bibich ★★ Export-oriented, avant-garde winery from nr Zadar.

Coronica, Moreno ★★★ Top MALVAZIJA (DYA) and Gran Malvazija **02** 03' 04' 05' and Gran Teran **03** from ISTRIA. Also Cab Sauv 03 Grabar. Classic.

Cult wines Expensive, highly regarded reds produced in minute quantities. Controversial pioneer Stagnum **03'** 04, unanimously excellent DINGAČ Bura **04' 05'**, powerful POSTUP Mare **04' 05'** (16 degrees!), new Merlotina 04' (Merlot) and outrageously expensive Medvid **03'** 04 05.

Dalmacija-vino ★ Giant co-op at Split: v.gd Faros.

Dalmatia Dalmacija. The coast of Croatia is a grower's paradise. Traditionally high in alcohol. Whites (Debit, Maraština) improving, reds improving fast.

Dingač 03' 04' 05' V'yd designation on PELJEŠAC's steep southern slopes. "Grand cru" for PLAVAC MALI. Made from partially dried grapes: full-bodied robust, dry (over)ripe red. Look for: Bura, KIRIDŽIJA, Radovič, and Skaramuča.

Enjingi, Ivan ★★★ Producer of excellent sweet botrytized and dry whites from Požega. GRAŠEVINA, Sivi Pinot, and superb white blend Venje.

Graševina Welschriesling. Best in SLAVONIJA. Look for Adžić, Djakovačka vina, ENJINGI, KRAUTHAKER, KUTJEVO, Vinarija Daruvar. From dry to top botrytis.

Grgić, Miljenko ★★★ "Paris tasting" winner (see Grgich Hills, California); produces PLAVAC and POŠIP back home at PELJEŠAC peninsula.

Hvar Beautiful island in mid-Dalmatia. Gd reds from PLAVAC MALI from steep southern slopes. Interesting native wines from plateau. Look for: IVAN DOLAC, Carić Faros, Plančić, ZLATAN PLAVAC, PZ Svirče, Tomić .

Istria N Adriatic peninsula. MALVAZIJA and TERAN reign here. Gd for Cab Sauv. Look for Arman Franc, Clai, CORONICA, Degrassi, Kabola, KOZLOVIĆ, MATOŠEVIĆ, Pilato.

Ivan Dolac Area on south slopes of HVAR. "*Grand cru*" for PLAVAC MALI.

Kiridžija, Vedran ★★ Producer of consistently gd DINGAČ **03' 04'** 05'.

Korak ★★ Producer of gd whites from PLEŠIVICA. Chard and Ries.

Kozlović ★★★ Gd white producer from ISTRIA. Esp MALVAZIJA. Also reds.

Krauthaker, Vlado ★★★ Top Croatian producer of dry whites **04' 05 06** from Kutjevo, esp Chard and GRAŠEVINA Mitrovac. Reds are ★★ **03'**.

Kutjevo Name shared by a town in SLAVONIJA, centre of GRAŠEVINA. Also the ★★→★★★ co-op, GRAŠEVINA and top botrytis.

Malvazija Malvasia 04' 05 **06' 07**. Planted in ISTRIA. A pleiad of private producers is producing character and style.

Matošević, Ivica ★★→★★★ Pioneer and leader from ISTRIA. MALVAZIJA Alba.

Mendek Selekcija **03'** 04'. Highly regarded and expensive red from PELJEŠAC.

Pelješac Beautiful peninsula and region in south DALMATIA. Some v.gd PLAVAC MALI. Home of POSTUP, DINGAČ. See also GRGIĆ, MENDEK, Miloš.

Pjenušac Sparkling. Look for Tomac, Peršurić, also Šenpjen.

Plavac Mali The best DALMATIAN red grape: wine of body, strength, and ageability. See PELJEŠAC. Promising at island of Brač (Murvica).

Plešivica Quality sub-region nr Zagreb, known for whites and sparkling. Look for: KORAK, Režek, Šember Tomac.

Pošip Best DALMATIAN white, mostly on island of Korčula.

Postup V'yd designation northwest of DINGAČ. Medium- to full-bodied red.

Prošek *Passito*-style dessert wine from DALMATIA.

Slavonija Sub-region in north for white. Look out for ENJINGI, Jakobovič, KRAUTHAKER, KUTJEVO.

Stolno vino Table wine. Not many v.gd wines are labelled "stolno".

Suho Dry. *Polusuho* is semi-dry; *poluslatko* is semi-sweet, *sladko* is sweet.

Teran Stout, dark red pride of ISTRIA, Refosco grape. Try CORONICA.

Vinoplod ★ Co-op from Šibenik. Best is BABIĆ **03' 04'** 05'.

Vrhunsko vino A fairly rigorous designation for high-quality wines.

Vugava Rare white from island of Vis. Linked to Viognier. Try Lipanović.

Zdjelarević ★★ White wines from SLAVONIJA, esp Chard **05' 06'**.

Žlahtina Native white from island of Krk. Look for Katunar, Toljanić.

Zlatan Otok ★★★ HVAR-based winery of Zlatan Plenković, uncrowned king of PLAVAC MALI and Croatian winemaker of the yr 2007. His Zlatan Plavac Grand Cru **03'** 04' is among top Croatian reds.

Bosnia & Herzegovina

Since the civil war ended in 1995, wine production in Bosnia & Herzegovina has been dominated by small independent family operations.

Blatina Native red grape and wine.

Kameno Vino White of unique, irrigated desert v'yd in Neretva Valley.

Mostar The area around Mostar, the unofficial capital city of Herzegovina, has been the heartland of Herzegovinian wine production since World War II.

Cellars such as Ljubuski (the oldest in the country) and Citluk are producing gd-quality ZILAVKA white and slightly less impressive BLATINA red.

Samotok Light red (rosé/*ruzica*) wine from run-off juice (and no pressing).
Zilavka White grape. Potentially dry and pungent. Fruity; faint apricot flavour.

Serbia

Strengths include light, fruity reds made from the Prokupac grape, but international varieties, notably Cabernet Sauvignon and, in the Zapadna Morava region, Sauvignon Blanc, are doing well.

Montenegro

13 July State-run co-op; high-tech Italian kit. VRANAC is gd quality.
Crmnica Lakeside/coastal v'yds esp for Kadarka grape (see Hungary).
Duklja Late-harvested, semi-sweet version of VRANAC.
Krstač Montenegro's top white grape and wine; esp from CRMNICA.
Vranac Local vigorous and abundant red grape and wine. Value.

Macedonia

Macedonia is a warm, mountainous country in southeastern Europe, which gained independence in 1991. It has 22,400 ha of vineyards and a wine tradition dating back to Alexander the Great. At its peak in the 1980s it produced two-thirds of Yugoslavia's wine. Today the industry is fully privatized, with 38 wineries and a wine law conforming to EU standards.

Bovin ★ First winery to be privatized. Rustic reds.
Cekorov ★★ Tiny 3-ha family estate. VRANEC (03) is one of the best.
Fonko ★ Young winery, best known for Chard and Bucephall VRANEC.
Kratosija Local red grape also found in Montenegro; sound wines.
Pivka ★ Private winery in TIKVEŠ region. Gd VRANEC.
Popov ★ Small family winery. Decent VRANEC/Cab Sauv and Villa Luna white.
Povardarie (Vardar Valley) Main wine region with 85% of production. Other 2 are Pcinja-Osogovo and Pelagonija-Polog.
Skovin ★→★★ Large producer with 450 ha v'yds. Decent reds.
Smederevka Widely planted native white grape, noted for high acidity and nutty characters, also found in Serbia and Hungary.
Stanušina Indigenous light-coloured red grape making pale, fruity wines.
Temjanika Local name for Muscat Frontignan.
Tikveš ★ Macedonia's largest winery in region of same name.
Vranec Local name for Montenegro's red Vranac (qv); with SMEDEREVKA, accounts for 80% of production.
Zilavka Well-regarded local white variety.

The Czech Republic & Slovakia

Czech Republic

In the Czech Republic vines are grown in two wine regions: Bohemia and Moravia. With a general economic boom underway, much ready cash is available and the middle classes are steadily moving away from their beloved beer, while the new financial elite is busy building state-of-the-art wineries with its new-found wealth. Wine producers are upbeat.

Bohemia

720 ha in 2 demarcated wine sub-regions: Mělnická and Litoměřická. Same latitude and similar wines to east Germany. Best in the Elbe Valley (north of Prague), notably at Mělník (Ries, Ruländer, Traminer, and exemplary Pinot N). V'yd renewal, esp round Prague, inc several small boutique wineries. Producers include: Lobkowicz-Mělník (oak-aged reds, barrel-fermented Chard, *méthode traditionnelle* Ch Mělník). Kosher wine production in Chrámce. Sparkling wine is mostly tank-fermented using grapes from Austria. The market is dominated by the two biggest players, Bohemia Sekt in Starý Plzenec (Henkell-Söhnlein) and Soare Sekt in Jablonec (Schloss Wachenheim).

Moravia

18,000 ha in 4 demarcated wine sub-regions: Znojemská (Znojmo), Mikulovská (Mikulov), Velkopavlovická (Velké Pavlovice) and Slovácko. V'yds situated in southeast along Austrian and Slovak borders: similar grapes. Look for: Springer and Stapleton & Springer (both Bořetice), Krist (Milotice), Sonberk (Pouzdřiany), Spielberg (Archlebov), Nové vinařství (Drnholec), and Reisten (Pavlov), all young and dynamic among established giants Znovín Znojmo, Vinné Sklepy (Valtice), Vinselekt-Michlovský (Rakvice) and Moravské vinařské závody (Bzenec). Icing on the cake is Icewine and straw wine. Beware outrageously priced 20-cl bottles.

Slovak Republic

There are roughly 17,000 ha on v'yds in six wine regions: Malokarpatská (Little Carpathians), Juhoslovenská (Southern Slovakia), Nitrianská (Nitra), Stredoslovenská (Central Slovakia), Východoslovenská (Eastern Slovakia), and the smallest Tokajská (Tokaj) region, neighbouring Hungary's Tokaj. Classic central European and international varieties. Leading producers: Ch Belá (Mužla) with Müller-Scharzhof (of Germany's Saar) involvement, Masaryk (Skalica), Matyšák (Pezinok), Mrva & Stanko (Trnava), J J Ostrožovič (V Trňa, Tokaj), Pavelka-Sobolič (Pezinok), Villa Vino (Rača), Víno Nitra (Nitra), and Karpatská Perla (Šenkvice). For sparkling wine: J E Hubert and Pálffy Sekt.

Romania

Romania joined the EU in 2007 and the wine industry has benefited from considerable EU investment to upgrade winery equipment and replant vineyards. This, and international winemaking expertise, has also helped raise standards. Romania remains one of the world's biggest producers and consumers of wine, but its v'yd area continues to fall, to around 180,000 ha in 2006. Increasing wealth within Romania means the domestic market consumes almost all the country's production, and it is now a net importer. The country is divided into seven different zones with 28 controlled appellations of origin.

Băbească Neagră Traditional "black grandmother grape" of the MOLDOVAN Hills, esp Nicoresti area; light body and ruby-red colour.

Banat Small wine region on western border, with 2 DOCS: Banat itself and Recas, ITALIAN RIES, Sauv Bl, MUSCAT OTTONEL, local Ries de Banat; light red Cadarca, Cab Sauv, MERLOT.

Blaj Wine region in TÂRNAVE (TRANSYLVANIA), dry or off-dry whites.

Bohotin East Moldavia region known for aromatic rosé Busuioacă de Bohotin.

Burgund Mare Romanian name for Blaufränkisch (Kékfrankos in Hungary).

Carl Reh ★★ Innovative German-owned winery with 190-ha v'yd in Oprisor. V.gd reds, esp La Cetate (**03 05** 06′). Val Duna is export label for gd varietal whites.

Cotnari Region in northeast with v.gd botrytis conditions. Famous for over 500 yrs for medium to sweet GRAŞĂ, FETEASCĂ ALBĂ, TĂMÂIOASĂ, and dry Frâncuşă.

Cotnari Winery 1,200 ha in COTNARI region. Wines range from dry to v. sweet, inc v.gd collection wines.

Cramele Recaş ★★ British-Romanian firm with 700 ha v'yds in BANAT region. PINOT N with potential. V.gd Sauv Bl.

Crişana & Maramures Western region inc DOCs of Crişana and historical Miniş (since 15th century): esp red Cadarca; crisp, white Mustoasă.

Davino Winery 40 ha in DEALU MARE. V.gd Dom Ceptura white (**06**) and red (**04** 05).

Dealu Mare (Dealul Mare) "The Big Hill". Important well-situated area in southeastern Carpathian foothills. Excellent reds, esp FETEASCĂ NEAGRĂ, Cab Sauv, MERLOT, PINOT N. Whites from TĂMÂIOASĂ.

Dobrogea Sunny, dry, Black Sea region. Includes DOC regions of MURFATLAR, Badabag, and Sarica Niculitel. Famous for sweet late-harvest Chard and increasingly for full-bodied reds.

DOC Denumire de Origine Controlata. Classification for higher-quality wines with denomination of origin. DOC-CMD means picked fully ripe; DOC-CT is late harvest; DOC-CÎB is noble late harvest, or botrytized.

Domeniile Tohani Winery Major holding in DEALU MARE specializing in red wines (inc FETEASCĂ NEAGRĂ, Cab Sauv, PINOT N, MERLOT) and sweet Dollete.

Domeniul Coroanei Segarcea Former crown dom in southwest with 320 ha. Gd lively whites, inc FETEASCĂ REGALĂ, Sauv Bl, Muscat Frontignan Rosé.

Drăgăşani Region on river Olt south of Carpathians. Traditional (white: Crâmposie Selectionată; reds: Novac, Negru de Drăgăşani) and international varieties. Gd MUSCAT OTTONEL.

Fetească Albă Romania's third-most-planted white grape with faintly Muscat aroma. Same as Hungary's Leányka, with gd potential for sparkling.

Fetească Neagră "Black maiden grape" with potential as showpiece variety. Difficult to handle, but can give deep, full-bodied wines with character.

Fetească Regală A cross of FETEASCĂ ALBĂ with GRAŞĂ (gd for sparkling and recently some successful barrel-fermented versions). Most-planted white.

Graşă Local Romanian grape whose name means "fat". Prone to botrytis and v. important grape in COTNARI. Grown as Kövérszölö in Hungary's Tokaj region.

Halewood Winery ★★ British venture producing gd wines, esp reds. V'yds in DEALU MARE: fine FETEASCĂ NEAGRĂ, PINOT N. Also TRANSYLVANIA and MURFATLAR.

Huşi Wine region in Moldava, whites, inc local Zghihara and sweet aromatic pink Busuioacă de Bohotin.

Iaşi Region for fresh acidic whites (FETEASCĂ ALBĂ, also RIES ITALIAN, ALIGOTÉ, sparkling MUSCAT OTTONEL). Reds: FETEASCĂ NEAGRĂ, MERLOT, Cab Sauv.

Iordana High acid, low alcohol local white grown in Apold for sparkling wines.

Jidvei Winery in sub-region of the same name in TRANSYLVANIA (TÂRNAVE). Fair whites: FETEASCĂ, ITALIAN RIES, Sauv Bl, Traminer Roz, and sparkling.

Lacrima lui Ovidiu "Ovid's Tear": sweet fortified wine aged for many yrs in oak barrels until amber coloured, from MURFATLAR.

Merlot Romania's widely planted, red variety.

Moldova (Moldovia) Western part of former Romanian province (eastern part became Republic of Moldova see page 000). Largest wine region, lying northeast of Carpathians. DOC areas include BOHOTIN, COTNARI, Dealu Bujorului, HUŞI, IAŞI, ODOBEŞTI, Coteşti, Nicoreşti.

Muntenia and Oltenia Hills Major wine region covering the DOC areas of DEALU MARE, Dealurile Olteniei, DRĂGĂŞANI, PIETROASA, Sâmbureşti, Stefaneşti.

Murfatlar Area with v'yds in DOBROGEA nr Black Sea; v.gd Chard, Pinot Gris, and Cab Sauv. Sub-regions are Cernavoda and Megidia.

Murfatlar Winery ★★ Largest bottled-wine producer with around 3,000 ha. V.gd labels Trei Hectare (FETEASCĂ NEAGRĂ, Cab Sauv, Chard) and Ferma Nouă

(MERLOT, Sauv Bl).

Muscat Ottonel Muscat of eastern Europe; a Romanian speciality, esp in cool TRANSYLVANIA and in Moldava dry to sweet wines.

Odobeşti Ancient wine region in Vrancea. Local Galbenă de Odobeşti variety makes everyday whites.

Pietroasa Area in DEALU MARE known for producing sweet whites, esp TĂMÂIOASĂ ROMÂNEASCĂ.

Pinot Noir Grown for over 100 yrs, originally as sparkling base. Newer plantings of French clones show promise.

Prince Stirbey ★★ **05 06** 20-ha estate in DRĂGĂŞANI returned to Austrian-Romanian noble family (Kripp-Costinescu). V.gd dry from local Crâmposie Selectionată, FETEASCĂ REGALĂ, and TĂMÂIOASĂ ROMÂNEASCĂ.

Riesling, Italian Widely planted Welschriesling, starting to show potential.

SERVE ★★→★★★ French-founded DEALU MARE winery and v'yds. Excellent Terra Romana label, esp Cuvée Charlotte **03'** 04 (blend of FETEASCĂ NEAGRĂ, Cab Sauv, MERLOT).

Tămâioasă Românească White "frankincense" grape, with exotic aroma and taste belonging to Muscat family. Often makes fine botrytis wines in COTNARI and PIETROASA.

Târnave (also Tîrnave) Cool region in TRANSYLVANIA, known for Sauv Bl and FETEASCĂ REGALĂ. Dry aromatic wines (esp Pinot Gr, Gewurz) and sparkling. See JIDVEI, BLAJ.

Transylvania Cool mountain plateau in centre of Romania. V'yds often steep and mostly producing white wines with gd acidity from FETEASCĂ ALBA, FETEASCĂ REGALĂ, MUSCAT, Traminer, ITALIAN RIES. Sub-regions include TÂRNAVE, Alba-Iulia, Lechinta, Aiud, and Apold.

Valea Călugărească "Valley of the Monks", part of DEALU MARE and site of research winery. Nice MERLOT, Cab Sauv, PINOT N, RIES, Pinot Gr.

Vanju Mare Warm region in southwest noted for full-bodied reds.

Vinarte Winery ★★→★★★ **01 03** 05 Italian investment covering 3 doms: Villa Zorilor in DEALU MARE, Castel Bolovanu in DRĂGĂŞANI Terase Danubiane in VANJU MARE.

Vincon Vrancea Winery Largest firm in VRANCEA region.

Vinia One of Romania's largest wineries at IAŞI. Major producer of COTNARI wines. Also whites and light reds.

Vin cu Indicatie Geografica Equivalent to VDP. Also known as Vin de Regiune.

Vin de masă Table wine.

Vinterra Dutch/Romanian venture reviving FETEASCĂ NEAGRĂ; also makes gd PINOT N, MERLOT.

Vrancea Important county in MOLDOVA covering Panciu, ODOBEŞTI, and Coteşti.

Greece

Greece emerged in the 1990s as an international player in the wine world. Variety of climates, terroirs, and indigenous grapes are on its side. Now Greek producers are finally becoming more extrovert. The wines are getting good reactions from North America and Russia, and there are new and experimental styles emerging, as well as an increasing focus on viticulture. It seems that the term "Greek Wine Revolution", coined in the 1990s, was used far too early.

Aghiorghitiko NEMEA's red grape leading Greek wine out of anonymity, now planted almost everywhere, even in the north.

Aivalis ★★★ Boutique NEMEA producer: extracted AGHIORGHITIKO. Top (and pricey) wine is "4", from 120+-yr-old vines.

Alpha Estate ★★★ Impressive estate in cooler-climate Amindeo. V.gd barrel-aged Merlot/Syrah/XINOMAVRO blend, pungent Sauv Bl, unfiltered XINOMAVRO from ungrafted vines. Top wine: Alpha 1 that demands ageing. ★★★★ soon?

Antonopoulos ★★→★★★ PATRAS-based winery, with top-class MANTINIA, crisp Adoli Ghis, Lafon-(Burgundy)-like Chard, and Cab-based Nea Dris (97 98 00 01 02 03). Top wine: violet-scented Vertzami/Cab Fr.

Arghyros ★★→★★★ Top SANTORINI producer with exemplary but expensive VINSANTO aged 20 yrs in cask. Exciting KTIMA white, a popular oak-aged Vareli white, and new fragrant (dry) Aidani.

Assyrtiko One of the v. best white grapes of the Mediterranean, balancing power, minerality, extract, and high acid.

Avantis ★★★ Boutique winery in Evia with (red) v'yds in Boetia. Dense Syrah, Aghios Chronos Syrah/Viognier, pungent Sauv Bl and rich MALAGOUSIA. Top wine: elegant single-v'yd Avantis Collection Syrah 02 03 04.

Biblia Chora ★★★ Polished New World-style wines. Highly sought-after Sauv Bl/ASSYRTIKO. Floral Syrah Rosé. Oaked Ovilos (white) Sem/ASSYRTIKO is extremely noteworthy. Tangy red Areti cask-aged AGHIORGHITIKO.

Boutari, J & Son ★→★★ Producers in NAOUSSA. Excellent-value wines, esp Grande Reserve NAOUSSA, popular MOSCHOFILERO. Top Santorini Kalisti, single-v'yd Skalani from CRETE.

Cambas, Andrew ★ Brand owned by BOUTARI. Chard and Cab Sauv.

Carras, Domaine ★→★★ Estate at Sithonia, Halkidiki, with its own OPAP(Côtes de Meliton). Ch Carras 01 03. Underperforming.

Cava Legal term for cask-aged still white and red table wines – eg Cava Amethystos Kosta Lazaridi, Cava Hatzimihali.

Cephalonia (Kephalonia) Ionian island: excellent, floral white Robola, emerging styles of sweet Muscat, MAVRODAPHNE.

Creta-Olympias ★★ V.gd Cretan producer. Inexpensive Nea Ghi range, v.gd-value spicy white Xerolithia, red Mirabelo. New Pirorago 04 Syrah/Cab Sauv/Kotsifali blend.

Crete Quality improves led by Ekonomou, LYRARAKIS, Douloufakis, MANOUSSAKIS.

Dougos ★★ From the Olympus area, producing interesting Rhône blends.

Driopi ★★★ New venture of TSELEPOS in high NEMEA. Initial vintages are serious (esp single-v'yd KTIMA) and of the high-octane style.

Emery ★→★★ Historic RHODES producer, specializing in local varieties. Brands Villaré, Grand Rosé. V.gd-value Rhodos Athiri. Sweet Efreni Muscat.

Gaia ★★★ Top-quality NEMEA-based producer and winery on SANTORINI. Fun Notios label. New World-like AGHIORGHITIKO. Thought-provoking but top-class dry white *Thalassitis Santorini*. Top wine Gaia Estate (97 98 99 00 01 03 04 05). New Anatolikos dessert (sun-dried) NEMEA.

Gentilini Cephalonia ★★→★★★ Exciting whites inc v.gd Robola. New Unique Red Blend and serious Syrah.

Georgakopoulos Central Greece ★★ Full-throttle, New World-style reds Blanc de Noir Cab Sauv and rich unoaked Chard.

Gerovassiliou ★★★ Perfectionist miniature estate nr Salonika. Look for benchmark ASSYRTIKO/MALAGOUSIA, smooth Syrah/Merlot blend. Herby, red Avaton 03 from rare indigenous varieties. Top wine: Syrah (01 02 03 04). For many, the trend-setter for Greek wines.

Goumenissa (OPAP) ★→★★ XINOMAVRO and Negoska oaked red from MACEDONIA. Esp Aidarinis, BOUTARI, Ligas, and Tatsis Bros.

Hatzidakis ★★★ Low-tech but high-class producer. Stunning range across the board. Try the excellent Nihteri.

Hatzimichalis, Domaine ★→★★★ Large v'yds and merchant in Atalanti. Huge range. Greek and French varieties. Top red Rahes Galanou Merlot/Cab Fr.

Katoghi-Strofilia ★★→★★★ V'yds and wineries in Attica, Peloponnese, and north Epirus. Greek varieties but also Chard, Cab Sauv, and floral Traminer. Katogi is a historic brand, the first-ever premium Greek wine. Top wine: KTIMA Averoff.

Katsaros ★★→★★★ Small organic winery of v. high standards on Mt Olympus. KTIMA red, a Cab Sauv/Merlot has staying power. Supple Chard.

Kir-Yanni ★★→★★★ High-quality v'yds in NAOUSSA and at Amindeo. Vibrant white Samaropetra; complex and ageworthy Dyo Elies red; top NAOUSSA Ramnista (**97 98** 99 00 01 03 04).

Kouros ★ Reliable, well-marketed white PATRAS and red NEMEA from KOURTAKIS.

Kourtakis, D ★★ Athenian merchant with mild RETSINA and gd NEMEA.

Ktima Estate, farm. Term not exclusive to wine.

Lazaridis, Domaine Kostas ★★→★★★ V'yds and wineries in Drama and Kapandriti (nr Athens and sold under the Oenotria Land label). Quality Amethystos label (white, red, rosé). Top wine: unfiltered red CAVA Amethystos (**97 98 99** 00 01 02 03). Bordelais Michel Rolland's first Greek consultancy.

Lazaridis, Nico ★★→★★★ Spectacular post-modernist winery and v'yds in Drama, Kavala and Mykonos. Gd Ch N Lazaridis (white, rosé, and red). Top wine: Magiko Vouno white, red. New (ultra-premium) range under Perpetuus brand.

Lemnos (OPAP) Aegean island: co-op dessert wines, deliciously fortified, lemony Muscat of Alexandria. Also try the dry Muscats by Kyathos-Honas winery.

Lyrarakis ★★→★★★ A v.gd producer from CRETE. Whites from the rare Plyto and Dafni varieties, as well as a deep, complex blend of Syrah and Kotsifali.

Malagousia Rediscovered perfumed white grape.

Manoussakis ★★★ Impressive newcomer from CRETE, with Rhône-inspired blends. Delectable range under Nostos brand, led by Roussanne and Syrah.

Mantinia (OPAP) High central Peloponnese region. Fresh, grapey MOSCHOFILERO.

Matsa, Château ★★→★★★ Historic and prestigious small estate in Attica. Top wine: Ktima ASSYRTIKO/Sauv Bl. Excellent MALAGOUSIA.

Mavrodaphne (OPE) "Black laurel", and red grape. Cask-aged port/recioto-like, concentrated red; fortified. Speciality of PATRAS, north Peloponnese. Dry versions (eg ANTONOPOULOS) are increasing, with much promise.

Mercouri ★★→★★★ Peloponnese family estate. V.gd Refosco, delicious RODITIS. New CAVA. Classy Refosco dal Penducolo red, fine sweet Belvedere Malvasia.

Mezzo Sweet wine produced in SANTORINI from sun-dried grapes, lighter and less sweet than VINSANTO. Some dispute over style – some producers (eg SIGALAS) use the term for wine made from the red Mandilaria variety, while others (eg ARGHYROS) use the same white varieties as VINSANTO.

Mitravelas ★★→★★★ Outstanding new entry in NEMEA, promising great things.

Moraitis ★★ Small quality producer on the island of Paros. V.gd smoky (white) Monemvasia, Ktima (white) Monemvasia/ASSYRTIKO, (red) tannic Moraitis Reserve 01 Monemvasia/Mandelaria blend.

Moschofilero Pink-skinned, rose-scented, high-quality, high-acid grape.

Naoussa (OPAP) r High-quality region for XINOMAVRO. One of two Greek regions where a *cru* notion may soon develop.

Nemea (OPAP) r Region in east Peloponnese producing dark, spicy AGHIORGHITIKO wines. Recent investment has moved it into higher gear. High Nemea merits its own appellation. Koutsi is front-runner for *cru* status.

Nemeion A new KTIMA in NEMEA, setting new pricing standards for the appellation, with wines to match.

Oenoforos ★★ Gd Peloponnese producer with high v'yds. Extremely elegant RODITIS (white). Also delicate white Lagorthi, nutty Chard (Burgundian, limited release, magnum only), crisp Ries, and stylish Syrah.

OPAP "Appellation of Origin of Higher Quality". In theory equivalent to French VDQS, but in practice where many gd appellations and wines belong.

OPE "Appellation of Origin Controlled". In theory equivalent to French *apppelation contrôlée* but mainly reserved for Muscat and MAVRODAPHNE.

Papaïoannou ★★→★★★ Reliable NEMEA grower. Classy red (inc Pinot N); flavourful white. Top wine: KTIMA Papaioannou Palea Klimata (old vines) **97 98** 00 01 03 04 and Microklima (a micro-single v'yd) **01**.

Patras (OPAP) White wine (based on RODITIS) and wine town facing the Ionian Sea. Home of MAVRODAPHNE. Rio-Patras (OPE) sweet Muscat.

Pavlidis ★★★ Ambitious new v'yds and winery at Kokkinogia nr Drama. Gd ASSYRTIKO/Sauv Bl, v.gd ASSYRTIKO. New Syrah and Tempranillo.

Rapsani Interesting oaked red from Mt Olympus. Rasping until rescued by TSANTALIS, but new producers, like Liappis, are moving in.

Retsina Attica speciality white with Aleppo pine resin added. Domestic consumption waning.

Rhodes Easternmost island. Home to creamy (dry) Athiri white grape. Top wines include Caïr (co-op) Rodos 2400 and Emery's Villare. Also some sparkling.

Roditis White grape grown all over Greece. Gd when yields are low.

Samos (OPE) Island nr Turkey famed for sweet, golden Muscat. Esp (fortified) Anthemis, (sun-dried) Nectar. Rare old bottlings can be ★★★★.

Santorini Volcanic island north of CRETE: luscious, sweet VINSANTO and MEZZO, mineral-laden, *bone-dry white from fine Assyrtiko*. Oaked examples can be gd. Top producers include GAIA, HATZIDAKIS, SIGALAS. Try ageing everything.

Semeli ★★→★★★ Estates nr Athens and NEMEA and a new winery in MANTINIA under the Nassiakos name. Value Orinos Helios (white and red) and NEMEA's only Grande Reserve, released after 4 yrs.

Sigalas ★★→★★★ Top SANTORINI estate producing leading oaked SANTORINI Bareli. Stylish VINSANTO. Also rare red, Mourvèdre-like Mavrotragano.

Skouras ★★→★★★ Innovative Peloponnese wines. First to introduce screwcaps on Chard Dum Vinum Sperum with most of the white range following suit. New wine: Synoro (Cab Fr dominated). Top wine: High Nemea Grande Cuvée 03.

Spiropoulos, Domaine ★★ Organic producer in MANTINIA. Oaky, red Porfyros (AGHIORGHITIKO, Cab Sauv, Merlot). Sparkling Odi Panos has potential.

Tetramythos ★★ Exploring the possibilities of cool-climate parts of Peloponnese, a new and promising venture. The winery was burnt in the great summer fires of 07, but the comeback is assured.

TO "Regional Wine", French VDP equivalent. Most exciting Greek wine category•.

Tsantalis ★→★★★ Merchant and v'yds at Agios Pavlos. AC wines. Gd red Metoxi, Rapsani Reserve, and Grande Reserve, and gd-value *Organic Cab Sauv* and excellent Avaton. The top-of-the-range Kormilitsa (red, white, and Gold Collection) are making waves in the Kremlin.

Tselepos ★★→★★★ Top-quality Mantinia producer and Greece's best Gewurz. Other wines: fresh, oaky Chard, v.gd Cab Sauv/Merlot, single-v'yd Avlotopi Cab Sauv. Top wine: single-v'yd Kokinomylos Merlot.

Vinsanto Sweet wine style produced in SANTORINI, from sun-dried ASSYRTIKO and Aidani. Require long ageing, both in oak and bottle. The best and oldest Vinsantos are ★★★★ and practically indestructible. See also MEZZO.

Voyatzi Ktima ★★ Small estate nr Kozani. Aromatic white, classy elegant red.

Xinomavro The tastiest of indigenous red grapes – though name means "acidic-black". Grown in the cooler north, it is the basis for NAOUSSA, GOUMENISSA, and Amindeo. High potential: Greece's answer to Nebbiolo.

Zitsa Mountainous Epirus AC. Delicate Debina white, still or sparkling.

To decipher codes, please refer to "Key to symbols" on the front flap of jacket, or "How to use this book" on p.10.

GREECE

Cyprus

The wine industry of Cyprus has faced great challenges during recent years. Until the mid-1990s the industry centred on the production of high-volume wines for Eastern Europe, "Sherry lookalikes" for the UK, and concentrated grape must for various uses. Today those markets have collapsed. Cyprus is now a member of the EU and, as such, can no longer restrict imports of wine from other EU countries. It has been estimated that about 13% of the wine currently drunk in Cyprus is imported. The industry has responded by improving the quality dramatically, searching out better native grapes, and increasing plantings of international varieties. It remains to be seen if these changes are enough.

Commandaria A sweet and deliberately oxidized wine. The greatest Cypriot wine, almost certainly the wine with the longest heritage in the world. (The poet Hesiod wrote of its ancestor in 800 BCE.) Produced in hills north of Limassol. Region limited to 14 villages. Made from sun-dried XYNISTERI and MAVRO grapes. Best (as old as 100 years) is superb.

ETKO One of largest producers. Range includes Salera (red and white), also Shiraz, Merlot, and Chard. Best: Ino Cab Sauv.

KEO Large, go-ahead firm. Interested in planting of international grapes and re-discovery of undervalued native varieties. Range includes single-estate wines Ktima Mallia (red and white), Anerada (white), also Heritage (red), oak-aged MARATHEFTIKO. Production moved from Limassol to regional wineries. COMMANDARIA St John and top-quality vintage COMMANDARIA.

Loel One of major producers. Reds: Orpho Negro. Mediterranean Cab Sauv and Mediterranean Chard, also COMMANDARIA Alasia and brandies.

Maratheftico Vines of superior quality make concentrated red wine, close to Cab Sauv; not easy to cultivate but possibly the future grape of Cyprus.

Mavro The black grape of Cyprus. Can produce quality if planted at high altitude; otherwise sound, acceptable wines. Easier to cultivate than MARATHEFTICO.

Opthalmo Black grape (red/rosé): lighter, sharper than MAVRO. Easier to cultivate than MARATHEFTICO.

Palomino Soft, dry white (LOEL, SODAP). V. drinkable ice-cold.

Pitsilia Region south of Mt Olympus. Some of best whites and COMMANDARIA.

SODAP A co-op winery and one of four largest producers. New ranges made using Australian consultancy: Island Vines (red and white is modern, fresh, made from a mix of native and international grapes); the white considered one of best expressions of XYNISTERI. Mountain Vines (white) is made from international varieties. Both are inexpensive. Also regional wines (red and white) from new Kamanterena winery at Paphos.

Xynisteri Native aromatic white grape of Cyprus, making delicate, fruity wines.

Malta

From the 08 vintage, DOK regulations will ban chaptalization and bring vineyard, winemaking, and labelling practices into line with those prevailing in the EU. Pioneering estate Meridiana (Antinori-backed) continues, since 1994, to make excellent, quintessentially Maltese Isis and Mistral Chardonnays, Astarte Vermentino/Chardonnay, Melqart Cabernet Sauvignon/Merlot, Nexus Merlot, *excellent Bel Syrah*, and premium Celsius Cabernet Sauvignon Res from island vines only. Volume producers of note are Delicata, Marsovin, and Camilleri.

Words within entries marked like this *Alter Ego de Palmer* indicate wines especially enjoyed by Hugh Johnson over the past 12 months (mid '07–'08).

England & Wales

Although the summer of 2007 may not have done UK wine-growers any favours (it was one of the wettest and coolest on record), the "fizz factor" still provides good news. English and Welsh sparkling wine seems to have caught the imagination of the British wine trade as well as the wine-drinking public. Major wine retailers report both increasing sales and increasing enquiries. With plantings of Champagne varieties officially topping the 35%-of-all-vineyards mark and well on their way to being 50% by June 2009, even the French have started to take notice and talk about the possibility of planting vines in England.

Astley Stourport-on-Severn, Worcestershire ★★ Wines continue to win awards and medals. Severn Vale o6 v. gd.

Breaky Bottom East Sussex ★★ Sparkling wines well worth trying, esp Cuvée Rémy Alexandre 99 and Cuvée Alex Mercier 03. Kir Royal also v.gd.

Camel Valley Cornwall ★★★ Lindo père et fils (Bob and Sam) continue to surprise and improve. Sam was Winemaker of the Year in 2007. 05 06 quality excellent, esp Rosé o6 sparkling and Bacchus o6.

Chapel Down Kent ★★★ Still UK's largest producer and with recent purchase of additional 40 ha to plant with Champagne varieties, should stay on top. 04, 05 and o6 all v.gd, esp *Pinot Reserve Sparkling 02* and Rosé o6. New winery planned for 2008/2009.

Denbies Surrey ★★ UK's largest v'yd with 107 ha at last now produces a gd range of interesting wines. Coopers Brook 04 (Chard blend) and Ortega 04 excellent. Also voted UK Wine Producer of the Year.

Nyetimber West Sussex ★★★ Recent plantings have brought total up to 104 ha, making this the second-largest UK v'yd. Quality slipped slightly with change of owner and winemaker, but getting back on track. Classic Cuvée 00 v gd.

RidgeView East Sussex ★★★ 04 Bubbly pioneer since 1993, still leader with fine dry cuvées labelled Merett. Fitzrovia Rosé 04 superb. 25% of company recently sold to another grower with large v'yds, which will see output rise to 325,000 bottles by 2014.

Sharpham Devon ★★ o6 Great range of wines (and also great cheeses). Dart Valley Reserve o6 and Barrel Fermented o6 best wines.

Stanlake Park Berkshire ★★ o6 Large range of wines of above-average quality. Gewurz o6 surprise silver medal winner, worth trying. Bacchus o6, Fumé o6, and Pinot Blush o6 also gd.

Three Choirs Gloucs ★★ 05 o6 UK's second-largest producer. Large range inc v. gd-value Classic Cuvée NV sparkling and Premium Selection Rosé o6.

Other noteworthy producers

A'Becketts Wiltshire Estate Rosé o6 and Estate Red o6 both worth trying.

Biddenden Kent Try Rosé Sparkling 05 and White Sparkling 01.

Brightwell Oxfordshire Up-and-coming producer. Try Crispin 05.

Hush Heath Estate Kent Balfour Brut Rosé 04 silver medal winner.

Meopham Valley Kent Sparkling 04 Silver Medal winner.

Polgoon Cornwall Rosé o6 under screwcap excellent.

Sandhurst Kent 04 Pinot Noir worthy winner of "Best Red" in 2007.

Wickham Hampshire Special Release Fumé o6 v.gd.

Yearlstone Devon "No 5" silver medal winner gd. Pity only still wines.

Asia, North Africa, Israel & Lebanon

Algeria The wine industry has seen drastic decline since independence in 1960 due to political and religious influences. Aggressive replanting (region naturally protected from phylloxera) now underway to raise annual production from 50 million to around 150 million litres. Important regions: Tlemcen (powerful reds, whites, rosé – Dom de Sebra), Mascara (Dom El Bordj, Dahra (reds, rosés – Dom de Khadra), Zaccar (Ch Romain), Médéa (Ch Tellagh), Tessala, Aïn-Bessem-Bouira.

China The 6th-largest wine producer in the world. (Blending with imports casts doubts.) Extreme climate necessitates burying vines against the cold. Frequent hailstorms, monsoon rains and poor soils haven't stopped 500 wineries being founded. Some 83% of production sold domestically and four-fifths is red. The Napa model of wine tourism is being copied, with spas (Bodegas Langes) and tourist facilities. Twenty-six provinces produce wine, the most productive being Xinjiang, Tianjin, Shandong, Jinlin, Hebei, and Henan, and high-altitude areas of Yunnan. Production dominated by Dynasty, Changyu, and Great Wall. Some premium producers now emerging: Huadong (Chard, Ries) in Shandong, Shanxi Grace in Shanxi (Merlot, Rosé, Chairman's Reserve, B'x blend, Chard), Lou Lan, Turpan (Merlot), Suntime Manas from Xinjiang, Dragon Seal (Reserve Cab Sauv) and Bodega Langes in Hebei. Others to watch: Ch Bolongbao (organic) in Hebei, Helen Mountain, Chang Baishan (Ice wine) in Jinlin.

India Just under 50 wineries make over 6m litres of wine. Production is centred at Maharashtra, with 36 wineries; this region is home to the successful Ch Indage (Chard, Cab Sauv, Shiraz, and *Omar Khayyam* sparkling wine) and the expanding Sula, producing Chenin Bl, Sauv Bl, Zin, and Merlot. Grover Vineyards is the other well-known producer, located in Bangalore, where Michel Rolland makes La Reserve Cab Sauv/Shiraz, Viognier. Other producers to watch: Dajeeba Wines, Flemingo Wines, McDowell, Mountain View, ND Wines, Rajdheer Wines and Sailo Wines.

Japan Home to more than 200 wineries, just 3% of Japanese wines are made locally; the rest are made with imported concentrate and bulk wine. The country has two main wine regions: Yamanashi (near Mount Fuji, the most important; and Nagano. Both are beset with climatic problems (summer rain and high humidity), and coupled with excessive soil fertility, this has led to producers researching new regions and indigenous varieties. Other smaller regions include Yamagata prefectures (north of Tokyo) and Hokkaido, the coldest wine region in the world, which in 2006 produced a gd vintage.

Japan has no appellation system, but some efforts are now being made regionally. The wine sector continues to draw interest from large Japanese breweries. Production is dominated by Mercian, Suntory, Sapporo (Polaire), Mann, and Kyowa Hakko Kogyo (Ste Neige).

Of indigenous varieties, Koshu (disc 1186) is the most prominent, making gd crisp, dry whites (gd producers: Grace, Katsunuma, Mercian). Other promising indigenous varieties include Shokoshi (Coco Farm, Katsunuma), the lighter red Yama Sauvignon (Mars) and Kai Noir – a hybrid (Grace). The Japanese government is currently seeking EU export approval for Koshu.

Red production is now moving toward lighter styles. The most interesting and expensive wines are from international varieties, such as Mann's Chard and Merlot from Nagano, *Mercian's Kikyogahara Merlot* and Hokushin Char,

Asahi Yoshu's Kainoir, and Jyonohira Cab Sauv. Smaller wineries to watch include Alps, Obuse, Marufuji, Takeda, Tsuno and Yamazaki.

Morocco Like Algeria, once a main supplier for France. The slopes of the Atlas Mountains (Meknes and Fez) have the best conditions. Chard, Syrah, Cab Sauv, and Merlot produce gd wine, while Cinsault, Carignan, and Grenache produce traditional reds and "Gris". Coastal v'yds source notable light, fruity wines. Best producer, Celliers de Meknes, makes 90% of Morocco's wine, of which 75% is red and 20% rosé. Cépages de Boulaouane, Cépages de Meknes and Société Thalvin also figure. Area under vine declined drastically following independence, but foreign investment has woken up the industry. Best labels include L'Excellence de Bonassia (aged Cab Sauv/Merlot), Ch Roslane's Les Coteaux de l'Atlas, Les Trois Domaines, Dom Riad Jamil, Ksar.

Tunisia Foreign investment here too. UCCV (Vieux Magon, Reine Elissa) still dominates production, but smaller wineries such as Domaine's Atlas (gd Punique, Ifrikia), Ceptunes, Kelibia, Kurbis, Lansarine, Neferis, Ch St Augustin produce gd wine. French-style winemaking using international varieties is giving way to New World tastes, but regional AOC classifications continue to gain popularity.

Turkey Twocompanies, Kavaklidere (gd white Angora, Selection red) and Doluca (gd Kav), dominate; both have had much recent success with international varieties, inc blending with indigenous grapes. Diren, Melen, Sarafin (v.gd international varieties), and Kocabag also make gd wine. The main area of production is Thrace/Marmara (40%); other districts are central/ east/southeast Anatolia and the Black Sea coast. Indigenous Emir and Narince produce gd whites; Bogazkere and Oküzgözü make powerful reds.

The Old Russian Empire

The Soviet legacy hangs heavily over the region's wine industries. Post-USSR, Russia continued to be the main wine market for Ukraine, Georgia, and Moldova. Recent Russian ban on Moldovan and Georgian wines means they must upgrade to reach other markets. Large ex-Soviet wineries dominate, but they blend with cheap, imported bulk wine – without saying so on the label. Some gd wines are produced by flying winemakers. Known authentic producers are listed below:

Ukraine Crimea has potential for first-class wines, but still unrealized. Production continues at historic Massandra (Yalta). Classic Pinot N brut sparkling from Novy Svet (Crimea, served at Tsar's coronation 1896) did well in blind tasting. Wineries: Sebastopol and Kotebel lead change and quality; Inkermann, Magarach for reds; Artyomovskoe for sparkling.

Georgia Possibly the oldest wine region: antique methods such as fermentation in clay vats (*kvevris*) still exist and a host of indigenous grape varieties remain untried. Reluctant to modernize, but newer techniques used for exports (Mukuzani, Tsinandali). Kakheti (east) makes two-thirds of Georgia's wine, especially lively, savoury red (*Saperavi grape*) and acceptable white (Tibaani, Rkatsiteli, Gurjaani). Foreign investors: Pernod Ricard with GWS brand; Bagrationi has cheap, drinkable sparkling wine – making new investments now. The ones to watch: Shumi, Suliko, Talisman. As the industry evolves, Georgia could be an export hit.

Words within entries marked like this *Alter Ego de Palmer* indicate wines especially enjoyed by Hugh Johnson over the past 12 months (mid '07–'08).

> **France to Russia**
> Château Le Grand Vostock is the Russian regional leader. Built in 2003 with French technology and equipment, and with a resident French winemaker, Le Grand Vostock produces top white and red blends of French varietals and Russian – Saperavi, Rkatsiteli.

Moldova Most important in size and potential, but poorest, with few signs of recovery. Post-USSR, became the main source of inexpensive wine to Russia. Has now lost Russian market and a large piece of its national income. Regions: Bugeac (most important), Nistrean, Codrean, Northern. Grapes include Cab Sauv, Pinot N, Merlot, Saperavi, Ries, Chard, Pinot Gris, Aligoté, Rkatsiteli. Top wineries: Cricova, Cahul, Hincesti (now with organic), Kazayak Purkar. With dependence on Russia broken, is worth watching. Appellations now in force.

Russia Market continues to grow in sophistication and at a fast pace. Krasnodar on northern Black Sea coast produces 60% of Russia's authentic wine. Australian winemaker at Myskhako (Novorossiysk) making gd Aligoté, Chard, Cab Sauv, and at Fanagoria (Temruk), the largest producer – Merlot and Cab Sauv. Also sweet Kagor from Vityazevo Winery (Anapa). Abrau Durso Brut (also Prince Golitsyn): classic sparkling since 1896.

Azerbaijan Production coming on line for new winery of French company Castel.

Israel & Lebanon

This corner of the eastern Mediterranean is buoyant with numerous new wineries. It is an area of similarities and contrasts, where regions are defined by war and religion. The terroir of Israel and Lebanon is similar, and distances between the Upper Galilee and the Bekaa Valley are small, but the winemaking philosophies are different. Israel is more New World, Lebanon more influenced by France. Both are making increasingly good wines, particularly reds.

Israel

Amphorae r w ★ Well-balanced Chard. Viognier of interest.

Barkan r w ★→★★ Barkan and Segal reds gd value at every price point.

Bazelet ha Golan Golan r ★ Gd Cab Sauv – ripe, rounded, approachable.

Binyamina r w ★ Traditional winery placing new emphasis on quality.

Carmel r w sp ★→★★★ Founded in 1882 by a Rothschild. Elegant Limited Edition (**02** 03' 04). Smoky, tarry Kayoumi Cab Sauv. Old-vine Carignan and Petite Sirah esp interesting. Luscious late-harvest Gewurz.

Castel Judean Hills r w ★★★ Small family estate in Jerusalem mountains. *Characterful complex Grand Vin* (**02** 03' 04). Second label, Petit Castel, gd value. Outstanding, well-balanced Chard – "C" Blanc du Castel.

> **Kosher wine**
> Most wine producing countries produce some kosher wine. Curiously in Israel not all the wine is kosher, but the best are: CASTEL, YARDEN, and YATIR produce good international wines that just happen to be kosher.
> Kosher means "pure". Basically this means that the winery workers have to be religious Jews and nothing un-kosher can be added. Otherwise procedures do not differ from traditional winemaking. However, kosher table wine should not be confused with the sweet red sacramental wines which gave kosher wines a bad name. Kosher wines are usually suitable for vegetarians and vegans.

Château Golan Golan r (w) ★★ Intense Eliad. Interesting Grenache/Syrah blend.
Chillag r Israel's most prominent female winemaker. Elegant Merlot.
Clos de Gat Judean Hills r w ★★→★★★ Classy estate. Spicy Syrah. Buttery Chard.
Dalton Upper Galilee r w ★→★★ Consistent wines. Reserve Cab Sauv best.
Ella Valley Judean Hills r w ★→★★ Well-made wines. Cab Fr showing finesse.
Flam r (w) ★★ Fine Cab Sauv, tight Merlot, earthy, herbal Syrah Cab.
Galil Mountain Upper Galilee r w ★★ Concentrated Yiron B'x blend; successful Pinot N. Unoaked Cab Sauv and Merlot very gd value.
Margalit r ★★★ Rich B'x blend, Enigma. Excellent Special Reserve.
Pelter r w (sp) ★→★★ New on the block. Promising. Cab/Shiraz best.
Recanati r w ★→★★ Gd competition wines, very New World in style.
Saslove r (w) ★→★★ Aviv reds are flavourful; Reserve red more sophisticated.
Sea Horse r (w) ★ Idiosyncrati garagiste specializing in Syrah and Zin.
Tabor Galilee r w ★ Crisp, aromatic Sauv Bl. All wines v.gd value.
Teperberg r w ★ Efrat reborn – new winery, new name, and better wines.
Tishbi r w ★ Grower turned winemaker. Still a family operation.
Tulip r (w) ★ The Shiraz has gd varietal character. Represents value.
Tzora r w ★ Kibbutz winery using fruit from Judean Foothills v'yds.
Vitkin r w ★→★★ Promising boutique. Carignan and Petite Sirah specialist.
Yarden Golan Heights r w sp ★★→★★★ Pioneering winery. Cab Sauv always gd; eagerly awaited rare B'x blend red Katzrin (00' 03'). Superb Heights Wine dessert and Blanc de Blancs sparkling. Gamla fruit-forward second label.
Yatir Judean Hills r (w) ★★★ Rich, velvety, concentrated reds. Yatir Forest (**01'** 03 04) outstanding. Second label Cab/Shiraz/Merlot is great value.

Lebanon

Château Musar r (w) ★★★ Unique, raisiny, long-lasting Cab Sauv/Cinsault/Carignan red (95 96 98). Legendary to some; past its best to others. Hochar red is fruitier. Oaky white from indigenous Obaideh and Merwah.
Clos St Thomas r (w) ★→★★ Deep but silky red wines. Les Emirs great value.
Domaine des Tourelles r w ★ Rebirth of old winery. Elegant Marquis des Beys.
Kefraya r w ★→★★★ Spicy, minerally Comte de M (00' 01 02) from Cab, Syrah, and Mourvèdre. Fruity, easy-drinking Les Bretèches. Quality dessert wine.
Kouroum r w ★ Sept Cépages is an interesting blend of 7 varieties.
Ksara r w ★★ 150 yrs old but still progressive. Excellent value wines.
Massaya r w ★★ Gold Reserve and Silver Selection examples of New Lebanon.
Wardy r w ★ Les Cèdres oaky red. Crisp, fresh Chard and Sauv Bl.

ASIA, NORTH AFRICA, ISRAEL & LEBANON

North America

Anderson Valley
Clear Lake
Clear Lake
Alexander Valley
Russian River Valley
Sonoma Valley
Napa Valley
Carneros
Sacramento
Sierra Foothills
Sacramento
El Dorado
Amador
Lodi
Calaveras

NEVADA

Lake Tahoe

San Francisco
Livermore Valley
Santa Clara Valley
Santa Cruz Mountains
Salinas
Carmel Valley
Arroyo Seco
San Lucas
Paso Robles

San Joaquin
Fresno

CALIFORNIA

Pacific Ocean

Edna Valley
Santa Maria Valley
SANTA BARBARA
Santa Ynez Valley
Santa Barbara

Los Angeles
Teme

More heavily shaded areas are the wine-growing regions

NB AVA   American Victicultural Area

California

C alifornia is on a roll. It seems hardly a week passes without the appearance of amazing new wine, made from a grape that was facing extinction a decade ago, from an obscure wine region. But that's California. Novelty is news and there is plenty of new wine on offer from the Golden State. California's Rhône Rangers started riding the vineyards in the 1980s but then it was all about Syrah. There's still plenty of good Syrah in California but you can also find many other Rhône varieties, like Viognier. It's a familiar story that in 1968 there were only 14 ha of Viognier planted in France and little more elsewhere. Today there are about 1,012 ha of Viognier growing in California. And California's thirst for new wines doesn't stop with the Rhône. Vermentino? Sure. Albariño? All over the place. If you are a more traditional wine drinker, not to worry. There's enough Cabernet Sauvignon, Chardonnay, Pinot Noir and Zinfandel to supply a thirsty world. In the end, California, now the fourth largest wine-producing region on the planet, does seem to have something for everyone – from $200 bottles of cult Napa Cabernet Sauvignon to $2 bottles of Central Valley gulpable red. Tolerance for high alcohol and palpable sweetness is assumed.

The principal Californian vineyard areas

Central Coast

An umbrella region stretching from San Francisco Bay south almost to Los Angeles. Important sub-AVAs include:

Arroyo Seco Monterey County. Excellent Ries both dry and late harvest, citrus Chard and Cab Sauv.

Edna Valley San Luis Obispo County. Cool winds whip through a gap in the coastal range off Morro Bay. Excellent minerally Chard.

Paso Robles San Luis Obispo County. Known for Zin. Promising plantings of Syrah and Rhône varieties.

Santa Lucia Highlands Monterey County. AVA above the Salinas Valley. Excellent Syrah and Ries; outstanding Pinot N.

Santa Maria Valley Santa Barbara County. Outstanding Pinot N, gd Chard, Viognier, and Syrah.

Santa Rita Hills New AVA in Santa Barbara County offering v gd Pinot N.

Santa Ynez Valley Santa Barbara County. Like Santa Maria but warmer inland regions. Rhône grapes, Pinot N, Chard in cool areas. Sauv Bl a gd bet.

North Coast

Lake, Mendocino, Napa, Sonoma counties, all north of San Francisco. Ranges from v. cool climate nr San Francisco Bay and the coast to very warm interior regions. Soils vary from volcanic to sandy loam. Includes following:

Alexander Valley Sonoma County. Fairly warm AVA bordering Russian River. Excellent Cab Sauv in a ripe, juicy style. Gd Sauv Bl nr the river.

Anderson Valley Mendocino County. Cool valley opening to the Pacific. Outstanding sparkling wine, v gd Gewurz and Pinot N.

Carneros Napa and Sonoma counties. Cool and foggy region bordering San Francisco Bay. Top site for Pinot N and Chard. V gd sparkling wine.

Dry Creek Valley Sonoma County. Relatively warm region offering distinctive Zin and Sauv Bl, with Cab Sauv a winner on rocky hillsides.

Lake County Warm to hot mountainous region centred around Clear Lake. Gd Zin, Sauv Bl nr the lake, and lush, fruity Cab Sauv on cooler hillsides.

Mendocino County Large region north of Sonoma County with a wide range of growing regions from hot interior valleys to cooler regions nr the coast.

Mount Veeder Napa County. High-altitude AVA (v'yds planted up to 730 m) best known for concentrated Cab Sauv and rich Chard.

Napa Valley Napa's v'yd land has become the most expensive outside of Europe. Great diversity of soil, climate, and topography in such a small area can produce a wide range of wines, esp the red Bordeaux varieties. Wines have achieved international acclaim, and are priced to match.

Oakville Napa County. Located in mid-valley, the heart of Cab Sauv County.

Redwood Valley Mendocino County. Warm interior region. Gd basic Cab Sauv, excellent Zin, everyday Chard, and Sauv Bl.

Russian River Valley Sonoma County. V. cool, often fog-bound until noon. Maybe best Pinot N in California; Zin and Cab Sauv on hillside v'yds. Green Valley is a small super-cool AVA located within the Russian River AVA.

Rutherford Napa County. Rivals Oakville as Cab Sauv heartland. Long-lived reds from hillside v'yds.

St Helena V.gd Cab Sauv with bright, elegant fruit and a silky mouthfeel.

Sonoma Coast Sonoma County. Trendy new region borders the Pacific. V. cool climate, v. poor soils. New plantings of Pinot N show great promise.

Sonoma Valley Varied growing regions produce everything from Chard to Zin. Sub-AVA Sonoma Mountain gd for powerful Cab Sauv.

Spring Mountain Napa County. v.gd Cab Sauv with pockets of delicious Sauv Bl at lower elevations, plus gd Ries.

Stags Leap Napa County. East of Napa River, distinctive Cab Sauv and Merlot.

Bay Area

Urban sprawl has wiped out most of the v'yds that once surrounded San Francisco bay, although still gd Cab Sauv and Sauv Bl in the Livermore AVA east of the bay and small amounts of outstanding Cab Sauv and Pinot N from Santa Cruz County, south of the Bay.

Central Valley

About 60% of California's v'yds are in this huge region that runs north to south for several hundred miles. Now shedding its image as a low-quality producer, as Valley growers realize they must go for quality to keep up. Lodi region in particular turning up v.gd Zin, Sauv Bl and Rhône, Spanish varieties.

Sierra Foothills

Vines were first planted here during Gold Rush in the 1850s. Best regions include:

Amador County Warm region famous for old Zin v'yds producing jammy, intense wines, as well as crisp Sauv Bl.

Fiddletown Amador County. High-elevation v'yds produce a more understated, elegant Zin than much of Amador.

Shenandoah Valley Amador County. Source of powerful Zins and increasingly well-regarded Syrah.

Recent vintages

Its size and wide range of microclimates make it impossible to produce a one-size-fits-all vintage report for California. Its climate is not as consistent as its "land of sunshine" reputation suggests. Although grapes ripen regularly, they are often subject to spring frosts, sometimes a wet harvest time, and (too often) drought. The following vintage assessment relies most heavily on evaluation of Cab Sauv from North Coast regions. For Chard, the best vintages are: 01 03 04.

2007 Early bud-break and a fairly mild summer growing season with a burst of heat in Aug followed by a cool Sept seemed to set the stage for a textbook-perfect harvest; then came rains in late Sept and Oct so results could be mixed, esp for Cab Sauv on the North Coast. Overall, winemakers are happy with the way the young wines are developing.

2006 Early results mixed; summer heat cut crop size. Long harvest ripening has led to balanced wines that look gd at this point.

2005 After sorting out this vintage some of the early promise has faded. Wines likely to be for short-term consumption.

2004 Scant winter rains and a warm spring led to bud-break and bloom at least three weeks early. Hopes were high until a prolonged heatwave hit the North Coast. Grapes ripened quickly with uneven quality. At best average.

2003 A difficult yr all around. Spring was wet and cool, with a series of heat spikes during the summer and some harvest rains. Overall, spotty.

2002 Average winter rainfall and slightly delayed bud-break with some frost damage. The growing season was cool, leading to an average-sized crop with superior quality and showing well with age.

2001 Excellent quality with Cab Sauv for ageing up to a decade.

2000 Scares included a threatened storm from the south in early Sept, but damage was minimal. Biggest harvest on record. OK quality.

1999 V. cold spring and summer created late harvest, but absence of autumn rain left crop unscathed. Intensely flavoured and coloured wines. Outstanding quality, which is looking even better with age.

1998 Erratic harvest stumbled into Nov. Wines are adequate to dismal.

1997 Huge crop that looked gd early. At peak now.

1996 Tiny crop, lots of structure, lacks aromatic charm.

1995 Another small crop, great vitality but slow to unfold. Gd Zins, great Cabs. Best vintage for cellaring since 90.

1994 Mild growing season; dry, late harvest. Drink Cab Sauv now.

1993 Average yr; drink now or, better, yesterday.

Abreu Vineyards Napa ★★★ Massive Cab Sauv that can be worth waiting for.

Acacia Carneros ★★★ (Pinot N) 03 04 05 CARNEROS pioneer in Chard and Pinot N, always reliable, recently emphasizing single-v'yd wines. Luscious Viognier.

Acorn Russian River Valley ★★→★★★ Outstanding Zin from Heritage vines. Also v gd Sangiovese and Syrah.

Alban Edna Valley ★★→★★★ Emphasis on Rhônes, inc excellent Viognier. Grenache, Roussanne and Marsanne also top-rated.

Alexander Valley Vineyards Sonoma ★★★ Fruit-forward, drink-me-now Cab Sauv and Zin, reliable Chard.

Alma Rosa Santa Rita Hills ★★★ Richard Sanford, a master wine whiz at Sanford and Benedict Winery, is back at a new stand and producing lovely Pinot Gr and Chard from organic v'yds. Also v gd Vin Gris from Pinot N. Pinot N coming soon.

Altamura Vineyards Napa ★★★ 97 99 00 01 02 03 04 Cab Sauv is one of NAPA's best, with a firm structure and deep flavours; also a gd Sangiovese.

Amador Foothills Winery Amador ★★★ Top Zin and a bright, zingy Sauv Bl; Syrah also gd.

Andrew Murray Sta Barbara ★★★ It's Rhônes around the clock here. Outstanding Viognier and Roussanne among the whites and a solid Syrah.

Araujo Napa ★★★96 97 99 00 02 03 04 Powerful but never over-the-top cult Cab Sauv made from historic Eisele v'yd.

Armida Sonoma ★★→★★★ RUSSIAN RIVER VALLEY winery with solid Merlot, gd Pinot N, and a zippy Zin made from DRY CREEK VALLEY grapes.

Arthur Earl Sta Barbara ★★★ Artisan bottlings of mostly Rhône varietals, splashing out with an occasional Italian. Quality steadily improving.

Au Bon Climat Sta Barbara ★★★→★★★★ Owner Jim Clendenen listens to his private drummer: ultra-toasty Chard, flavourful Pinot N, light-hearted Pinot Bl. Vita Nova label for B'x varieties, Podere Olivos for Italianates. See QUPÉ.

Babcock Vineyards Sta Barbara ★★★ V.gd Pinot N, Chard and Sauv Bl from cool climate v. nr the Pacific in SANTA YNEZ VALLEY. New Grand Cuvée Pinot N has moved quality up a notch.

Beaulieu Vineyard Napa ★★→★★★ 97 99 01 03 Not the jewel it was when André Tchelistcheff was setting the style for NAPA Cab Sauv half a century ago but still worth looking out for, esp the Georges de Latour Private Reserve Cab Sauv. Decent budget wines under the Beaulieu Coastal label.

Benessere Napa ★★★ Sangiovese and Syrah worth a try. New Super Tuscan-style blend called Phenomenon is outstanding.

Benziger Family Winery Sonoma ★★★ Move towards top quality continues at this family winery. Estate v'yds now biodynamic. Look for Merlot and Cab Sauv.

Beringer Blass (Foster's Wine Estates) NAPA ★→★★★ (Cab) 97 99 00 01 A NAPA classic. Single-v'yd Cab Sauv Reserves can sometimes be over the top, but otherwise worthy of ageing. Velvety, powerful Howell Mountain Merlot one of the best. Look for Founder's Estate bargain line from NORTH COAST and CENTRAL COAST grapes. Also owns CH ST JEAN, ETUDE, Meridian, ST CLEMENT, STAGS' LEAP WINERY, and Taz, a brawny ★★→★★★ Pinot from Santa Barbara.

Bernardus Carmel Valley ★★★ Impressive red Meritage wines from densely planted, high-altitude v'yd. Brilliant Sauv Bl.

Biale Napa ★★→★★★ Small Zin specialist using mostly NAPA fruit.

Boeger El Dorado ★★→★★★ First El Dorado winery after Prohibition. Mostly estate wines. Attractive Merlot, Barbera, Zin, and Meritage. More understated than many in SIERRA FOOTHILLS and always reliable.

Bogle Vineyards Yolo ★→★★★ Major growers in the Sacramento Delta, Bogle family makes an attractive line of consistently gd and affordable wines.

Bokisch Lodi ★★→★★★ The focus is on Spanish varieties at this family estate. Garnacha, Albariño and Tempranillo show gd varietal character. Tempranillo esp impressive.

Bonny Doon Sta Cruz Mtns ★★★ Original Rhône Ranger Randall Grahm has slashed production, selling off his budget brands to concentrate on single-v'yd biodynamic wines. He is also building a winery in Washington State to produce his brilliant *Pacific Rim Riesling*.

Bonterra See Fetzer.

Bouchaine Vineyards Napa, Carneros ★★→★★★ Winery has had some ups and downs since its founding in 1980. Now on an up-swing with classic, sleek Chard and juicy but serious single-v'yd Pinot N.

Bronco Wine Company San Joaquin Founded by Fred Franzia, the nephew of Ernest Gallo, Bronco farms about 14 ha in the CENTRAL VALLEY. Franzia draws on this vast supply for his well-known Charles Shaw Two Buck Chuck brand. Franzia also fields several other labels, inc NAPA Creek and NAPA Ridge. Quality is not the point: Franzia is selling wine as a popular beverage.

Buena Vista Napa, Carneros ★★→★★★ After stumbling for a few yrs, Buena Vista is back on track with v.gd Estate Cab Sauv and gd Sauv Bl from LAKE COUNTY. Chard worth a look. Now part of CONSTELLATION's global wine group.

Burgess Cellars Napa ★★★ (Cab) 97 **99** 00 01 02 03 Cab Sauv from Howell Mountain grapes is splendid sleek and powerful while remaining balanced.

Cain Cellars Napa ★★★ 97 **99** 00 01 Often overlooked, Cain Cellars remains one of NAPA's jewels with consistent bottlings of Cain Five, a supple and elegant red wine based on Cab Sauv and its 4 B'x cousins, from Spring Mountain grapes. Cain Cuvée (declassified Cain Five) can rival the big brother.

Cafaro Napa ★★★ V.gd Cab Sauv and Merlot with the Alta Tierra red blend, made from hillside grapes, outstanding.

Cakebread Napa ★★★ (Cab) 97 99 **00** 01 02 03 Quality seems to improve with each vintage, esp the powerful Cab Sauv, which recently has been more balanced than earlier versions. One of the best Sauv Bls in the state.

Calcareous Paso Robles ★★ New winery specializing in Rhône varietals. Gd Viognier and outstanding Tres Violet red (mostly Syrah) blend. Keep an eye on this newcomer.

Calera San Benito ★★★★ Josh Jensen fell in love with Pinot N while at Oxford, and still is. He makes 3 supple and fine Pinot Ns named after v'yd blocks in the dry hills of San Benito, inland from Monterey: Reed, Seleck, and Jensen; also intense, flowery Viognier.

Campion Winery Napa ,Carneros ★★→★★★ Pinot N guru Larry Brooks is making only single-v'yd Pinot N from several sites. In limited distribution, worth seeking out.

Caymus Napa ★★★→★★★★ 91 **97** 99 00 01 The Special Selection Cab Sauv is consistently one of California's most formidable: rich, intense, slow to mature. Also a regular bottling, balanced and a little lighter. Gd Chard from Mer Soleil winery in Monterey, owned by Caymus.

Ceago Vinegarden Lake ★★→★★★ Jim Fetzer well settled into his biodynamic ranch on Clear Lake in LAKE COUNTY, produces v.gd Sauv Bl and Cab Sauv.

Ceja Vineyards Napa ★★→★★★ Established 1999, one of few California wineries owned by Mexican former v'yd workers. Early wines look gd, esp balanced Cab Sauv and delicious Chard from v'yds in NAPA and Sonoma.

Chalk Hill Sonoma ★★→★★★ Cab Sauv with some ageing potential is reliable.

Chalone Monterey ★★★→★★★★ Historic mountain estate above the Salinas Valley in Monterey. Marvellous flinty Chard and rich, intense Pinot N. Also makes a gd Chenin Bl (unusual in California) and a tasty Pinot Bl.

Chappellet Napa ★★★ Lovely little estate with ageworthy Cab Sauv, esp Signature label. ***Chenin Bl: a Napa classic***, dry and succulent. Pleasing Chard; gd Cab Fr, Merlot and Moelleux.

Château Montelena Napa ★★★→★★★★ (Chard) 99 00 01 (Cab) **91 95** 96 97 99 00 That rare thing in California, an ageworthy Chard. The estate Cab Sauv is also capable of extended ageing.

Château Potelle Napa ★★★ Recently sold to Jess Jackson, founder of KENDALL-JACKSON. Not certain at time of writing if high standards for Chard, Cab Sauv and Zin (from PASO ROBLES) will be maintained.

Château St Jean Sonoma ★★→★★★ Pioneered single-v'yd Chard in California under Richard Arrowood in the 1970s, still outstanding; gd Sauv Bl. Cinq Cepage, made from the 5 B'x varieties, can be ★★★★ quality. SONOMA County Cab Sauv and Chard are gd budget buys.

Chimney Rock Napa ★★★→★★★★ (Cab) 97 99 STAGS LEAP AVA producer of elegant, sometimes understated Cab Sauv capable of long ageing.

Redrawing the California wine map
Just when you think you've got wine California mapped, the territory changes. The CENTRAL COAST is supposed to be about Chardonnay and Pinot Noir. Erase that. There is a wave of new wineries in PASO ROBLES and Santa Barbara that add a new dimension to the California wine map. Some are winemakers like DANIEL GEHRS, making small amounts of wine from several v'yds; others are long-time growers, like LAFOND in the SANTA RITA HILLS, now making their own wine. It is difficult to keep the maps up to date, but it is a treat for those of us who like to try exciting new wines.

Clark-Claudon Napa ★★★ Balanced, silky hillside Cab Sauv from estate v'yd on the eastern slope of Howell Mountain. v.gd unoaked Sauv Bl from Pope Valley.

Clautiere Paso Robles ★★ Yet another gd new CENTRAL COAST producer offering value for dollars. The Estate Cab Sauv reaches ★★★, also v.gd Mourvèdre and a fruit-forward Grenache.

Cline Cellars Carneros ★→★★ Originally Contra Costa (important v'yds still there), now in SONOMA/CARNEROS and still dedicated mostly to rustic-style Rhône blends and sturdy Zin.

Clos du Bois Sonoma ★★→★★★ Large-scale SONOMA producer of quaffable everyday wines, with the exception of a single-v'yd Cab Sauv (Briarcrest) and Calcaire Chard, which can be v.gd. Recently acquired by CONSTELLATION.

Clos du Val Napa ★★★★ **95 97** 99 00 01 Consistently elegant Cab Sauvs that are among the best ageing candidates in the state. Chard is a delight and a Sem/Sauv Bl blend called Ariadne is a charmer.

Clos LaChance Sta Cruz ★★ Relative newcomers showing gd Zin and bright Chard from sourced fruit and own v'yds.

Clos Pegase Napa ★★→★★★ Is it a winery or museum? Sometimes hard to tell, but at best a sleek Cab Sauv from v'yds nr Calistoga, and a minerally Chard from CARNEROS grapes.

Cohn, B R Sonoma ★★→★★★ Ex-rock'n'roller Bruce Cohn makes powerful estate Cab Sauv in SONOMA VALLEY with gd ageing potential.

Conn Creek Napa ★★★ v.gd Cab Sauv sourced from several NAPA v'yds; elegant wines with gd structure and long ageing potential.

Continuum Name of new NAPA enterprise of the Mondavi family.

Constellation ★→★★★★ Owns wineries in California, NY, Washington State, Canada, Chile, Australia and New Zealand. Produces 90 million cases annually, selling more than any other wine company in the world. Once a bottom feeder, now going for the top. Bought MONDAVI at end of 2004 and also owns FRANCISCAN, Estancia, Mount Veeder, SIMI, RAVENSWOOD, among others.

Corison Napa ★★★★ **91 95** 96 97 99 00 01 02 Cathy Corison is a treasure of a winemaker. While too many in NAPA follow the $iren call of over-extracted powerhouse wines delivering big numbers from critics but no satisfaction in the glass, Corison continues to quietly make supple, flavoursome Cab Sauv promising to age well.

Cosentino Napa ★★→★★★ Irrepressible winemaker-owner Mitch Cosentino always full tilt. Results sometimes odd, sometimes brilliant, never dull. Cab Sauv always worth a look; Chard can be v.gd.

Coturri & Sons, H Sonoma ★ Cultish following for organic, no-sulphite but unreliable wines. Zin is the best bet.

Cuvaison Napa ★★★ (Cab) **99** 00 02 Gd to sometimes v.gd Chard, Merlot, Syrah from CARNEROS. Impressive Cab Sauv from MOUNT VEEDER.

Dalla Valle Napa ★★★★ **97** 99 00 01 Hillside estate is that rare thing: a cult classic with a track record. Maya is a Cab Sauv-based brawny, and Pietre Rosso, from Sangiovese, is a brilliant showcase for that variety, rare in California.

Daniel Gehrs Sta Barbara ★★→★★★ Veteran winemaker producing small lots of wines from CENTRAL COAST v'yds. A terrific Tempranillo and a balanced and luscious Zin from SANTA YNEZ VALLEY.

David Bruce Sta Cruz Mtns ★★★ Legendary mountain estate is still on top of the game with powerful, long-lasting Chard and superb Pinot N.

David Noyes Wines Sonoma ★★★ Former RIDGE and KUNDE Estate winemaker out on his own and clearly having a gd time with elegant Pinot N and a delicious Tocai Friulano. The Dutton Ranch RUSSIAN RIVER Pinot N is a spicy delight.

Davis Bynum Sonoma ★★★ Superb single-v'yd Pinot N from RUSSIAN RIVER VALLEY occasionally rises to ★★★★. Chard is lean and minerally with silky mouthfeel.

Dehlinger Sonoma ★★★★ (Pinot) 01 **03** 04 Outstanding Pinot N from estate RUSSIAN RIVER VALLEY v'yd. Also gd Chard, Syrah. Even in bad yrs, Dehlinger manages to pull it off.

Delicato Vineyards San Joaquin ★→★★ One-time CENTRAL VALLEY jug producer has moved up-scale with purchase of Monterey v'yds and several new bottlings from Lodi. Watch this brand for gd quality at everyday price, esp the Clay Station Lodi bottlings.

Diamond Creek Napa ★★★★ **91** 94 **95** 99 00 01 Austere, stunning cult Cabs from hilly v'yd nr Calistoga go by names of v'yd blocks: Gravelly Meadow, Volcanic Hill, Red Block Terrace. Wines age beautifully. One of NAPA's jewels.

Domaine Carneros Carneros ★★★ Showy US outpost of Taittinger in NAPA, CARNEROS echoes austere style of its parent in Champagne (see France) but with a delicious dollop of California fruit. Vintage Blanc de Blancs v.gd. La Rêve the luxury *cuvée*. Still Pinot N and Chard also impressive.

Domaine Chandon Napa ★★→★★★ Napa branch of Champagne house. Look for the NV Reserve, Etoile, esp the rosé, and a gd selection of still wines.

Dominus Napa ★★★★ **95** 97 99 00 01 02 03 Christian Moueix of Pomerol produces red B'x blend that is slow to open but ages beautifully; packed with power inside a silk glove. Second wine is Napanook.

Dry Creek Vineyard Sonoma ★★ Sauv (Fumé) Bl set standard for California for decades. Still impressive. Pleasing Chenin Bl; gd Zin.

Duckhorn Vineyards Napa ★★★→★★★★ Known for dark, tannic, almost plummy-ripe, single-v'yd Merlots (esp Three Palms) and Cab Sauv-based blend Howell Mountain. New winery in ANDERSON VALLEY for Golden Eye Pinot N in a robust style more akin to Cab Sauv than Pinot. Makes a Zin/Cab Sauv blend in Paraduxx, a second NAPA winery.

Dunn Vineyards Napa ★★★★ **90 91** 95 97 99 01 Owner-winemaker Randy Dunn makes dark Cab Sauv from Howell Mountain, which ages magnificently, slightly milder bottling from valley floor. One of a few NAPA winemakers to resist the stampede to jammy, over-the-top wines to curry wine critics' favour.

Dutton-Goldfield Western Sonoma County ★★★ Winemaker-grower duo crafting outstanding Pinot N and Chard from top cool-climate sites; rapidly being recognized as modern California classics.

Duxoup Sonoma ★★★ Quirky DRY CREEK producer of excellent Rhône-style Syrah and inky, old-vine Charbono. A promising Sangiovese under Gennaio label. Limited production but worth seeking out.

Eberle Winery San Luis Obispo ★★→★★★ Powerful Cab Sauv and Zin with gd balance and a supple concentration. New Viognier is a treat.

Edna Valley Vineyard San Luis Obispo ★★★ Much improved in past few vintages; v.gd Chard, crisp and fruity, lovely Sauv Bl. Recent Syrah impressive.

Etude Napa ★★★ Founder Tony Soter now making wine in Oregon with gd initial success. BERINGER BLASS now owns Etude and continues producing rich and juicy Pinot N from CARNEROS fruit.

Failla Vineyards Napa ★★→★★★ Winery on the Silverado Trail in NAPA gaining a reputation for SONOMA COAST and RUSSIAN RIVER VALLEY Pinot N and Chard.

Far Niente Napa ★★★ (Cab) 99 00 01 Opulence is the goal in both Cab Sauv and Chard from luxury NAPA estate. Can go over the top.

Ferrari-Carano Sonoma ★★★ Anyone who has visited the DRY CREEK estate knows there is less to the wine than meets the eye, esp in the last few vintages. Still an occasional bullseye; Merlot the best bet.

Fess Parker Sta Barbara ★★★ Founded by actor who played title role in TV's *Daniel Boone*; son Eli is winemaker. Gd Chard in tropical-fruit style, impressive Pinot N and Syrah, surprisingly gd Ries. Parker Station Pinot N is a luscious little wine made from young vines.

Fetzer Mendocino ★★→★★★ A leader in the organic/sustainable-viticulture movement, Fetzer has produced consistent-value wines from least expensive range (Sundial, Valley Oaks) to **brilliant Reserve wines**. Also owns Bonterra Vineyards (all organic grapes) where Roussanne and Marsanne are stars. McNabb Ranch line now farmed biodynamically. Jekel and Five Rivers brands are now made at Fetzer.

Ficklin Vineyards Madera, Central Valley ★★★ Lush and delicious port-style dessert wines made from the classic Portuguese varieties.

Fiddlehead San Luis Obispo ★★★ Winemaker Kathy Joseph has a fine touch with balanced and elegant Pinot N. Also zippy Sauv Bl in a minerally B'x style.

Firestone Sta Barbara ★★ An old name for gd basic Chard and a tempting Ries. Winery now owned by nearby Foley Estates V'yds.

Fisher Sonoma ★★→★★★ Underrated but solid producer of gd Chard from SONOMA hillside grapes and a restrained Cab Sauv from NAPA grapes.

Flora Springs Wine Co Napa ★★★ Best are the 2 Meritage wines, red Trilogy and white Soliloquy, made from benchland v'yds above valley floor. Juicy Merlot also worth a look. Chard sometimes heavy on the oak.

Flowers Vineyard & Winery Sonoma ★★★ Intense, terroir-driven Pinot N and Chard from v. cool-climate vines only a few miles from the Pacific. Flowers has won early critical acclaim and is clearly a winery to watch.

Foley Estates Vineyard Sta Barbara ★★→★★★ Barely 10 yrs old, already known for balanced, delicious Chard and Pinot N, now owns Firestone , Merus (Napa) and Three Rivers.

Foppiano Sonoma ★★→★★★ One of the grand old families in California wine. You can count on the Zin every time but look esp for Petite Sirah, better known as "petty sir" among the California rearguard.

Forman Napa ★★★★ 97 99 00 01 Winemaker who found fame at STERLING in the 1970s now makes his own excellent Cab Sauv and Chard.

Foxen Sta Barbara ★★★ An impressive range of wines from this consistently gd producer. Wines range from Rhône style to Cab Fr to brilliant Pinot N.

Franciscan Vineyard Napa ★★★ Quality has been maintained under CONSTELLATION ownership, esp the top-of-the-line wines like the graceful red Magnificant and the Cuvée Sauvage Chard, one of the first California Chards using wild-yeast fermentation. Gd budget wines under Estancia label.

Freeman Russian River Valley ★★ New producer showing great promise with cool-climate Pinot N (Akiko's Cuvée from SONOMA COAST AVA) and RUSSIAN RIVER Pinot N. Keep an eye on this exciting new estate.

Freemark Abbey Napa ★★★ 97 00 01 Historic, currently underrated but consistent producer of stylish Cab Sauv (esp single-v'yd Sycamore and Bosché).

Fritz Dry Creek Valley ★★ Consistently gd Zin from DRY CREEK and RUSSIAN RIVER AVAs, sometimes rising to ★★★.

Frog's Leap Napa ★★★→★★★★ 99 00 01 02 03 Small winery, as charming as its name (and T-shirts) suggest. Lean, minerally Sauv Bl, toasty Chard, spicy Zin. Supple and delicious Merlot, Cab Sauv. Converting to organic and biodynamic with recent wines showing more depth and intensity. Not a coincidence.

Gallo, E & J San Joaquin ★→★★ California's biggest winery is an easy target, going back to the days of wines like Thunderbird. In the long view, Gallo has done more to open up the American palate to wine than any other winery. Gallo's 1960s Hearty Burgundy was a groundbreaking popular wine. It still does the basic commodity wines, but it has also created an imposing line of regional varieties, such as Anapauma, Marcellina, Turning Leaf and more, all wines of modest quality perhaps but predictable and affordable.

Gallo Sonoma Sonoma ★★→★★★ DRY CREEK VALLEY winery bottles several wines from SONOMA, NORTH COAST. Cab Sauv can be v.gd, esp the single-v'yd ones.

> **The Spanish are back**
> The first wine grapes in California were planted by Spanish missionaries coming north from Mexico in the 18th century. The Spanish have returned, or at least grape varieties usually associated with Spain seem to be the coming thing in California. Albariño, Galicia's quirky white wine grape, has found a new home in California, with, for example, tasty new bottlings from Bokisch and Randall Grahm's Ca' del Solo label. Tempranillo is also on the rise, with excellent offerings by Christine Andrew and Longoria V'yds. The Caballeros aren't challenging the Rhône Rangers yet, but they are trying.

Chard also better than average. Other wines made in SONOMA worth a try include Frei Brothers and McMurray, esp Pinot Gr.

Gary Farrell Sonoma ★★★→★★★★ Well established with some of the best Pinot N and Chard from the RUSSIAN RIVER VALLEY over the yrs. Shared space at Davis BYNUM; now has his own. Also look for Zin and Chard and a v.gd Sauv Bl.

Geyser Peak Sonoma ★★→★★★ Reliable, sometimes underrated producer of toasty Chard, powerful, sleek Cab Sauv, juicy Shiraz. A recent focus on Sauv Bl is welcome.

Gloria Ferrer Sonoma, Carneros ★★★ Built by Spain's Freixenet for sparkling wine, now producing spicy Chard and bright, silky Pinot N and other varietals, all from CARNEROS fruit. Bubbly quality remains high, esp the Brut Rosé and the Royal Cuvée, inspired by a visit from King Juan Carlos of Spain.

Grace Family Vineyard Napa ★★★★ 97 99 00 01 Stunning Cab Sauv. Shaped for long ageing. One of the few cult wines that may actually be worth the price.

Greenwood Ridge Mendocino ★★→★★★ Winery well above the floor of ANDERSON VALLEY offers engaging off-dry perfumed Ries. Reds, esp Cab Sauv and Pinot N, also v.gd.

Grgich Hills Cellars Napa ★★★→★★★★ Solid NAPA producer of supple Chard (which can age); balanced, elegant Cab Sauv; jammy, ripe Zin from SONOMA grapes. Gd Sauv Bl in minerally style. New biodynamic Sauv Bl impressive.

Groth Vineyards Napa ★★★★ 95 97 99 00 01 OAKVILLE estate Cab Sauv has been 4-star for a decade, with big, wrap-around flavours made for ageing.

Gundlach-Bundschu Sonoma ★★→★★★ Historic SONOMA VALLEY winery offers *memorable Gewurz*, Merlot, Zin. Much improved Cab Sauv.

Hagafen Napa ★★ One of the first serious California kosher producers. Gd Chard and Sauv Bl and palate-friendly Zin.

Halter Ranch Paso Robles ★★ A stylish Cab Sauv leads the list but Rhône-style Syrah, firm and peppery, is moving up fast.

Handley Cellars Mendocino ★★★ Winemaker Mila Handley makes excellent ANDERSON VALLEY Chard, Gewurz, Pinot N. Also v.gd DRY CREEK VALLEY Sauv Bl and Chard from her family's vines in SONOMA County; also a small amount of intense sparkling wine well worth a look.

Hanna Winery Sonoma ★★★ Has been reaching for 4-star status for yrs. Recent vintages of Cab Sauv and well-made Sauv Bl are excellent.

Hanzell Sonoma ★★★★ (Chard) 01 02 03 (Pinot N) 00 01 02 Pioneer (1950) small producer of outstanding terroir-driven Chard and Pinot N from estate vines. Always gd; quality level has risen sharply in the past few yrs. Deserves to be ranked with the best of California.

Harlan Estate Napa ★★★★ 97 99 00 01 03 Concentrated, sleek, cult Cab Sauv from small estate commanding luxury prices.

Harrison Clarke Santa Ynez ★★ All about Syrah and Grenache. Estate Syrah is worth seeking out and the Grenache has rich flavour profile and mouthfeel.

Hartford Court Sonoma ★★★ Part of KENDALL-JACKSON's Artisans & Estates group showing v.gd single-v'yd Pinot Ns, tight coastal-grown Chard, and wonderful old-vine RUSSIAN RIVER Zins.

HDV Carneros ★★★ Complex and layered Chard with a minerally edge from grower Larry Hyde's v'yd in conjunction with Aubert de Villaine of Dom de la Romanée-Conti (see France).

Heitz Napa ★★★→★★★★ 97 99 00 01 History-making deeply flavoured, minty Cab Sauv from Martha's V'yd. Bella Oaks and newer Trailside V'yd rival but can't match Martha. Some feel quality has slipped in recent vintages.

Heller Estate Carmel Valley, Monterey ★★★ 99 00 01 02 Dark, powerful Cab Sauv from organic v'yds acquiring California's cult status. Chenin Bl is charming.

The Hess Collection Napa ★★→★★★ Owner and art collector Donald Hess uses winery visiting area as a museum. Cab Sauv from MOUNT VEEDER AVA v'yds step up to new quality level; Chard crisp and bright; Hess Select label v.gd value.

Honig Napa ★★★ Big jump in quality after switching to organic farming. V.gd Cab Sauv in classic NAPA style and seriously delicious Sauv Bl lead the parade.

Hop Kiln Sonoma ★★★ A new direction for this well-regarded winery with a brand called HK Generations. Chard is superb, Pinot N excellent, both made from RUSSIAN RIVER VALLEY grapes. Also gd Zin.

Iron Horse Vineyards Sonoma ★★★→★★★★ RUSSIAN RIVER family estate producing *some of California's best bubbly*, esp a series of late-disgorged beauties. Chard from RUSSIAN RIVER VALLEY is v.gd and an above-average Cab Sauv from ALEXANDER VALLEY v'yds.

Ironstone Lodi & Calaveras County ★→★★ Long-time growers with a destination winery in SIERRA FOOTHILLS making honestly priced and easy-drinking wines from mostly CENTRAL VALLEY grapes. New Verdelho from Lodi is superb. Outstanding Lodi Tempranillo under new Christine Andrew label.

Jade Mountain Napa ★★→★★★ V.gd Rhône-style wines, esp Syrah, Mourvèdre.

Jessie's Grove Lodi ★★ Old Zin vines work well for farming family's venture.

Jordan Sonoma ★★★★ (Cab) 98 99 00 01 02 Extravagant ALEXANDER VALLEY estate models its Cab Sauv on supplest B'x. And it lasts. Minerally Chard is made in a Burgundian style.

Joseph Phelps Napa ★★★★ (Insignia) 95 97 99 00 01 Long-serving Phelps is one of the top Cab Sauv houses in California, esp the Insignia and Backus. Look for fine Rhône series under Vin du Mistral label. Expect great things from a Pinot N-only winery in coastal SONOMA. Beginning to farm biodynamically.

Joseph Swan Sonoma ★★★ Long-time RUSSIAN RIVER producer of intense Zin and classy Pinot N capable of ageing in the 10-yr range.

J Vineyards Sonoma ★★★ Part of JORDAN, now on its own in RUSSIAN RIVER VALLEY. Creamy classic Brut the foundation. Pinot N and Pinot Gr worth a look.

Kendall-Jackson Sonoma ★★→★★★ Staggeringly successful style aimed at widest market, esp broadly sourced off-dry toasty Chard. Even more noteworthy for the development of a diversity of wineries under the umbrella of Kendall-Jackson's Artisans & Estates (see HARTFORD COURT).

Kenwood Vineyards Sonoma ★★→★★★ (Jack London Cab) 99 00 01 Single-v'yd Jack London Cab Sauv, Zin (several) the high points of a consistent line. Sauv Bl is reliable value.

Kistler Vineyards Sonoma ★★★ (Chard) Still chasing the Burgundian model of single-v'yd Pinot N, most from RUSSIAN RIVER, with mixed success. Chards can be v. toasty, buttery, and over-the-top, though they have a loyal following.

Korbel Sonoma ★★ Largest US producer of *méthode champenoise* with focus on fruit flavours. Gd picnic wines.

Words within entries marked like this *Alter Ego de Palmer* indicate wines especially enjoyed by Hugh Johnson over the past 12 months (mid '07–'08).

Charles Krug Napa ★★→★★★ Historically important winery; wines on an upward trend under third generation of (the other) Mondavi family. New focus on red B'x styles showing gd results.

Kunde Estate Sonoma ★★★ Solid SONOMA VALLEY producer and noted grower with an elegant, understated Chard, flavourful Sauv Bl, peachy Viognier, and silky Merlot. All estate-bottled.

Lafond Santa Rita Hills ★★→★★★ Veteran grower in this exciting new appellation now making wine – and what took them so long? The Syrah is reminiscent of a southern Rhône, with bright minerality and long finish. Pinot N is also gd.

La Jota Napa ★★→★★★ Huge, long-lived Cab Sauv from Howell Mountain.

Lambert Bridge Dry Creek, Sonoma ★★★ Seductive Merlot, zesty Zin, and brilliant Sauv Bl in a "B'x meets New Zealand" style.

Lamborn Howell Mountain, Napa ★★★ V'yd planted on historic 19th-century site. Big juicy Zin, Cab Sauv coming along for this cult winery.

Landmark Sonoma ★★→★★★ Early promise of elegant Burgundian-style Chard blunted by oaky-toasty flavours in late 1990s. Now back on track.

Lane Tanner Sta Barbara ★★★ 01 02 03 Owner-winemaker makes v. personal and superb single-v'yd Pinot N (Bien Nacido, Sierra Madre Plateau) reflecting terroir with a quiet, understated elegance.

Lang & Reed Napa ★★★ Specialist focusing on delicious Loire-style Cab Fr.

Laurel Glen Sonoma ★★★★ (Cab) 91 94 95 Floral, well-etched and long-lived Cab Sauv with a sense of place from steep v'yd on SONOMA MOUNTAIN.

Lava Cap El Dorado ★★ SIERRA producer making a wide range of mostly estate wines. Cab Sauv is gd, but Zin is outstanding.

Livingston Moffett St Helena, Napa ★★★ Noteworthy Cab Sauv from RUTHERFORD Ranch v'yds. Syrah also v.gd.

Lockwood Monterey ★ South Salinas Valley v'yd. Gd value in Chard, Sauv Bl.

Lohr, J Central Coast ★★→★★★ Large winery with extensive v'yds; v.gd PASO ROBLES Cab Sauv Seven Oaks. Recent series of Meritage-style reds best yet. Commodity line is Cypress.

Long Meadow Napa ★★★ Elegant, silky Cab Sauv better with each vintage. V'yd is organically farmed. Potential cult status.

Longoria Winery Sta Barbara (★★→★★★) Rick Longoria makes brilliant Pinot N from top v'yds in the area. New Albariño is brilliant.

Louis M Martini Napa ★★→★★★ Long history-making, ageworthy Cab Sauv, Zin. On downslide for several yrs. Now on the way back after purchase by GALLO in 2002 with recent bottlings of Cab Sauv showing v. well.

MacRostie Sonoma, Carneros ★★★ Toasty, ripe Chard with some complexity is flagship. Also Merlot, Pinot N from single v'yds. New Syrah is v.gd.

Mahoney Vineyards Napa, Carneros ★★→★★★ Founder of Carneros Creek, one of the CARNEROS pioneers and an early Pinot N enthusiast, now producing under own label. V.gd Vermentino, excellent single-v'yd Pinot N.

Marcassin Sonoma Coast Cult queen Helen Turley's own tiny label. Worth so much at auction that few ever drink it. Concentrated Chard and dense Pinot N. Chard so densely concentrated those who do taste it never forget.

Marimar Torres Estate Sonoma ★★★★ (Chard) 01 02 03 04 (Pinot N) 00 01 02 03 Several bottlings of Chard and Pinot N from Don Miguel estate v'yd in Green Valley. *The Chard is complex and sometimes rather edgy*, with gd ageing potential. New Acero Don Miguel Chard is unoaked and a lovely expression of Chard fruit. New unfiltered Pinot N from the Doña Margarita v'yd, only a few miles from the ocean, is intense and surprisingly rich for young vines. V'yds now farmed organically and moving toward biodynamics.

Markham Napa ★★★ Underrated producer of elegant Merlot and solid Cab Sauv.

Martinelli Russian River ★★★ Family growers from fog-shrouded western hills of

SONOMA, famous for old-vine Jackass Hill Vineyard Zin.

Matanzas Creek Sonoma ★★ Excellent Sauv Bl has slipped of late. Merlot outstanding; Chard gd. Owned by KENDALL-JACKSON.

Mayacamas Napa ★★★ Pioneer boutique v'yd with rich Chard and firm (but no longer steel-hard) Cab Sauv, capable (and worthy of) long ageing.

Merry Edwards Russian River ★★★★ Superstar consultant has planted her own Pinot N v'yd in RUSSIAN RIVER district and buys in grapes. Her Pinot N is "must drink". Also lovely, true-to-varietal Sauv Bl.

Merryvale Napa ★★★ Best at Cab Sauv and Merlot, which have elegant balance and supple finish. Sauv Bl can be v.gd.

Mettler Family Vineyards Lodi ★★ Long-time growers now producing a sleek and tangy Cab Sauv and a powerful Petite Sirah.

Peter Michael Sonoma ★★★→★★★★ Stunning, complex Chard from Howell Mountain in a powerful style, and a more supple ALEXANDER VALLEY bottling. Cab Sauv on the tight side.

Michel-Schlumberger Sonoma ★★→★★★ Excellent ageing potential in supple Cab Sauv usually blended with Merlot from hillside vines in DRY CREEK.

Milano Mendocino ★★ Small producer of Zin, Cab Sauv, worth seeking out.

Mitchell Katz Livermore Valley ★★→★★★ An upcoming winery in Livermore winery. Makes v.gd Cab Sauv and a blockbuster Petite Sirah. Watch for more.

Monteviña Amador ★★ Reliable producer of fruit-forward Zin and a v.gd Barbera. Top of line Terra d'Oro.

Monticello Cellars Napa ★★★ 97 99 01 Top Cab Sauv and Chard under Corley label, basic line under Monticello.

Morgan Monterey ★★★★ Top-end, single-v'yd Pinot Ns and Chards from SANTA LUCIA HIGHLANDS v'yds. Esp fine unoaked Chard Metallico. Estate Double L v'yd farmed organically. New Rhônish entry Côtes du Crows is charming.

Mount Eden Sta Cruz Mts ★★★ Founded by California wine guru Martin Ray in the 1940s, Mount Eden produces ageworthy Chard – rare in California – and intense Pinot N.

Mount Veeder ★★★ Powerful mountain Cab Sauv repays cellar time. Owned by CONSTELLATION.

Mumm Napa Valley Napa ★★★ Stylish bubbly, esp delicious Blanc de Noirs and a rich, complex DVX single-v'yd fizz to age a few yrs in the bottle.

Murphy-Goode Sonoma ★★ Large ALEXANDER VALLEY estate. Sauv Bl, Zin are tops. Tin Roof (screwcap) line offers refreshing Sauv Bl and Chard *sans* oak, in contrast to lavishly oaked Reserve line.

Nalle Sonoma ★★★ Doug Nalle makes lovely Zins from DRY CREEK fruit, juicy and delicious young will also mature gracefully. Try new bottlings of Pinot N.

Napa Wine Company Napa ★★★ Largest organic grape-grower in NAPA sells most of the fruit and operates a custom crush facility for several small premium producers. Offers v.gd Cab Sauv under own label.

Navarro Vineyards Mendocino ★★★→★★★★ Modern ANDERSON VALLEY pioneer producing Ries and Gewurz ranking with the best of the New World. Also Pinot N in 2 styles, homage to Burgundy from ANDERSON VALLEY grapes, plus a brisk and juicy bottling from bought-in grapes.

Newton Vineyards Napa ★★★→★★★★ (Cab) 97 **99** 00 01 (Merlot) **99** 00 01 02 Mountain estate makes excellent Merlot that outshines the supple Cab Sauv. Peter Newton died 2008

Nickel & Nickel Napa Specialist in exceptional terroir-driven single-v'yd Cab Sauv from NAPA and SONOMA.

Niebaum-Coppola Estate Napa ★★★ (Rubicon) **99 00** 01 "Godfather" Coppola has proven he is as serious about making wine as making movies. Rubicon, a B'x blend, is best on the list; Edizione Pennino concentrates on delightfuly old-fashioned Zin. Budget Diamond series made at recently purchased Ch Souverain in SONOMA.

Ojai Sta Barbara ★★★ Former AU BON CLIMAT partner Adam Tolmach makes range of v.gd wines, esp Syrah and a few other Rhônes from CENTRAL COAST v'yds.

Opus One Napa ★★★★ There have been a lot of in-and-out yrs at Opus, with wines rarely living up to the hype for this red B'x blend. Perhaps new partnership under CONSTELLATION will set it straight. Again, maybe not.

Pahlmeyer Napa ★★★ Cultish producer of dense, tannic Cab Sauv and more supple Merlot.

Paradigm Napa ★★★ Westside OAKVILLE v'yd with an impressive Merlot and a bright, supple Cab Sauv.

Paraiso Monterey ★★ Luscious Ries and Pinot Bl. Bright and balanced Pinot N from SANTA LUCIA HIGHLANDS fruit and a supple Syrah.

Parry Cellars Napa ★★★ Newcomer producing small amounts of graceful, elegant Cab Sauv from a v'yd on the Silverado Trail.

Patianna Vineyards Russian River ★★★ Biodynamic v'yds farmed by Patty FETZER. Also sources grapes from organic v'yds in MENDOCINO. Lovely Sauv Bl and v.gd Syrah are main strengths.

Paul Dolan Mendocino ★★★ Pioneer of organic and biodynamic farming when he was winemaker at Fetzer, Dolan's own brand offers outstanding Zin, Syrah, Cab Sauv, Chard and Sauv Bl from organic, biodynamic NORTH COAST v'yds.

Peachy Canyon Paso Robles ★★→★★★ Zin specialists, focusing on bold single-v'yd bottlings; look for Old Schoolhouse and Snail V'yd.

Pedroncelli Sonoma ★★ Old hand in DRY CREEK producing bright, elbow-bending Zin, Cab Sauv, and a solid Chard.

Periano Lodi ★★ Gd example of the new look of Lodi wines. Outstanding Barbera, brilliant Viognier, and v.gd Chard.

Perry Creek El Dorado ★★→★★★ An extraordinary Syrah and above-average Cab Sauv from high-elevation vines .

Philips, R H Yolo, Dunnigan Hills ★→★★★ The only winery in the Dunnigan Hills AVA makes a wide range of wines. Excellent job with Rhône varieties under the EXP label and gd-value Toasted Head Chard.

Philip Togni Vineyards Napa ★★★→★★★★ **99 00 01** Veteran NAPA winemaker makes v. fine long-lasting Cab Sauv from SPRING MOUNTAIN.

Pine Ridge Napa ★★★ Tannic and concentrated Cab Sauvs from several NAPA AVAs. The just off-dry Chenin Bl is a treat.

Preston Dry Creek Valley, Sonoma ★★★ Lou Preston is a demanding terroirist, making outstanding DRY CREEK VALLEY icons like Zin and fruity, marvellous Barbera. His Sauv Bl is delicious. New line of Rhône varietals looking gd.

Pride Mountain Napa ★★★ Top hillside location on SPRING MOUNTAIN contributes bright fruit characters to fine B'x-variety offerings; ageing potential.

Provenance Napa ★★★ Lovely, elegant, and supple Cab Sauv from heart of NAPA estate. Winemaker Tom Rinaldi also makes superb Hewitt V'yd Cab Sauv.

Quady Winery San Joaquin Imaginative Madera Muscat dessert wines include celebrated orangey Essencia, rose-petal-flavoured Elysium, and Moscato d'Asti-like Electra. Recently introduced Vya Vermouth, an excellent aperitif.

Quintessa Napa ★★★ Homage to Bordeaux blend from a biodynamic estate on the Silverado Trail. Wines started on a high note, continue to improve. Winery developed by the Huneeus family of Chile, now linked to CONSTELLATION.

Quivira Sonoma ★★★ Focus on classic and v. drinkable Dry Creek Zin; also a range of delicious Rhône varietals. V'yds farmed biodynamically.

Qupé Sta Barbara ★★★ Never-a-dull-moment cellar-mate of AU BON CLIMAT.

CALIFORNIA

Marsanne, Pinot Bl, Syrah are all well worth trying.

Rafanelli, A Sonoma ★★★→★★★★ Extraordinary DRY CREEK Zin is strong suit. It will age, but it's so delightful when young, why bother?

Ramey Wine Cellars Russian River ★★★→★★★★ Outstanding single-v'yd Cab Sauv from NAPA, and rich and complex Chard from cooler v'yds.

Kent Rasmussen Carneros ★★★ Crisp, lingering Chard and delicious Pinot N. Ramsay is an alternative label for small production lots.

Ravenswood Sonoma ★★★ Joel Peterson pioneered single-v'yd Zin. Later added a budget line of SONOMA and Vintners Reserve Zin and Merlot. Now owned by CONSTELLATION, but quality appears to be holding firm.

Raymond Vineyards and Cellar Napa ★★★ 99 00 01 Balanced and understated Cab Sauv from family v'yds with potential for long-term ageing.

Ridge Sta Cruz Mts ★★★★ (Cab) 91 95 97 99 00 01 Founder and winemaster Paul Draper continues to work his magic here. Supple and harmonious Monticello Cab Sauv from estate is superb. Also outstanding single-v'yd Zin from SONOMA, NAPA, SIERRA FOOTHILLS, and PASO ROBLES. Most Zin has gd ageing potential. Outstanding Chard from wild-yeast fermentation often overlooked.

Robert Keenan Winery Napa ★★★ Winery on SPRING MOUNTAIN: supple, restrained Cab Sauv, Merlot; also Chard.

Robert Mondavi Napa ★★→★★★★ Brilliant innovator bought in 2004 by CONSTELLATION, has wine at all price/quality ranges. At the top are the NAPA VALLEY Reserves (bold, prices to match), NAPA VALLEY appellation series (eg CARNEROS Chard, OAKVILLE Cab Sauv, etc), NAPA VALLEY (basic production). At the low end are various CENTRAL COAST wines and Robert Mondavi-Woodbridge from Lodi. While the v. top wines may be holding their quality level, mid-ranges seem to be slipping.

Rochioli, J Sonoma ★★★→★★★★ Long-time RUSSIAN RIVER grower sells most fruit to GARY FARRELL and other top Pinot N producers, but holds back enough to make lovely complex Pinot N under his own label. Also v.gd Zin.

Roederer Estate Mendocino ★★★★ ANDERSON VALLEY branch of Champagne house. Supple, elegant house style. Easily one of the top 3 sparklers in California and hands-down the best rosé. Top-of-the-line luxury *cuvée* L'Ermitage superb.

Rosenblum Cellars San Francisco Bay ★★→★★★★ Makes a wide range of Zins and Rhône varietals from v'yds up and down the state. Quality varies, but always well above average.

Rutz Cellars Sonoma ★★→★★★ Early Chard outstanding but has strayed into over-the-top bottlings of late. V.gd Pinot N from RUSSIAN RIVER v'yds.

Saddleback Cellars Napa ★★★→★★★★ (Cab) 95 97 99 00 01 Owner-winemaker Nils Venge is a legend in NAPA. Lush Zin and long-lived Cab Sauv. In some vintages he makes a super Sauv Bl.

St Clement Napa ★★★→★★★★ (Cab) 99 00 01 Long-time NAPA producer has a new life under BERINGER BLASS ownership, with a turn towards terroir-based wines. Supple, long-lived Oroppas, a Cab Sauv-based blend, is the go-to wine here. Merlot and Chard also outstanding.

St Francis Sonoma ★★★ 99 00 01 Deep and concentrated Cab Sauv from single v'yds. Look for the Wild Oak V'yd Chard finished with a nod to Burgundy. The old-vine Zin is super.

Saintsbury Carneros ★★★→★★★★ (Pinot N) 00 01 02 03 Outstanding Pinot N, denser than most from CARNEROS. Chard full-flavoured, nicely balanced. Garnet Pinot N, made from younger vines, is a light-hearted quaff.

St-Supéry Napa ★★→★★★ Sleek and graceful Merlot; Cab Sauv can be outstanding, as is red Meritage. Sauv Bl one of best in state. Sources some grapes from warmer Pope Valley east of NAPA VALLEY. French-owned (Skalli).

Sanford Sta Barbara ★★→★★★ Founder Richard Sanford was one of the first to plant Pinot N in Santa Barbara, but wines have hit a rough patch under new owners. The Pinot N and Sauv Bl are still worth a look.

Santa Cruz Mountain Vineyard Sta Cruz ★★→★★★ (Cab Sauv) **97 99** 00 01 Produces wines of strong varietal character from estate grapes, inc v.gd Pinot N and an exceptional Cab Sauv – big, concentrated, ageworthy.

Sattui, V Napa ★★ King of direct-only sales (ie winery door or mail order). Wines made in a rustic, drink-now style. Reds are best, esp Cab Sauv, Zin.

Sausal Sonoma ★★→★★★ ALEXANDER VALLEY estate noted for its Zin and Cab Sauv. Century Vine Zin is a stunning example of old-vine Zin.

Schramsberg Napa ★★★★ Sparkling wine that stands the test of time. The first to make a true *méthode champenoise* in the state in commercial quantity. Historic caves. Reserve is splendid; ***Blanc de Noirs outstanding***. Luxury *cuvée* J Schram is America's Krug. Mirabelle is second label for palate-pleasing bubbly. Now making a v.gd Cab Sauv from mountain estate vines.

Schug Cellars Carneros ★★★ German-born and -trained owner-winemaker dabbles in other wines but outstanding CARNEROS Chard and Pinot N are his main interests.

Screaming Eagle ★★★★ Napa Small lots of cult Cab Sauv at luxury prices for those who like that kind of thing.

Sebastiani Sonoma ★ Former jug-wine king has tried to go upscale with v'yd wines with limited critical success.

Seghesio Sonoma ★★★ Respected family winery has a double focus: Italian varietals and Zin. The Zins are superb, drinkable when young, taking on new depth with age. The Italians are a cut above most California efforts in that line, esp Barbera and Sangiovese.

Selene Napa ★★★→★★★★ Ace winemaker Mia Klein makes rich concentrated B'x varietal wines. Hyde V'yd Sauv Bl is super; Chester V'yd red blend a must.

Sequoia Grove Napa ★★★ Estate Cab Sauvs are intense and long-lived, and the trend in the past few yrs is clearly upwards. Chard is balanced and has ageing potential most yrs.

Shafer Vineyards Napa ★★★★ (Cab Sauv) **90 91 95 97** 99 00 01 02 03 (Merlot) **00** 01 03 This California "first growth" gets top marks for deep yet supple Cab Sauv, esp the Hillside Select and Merlot. CARNEROS Chard (Red Shoulder Ranch) breaking out of oak shackles.

Sierra Vista El Dorado ★★→★★★ Dedicated Rhône-ist in SIERRA FOOTHILLS. Style is elegant, mid-weight, and fruit-driven, with emphasis on varietal typicity.

Signorello Napa ★★★ Fairly high-end Cab Sauvs and Chards, noteworthy Pinot N from RUSSIAN RIVER, v.gd Sem/Sauv Bl blend is best value. A bit less oak?

Silverado Vineyards Napa ★★★→★★★★ (Cab) **97 99** 00 01 02 Showy hilltop STAGS LEAP district winery offering supple Cab Sauv, lean and minerally Chard, and distinctive Sangiovese.

Silver Oak Napa/Sonoma ★★★→★★★★ Separate wineries in NAPA and ALEXANDER VALLEYS make Cab Sauv only. NAPA wines can be heavy on the oak. ALEXANDER VALLEY a bit more supple than NAPA

Simi Sonoma ★★→★★★ Up-and-down historic winery makes a wide range of varietals. Long-lived Cab Sauv and v.gd Chard still the heart of the matter.

Sinskey Vineyards Napa ★★★ Ex-ACACIA partner started winery. Chard with a gd acidic bite and luscious Pinot N are the highlights.

Smith & Hook Monterey ★★→★★★ Rich, fruity Pinot N from STA LUCIA HIGHLANDS v'yd leads the way followed by a gd Chard. Budget line is Hahn Estate.

Smith-Madrone Napa ★★ High up on SPRING MOUNTAIN, the Smith brothers make ***one of the state's best Ries*** in an aromatic off-dry style. V'yds are dry-farmed.

Sonoma-Cutrer Vineyards Sonoma ★★ Chard specialist has rarely lived up to

CALIFORNIA

expectations in the past but seems to be on track with latest bottlings, esp the RUSSIAN RIVER Ranches.

Spencer Roloson ★★ Négociant-producer of stylish Zin and Tempranillo from single v'yds. New Viognier from Lodi is charming.

Spottswoode Napa ★★★★ **95 96** 97 99 00 01 *Outstanding Cab Sauv* from estate v'yd is long-lasting, balanced, and harmonious. Another California "first growth". Brilliant Sauv Bl is a bonus.

Spring Mountain Napa ★★★→★★★★ Historic mountain estate on a winning path; excellent Cab Sauv with gd structure and depth and outstanding Sauv Bl.

Staglin Napa ★★★**99** 00 01 Silky, elegant Cab Sauv from RUTHERFORD Bench.

Stag's Leap Wine Cellars Napa ★★★★ **95 97** 99 00 01 Celebrated for silky, seductive Cab Sauvs (SLV, Fay, top-of-line Cask 23) and Merlots. Gd Chard is often overlooked. Holding the line for balance and harmony against the onslaught of over-the-top, super-concentrated NAPA Cabs. Recently purchased by partnership of Pierro Antinori and Ch Ste Michelle.

Stags' Leap Winery Napa ★★ Historic estate being revived by BERINGER BLASS. Historically important for Petite Sirah.

Steele Wines Lake ★★→★★★ Jed Steele is a genius at sourcing v'yds for a series of single-v'yd wines under main label and a second label called Shooting Star. Chard can get a little oaky, but Pinot N and some speciality wines, such as Washington State Aligoté, are outstanding. New budget line is Writer's Block, featuring an earthy and powerful Grenache.

Sterling Napa ★★→★★★ Scenic NAPA estate producing basic Chard and understated single-v'yd Cab Sauv. Sterling has never seemed to fulfil potential, despite gd v'yd sources.

Stony Hill Napa ★★★★ (Chard) **90 91 95 97** 99 00 Amazing hillside Chard for past 50 yrs, made in an elegant "homage to Chablis" style. Most wine sold from mailing list. Wines are v. long-lived.

Storybook Mountain Napa ★★ Dedicated Zin specialist makes taut and tannic Estate (not to everyone's taste) and Reserve wines from Calistoga v'yd.

Strong Vineyard Sonoma ★→★★ Cab Sauv from single-v'yd bottlings gd to v.gd; gd RUSSIAN RIVER Pinot N and a pleasing heritage-vine Zin.

Sutter Home Napa ★→★★ Famous for white Zin and rustic AMADOR red Zin. New upscale Signature Series and Trinchero Family Estates a step up, esp Cab Sauv.

Tablas Creek Paso Robles ★★★ Joint venture between owners of Ch Beaucastel and importer Robert Hass. V'yd based on cuttings from Châteauneuf v'yds. *Côtes de Tablas in both red and white* is amazingly gd, as is the Tablas Creek Esprit. These are must-drink wines for Rhônistas.

Talbott, R Monterey ★★★ Chard from single v'yds in MONTEREY is the name of the game, with the famed Sleepy Hollow v'yd in the SANTA LUCIA HIGHLANDS AVA at the heart. Approach is Burgundian.

The Terraces Napa ★★★ Supple and elegant Cab Sauv and Zin from several small v'yd plots in the eastern foothills of NAPA.

Thomas Fogarty Sta Cruz Mts ★★→★★★ Go here for a rich, complex Chard that ages fairly well. Also gd Pinot N from estate v'yds and a delightful Gewurz from Monterey grapes.

Trefethen Napa ★★★ Respected long-serving family winery. Gd off-dry Ries, balanced Chard for ageing, although recent releases have not shown as well. Cab Sauv shows increasing complexity, esp top-of-the-line Halo.

Tres Sabores Rutherford ★★★ Newcomer making 3 different Zins all from the same RUTHERFORD organically farmed hillside v'yds. Wines are consistently balanced and elegant, emphasizing different elements of the v'yd.

Truchard Carneros ★★★→★★★★ Merlot in CARNEROS? For sure. From the warmer north end of CARNEROS comes one of the flavoury, firmly built Merlots that give the AVA identity. Cab Sauv and Syrah even better, and the tangy lemony Chard is a must-drink. New bottlings of Tempranillo outstanding as is a Roussanne.

Turley Alexander Valley ★★★ Former partner in FROG'S LEAP, now specializing in hefty, heady, single-v'yd Zin and Petite Sirah from old vines.

Viader Estate Napa ★★★★ (Cab Sauv) 95 97 99 00 01 A blend of Cab Sauv and Cab Fr from Howell Mountain hillside estate. Powerful wines, yet balanced and elegant in best yrs. This is a classic NAPA mountain red. Ages well. Also look for new series of small-lot bottlings, inc Syrah, Tempranillo.

Volker Eisele Family Estate Napa ★★★→★★★★ 95 97 99 00 01 Sleek, luscious blend of Cab Sauv and Cab Fr from the little-known Chiles Valley AVA. Also look for a spicy Sauv Bl.

Wellington Sonoma ★★→★★★ Vivid old-vine Zin and sleek, powerful Cab Sauv.

Wente Vineyards Livermore and Monterey ★★→★★★ Historic specialist in whites, *esp Livermore Sauv Bl* and Sem. But Livermore estate Cab Sauv is also v.gd. Monterey sweet Ries can be exceptional. A little classic sparkling.

Williams Selyem Sonoma Intense smoky RUSSIAN RIVER Pinot N, esp Rochioli and Allen v'yds. Now reaching to SONOMA COAST, MENDOCINO for grapes. Cultish favourite can sometimes lose its balance and fall.

Willowbrook Sonoma ★★★ Newcomer makes impressive entrance with three single-v'yd Pinot Ns; wines are stylish and elegant with bright opening fruit and deep flavours in the middle and finish. Keep an eye on this producer.

York Creek Spring Mtn, Napa ★★★ Exceptional v'yd owned by Fritz Maytag, father of micro-brew revolution in US with his Anchor Steam beer. Sells to RIDGE and others. Now has own label. Mostly gd, always interesting.

Zaca Mesa Sta Barbara ★★→★★★ Now turning away from Chard and Pinot N to concentrate on estate Rhône grapes (esp Viognier) and blends (Cuvée Z).

Zahtila Vineyards Napa ★★★ Newcomer in north NAPA specializes in elegant and inviting Cab Sauv and intense Zin (one from Oat Hill estate v'yd nr Calistoga). Also makes DRY CREEK and RUSSIAN RIVER Zins from SONOMA COUNTY. To watch.

ZD Napa ★★ Overdose of American oak can spoil the Chard; Cab Sauv more restrained.

The Pacific Northwest

To simplify for visitors: think of Oregon as Burgundy and Washington as Bordeaux plus lots of other places. And expect high standards in both. Winemakers and growers are continuing to raise the quality bar while exploring new growing regions and varietals. The introduction of new clones of Pinot Noir and Chardonnay has been esp important in Oregon, and new Bordeaux clones are adding complexity to Washington State red wines as well. Both Pinot Noir and Pinot Gris are evolving in Oregon – some Pinot Noir taking on a more robust character – and Cabernet Franc and Syrah are coming into their own in Washington. Expect some gd new wines from Idaho in the next decade, as winemakers become more familiar wih v'yd sites. Overall, the Pacific Northwest continues to produce some of the most exciting wines in America.

Recent vintages

Any general discussion of vintages is difficult because of the wide variation in climate over the area and the jumble of microclimates in small regions.

2007 Not an easy vintage across the Northwest; rain and even some hail during harvest caused problems but, as always, those growers and wineries that paid attention will get it right.

2006 The century is young, but when talk turns to vintage of the century, this is it so far for Oregon. Incredible quality across the board. Washington and Idaho reporting similar quality.

2005 This is turning out to be a rather amazing vintage, if the winery paid attention. It was a cool harvest with some rain, but if the grapes were picked at the right time, the wines are looking v.gd. Oregon Pinot N, Washington Cab Sauv, Merlot, could be exceptional.

2004 Rain during flowering led to a small crop in some cases, but in general grape quality was high. Wines range from below average to well above average, depending on the site.

2003 A potentially mixed vintage after a season of heat and water stress.

2002 Wines with full expression and elegance.

2001 Lower acidity and less concentration than previous three yrs.

Oregon

Abacela Vineyards Umpqua Valley ★★★ New producer is performing well in unfashionable area of Oregon. Tempranillo, Dolcetto, Cab Fr, Syrah stand out.

Adelsheim Vineyard Yamhill County ★★★→★★★★ **02 04** 05 Oregon Pinot N veteran remains on top of the game with elegant Pinot N. New Dijon clone Chard, Ries, top Pinots Gr and Bl: clean, bracing.

Amalie Robert Estate Willamette ★★★ Promising new estate winery with a minerally, terroir-driven Pinot N and luscious Chard.

Amity Willamette ★★→★★★ 02 04 Pioneer in Oregon with exceptional Ries and Pinot Bl. The Pinot often rises to ★★★.

Andrew Rich (Tabula Rasa) Willamette ★★ Ex-California winemaker. Small lots of artisan wines, inc a supple Pinot N and exceptional Syrah.

Anne Amie Willamette ★★★ Outstanding Winemaker's Selection Pinot N, balanced and harmonious; v.gd Pinot Gr as well.

Archery Summit Willamette ★★★ Powerful Pinot N bottlings from several v'yds in the Red Hills AVA; made in a bold style that has won a loyal following.

Argyle Yamhill County ★★→★★★ V.gd Ries and v. fine Pinot N lead the way; also bargain bubbly. Winery founded by Aussie superstar winemaker Brian Croser.

Beaux Frères Yamhill County ★★★ Pinot N has more concentration than most Oregon offerings. Part-owned by critic Robert Parker.

Bethel Heights Willamette ★★→★★★ **01 02 04** 05 Deftly made estate Pinot N. Chard one of best in state; gd Pinot Bl, Pinot Gr.

Brick House Yamhill County ★★★ 01 02 Huge estate Pinot N. Dark and brooding; Estate Select a leaner, more balanced version.

Cameron Yamhill County ★★ (Pinot N) Eclectic producer of powerful, unfiltered Pinot N, Chard: some great. Also v.gd Pinot Bl.

Carabella Willamette ★★ Dijon Clone 76 Chard is outstanding, with a silky mouthfeel and just a touch of oak.

Chehalem Yamhill County ★→★★ Outstanding Chard with ageing potential, as well as a new, drink-me-now, no-oak Chard. V.gd Ries, Pinot Gr.

Cooper Mountain Willamette ★★★→★★★★ Complex Pinot N on a steady upward curve. Certified biodynamic v'yds.

Domaine Drouhin Willamette ★★★→★★★★ **01 02** 03 04 *Outstanding Pinot N*, silky and elegant, improving with each vintage. Chard also a winner.

Domaine Serene Willamette ★★★★ **00** 01 02 04 05 Burgundian approach to single-v'yd Pinot N is usually well ahead of the pack. Bottled unfiltered.

Elk Cove Vineyards Willamette ★★→★★★★ V.g Ries inc late-harvest. Top Pinot N.

Erath Vineyards Yamhill County ★★→★★★ **01 02** Oregon pioneer, founded 1968. V.gd Chard, Pinot Gr, Gewurz, Pinot Bl. Pinots and Ries age well.

Evesham Wood Willamette ★★★ Small family winery with fine Pinot N, Pinot Gr, and dry Gewurz. Pinot N leaping ahead in recent vintages. Organic.

Eyrie Vineyards Willamette ★★★ **00 01 02** Pioneer (1965) winery. Chards and Pinot Gr: rich yet crisp. All wines age beautifully.

Foris Vineyards Rouge Valley ★→★★ A lovely Pinot Bl and a classic red-cherry Pinot N top the list. One of the best in the south of the state.

Four Graces Willamette ★★→★★★ Opening act for this new winery is an exceptional estate Pinot N offering bright, lively fruit and gd mouthfeel; also check out the Pinot Bl and Pinot Gr. A winery to watch.

Freja Willamette ★★★ Only estate-grown Pinot N, the best notable. Wines are silky on the palate but with an underlying power, clearly in homage to Burgundy.

Henry Estate Rouge Valley ★→★★★ Big Cab Sauv and a light, crisp Müller-T bargain.

Ken Wright Cellars Yamhill County ★★★ **00 01** 02 Highly regarded Pinot N and a v.gd Chard from single v'yds.

King Estate South Willamette ★★★→★★★★ **02** 03 04 05 One of Oregon's largest wineries, is now certified organic. Lovely and constantly improving Pinot N, outstanding Chard.

Lachini Vineyards ★★★ New producer of outstanding Pinot N and v.gd Pinot Gr. V'yds farmed biodynamically. A coming star.

Lange Winery Yamhill County ★★→★★★ Rich and silky Pinot N, backed by a v.gd Pinot Gr and excellent Chard.

Oak Knoll Willamette ★★ Pinot is the big story at this popular winery, with intense but balanced bottlings. Also a v.gd off-dry Ries.

Panther Creek Willamette ★→★★ Concentrated, meaty, v'yd Pinot N.

Patricia Green Cellars Yamhill County ★★→★★★ Exciting, single-v'yd Pinot N is the heart of the story here. Started on a high note and improving with each vintage. Small production, but worth seeking out.

Penner-Ash Yamhill County ★★★ REX HILL winemaker Lynn Penner-Ash and her husband are making great Pinot N in a bolder style than many in Oregon.

Ponzi Vineyards Willamette ★★→★★★ **01 02 03** Long-established with consistently outstanding Pinot N and v.gd Pinot Gr and Chard.

Resonance Yamhill Carlton ★★ Veteran growers Kevin and Carla Chambers now out with their own Pinot N and it's a beauty. Track it down. Organic and biodynamic grapes.

Rex Hill Willamette ★★★→★★★★ Excellent Pinot N, Pinot Gr, and Chard from several north Willamette v'yds. Reserve wines can hit ★★★★.

RoxyAnn Rouge River ★★ Solid new producer with an esp gd Viognier and excellent Pinot Gr. Claret red blend is a pleasing quaff.

Sokol Blosser Willamette ★★★→★★★★ Superb wines throughout with an esp outstanding Pinot N, Chard, and Gewurz, balanced and harmonious.

Soter Yamhill Carlton ★★★ Tony Soter has moved his winemaking skills from California to Oregon and he got it right with first release, Mineral Springs V'yd Pinot N, a superb wine, balanced and harmonious with a long, lyrical finish.

Spangler Vineyards Rouge Valley ★★ Leading the list here is an elegant and pleasing Cab Fr; reserve Cab Sauv also v.gd.

Torii Mor Yamhill Co ★★★ V.gd single-v'yd Pinot N bottlings and superior Pinot Gr.

Tyee S Willamette ★★ Artisan producer of v.gd Pinot N, Pinot Gr, tasty Gewurz.

Van Duzer Winery Willamette ★→★★ Bright, fruity Pinot N, delicious Pinot Gr, from hillside v'yds in a v. cool part of Willamette Valley. Steadily improving.

Willakenzie Estate Yamhill County ★★★ Specialist in small lots of Pinot N, Pinot Gr, Pinot Bl and Pinot Meunier with a minuscule amount of Gamay Noir. Wines can be outstanding and are always worth a look.

Willamette Valley Vineyards Willamette ★★→★★★ Gd Ries, Chard and v.gd Pinot N. New clonal selection Chard raises the quality bar.

Washington & Idaho

Alexandria Nicole Cellars Columbia Valley Washington ★★→★★★ Newish artisan estate in the Horse Heaven Hills AVA produces a number of wines, inc B'x varietals, Rhônes and a zingy Cab Fr rosé.

Andrew Will Puget Sound, Washington ★★★★ 95 97 00 01 Owner Chris Camarda sources B'x varietals from Red Mountain, making outstanding single-v'yd reds: balanced, elegant, tremendous ageing potential.

Arbor Crest Spokane, Washington ★★ The top draw here is the Chard, followed closely by a floral Sauv Bl.

Badger Mountain Columbia Valley, Washington ★★ Washington's first organic v'yd, producing gd Cab Sauv and Chard. Also a new line of "no sulfites" organic wines.

Barnard Griffin Columbia Valley, Washington ★★→★★★ Small producer: well-made Merlot, Chard (esp barrel-fermented), Sem, Sauv Bl. Top Syrah. Crowd-pleasing Sangiovese rosé is new on the list.

Basel Cellars Walla Walla Valley, Washington ★★★ Newcomer sweeping the board with exciting B'x varieties and a brilliant Syrah. A great beginning.

Bergevin Lane Columbia Valley Washington ★★ Gd beginning for another new Washington winery with Syrah out in front.

Brian Carter Cellars Woodinville, Washington ★★→★★★ Limited production of gd to v.gd blends, inc a white blend of aromatic varietals, a Sangiovese-based Super Tuscan, two Bordeaux blends and a Rhône blend.

Bunnell Cellars Yakima Valley ★★★ A series of single-v'yd Syrahs are best-foot-forward here, plus a v.gd Viognier. New wine under RiverAerie label called Fete is a lively Bordeaux blend.

Buty Walla Walla Valley, Washington★★★ Winery founded in 2001 with emphasis on B'x blends and Syrah with pleasing results. Cab Sauv/Syrah blend called Reviviva of the Stones is popular favourite.

Cayuse Walla Walla Valley, Washington ★★→★★★ Several bottlings of gd to v.gd Syrah and an outstanding B'x blend have buyers calling. Biodynamic grapes.

Château Ste-Michelle Woodinville, Washington ★★→★★★★ Washington's largest winery; also owns COLUMBIA CREST, Northstar (top Merlot), Dom Ste-Michelle, and Snoqualmie, among others. Major v'yd holdings, first-rate equipment, and skilled winemakers keep wide range of varieties in front ranks. V.gd v'yd-designated Cab Sauv, Merlot, and Chard. Links with Loosen and Antinori.

Chinook Wines Yakima Valley, Washington ★★★ (Cab Sauv) 99 00 01 02 03 Elegant Merlot and Cab Sauv; outstanding Cab Fr and a delicious Cab Fr rosé.

Columbia Crest Columbia Valley, Washington ★★→★★★ Separately run CHÂTEAU STE-MICHELLE label for gd value wines. Cab Sauv, Merlot, Syrah, and Sauv Bl best. Also v.gd reserve wines.

Columbia Winery Woodinville, Washington ★★★ Pioneer (1962, as Associated Vintners) and still a leader, with balanced, stylish, understated single-v'yd wines. Marvellous Syrah.

DeLille Cellars Woodinville, Washington ★★★→★★★★ 98 99 00 01 02 A B'x specialist producing v.gd to excellent wines under 4 labels: Chaleur Estate Red, D2, Harrison Hill, Chaleur Estate Blanc. New addition is Syrah, Doyenne.

Di Stefano Woodinville, Washington ★★→★★★ Best bet is B'x red, inc a v.gd, elegant Cab Sauv; also a bright and juicy Syrah.

Dunham Cellars Walla Walla, Washington ★★→★★★ Artisan producer focusing on long-lived Cab Sauv and superb Syrah.

Forgeron Walla Walla ★★ New producer making small lots of single-v'yd wines; v.gd Syrah in a juicy style and notable Roussanne and Pinot Gr.

Glen Fiona Walla Walla, Washington ★★→★★★ Syrah/Syrah blends from Rhône specialist, esp Syrah/Cinsault/Counoise *cuvée*. Can be v.gd and built to last.

Hedges Cellars Yakima Valley, Washington ★★★→★★★★ Outstanding B'x reds from Red Mountain AVA. Fumé is a delicious and v. popular blend of Chard and Sauv Bl.

The Hogue Cellars Yakima Valley, Washington ★→★★ Large, reliable producer known for excellent, gd-value wines, esp Ries, Chard, Merlot, Cab Sauv. Produces quintessential Washington Sauv Bl.

Hyatt Vineyards Yakima Valley, Washington ★★→★★★ Stylish Merlot is among the state's best. Seek Black Muscat Icewine when conditions are right.

Indian Creek Idaho ★→★★ Top wine here is Pinot N backed by a v.gd Ries and successful Cab Sauv.

Kiona Vineyards Yakima Valley, Washington ★→★★ Solid wines from Red Mountain AVA, esp Cab Sauv; gd value and quality.

Lake Chelan Winery Columbia Valley, Washington ★★ A promising new winery with range of wines inc gd Cab Sauv, an attractive Syrah and a floral Ries.

L'Ecole No 41 Walla Walla ★★★→★★★★ (Merlot) 00 01 02 Blockbuster but balanced reds (Merlot, Cab Sauv, and super Meritage blend) with forward, ageworthy fruit. Gd barrel-fermented Sem.

Leonetti Walla Walla ★★★→★★★★ 99 00 01 *Harmonious Cab Sauv*: fine and big-boned. Bold and ageworthy Merlot. Splendid wines in great demand.

Long Shadows Columbia Valley ★★→★★★ Former Château Ste-Michelle CEO Allen Shoup has leading international winemakers producing Washington wine under a separate label. v.gd early releases inc Poet's Leap Ries; Pirouette, an amazing red; Chester-Kidder, a more concentrated, New Worldish red; and a bold Australian-style Syrah.

McCrea Puget Sound ★★★ A Rhône pioneer making small lots of gd to v. fine Viognier, Syrah, and Grenache even a rare varietal bottling of Counoise.

Nicolas Cole Cellars Columbia Valley, Washington ★★→★★★ Limited bottlings of balanced and elegant B'x-style reds and Rhônes that show promise of ageing.

Nota Bene Cellars Puget Sound, Washington ★★→★★★ Amazing red wines from B'x varietals sourced in Red Mountain AVA and other top Washington v'yds. Wines are built to last. Worth seeking out.

Owen Roe Washington ★★→★★★ Look for the Yakima Valley Chard and Ries; reds, esp B'x varieties, from Columbia Valley are v.gd.

Pepper Bridge Walla Walla Valley Washinton ★★→★★★ B'x-style Cab Sauv and Merlot. Series of limited-release, single-v'yd Cab Sauv can be exceptional.

Quilceda Creek Puget Sound, Wahinton ★★★→★★★★ (Cab) 99 00 01 Expertly crafted Columbia Valley Cab Sauv. Wines are beautifully balanced to age.

Reininger Walla Walla, Washington ★★→★★★ Small producer of fine Merlot and exceptional Syrah. Helix Columbia Valley Merlot is best.

Robert Karl Columbia Valley, Washington ★★→★★★ Spokane-based winery making small lots of single-v'yd wines from the Horse Heaven Hills AVA in the Columbia Valley. Both the Merlot and Cab Sauv can hit ★★★.

Ste Chapelle Snake River Valley, Idaho ★★ Pleasant, forward Chard, Cab Sauv, Merlot, and Syrah. Also v.gd Ries and Gewurz in dry Alsace style. Attractive sparkling wine: gd value and improving quality.

Sandhill Winery Columbia Valley, Washington ★★★ Estate-only wines from the

---

The "new" wines of Oregon

Twenty yrs ago there were about 50 wineries in Oregon. Today there are more than 350. Only a few years ago, most Oregon wine was made in the Williamette Valley AVA in northern Oregon. Now wine is made all through southern Oregon where a new Southern Oregon AVA, with several sub-appellations, has been established. There's a lot to follow here.

Red Mountain AVA. Outstanding Cab Sauv and Merlot and a v.gd Pinot Gr. Cinnamon Teal Red Table Wine is a local favourite.

Saviah Cellars Walla Walla Valley, Washington ★★ V.gd B'x blends from small family winery; outstanding Syrah.

Sawtooth Cellars Idaho ★★ Gd Cab Sauv with latest Syrah and Viognier v.gd.

Seven Hills Walla Walla Valley, Washington ★★→★★★ Known for balanced and elegant wines; Ciel du Cheval B'x blend v.gd.

Woodward Canyon Walla Walla, Washington ★★★→★★★★ (Cab) 98 99 **01** 02 Established in 1981, the winery is well known for intense but elegant Cab, Chard, and Merlot. Old-vine Cab Sauv is stunning.

East of the Rockies

While winemaking and grape-growing are still relatively newborn concerns in the eastern United States, they are evolving at an astonishing rate. New York State now boasts more than 250 wineries (up from 150 in 2002). Ohio has increased from 60 to 104 during the same period, while Virginia expanded its number of wineries from 65 to 126. Quality continues to rise impressively throughout the region. New York's Finger Lakes viticultural area may well be the best source of Riesling in the nation. While Merlot first put New York's Long Island area on the vinous map, Cabernet Sauvignon and Franc, and Syrah are currently making great strides. Virginia is having considerable success with Cabernet Franc, Viognier and other Rhône grapes. New York is the nation's third largest grape-growing state (after Washington), with Michigan and Pennsylvania occupying fourth and fifth positions.

Recent vintages

2001 and 2002 were excellent yrs, but 2000 and 2003 generally disappointing. 2004, 2005 and 2006 were gd. 2007 is shaping up to be as outstanding as 1995 and 1998, the best overall vintages in the East so far.

Anthony Road Finger Lakes, NY ★★★ Fine Ries; Pinot Gr, late-harvest Vignoles.

Barboursville Virginia ★★★★ Oldest of the state's modern-era wineries (founded 1976), owned by the Zonin family (see Italy). Excellent Chard, Cab Fr, Barbera, Nebbiolo, Pinot Gr and , and *Malvaxia*. Elegant inn and restaurant.

Bedell Long Island, NY ★★★ **02** 03 04 05 06 07 Now owned by CEO of New Line Cinema (and producer of *Lord of the Rings* trilogy), makes outstanding small-batch series of varietally labelled wines inc Chard, Gewurz and Cab Fr.

Breaux Virginia ★★★ 05 06 07 Beautiful 35-ha v'yd an hour from Washington, DC. Gd Chard, Merlot.

Chamard ★★ 03 04 05 06 Connecticut's best winery. AVA is Southeastern New England.

Channing Daughters ★★ 05 06 07 LONG ISLAND's innovative South Fork estate, with excellent and eclectic white blends (e. Tocai Friulano) inspired by Italy.

Château LaFayette Reneau Finger Lakes, NY ★★★★ 04' 05' 06 07 Stylish Chard, Ries, and top-notch Cab Sauv. Stunning lakeside setting.

Chrysalis Virginia ★★★★ Top Viognier, v.gd Petit Manseng, and native Norton.

Clinton Vineyards Hudson River, NY ★★ **05 06** 07 Clean, gd dry Seyval. Exceptional sparkling, also fine cassis, wild black raspberry and peach wines.

Debonné Vineyards Lake Erie, Ohio ★★ 05 06 07 Largest OHIO estate winery. Chard, Ries, Pinot Gr, and some hybrids: Chambourcin and Vidal.

Ferrante Winery Harpersfield, Ohio Venerable estate (since 1937) has emerged as quality leader with fine Chard, Cab Sauv, Ries, and superb Icewine.

Finger Lakes Beautiful cool upstate NY region, with over 100 wineries source of most of state's wines. Top wineries: ANTHONY ROAD, CH LAFAYETTE RENEAU, DR. FRANK, FOX RUN, HERON HILL, KING FERRY, Lakewood, LAMOREAUX LANDING, RED NEWT, STANDING STONE, Swedish Hill, and WIEMER.

Firelands Lake Erie, Ohio ★★ OHIO estate making Cab Sauv, Gewurz, Pinot Gr. Notable Icewine.

Fox Run Finger Lakes, NY ★★★ 04 05 06 07 Some of region's best Chard, Gewurz, Ries, and Pinot N. Gd café for lunch or light refreshment.

Frank, Dr. Konstantin (Vinifera Wine Cellars) Finger Lakes, NY ★★★★ 02 04 05 06 07 Continues to set the pace for serious winemaking. The late Dr. F was a pioneer in growing European vines in the FINGER LAKES. Excellent Ries, Gewurz; gd Chard, Cab Sauv, and Pinot N. Also v.gd Ch Frank sparkling.

The Hamptons (aka **South Fork**) LONG ISLAND AVA. The top winery is moneyed WÖLFFER ESTATE. Showcase Duck Walk owns 52 ha of vines, CHANNING DAUGHTERS now competitive.

Hermann J Wiemer Finger Lakes, NY ★★→★★★ 05 06 07 Creative, German-born owner/winemaker. *Outstanding Ries*; v.gd Chard. Winemaker Fred Merwarth recently took over operations from eponymous founder.

Heron Hill Finger Lakes ★★ Great Ries and dessert wines by Thomas Laszlo.

Horton Virginia ★★★ 06 07 Established early 1990s. Gd Viognier, Mourvèdre, Cab Fr, Norton.

Hudson River Region America's oldest wine-growing district (37 producers) and NY's first AVA. Straddles the river, 2 hours' drive north of Manhattan.

Jefferson Virginia ★★★ 04 05 06 07 Nr Thomas Jefferson's Monticello estate. Fine Pinot Gr, Viognier, Chard, Petit Verdot, Merlot, B'x blend.

Keswick Virginia ★★★ 04 05 06 Elegant Chard, v.gd Viognier, Touriga, and Cab-based blend.

King Family Estate/Michael Shaps Wines Virginia ★★★★ Excellent Chard, Merlot, Cab Fr, exceptional B'x blend, and superb Viognier by Burgundy-trained oenologist.

King Ferry Finger Lakes, NY ★★★ 05 06 07 Label is Treleaven. Great Ries, stylish Chards.

Kluge Virginia ★★★ 04 05 06 07 Showplace moneyed estate, ambitious wines include Viognier, *good brut sparkling*, and B'x blend.

Lake Erie Largest grape-growing district in the eastern US; 10,117 ha along shore of Lake Erie, includes portions of NY, PENNSYLVANIA, and OHIO. Also name of a tri-state AVA: NY's sector has 16 wineries, PENNSYLVANIA's 7 and OHIO's 32. OHIO's Harpersfield sets standards for quality.

Lamoureaux Landing Finger Lakes, NY ★★★ 03 04 05 06 07 Among NY's best Chard, Ries, and Cab Fr from striking Greek-revival winery.

Lenz Long Island NY ★★★ 04 05 06 07 Classy winery of NORTH FORK AVA. *Fine austere Chard* in the Chablis mode as well as rich barrel-fermented one, also notable Gewurz, Merlot, and sparkling wine.

Linden Virginia ★★★★ 02 04 05 06 07 Small (5,000 cases) VIRGINIA producer in mountains 100 km (62 miles) west of Washington, DC. Impressive Sauv Bl, Cab Fr, Petit Verdot, and B'x-style "claret".

Long Island, New York Exciting wine region and a hothouse of experimentation. Currently 1,200 ha, all vinifera (35% Merlot) and3 AVAs (Long Island, NORTH FORK, THE HAMPTONS). Most of its 43 wineries are on the NORTH FORK. Best varieties: Chard, Cab Sauv, Merlot. A long growing season; almost frost-free but hurricane-prone. Autumnal migrations of voracious birds a serious threat

Words within entries marked like this *Alter Ego de Palmer* indicate wines especially enjoyed by Hugh Johnson over the past 12 months (mid '07–'08).

EAST OF THE ROCKIES

to grapes. The young generation of wineries incl: Bridge, Comtesse Thérèse, Diliberto (gd reds), Martha Clara, Old Fields Shinn (owned by proprietors of Manhattan restaurant Home), Sherwood House (Chard and Merlot).

Maryland Has more than 30 wineries in 4 distinct growing regions. Best-known producer and oldest family-run winery is Boordy Vineyards, making v.gd Vidal Blanc, Chard and Cab Sauv. Basignani for gd Cab Sauv, Ries, and Seyval. Fiore: gd Chambourcin, Merlot, and Cab Sauv. Sugarloaf: gd Cab Fr. Elk Run for gd Pinot Gr and Gewurz.

Michigan Impressive cool-climate Ries and Gewurz, gd Pinot N, and Cab Fr are emerging; 52 wineries using Michigan grapes and 4 AVAs (728 ha of wine grapes, two-thirds of them vinifera). Best include Black Star, Brys, Château Chantal, Château Grand Traverse, Peninsula Cellars (esp dry Gewurz), Tabor Hill and Willow. Mawby known for outstanding sparkling. Fenn Valley, St. Julian and Lemon Creek have large following. Up-and-coming: Dom Berrien, Cherry Creek, Left Foot Charley, Longview.

Millbrook Hudson River, NY ★★ 04 05 06 07 Chards modelled on Burgundy; Cab Fr can be delicious.

Naked Mountain Virginia 06 07 Est 1981; known for big, buttery Chard.

Niagara Escarpment NY Newest AVA (Sept 2005); Currently 12 wineries, 10 more in the wings.

North Carolina Look for Chard, Viognier, Cab Fr. 70 wineries, inc Childress, Duplin (for Muscadine), Hanover Park, Iron Gate, Lassie, Laurel Gray, Old North State, RagApple, RayLen, Shelton. Biltmore is most visited winery in the US.

North Fork LONG ISLAND AVA (of 3). Top wineries: Bedell, Jamesport, Lieb, LENZ, PALMER, PAUMANOK, PELLEGRINI, PINDAR, Raphael. 2hrs' drive from Manhattan.

Ohio 104 wineries with more coming, 5 AVAs, notably LAKE ERIE and Ohio Valley. Notable progress with Pinot Gr, Ries, Pinot N, Cab Fr, Icewine.

Palmer Long Island, NY ★★ 04 05 06 07 Superior NORTH FORK producer; byword in Darwinian metropolitan market. Tasty Chard, Sauv Bl, Chinon-like Cab Fr.

Paumanok Long Island, NY ★★★★ 01 04 05 06 07 NORTH FORK winery; impressive Ries, Chard, Merlot, Cab Sauv; v.gd Chenin Bl; late-harvest botrytized Sauv Bl.

Pellegrini Long Island, NY ★★★★ 02 04 05 06 07 An enchantingly designed winery on NORTH FORK. Opulent Merlot, stylish Chard, B'x-like Cab Sauv.

Pennsylvania 90 wineries, with quality rapidly rising. Leading estates include pioneering Chaddsford (esp Barbera and Rubino, a Cab/Sangiovese blend), Allegro (worthy Chard, Cab Sauv, Merlot), Pinnacle Ridge (excellent sparkling and Cab Franc), and Manatawny Creek (noteworthy Cabs Fr and Sauv, and Bordeaux-style blend).

Pindar Vineyards Long Island, NY ★★★ 01 04 05 06 07 116-ha operation at NORTH FORK (island's largest). Range of blends and popular varietals, inc Chard, Merlot, sparkling, v.gd B'x-style red blend, Mythology. Visits.

Pollack Virginia One of the state's most promising new wineries, Chard, Cab Fr, B'x blend, Viognier.

Red Newt Finger Lakes, NY ★★★ 04 05 06 07 Turns out top Chard, Ries, and some of the best reds in the east, esp Cab Fr, Merlot, and B'x-inspired red blend.

Sakonnet Little Compton, Rhode Island ★★ 06 07 Largest New England winery. V. drinkable wines; delicious sparkling brut *cuvée*.

Standing Stone Finger Lakes, NY ★★ 06 07 One of the region's finest wineries with v.gd Ries, Gewurz, and B'x-type blend.

Tomasello New Jersey ★★ Gd Chambourcin, Pinot N, Cab Sauv, and Merlot.

Unionville Vineyards New Jersey ★★ Nice Chard and gd B'x-style red.

Valhalla Virginia ★★★ 04 05 06 07 V'yd at 600 m (2,000 ft) atop a granite mountain yields fine Alicante Bouschet, spicy Sangiovese, and gd red blend of all 5 B'x grapes.

Veritas Virginia ★★★ 04 05 06 07 Gd Chard, Cab Fr, Viognier, gutsy Petit Verdot.

Villa Appalaccia Virginia ★★★ 04 05 06 07 Italian-inspired winery in the Blue Ridge Mountains making limited amounts (3,000 cases total) of Primitivo, Sangiovese, Malvasia, Pinot Gr.

Virginia With 126 bonded wineries and 6 AVAs, Virginia is turning out some of the best wines in the east, with an emphasis on vinifera. The modern winemaking era now encompasses virtually every part of the state, some less than an hour's drive from Washington, DC.

Wagner Vineyards Finger Lakes, NY ★★ 04 05 06 07 Chard, dry and sweet Ries, B'x blend, and Icewine. Also has micro-brewery and restaurant.

Westport Rivers Southeast New England ★★ 05 06 07 Massachusetts house established in 1989. Gd Chard and elegant sparkling.

Whitehall Virginia ★★★★ 04 05 07 A handsome estate nr historic Charlottesville. Outstanding Viognier, noteworthy Pinot Gr, lush Petit Manseng, top Chard, Cab Fr, Touriga Nacional, and Cab Sauv blend.

Wölffer Estate Long Island, NY ★★★★ 04 05 06 07 Fine Chard, vibrant rosé and gd Merlot from talented German-born winemaker.

Wollersheim Wisconsin ★★ 06 07 Winery specializing in variations of Maréchal Foch. Prairie Fumé (Seyval Bl) is a commercial success.

Southeast & central states

Missouri Continues to expand, with over 50 producers in 3 AVAs: **Augusta**, **Hermann**, and **Ozark Highlands.** Best wines are Seyval Blanc Vidal, Vignoles (sweet and dry versions), and Chambourcin. **Stone Hill** in Hermann produces v.gd Chardonel (a frost-hardy hybrid of Seyval Blanc and Chard), Norton, and gd Seyval Blanc and Vidal Blanc. **Hermannhof** is also drawing notice for Vignoles, Chardonel, and Norton. Also notable: **St James** for Vignoles, Seyval, Norton; **Mount Pleasant** in Augusta for rich "port" and Norton; **Adam Puchta** for gd port-style wines and Norton, Vignoles, Vidal Blanc; **Augusta Winery** for Chambourcin, Chardonel, Icewine; **Les Bourgeois**, gd Syrah, Norton, Chardonel, Montelle, v.gd Cynthiana and Chambourcin.

Georgia There are now over a dozen wineries here. Look for: **Three Sisters** (Dahlonega), **Habersham Vineyards**, and **Ch Elan** (Braselton), which features southern splendour with v'yds, wine, and a resort.

The Southwest

Although southwest wineries tend to be modest, interest in production continues to grow. In the early 1970s, Texas boasted one winery; it now has over 12 while New Mexico holds at 30, Colorado has over 65, up from 16 only 12 years ago. Arizona has 20 and Oklahoma has over 25.

Texas

Becker Vineyards Stonewall ★★★ V.gd Cab Sauv, Sauv Bl, Viognier, Chenin Bl.

Cap Rock Lubbock Gd Merlot, Cab Sauv and blends, esp Bush Royal.

Delaney Vineyards Nr Dallas ★ Gd Cynthiana and Chard.

Driftwood Vineyards Texas Hill ★★ V.gd Muscat Canelli, Viognier, Sangiovese.

Dry Comal New Braunfels V.gd French Colombard, Shiraz, Merlot.

Fredericksburg Winery V.gd Orange Muscat, gd "port"and "sherry" styles.

Grape Creek Stonewall V.gd Pinot Grigio.

Haak Vineyard & Winery Galveston County ★ V.gd Blanc du Bois and Madeira.

Kiepersol Estates Vineyards Tyler Excellent Sangiovese, Syrah, Cab Sauv, Sem.

Llano Estacado Nr Lubbock ★★★ The pioneer with v.gd Chard, Cellar Select Port, and Viviano, a Tuscan-style red blend.

Lost Creek Vineyard Texas Hill Country Gd Chard, Blanc du Bois and blends.

McPherson Cellars Lubbock Continues growth with excellent Sangiovese, Viognier and Syrah.

Messina Hof Wine Cellars Bryan ★★★ Continues on award-winning trail with excellent Ries, Cab Sauv, Muscat Canelli and port-style wines.

Pheasant Ridge Nr Lubbock V.gd Chard and Cab Sauv.

Sister Creek Boerne Boutique winery with gd Pinot N, Chard, Muscat Canelli.

Spicewood Vineyards Spicewood V.gd Chard, Merlot.

Stone House Spicewood Gd blends and port-style wines.

New Mexico, etc.

New Mexico Emphasis on vinifera, though some French hybrids still used. **Black Mesa:** ★★ V.gd Cab Sauv, Seyval Blanc, Merlot, Ries. **Casa Rondeña:** ★★ V.gd Cab Fr, Meritage (red). **Corrales:** ★★ V.gd Cab Sauv, Merlot, Muscat Canelli. **Gruet:** ★★★ *Excellent sparkling*; v.gd Chard. **La Chiripada:** ★★ V.gd Ries, Chard and blends; gd port-style wine. **Ponderosa Valley:** ★★ V.gd Ries, Tempranillo, Syrah and blends. **La Viña:** ★★ V.gd Chard, Zin; gd blends. **St Clair, Blue Teal, Mademoiselle Vineyards, D H Lescombes,** and **Santa Rita Cellars** all under winemaker **Florent Lescombes** have a gd variety of wines, esp Muscat Canelli and Shiraz. **Luna Rosa:** V.gd Zin, Symphony, Shiraz. **Tierra Encantada:** New, with gd Tempranillo, Chambourcin.

Colorado Focus on vinifera grapes, with over 250 ha planted, ranging from the Grand Valley on the Western Slope, over the Rocky Mountains to the Front Range. **Carlson Cellars:** ★★★ V.gd Orange Muscat, Gewurz, Ries, fruit wines. **Canyon Wind:** Gd Chard, Cab Sauv. **Creekside Cellars:** Gd Chard and blends. **Garfield Estates:** V.gd Sauv Bl and Cab Fr. **Plum Creek:** ★★★ V.gd Cab Sauv, Ries Sauv Bl; Chard. **Two Rivers:** V.gd Cab Sauv, Chard, Merlot. **Verso Cellars:** V.gd Cab Sauv. **Balistreri:** Gd Cab Sauv, Syrah, Sangiovese. **Debeque Canyon:** V.gd Malbec. **Winery at Holy Cross:** V.gd Ries, gd Cab Sauv, Merlot. **Spero:** Gd Merlot and Cab Fr. **Bookcliff:** V.gd Chard, Merlot.

Arizona Callaghan Vineyards: ★★ V.gd Syrah, Cab Sauv, blends. **Dos Cabezas:** ★ V.gd Cab Sauv, Petite Sirah, Sangiovese. **Colibri:** Gd Viognier, Roussanne, Syrah. **Granite Creek:** V.gd late harvest Zin. **Echo Canyon:** Gd Syrah, Triad.

Oklahoma Vinifera emphasis but hybrids and native American grapes also grown. **Deer Creek** Edmond: Gd Muscat Canelli, Cab Sauv. **Greenfield Vineyard** Chandler: Gd Merlot, Sauv Bl. **Stone Bluff Cellars** Haskell: Gd Vignoles, Cynthiana, Chardonel. **Panther Hills** Bessie: ★★ Boutique V.gd Cab Sauv, gd Pinot N. **Tidal School Vineyards** Drumright: The largest; gd blends. **Oak Hills Winery** Chelsea: V.gd Catawba, Traminette. **Nuyaka Creek** Bristow: Gd grape, fruit wines and pleasing cordial-style selections, esp Petite Pecan. **Summerside** Vinita: Gd Chambourcin, Cynthiana.

Utah Spanish Valley (Moab): V.gd Ries and Cab Sauv.

Nevada Pahrump Valley Nr Las Vegas: Gd Symphony. **Tahoe Ridge** (North Nevada): Gd Sem. **Churchill Vineyards**: New, with gd Ries, Sem, Chard.

To decipher codes, please refer to "Key to symbols" on the front flap of jacket, or "How to use this book" on p.10.

Canada

Recent vintages

All vintages between 99 and 02 are drinking well right now. 03 wines are not recommended as crops were damaged by a serious wildfire. The better 04s and 05s are definitely worth cellaring for up to five years.

British Columbia

The biggest concentration of wineries is in the warm, dry Okanagan Valley around a vast lake, 400 km (245 miles) east of Vancouver, esp in the desert-like southernmost part of the region. Climatic conditions here are similar to neighbouring Washington State. There are over 133 wineries in five appellations: Okanagan Valley, Fraser Valley, Similkameen Valley, Vancouver Island, Gulf Islands. Up-and-coming: Arrowleaf (Pinot Gr), Joie (Chard), Prospect (Sauv Bl, Pinot Gr), See Ya Later Ranch (sparkling, Ries), Wild Goose (Ries Gewurz).

Blue Mountain Excellent Pinot N and sparkling.

Cedar Creek ★→★★★ Outstanding Chard, Pinot N, Meritage, and Merlot.

> **The Niagara Wine Trail**
> The Niagara Wine Trail is the fastest-growing wine region in New York, outpacing Long Island and the Finger Lakes. A few years ago it had three wineries, while today there are 12, with 12 more in the works to open as soon as possible (depending on the complicated government licensing process). It lies just east of Niagara Falls – one of the world's great wonders and tourist attractions – and just across the river from Ontario, Canada (which itself now has about 100 wineries and a solid reputation for quality). The US side of the grape-growing region is now an official American Viticultural Area known as the Niagara Escarpment, based on unique climatic and geographical distinctions such as Lake Ontario to the north and a limestone bluff (the Niagara Escarpment) to the south.

Golden Mile ★★ 04 05 06 Gd Pinot N and Chard.

Inniskillin Okanagan ★★★ Excellent Chard, Viognier, Pinot Bl.

Jackson-Triggs Okanagan ★★★ **02** 04 05 06 07 V.gd Cab Sauv, Meritage, Shiraz, Ries, Icewine.

Lake Breeze Gd Pinot Gr, Gewurz.

Mission Hill ★→★★★★ Acclaimed Chard, Sauv Bl/Sem, Ries, Icewine, Syrah, Merlot, and flagship Oculus. High culinary standards on dining terrace.

Osoyoos Larose Remarkably fine B'x blend red.

Quails' Gate ★★ Ries, Late Harvest Optima, Pinot N and Old Vines Foch.

Sumac Ridge ★★ **02 04** 05 06 07 Gewurz, Sauv Bl, sparkling Stellar's Jay among region's best. Notable Meritage. (Owned by CONSTELLATION.)

Tantalus ★★★ Excellent Ries.

Ontario

Includes Canada's largest viticultural area, Niagara Peninsula. Around 100 wineries. Moderating air currents from lakes Ontario and Erie extend growing season and diverse soils create a range of distinctive terroirs. Emerging quality-driven wineries include: Hidden Bench, Megalomaniac and Charles Baker. Icewine is the region's international flagship. Wines are often labelled with one of 12 sub-appellations located within the larger Niagara Peninsula but the Liquor Board permits some outrageous label scams.

Cave Spring Cellars ★★★ Benchmark Ries, sophisticated Chard from old vines, exceptional Late Harvest and Icewines.

Château des Charmes ★★★ Showplace ch-style winery. Fine Chard, B'x-style blend, Icewines, sparkling.

Creekside ★★→★★★ Consistently top producer of fine Pinot N, Sauv Bl, B'x-blend. Same winemaking team producing estate wines for Canadian sports legends Wayne Gretzky and Mike Weir.

Henry of Pelham ★★★ Respected family-owned winery with elegant Chard and Ries; B'x-style reds, distinctive Baco Noir, Icewine.

Hillebrand Estates ★→★★★ Large producer of gd sparkling, excellent Ries under Thirty Bench label.

Inniskillin ★★★ Important producer that spearheaded birth of modern Ontario wine industry. Skilful Burgundy-style Chards, Pinot N, Bx-style red; Icewine specialist.

Jackson-Triggs ★★★ State-of-art winery, Ries, Chard, and B'x-style reds.

Le Clos Jordanne ★★★★ Best-of-class Pinot N and Chard from organic v'yds.

Malivoire Small, innovative gravity-flow winery with v.gd Pinot N, Chard, and Gamay. Some organic.

Peninsula Ridge ★★★ Established in 2000. Gd Chard, Sauv Bl, and B'x varieties.

Pillitteri Large family-owned winery with gd Cab Fr and Merlot. Prolific Icewine producer.

Stratus ★★★ Hi-tech winery, flagship white and red multi-varietal blends; excellent Icewine.

Tawse ★★★ Opened 2005, much admired Chard, Pinot N and Cab Fr.

Vincor International ★→★★ Now owned by CONSTELLATION. Wineries include JACKSON-TRIGGS, INNISKILLIN, Nk'Mip, LE CLOS JORDANNE, OSOYOOS LAROSE.

Vineland Estates ★★★ Dry and semi-dry Ries; Vidal Icewine gd. Chard, Cab Sauv, Sauv Bl, and B'x-style red.

Vintners Quality Alliance (VQA) Provincially controlled appellation body guaranteeing 100% regional grapes with strict rules concerning grape production/winemaking.

To decipher codes, please refer to "Key to symbols" on the front flap of jacket, or "How to use this book" on p.10.

Central & South America

More heavily shaded areas are the wine-growing regions

Chile

There's a certain air of confidence about the modern Chilean wine industry. The strong peso may have affected sales in certain markets, but this doesn't seem to have deterred the producers from continuing to expand their horizons and improve their wines, nor of outsiders from investing – the Liger-Belair family of Vosne-Romanée is just one of several producers now working in the country. Ten years ago, visitors to a winery would be given a lengthy tour of the spanking new cellar followed by a tasting. Today, they are whisked straight into the vineyard to see new organic projects, biodynamic trials, experiments on irrigation (still a necessity in most of this arid country), and soil tests. Expansion into new regions continues apace. More than 1,000 km to the south of Santiago, there are new plantings of white varieties and Pinot Noir in Osorno in the Chilean Lake District and on Chiloé Island, while farther north, Choapa between Aconcagua and Limarí, is already looking promising for Syrah and Cabernet Sauvignon.

These two varieties are currently the most impressive in the Chilean red portfolio. Carmenère, once seen as the country's USP, is moving away from the rather intense and forceful style into something more interesting and drinkable, and its success in cool climates such as Elqui has been a revelation. While smatterings of Gewurztraminer, Riesling and Viognier show the potential for other white wine styles, Sauvignon Blanc and Chardonnay remain the top dogs, with the most refined examples coming from San Antonio and Casablanca.

South American vintages

Vintages do differ but not to the same extent as in Europe. Whites are almost without exception at their best within two years of vintage, reds within three years. The most ambitious reds (Chilean Cabernet-based wines, Argentine Cabernets and Malbecs) can confidently be kept for a decade or more but it is debatable whether they improve rather than get older beyond their fifth year. Curiously, odd years have been the best for Chilean reds in recent years, although currently the producer is of far greater importance than the vintage.

Aconcagua Northernmost quality region. Inc CASABLANCA, Panquehue, SAN ANTONIO.

Almaviva ★★★ Expensive but classy, claret-style MAIPO red – a joint venture between CONCHA Y TORO and BARON PHILIPPE DE ROTHSCHILD.

Altaïr ★★→★★★ Ambitious joint venture between Ch Dassault (St-Emilion) and SAN PEDRO. Pascal Chatonnet of B'x is consultant; *grand vin* (mostly Cab Sauv, Carmenère) complex and earthy, second wine Sideral for earlier drinking.

Anakena Cachapoal ★→★★ Solid range. Flagship wines under Ona label include punchy Syrah; Single V'yd bottlings and Reserve Chard also gd. Look out for Viognier and ONA Pinot N.

Antiyal ★★→★★★ Alvaro Espinoza's own estate, making fine, complex red from biodynamically grown Cab Sauv, Syrah, Carmenère. Second wine Kuyen.

Apaltagua ★★→★★★ Carmenère specialist drawing on old-vine fruit from Apalta (Colchagua). Grial is rich, herbal flagship wine.

Aquitania, Viña ★★→★★★ Chilean/French joint venture involving Paul Pontallier and Bruno Prats from B'x (Paul Bruno was old label) making v.gd Lazuli Cab Sauv (MAIPO) and Sol de Sol Chard from Malleco.

Arboleda, Viña ★★ Part of the ERRÁZURIZ/CALITERRA stable, with whites from Leyda and CASABLANCA and reds from ACONCAGUA, inc polished Cab Sauv/Merlot/Carmenère blend Seña and excellent varietal Carmenère.

Baron Philippe de Rothschild ★→★★ B'x company making simple varietal range, better Escudo Rojo red blend. Also see ALMAVIVA.

Bío-Bío Promising southern region. Potential for gd whites and Pinot N.

Botalcura ★★→★★★ Curicó venture involving French winemaker Philippe Debrus, formerly of VALDIVIESO. Grand Reserve Cab Fr is the star.

Calina, Viña ★→★★ Kendall-Jackson (California) venture. Better reds than whites, with Cab Sauv/Merlot blend Bravura the pick.

Caliterra ★→★★ Sister winery of ERRÁZURIZ. Chard and Sauv Bl improving (more CASABLANCA grapes), reds becoming less one-dimensional, esp Tribute range and new flagship red Cenit.

Cánepa, José Colchagua ★★ Solid range. Lemony Sem, spicy Zin among the more unusual wines. Best include juicy Malbec and fragrant Syrah Res.

Carmen, Viña ★★→★★★ MAIPO winery; same ownership as SANTA RITA. Ripe, fresh Special Res CASABLANCA Chard and late-harvest MAIPO Sem top whites. Reds even better; esp RAPEL Merlot, MAIPO Petite Sirah, Gold Res Cab Sauv.

Carta Vieja ★→★★ MAULE winery owned by one family for 6 generations. Reds better than whites; but Gran Reserva Chard is gd.

Casablanca Cool-climate region between Santiago and coast. Little water: drip irrigation essential. Top-class Chard, Sauv Bl; promising Merlot, Pinot N.

Casablanca, Viña ★→★★ RAPEL and MAIPO fruit used for some reds; but better wines – Merlot, Sauv Bl, Chard, Gewurz – from CASABLANCA. Also look for super-*cuvée* Neblus and new Nimbus Estate varietals.

Casa Lapostolle ★★→★★★★ Impressive French-owned, Michel Rolland-inspired winery. Gd across the board, with new Sem highlight of the whites and Borobo red blend, Cuvée Alexandre Merlot and Syrah, and Carmenère-based *Clos Apalta* pick of the reds.

Casa Marín ★★★ Dynamic San Antonio white specialist, v.gd Gewurz and superb Sauv Bl. Syrah and Pinot N promising.

Casa Rivas Maipo ★★ Part of group that includes TARAPACA, VIÑA MAR, Missiones de Rengo. Best: Sappy Sauv Bl; gentle, citrus Chard Res; blackcurrant-pastille-y Cab Sauv; generously fruity Maria Pinto Syrah/Cab Sauv Res.

Casas del Bosque ★→★★★ CASABLANCA winery, also using Cab Sauv from Cachapoal for elegant range inc juicy underrated Sauv Bl, svelte Pinot N and peppery Syrah Res.

Casa Silva ★★ Colchagua estate with solid range topped by silky, complex Altura red and Quinta Generación Red and White. Also commendable Doña Dominga range; Carmenère is v.gd.

Casas del Toqui ★→★★★★ RAPEL venture by Médoc Ch Larose-Trintaudon under the Las Casas del Toqui and Viña Alamosa labels. Silky top-end Leyenda red blend and Prestige Cab Sauv.

Concha y Toro ★→★★★ Mammoth, quality-minded operation. Best: subtle Amelia Chard (CASABLANCA); *grippy Don Melchor Cab Sauv*; Terrunyo; Winemaker Lot single-v'yd range; and new, complex Carmin de Peumo (Carmenère). Marqués de Casa Concha, Trio, Explorer, Casillero del Diablo offer v.gd value. Maycas del Limarí is new winery in the north. See also BARON PHILIPPE DE ROTHSCHILD, CONO SUR, TRIVENTO (Argentina).

Cono Sur Chimbarongo, Colchagua ★★→★★★ V.gd Pinot N, headed by Ocio. Other top releases appear as 20 Barrels selection; new innovations under Visión label (BÍO-BÍO Ries is superb). Also dense, fruity Cab Sauv, delicious Viognier, rose-petal Gewurz, impressive new Syrah. Style is aimed at drinkability, not muscle. Second label Isla Negra; owned by CONCHA Y TORO.

Córpora Dynamic organization that owns GRACIA DE CHILE, Augustinos (peppery Grand Reserve Malbec), Veranda (joint venture with Boisset of Burgundy), PORTA and now Canata in BÍO-BÍO. See also GRACIA DE CHILE.

Cousiño Macul ★★→★★★ MAIPO producer now relocated to Buin. Now more modern in style, but better? Reliable Antiguas Res Cab Sauv; zesty Sauvignon Gris; new top-of-the-range blend Lota. Cab Sauv rosé v. refreshing.

Cremaschi Furlotti ★→★★★ MAULE red specialist impressing with herby Syrah and heady Limited Edition (Cab Sauv-based) and Venere (Carmenère-based) blends.

de Martino Maipo ★★→★★★ Ambitious Carmenère pioneer; one of west MAIPO's best wineries, esp for Gran Familia Cab Sauv and Legado range.

Domus Maipo ★★→★★★ Ambitious winery making gd Chard and v.gd Domus Aurea Cab Sauv; sister Cabs Stella Aurea and Peñalolen also tasty.

Echeverría ★★ Boutique Curicó (MAULE) winery. Reliable Res Cab Sauv; gd oaked and unoaked Chard; improving Sauv Bl; elegant, fragrant Carmenère.

Edwards, Luís Felipe ★★ Colchagua winery. Citrus Chard, silky Res Cab Sauv. Shiraz and plump Doña Bernarda are specialities. Amazing new high-altitude, super-steep v'yds will come on stream in next few yrs: enormous potential.

El Principal, Viña ★★★ Pirque (MAIPO) estate that has gone rather quiet under new ownership. Earlier vintages of B'x-blend El Principal and second wine Memorias are excellent.

Emiliana Orgánico ★→★★★ Organic/biodynamic specialist involving Alvaro

CENTRAL & SOUTH AMERICA

NB Vintages in colour are those you should choose first for drinking in 2009.

Espinoza (see ANTIYAL). Complex, Syrah-heavy "G" and Coyam show almost Mediterranean-style wildness; cheaper Adobe and Novas ranges v.gd for affordable complexity. See also GEO WINES.

Errázuriz ★→★★★ Main winery in ACONCAGUA's Panquehue district, with whites coming from CASABLANCA. Complex Wild Ferment Chard; brooding La Cumbre Syrah; complex Don Maximiano Cab Sauv; new KAI Carmenère. See also ARBOLEDA, CALITERRA, Seña, VIÑEDO CHADWICK.

Estampa, Viña ★★ Colchagua blend specialists, for reds and whites. Savoury Syrah-based Gold Assemblage pick of solid range.

Falernia, Viña ★★ Winery in far north Elqui Valley, v'yds lie at around 2,000 m. Alta Tierra Syrah and Chard show potential; gd Sauv Bl, Carmenère, Merlot.

Fortuna, Viña La Lontué Valley ★★ Established winery with attractive range.

Garcés Silva Leyda ★★→★★★ Exciting SAN ANTONIO bodega making excellent, full-bodied Sauv Bl and commendable Pinot N and Chard under the Amayna label.

Geo Wines Umbrella under which Alvaro Espinoza makes wines for several new wineries. Look for earthy Chono San Lorenzo MAIPO red blend and tangy Quintay BÍO-BÍO Ries.

Gracia de Chile ★→★★ Winery with v'yds from ACONCAGUA down to BÍO-BÍO. Reserva Lo Mejor Cab Sauv and Syrah (both ACONCAGUA), BÍO-BÍO Sauv Bl are best.

Hacienda Araucano ★★→★★★ The Lurton brothers' Chilean enterprise. Complex Gran Araucano Sauv Bl (CASABLANCA), refined Carmenère/Cab Sauv blend Clos de Lolol, and heady Alka Carmenère. Look out for new Humo Blanc Pinot N.

Haras de Pirque ★★→★★★ Pirque (MAIPO) estate. Smoky Sauv Bl, stylish Chard, dense Cab Sauv/Merlot. Top wine Albis (Cab Sauv/Carmenère) is solid, smoky red made in joint venture with Antinori (see Italy).

Leyda, Viña ★★→★★★ SAN ANTONIO pioneers producing elegant Chard (Lot 5 Wild Yeasts is the pick), lush Pinot N (esp Lot 21 *cuvée* and lively rosé), tangy Garuma Sauv Bl. Now owned by SAN PEDRO.

Limari Northerly, high-altitude region, so quite chilly (for Chile); already impressing with Syrah and Chard.

Loma Larga ★★→★★★ New CASABLANCA venture impressing with Sauv Bl, Pinot N, Cab Fr and Syrah. V. classy wines.

Maipo Famous wine region close to Santiago. Chile's best Cab Sauvs often come from higher, eastern sub-regions such as Pirque and Puente Alto.

Matetic San Antonio ★★★ Decent Pinot N and Chard from exciting winery. Stars are fragrant, zesty Sauv Bl and spicy, berry EQ Syrah. Second label Coralillo.

Maule Southernmost region in Central Valley. Claro, Loncomilla, Tutuven valleys.

Montes ★★→★★★★ Highlights of a first-class range are Alpha Cab Sauv, B'x-blend Montes Alpha M, *Folly Syrah from Apalta* and Purple Angel, Carmenère at its most intense. Also promising new Leyda Sauv Bl and Pinot N.

MontGras ★★→★★★ State-of-the-art Colchagua winery with fine limited-edition wines, inc Syrah and Zin. High-class flagships Ninquén Cab Sauv and Altu Ninquén Syrah. Gd value organic Soleus and excellent Amaral (Leyda) whites.

Morandé ★★ Gd value range inc César, Cinsault, Bouschet, Carignan. Limited Edition range inc a spicy Syrah/Cab Sauv, inky Malbec; top wine is Cab Sauv-based House of Morandé.

Neyen ★★★ New project in Alpata for Patrick Valette of St Emilion, making intense old-vine Carmenère/Cab Sauv blend.

Odfjell ★→★★★ MAIPO-based, Norwegian-owned red specialist. Top wine: Aliara Cab Sauv. Orzada range, inc v.gd entry-level Armador. Wines of character.

Words within entries marked like this *Alter Ego de Palmer* indicate wines especially enjoyed by Hugh Johnson over the past 12 months (mid '07–'08).

Pérez Cruz ★★★ MAIPO winery with Alvaro Espinoza (see ANTIYAL) in charge of winemaking. Fresh, spicy Syrah, aromatic Cot, and stylish Quelen and Liguai red blends.

Porta, Viña ★→★★ MAIPO winery. Range inc supple, spicy Cab Sauv. See CÓRPORA.

Rapel Central quality region divided into Colchagua and Cachapoal valleys. Great "Merlot" (much is actually Carmenère). Watch for sub-region Marchihue.

La Rosa, Viña ★★ Reliable RAPEL Chard, Merlot, and Cab Sauv under La Palmeria and Cornellana labels. Don Reca reds are the stars, plus Ossa Sixth Generation red blend.

San Antonio Coastal region west of Santiago benefiting from sea breezes; v. promising for whites, Syrah, and Pinot N. Leyda is a sub-zone.

San Pedro ★→★★★ Massive Curicó-based producer. 35 South (35 Sur) for affordable varietals; Castello de Molina a step up. Best are 1865 reds and elegant Cabo de Hornos. See also ALTAÏR, TABALÍ, VIÑA LEYDA.

Santa Carolina, Viña ★★→★★★ Historic bodega. Quality ladder goes varietal, Reserva, Barrica Selection, Reserva de Familia, and new VSC Cab Sauv/Syrah/Petit Verdot blends. Syrah and Carmenère gd at all levels.

Santa Inés ★★ Successful small family winery in Isla de MAIPO making ripe, blackcurranty Legado de Armida Cab Sauv. Part of DE MARTINO stable.

Santa Mónica ★→★★ Rancagua (RAPEL) winery; the best label is Tierra del Sol. Ries, Sem, and Merlot under Santa Mónica label also gd.

Santa Rita ★★→★★★ Quality-conscious MAIPO bodega. Best: Casa Real MAIPO Cab Sauv; but Triple C (Cab Sauv/Cab Fr/Carmenère) and Floresta range nearly as gd.

Selentia ★★ New Chilean/Spanish venture. Res Special Cab Sauv is fine.

Seña See VIÑA ARBOLEDA.

Tabalí Limarí ★★ Winery partly owned by SAN PEDRO, making refined Chard and earthy, peppery Syrah. Look out for fine newcomers Viognier and Pinot N.

Tarapacá, Viña ★★ MAIPO winery improved after investment, but inconsistent.

Terramater ★→★★ Wines from all over Central Valley, inc v.gd Altum range. Patrick Valette now consults here.

Terranoble ★→★★ Talca winery specializing in grassy Sauv Bl and light, peppery Merlot. Range now includes v.gd spicy Carmenère Gran Res.

Torreón de Paredes ★→★★ Attractive, crisp Chard, ageworthy Res Cab Sauv from this RAPEL bodega. Flagship Don Amedo Cab Sauv could be better.

Torres, Miguel ★★→★★★ Fresh whites and gd reds, esp sturdy *Manso del Velasco single-v'yd Cab Sauv* and Cariñena-based Cordillera. Conde de Superunda is rare top *cuvée*. See also Spain.

Undurraga ★→★★ MAIPO estate known for its Pinot N. Top wines: Res Chard, refreshing, limey Gewurz, peachy Late Harvest Sem. New TH range (Terroir Hunter - the start of a new forward-looking policy) more form than content so far, but they seem serious about it.

Valdivieso ★→★★★ Major producer impressing in recent yrs with Reserve and Single-V'yd range from top terroirs around Chile. NV red blend Caballo Loco, and wonderfully spicy new Carignan-based Eclat.

Vascos, Los ★→★★★ Lafite-Rothschild venture moving from B'x wannabe to more successful yet still elegant style. Top Le Dix and Grande Réserve.

Ventisquero, Viña ★→★★★ Thrusting young winery, with wines from throughout Chile. Labels include Chileno and Yali; top wine is Pangea, a rich but fragrant Apalta Syrah made with help from Australian John Duval.

Veramonte ★★ Whites from CASABLANCA fruit, red from Central Valley grapes – all gd. Top wine: Primus red blend.

Villard ★★ Sophisticated wines made by French-born Thierry Villard. Gd MAIPO reds, esp heady Merlot, Equis Cab Sauv, and CASABLANCA whites.

Mar, Viña Casablanca ★→★★ B'x-style reds are a little scrawny, but Pinot N, Sauv Bl, and Chard all show CASABLANCA at its best. See CASA RIVAS.

Viñedo Chadwick Maipo ★★★ Stylish Cab Sauv improving with each vintage from v'yd owned by Eduardo Chadwick, chairman of ERRÁZURIZ.

Viu Manent ★→★★ Emerging Colchagua winery. Dense, fragrant Viu 1 tops range; Secreto Malbec and Viognier alsovgd. Late Harvest Sem top notch.

Von Siebenthal ★★★ Small (in Chilean terms) Swiss-owned ACONCAGUA winery. V.gd Carabantes Syrah and B'x-inspired reds, the best of which is elegant Cab Sauv/Petit Verdot/Carmenère blend Montelig.

Argentina

The number of high-class Argentine reds, especialy those based on old-vine Malbec, continues to expand. Cabernet Sauvignon, once the also-ran to Malbec, is finally showing its mettle, and the two blend together extremely well. What remains to be seen is whether this high-end success can be duplicated lower down the scale and in the white wines as well.

Mendoza remains the largest and most exciting province, and with vineyards rising from 500m up to over 1500m, there's a site suited to every grape variety. Further south, Rio Negro and Neuquén are regions to keep an eye on for lighter, more fragrant wines, while to the north, Salta boasts the highest vineydards in the world, some excellent reds and delightful whites made from the aromatic Torrontes.

Achaval Ferrer ★★★→★★★★ MENDOZA. Super-concentrated Altamira, Bella Vista, and Mirador single-v'yd Malbecs and Quimera Malbec/Cab/Merlot blends.

Alta Vista ★→★★★ French-owned MENDOZA venture specializing in Malbec. Dense, spicy Alto among best wines in the country. Also fresh, zesty Torrontés. Sister winery Navarrita makes fine Winemakers Selection Malbec.

Altos las Hormigas ★★★ Italian-owned Malbec specialist, wines made by consultant Alberto Antonini (ex-Italy's Antinori). Best: Viña las Hormigas Res.

Antucura ★★★ Valle de Uco bodega with beautifully balanced, spicy Cab Sauv/Merlot blend. Calvulcura is second label.

Argento ★→★★ CATENA offshoot making gd commercial wine under the Libertad, Malambo and Argento labels.

Balbi, Bodegas ★★ Pernod Ricard-owned San Rafael producer. Juicy Malbec, Chard, and delicious Syrah (red and rosé). Red blend Barbaro also v.gd.

Bianchi, Valentin ★ San Rafael red specialist. Enzo Bianchi (Cab Sauv/Merlot/Malbec) is excellent flagship. Gd-value Elsa's V'yd inc meaty Barbera. Pithy Sauv Bl; also decent sparkling.

Fin del Mundo, Bodega del ★★ First winery in the province of Neuquén; Malbec a speciality, top wine Special Blend is Merlot/Malbec/Cab Sauv.

Bressia ★★→★★★ Tiny new winery already on form with classy Malbec-dominated Profundo from Agrelo and Conjuro Malbec from Tupungato.

Cabernet de los Andes ★★ Promising organic (and partly biodynamic) Catamarca estate with big, fragrant, balanced reds under Vicien and Tizac labels.

Canale, Bodegas Humberto ★★ Premier Río Negro winery known for its Sauv Bl and Pinot N, but Merlot and Malbec (esp Black River label) are the stars.

Cassone, Bodega ★★ Mendoza enterprise now benefiting from Alberto Antonini's winemaking expertise (ALTOS LAS HORMIGAS, Renacer, Melipal). Watch out for Obra Prima Malbec.

Catena Zapata, Bodega ★★→★★★★ Consistently gd range rises from Alamos through Catena, Catena Alta, to flagship Nicolas Catena Zapata and new Malbec Argentino, plus occasional single-v'yd Malbecs. Also joint venture with the Rothschilds of Lafite: seriously *classy Caro* and younger Amancaya; see ARGENTO; LUCA/TIKAL.

Chakana ★★ Agrelo winery to watch for joyful Malbec, Cab Sauv, Syrah, Bonarda.

Chandon, Bodegas ★→★★ Makers of Baron B and M Chandon sparkling under Moët & Chandon supervision; promising Pinot N/Chard blend. See TERRAZAS.

Clos de los Siete ★★ Seven parcels of French-owned vines in MENDOZA, run by Michel Rolland (see France). A juicy Malbec already exists, but each site will produce its own wine (see MONTEVIEJO).

Cobos, Viña ★★★ Stunning Marchiori V'yd old-vine Malbec from Paul Hobbs.

Colomé, Bodega ★★→★★★ SALTA bodega owned by California's Hess Collection. Pure, intense, biodynamic Malbec-based reds, lively Torrontés.

Dominio del Plata ★→★★★ Ex-CATENA husband and wife winemakers produce superior wines under the Crios, Susana Balbo, BenMarco, Anubis and Budini labels. Nosotros is bold Malbec/Cab Sauv flagship.

Doña Paula ★ Luján de Cuyo estate owned by Santa Rita (see Chile). Elegant, structured Malbec; modern fleshy Cab Sauv; tangy Los Cardos Sauv Bl.

Etchart ★★→★★★ Reds gd, topped by plummy Cafayate Cab Sauv. Torrontés also one of the best, with intriguing late-harvest Tardio.

Fabre Montmayou ★★ French-owned Luján de Cuyo (MENDOZA) bodega; fine reds and advice from Michel Rolland (see France). Also decent Chard. Infinitus is sister bodega in Río Negro making supple Gran Res Merlot.

Familia Schroeder ★★ Confident NEUQUÉN estate impressing with reds and whites.v.gd Saurus Select range includes sappy Sauv Bl, earthy Merlot and fragrant Malbec.

Familia Zuccardi ★→★★★ Dynamic MENDOZA estate producing gd-value Santa Julia range, led by new blend Magna, better Q label (impressive Malbec, Merlot, Tempranillo), and deep yet elegant Zeta (Malbec/Tempranillo).

La Anita, Finca ★★→★★★ MENDOZA estate making high-class reds, esp Syrah and Malbec, and intriguing whites, inc Sem and Tocai Friulano.

El Retiro, Finca ★→★★ MENDOZA bodega for gd Malbec, Bonarda, Tempranillo.

Flichman, Finca ★★ Long-established company. Gd-value Syrah. Best: Dedicado blend (mostly Cab Sauv/Syrah). Paisaje de Tupungato (B'x blend), Paisaje de Barrancas (Syrah-based) v.gd.

Las Moras, Finca ★★ San Juan bodega with chunky Tannat, chewy Malbec Res, and plump, fragrant Malbec/Bonarda blend Mora Negra.

Sophenia, Finca Tupungato bodega. Advice from Michel Rolland (see France). Malbec and Cab Sauv shine; gd Altosur entry-level range; top Synthesis.

Kaikén ★★→★★★ Mendoza venture for Aurelio Montes (see Chile) making user-friendly range topped by Ultra Cab Sauv and Malbec.

Luca/Tikal ★★★ Classy boutique wineries owned by Nicolas CATENA's children. Winemaker Luis Reginato also makes excellent La Posta del Vinatero range.

Luigi Bosca ★★→★★★ Small MENDOZA bodega with 3 tiers of quality – Finca La Linda, Luigi Bosca Res, and a top level that includes esp gd Finca Los Nobles Malbec/Verdot and Cab Sauv/Bouchet, plus impresive Gala blends.

Lurton, Bodegas J & F ★→★★★ MENDOZA venture of Lurton brothers. Juicy, concentrated Piedra Negra Malbec and complex, earthy Chacayes (Malbec) head range; new Flor de Torrontés more serious than most.

Marguery, Familia Top-class Malbec from old vines in the Tupungato district.

Masi Tupungato ★★→★★★ MENDOZA enterprise for the well-known Valpolicella producer (see Italy). Passo Doble is fine *ripasso*-style Malbec/Corvina/Merlot blend; Corbec is even better Amarone lookalike (Corvina/Malbec).

Mendel ★★★ Former TERRAZAS winemaker Roberta de la Mota makes plummy Malbec and graceful Unus blend from old Luján de Cuyo vines.

Mendoza Most important province for wine (over 70% of plantings). Best sub-

CHILE/ARGENTINA

regions: Agrelo, Valle de Uco (includes Tupungato), Luján de Cuyo, Maipú.

Monteviejo ★★→★★★★ One of the v'yds of CLOS DE LOS SIETE, now with top-class range of reds headed by wonderfully textured Monteviejo blend (Malbec/Merlot/Cab Sauv/Syrah); Lindaflor Malbec also v.gd.

Navarro Correas ★★ Gd if sometimes over-oaked reds, esp Col Privada Cab Sauv. Also reasonable whites, inc v. oaky Chard and Deutz-inspired fizz.

Neuquén Patagonian region to watch: huge developments since 2000.

Nieto Senetiner, Bodegas ★★ Luján de Cuyo-based bodega. Quality rises from tasty entry-level Santa Isabel through Reserva to top-of-range Cadus reds.

Noemia ★★★ Old-vine RÍO NEGRO Malbec from Hans Vinding-Diers and Noemi Cinzano. J Alberto and A Lisa new second labels. (Chacra Pinot N from nearby is another promising Vinding-Diers project.)

Norton, Bodegas ★★ Old bodega, now Austrian-owned. Gd whites; v.gd reds, esp Malbec, *excellent value Privada (Merlot/Cab Sauv/Malbec)* and new Malbec-based Gernot Langes icon.

O Fournier ★→★★★ Spanish-owned Valle de Uco bodega. Urban v.gd entry-level range; then come B Crux and Alfa Crux, both fine Tempranillo/Merlot/Malbec blends. Also fragrant but rare Syrah. Now producing Chilean wines too.

Peñaflor ★→★★★ Argentina's biggest wine company. Labels include Andean Vineyards and, finer, TRAPICHE, LAS MORAS, SANTA ANA and MICHEL TORINO.

Poesia ★★→★★★★ Exciting Luján de Cuyo producer under same ownership as Clos l'Eglise of B'x; stylish Poesia (Cab Sauv/Malbec), chunkier but fine Clos des Andes (Malbec), and juicy Pasodoble Malbec/Syrah/Cab Sauv blend.

Pulenta Estate ★★→★★★ Luján de Cuyo winery. Gd Sauv Bl and v.gd reds. Best: Gran Corte (Cab Sauv/Malbec/Merlot/Petit Verdot), Cab Fr and Malbec.

Río Negro Patagonia's oldest wine region, gd for Pinot N and Malbec.

Ruca Malen ★★→★★★ Promising red wine specialist with v'yds in Luján de Cuyo and the Uco Valley. Kinien is top range.

Salentein, Bodegas ★★ MENDOZA bodega, impressing with Cab Sauv, Malbec, Merlot, Primus Pinot N. Finca El Portillo (a separate estate) gd for cheaper wines; also Bodegas Callia in San Juan, where Shiraz is the focus.

Salta Northerly province with some of the world's highest v'yds. Sub-region Cafayate renowned for Torrontés.

San Juan Second largest wine region, home to promising Shiraz and Tannat.

San Pedro de Yacochuya ★★★ SALTA collaboration between Michel Rolland (see France) and the ETCHART family. Ripe but fragrant Torrontés; dense, earthy Malbec; and powerful, stunning Yacochuya Malbec from oldest vines.

Santa Ana, Bodegas ★→★★ old-established firm at Guaymallen, MENDOZA. New La Mascota range a distinct improvement, with weighty Cab Sauv being the pick; also bright, friendly Cepas Privadas Viognier.

San Telmo Modern winery making fresh, full-flavoured Chard, Chenin Bl, Merlot. Best: Malbec and Cab Sauv Cruz de Piedra-Maipú.

Soluna ★★ Ambitious new Fairtrade project making Malbec in Luján de Cuyo; top wine fleshy Primus.

Tacuil, Bodegas ★★→★★★ 33 de Davalos is spicy Cab Sauv/Malbec blend.

Terrazas de los Andes ★★→★★★ CHANDON enterprise for still wines made from Malbec, Cab Sauv, Chard, Syrah. Three ranges: entry-level Terrazas (juicy Cab Sauv is the star), mid-price Res, and top-of-the-tree Afincado. Joint venture with Ch Cheval Blanc of B'x making superb Cheval des Andes blend.

Torino, Michel ★★ Rapidly improving organic Cafayate enterprise; Don David Malbec and Cab Sauvvgd. Altimus is rather oaky flagship.

Toso, Pascual ★★→★★★ Californian Paul Hobbs heads a team making g. value, tasty range inc ripe but finely structured Magdalena Toso (mostly Malbec).

Trapiche ★★→★★★ PEÑAFLOR premium label in ascending order of quality: Astica,

Trapiche (Oak Cask Syrah), Fond de Cave (gd Malbec Reserva), Medalla (Cab Sauv), pricy red blend Iscay, and trio of single-v'yd Malbecs.

Trivento ★→★★ Owned by Concha y Toro of Chile, making gd-value range, with Viognier standing out; also under Otra Vida label.

Val de Flores ★★★★ Another Michel Rolland-driven enterprise close to CLOS DE LOS SIETE for compelling yet elegant (and biodynamic) old-vine Malbec.

Viniterra ★→★★ Clean, modern wines under Omnium, Bykos, Viniterra labels.

Weinert, Bodegas ★→★★ Potentially fine reds, esp Cavas de Weinert blend (Cab Sauv/Merlot/Malbec), are often spoiled by extended ageing in old oak.

Other Central & South American wines

Bolivia With just a handful of wineries, this hot, humid country is not a major wine producer. Even so, wines such as Cepas de Altura Cab Sauv from **Vinos y Viñedos La Concepción** wines show what is possible. The v'yds, 1,000 km south of La Paz, are the highest in the world.

Brazil New plantings of better grapes are transforming a booming industry in a wine-conscious country. International investment, esp in Rio Grande do Sul and Santana do Liuramento, notably from France and Italy, are significant. The sandy Frontera region and Sierra Gaucha hills (Italian-style sparkling) to watch. Continuous harvesting is possible in some equatorial v'yds. Of the wines that do leave Brazil, 95% are made by **Vinicola Aurora (Bento Gonçalves)**, sometimes under the **Amazon** label. Look out for **Rio Sol, Miolo**.

Mexico Oldest Latin American wine industry is reviving, with investment from abroad (eg Freixenet, Martell, Domecq) and California influence via UC Davis. Best in Baja California (with Valle de Guadeloupe among the best sub-zones), Querétaro, and on the Aguascalientes and Zacatecas plateaux. Lack of water is a problem countrywide. Top Baja C producers are **Casa de Piedra** (impressive Tempranillo/Cab Sauv), **L A Cetto** (Valle de Guadeloupe, the largest, esp for Cab Sauv, Nebbiolo, Petite Sirah), **Doña Lupe** (organic specialist), **Bodegas Santo Tomás** (working with California's Wente Brothers to make Duetto, grapes from both sides of the border), **Monte Xanic** (with Napa award-winning Cab Sauv), **Bodegas San Antonio, Cavas de Valmar.**

Peru Viña Tacama exports some pleasant wines, esp the Gran Vino Blanco white; also Cab Sauv and classic-method sparkling. Chincha, Moquegua, and Tacha regions are making progress, but phylloxera is a serious problem.

Uruguay Point of difference here is the rugged, tannic grape Tannat, producing a sturdy, plummy red, best blended with Merlot and Cab Sauv. **Carrau/Castel Pujol** is among the most impressive wineries: Amat Gran Tradición 1752 and Las Violetas Reserva show Tannat at its most fragrant. Juanicó is equally impressive, with flagship red blend Preludio and joint venture with Bernard Magrez of Ch Pape Clément to produce Gran Casa Magrez de Uruguay. Others: Bouza, Bruzzone & Sciutto, Casa Filguera, Castillo Viejo, De Lucca, Los Cerros de San Juan, Dante Irurtia, Pisano (working with Boisset of Burgundy under the Viña Progreso label), Carlos Pizzorno, and Stagnari.

To decipher codes, please refer to "Key to symbols" on the front flap of jacket, or "How to use this book" on p.10.

Australia

More heavily shaded areas are
the wine-growing regions

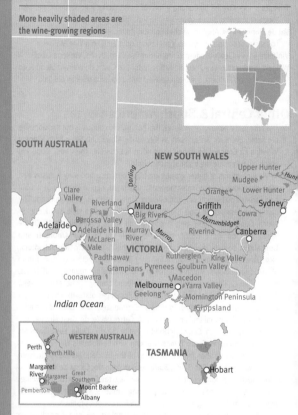

As the 2008 vintage approached, a deadly combination of severe drought and apparent climate change was sweeping across the industry like a Californian wildfire. The main artery for the eastern half of Australia, the Murray Darling water system, is buckling at the knees, with the lowest ever inflows over the past five years. Crop estimates by informed observers suggested a harvest of 1.2 m tonnes until the vintage was underway when the estimate was lifted to 1.6 m tonnes.

The outlook for 2009 is nonetheless bleak, especially for the volume brands such as Jacob's Creek, Yellowtail, *et al*. Barring a miracle, there will be even less water (and fewer grapes) for these once low-priced grapes needed for these wines. Winery fixed costs will rise as the grape intake is cut in half and a remorselessly increasing A$ will add to export costs.

There may be a silver lining. Australia has already identified regional wines with both quality and a sense of place as the future for the industry. As bulk wine is imported (a year ago it was being exported) for low-price wines on the domestic market, more of the best wines will be exported. Cheap and cheerful may no longer be the export banner.

Recent vintages

New South Wales (NSW)

2007 The earliest vintage ever recorded for all regions; full flavour across white and red wines.

2006 A burst of extreme heat around Christmas in some regions did not leave a lasting mark on a vintage of overall high quality.

2005 A very good to exceptional year across almost all districts, especially the Hunter, Mudgee, and Orange.

2004 Hunter Valley suffered; other regions good to very good outcomes.

2003 Continued drought broken by heavy rain in Jan/Feb; variable outcomes.

2002 Heavy Feb rain caused problems in all but two areas. Riverina outstanding.

2001 Extreme summer heat and ill-timed rain set the tone; remarkably, Hunter Valley Semillon shone.

2000 A perfect growing season for the Hunter Valley, but dire for the rest of the state; extreme heat followed by rain during the harvest.

Victoria (Vic)

2007 Broke the record for the earliest vintage; frost and bushfire smoke taint hit some regions hard.

2006 One of the earliest and most compressed vintages on record; paradoxically fruit flavour came even earlier. A charmed year.

2005 Rain up to end of Feb was followed by a freakish three-month Indian summer giving superb fruit.

2004 Near perfect weather throughout ripened generous yields.

2003 Overall, fared better than other states, except for bushfire-ravaged Alpine Valleys.

2002 Extremely cool weather led to tiny yields, but wines of high quality.

2001 Did not escape the heat; a fair to good red vintage, whites more variable.

2000 Southern and central regions flourished in warm and dry conditions; terrific reds. Northeast poor; vintage rain.

South Australia (SA)

2007 Devastating frosts hit the Limestone Coast repeatedly. A dry, warm vintage favoured red wines across the board.

2006 A great Cabernet year; for other reds those picked before Easter rains did best. Here, too, flavour ripeness came early.

2005 Clare Valley, Coonawarra, Wrattonbully, and Langhorne Creek did best in what was a large but high-quality vintage with reds to the fore.

2004 Excellent summer and autumn weather helped offset large crops (big bunches/berries); heavy crop-thinning needed.

2003 A curate's egg. The good: Limestone Coast and Clare Riesling (yet again); the bad: rain-split Shiraz.

2002 Very cool weather led to much reduced yields in the south and to a great Riverland vintage in both yield and quality. Fine Riesling again.

2001 Far better than 2000; Clare Valley Riesling an improbable success.

2000 The culmination of a four-year drought impacted on both yield and quality, the Limestone Coast Zone faring the best.

Western Australia (WA)

2007 A v. warm quickfire vintage made white quality variable, reds better.

2006 Complete opposite to Eastern Australia; a cool, wet and late vintage – gave good whites, dubious reds.

2005 Heavy rain in late March and April spoiled what would have been the vintage of a generation for Cabernet and Shiraz in the south; whites uniformly excellent.

2004 More of the same; mild weather, long autumn. Good flavours, some lacking intensity.

2003 An in-between year, with ill-timed rainfall nipping greatness in the bud.

2002 Best since 84 in Swan District. In the south, quality is variable.

2001 Great Southern, the best vintage since 95; good elsewhere.

2000 Margaret River excellent, variation elsewhere; the Swan Valley ordinary.

Adelaide Hills SA Best SAUV BL region: cool, 450-m sites in Mt Lofty ranges.

Alkoomi Mount Barker, WA r w ★★★ (RIES) **01 02 03** 04 06' (CAB SAUV) **97** 99 01 02' 04 05 A veteran of 35 yrs making fine RIES and long-lived reds.

All Saints Rutherglen, Vic r w br ★★ Historic producer making creditable table wines; great fortifieds.

Alpine Valleys Vic Geographically similar to KING VALLEY and similar use of grapes.

Amberley Estate Margaret R WA r w ★★ Successful maker of a full range of regional styles now improving. Now a tiny part of Constellation.

Angove's SA r w (br) ★→★★ Large, long-established MURRAY VALLEY family business. Good-value range of white and red varietals.

Annie's Lane Clare V, SA r w ★★→★★★ Part of FWE. Consistently gd, boldly flavoured wines; flagship Copper Trail excellent, esp RIES.

Ashbrook Estate Margaret R, WA r w ★★★ Minimum of fuss; consistently makes 8,000 cases of exemplary SEM, CHARD, SAUV BL, VERDELHO, and CAB SAUV.

Ashton Hills Adelaide Hills, SA r w (sp) ★★★ Fine, racy, long-lived RIES and compelling PINOT N crafted by Stephen George from 25-yr-old v'yds.

Bailey's NE Vic r w br ★★ Rich SHIRAZ, and magnificent dessert Muscat (★★★★) and "Tokay". Part of FWE.

Balgownie Estate Bendigo and Yarra V, Vic r w ★★→★★★ Rejuvenated producer of v. well-balanced wines now with separate YARRA VALLEY arm.

Balnaves of Coonawarra SA r w ★★★ Grape-grower since 1975; winery since 1996. V.gd CHARD; excellent supple, medium-bodied SHIRAZ, MERLOT, CAB SAUV.

Bannockburn Geelong r w ★★★ (CHARD) **00 02'** 03 04 05' 06 (PINOT N) **02' 03'** 04' 05' 06 Intense, complex CHARD and PINOT N produced using Burgundian techniques. New winemaker Michael Glover is a whizz.

Banrock Station Riverland, SA r w ★→★★ Almost 1,600-ha property on MURRAY River, 243-ha v'yd, owned by HARDYS. Impressive budget wines.

Barossa Valley SA Australia's most important winery (but not v'yd) area; grapes from diverse sources make diverse wines. Local specialities: v. old-vine SHIRAZ, Mourvèdre, and GRENACHE.

Bass Phillip Gippsland, Vic r ★★★→★★★★ (PINOT N) **91'** 94' **96** 97' **99'** 02' 03 04 05' Tiny amounts of stylish, eagerly sought-after PINOT N in 3 quality grades; v. Burgundian in style, though quality can be erratic.

Bay of Fires N Tas r w sp ★★★ Pipers River outpost of HARDYS empire. Produces stylish table wines and Arras super-*cuvée* sparkler.

Beechworth Vic Trendy region; Castagna and GIACONDA are best-known wineries.

Bellarmine Wines Pemberton WA w (r) ★★★ German Schumacher family is long-distance owner of this 20-ha v'yd: (*inter alia*) startling Mosel-like RIES at various sweetness/alcohol levels, at ridiculously low prices.

Bendigo Vic Widespread 34 small v'yds, some v.gd quality. Notable: BALGOWNIE, PONDALOWIE, Passing Clouds, Turner's Crossing, and Water Wheel.

Best's Grampians, Vic r w ★★→★★★ (SHIRAZ) **94'** 97' 98 01' 02' 03' 04' 05' 06'

Conservative old family winery; v.gd mid-weight reds. ***Thomson Family Shiraz*** from 120-yr-old vines is superb.

Big Rivers Zone NSW and Vic The continuation of South Australia's Riverland, inc the MURRAY Darling, Perricoota and Swan Hill regions.

Bindi Macedon, Vic r w ★★★→★★★★ Ultra-fastidious, terroir-driven maker of outstanding, long-lived PINOT N and CHARD.

Bloodwood, Orange, NSW r w ★★★ Old dog (1983) in up-and-coming cool, high-altitude, andpicturesque region. CHARD, RIES, and Big Men in Tights Rosé gd.

Blue Pyrenees Pyrenees, Vic r w sp ★★ 180 ha of mature v'yds are being better utilized across a broad range of wines.

Boireann Granite Belt Qld r ★★→★★★★ Consistently the best producer of red wines in Queensland (in tiny quantities).

Botobolar Mudgee, NSW r w ★★ Marvellously eccentric little organic winery.

Brand's of Coonawarra Coonawarra, SA r w ★★★ 90' 91' 94 96' 98' 02 03 04 05' 06'Owned by MCWILLIAM'S. Super-premium Stentiford's SHIRAZ (100-yr-old vines) and Patron's CAB SAUV are tops.

Bremerton Langhorne Creek, SA r w ★★ Regularly produces attractively priced red wines with silky, soft mouthfeel and stacks of flavour.

Brini Estate McLaren Vale, SA r ★★→★★★ Family grape-growers for 50 yrs now have pick of the crop contract-made into velvety SHIRAZ and GRENACHE.

Brokenwood Hunter V, NSW r w ★★★ (ILR Res SEM) 99' 03' 04 05' 06 07 (Graveyard SHIRAZ) 85' 86' 87' 93' 97' 98' 00' 02' 03' 05' (SEM) and Cricket Pitch SEM/SAUV BL fuel sales.

Brookland Valley Margaret R, WA r w ★★→★★★ Superbly sited winery (with a restaurant) doing great things, esp with SAUV BL. Owned by HARDYS.

Brown Brothers King V, Vic r w dr br sp sw ★→★★★ (Noble RIES) 99' 00 02' 04 05 Old family firm, with new ideas. Wide range of delicate, varietal wines, many from cool mountain districts, inc CHARD and RIES. Dry white Muscat is outstanding. CAB SAUV blend is best red.

Buller Rutherglen, Vic br ★★★★ Rated for superb Rare Liqueur Muscat and "Tokay" (Muscadelle).

Leo Buring Barossa, SA w ★★★ 73' 79' 84' 91' 94' 95 98 02 04' 05' 06 Part of FWE. Happily, now exclusive RIES producer; Leonay top label, ages superbly. Has moved to screwcap.

By Farr/Farr Rising Geelong, Vic r w ★★★ Father Gary and son Nick's own, after departure from BANNOCKBURN. CHARD and PINOT N are minor masterpieces.

Cabernet Sauvignon 28,227 ha; 183,057 tonnes. Grown in all wine regions, best in COONAWARRA. From herbaceous green pepper in coolest regions, through blackcurrant and mulberry, to dark chocolate and redcurrant in warmer areas.

Campbells' Rutherglen, Vic r br (w) ★★ Smooth, ripe reds and gd fortified wines; Merchant Prince Rare Muscat and Isabella Rare Tokay v.gd.

Canberra District NSW Both quality and quantity on the increase; altitude-dependent, site selection important.

Capel Vale Geographe, WA r w ★★★ V. successful with gd whites, inc RIES. Also top-end SHIRAZ and CAB SAUV.

Cape Mentelle Margaret R, WA r w ★★★ Robust CAB SAUV gd, CHARD even better; also ZIN and v. popular SAUV BL/SEM. LVMH Veuve Clicquot owner; also Cloudy Bay (see New Zealand).

Capercaillie Hunter V, NSW r w ★★→★★★ Veteran Alasdair Sutherland goes from strength to strength, supplementing local grapes with purchases from elsewhere, inc ORANGE, MCLAREN VALE, etc.

Words within entries marked like this ***Alter Ego de Palmer*** indicate wines especially enjoyed by Hugh Johnson over the past 12 months (mid '07–'08).

AUSTRALIA

> **Genetic selection (GS) or manipulation (GM)**
> There is a world of difference between GS and GM but the two are often
> confused. A prime example of GS is clonal selection, accepted in all parts
> of the wine world as both legitimate and important. While GM might well
> result in vines resistant to mildews and/or botrytis (with obvious
> environmental and cost benefits), Australia, like France, has resolutely
> turned its back on GM. It nonetheless has massive indirect benefits: take
> yeast as an example. GM is used to produce a yeast which enhances the
> aroma and flavour of SAUV BL. Researchers then go back into the natural
> (wild) population of *S. cerevisiae* and select a strain with similar genes to
> its GM counterpart. Here theory becomes reality, because such a yeast is
> now being used in a number of countries, including Australia.

Carlei Estate Yarra V, Vic r w ★★ Mercurial winemaker Sergio Carlei sources PINOT
N and CHARD from various v'yds and cool regions to make wines with abundant
character.

Casella Riverina, NSW r w ★ The (yellow tail) phenomenon has swept all before it
with multimillion-case sales in US. Like Fanta: soft and sweet.

Centennial Vineyards Southern Highlands, NSW r w ★★ So far, sources much of
its best grapes from ORANGE, but the winemaking skills and a large investment
chequebook are there.

Central Ranges Zone NSW Encompasses MUDGEE, ORANGE, and Cowra regions,
expanding in high-altitude, moderately cool to warm climates.

Chain of Ponds Adelaide Hills, SA r w ★★ Impeccably made, full, flavoursome
wines. SEM, SAUV BL, and CHARD to the fore.

Chalkers Crossing Hilltops, NSW r w ★★→★★★ Beautifully balanced cool-climate
wines made by French-trained Celine Rousseau.

Chambers' Rosewood NE Vic br (r w) ★★→★★★ Viewed with MORRIS as the
greatest maker of "Tokay" and Muscat.

Chardonnay 366,976; tonnes 32151 ha. Best known for fast-developing, buttery,
peachy, sometimes syrupy wines, but cooler regions produce more elegant,
tightly structured, ageworthy examples. Oak is less heavy-handed.

Charles Melton Barossa, SA r w (sp) ★★★ Tiny winery with bold, luscious reds,
esp Nine Popes, an old-vine GRENACHE/SHIRAZ blend.

Cheviot Bridge Long Flat, SE Aus r w ★★ Part of new corporate empire that bought
the Long Flat brand from TYRRELL'S.

Clarendon Hills McLaren Vale, SA r (w) ★★★ Monumental (and expensive) reds
from small parcels of contract grapes around Adelaide.

Clare Valley (Clare V), SA Small high-quality area 145 km north of Adelaide. Best
for RIES; also SHIRAZ and CAB SAUV.

Clonakilla Canberra District, NSW r w ★★★ Deserved leader of the
SHIRAZ/Viognier brigade. RIES and other wines also v.gd.

Coldstream Hills Yarra V, Vic r w (sp) ★★★ (CHARD) **96' 02' 03** 04' 05' 06' (PINOT N)
92' 96' **02'** 04' 05' 06' Established in 1985 by wine critic James Halliday.
Delicious PINOT N to drink young, and Reserve to age leads Australia. V.gd
CHARD (esp Res), fruity CAB SAUV, MERLOT. Part of FWE.

Coonawarra SA Southernmost v'yds of state: home to most of Australia's best
CAB SAUV; successful CHARD, RIES, and SHIRAZ. Perhaps finest of doubtful
veracity except for CAB.

Coriole McLaren Vale, SA r w ★★→★★★ (Lloyd Reserve SHIRAZ) **90' 91' 96'** 97 **98'**
02' 04 05' 06' To watch, esp for old-vine SHIRAZ Lloyd Reserve.

Craiglee Macedon, Vic r w ★★★ (SHIRAZ) **93' 96'** 97' 98' 00 02' 04' 05' 06' Re-
creation of famous 19th-century estate. Fragrant, peppery SHIRAZ, CHARD.

Crawford River Henty, Vic w r ★★★ John Thomson consistently produces some of Australia's best RIES from this ultra-cool region.

Cullen Wines Margaret R, WA r w ★★★★ (CHARD) **99' 00' 02' 03'** 04' 05' 06' (CAB SAUV/MERLOT) **87' 90' 94' 95'** 96 98' 99' 01' 04' 05' Vanya Cullen makes strongly structured substantial but subtle SEM/SAUV BL, bold CHARD and outstanding CAB SAUV: all real characters.

Cumulus Orange, NSW r w ★★ By far the largest v'yd owner and producer in the region but continues to have unsettled management.

Cuttaway Hill Southern Highlands, NSW ★★ r w Leads the region in the production of estate-grown wines, esp CHARD, SAUV BL, Pinot Gr.

Dalwhinnie Pyrenees, Vic r w ★★★ (CHARD)**98 00' 03'** 04' 05 (SHIRAZ) **98** 99' 00' 02 03 04' 05' Rich CHARD and SHIRAZ. CAB SAUV best in PYRENEES.

d'Arenberg McLaren Vale, SA r w (sw br sp) ★★→★★★ Old firm with new lease of life; sumptuous SHIRAZ and GRENACHE, lots of varieties and wacky labels.

Deakin Estate Murray Darling r w ★ Part of KATNOOK group, producing large volumes of v. decent varietal table wines.

De Bortoli Griffith, NSW r w d dr sw (br) ★→★★★ (Noble SEM) Irrigation-area winery. Standard red and white but splendid sweet botrytized Sauternes-style Noble SEM. See also next entry.

De Bortoli Yarra V, Vic r w ★★→★★★ (CHARD) **02' 04 05'** 06' (SHIRAZ) **02' 04'** 05' 06' YARRA VALLEY's largest producer. Main label is v.gd; second label Gulf Station and third label Windy Peak v.gd value.

Delatite Upper Goldburn (r) w (sp) ★★★ (RIES) **01** 02' 04 05 06' 07' RIES, Gewurz, and SAUV BL are specialities of this cool mountainside v'yd.

Devil's Lair Margaret R, WA r w ★★★ Opulently concentrated CHARD and CAB SAUV/MERLOT. Fifth Leg is fast-growing trendy second label. Part of FWE.

New varieties and varietal choice

In the past 20 yrs or so the number of varieties in commercial production has quadrupled. Vines from Russia to Portugal – and every country in between – have sprung up everywhere; the varietal count is now in excess of 115. There is Italian Fiano, and French Aucerot and Petit Meslier among the whites, and Russian Saperavi and Italian Marzemino among the reds. So far choice seems to have been somewhat haphazard, but the need for varieties that perform well in warm-to-hot climates will clarify people's ideas.

Diamond Valley Yarra V, Vic r w ★★→★★★ (PINOT N) **98' 01' 02' 04'** 05' 06' Outstanding PINOT N in significant quantities; others gd, esp CHARD.

Domaine A S Tas r w ★★★ Swiss owners/winemakers Peter and Ruth Althaus are ultimate perfectionists; SAUV BL (Fumé Blanc) and CAB SAUV are picks.

Domaine Chandon Yarra V, Vic sp (r w) ★★★ Classic sparkling wine from grapes grown in cooler wine regions, supported by owner Moët & Chandon. Well known in UK as Green Point (label also used for table wine).

Dominique Portet Yarra V, Vic r w ★★→★★★ After 25-yr career at TALTARNI, now in his own winery for the first time, going from strength to strength.

Eden Hall Eden V, SA r w ★★ Substantial v'yd planted in 1996 on historic property making excellent SHIRAZ/Viognier, CAB SAUV and RIES.

Eden Valley Eden V, SA Hilly region home to HENSCHKE and PEWSEY VALE; RIES and SHIRAZ of v. high quality.

Elderton Barossa, SA r w (sp br) ★★ Old vines; flashy, rich, oaked CAB SAUV and SHIRAZ.

Evans & Tate Margaret R, WA r w ★★→★★★ In October 2007 finally acquired (from receivers) by a syndicate headed by MCWILLIAMS. Wine quality has remained remarkably stable during its extended financial woes.

Ferngrove Vineyards Great Southern, WA r w ★★★ Cattle farmer Murray Burton's syndicate has established 223 ha since 1997; great RIES, Malbec.

Freycinet Tas r w (sp) ★★★ (PINOT N) **95' 96'** 00' 01' **02' 03'** 04 East coast winery producing voluptuous, rich PINOT N and gd CHARD.

FWE (Fosters Wine Estates) Official name of the merged Beringer Blass and Southcorp wine groups. Has 41 brands in Australia, more than any other, excluding the virtual brands (which use contract grapes, contract wineries, contract staff) that come and go like mushrooms after rain.

Gapsted Wines Alpine V, Vic r w ★★ Brand of large winery that crushes grapes for 50 growers; own label commendable.

Geelong Vic Once-famous area destroyed by phylloxera, re-established in the mid-1960s. V. cool, dry climate: firm table wines from gd-quality grapes. Names inc BANNOCKBURN, BY FARR, Curlewis, SCOTCHMANS HILL.

Gemtree Vineyards McLaren Vale, SA r (w) ★★ Top-class SHIRAZ alongside Tempranillo, Bordeaux blends and other exotica, linked by quality.

Geoff Merrill McLaren Vale, SA r w ★★ Ebullient maker of Geoff Merrill and Mt Hurtle. A questing enthusiast; his best are excellent, others unashamedly mass-market oriented. TAHBILK OWNS 50%.

Geoff Weaver Adelaide Hills, SA r w ★★★ An 8-ha estate at Lenswood. V. fine SAUV BL, CHARD, RIES, and CAB SAUV/MERLOT blend. Marvellous label design.

Giaconda Beechworth, Vic r w ★★★ (CHARD) Australia's answer to Kistler (see California). CHARD is considered by many to be the best in Australia – certainly the 96 is one of the all-time greats. PINOT N is v. variable; newly introduced SHIRAZ better.

Glaetzer Wines Barossa, SA r ★★★ Hyper-rich, unfiltered, v. ripe old-vine SHIRAZ headed by iconic Amon-Ra. V.gd examples of high-octane style much admired by US critics.

Goulburn Valley (Goulburn V), Vic V. old (TAHBILK) and relatively new (MITCHELTON) wineries in temperate mid-Victoria region. Full-bodied table wines.

Goundrey Wines Great Southern, WA r w ★★ Recent expansion has caused quality to be variable. Now part of Constellation.

Grampians Vic Region previously known as Great Western. Temperate region in central west of state. High quality, especially SHIRAZ.

Granite Belt Qld High-altitude, (relatively) cool region just north of Queensland/NSW border. Esp spicy SHIRAZ and rich SEM.

Granite Hills Macedon, Vic r w ★★→★★★ 30-yr-old family v'yd and winery has regained original class with fine elegant RIES and spicy SHIRAZ.

Grant Burge Barossa, SA r w (sp sw br) ★★→★★★ 400,000 cases of silky-smooth reds and whites from the best grapes of Burge's large v'yd holdings.

Great Southern WA Remote, cool area; FERNGROVE and GOUNDREY are the largest wineries. Albany, Denmark, Frankland River, Mount Barker, and Porongurup are official sub-regions.

Greenstone Vineyard Heathcote, Vic r ★★ A partnership between David Gleave MW (London), Alberto Antonini (Italy) and Australian viticulturist Mark Walpole; great SHIRAZ, nascent Sangiovese.

Grenache 2,097 ha; 25,418 tonnes. Produces thin wine if overcropped, but can do much better. Growing interest in old BAROSSA and MCLAREN VALE plantings.

Grosset Clare, SA r w ★★★→★★★ (RIES) **97' 99'** 00' 01 **02' 03'** 04' 05 06' 07 (Gaia) **90' 91' 92 94' 96' 98' 99** 01' 02' 03' 04' 05' Fastidious winemaker. Foremost Australian RIES, lovely CHARD, PINOT N, and exceptional Gaia CAB SAUV/MERLOT from dry v'yd high on Mount Horrocks.

Haan Wines Barossa, SA r w ★★★ Low yields and meticulous winemaking ensure top results for Viognier, MERLOT, SHIRAZ, and B'x blend (Wilhelmus).

Hanging Rock Macedon, Vic r w sp ★→★★★ (Heathcote SHIRAZ) 00' 01' 02' 03' 04 (05) Has successfully moved upmarket with sparkling Macedon and HEATHCOTE SHIRAZ; bread and butter comes from contract winemaking.

Hardys r w sp (sw) ★★→★★★★★ (Eileen CHARD) 01' 02' 03' 04' 05' (06') (Eileen Shiraz) 70' 96' 98' 02' 04' 05' (06') Historic company blending wines from several areas. Best are Eileen Hardy and Thomas Hardy series and (Australia's best) "Vintage Ports". Part of Constellation, world's largest wine group.

Heathcote Vic The 500-million-yr-old, blood-red Cambrian soil has seemingly unlimited potential to produce reds, especially SHIRAZ, of the highest quality.

Heathcote Estate Heathcote, Vic r ★★★ SHIRAZ specialist brimming with potential for small group of owners/executive winemakers; overlaps with YABBY LAKE.

Heggies Eden V, SA r w dr (sw w) ★★ V'yd at 500 m owned by S SMITH & SONS, like PEWSEY VALE with v.gd RIES, but adds Viognier esp and CHARD to its portfolio.

Henschke Eden Valley, SA r w ★★★★ (SHIRAZ) 58' 61' 84' 86' 88 90' 91' 93' 96' 98' 99' 01' 02' 04' 05 (06') (CAB SAUV) 80' 85' 86' 88 90' 91' 93 94 96' 98 99' 01' 02' (04' 05 (06') A 139-yr-old family business, perhaps Australia's best, known for delectable Hill of Grace (SHIRAZ), v.gd CAB SAUV and red blends, and value whites, inc RIES. Lenswood v'yds in ADELAIDE HILLS add excitement. Fervent opponent of corks for reds, too.

Regions: Geographical Indications

The process of formally defining the boundaries of the zones, regions, and sub-regions, known compendiously as Geographic Indications (GIs), continues. These correspond to the French ACs, and AVAs in the United States. It means every aspect of the labelling of Australian wines has a legal framework that, in all respects, complies with EU laws and requirements. The most recent GI is New England Australia, a quixotic appellation name derived from the long-term geographical name, but with "Australia" appended to head off international legal challenges.

Hewitson SE Aus r (w) ★★★ The virtual winery of ex-PETALUMA/ex-flying winemaker Dean Hewitson, sourcing parcels of 60–100-yr-old vines and making wines (with great skill) in rented space.

Hollick Coonawarra, SA r w (sp) ★★→★★★ (CAB SAUV/MERLOT) 91' 96' 98' 99 01' 02' 03 05' Has expanded estate v'yds, most recently in WRATTONBULLY. Main focus on CAB SAUV, SHIRAZ and MERLOT. Top-class restaurant too.

Hope Estate Lower Hunter V, NSW ★★ Snapped up Rothbury Estate Winery from FWE; also owns Virgin Hills and Western Austalia v'yds.

Houghton Swan V, WA r w ★→★★★ The most famous old winery of Western Australia. Soft, ripe ***Supreme is top-selling, ageworthy white***; a national classic. Also excellent CAB SAUV, VERDELHO, SHIRAZ, etc sourced from MARGARET RIVER and GREAT SOUTHERN. See HARDYS.

Howard Park Mount Barker and Margaret R, WA r w ★★★ (RIES) 91' 95' 97' 99' 02' 03' 05' 06' (CAB SAUV) 88' 90 94' 96' 98' 99' 01' 02' 03' 04 05' (CHARD) 98' 02' 03 04' 05 06' Scented RIES, CHARD; spicy CAB SAUV. Second label: MadFish Bay is excellent value.

Hunter Valley Hunter Valley, NSW Great name in NSW. Broad, soft, earthy SHIRAZ and gentle SEM that live for 30 yrs. CAB SAUV not important; CHARD is.

Huntington Estate Mudgee, NSW r w ★★ (CAB SAUV) 94' 95' 96' 97' 99' 01' 02' 35-yr-old v'yds (mainly SHIRAZ and CAB SAUV) on some of the best soil in the region, recently acquired by quality-conscious neighbour Abercorn. Separate identity will be retained.

Jacob's Creek (Orlando), Barossa, SA r w sp (br sw) ★→★★★ Great pioneering company, now owned by Pernod Ricard. Almost totally focused on 3 tiers of Jacob's Creek wines, covering all varieties and prices, all tied historically to Jacob Gramp and his eponymous creek.

Jasper Hill Heathcote, Vic r w ★★→★★★ (SHIRAZ) 85' 90' 91' 96' 97' 98' 99' 00' 04' 05' Emily's Paddock SHIRAZ/Cab Fr blend and Georgia's Paddock SHIRAZ from dry-land estate are intense, long-lived, and much admired.

Jim Barry Clare V, SA r w ★★→★★★ Some great v'yds provide gd RIES, McCrae Wood SHIRAZ, and richly robed and oaked The Armagh.

John Duval Wines Barossa, SA r ★★★ The eponymous business of former chief red-winemaker for Penfolds (and Grange), making delicious reds that are supple and smooth, yet amply structured.

Kaesler Barossa, SA r (w) ★★→★★★ Old Bastard SHIRAZ outranks Old Vine SHIRAZ. Wine in the glass gd, too (in heroic style).

Katnook Estate Coonawarra, SA r w (sp sw w) ★★★ (Odyssey CAB SAUV) 91' 92' 94' 96' 97' 98' 00 01' 02' Excellent pricey icons Odyssey and Prodigy SHIRAZ.

Keith Tulloch Hunter V, NSW r w ★★★ Ex-Rothbury winemaker fastidiously crafting elegant yet complex SEM, SHIRAZ, etc.

Killikanoon Clare V, SA ★★→★★★ r w RIES and SHIRAZ have been awesome performers in shows over past yrs. In Sept 2007 acquired National Trust ranked Seppeltsfield and SEPPELT fortified wines, inc 100-yr-old annual release of legendary Para Liqueur.

Kingston Estate SE Aus ★→★★ Kalaedoscopic array of varietal wines from all over the place, consistency and value providing the glue.

King Valley Vic Altitude between 155 m and 860 m has massive impact on varieties and styles, and prolonged legal wrangling over GI boundaries. 29 wineries headed by BROWN BROS, and important supplier to many others.

Knappstein Wines Clare V, SA r w ★★→★★★ Reliable RIES, CAB SAUV/MERLOT, SHIRAZ, and CAB SAUV. Owned by LION NATHAN.

Lake Breeze Langhorne Ck, SA r (w) ★★ Long-term grape-growers turned winemakers, producing succulently smooth SHIRAZ and CAB SAUV.

Lake's Folly Hunter V, NSW r w ★★★★ (CHARD) 89' 97' 99' 00' 02' 03' 04' 05' 06' (CAB SAUV) 69 81 89' 91 93 97' 98' 00 02 03' 05' Founded by Max Lake, the pioneer of HUNTER CAB SAUV. New owners since 2000. CHARD usually better than CAB SAUV these days.

Lamont's Swan V, WA r w ★★ Winery and superb restaurant owned by Corin Lamont (daughter of legendary Jack Mann) and husband. Delicious wines.

Langmeil Barossa, SA r w ★★★ Owns the oldest block of SHIRAZ (planted in 1846) in the world plus other old v'yds making opulent SHIRAZ's without excessive alcohol.

Leasingham Clare V, SA r w ★★→★★★ Important mid-sized quality winery bought by HARDYS in 1987. Gd RIES, SHIRAZ, and CAB SAUV/Malbec blend. Various labels.

Leeuwin Estate Margaret R, WA r w ★★★★ (CHARD) 82' 85' 87' 89 92' 95' 97' 98 99' 01' 02' 03 04' 05' (06) Leading Western Australia estate, lavishly equipped. Superb, ageworthy (and expensive) *Art Series Chard*. SAUV BL, RIES, and CAB SAUV also gd.

Limestone Coast Zone SA Important zone inc Bordertown, COONAWARRA, Mount Benson, Mount Gambier, PADTHAWAY, Robe, and WRATTONBULLY. All regions suffered significant frost damage in 2006/2007.

Lindemans r w ★→★★ One of the oldest firms, now owned by FWE. Low-price Bin range (esp Bin 65 CHARD) now its main focus, a far cry from former glory.

Lion Nathan New Zealand brewery; owns KNAPPSTEIN, MITCHELTON, PETALUMA, ST HALLET, Smithbrook, STONIER and TATACHILLA.

Macedon and **Sunbury** Vic Adjacent regions, Macedon at higher elevation, Sunbury nr Melbourne airport. CRAIGLEE, GRANITE HILLS. HANGING ROCK, VIRGIN HILLS,

Majella Coonawarra, SA r (w) ★★★→★★★★ Rising to the top of COONAWARRA cream. The Malleea is outstanding CAB SAUV/SHIRAZ super-premium red. SHIRAZ and CAB SAUV also v.gd.

Margaret River WA Temperate coastal area south of Perth, with superbly elegant wines. Australia's most vibrant tourist wine (and surfing) region.

McGuigan Simeon Hunter V, NSW ★→★★ Nominal Hunter base of Australia's fifth-largest wine group, recently adding Miranda to its collection. Has been buffeted by stormy financial climate but shows signs of riding out the storm.

McLaren Vale SA Historic region on the southern outskirts of Adelaide. Big, alcoholic, flavoursome reds have great appeal to US, but Coriole, WIRRA WIRRA, and others show flavour can be gained without sacrificing elegance.

McWilliam's Yarra V, Vic; Coonawarra SA; Margaret River, WA r w (sw br) ★★→★★★ Still family-owned (Gallo lurking with 10% of shares) but has reinvented itself with great flair, always over-delivering. Elizabeth SEM the darling of Sydney, cheaper Hanwood blends in many parts of the world. Elizabeth and Lovedale SEMS so consistent and ageworthy that vintages irrelevant. In Oct 2007 added EVANS & TATE to its empire.

Merlot Was the star of the new millennium; from 9,000 tonnes in 1996 to 90,402 tonnes in 2007. Grown everywhere, but shouldn't be, and beginning to show signs of fading.

Mitchell Clare V, SA r w ★★→★★★ (RIES) 00' 01' 03 04 05' 06' Small family winery for excellent CAB SAUV and firmly structured dry RIES, under screwcap since 00.

Mitchelton Goulburn V, Vic r w (sw w) ★★ Reliable producer of RIES, SHIRAZ, CAB at several price points, plus speciality of Marsanne and Roussanne.

Mitolo McLaren Vale; Barossa, SA r ★★★ One of the best "virtual wineries" (ie contract v'yds, contract wineries, contract winemaker), paying top dollar for top-quality SHIRAZ and CAB; quality oak and winemaking by Ben GLAETZER. Heroic but (virtually) irresistible wines.

Moorilla Estate Tas r w (sp) ★★★ Senior winery on outskirts of Hobart on Derwent River: v.gd RIES, Gewurz, and CHARD; PINOT N now in the ascendant. Superb restaurant.

Moorooduc Estate Mornington Pen, Vic r w ★★★ Stylish and sophisticated (wild yeast, etc) producer of top-flight CHARD and PINOT N.

Mornington Peninsula Vic Exciting wines in new cool coastal area 40km south of Melbourne; 1,000 ha. Many high-quality, boutique wineries.

Morris NE Vic br (r w) ★★→★★★★ Old winery at RUTHERGLEN for some of Australia's greatest dessert Muscats and "Tokays". Offered for sale by Orlando late 2007.

Moss Wood Margaret R, WA r w ★★★★ (CAB SAUV) 77' 80' 85' 88 90' 91' 94 95' 96' 99' 01' 02 04' (05) To many, the best MARGARET RIVER winery (11.7 ha). SEM, CAB SAUV, CHARD, all with rich fruit flavours.

Mount Horrocks Clare V, SA w r ★★★→★★★★ Finest dry RIES and sweet Cordon Cut RIES; CHARD best in region.

Mount Langi Ghiran Grampians, Vic r w ★★★ (SHIRAZ) 81 84 88 89' 93' 95 96' 98 03' 04' 05' Esp for superb, rich, peppery, Rhône-like SHIRAZ, one of Australia's best cool-climate versions. Now owned by YERING STATION.

Mount Mary Yarra V, Vic r w ★★★★ (PINOT N) 97' 99 00' 02' 05' 06' (Quintet) 88' 90' 92' 94 95' 96' 97' 98' 99 00' 02 03 04' The late Dr. John Middleton made tiny amounts of suave CHARD, vivid PINOT N, and (best of all) CAB SAUV blend: *Australia's most Bordeaux-like "claret"*. All age impeccably. His family go on.

Mudgee NSW Long-established region northwest of Sydney. Big reds, surprisingly fine SEM, and full CHARD.

AUSTRALIA

Murdock Coonawarra, SA r ★★★ Long-term grower now making classic CAB SAUV.

Murray Valley SA, Vic, NSW Vast irrigated v'yds. Now at the epicentre of the drought/climate-change firestorm.

Neagles Rock Clare V, SA r w ★★★ Husband and wife industry veterans who took the plunge into winery ownership, making every post a winner. RIES, SHIRAZ and Sangiovese all v.gd.

Ninth Island See PIPERS BROOK.

O'Leary Walker Wines Clare V, SA r w ★★★ Two whizz-kids have mid-life crisis and leave BERINGER BLASS to do their own thing – v. well.

Orange NSW Cool-climate, high-elevation region giving lively CHARD, CAB SAUV, MERLOT, SHIRAZ.

Padthaway SA Large area developed as overspill of COONAWARRA. Cool climate; gd CHARD and excellent SHIRAZ (Orlando). Severe frost damage in 2006.

Paringa Estate Mornington Pen, Vic r w ★★★★ Maker of quite spectacular CHARD, PINOT N, and (late-picked) SHIRAZ, winning innumerable trophies.

Parker Estate Coonawarra, SA r ★★★ Small estate making v.gd CAB SAUV, esp Terra Rossa First Growth. Acquired by YERING STATION mid-2004.

Pemberton WA Region between MARGARET RIVER and GREAT SOUTHERN; initial enthusiasm for PINOT N replaced by MERLOT and SHIRAZ.

Penfolds Originally Adelaide, now everywhere r w (sp br) ★★–★★★★ (Grange) (Bin 707)(Grange) 52' 53' 55' 62' 63' 66' 71' 76' 78' 80' 83' 86' 90' 91' 94' 96' 98' 99' 01' 02' 03 (Cab S Bin 707) 64' 76' 86' 90' 91' 96' 02' 04' 05' (06') Consistently Australia's best red wine company, if you can decode its labels. Its Grange (was called Hermitage) is deservedly ★★★★. Yattarna CHARD was released in 98. Bin 707 CAB SAUV not far behind. Has hugely impressive 04, 05, and 06 reds coming up for release over the next 3 yrs.

Penley Estate Coonawarra, SA r w ★★★ High-profile, no-expense-spared winery. Rich, textured, fruit-and-oak CAB SAUV; SHIRAZ/CAB SAUV blend; CHARD.

Perth Hills WA Fledgling area 19 miles east of Perth with a larger number of growers on mild hillside sites. Millbrook and Western Range best.

Petaluma Adelaide Hills, SA r w sp ★★★★ (RIES) 80' 02' 03 04' 05' 06' (CHARD) 92' 01' 02 03' 04' 05' (CAB SAUV COONAWARRA) 79' 90' 91' 95' 98' 99 00' 03' 05' Created by the fearsome intellect and energy of (now retired) Brian Croser. Red wines richer from 1988 on. Fell prey to LION NATHAN 2002.

Peter Lehmann Wines Barossa, SA r w (sp br sw w) ★★–★★★ Defender of BAROSSA faith; fought off Allied-Domecq by marriage with Swiss Hess group. Consistently well-priced wines in substantial quantities. Try Stonewell SHIRAZ and Reserve Bin SEM and RIES with 5 yrs age.

Pewsey Vale Adelaide Hills, SA w ★★★→★★★★ Glorious RIES, especially The Contours, released with screwcap, 5 yrs bottle-age and multiple trophies.

Pierro Margaret R, WA r w ★★★ (CHARD) 96' 99' 00' 01' 02' 03 05' (06) Highly rated producer of expensive, tangy SEM/SAUV BL and v.gd barrel-fermented CHARD.

Pinot Noir 4,302 ha; 26,253 tonnes. Mostly used in sparkling. Exciting wines from south Victoria, TASMANIA, and ADELAIDE HILLS; plantings are increasing.

Pipers Brook Tas r w sp ★★★ (RIES) 98' 99' 00' 01' 02' 04' 06 (CHARD) 97 99' 00' 02' 05' Cool-area pioneer; v.gd RIES, PINOT N, restrained CHARD, and sparkling from Tamar Valley. Second label: Ninth Island. Owned by Belgian Kreglinger family, owners of Vieux-Ch-Certan (see Châteaux of Bordeaux).

Pirramimma McLaren Vale, SA r w ★★ Century-old family business with large v'yds moving with the times; snappy new packaging, the wines not forgotten.

Pirie Estate N Tas r w sp ★★→★★★ A phoenix arisen, with its own brand

and responsibility for TAMAR RIDGE and Rosevears Estate.

Plantagenet Mount Barker, WA r w (sp) ★★★ (r) 95 98' 01' 03 05' The region's elder statesman: wide range of varieties, esp rich CHARD, SHIRAZ, and vibrant, potent CAB SAUV.

Pondalowie Bendigo, Vic r ★★★ Flying winemakers with exciting SHIRAZ/ Viognier/Tempranillo in various combinations.

Primo Estate Adelaide Plains, SA r w dr (w sw) ★★★ Joe Grilli is a miracle-worker given the climate; successes include v.gd botrytized RIES, tangy Colombard, and potent Joseph CAB SAUV/MERLOT.

Pyrenees Vic Central Victoria region producing rich, often slightly minty reds.

Red Hill Estate Mornington Pen, Vic r w sp ★★→★★★ One of the larger and more important wineries; notably elegant wines.

Redman Coonawarra, SA r ★★★ Famous old name in COONAWARRA; red specialist: SHIRAZ, CAB SAUV, CAB SAUV/MERLOT. Wine fails to do justice to v'yd quality.

Redheads MacLaren V, SA r ★★ Tiny "studio" for super-concentrated reds.

Richmond Grove Barossa r w ★→★★★ Master winemaker John Vickery produces great RIES at bargain prices; other wines are OK. Owned by Orlando Wyndham.

Riesling 4,333 ha; 31,003 tonnes. Has a special place in the BAROSSA, EDEN, and CLARE VALLEYS. Usually made bone-dry; can be glorious with up to 20 yrs bottle-age. Screwcaps now the only accepted closure.

Riverina NSW Large-volume irrigated zone centred around Griffith. Its water supply will be better than the Murray Valley over 2008 and 2009. Thereafter it will be in the lap of the gods.

Robert Channon Wines Granite Belt, Qld r w ★→★★ Lawyer turned *vigneron* has 6.8 ha of permanently netted, immaculately trained v'yd producing v.gd VERDELHO (plus usual others).

Talking Strine

You thought it was just the British who talk about the weather? When two Australian winemakers meet, the first question they ask is "Had any rain?" And the answer, usually, is "Not much." Unless they're from the Hunter Valley, where the dams are overflowing. Drought, what drought?

Rockford Barossa, SA r w sp ★★→★★★★ Small producer from old, low-yielding v'yds; reds best, also iconic sparkling Black SHIRAZ.

Rosemount Estate Upper Hunter, V, McLaren Vale, Coonawarra, SA r w (sp) ★★ Rich Roxburgh CHARD, MCLAREN VALE Balmoral Syrah, MUDGEE Mountain Blue CAB SAUV/SHIRAZ, and COONAWARRA CAB SAUV lead the wide range. Part of FWE.

Rutherglen and **Glenrowan** Vic Two of 4 regions in the northeast Victoria Zone, justly famous for weighty reds and magnificent, fortified dessert wines.

St Hallett Barossa, SA r w ★★★ (Old Block) 86' 90' 91' 96 98' 99 01 02' 04' 05' 06' Old Block SHIRAZ the star; rest of range is smooth, stylish. LION NATHAN-owned.

St Sheila's SA p sw sp 36 22 38 Full-bodied fizzer. Ripper grog, too.

Saltram Barossa, SA r w ★★→★★★ Mamre Brook (SHIRAZ, CAB SAUV, CHARD) and No 1 SHIRAZ are leaders. Metala is associated Stonyfell label for Langhorne Creek CAB SAUV/SHIRAZ. An FWE brand.

Sandalford Swan V, WA r w (br) ★→★★ Fine old winery with contrasting styles of red and white single-grape wines from SWAN and MARGARET RIVER areas.

Sauvignon Blanc 4,606 ha; 36,517 tonnes. Usually not as distinctive as in New Zealand, but amazingly popular. Many styles, from bland to pungent.

Scotchmans Hill Geelong, Vic r w ★★ Makes significant quantities of stylish PINOT N, gd CHARD, and spicy SHIRAZ.

AUSTRALIA

NB Vintages in colour are those you should choose first for drinking in 2009.

Pannell, SC Mclaren Vale, SA r ★★★ Ex-HARDY wunderkind turned flying winemaker, Steve Pannell has produced a dazzling array of SHIRAZ- and GRENACHE-based wines for his own label.

Semillon 6,487 ha; 75,198 tonnes. Before the arrival of CHARD, Sem was the HUNTER VALLEY's answer to South Australia's RIES. Traditionally made without oak and extremely long-lived. Brief affair with oak terminated.

Seppelt Bendigo, Grampians, Henty r w sp br (sw w) ★★★ (St Peter's SHIRAZ) 71' **85' 86' 91' 96'** 97' 99' 02' 03' 04' 05' (06) Has been broken up and sold by FWE, notably SEPPELTSFIELD (see below) and amazing range of 100+-yr-old fortifieds. GRAMPIANS winery and table wines retained with Seppelt table wine brand, notably SHIRAZ, all sourced from premium Victoria regions.

Seppeltsfield Cellar Doors Barossa SA National Trust Heritage Winery purchased by Kilikanoon shareholders in 2007 and being restored to full working order. Priceless stocks of fortified wines in barrels dating back to 1878 still under the vigilant care of long-term winemaker, James Godfrey.

Setanta Wines Adelaide Hills, SA r w ★★★ The Sullivan family, first-generation Australians ex-Ireland, produce wonderful RIES, CHARD, SAUV BL, SHIRAZ and CAB SAUV with Irish mythology labels of striking design.

Sevenhill Clare V, SA r w (br) ★★ Owned by the Jesuitical Manresa Society since 1851. Consistently gd wine; SHIRAZ and RIES can be outstanding.

Seville Estate Yarra V, Vic r w ★★★ (SHIRAZ) **91' 94** 97' 00' 02' 03' 04' 05' 06 Ownership changes have not affected quality of CHARD, SHIRAZ, PINOT N.

Shadowfax Geelong, Vic r w ★★→★★★ Stylish new winery, part of Werribee Park; also hotel based on 1880s mansion. V.gd CHARD, PINOT N, SHIRAZ.

Shantell Yarra V, Vic r w ★★→★★★ Underrated producer with 30-yr-old v'yd. SEM, CHARD, PINOT N, CAB SAUV.

Shaw & Smith Adelaide Hills, SA w (r) ★★★ Founded by Martin Shaw and Australia's first MW, Michael Hill Smith. Crisp SAUV BL, complex, barrel-fermented M3 CHARD, and, of course, SHIRAZ.

Shelmerdine Vineyards Heathcote, Yarra V, Vic r w ★★ →★★★ Well-known family with high-quality wines from estate in the YARRA VALLEY and HEATHCOTE, the latter with unusual elegance and relatively low alcohol levels.

Shiraz 48,794 ha; 366,976 tonnes. Hugely flexible: velvety/earthy in the HUNTER; spicy, peppery, and Rhône-like in central and south Vic; or brambly, rum-sweet, and luscious in BAROSSA and environs (eg PENFOLDS' Grange).

Sirromet Queensland Coast r w ★★ A striking (100-ha) 75,000-case winery, with a 200-seat restaurant; biggest of many such new ventures. Wines from 100-plus ha of estate v'yds in GRANITE BELT consistently gd.

Smith, S & Sons (alias Yalumba) Barossa, SA r w sp br (sw w) ★★→★★★ Big old family firm with considerable verve. Full spectrum of high-quality wines, inc HEGGIES, PEWSEYVALE and YALUMBA. Angas Brut, a gd-value sparkling wine, and Oxford Landing varietals are now world brands.

South Burnett Queensland's second region: 15 wineries and more births (and some deaths) imminent, symptomatic of southeast corner of the state.

South Coast NSW Zone Includes Shoalhaven Coast and Southern Highlands.

Southcorp The former giant of the industry; now part of FWE. Owns LINDEMANS, PENFOLDS, ROSEMOUNT, Seaview, SEPPELT, WYNNS and many others.

Southern NSW Zone inc CANBERRA, Gundagai, Hilltops, Tumbarumba.

Stanton & Killeen Rutherglen, Vic br r ★★★ The sudden and untimely death of Chris Killeen in 2007 was a major blow to this fine maker of fortified and dry red wines, but his children will carry on as the fourth generation.

Stefano Lubiana S Tas r w sp ★★→★★★ Beautiful v'yds on the banks of the Derwent River 20 minutes from Hobart. Sparkling wine specialist, but also v.gd table wines inc PINOT N.

Stella Bella Margaret R, WA r w ★★★ Avant-garde label designs and names shouldn't obscure deadly serious commitment to quality. CAB SAUV, SEM/SAUV BL, CHARD, SHIRAZ, Sangiovese/CAB all shine.

Stonehaven Padthaway, SA r w ★★ First large (A$20 million) winery in PADTHAWAY region, built by HARDYS, servicing whole LIMESTONE COAST ZONE production.

Stonier Wines Mornington Pen, Vic r w ★★★ (CHARD) oo' **01 02** 03' 04 **04'** 05' 06' (PINOT N) oo' **02'** 03 04' **05'** 06' Consistently v.gd; Reserves outstanding, notable for their elegance. Owned by LION NATHAN.

Summerfield Pyrenees, Vic r (w) ★★ Consistent producer of estate-grown, blockbuster SHIRAZ and CAB SAUV, esp in Reserve appellation.

Sunbury see MACEDON.

Swan Valley (Swan V), WA Located 20 minutes north of Perth. Birthplace of wine in the west. Hot climate makes strong, low-acid table wines; being rejuvenated for wine tourism.

Tahbilk Goulburn V, Vic r w ★★–→★★★ (Marsanne) 74' 75' **82' 92' 97' 98' 99' 01' 03'** 05' 06' (SHIRAZ) 68' **71' 76' 86 98' 00** 02' 03 04' 05 Beautiful historic family estate: long-ageing reds, also RIES and Marsanne. Reserve CAB SAUV outstanding; value for money ditto. Rare 1860 Vines SHIRAZ, too.

Taltarni Pyrenees, Vic r w (sp) ★★ New management and winemaking team producing more sophisticated reds, esp Cephas.

Tamar Ridge N Tas r w (sp) ★★–→★★★ Public-company ownership, Dr. Richard Smart as viticulturist, Dr. Andrew Pirie as CEO/chief winemaker, and 230-+ ha of vines make this a major player in TASMANIA.

Tapanappa SA r ★★ New WRATTONBULLY collaboration between Brian Croser, Bollinger, and J-M Cazes of Pauillac (see France). To watch. Croser has bought back his old PETALUMA winery (not the brand) as home base.

Tarrawarra Yarra V, Vic r w ★★★ (CHARD) **oo 01'** 02' 03' 04' 05' 06' (PINOT N) oo 01' 02' 03 04' 05 06 Has moved from idiosyncratic to elegant, mainstream CHARD and PINOT N. Tin Cows is the second label.

Tarrington Henty, Vic r w ★★★ Cameo winery producing jewel-like CHARD (intense, no oak) and PINOT N in minuscule quantities.

Tasmania Production continues to surge, but still tiny. Great potential for sparkling, CHARD, PINOT N, and RIES in cool climate. Only region to report excess demand for grapes in 2006; frost will exacerbate imbalance in 2007.

Tatachilla McLaren Vale, SA r w ★★–→★★★ Significant production of nice whites and v.gd reds. Acquired by LION NATHAN in 2002.

Taylors Wines Clare V, SA r w ★★–→★★★ 580,000-case production of much-improved RIES, SHIRAZ, CAB SAUV. Exports under Wakefield Wines brand (trademark issues with Taylors of Oporto) with much success.

Ten Minutes by Tractor Mornington Pen, Vic r w ★★ Amusing name and sophisticated packaging rapidly growing under new (single) owner Martin Spedding. SAUV BL, CHARD, PINOT N are all gd.

T'Gallant Mornington Pen, Vic w (r) ★★ Improbable name and avant-garde labels for Australia's top Pinot Gr producer. Quixotic acquisition by FWE.

The Islander Estate Kangaroo Island, SA r w ★★ New, full-scale development by Jacques Lurton, planned as likely retirement venture. Flagship estate wine an esoteric blend of Sangiovese, Cab Fr, and Malbec. Watch this space.

Torbreck Barossa, SA ★★★★ r (w) The most stylish of the cult wineries beloved of the US; focus on old-vine Rhône varieties led by SHIRAZ.

Tower Estate Hunter V, NSW r w ★★★–→★★★★ Offers luxury convention facilities and portfolio of 10 wines made from grapes grown in the best parts of Australia. Impressive stuff. The creation of the late Len Evans (d. 2006).

AUSTRALIA

Trentham Estate Murray Darling (r) w ★→★★ 60,000 cases of family-grown and -made, sensibly priced wines from "boutique" winery on Murray River; gd restaurant, too. Deserves to survive, and hopefully will.

Turkey Flat Barossa, SA r p ★★★ Icon producer of rosé, GRENACHE, and SHIRAZ from core of 150-yr-old v'yd. Top stuff; controlled alcohol and oak.

Two Hands Barossa, SA r ★★→★★★ Savvy wine execs have created v. successful virtual winery with top SHIRAZ from PADTHAWAY, MCLAREN VALE, Langhorne Csreek, BAROSSA, and HEATHCOTE stuffed full of alcohol, rich fruit, oak, and the kitchen sink.

Tyrrell's Hunter V, NSW r w ★★★ (SEM) 94' 97' 98' 99' 00' 01' 03' 05' (CHARD Vat 47) 97' **98 99' 00'** 02' 04' 05' Australia's greatest maker of SEM, Vat 1 now joined with a series of individual v'yd or sub-regional wines, one or more of which will stand out in any given vintage, hence the unusual vintage ratings for the sems. Vat 47, too, continues to defy the climatic odds, albeit in a different style to LAKE'S FOLLY.

Upper Hunter NSW Established in early 1960s; irrigated vines (mainly whites), lighter and quicker developing than Lower Hunter's.

Vasse Felix Margaret R, WA r w ★★★ (CAB SAUV) **96 97** 98' 99' **01** 02 03' 04' 05' With CULLEN, pioneer of MARGARET RIVER. Elegant CAB SAUV, notable for mid-weight balance.

Verdelho 1,603 ha, 18,627 tonnes. Old white grape made in large volumes, unoaked and slightly sweet; cash cow.

Voyager Estate Margaret R, WA r w ★★★ 35,000 cases of estate-grown, rich, powerful SEM, SAUV BL, CHARD, CAB SAUV/MERLOT.

Wendouree Clare V, SA r ★★★★ Treasured maker (tiny quantities) of Australia's most powerful and concentrated reds, based on SHIRAZ, CAB SAUV, Mourvèdre, and Malbec. Immensely long-lived, so much so that any wine less than 20 yrs old will not have reached maturity, and all of the six different wines would justify slightly different ratings.

West Cape Howe Denmark, WA w r ★★★ 55,000 cases of dazzling RIES, SAUV BL, CHARD, SHIRAZ/VIOGNIER, CAB SAUV and Tempranillo. Amazing.

Willow Creek Mornington Pen, Vic r w ★★★ Impressive producer of CHARD and PINOT N in particular, with echoes of Burgundy. Perhaps it's the wine list at the excellent Salix restaurant with all 31 *grand cru* v'yds on offer.

Wilson Vinyard Clare V, SA r w ★★ Stylish RIES from Clare and adjoining Polish Hill River; Hand Plunge SHIRAZ and CAB SAUV often of same quality.

Wirra Wirra McLaren Vale, SA r w (sp sw w) ★★★ (RSW SHIRAZ) 98' 99' 01' 02' 04' 05' 06' (CAB SAUV) 97' 98' **99** 01' 02' 04' 05' 06' High-quality wines making a big impact. RSW SHIRAZ has edged in front of CAB SAUV; both superb. Angelus CAB SAUV now Dead Ringer in export markets.

Wolf Blass Barossa, SA r w (sp, sw, br) ★★★ (CAB SAUV blend) **90' 91' 94** 96' 98' 02' 04 05' (06') Founded by the ebullient Wolf Blass, now swallowed up by FWE (see also Beringer Blass, California). It is well served by winemakers Chris Hatcher (chief) and Caroline Dunn (reds).

Woodlands Margaret R, WA r (w) ★★★→★★★★ 7 ha of 30-plus-yr-old CAB SAUV among top v'yds in region, joined by younger but still v.gd plantings of other B'x reds. Still family-owned and run, but consultancy advice has lifted quality to sensational levels, esp single-barrel Réserve du Cave releases.

Wrattonbully SA Important grape-growing region in LIMESTONE COAST ZONE for 30 yrs; profile lifted by recent arrival of TAPANAPPA.

Wynns Coonawarra, SA r w ★★★ (SHIRAZ) 55' 63 86' **90' 91' 94' 96'** 97 98' 99' 00 02 04 05' (CAB SAUV) 57' 60' 82' **85' 86'** 90' 91' 94' 96' 98' 99' 00 02 04 05' SOUTHCORP-owned COONAWARRA classic. RIES, CHARD, SHIRAZ, and CAB SAUV are all v.gd, esp John Riddoch CAB SAUV and Michael SHIRAZ.

Yabby Lake Mornington Pen, Vic r w ★★★ Joint venture between movie-distribution magnate Robert Kirby, Larry McKenna (ex-Martinborough), and Tod Dexter (ex-STONIER) (affiliated to HEATHCOTE estate), utterly driven by the goal of quality.

Yalumba See S SMITH & SONS.

Yarra Burn Yarra V, Vic r w sp ★★→★★★ Estate making SEM, SAUV BL, CHARD, sparkling PINOT N/CHARD/Pinot Meunier. Acquired by HARDYS in 1995. Bastard Hill CHARD and PINOT N legitimate flag-bearers.

Yarra Valley Superb historic area nr Melbourne. Growing emphasis on v. successful PINOT N, CHARD, SHIRAZ, and sparkling. Lower-altitude v'yds, unprecedented frost damage in Nov 2006, followed by the discovery of phylloxera, so far a single isolated patch.

Yarra Yarra Yarra V, Vic r w ★★★ Recently increased to 7 ha, giving greater access to fine SEM/SAUV BL and CAB SAUV, each in classic B'x style.

Yarra Yering Yarra V, Vic r w ★★★→★★★★ (Dry Reds) 80' 81' 82' **83 84 85** 90' 91' **93' 94' 95 96 97' 99' 00' 01** 02' 03 04' 05' 06' Best-known Lilydale boutique winery. Esp racy, powerful PINOT N; deep, herby CAB SAUV (Dry Red No 1); SHIRAZ (Dry Red No 2). Luscious, daring flavours in red and white. Also fortified "Port-Sorts" from the correct grapes.

Yeringberg Yarra V, Vic r w ★★★ (Marsanne) **91' 92 94' 95** 97 98 00 02' 04 05' 06'(CAB SAUV) 77' **80 81' 84' 88' 90** 97' **98 00' 02'** 04 05' Dreamlike, historic estate still in the hands of founding family. Makes small quantities of v. high-quality Marsanne, Roussanne, CHARD, CAB SAUV and PINOT N.

Yering Station/Yarrabank Yarra V, Vic r w sp ★★★ On site of Victoria's first v'yd; replanted after 80-yr gap. Extraordinary joint venture: Yering Station table wines (Reserve CHARD, PINOT N, SHIRAZ VIOGNIER); Yarrabank (esp fine sparkling wines for Champagne Devaux). Decimated by frost, but has enough stock to weather the storm.

Zema Estate Coonawarra, SA r ★★→★★★ One of the last bastions of hand-pruning in COONAWARRA; silkily powerful, disarmingly straightforward reds.

AUSTRALIA

*Words within entries marked like this **Alter Ego de Palmer** indicate wines especially enjoyed by Hugh Johnson over the past 12 months (mid '07–'08).*

New Zealand

**More heavily shaded areas are the
wine-growing regions**

Northland

Auckland
Auckland ○ ○ Waiheke Island

Waikato

Gisborne

Hawke's
Bay

Wairarapa
(incl Martinborough)
Nelson
Nelso ○ ○ **Wellington**
Marlborough ○ **Blenheim**

Canterbury Waipara
○ **Christchurch**

Tasman Sea

Central Otago

○ *Pacific Ocean*
Dunedin

N ew Zealand often wins trophies for the best Sauvignon Blanc and
Pinot Noir in international competitions, yet its 550 wineries produce
just 0.5% of the world's wine. The area of bearing vineyards has tripled in
the past decade. The key export is Sauvignon Blanc from the sunny but
nocturnally chilly Marlborough region. Top models – Saint Clair Wairau
Reserve Sauvignon Blanc is the current showstopper – are strikingly
aromatic and mouth-wateringly crisp, with pungent tropical fruit and
herbaceous flavours. Half the country's exports, depressingly, are of this
predictable variety. Pinot Noir is typically scented, vibrant and supple,
with drink-young appeal. The sturdy, well-rounded Chardonnays from
Gisborne and Hawke's Bay are less fashionable, as are Hawke's Bay's
often stylish blends of Merlot and Cabernet Sauvignon. Fast-emerging
stars are Pinot Gris (mouth-filling and soft in the north, lighter and crisper
in the south), and Syrah, yielding perfumed, peppery, richly varietal reds
in Hawke's Bay and on Waiheke Island.

Recent vintages

2007 Biggest-ever harvest, although low-cropping in the smaller regions.
Notably dry autumn yielded excellent wines in Hawke's Bay and Gisborne,
and punchy, ripe, slightly lower-alcohol Marlborough Sauvignon Blanc.

2006 Record crop. In the North Island some reds were caught by autumn rains.
Average to good Marlborough Sauvignon; some lack pungency.

2005 Much lower-yielding than 2004, due to exceptionally cold, wet, early
summer. Late summer and autumn variable but often good. Excellent
Marlborough Sauvignon Blanc and Pinot Noir.

Words within entries marked like this *Alter Ego de Palmer* indicate wines
especially enjoyed by Hugh Johnson over the past 12 months (mid '07–'08).

2004 Record crop, reflecting fast-expanding vineyard area and heavy yields. Exceptionally wet Feb, but cool, dry autumn. Variable quality, with some Sauvignon Blanc lacking depth.

2003 Frost-affected season, yielding the lightest crop yet. Unripe flavours in some wines; excellent intensity in others.

Akarua Central Otago ★★ Respected producer with powerful, concentrated Cadence Pinot N, creamy, buttery Chard, and full-bodied, dry, spicy Pinot Gr. Supple, charming, second-tier Pinot N, labelled Gullies.

Allan Scott Marlborough ★★ Excellent Ries (from vines up to 30 yrs old), gd Chard, Sauv Bl; sturdy spicy Pinot N.

Alpha Domus Hawke's Bay ★★ Gd Chard and concentrated reds, especially savoury Merlot-based The Navigator, and notably dark rich Cab Sauv-based The Aviator. Top wines labelled AD.

Amisfield Central Otago ★★ Impressive fleshy, smooth Pinot Gr and floral, complex Pinot N. Lake Hayes is lower-tier label.

Astrolabe Marlborough ★★ Label owned by WHITEHAVEN winemaker Simon Waghorn. Strikingly intense harmonious Sauv Bl.

Ata Rangi Martinborough ★★★ Small but highly respected winery. Outstanding *Pinot N (03 05 06') is one of NZ's greatest* and v.gd young-vine Crimson Pinot N. Rich, concentrated Craighall Chard and Lismore Pinot Gr.

Auckland Largest city in NZ. Henderson, Huapai, Kumeu, Matakana, Clevedon, Waiheke Island districts – pricey, variable B'x-style reds and ripe, rounded Chard – nearby.

Awatere Valley Marlborough Important sub-region, slightly cooler than the larger WAIRAU VALLEY, with racy herbaceous, minerally Sauv Bl and scented, slightly leafy Pinot N.

Babich Henderson (Auckland) ★★→★★★ Mid-size family firm, established 1916; quality, value. AUCKLAND, HAWKE'S BAY, and MARLBOROUGH v'yds. Refined, slow-maturing Irongate Chard (04) and tight elegant Irongate Cab Sauv/Merlot/Cab Franc (single v'yd). Ripe, dry MARLBOROUGH Sauv Bl.

Benfield & Delamare Martinborough ★★ Tiny winery, surrounded by Pinot N, producers of elegant, long-lived B'x-style reds.

Bilancia Hawke's Bay ★★ Small producer of classy Syrah (inc brilliant, hill-grown La Collina) and rich Viognier, Pinot Gr.

Blackenbrook Nelson ★★ Small winery with perfumed, rich Gewurz, Pinot Gr, Ries; punchy Sauv Bl; promising Pinot N.

Brancott Vineyards ★→★★★ Brand used by PERNOD RICARD NEW ZEALAND in US.

Brightwater Nelson ★★ Impressive whites, especially crisp, flavour-packed Ries and Sauv Bl. Top wines labelled Rutherford.

Brookfield Hawke's Bay ★★ Outstanding "gold label" Cab Sauv/Merlot; gd Chard, Pinot Gr, and Gewurz. *Hillside Syrah is a winner*.

Cable Bay Waiheke Island ★★ Mid-sized producer with tight, refined Waiheke Chard and spicy, savoury, Five Hills red; subtle, finely textured MARLBOROUGH Sauv Bl. Second label is Culley.

Canterbury NZ's fifth largest wine region; most top v'yds in warm, sheltered Waipara district. Long, dry summers favour Pinot N, Ries.

Carrick Central Otago ★★ Bannockburn winery with flinty, flavourful whites (Pinot Gr, Sauv Bl, Chard, Ries) and densely packed Pinot N, built to last.

Central Otago (r) 06 (w) 06 Fast-expanding, cool mountainous region (now NZ's fourth largest) in southern South Island. Scented, crisp Ries and Pinot Gr; Pinot N perfumed and silky, with intense character. Best drunk young.

Chard Farm Central Otago ★★ Fresh, vibrant Ries, Pinot Gr, and *perfumed, graceful, supple Pinot N*.

Church Road Hawke's Bay ★★→★★★ PERNOD RICARD NEW ZEALAND winery. Rich, refined Chard and elegant, distinctly Bordeaux-like Merlot/Cab Sauv. Top Reserve wines; prestige, claret-style red, Tom (02).

Churton Marlborough ★★ Subtle, complex, finely textured Sauv Bl; fragrant, spicy, v. harmonious Pinot N.

Clearview Hawke's Bay ★★→★★★ Burly, lush, supercharged Reserve Chard; dark, rich Reserve Cab Fr, Enigma (Merlot-based), Old Olive Block (Cab Sauv blend).

Clifford Bay Marlborough ★★ Single-v'yd, AWATERE VALLEY producer of fresh, lively Chard, Ries, Pinot N. Scented, intense Sauv Bl is best. Now linked to Vavasour.

Clos Henri Marlborough ★★→★★★ Established by Henri Bourgeois (see France). First vintage 2003. Deliciously weighty, rich, rounded Sauv Bl and vibrant, supple Pinot N.

Cloudy Bay Marlborough ★★★ Large-volume Sauv Bl (dry, finely textured), Chard (robust, complex, crisp), and Pinot N (floral, supple) are v.gd. Pelorus sparkling toasty, rich. Rarer Gewurz, Late-Harvest Ries, and Te Koko (oak-aged Sauv Bl) now the finest wines. Pinot Gr is in the wings.

Cooper's Creek Auckland ★★ Excellent Swamp Reserve Chard; v.gd Sauv Bl, Ries; top-value Viognier; floral slightly spicy Arneis (NZ's first).

Corbans Auckland ★→★★★ Established 1902, now PERNOD RICARD N Z brand. Best wines: Cottage Block; Private Bin. Quality from basic to outstanding.

Craggy Range Hawke's Bay ★★→★★★ Mid-sized winery with v'yds in MARTINBOROUGH and HAWKE's BAY. Restrained Sauv Bl, stylish Chard, Pinot N; strikingly dense, ripe firm Merlot and Syrah from GIMBLETT GRAVELS. To follow.

Daniel Le Brun Marlborough ★★ Best known for citrus, yeasty Brut NV. Now a brand of Lion Nathan.

Delegat's Auckland ★★ Large, fast-expanding company, still mostly family-owned. V'yds and new NZ$73-million winery at MARLBOROUGH. Reserve Chard, Merlot, and Cab Sauv/Merlot offer v.gd quality and value. Hugely successful Oyster Bay brand: fresh fruit-driven Chard and Sauv Bl, elegant Pinot N.

Delta Marlborough ★★ Promising new producer with substantial, graceful Pinot N. Top label: Hatter's Hill.

Deutz Auckland ★★★ Champagne company gives name to fine sparkling from MARLBOROUGH by PERNOD RICARD NEW ZEALAND. NV: lively, yeasty, flinty. Vintage Blanc de Blancs: finely focused, citrus, piercing.

Dog Point Marlborough ★★ Grape-grower Ivan Sutherland and winemaker James Healy (both ex-CLOUDY BAY) produce unusually complex, finely textured, oak-aged Sauv Bl (Section 94), Chard, and Pinot N.

Dry River Martinborough ★★★ Tiny winery, now American-owned. Penetrating, long-lived Chard, Ries, Pinot Gr, Gewurz, and notably ripe, powerful, slowly evolving Pinot N (03' 04).

Escarpment Martinborough ★★ Sturdy, Alsace-like Pinot Gr and complex, leafy Pinot N from Larry McKenna, ex-MARTINBOROUGH VINEYARD. Top label: Kupe.

Esk Valley Hawke's Bay ★★→★★★ Owned by VILLA MARIA. Some of NZ's most voluptuous Merlot-based reds (especially Reserve label 02' 04), excellent Merlot rosé (NZ's best), satisfying Chards, Chenin Bl and Sauv Bl.

Fairhall Downs Marlborough ★★ Single-v'yd wines from elevated site. Weighty, dry Pinot Gr, intense, racy Sauv Bl and perfumed, smooth Pinot N.

Felton Road Central Otago ★★★ Star winery in warm Bannockburn area. Bold, supple Pinot N Block 3 and 5 and light, intense Ries outstanding; excellent Chard and regular Pinot N.

Fiddler's Green Waipara ★★ Flavourful, crisp, cool-climate Chard, Ries and Sauv Bl; vibrant, cherryish Pinot N.

Forrest Marlborough ★★ Mid-size winery; easy-drinking Chard, Sauv Bl, excellent Ries; gorgeous botrytized Ries; flavour-crammed HAWKE'S BAY Cornerstone

Vineyard Cab Sauv/Merlot/Malbec. V.gd new flagship range, labelled John Forrest Collection.

Foxes Island Marlborough ★★ Small producer of rich, smooth Chard, finely textured Sauv Bl, and elegant, supple Pinot N.

Framingham Marlborough ★★ Owned by PERNOD RICARD NEW ZEALAND. Superb aromatic whites, *notably intense zesty Ries*, and lush slightly sweet Pinot Gr, Gewurz. Subtle, dry Sauv Bl. Scented, silky Pinot N.

Fromm Marlborough ★★★ Swiss-founded, focusing on v. powerful red wines. Sturdy, firm, long-lived Pinot N, esp under Fromm Vineyard and Clayvin Vineyard labels. Also unusually *stylish Clayvin Chard*. Earlier-drinking La Strada range also v.gd.

Gibbston Valley Central Otago ★★ Pioneer winery with popular restaurant. Greatest strength is Pinot N, especially robust, exuberantly fruity Reserve (**05** 06). Racy local whites, especially zingy, flavour-packed, medium-dry Ries.

Giesen Canterbury ★ German family winery. Gd, slightly honeyed Ries; bulk of production is average-quality MARLBOROUGH Sauv Bl. Offered for sale in 2007.

Gimblett Gravels Hawke's Bay Defined area with v. free-draining soils, noted for rich, ripe, B'x-style reds and Syrah.

Gisborne (r) **06 07'** (w) **06 07'** NZ's third-largest region. Abundant sunshine and rain, with fertile soils. Key strength is Chard (typically deliciously fragrant, ripe, and soft in its youth). Gd Gewurz and Viognier; Merlot more variable.

Goldwater Waiheke Island ★★→★★★ Region's pioneer Cab Sauv/Merlot Goldie (**00' 02 04**) has Médoc-like finesse. Also crisp, citrus Chard and solid Sauv Bl, from MARLBOROUGH. Sold in 2006 to NZ Wine Fund (also owns VAVASOUR).

Gravitas Marlborough ★★ Solid Chard (Reserve and Unoaked), subtle, sustained Sauv Bl and graceful, flowing Pinot N.

Greenhough Nelson ★★→★★★ One of region's top producers, with immaculate and deep-flavoured Ries, Sauv, Chard, Pinot N. Top label: Hope Vineyard.

Grove Mill Marlborough ★★→★★★ Attractive whites, inc vibrant Chard; excellent Ries, Sauv, and slightly sweet Pinot Gr. Gd, lower-tier Sanctuary brand. First winery to earn CarboNZero certification.

Hans Herzog Marlborough ★★★ Established by Swiss immigrants. Power-packed, pricey, but classy Merlot/Cab Sauv, Montepulciano, Pinot N, Chard, Viognier and Pinot Gr. Sold under Hans brand in Europe and US.

Hawke's Bay (r) **02' 04** 05' 06 (w) NZ's second-largest region. Long history of winemaking in sunny climate; shingly and heavier soils. Full, rich Merlot and Cab Sauv-based reds in gd vintages; Syrah a fast-rising star; powerful Chard; rounded Sauv Bl; NZ's best Viognier.

Highfield Marlborough ★★ Japanese owned with quality Ries, Chard, Sauv Bl, and Pinot N. Elstree sparkling disappointing in 02 and 03.

Huia Marlborough ★★ Mouth-filling, subtle wines that age well, inc savoury, rounded Chard and perfumed, well-spiced Gewurz.

Hunter's Marlborough ★★→★★★ Pioneering winery with intense, immaculate Sauv Bl. *Fine, delicate Chard*. Excellent sparkling (Miru Miru), Ries, Gewurz; light, elegant Pinot N.

Isabel Estate Marlborough ★→★★★ Family estate with formerly outstanding Pinot N, Sauv Bl, and Chard, but lately less exciting.

Jackson Estate Marlborough ★★ Consistently lively, full-flavoured Sauv Bl, attractive, fruit-driven Chard, and sweet-fruited and supple Pinot N (much improved since 05).

Johanneshof Marlborough ★★ Small, low-profile winery with outstandingly perfumed, lush Gewurz. Other wines more variable.

Kaituna Valley Canterbury ★★→★★★ Small producer with v'yds nr Christchurch and in MARLBOROUGH. Consistently v. powerful, multi-award-winning Pinot N.

NEW ZEALAND

Karikari Northland ★★ NZ's northernmost v'yd and winery, American owned, with rich, ripe Bordeaux-style reds, Pinotage, and Syrah.

Kathy Lynskey Marlborough ★★ Gd aromatic whites (Gewurz, Pinot Gr); ripe, passion fruit/lime Sauv Bl; stylish Pinot N (Castro Reserve powerful, firm; Block 36 Reserve floral, charming).

Kemblefield Hawke's Bay ★→★★ US-owned winery. Solid reds; ripely herbal, oak-aged Sauv Bl; soft, peppery Gewurz, and fleshy, lush Chard.

Kim Crawford Hawke's Bay ★★ Now part of US-based Constellation empire. Numerous labels, inc rich, oaky GISBORNE Chard and scented, strong-flavoured MARLBOROUGH Sauv Bl. Top range labelled SP (Small Parcel).

Kumeu River Auckland ★★→★★★ Rich, refined Kumeu Estate Chard (**06'** 07) single-v'yd Mate's Vineyard Chard even more opulent. Two new, single-v'yd Chards in 06 (Coddington is powerful, peachy; Hunting Hill tight, elegant). Second label: Kumeu River Village.

Lake Chalice Marlborough ★★ Small producer with fresh, vibrant, creamy Chard and incisive, slightly sweet Ries; Sauv Bl of excellent quality. Platinum premium label.

Lawson's Dry Hills Marlborough ★★→★★★ Weighty wines with intense flavours. Unusually complex Sauv Bl and opulent Gewurz; gd Pinot Gr and Ries.

Lincoln Auckland ★ Long-established family winery. Gd-value varietals of improving quality: buttery GISBORNE Chard (top label Reserve). New export brand: Promised Land.

Lindauer See PERNOD RICARD NEW ZEALAND.

Longridge ★ Former CORBANS brand, now owned by PERNOD RICARD NZ. Reliable wines (inc citrus, lightly oaked Chard) typically from HAWKE'S BAY.

Margrain Martinborough ★★ Small winery with firm, concentrated Chard, Ries, Pinot Gr, Gewurz, and Pinot N, all of which reward bottle-age.

Marlborough (r) 05' **06** 07' (w) 07' NZ's largest region (more than half of all plantings). Warm days and cold nights give aromatic, crisp whites. Intense Sauv Bl, from sharp, green capsicum to ripe tropical fruit. Fresh, limey Ries; v.

Sustainability

During the "food miles" debate, British consumers have been urged to switch from New Zealand to French wines, on environmental grounds. Yet an influential study by Lincoln University, near Christchurch, proved that New Zealand agriculture is so energy-efficient that its products, even after being shipped to the other side of the world, have racked up lower carbon emissions than the same goods produced in Europe.

"While we reject the specious argument around 'food miles', this catchphrase underlines the hold environmental issues have on consumer thinking in key markets," says New Zealand Winegrowers. "In short, the importance of sustainability has never been clearer."

Over 60% of New Zealand's vineyard area, and 70% of its wine volume, are now covered by the industry's Sustainable Winegrowing system. Due to heavy compliance costs, however, until recently most small wineries have been reluctant to join the initiative.

Sustainable Winegrowing itself has come under attack from the Soil and Health Association of New Zealand: "Really, they are misusing the word, because Sustainable Winegrowing is not sustainable." About NZ$1,000 of fungicides, herbicides and insecticides are applied per hectare per year in New Zealand vineyards. The industry recently adopted the goal of having all New Zealand grapes and wine produced under independently audited sustainability schemes by 2012.

promising Pinot Gr and Gewurz; Chard leaner, more appley than HAWKE'S BAY. High-quality sparkling and botrytized Ries. Pinot N underrated, top examples among NZ's finest.

Martinborough (r) 03'06' (w) 06'07 Small, high-quality area in south WAIRARAPA (foot of North Island). Warm summers, dry autumns, gravelly soils. Success with white grapes, but most renowned for sturdy, rich, long-lived Pinot N.

Martinborough Vineyard Martinborough ★★★ Distinguished small winery; *one of NZ's top Pinot Noirs (03'06')*. Rich, biscuity Chard and intense Ries.

Matakana Estate Auckland ★→★★ Largest producer in Matakana district. Average to gd Chard, Pinot Gr, Sem, Syrah, and Merlot/Cab Sauv blend.

Matariki Hawke's Bay ★★ Stylish white and red, large v'yds in stony Gimblett Road. Rich Sauv Bl; tight, concentrated Chard; robust Quintology red blend.

Matua Valley Auckland ★★→★★★ Producer of NZ's first Sauv Bl in 1974. Now large company owned by Beringer Blass (see California), with v'yds in 4 regions. Top range Ararimu includes fat, savoury Chard and dark, rich Merlot/Cab Sauv. Numerous attractive GISBORNE (esp Judd Chard), HAWKE'S BAY, and MARLBOROUGH wines (Shingle Peak). Shingle Peak Sauv Bl top value.

Maven Marlborough ★★ Young, quality-focused producer with eye-catching labels – several different for each vintage of each wine. Ripe, tropical fruit Sauv Bl (Reserve is partly barrel-fermented).

Mills Reef Bay of Plenty ★★→★★★ The Preston family produces impressive wines from HAWKE'S BAY grapes. Top Elspeth range include dense, rich B'x-style reds and Syrah. Reserve range reds also impressive and outstanding value.

Millton Gisborne ★→★★★ Region's top small winery: mostly organic. Hill-grown, single-v'yd Clos de Ste Anne Chard is superbly concentrated and full of personality. Rich, long-lived Chenin Bl is NZ's finest (honeyed in wetter vintages; tight, pure and long-lived in drier seasons).

Mission Hawke's Bay ★→★★ NZ's oldest wine producer, established 1851, still run by Catholic Society of Mary. Solid varietals: creamy-smooth Chard is especially gd value. Reserve range includes B'x-style reds and Chard. Top label: Jewelstone (v. classy, concentrated Chard).

Monkey Bay ★ NOBILO brand, modestly priced and v. popular in US. Easy-drinking, dryish Chard; gently sweet Sauv Bl; leafy, slightly sweet Cab/Merlot; fresh, fruity Merlot.

Montana Auckland ★→★★★ Formerly name of NZ wine giant, now a key brand of PERNOD RICARD NEW ZEALAND. Top wines are Letter Series (eg "B" Brancott Sauv Bl). Terroir Series is second tier, followed by Reserve. Big-selling varietals include smooth, peachy, lightly oaked GISBORNE Chard and crisp, grassy MARLBOROUGH Sauv Bl.

Morton Estate Bay of Plenty ★→★★ Respected mid-size producer with v'yds in HAWKE'S BAY and MARLBOROUGH. Refined Black Label Chard is one of NZ's best (02'04). White Label Chard also v.gd and top value.

Mount Riley Marlborough ★→★★ Fast-growing company. Easy-drinking Chard; punchy Sauv Bl; dark, flavoursome Merlot/Malbec. Top wines labelled Seventeen Valley. All gd value.

Mt Difficulty Central Otago ★★ Quality producer in relatively hot Bannockburn area. Best known for v. refined, intense Pinot N (Roaring Meg is for early consumption; Single V'yd Pipeclay Terrace is dense, lasting).

Muddy Water Waipara ★★ Small, high-quality producer with beautifully intense Ries, minerally Chard, and savoury, subtle Pinot N.

Mud House Marlborough ★→★★ Punchy, vibrant Sauv Bl (more herbaceous than WAIPARA Hills version). Purchased in 2006 by WAIPARA HILLS.

Nautilus Marlborough ★★ Small range of distributors Négociants (NZ), owned by S Smith & Sons (see Australia). Top wines include stylish, finely balanced

NEW ZEALAND

Sauv Bl, savoury Pinot N, and fragrant sparkler. Lower-tier: Twin Islands.

Nelson (r) **06** 07 (w) **06** 07 Small, fast-growing region west of MARLBOROUGH; climate wetter but equally sunny. Clay soils of Upper Moutere hills and silty Waimea Plains. Strengths in aromatic whites, esp Ries, Sauv Bl, Pinot Gr, Gewurz; also gd Chard and Pinot N.

Neudorf Nelson ★★★ A top smallish winery. Powerful yet elegant Moutere Chard (03' **04** 05) is one of NZ's greatest; superb, v. savoury Moutere Pinot N. Sauv Bl and Ries also gd.

Ngatarawa Hawke's Bay ★★→★★★ Mid-sized. Top Alwyn Reserve range, inc powerful Chard, Cab Sauv, Merlot. Mid-range Glazebrook also excellent.

Nga Waka Martinborough ★★ Steely whites of high quality. Outstanding Sauv Bl; piercingly flavoured Ries; robust, savoury Chard. Pinot N scented and supple.

Nobilo Auckland ★→★★ NZ's second largest wine company, now owned by Constellation (US-based). MARLBOROUGH Sauv Bl is gd but sharply priced. Superior varietals labelled Icon. v.gd Drylands Sauv Bl. Cheaper wines labelled Fernleaf and Fall Harvest. See also SELAKS, MONKEY BAY.

Olssens Central Otago ★★ Consistently attractive Pinot N, from first Bannockburn v'yd. Softly seductive, rich Jackson Barry Pinot N is middle-tier; top wine is bold Slapjack Creek Reserve Pinot N.

Omaka Springs Marlborough ★→★★ Punchy, herbaceous Sauv Bl (especially Falveys), solid Ries, Chard, and leafy reds.

Palliser Martinborough ★★→★★★ One of the area's largest and best wineries. Superb tropical-fruit Sauv Bl in favourable seasons (rare lately), excellent Chard, Ries, Pinot N. Top wines: Palliser Estate. Lower tier: Pencarrow.

Pask, C J Hawke's Bay ★★ Mid-size winery, extensive v'yds in GIMBLETT GRAVELS. Gd to excellent Chard. Cab Sauv, Syrah and Merlot-based reds now consistently impressive. Top wines labelled Declaration.

Pegasus Bay Waipara ★★→★★★ Small but distinguished range: notably taut, cool-climate Chard; lush, complex, oaked Sauv Bl/Sem; *rich, zingy, medium Ries*. Merlot-based reds are region's finest. Pinot N lush and silky (especially Prima Donna). Second label: Main Divide.

Peregrine Central Otago ★★ Crisp, cool-climate Ries, Pinot Gr, Gewurz of variable quality, and beautifully rich, silky, gd-value Pinot N.

Pernod Ricard New Zealand Auckland ★→★★★ NZ wine giant, formerly called MONTANA. Wineries in AUCKLAND, GISBORNE, HAWKE'S BAY, and MARLBOROUGH. Extensive co-owned v'yds for MARLBOROUGH whites, inc top-value MONTANA Sauv Bl, Ries, and Chard (Reserve range esp gd). Strength in sparkling, inc DEUTZ, and stylish, fine-value Lindauer. Elegant CHURCH ROAD reds and quality Chard. Other key brands: CORBANS, LONGRIDGE, Saints. STONELEIGH, Triplebank offers intense, racy AWATERE VALLEY wines.

Providence Auckland ★★★ Rare, Merlot-based red from Matakana district. Perfumed, lush, and silky; v. high-priced.

Quartz Reef Central Otago ★★ Quality producer with weighty, flinty Pinot Gr; substantial rich Pinot N; *yeasty, lingering, Champagne-like sparkler Chauvet*.

Rimu Grove Nelson ★★ Small, American-owned, coastal v'yd. Concentrated, minerally Chard and Pinot Gr; rich, spicy Pinot N.

Rippon Vineyard Central Otago ★★ Stunning v'yd on shores of Lake Wanaka. Fine-scented, fruity Pinot N and slowly evolving whites, inc steely, appley Ries.

Rockburn Central Otago ★★ Crisp, racy Chard, Pinot Gr, Gewurz, Ries, Sauv Bl. Fragrant, supple, rich Pinot N is best.

Sacred Hill Hawke's Bay ★★→★★★ Middle-size producer, partly Chinese-owned. Distinguished Riflemans Chard (powerful, from cool, elevated site) and Brokenstone Merlot. Punchy, off-dry MARLBOROUGH Sauv Bl. Other brands: Gunn Estate (bold, lush Skeetfield Chard), Wild South (Marlborough range).

Saint Clair Marlborough ★★→★★★ Fast-growing, export-led producer with substantial v'yds. Prolific award winner. Punchy Sauv Bl, fragrant Ries, easy Chard, and plummy, early-drinking Merlot. Rich Reserve Chard, Merlot, Pinot N. Exceptional Wairau Reserve Sauv Blanc. Bewildering array of second-tier Pioneer Block wines (incl 8 Sauv Bls). Vicar's Choice is lower tier, gd value.

St Helena Canterbury ★ The region's oldest winery, founded near Christchurch in 1978. Light, supple Pinot N (Reserve is bolder). Chard variable but gd in better vintages. MARLBOROUGH Sauv Bl solid.

Seifried Estate Nelson ★★ Region's biggest winery, founded by an Austrian. Known initially for well-priced Ries and Gewurz; now also producing gd-value, often excellent Sauv Bl and Chard. Best wines: Winemakers Collection.

Selaks Marlborough ★→★★ Mid-size family firm bought by NOBILO in 1998. Moderately priced, fruit-driven Marlborough Sauv Bl, Ries, and Chard under Premium Selection label are its strengths; reds are mostly plain but improving. Top wines: Founders Reserve.

Seresin Marlborough ★★→★★★ Established by NZ film producer Michael Seresin. Stylish, concentrated Sauv Bl, Chard, Pinots N and Gr, Ries, Noble Ries. Second tier: Momo (gd quality, value).

Sileni Hawke's Bay ★★ Architecturally striking winery with extensive v'yds and classy Chard and Merlot. Top wines: EV (Exceptional Vintage), then Estate Selection, and Cellar Selection. Rich, smooth Marlborough Sauv Bl (esp The Straits).

Southbank Hawke's Bay ★→★★ Fast-growing new producer. Creamy, rich HAWKE'S BAY Chard and penetrating MARLBOROUGH Sauv Bl are best.

Spy Valley Marlborough ★★ High-achieving company with extensive v'yds. Sauv Bl, Chard, Ries, Gewurz, Pinot Gr, and Pinot N are all v.gd and priced right. Superb new top selection: Envoy.

Staete Landt Marlborough ★★ Dutch immigrants, producing v. refined Chard, Sauv Bl, and Pinot Gr; and graceful, supple Pinot N.

Stonecroft Hawke's Bay ★★→★★★ Small winery. NZ's first serious Syrah (since 1989), more Rhône than Oz. Outstanding Chard, v. rich Old Vine Gewurz.

Stoneleigh Former CORBANS brand, now owned by PERNOD RICARD NEW ZEALAND. Impressive MARLBOROUGH whites (inc punchy, tropical fruit Sauv Bl, refined, medium-dry Ries and creamy-smooth Chard) and Pinot N, esp Rapaura Res.

Stonyridge Waiheke Island ★★★★ Boutique winery. Famous for exceptional B'x-style red, Larose (99 **00'** 04' 05' 06'). Also powerful, dense Rhône-style blend Pilgrim and supercharged Luna Negra Malbec. Second label: Fallen Angel.

Tasman Bay Nelson ★→★★ Best known for creamy-smooth Chard. Top, single-v'yd wines sold as Spencer Hill.

Te Awa Hawke's Bay ★★ US-owned estate v'yd. Classy Chard and Boundary (Merlot-based blend); gd Longlands labels. Now linked to Dry River.

Te Kairanga Martinborough ★→★★ One of district's larger wineries. Big, flinty Chard (richer Reserve); perfumed, supple Pinot N (complex, powerful John Martin Reserve; Runholder is middle tier).

Te Mata Hawke's Bay ★★★→★★★★ Prestigious winery. Fine, powerful Elston Chard; super-stylish Coleraine (Merlot/Cab Sauv/Cab Fr blend) (98' **00'** 02' 05'). Syrah and Viognier among NZ's finest. Woodthorpe range for early drinking (v.gd Chard, Sauv Bl, Gamay Noir, Merlot/Cab, Syrah/Viognier).

Te Motu Waiheke Island ★★ Top wine of Waiheke Vineyards, owned by Dunleavy and Buffalora families. Concentrated mellow red. Dunleavy second label.

Terra Vin Marlborough ★★ Weighty, dry, tropical-fruit-flavoured Sauv Bl/Sem and rich, firmly structured, complex Pinot N, esp Hillside Selection.

Te Whau ★★★ Tiny Waiheke Island winery/restaurant. Beautifully ripe, long Chard and savoury, earthy, complex red, The Point (B'x blend).

NEW ZEALAND

Tohu ★→★★ Maori-owned venture with extensive v'yds. Punchy, racy Sauv Bl (Mugwi is esp powerful) and moderately complex Pinot N, both from MARLBOROUGH; full-flavoured GISBORNE Chard.

Torlesse Waipara ★→★★ Small, gd-value CANTERBURY producer of fresh, flinty Ries and firm, toasty, citrus Chard. Mid-weight Pinot N. Top range: Omihi Road.

Trinity Hill Hawke's Bay ★★→★★★ Firm, concentrated reds and top-flight GIMBLETT GRAVELS Chard. Homage range: v. powerful, concentrated and expensive (Chard, Syrah, Merlot-based). V. promising Tempranillo. Scented, soft, rich Pinot Gr and Viognier among NZ's best.

Unison Hawke's Bay ★★→★★★ Red specialist with dark, spicy, flavour-crammed blends of Merlot, Cab Sauv, Syrah. Selection label is oak-aged the longest. Also fragrant, fleshy, flavour-crammed Syrah.

Vavasour Marlborough ★★ Based in AWATERE VALLEY. Immaculate, intense Chard and Sauv Bl; promising Pinot N and Pinot Gr. Dashwood is the second label (aromatic, vibrant Sauv Bl is top value). Linked to GOLDWATER and CLIFFORD BAY.

Vidal Hawke's Bay ★★→★★★ Part of VILLA MARIA. Distinguished Res Chard and Res Merlot/Cab Sauv. Mid-priced Merlot/Cab Sauv is gd value. Top Syrahs (Res and Soler) outstanding. Excellent Marlborough Sauv Bl, Ries and Pinot N.

Villa Maria Auckland ★★→★★★ NZ's largest family-owned wine company, includes VIDAL and ESK VALLEY. Top ranges: Reserve (express regional character) and Single Vineyard (reflect individual sites); Cellar Selection: middle tier (less oak) is often excellent; third-tier Private Bin wines can be v.gd and top value (esp Ries, Sauv Bl, Gewurz, Pinot Gr, Pinot N). Brilliant track record in competitions. Other brands: Thornbury, Northrow.

Vinoptima Gisborne ★★→★★★ Small Gewurz specialist, owned by Nick Nobilo (ex-NOBILO wines). Top vintages (04 06) are full of power and personality. Also gorgeous Noble Late Harvest (04).

Waimea Nelson ★★ Emerging as one of region's top and best-value producers. Punchy, ripe, dry Sauv Bl, rich, softly textured Pinot Gr, gd Ries (Classic is honeyed, medium style). Top range: Bolitho SV.

Waipara Hills Canterbury ★★ Publicly owned, sizeable producer of MARLBOROUGH and CANTERBURY wines, esp intense, ripe MARLBOROUGH Sauv Bl. Top-flight Waipara Ries and Pinot Gr. Also owns MUD HOUSE (more herbaceous Sauv Bl).

Waipara Springs Canterbury ★★ Small producer of lively, cool-climate Ries, Sauv Bl, and Chard; impressive top range: Premo (incl arrestingly rich 06 Pinot N).

Wairarapa NZ's sixth largest wine region. Includes East Taratahi and Gladstone. See also MARTINBOROUGH.

Wairau River Marlborough ★★ Intense, racy Sauv Bl; full-bodied, well-rounded Pinot Gr; perfumed, softly mouth-filling Gewurz. Home Block is top label.

Wairau Valley MARLBOROUGH's largest district, with most of the region's v'yds and the vast majority of its wineries.

Waitaki Valley New region in North Otago. Promising Pinot N (slightly herbal), Pinot Gr and Ries.

Wellington Capital city and official name of region; includes WAIRARAPA, Te Horo, MARTINBOROUGH.

Whitehaven Marlborough ★→★★ Scented, v. pure and harmonious Sauv Bl. Solid Chard and Ries. Gallo is part-owner.

Wither Hills Marlborough ★★→★★★ Rich, toasty Chard; huge-selling, fragrant, fleshy Sauv Bl (06 very controversial in NZ, due to marked variation between show samples and retail bottlings); serious, concentrated, spicy Pinot N. Owned since 2002 by Lion Nathan. Second tier: Shepherds Ridge.

Wooing Tree Central Otago ★★ Young producer at Bannockburn. Rich Pinot N.

South Africa

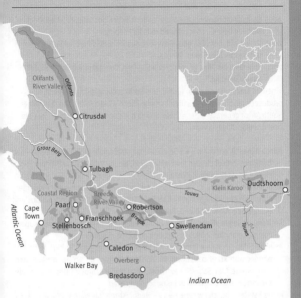

Olifants
River Valley
Olifants

○ Citrusdal

Groot Berg

○ Tulbagh

Coastal Region   Breede
River Valley   *Touws*   Klein Karoo   Oudtshoorn ○

Cape
Town ○   Paarl ○   ○ Robertson
   ○ Franschhoek   *Breede*
  Stellenbosch   ○ Swellendam

Atlantic Ocean

    ○ Caledon
     Overberg
Walker Bay   ○ Bredasdorp   *Indian Ocean*

Touws

Visitors to South Africa can expect a glorious surprise in the quality,
variety and value of its new generation of wines. Its top labels are now
equal to California's best and must give Australia food for thought. The
average standard is high and prices very moderate. No longer is there a
feeling that a country new to the modern wine world is feeling its way.

With this confidence comes new exploration of its most-planted white
grape, Chenin Blanc, once despised, now ready to be recognized as the
country's most versatile variety and hopefully to take over from its often
pedestrian Sauvignon Blanc as the essential national refreshment. The
unique national red, Pinotage, leaves most visitors unmoved. Cabernet
and its cousins are the reds that truly succeed here, particularly in the
classic central regions of Stellenbosch and Franschock, with Pinot Noir
a revelation in the new vineyards behind Walker Bay.

There is much more. Rhône varieties are shaping up well and one or
two Italians show promise. There is bright Riesling, fragrant Viognier, fine
Semillon and all sorts of tentative blends. Chardonnay needs no help or
explanation. It simply works here – sometimes brilliantly. There is little
need to import champagne either, méthode cap classique is a huge success.

Can South Africa absorb such a cornucopia? No chance, without
serious exports. The rest of the world should seize the opportunity with
both hands.

Recent vintages

2007 An almost perfect run-up to harvest: cool, wet winter; dry, largely disease-
free summer. A general heatwave – soaring above 40ºC – just before
picking rushed the ripening and pushed up alcohol.

2006 Dry, warm winter but a trouble-free, hot, longer summer than 2005 – by about two weeks – with average yields, slightly lower alcohols; the fourth sound vintage in a row.

2005 Early, short harvest after an exceptionally dry, hot season. Small, thick-skinned berries, concentrated reds for keeping.

2004 Drawn-out, hot year, above-average quality across most varieties. Intense reds, especially Shiraz, Pinotage.

2003 Excellent: hot, dry, generally disease-free. Concentrated, rich reds, for longer keeping.

Vineyard practices and cellar techniques are improving each vintage: a producer's reputation is usually a better guide to wine quality than the vintage. South Africa generally experiences warm to hot summers. Most dry whites are best drunk within 2–3 years.

Adoro Wines St'bosch r w ★★★ South African stablemate of Speyside single-malt BenRiach. Trio of elegant food wines (Red, Naudé White, Sauv Bl) from cooler sites. Laudably modest alcohols.

Alto Estate St'bosch r ★★ Historic DISTELL-owned property on Helderberg Mountain slopes. Ageworthy Cab Sauv (00 01' 02 03 04), spicy Shiraz, and evergreen B'x/Shiraz blend, Rouge (aka "Estate").

Anthony de Jager Wines Paarl r ★★★ FAIRVIEW winemaker's own label; supple, complex Homtini Shiraz, spiced with dollop of Viognier.

Anwilka St'bosch r ★★★ Bordeaux notables Bruno Prats and Hubert de Boüard partner with KLEIN CONSTANTIA in high-end venture on 40 ha in Helderberg area. Svelte Cab Sauv/Shiraz blend, sold mainly through Bordeaux trade; second label and new cellar being contemplated.

Asara Estate St'bosch r w sw ★★→★★★ Hedonist-friendly winery and 5-star hotel (tapas bar, cigar/whisky lounges, etc); varied range holds pleasant surprises such as Amarone-style Pinotage.

Ashbourne See HAMILTON RUSSELL.

Ataraxia Mountain Vineyards Walker Bay r w ★★★ Kevin Grant, ex-HAMILTON RUSSELL, now gone solo to rave local/international reviews. Penetrating, minerally Chard among South Africa's best.

Axe Hill Calitzdorp sw ★★★→★★★★ Outstanding tiny specialist producer of port-style. Restrainedly opulent Cape Vintage (Touriga Nacional/Tinta Barroca 00' 01 02' 03' 04 05); solera-aged Dry White Port from Chenin Bl.

Backsberg Estate Cellars Paarl r w (sw) ★★→★★★ Resurgent family enterprise; first in South Africa to claim to be carbon neutral. Spread of 20+ labels in 6 ranges, inc kosher and organic. Quirky Elbar red blend and wooded John Martin Res Sauv Bl among standouts.

Beaumont Wines Walker Bay r w (sw) ★★★ Charming, rustic family winery making characterful and distinctive Chenin Bl, Pinotage, Shiraz, Mourvèdre, and Sem/Sauv Bl botrytis dessert Goutte d'Or.

Bellingham r w ★→★★ Revamp of DGB's enduring high-volume brand bins varietal Spitz range and ushers in new blended lines, Legends and Fusion; showy Maverick quintet promoted to flag bearer.

Beyerskloof St'bosch r (sp sw) ★★→★★★★ Top grower/producer of Pinotage in Cape: 7 versions of grape on offer, inc powerful Res, Synergy Res blend, and new Brut sparkling. Even Pinotage burgers, in popular new restaurant. Only B'x-style Field Blend (previously "Beyerskloof") 00 01 02 03' is Pinotage-free.

Bilton Wines St'bosch r (w) ★★★ Improved selection of modern, accessible reds: best are B'x/Shiraz blend Matt Black; fruit-rich Merlot.

Boekenhoutskloof Franschhoek r w (sw) ★★→★★★★ Highly rated grower/producer, consistently ranked top Cape label by some local critics; specializing in unfiltered, native-yeast ferments. Rich, ripe reds: spicy Syrah 01' 02' **03** 04' 05; *intense, minerally* Cab Sauv **01'** 02 03 04' 05; supple Chocolate Box blend. Also *fine Sems dry* and botrytis, and gd-value second label Porcupine Ridge.

Bon Courage Estate Robertson r w sw sp ★★→★★★ Extensive range led by improving Inkará reds, stylish MCCs, and pair of outstanding desserts (botrytis Ries and White Muscadel). Easy-drinkers in new Like Father Like Son range.

Boplaas Family Vineyards Calitzdorp r w sw ★★→★★★ Family winery best known for port-styles (esp Vintage Res port-style 99' **01** 03 04' 05') and Cape Tawny). Now also Family Res (unfortified) range, from cooler areas.

Boschendal Wines Paarl r w sp ★★→★★★ Famous old estate (estb 1685) showing new élan under DGB ownership. Catholic offering topped by Cecil John Res range (meaty Shiraz, steel-edged Sauv Bl) and Res Collection (forceful Grand Res red, fleshy Shiraz). Old favourites like B'x-style red Lanoy still satisfy.

Bouchard Finlayson Walker Bay r w ★★★ Among handful of outstanding South African Pinot N growers, with solid reputation for 2 top labels: Galpin Peak (**00** 01 02') 03 04 05) and barrel selection Tête de Cuvée (**99 01'** 03' 05'). Also impressive Chards (oaked and unwooded), and red blend Hannibal.

Buitenverwachting Constantia r w sp ★★→★★★ Cape *grande dame*, reclining imposingly on Constantia Mountain slopes since 1796; standout Sauv Bl, Husseys Vlei Chard, restrained B'x blend Christine (99 **00 01'** 02 03), and, returning after a hiatus, botrytis dessert Noblesse.

Cabrière Franschhoek (r) sp ★★ Reliable NV MCC sparkling under Pierre Jourdan label (Brut Sauvage; Belle Rose). Fine Pinot N in some yrs.

Camberley Wines St'bosch r (sp) ★★→★★★ Family-run red specialist: striking Shiraz (and now savoury Sparkling Shiraz); impressive, full B'x blend Philosopher's Stone; massive, plummy Pinotage.

Capaia Wines Philadelphia r w ★★→★★★ Recent French-German-Austrian collaboration; supple, rich-berry Capaia B'x blend winning local plaudits.

Cape Bay ★★ NEWTON JOHNSON family's successful, easy-priced export range.

Cape blend Still somewhat nebulous category; here denoting a red blend with some proportion of Pinotage.

Cape Chamonix Wine Farm Franschhoek r w sp ★★→★★★ Recently improved reds: Pinot N; B'x-style red Troika; excellent Chard and Sauv Bl reserves; elegant Chard-based MCC sparkling.

Cape Point Vineyards Cape Point (r) w ★★★→★★★★ Premium mostly white wine label, from Atlantic-cooled v'yds on tip of Cape Town's Peninsula. Elegant, complex flagship Sauv Bl/Sem blend Isliedh; outstanding, minerally Sem; exhilarating Sauv Bls.

Cape Winemakers Guild (CWG) Stages a benchmarking annual auction of limited, premium bottlings by 38 of South Africa's top growers.

Cederberg Private Cellars Cederberg r w ★★→★★★ Family-tended v'yds in soaring Cederberg mountain chain. Old-vines intensity in V Generations Cab Sauv and Chenin Bl; also supple Shiraz and zingy Sauv Bl.

Cloof Darling r w ★★→★★★ Rising label, powered by beefy wines from dryland bush vines; best is concentrated Crucible Shiraz. Offbeat names (Inkspot, Very Sexy Shiraz, Dark Side) leaven the intensity.

The Company of Wine People r w (sp) ★→★★★ A 2.5-million-case-a-yr STELLENBOSCH operation with 50+ labels in a dozen tiers. Best: Kumkani and Kumkani Reflections ranges, with elegant Triple J Shiraz, peachy Chard/Viognier, powerful single-v'yd Sauv Bl Lanner Hill and dry white VVS (Viognier/Verdelho/Sauv Bl). See also THANDI.

SOUTH AFRICA

Constantia South Africa's original – still highly reputed – fine-wine growing area; home of the celebrated sweet Muscat-based wines of the 18th and 19th centuries, revived in recent yrs by GROOT and KLEIN CONSTANTIA.

Constantia Uitsig Constantia (r) w (sp) ★★→★★★ Premium v'yds and tourism destination, partly black-owned. Mainly white wines, all excellent; also new all-Chard MCC sparkling, and B'x-style Constantia Red.

Cordoba Winery St'bosch r (w) ★★→★★★ Highly regarded winery/v'yds on Helderberg Mountain. Usually late-developing, Cab Fr-based blend Crescendo; plus Merlot.

Dalla Cia Wine & Spirit Company St'bosch r w ★★→★★★ Striking, fine B'x blend Giorgio; unoaked Chard and Sauv Bl. Also intense grappa-style digestifs.

Danie de Wet See DE WETSHOF.

David Frost Estate Paarl r ★★★ South African golfing legend's increasingly respected small range of reds led by Cab Sauv and *B'x blend Par Excellence*.

Delaire Winery St'bosch r w ★★ Makeover nearing completion at spectacular eyrie on Helshoogte Pass, owned by jeweller Laurence Graff. Best: Driven by Cab (B'x blend) and Botmaskop (previously Cab Sauv, now B'x/Shiraz blend).

Delheim St'bosch r w sw ★★→★★★ Eco-minded family winery. Acclaimed Vera Cruz Shiraz; plummy Grand Res Cab (00 01 03 04'). Also Chard Sur Lie and botrytis Edelspatz, from single-v'yd Ries.

De Krans Calitzdorp r w sw ★★→★★★ Old family-run Karoo v'yds make rich, impressive port-styles (esp Vintage Res port-style 99 01 02 03' 04' 05'). Also flavourful unfortified Tinta Barocca, Tempranillo, and Touriga Nacional.

De Toren Private Cellar St'bosch r ★★★ Elegant B'x blend Fusion V 01 02 03' 04 05' and earlier-maturing Merlot-based blend "Z".

De Trafford Wines St'bosch r w sw ★★★★ Exceptional boutique grower. David Trafford has international reputation, and knack, for bold but elegant wines. Brilliant B'x/Shiraz blend Elevation 393 (00 01 03' 04 05); Cab Sauv (00 01 03' 04 05); Shiraz. Also soupçons of Pinot N, Merlot, oaked Chenin Blanc, and Vin de Paille-style Straw Wine (also Chenin Bl) all worth cellaring.

DeWaal Wines r w ★★→★★★ HQ at Uiterwyk, old family estate nr STELLENBOSCH. Pinotage a forte: Top of the Hill among South Africa's best, from 50+-yr-old vines. V.gd Shiraz and CAPE BLEND.

De Wetshof Estate Robertson (r) w (sw) ★★ Chard pioneer and still exponent; toasty Bateleur, *Bon Vallon* (South Africa's first unwooded version) and Limestone Hill (under Danie de Wet label) stand out. Also promising Pinot N.

DGB Well-established Wellington-based producer/wholesaler; brands include BOSCHENDAL, BELLINGHAM, and Douglas Green.

Diemersdal Estate Durbanville r w (sw) ★★→★★★ Younger generation injecting dynamism into family farm. V.gd B'x red and Sauv Bl in new M M Louw range; single-v'yd Sauv Bl; Chard Res. Exciting West Coast joint venture, SIR LAMBERT.

Diemersfontein Wines Wellington r (w) ★★ Flagship Carpe Diem range noted for full-throttle Pinotage; now joined by equally unretiring wooded Chenin Bl.

Distell South Africa's biggest drinks company, headquartered in STELLENBOSCH. Owns many brands, spanning quality scales: Ch Libertas, FLEUR DU CAP, MONIS, NEDERBURG, Tassenberg, Two Oceans, ZONNEBLOEM, etc. Also interests in various top STELLENBOSCH wineries, inc ALTO, NEETHLINGSHOF, and STELLENZICHT.

Dornier Wines St'bosch r w ★★→★★★ Architectural showpiece in a sylvan setting. Stylish flagships Dornier Donatus (B'x red) and Donatus White (Chenin Bl/Sem); Merlot and Pinotage are plush and fruity.

Words within entries marked like this *Alter Ego de Palmer* indicate wines especially enjoyed by Hugh Johnson over the past 12 months (mid '07–'08).

> **From the nursery**
> South African wineries are multiplying at the rate of more than one a week. A selection of recent start-ups worth watching:
>
> **Belfield** Family label from ELGIN; leafy, lovely Cabernets and B'x red.
>
> **De Morgenzon** Supercharged Chenin Bl from old STELLENBOSCH single-v'yd; star winemaker Teddy Hall consulting.
>
> **Edgebaston** Finlayson family (GLEN CARLOU) own-label; Chard, Shiraz, and great GS Cab Sauv honouring legendary winemaker George Spies.
>
> **Glenelly Estate** Major investment by May-Eliane de Lencquesaing (Pichon-Lalande, B'x), kicking off with second-label B'x/Shiraz blend, Glenelly Hill.
>
> **The Goose** Top South African golfer Retief Goosen's proprietary label, from cool-climate Langkloof grapes.
>
> **Metzer Wines** Jocund name – The Kitchen Sink – belies serious, assured Syrah by Wade Metzer.
>
> **Silverthorn** Graceful, oak-enriched Chard MCC sparkling, by STEENBERG cellarmaster John Loubser.
>
> **Sir Lambert** DIEMERSDAL and West Coast partners; crisp, nettly Sauv Bl from new appellation Lamberts Bay.

Durbanville Hills Durbanville r w ★★→★★★ Maritime-cooled v'yds co-owned by giant DISTELL. Best is eponymous range (esp Caapmans Cab Sauv/Merlot, Sauv Bl); also Rhinofields Res range with gd Chard, contrasting Sauv Bls.

Du Toitskloof Winery Rawsonville r w sw ★→★★ Regular winner of local gd-value awards. Super-quaffable Sauv Bl, delicious fortified desserts.

Elgin Cooler upland v'yds east of Cape Town; burgeoning corps of vintners; winemaker Ross Gower and viticulturist Paul Wallace have eponymous labels; South Hill, Oak Valley, Iona worth seeking out.

Ernie Els Wines St'bosch r ★★★→★★★★ South African golfing great's joint venture with Jean Engelbrecht (RUST EN VREDE). Rich, aromatic eponymous B'x blend (01 02' 03 04' 05) among Cape's priciest wines. Also standout Engelbrecht-Els Proprietor's Blend, mainly Cab Sauv/Shiraz. V.gd Guardian Peak range, inc SMG (Syrah/Mourvèdre/Grenache) and opulent Cab.

Estate Wine Official term for wines grown, made, and, from this yr, bottled on "units registered for the production of ESTATE WINE". Not a quality designation.

Fairview Paarl r w sw ★★→★★★★ Dynamic, export-savvy proprietor Charles Back produces never-ending innovations with emphasis on Rhône and, latterly, Italian varieties; open, generous, ready-to-drink wines. Top range is single-v'yd Red Seal. Regular labels include Cape's first and still v.gd Viognier. Successful with Goats do Roam range: Rhône and B'x blends Goat-Roti, Bored Doe, etc – taunting, gimmicky labels that usually over-deliver. Back is now stakeholder in Citrusdal Cellars, blessed with old vines and snowline v'yds in Piekenierskloof and Cederberg appellations. See also SPICE ROUTE.

FirstCape Vineyards r w ★★ One of South Africa's outstanding recent export successes. Joint venture of NEWTON JOHNSON, BrandPhoenix in UK, and 5 local co-ops; now headquartered in Simondium nr PAARL. V.gd price/quality in 4 ranges, inc new Café Collection. Lots of easy/early fun.

Flagstone Winery Somerset West r w ★★→★★★★ Hotbed of innovation, now in ambit of giant Constellation, founder and prime mover Bruce Jack retains winemaking/marketing control. Two dozen labels in 4 ranges, many named with cheerful idiosyncrasy (eg Love Handles Shiraz). Grapes sourced from many individual, often far-flung v'yds. Best: Bowwood Cab Sauv/Merlot; Mary Le Bow B'x/Shiraz. Regular youthful standouts: The Berrio Sauv Bl; Dark Horse Shiraz; Longitude red blend. New collaboration with Riebeek Cellars,

Springtree, aims to catapult Fish Hoek brand into international big leagues.

Franschhoek Booming French-founded neighbour to STELLENBOSCH. Many wineries (and restaurants).

Fleur du Cap St'bosch r w sw ★★→★★★ DISTELL's flagship label; includes v.gd Unfiltered Collection (Cab Sauv, Chard; Sem; and Sauv Bl and Viognier limited releases). Also plush new B'x blend Laszlo, racy botrytis Ries.

The Foundry St'bosch r w ★★★ MEERLUST winemaker Chris Williams' small-scale production, buying in site-specific parcels for outstanding Syrah and Viognier.

Gilga Wines St'bosch r ★★→★★★ Boutique label; intense Syrah; floral Shiraz-based blend Amurabi.

Glen Carlou Paarl r w ★★★ First-rate winery and v'yds owned by Donald Hess, with fine-art gallery and new Zen Restaurant. Standout, spicy Syrah (02 03 04' 05 06); Gravel Quarry Cab Sauv; also fine B'x blend Grand Classique (00 01 02 03 04) and full Pinot N. Two excellent Chards, led by Quartz Stone label.

Goats do Roam See FAIRVIEW.

Graham Beck Wines Robertson/Franschhoek r w sp (sw) ★★→★★★ Avant-garde properties of mining tycoon Graham Beck, making *classy MCC sparkling inc vintage Blanc de Blancs Chard*. Also outstanding "ultra premium" The Ridge; Coffeestone Cab Sauv; The William CAPE BLEND; Pheasants' Run Sauv Bl; and sumptuous dessert Rhona Muscadel. V.gd Viognier.

Grangehurst Winery St'bosch r ★★→★★★ Small, top red specialist, mostly buying in grapes. Cape blend Nikela (98 99 00 01); v.gd Pinotage (97 98 99 01); concentrated Cab Sauv/Merlot; Shiraz/Cab Sauv.

Groot Constantia Constantia r w (sp sw) ★→★★ Historic estate nr Cape Town. Legendary red and white Muscat desserts in early 19th century; Grand Constance revives tradition. V.gd B'x blend Res; Chard in Gouverneurs range.

Groote Post Vineyards Darling r w ★★→★★★ Coastal, cool-climate benefits for Chard (oaked and unwooded) and intense Shiraz; also Sauv Bl Res.

Hamilton Russell Vineyards **(HRV)** Walker Bay r w ★★★★ Cape's Burgundian-style specialist estate at Hermanus. Fine Pinot N 01' 03' 04 05 06; classy Chard 02 03 04 05' 06. Small yields, French-inspired vinification, careful barrelling. Also gd Sauv Bls and Pinotages under HRV-owned Southern Right and Ashbourne labels.

Hartenberg Estate St'bosch r w ★★★ Cape front-ranker. The McKenzie B'x blend; always serious Shiraz (01 02 03 04' 05); also flagship single-site The Stork Shiraz (03 04'); fine Merlot. Award-winning Chards, top is The Eleanor.

Havana Hills Durbanville r w ★★→★★★ Well-structured, fruity reds in Du Plessis range: Médoc-style Du Plessis red, Shiraz Res. Flagship is B'x blend Kobus.

Ingwe St'bosch r w ★★→★★★ Alain Moueix (see France) among early 90s French investors; elegant Merlot-based blend Ingwe; Sauv Bl/Sem Amehlo white.

Jack & Knox Winecraft Somerset West r w ★★ Bruce Jack (FLAGSTONE) and Graham Knox (Siyabonga) collaboration. Excellent Green on Green Sem; promising Coincidence Chard.

J C le Roux St'bosch sp ★★ South Africa's largest sparkling-wine house, DISTELL owned. Best are Pinot N, Scintilla (Chard/Pinot N), and Pinot N Rosé, all MCC.

Jean Daneel Wines Napier r w (sp) ★★★ Outstanding Signature Series, esp Chenin Bls ("regular" and new *Directors' Signature in powerful Savennières style*), Cab Sauv/Merlot, Chard MCC sparkling.

Joostenberg Wines Paarl r w sw ★★→★★★ Family winery noted for Chenin Bl botrytis dessert; also v.gd Cab Sauv/Merlot/Shiraz blend Bakermat; esp gd Shiraz/Viognier.

Jordan Winery St'bosch r w ★★★★ Enduring excellence, value. Flagship Chard Nine Yards Res; B'x blend Cobblers Hill (00 01 03 04'); Cab Sauv; Merlot; Sauv Bl; and Ries botrytis dessert Mellifera.

J P Bredell Wines St'bosch r (w) sw ★★→★★★ Rich Bredell's Cape Vintage Res (97 98 00 01 03) port-style a local benchmark; excellent Late Bottled Vintage. Also sturdy unfortified reds, inc quaffing-style Helderzicht V'yd Collection.

Kaapzicht Estate St'bosch r w ★★★ Family-run red wine specialist. Signature is ripe, concentrated Steytler Vision (Pinotage/Cab Sauv/Merlot) 00 **01'** 02' 03' 04; Steytler and Kaapzicht Pinotages. Well-crafted Kaapzicht Cab Sauvs.

Kanonkop Estate St'bosch r ★★→★★★★ Grand local status past 3 decades, mainly with 2 labels: oak-polished Pinotage (01 02 03' 04 05) and, with a fanatical following, B'x blend Paul Sauer (00 01 02 03 04'), plus Cab Sauv. Second label is CAPE BLEND Kadette.

Kanu Wines St'bosch r w sw ★★→★★★ Best known for barrel-aged Chenin Bl; also v. gd B'x red Keystone, Chard, and botrytis Chenin Bl Kia-Ora.

Ken Forrester Wines St'bosch r w sw ★★→★★★ Vintner/restaurateur Ken Forrester and wine-grower Martin MEINERT collaboration. Benchmark Chenin Bl in Ken Forrester range; also outstanding, luscious off-dry FMC version, from old bush vines. Hearty but fine Grenache/Shiraz Gypsy. Sumptuous botrytis Chenin Bl named "T".

Klein Constantia Estate Constantia r w sw ★★→★★★★ From 1986, with luscious (non-botrytis) Vin de Constance (98 99 **00'** 01 02), re-created legendary 18th-century Muscat dessert. Other stars in recently revamped and expanded portfolio: elegant Sem/Sauv blend Mme Marlbrook, partnering beefed-up Marlbrook red; limited-release Perdeblokke Sauv Bl; ageworthy Ries; chalky Sauv Bl. Classy sundowners in KC range. See also ANWILKA.

Kleine Zalze Wines St'bosch r w ★★→★★★ Shiraz tops v.gd Family Res and V'yd Selection reds, inc Cab Sauv and Merlot. Also multi-awarded barrel-fermented and unwooded Chenin Bl and Chard.

Krone sp ★★ Two fine, light brut MCCs, Borealis and Rosé, from Chard/Pinot N, by one of Cape's oldest estates, Twee Jonge Gezellen at Tulbagh.

Kumala r w (sp) ★ Hugely successful Constellation-owned export label poised for quality boost under aegis of Bruce Jack, of sister brand FLAGSTONE.

KWV Paarl r w sw (sp) ★→★★★ Formerly South Africa's national wine co-op and controlling body, now a partly black-owned group. Top ranges are Cathedral Cellar (best are Cab Sauv, B'x red Triptych, Shiraz, Chard), Laborie and KWV Res. Gd early notices for new oak-driven Café Culture Pinotage. Regular KWV labels include B'x/Shiraz blend Roodeberg, a Cape institution; vast range of reds, whites, sparkling, port-styles, and fortified desserts.

La Motte Franschhoek r w ★★→★★★ Diversified, increasingly organic farming venture (floriculture, ethereal oils) by the Ruperts, a leading Cape wine (and international business) family. Fine, distinctive Pierneef Collection Shiraz/ Viognier and assertively fruity Sauv Bl. Also excellent B'x-style red Millennium, stylish Shiraz.

Lanzerac Wines St'bosch r w ★★ Old v'yds (and grand hotel) expensively refurbished, replanted by banking/retailing magnate Christo Wiese. Pinotage remains speciality, inc new limited-release Res.

L'Avenir St'bosch r w (sw) ★★→★★★ Punning pseudo-French labelling (Vin de Meurveur, Vin d'Erstelle) now discontinued but historic focus on (and success with) Pinotage and Chenin Bl continue under Chablis eminence Michel Laroche. New entry-level By L'Avenir range offered in screwcap format.

Le Riche Wines St'bosch r (w) ★★★ Fine Cab Sauv-based boutique wines, hand-crafted by respected Etienne le Riche. Recently a Chard. Also Grand Vin de Terroir, vinified in Bergerac.

Long Mountain Wine Company r w (sp) ★ Pernod Ricard label, recently buying grapes more widely. New Premium Res range a step up.

L'Ormarins Private Cellar Franschhoek r w ★★★ Total revamp (v'yds, infrastructure, branding) under hands-on billionaire Johann Rupert culminates in impressive new 3-tier portfolio. Tethered flamboyance in flagship Anthonij Rupert line, mainly B'x varietal reds plus *Chard Res Serruria* and white blend Nemesia; L'Ormarins range features vastly improved Optima B'x red; Italian-themed Terra del Capo line-up inc soft Sangiovese/Merlot. French savant Michel Rolland consults.

Lourensford St'bosch r w ★★ Vast v'yds, winery/tourism project – 300+ ha under vine alone – owned by business heavyweight Christo Wiese (LANZERAC). Best bottlings: peachy Viognier, botrytis dessert from Sem, flagship Cab Sauv/ Shiraz blend Seventeen Hundred. Entry-level Eden Crest and Five Heirs labels.

Meerlust Estate St'bosch r w ★★★ Prestigious v'yds and cellar, probably South Africa's best-known quality red label, still in the control of the Myburgh family after 250 yrs. Hallmark elegance and restraint continue under new winemaker Chris Williams. *Flagship Rubicon* (**97 98** 99 00 01' 03'), one of Cape's first B'x blends; also excellent Merlot and occasional Cab Sauv; individual Chard and Pinot N. Gd-value 2nd label Red, for yrs when Rubicon "declassified".

Meinert Wines St'bosch r ★★→★★★ Small-scale producer/consultant Martin Meinert makes 2 fine blends, Devon Crest (B'x) and Synchronicity (B'x/Pinotage), and understated Merlot from Devon Valley v'yds.

Méthode Cap Classique (MCC) South African term for classic-method sparkling wine. The best have real style.

Monis Wines Paarl sw ★★ DISTELL-owned: enduring quality from oldest (1906) fortified wine producer of tawny-port-styles and Muscadels.

Môreson Franschhoek r w sp ★★ Powerful, prize-winning Pinotage, elegant B'x blend Magia, fine Premium Chard; tasty easy-drinkers in Pinehurst range.

Morgenhof Estate St'bosch r w sw (sp) ★★★ Old property (1692), transformed into splendid wine/tourism venue by Anne Cointreau (of Cognac/ liqueur family). Reputation for Merlot, B'x red Première Sélection, and Chenin Bl. Also toasty Brut Res MCC and Chard. Gd everyday Fantail range.

Morgenster Estate St'bosch r ★★★ Immaculate Italian-owned, French-toned wine and olive farm, Pierre Lurton of Cheval Blanc consulting. Two classically styled B'x blends: fine, supple Morgenster (00 **01** 03 04), similarly restrained second label Lourens River Valley.

Mountain Oaks Winery Worcester r w ★★ Exciting, organic boutique tucked away in Slanghoek Valley. V.gd Pinotage and new Cab Sauv/Cab Fr; Chard and Chenin Bl (oaked and unwooded).

Mulderbosch Vineyards St'bosch r w (sw) ★★★ Penetrating – usually scintillating too – Sauv Bl. Two Chards: oak-fermented and fresh, less oaky. V.gd barrel-fermented Chenin Bl subtitled Steen op Hout. Easy, B'x-style blend, Faithful Hound; new botrytis Sauv Bl.

Mvemve Raats St'bosch r ★★ Boutique-scale partnership between Mzokhona Mvemve, South Africa's first university-qualified black winemaker, and Bruwer Raats (RAATS FAMILY). Complex B'x blend De Compostella. Also promising Sagila range, by Mvemve working solo.

Namaqua Wines Olifants River r w sw sp ★ Formerly Vredendal Winery, owns one of southern hemisphere's largest temperature-controlled cellars; 9 million cases, mostly white, in Gôiya, Namaqua, and Spruitdrift ranges; also B4 and Inanda sparkling.

Nederburg Wines Paarl r w sw s/sw sp ★→★★★ Among South Africa's biggest (1 million+ cases per annum) and best-known brands, owned by DISTELL, restored to form. Stages annual wine event, the Nederburg Auction. Excellent new Manor House label (esp Cab); reliable Classic Range reds inc Edelrood and Baronne blends; Cab Sauv; botrytis dessert Noble Late Harvest. Also inexpensive quaffers in Lifestyle segment. Small quantities of v.gd Private

Bins for auction, inc reputed Chenin Bl botrytis Edelkeur (**02** 03' 04' 05 06).

Neethlingshof Estate St'bosch r w sw ★★ Tourist magnet (restaurants, family friendly) co-owned by DISTELL. Best in flagship Lord Neethling range (esp botrytis Ries); v.gd new Sauv Bl Res; flowery Gewurz.

Neil Ellis Wines St'bosch r w ★★★ Veteran winemaker Neil Ellis sources special cooler-climate parcels for site expression. Top-flight Vineyard Selection Cab Sauv (00' 01 03 04' 05), Syrah, oak-fermented Sauv Bl. Premium range inc v.gd Cab Sauv, Pinotage, Shiraz (unoaked), Sauv Bls, Groenekloof and ELGIN.

Newton Johnson Wines Walker Bay r w ★★→★★★ Hemel-en-Aarde cellar and restaurant with breathtaking view. Own and sourced grapes yield one of few v.gd Cape Pinot Ns; *outstanding Chard*; intense Sauv Bl; peppery Shiraz/Mourvèdre; food-style rosé. See also CAPE BAY, FIRSTCAPE.

Nitida Cellars Durbanville r w ★★→★★★ Expanding v.gd range, sea-cooled v'yds; fresh, vital Sauv Bls and Sem. Also gd Cab Sauv, B'x-style red Calligraphy, elegant new Sauv Bl/Sem blend Coronata.

The Observatory Cellars Swartland r (w) ★★→★★★ Rhône-influenced boutique in Perdeberg foothills, with organic/biodynamic methods. Perfumed Syrah; juicy Carignan/Syrah, elegant Pinotage/Syrah; singular Chenin Bl/Chard.

Overgaauw Estate St'bosch r w ★★→★★★ Van Velden family team, now led by scion David. Dependable, classically styled Merlot, B'x blend Tria Corda, Cab Sauv; 2 excellent port-styles. Everyday fare in new Shepherd's Cottage line.

Paarl Town and demarcated wine region ±50 km northeast of Cape Town. Microwineries to multinational conglomerates; divergent styles and approaches; best results with Mediterranean varieties (r and w), Cab Sauv.

Paul Cluver Wines Elgin r w sw ★★→★★★ Leading winery, on vast and scenic De Rust estate; convincing Pinot N, elegant Chard, always gorgeous botrytis Ries **03' 04 05' 06'**; unique forest amphitheatre for summer concerts.

Plaisir de Merle Paarl r w ★★★ Grand, DISTELL-owned cellar and v'yds. Much improved range now headlined by outstanding Cab Fr (03' 04 05), Grand Plaisir B'x/Shiraz blend. Other reds, Sauv Bl, and Chard also excellent.

Pongràcz sp ★★ DISTELL-owned MCC brand; vintaged Desiderius and popular NV Pongràcz, both Chard/Pinot N.

Quoin Rock Winery St'bosch r w (sw) ★★→★★★ Classically styled, inc grapes from southerly Cape Agulhas v'yds. Picks are elegant Syrah, Merlot, and white flagship Oculus (Sauv Bl). Second label is Glenhurst.

Raats Family St'bosch r w ★★→★★★ Deep-scented, minerally Cab Franc, and 2 Chenin Bls, oaked and unoaked, both worth keeping a few yrs.

Raka Walker Bay r w ★★→★★★ Run by seafaring Dryer family; powerful, personality-packed wines, inc award-winning Biography Shiraz, plus hearty, opulent Figurehead CAPE BLEND, deep-flavoured Merlot, and racy Sauv Bl.

Remhoogte Estate St'bosch r w ★★→★★★ Boustred family partnered by consultant Michel Rolland; trio of classically styled CAPE BLENDS: Bonne Nouvelle, ESTATE WINE, Aigle Noir. New easy-sipping Chenin Bl.

Rijk's Private Cellar Tulbagh r w ★★→★★★ Small-scale, big-impact winery. Emphasis on blends, eg Cab Sauv-powered Bravado, Shiraz/Mourvèdre The Crossing, and Sem/Sauv Bl. Depth, intensity remain signatures.

Robertson District Low-rainfall inland valley; lime soils; historically gd Chard, dessert styles (notably Muscat); more recently Sauv Bl, Shiraz, Cab Sauv; proliferation of family-run boutiques (best include Quando, Arendsig); condusive climate for organic production (eg Bon Cap).

Robertson Winery Robertson r w sw ★→★★ Gd value from co-op-scale (29,000 tons p.a.) winery. Best is No. 1 Constitution Rd Shiraz; also v.gd Vineyard Selection range: Shiraz, Pinotage, and Chard. Ries Noble Late Harvest can be superb. See Robertson District above.

Rudera Wines St'bosch r w (sw) ★★★ Local stardom for Chenin Bl. Various labels, styles, all outstanding: Also excellent Cab Sauv, Syrah.

Rupert & Rothschild Vignerons r w ★★★ Top v'yds, cellar at Simondium, PAARL. Joint venture between the Rothschilds and the Ruperts, 2 old French and South African wine families. Roving French guru Michel Rolland advises. Mellow, impressive B'x blend Baron Edmond 98 00 01 03; Chard Baroness Nadine is a deep-flavoured classic.

Rustenberg Wines St'bosch r w (sw) ★★★→★★★★ Prestigious old winery, producing continuously for more than a century. Flagship is single-v'yd unfiltered Cab Sauv Peter Barlow 99' 01' 03 04. *Outstanding B'x blend John X Merriman*; new, savoury Syrah; single-v'yd Chard Five Soldiers. Also top second label Brampton.

Rust en Vrede Estate St'bosch r ★★★ Revival underway under new owner (and ERNIE ELS partner) Jean Engelbrecht and ex-DISTELL winemaker Coenie Snyman. Strong, individual reds led by Cab Sauv-based ESTATE WINE, Cab Sauv, and Shiraz.

Sadie Family Swartland r w ★★★★ Biodynamically grown, trendily/traditionally-made (wild-yeasts, no fining/filtration) Columella (Shiraz, partnered with Mourvèdre) 01 02' 03 04 05' a Cape benchmark. Complex, intriguing white blend Palladius. Star winemaker Eben Sadie also grows a rated red blend, Dits del Terra, in Priorat, Spain, and, locally, the Sequillo range in partnership with Cape Wine Master Cornel Spies.

Saronsberg Cellar Tulbagh r w ★★→★★★ Growing following for Rhône varieties and blends, inc Shiraz and Viognier-seasoned Full Circle. Detour into B'x territory via red blend Rooi, in new jazzily packaged Provenance range.

Saxenburg St'bosch r w (sw sp) ★★→★★★ Swiss-owned v'yds and winery jointly run with French Ch Capion. Roundly oaked reds and Chard in high-end Private Collection; flagship Shiraz Select 98 00 01 02 03'; well-flavoured easy-drinkers in Guinea Fowl range.

Ses'Fikile Somerset West r w ★★ Front-ranker among Cape's new black-controlled wine ventures; all-woman business in partnership with FLAGSTONE. Much expanded line-up; best in Matriarch range.

Signal Hill Cape Town r w sw ★★→★★★ French flair in lively range, widely sourced grapes, inc tiny parcels in/around Cape Town city-centre; Jean-Vincent Ridon assisted by winemakers Khulekani Buthelezi and Wade METZER (see also METZER WINES). Malbec, Petit Verdot, Furmint (Tokaji lookalike Mathilde Aszú), Muscat and Pinotage all feature; several ageworthy desserts.

Simonsig Estate St'bosch r w sp sw ★★→★★★ Consistency and value among hallmarks of Malan family winery. Extensive but serious top-end range inc red B'x blend Tiara, much decorated Merindol Syrah 01' 02 03 04 05, Red Hill Pinotage 01 02 03' 04 05, v.gd Chard, and dessert-style Gewurz. First (30 yrs ago) MCC, Kaapse Vonkel, from Chard/Pinot N.

Solms-Delta Franschhoek r w ★★→★★★ Neuroscientist Mark Solms and veteran winemaker Hilko Hegewisch power this rising star. Intriguing, intelligent wines; best inc Amarone-style Shiraz Africana, sophisticated dry Rosé Lekkerwijn, scented Ries blend Koloni.

Southern Right See HAMILTON RUSSELL.

Spice Route Winery Swartland r w ★★★ Charles Back (FAIRVIEW)-owned cellar; hearty Rhône-style reds, esp intricate Malabar blend; also scented Viognier. Non-Rhône offerings inc beautiful old-vines Chenin Bl and classy Pinotage.

Spier Wines St'bosch r w ★★→★★★ A serious player (500,000+ cases per annum), owner of several widely exported brands, notably Spier and Savanha, each with tiers of quality. Most excitement in Spier's Private Collection and Vintage Selection ranges.

Springfield Estate Robertson ★★★ Cult wines, traditionally vinified, oozing personality. Exceptional softer-style Cab Sauvs (Whole Berry and Méthode Ancienne); B'x red Work of Time; opulent Méthode Ancienne Chard. All unfiltered, unfined, native yeast fermented. Unoaked Wild Yeast Chard; consistent Sauv Bls labelled Special Cuvée and Life From Stone.

Stark-Condé Wines St'bosch r ★★–★★★★ Ripe, full, single-v'yd Cab Sauv and Syrah, hand-crafted in Jonkershoek Valley by boutique grower José Conde.

The Stables r w (sp) ★–★★★ KwaZulu-Natal's first registered wine estate, family run, welcoming; mix of Kwa-Zulu-Natal and Western Cape v'yds.

Steenberg Vineyards Constantia r w (sp) ★★★–★★★★★ Top-league winery and v'yds, now under rising star winemaker Ruth Penfold. Best known for arresting Sauv Bls, esp flinty single-v'yd Res. Serious, elegant Merlot; red flagship blend Catharina; waxy Sem. Terrific new Sauv Bl/Sem mix Magna Carta. Fine Nebbiolo, one of handful in South Africa.

Stellenbosch (St'bosch) Oak-shaded university town, second oldest in South Africa, and demarcated wine district 50 km east of Cape Town. Heart of the wine industry – the Napa of the Cape. Many top estates, esp for reds, tucked into mountain valleys and foothills; extensive wine routes, many restaurants.

Stellenzicht Vineyards St'bosch r w ★★ DISTELL co-owned Helderberg winery and v'yds; excellent, sturdy Syrah; v.gd barrelled Sem; and, in Cellarmaster's Release range, Cab Sauv and new Pinotage.

Stormhoek r w ★★ UK-South African partnership, phenomenal growth fuelled by clever use of the internet. Recently expanded range inc v.gd Terraces Cab Sauv and Guava Pinotage; also Couture Rosé, served on the rocks.

Tanzanite w sp ★★ *Polished, tempting MCC to swallow.*

Thandi Wines St'bosch r w ★–★★★ Early black joint wine venture now under aegis of THE COMPANY OF WINE PEOPLE. Best: Cab Sauv, Merlot/Cab Sauv, and Chard.

Thelema Mountain Vineyards St'bosch r w (sw) ★★★–★★★★ After 3 decades, winemaker Gyles Webb and Thelema's star is undimmed. Cab Sauv 00' 03 04 05; *The Mint Cab Sauv shows off Thelema's trademark sweet minty intensity*; rich Merlot Res, 2 elegant Shiraz (Thelema v'yd), and Arumdale (ex-ELGIN v'yd); excellent Chard, and Sauv Bl and Sutherland Sauv Bl from ELGIN v'yd. Individual, spicy, rich Ed's Res Chard.

Tokara St'bosch r w (sw) ★★★ Showcase winery/v'yds under Gyles Webb (THELEMA). Best are B'x-inspired Red (Cab Sauv-based) and White (Sauv Bl/Sem); elegant Chard; Sauv Bls, one from fledgling ELGIN vines. Entry-level range Zondernaam puts many top-tier labels to shame. Excellent restaurant. Winemaker Miles Mossop's own label shows pedigree.

Twee Jonge Gezellen See KRONE.

Uva Mira Vineyards St'bosch r w ★★–★★★★ Lofty Helderberg sites yielding outstanding Chard, v.gd Shiraz (both single v'yd); gd B'x/Shiraz and Sauv Bl.

South Africa's top 10 wineries
BOEKENHOUTSKLOOF
DE TRAFFORD WINES
FAIRVIEW
HAMILTON RUSSELL VINEYARDS
KANONKOP ESTATE
NEIL ELLIS WINES
RUSTENBERG WINES
SADIE FAMILY
THELEMA MOUNTAIN VINEYARDS
VERGELEGEN

SOUTH AFRICA

Veenwouden Private Cellar Paarl r (w) ★★→★★★ Expanded offering inc Tempranillo/Cab Sauv and Viognier/Chenin Bl under Thornhill label. Best remain Merlot and B'x-style red Classic.

Vergelegen Somerset West r w (sw) ★★★★ To many still the front-running South African winery. A great mansion, immaculate v'yds and wines, serially awarded cellar door. Flagship is powerful, luxury-priced "V" **01'** 03 04 (single-v'yd Cab); B'x blend Vergelegen is lower keyed but still sumptuous; ditto Cab Sauv, Merlot, approachable Shiraz. "White" (and new barrel-selected Auction Res) are minerally, oak-fermented Sem blends. Superb, lemony Chard Res; standout, racy Sauv Bl Res (aka Schaapenberg); botrytis Ries dessert. Even quaffing Mill Race Red is rung above the norm.

Vilafonté r ★★★ First US-South African joint venture; now based in STELLENBOSCH town; California's Zelma Long (ex-Simi) and Phil Freese (ex-Mondavi viticulturalist) partnering WARWICK's Mike Ratcliffe. Top international notices for fine, supple B'x blends: firmly structured Series C, accessible Series M.

Villiera Wines St'bosch r w sp sw ★★→★★★ Grier family v'yds and winery with excellent quality/value range. Cream of (extensive) crop: B'x red Monro; Bush Vine Sauv Bl; Chenin Bl in serious Cellar Door range; 5 MCC bubblies (inc sulphur-free Brut Natural); 2 botrytis desserts from Ries and Chenin Bl. Recently established boutique-scale Dom Grier nr Perpignan, bottling a range of Côtes du Roussillon and VDP.

Vins d'Orrance Cape Town r w ★★→★★★ Excellent small-scale producer of Syrah Cuvée Ameena, complex Chard Cuvée Anaïs.

Vredendal Winery See NAMAQUA WINES.

Vriesenhof Vineyards St'bosch r w (sw) ★★★ Three labels, vinified by veteran Jan Coetzee: Vriesenhof (inc flagship B'x blend Kallista; Pinot N; Pinotage-based Enthopio); Talana Hill (B'x red Royale and Chard); and Paradyskloof easy-drinkers (Pinotage, Chard, etc).

Warwick Estate St'bosch r w ★★→★★★ Steered by dynamic Ratcliffe family (scion Mike also partner in US-South African project VILAFONTÉ). Pinotage blend Three Cape Ladies joined by B'x red First Lady. Also fine B'x red Trilogy (aka Estate Res); Cab Fr; Chard; Prof Black Sauv Bl.

Waterford Estate St'bosch r w sw ★★→★★★ Outstanding v'yds and hewn-stone winery, with top-rank status under veteran Kevin Arnold. Eponymous Shiraz (01 **02'** 03 04) is Cape classic; minerally Cab Sauv (01 02 03' 04), and Chard. Superb new flagship, The Jem, is intricate Cab Sauv-based blend, among South Africa's priciest wines.

Welgemeend Estate Paarl r ★★→★★★ Boutique winery, owned by Gauteng-based consortium. B'x blend (South Africa's first) Estate Res; Malbec-based Douelle.

Weltevrede Estate Robertson r w (sp) sw ★★ Building a reputation for well-crafted, individual Chard, Sauv Bl and Syrah emphasizing the farm's diverse soils. Gd Philip Jonker Brut sparkling.

Wine of Origin South Africa's "AC", but without French crop-yield etc restrictions. Certifies vintage, variety, region of origin.

The Winery of Good Hope St'bosch r w ★★→★★★ Australian-French-South African winemaking team for this premium brand. Flagship range is Radford Dale: top-notch Gravity (red blend, varying with vintage) and Chard; also promising new Shiraz/Merlot. First-rate Chenin Bl in Vinum range; Swartland grapes star in opulent Black Rock white and red blends.

Zonnebloem r w sw ★★ Reliable, easy-drinking range by DISTELL, widely sourced. Best is B'x red Lauréat. Occasional Limited Editions worth sampling.

Zorgvliet Wines St'bosch r w ★★→★★★ Vinous arm of diversified lifestyle group Zorgvliet Portfolio. 20+ labels in 4 ranges, topped by pricey B'x red Richelle. Silver Myn Cab Fr and Petit Verdot also gd.

Wine & food

Food these days is becoming almost as complicated as wine. We take Japanese for granted, Chinese as staple, look to Italian for comfort and then stir the pot with this strange thing called Fusion Rules. Don't try to be too clever; wine you like with food you like is safest.

In this year's wine & food section we look at the pleasures and puzzles of matching modern food to modern wine; as always, I suggest particular wines for particular dishes. These are personal choices, based on decades of experimentation and many suggestions from friends; at the very least they may ease menu stress, both at home and in restaurants.

Before the meal – apéritifs

The conventional apéritif wines are either sparkling (epitomized by Champagne) or fortified (epitomized by sherry in Britain, port in France, vermouth in Italy, etc.). A glass of white or rosé (or in France red) table wine before eating is presently in vogue. It calls for something light and stimulating, fairly dry but not acidic, with a degree of character; rather Riesling or Chenin Blanc than Chardonnay. Sauvignon Blanc has become a cliché.

Warning: Avoid peanuts; they destroy wine flavours. Olives are too piquant for many wines; they need sherry or a Martini. Eat almonds, pistachios, cashews or walnuts, plain crisps or cheese straws instead.

First courses

Aïoli A thirst-quencher is needed for its garlic heat. Rhône, sparkling dry white; Provence rosé, Verdicchio. And marc or grappa, too, for courage.

Antipasti Dry or medium white: Italian (Arneis, Soave, Pinot Grigio, Prosecco, Vermentino); light but gutsy red (Dolcetto, Franciacorta, young Chianti).

Artichoke vinaigrette An incisive dry white: New Zealand Sauv Bl; Côtes de Gascogne or a modern Greek; young red: Bordeaux, Côtes du Rhône.
  with hollandaise Full-bodied slightly crisp dry white: Pouilly-Fuissé, Pfalz Spätlese, or a Carneros or Yarra Valley Chard.

Asparagus A difficult flavour for wine, being slightly bitter, so the wine needs plenty of its own. Sauv Bl echoes the flavour. Semillon beats Chard, especially Australian, but Chard works well with melted butter or hollandaise. Alsace Pinot Gr, even dry Muscat is good, or Jurançon Sec.

Aubergine purée (Melitzanosalata) Crisp New World Sauv Bl e.g. from South Africa or New Zealand; or modern Greek or Sicilian dry white. Or try Bardolino red or Chiaretto. Baked aubergine dishes can need sturdier reds: Shiraz, Zin.

Avocado with seafood Dry to medium or slightly sharp white: Rheingau or Pfalz Kabinett, Grüner Veltliner, Wachau Ries, Sancerre, Pinot Gr; Sonoma or Australian Chard or Sauv Bl, or a dry rosé. Or Chablis Premier Cru.
  with mozzarella and tomato Crisp but ripe white with acidity: South African Chenin Blanc, Soave.

Bisques Dry white with plenty of body: Pinot Gr, Chard, Gruner Veltliner. Fino or dry amontillado sherry, or Montilla. West Australian Sem.

Bouillabaisse Savoury dry white, Marsanne from the Midi, Rhône or Australia, Corsican or Spanish rosé, or Cassis, Verdicchio.

Carpaccio, beef Seems to work well with most wines, inc reds. Top Tuscan is appropriate, but fine Chards are good. So are vintage and pink Champagnes.

salmon Chard or Champagne.

tuna Viognier, California Chard or New Zealand Sauv Bl.

Caviar Iced vodka. Champagne, if you must, full-bodied (e.g. Bollinger, Krug).

Ceviche Australian Ries or Verdelho, New Zealand Sauv Bl.

Charcuterie Young Beaujolais-Villages, Loire reds such as Saumur, New Zealand or Oregon Pinot N. Young Argentine or Italian reds. Bordeaux Blanc can work well too, as can light Chard like Côte Chalonnaise.

Chorizo Austrian Ries, good white Graves, Grüner Veltliner

Chowders Big-scale white, not necessarily bone dry: Pinot Gr, Rhine Spätlese, Albariño, Australian Sem, buttery Chard. Or fino sherry.

Consommé Medium-dry amontillado sherry or sercial madeira.

Crostini Morellino di Scansano, Montepulciano d'Abruzzo, Valpolicella, or a dry Italian white such as Verdicchio or Orvieto.

Crudités Light red or rosé: Côtes du Rhône, Minervois, Chianti, Pinot N; or fino sherry. For whites: Alsace Sylvaner or Pinot Blanc.

Dim-Sum Classically, China tea. For fun: Pinot Grigio or Ries; light red (Bardolino or Loire). NV Champagne or good New World fizz.

Eggs See also Soufflés. These present difficulties: they clash with most wines and can ruin good ones. But local wine with local egg dishes is a safe bet. So ★→★★ of whatever is going. Try Pinot Bl or not too oaky Chard. As a last resort I can bring myself to drink Champagne with scrambled eggs.

quail's eggs Blanc de Blancs Champagne.

seagull's (or gull's) eggs Mature white burgundy or vintage Champagne.

oeufs en meurette Burgundian genius: eggs in red wine calls for a glass of the same.

Escargots Rhône reds (Gigondas, Vacqueyras), St-Véran or Aligoté. In the Midi, very good Petits-Gris go with local white, rosé or red. In Alsace, Pinot Bl or the dry Muscat.

Fish terrine Pfalz Ries Spätlese Trocken, Grüner Veltliner, Chablis Premier Cru, Clare Valley Ries, Sonoma Chard; or manzanilla.

Foie gras Sweet white. In Bordeaux they drink Sauternes. Others prefer a late-harvest Pinot Gr or Ries (inc New World), Vouvray, Montlouis, Jurançon Moelleux or Gewurz. Tokáj Aszú 5 puttonyos is a Lucullan choice. Old dry amontillado can be sublime. With hot foie gras, mature vintage Champagne. But not on any account Chard or Sauv Bl.

Gazpacho A glass of manzanilla or fino before and after. Or Sauv Bl.

Goat's cheese, warm Sancerre, Pouilly-Fumé or New World Sauv Bl.

chilled Chinon, Saumur-Champigny or Provence rosé. Or strong red: Ch Musar, Greek, Turkish, Australian sparkling Shiraz.

Gravadlax Akvavit or iced sake. Or Grand Cru Chablis; California, Washington or Margaret River Chard; or Mosel Spätlese (not Trocken).

Guacamole California Chard, Sauv Blanc, dry Muscat or NV Champagne. Or Mexican beer.

Haddock, smoked, mousse or brandade A wonderful dish for showing off any stylish full-bodied white, inc Grand Cru Chablis or Sonoma, South African or New Zealand Chard.

Ham, raw or cured See also Prosciutto. Alsace Grand Cru Pinot Gr or good, crisp Italian Collio white. With Spanish *pata negra* or *jamon*, fino sherry or tawny port. See also Ham, cooked.

Herrings, raw or pickled Dutch gin (young, not aged) or Scandinavian akvavit, and cold beer. If wine essential, try Muscadet.

Houmous Pungent, spicy dry white, e.g. Furmint or modern Greek white.

Mackerel, smoked An oily wine-destroyer. Manzanilla sherry, proper dry Vinho Verde or Schnapps, peppered or bison-grass vodka. Or good lager.

Mayonnaise Adds richness that calls for a contrasting bite in the wine. Côte Chalonnaise whites (e.g. Rully) are good. Try New Zealand Sauv Bl, Verdicchio or a Spätlese trocken from the Pfalz.

Mezze A selection of hot and cold vegetable dishes. Sparkling is a good all-purpose choice, as is rosé from the Languedoc or Provence. Fino sherry is in its element.

Minestrone Red: Chianti, Zin, Teroldego, Rhône Syrah, etc. Or fino.

Mozzarella with tomatoes, basil Fresh Italian white, e.g. Soave, Alto Adige. Vermintino from the coast. Or simple Bordeaux Blanc. See also Avocado.

Oysters, raw NV Champagne, Chablis Premier Cru, Muscadet, white Graves, Sancerre or Guinness. Or even light, cold Sauternes.

    cooked Puligny-Montrachet or good New World Chard. Champagne is good with either.

Pasta Red or white according to the sauce or trimmings:

    cream sauce Orvieto, Frascati, Alto Adige Chard.

    meat sauce Montepulciano d'Abruzzo, Salice Salentino, Merlot.

    pesto (basil) sauce Barbera, Ligurian Vermentino, New Zealand Sauv Bl, Hungarian Furmint.

    seafood sauce (e.g. vongole) Verdicchio, Soave, white Rioja, Cirò, Sauv Bl.

    tomato sauce Chianti, Barbera, south Italian red, Zin, South Australian Grenache.

Pastrami Alsace Ries, young Sangiovese or Cab Fr.

Pâté

    chicken liver Calls for pungent white (Alsace Pinot Gr or Marsanne), a smooth red like a light Pomerol, Volnay or New Zealand Pinot N, or even amontillado sherry.

    duck pâté Châteauneuf-du-Pape, Cornas, Chianti Classico, Franciacorta.

    fish pâté Muscadet, Mâcon-Villages, Australian or South African Chard (unoaked).

    pâté de campagne A dry white ★★: good vin de pays, Graves, Fumé Blanc.

Peperonata Dry Australian Ries, Western Australia Sem or New Zealand Sauv Bl. Tempranillo or Grenache.

Pipérade Navarra rosado, Provence or Southern French rosés. Or dry Australian Ries. For a red: Corbières.

Pimentos, roasted New Zealand Sauv Bl, Spanish Chard or Valdepeñas.

Pizza Any ★★ dry Italian red. Or Rioja, Australian Shiraz, southern French red or Douro red.

Prawns, shrimps, or langoustines Fine dry white: burgundy, Graves, New Zealand Chard, Washington Ries, Pfalz Ries, Australian Ries – even fine mature Champagne. ("Cocktail sauce" kills wine, and in time, people.)

Prosciutto (also with melon, pears or figs) Full dry or medium white: Orvieto, Lugana, Sauv Bl, Grüner Veltliner, Tokay Furmint, white Rioja, Australian Sem, or Jurançon Sec.

Quiches Dry full-bodied white: Alsace, Graves, Sauv Bl, dry Rheingau; or young red (Tempranillo, Periquita), according to ingredients.

Risotto Pinot Gr from Friuli, Gavi, youngish Sem, Dolcetto or Barbera d'Alba.

    with fungi porcini Finest mature Barolo or Barbaresco.

    with mushrooms Cahors, Madiran, Barbera, or New World Pinot N.

Salade niçoise Very dry, ★★, not too light or flowery white or rosé: Provençal, Rhône, or Corsican; Catalan white; Fernão Pires, Sauv Bl.

Salads As a first course, especially with blue cheese dressing, any dry and appetizing white wine.

    Caesar salad Spanish or southern French rosé; neutral, crisp whites, preferably from near Rome.

NB Vinegar in salad dressings destroys the flavour of wine. If you want salad at a meal with fine wine, dress the salad with wine or a little lemon juice instead of vinegar.

Salami Barbera, top Valpolicella, genuine Lambrusco, young Zin, Tavel or Ajaccio rosé, Vacqueyras, young Bordeaux, Chilean Cab Sauv, Argentine Malbec.

Salmon, smoked A dry but pungent white: fino (esp manzanilla) sherry, Alsace Pinot Gr, Chablis Grand Cru, Pouilly-Fumé, Pfalz Ries Spätlese, vintage Champagne. If you must have a red, try a lighter one such as Barbera. Vodka, schnapps or akvavit.

Shark's fin soup Add a teaspoon of Cognac. Sip amontillado.

Soufflés As show dishes these deserve ★★★ wines.

    cheese Red burgundy or Bordeaux, Cab Sauv (not Chilean or Australian), etc. Or fine white burgundy.

    fish Dry white: ★★★ Burgundy, Bordeaux, Alsace, Chard, etc.

    spinach (tougher on wine) Mâcon-Villages, St-Véran, or Valpolicella. Champagne can also be good with all textures of soufflé.

Tapas Perfect with fino sherry, which can cope with the wide range of flavours in both hot and cold dishes.

Tapenade Manzanilla or fino sherry, or any sharpish dry white or rosé.

Taramasalata A rustic southern white with personality; not necessarily Retsina. Fino sherry works well. Try white Rioja or a Rhône Marsanne. The bland supermarket version submits to fine delicate whites or Champagne.

Tortilla Rioja crianza, fino sherry, or white Mâcon-Villages.

Trout, smoked Sancerre, California or South African Sauv Bl. Rully or Bourgogne Aligoté, Chablis or Champagne. Light German Riesling Kabinett.

Vegetable terrine Not a great help to fine wine, but California, Chilean or South African Chard makes a fashionable marriage, Chenin Blanc such as Vouvray a lasting one.

Whitebait Crisp dry whites: Greek, Touraine Sauv Bl, Verdicchio or fino sherry.

Fish

Abalone Dry or medium white: Sauv Bl, Côte de Beaune blanc, Pinot Gr, Grüner Veltliner. Chinese style: vintage Champagne.

Anchovies, marinated The marinade will clash with pretty well everything. Keep it light, white, dry, and neutral.

    in olive oil, or salted A robust wine: red, white or rosé – try Rioja.

Bass, sea Weissburgunder from Baden or Pfalz. Very good for any fine/delicate white, e.g. Clare dry Ries, Chablis, white Châteauneuf-du-Pape. But strengthen the flavours of the wine according to the flavourings of the fish: **ginger, spring onions** more powerful Ries; **porcini** top Alsace Pinot Bl.

Beurre blanc, fish with A top-notch Muscadet-sur-lie, a Sauv Bl/Sem blend, Chablis Premier Cru, Vouvray or a Rheingau Ries.

Brandade Chablis Premier Cru, Sancerre Rouge or New Zealand Pinot N.

Brill Very delicate: hence a top fish for fine old Puligny and the like.

Cod, roast good neutral background for fine dry/medium whites: Chablis, Meursault, Corton-Charlemagne, cru classé Graves, Grüner Veltliner, German Kabinett or dry Spätlesen, or a good lightish Pinot N.

Crab Crab and Riesling are part of the Creator's plan.

    Chinese, with ginger and onion German Ries Kabinett or Spätlese Halbtrocken. Tokay Furmint, Gewürz.

    cioppino Sauv Bl; but West Coast friends say Zin. Also California sparkling.

    cold, dressed Alsace, Austrian or Rhine Ries; dry Australian Ries or Condrieu.

softshell Chard or top-quality German Ries Spätlese.

Thai crabcakes Pungent Sauv Bl (Loire, South Africa, Australia, New Zealand) or Ries (German Spätlese or Australian).

with black bean sauce A big Barossa Shiraz or Syrah. Even Cognac.

with chilli and garlic Quite powerful Ries, perhaps German Grosses Gewächs or equivalent.

Curry A generic term for a multitude of flavours. Ries is a good bet. Or Sauv Bl.

Eel, smoked Ries, Alsace or Austrian according to the other ingredients. Or fino sherry, Bourgogne Aligoté. Schnapps

Fish and chips, fritto misto, tempura Chablis, white Bordeaux, Sauv Bl, Pinot Bl, Gavi, fino, montilla, Koshu, tea; or NV Champagne and Cava.

Fish baked in a salt crust Full-bodied white or rosé; Rioja, Albariño, Sicily, Côtes de Lubéron or Minervois.

Fish pie (with creamy sauce) Albariño, single-vineyard Soave Classico, Alsace Pinot Gr or Ries.

Haddock Rich dry whites: Meursault, California or New Zealand Chard, Marsanne or Albariño.

Hake Sauv Bl or any fresh fruity white: Pacherenc, Tursan, white Navarra.

Halibut As for turbot.

Herrings, fried/grilled Need a white with some acidity to cut their richness. Rully, Chablis, Bourgogne Aligoté, Greek, dry Sauv Bl. Or cider.

Kedgeree Full white, still or sparkling: Mâcon-Villages, South African Chard, . Grüner Veltliner, or (at breakfast) Champagne.

Kippers A good cup of tea, preferably Ceylon (milk, no sugar). Scotch? Dry oloroso sherry is surprisingly good.

Lamproie à la Bordelaise 5-yr-old St-Emilion or Fronsac. Or Douro reds with Portuguese lampreys.

Lobster, richly sauced Vintage Champagne, fine white burgundy, cru classé Graves, California Chard or Australian Ries, Pfalz Spätlese.

cold NV Champagne, Alsace Ries, Chablis Premier Cru, Condrieu, Mosel Spätlese, Penedès Chard, or a local fizz.

Mackerel, grilled Hard or sharp white: Sauv Bl from Touraine, Gaillac, Vinho Verde, white Rioja or English white. Or Guinness.

with spices White with muscle : Austrian Ries, Grüner Veltliner, German Grosses Gewächs.

Monkfish Often roasted, which needs fuller rather than leaner wines. Try New Zealand Chard, New Zealand/Oregon Pinot N or Chilean Merlot.

Mullet, red A chameleon, adaptable to good white or red, especially Pinot N.

Mullet, grey Verdicchio, Rully or unoaked Chard.

Mussels Muscadet-sur-lie, Chablis Premier Cru, Chard.

stuffed, with garlic See Escargots.

Paella, shellfish Full-bodied white or rosé, unoaked Chard.

Perch, sandre Exquisite fishes for finest wines: top white burgundy, Alsace Ries Grand Cru or noble Mosels. Or try top Swiss Fendant or Johannisberg.

Salmon, seared or grilled Pinot N is the fashionable option. Merlot or light claret not bad. Or fine white burgundy: Puligny- or Chassagne-Montrachet, Meursault, Corton-Charlemagne, Chablis Grand Cru; Grüner Veltliner, Condrieu, California, Idaho or New Zealand Chard, Rheingau Kabinett/ Spätlese, Australian Ries.

fishcakes Call for similar (as for above), but less grand, wines.

Sand-dabs This sublime fish can handle your fullest Chard (but not oaky).

Sardines, fresh grilled Very dry white: Vinho Verde, Soave, Muscadet, or modern Greek (esp from Santorini).

Sashimi If you are prepared to forego the wasabi, sparkling wines will go. Or

Washington or Tasmanian Chard, Chablis Grand Cru, Rheingau Ries English Seyval Bl. Otherwise, iced sake, fino sherry, or beer. Trials have matched 5-putt Tokáj with fat tuna, sea urchin and anago (eel).

Scallops An inherently slightly sweet dish, best with medium-dry whites.

in cream sauces German Spätlese, Montrachet, or top Australian Chard.

grilled or seared Hermitage Blanc, Grüner Veltliner, Entre-Deux-Mers, vintage Champagne, or Pinot N.

with Asian seasoning New Zealand, South African Chenin Blanc, Verdelho, Australian Ries, or Gewurz.

Shellfish Dry white with plain boiled shellfish, richer wines with richer sauces.

with plateaux de fruits de mer: Chablis, Muscadet, Picpoul de Pinet, Alto Adige Pinot Blanc.

Skate/raie with brown butter White with some pungency (e.g. Pinot Gr d'Alsace), or a clean straightforward wine like Muscadet or Verdicchio.

Snapper Sauv Bl if cooked with Oriental flavours; white Rhône or Provence rosé with Mediterranean flavours.

Sole, plaice, etc.: plain, grilled, or fried Perfect with fine wines: white burgundy or its equivalent.

with sauce According to the ingredients: sharp dry wine for tomato sauce, fairly rich for creamy preparations.

Sushi Hot wasabi is usually hidden in every piece. German QbA trocken wines, simple Chablis, or NV brut Champagne. Or, of course, sake or beer.

Swordfish Full-bodied dry white of the country. Nothing grand.

Tagine, with couscous North African flavours need substantial whites to balance – Austrian, Rhône – or crisp, neutral whites that won't compete. Preserved lemon demands something with acidity. Go easy on the oak.

Trout, grilled or fried Delicate white wine, e.g. Mosel (especially Saar or Ruwer), Alsace Pinot Bl.

Tuna, grilled or seared Generally served rare, so try a red: Cab Fr from the Loire, or Pinot N. Young Rioja is a possibility.

Turbot Serve with your best rich dry white: Meursault or Chassagne-Montrachet, Corton-Charlemagne, mature Chablis or its California, Australian or New Zealand equivalent. Condrieu. Mature Rheingau, Mosel or Nahe Spätlese or Auslese (not trocken).

Meat, poultry, game

Barbecues The local wine: Australian, South African, Argentina are right in spirit. Check out the marinades:

Asian flavours (lime, coriander, etc.): rosé, Pinot Gr, Ries.

Chilli: Shiraz, Zin, Pinotage, Malbec.

Middle Eastern (cumin, mint): crisp dry whites, rosé.

Oil, lemon, herbs: Sauv Bl.

Red wine: Cab, Merlot, Malbec, Tannat.

Tomato sauces: Zin, Sangiovese.

Beef, boiled Red: Bordeaux (Bourg or Fronsac), Roussillon, Gevrey-Chambertin, or Côte-Rôtie. Medium-ranking white Burgundy is good, e.g. Auxey-Duresses. Or top-notch beer. Mustard softens tannic reds, horseradish kills everything – but can be worth the sacrifice.

roast An ideal partner for fine red wine of any kind. See above for mustard.

stew Sturdy red: Pomerol or St-Emilion, Hermitage, Cornas, Barbera, Shiraz, Napa Cab Sauv, Ribera del Duero or Douro red.

Beef Stroganoff Dramatic red: Barolo, Valpolicella Amarone, Cahors, Hermitage, late-harvest Zin – even Moldovan Negru de Purkar.

Boudin Blanc Loire Chenin Bl, especially when served with apples: dry Vouvray, Saumur, Savennières. Mature red Côtes de Beaune, if without apple.

Boudin Noir (blood sausage) Local Sauv Bl or Chenin Bl – especially in the Loire. Or Beaujolais Cru, especially Morgon. Or light Tempranillo.

Cabbage, stuffed Hungarian Cab Fr/Kadarka; village Rhônes; Salice Salentino, Primitivo and other spicy southern Italian reds. Or Argentine Malbec.

Cajun food Fleurie, Brouilly, or New World Sauv Bl.

    with gumbo: amontillado or Mexican beer.

Cassoulet Red from southwest France (Gaillac, Minervois, Corbières, St-Chinian or Fitou) or Shiraz. But best of all Beaujolais Cru or young Tempranillo.

Chicken/turkey/guinea fowl, roast Virtually any wine, including very best bottles of dry to medium white and finest old reds (especially burgundy). The meat of fowl can be adapted with sauces to match almost any fine wine (e.g. *coq au vin* with red or white burgundy). Try sparkling Shiraz with strong, sweet, or spicy stuffings and trimmings.

Chicken Kiev Alsace Ries, Collio, Chard, Bergerac rouge.

Chilli con carne Young red: Beaujolais, Tempranillo, Zin, Argentine Malbec.

Chinese food

    Canton or Peking style Rosé, or dry to medium-dry white – Mosel Ries Kabinett or Spätlese trocken – can be good throughout a Chinese banquet. Gewürz often suggested but rarely works (but brilliant with ginger), yet Chasselas and Pinot Gr are attractive alternatives. Dry or off-dry sparkling (especially Cava) cuts the oil and matches sweetness. Eschew sweet/sour dishes but try St-Emilion ★★, New World Pinot N, or Châteauneuf-du-Pape with duck. I often serve both white and red wines concurrently during Chinese meals.Champagne becomes a thirst quencher.

    Szechuan style Verdicchio, Alsace Pinot Bl, or very cold beer.

Choucroute garni Alsace Pinot Bl, Pinot Gr, Ries, or beer.

Cold roast meat Generally better with full-flavoured white than red. Mosel Spätlese or Hochheimer and Côte Chalonnaise are very good, as is Beaujolais. Leftover cold beef with leftover vintage Champagne is bliss.

Confit d'oie/de canard Young tannic red Bordeaux, California Cab Sauv and Merlot, and Priorato cut richness. Alsace Pinot Gr or Gewürz match it.

Coq au vin Red burgundy. In an ideal world, one bottle of Chambertin in the dish, two on the table.

Curry See Indian dishes.

Duck or goose Rather rich white: Pfalz Spätlese or off-dry Alsace Grand Cru. Or mature gamey red: Morey-St-Denis, Côte-Rôtie, Bordeaux, or Burgundy. With oranges or peaches, the Sauternais propose drinking Sauternes, others Monbazillac or Ries Auslese. Mature weighty vintage Champagne is good, too, and handles red cabbage surprisingly well.

    Peking See Chinese food.

    wild duck Big-scale red: Hermitage, Bandol, California or South African Cab Sauv, Australian Shiraz – Grange if you can afford it.

    with olives Top-notch Chianti or other Tuscans.

Frankfurters German, NY Riesling, Beaujolais, light Pinot N. Or Budweiser (Budwar) beer.

Game birds, young, plain-roasted The best red wine you can afford.

    older birds in casseroles Red (Gevrey-Chambertin, Pommard, Santenay or Grand Cru St-Emilion, Napa Valley Cab Sauv or Rhône).

    well-hung game Vega Sicilia, great red Rhône, Château Musar.

    cold game Mature vintage Champagne.

Game pie, hot Red: Oregon Pinot Noir.

cold Good quality white burgundy, cru Beaujolais, or Champagne.

Goulash Flavoursome young red: Hungarian Kékoportó, Zin, Uruguayan Tannat, Morellino di Scansano, young Australian Shiraz.

Grouse See Game birds – but push the boat right out.

Haggis Fruity red, e.g. young claret, young Portuguese red, New World Cab Sauv or Malbec, or Châteauneuf-du-Pape. Or, of course, malt whisky.

Ham, cooked Softer red burgundies: Volnay, Savigny, Beaune; Chinon or Bourgueil; sweetish German white (Rhine Spätlese); Tokaj Furmint or Czech Frankovka; lightish Cab Sauv (e.g. Chilean), or New World Pinot N. And don't forget the heaven-made match of ham and sherry. See ham, raw or cured.

Hamburger Young red: Australian Cab Sauv, Chianti, Zin, Argentine Malbec, Tempranillo. Or Coke or Pepsi (not 'Diet', but 'Max').

Hare Jugged hare calls for flavourful red: not-too-old burgundy or Bordeaux, Rhône (e.g. Gigondas), Bandol, Barbaresco, Rib del Duero, Rioja Reserva. The same for saddle, or for hare sauce with pappardelle. This could be the moment for a Supertuscan.

Indian dishes Medium-sweet white, very cold: Orvieto abboccato, South African Chenin Bl, Alsace Pinot Bl, Torrontes, Indian sparkling, Cava or NV Champagne. Or emphasize the heat with a tannic Barolo or Barbaresco, or deep-flavoured reds such as Châteauneuf-du-Pape, Cornas, Australian Grenache or Mourvèdre, or Valpolicella Amarone.

Kebabs Vigorous red: modern Greek, Corbières, Chilean Cab Sauv, Zin, or Barossa Shiraz. Sauv Bl, if lots of garlic.

Kidneys Red: St-Emilion or Fronsac: Nuits-St-Georges, Cornas, Barbaresco, Rioja, Spanish or Australian Cab Sauv, top Alentejo.

Lamb, roast One of the traditional and best partners for very good red Bordeaux – or its Cab Sauv equivalents from the New World. In Spain, the partner of the finest old Rioja and Ribera del Duero Reservas.

cutlets or chops As for roast lamb, but a little less grand.

Liver Young red: Beaujolais-Villages, St-Joseph, Médoc, Italian Merlot, Breganze Cab Sauv, Zin, Tempranillo, Portuguese Bairrada.

Calf's Red Rioja crianza, Salice Salentino Riserva, Fleurie.

Meatballs Tangy medium-bodied red: Mercurey, Crozes-Hermitage, Madiran, Morellino di Scansano, Langhe Nebbiolo, Zin, Cab Sauv.

spicy Middle-Eastern style Simple, rustic red.

Moussaka Red or rosé: Naoussa from Greece, Sangiovese, Corbières, Côtes de Provence, Ajaccio, New Zealand Pinot N, young Zin, Tempranillo.

Osso buco Low tannin, supple red, such as Dolcetto d'Alba or Pinot N. Or dry Italian white such as Soave and Lugana.

Oxtail Rather rich red: St-Emilion, Pomerol, Pommard, Nuits-St-Georges, Barolo or Rioja Reserva, Ribera del Duero, California or Coonawarra Cab Sauv, Châteauneuf-du-Pape, mid-weight Shiraz.

Paella Young Spanish wines: red, dry white or rosé: Penedès, Somontano, Navarra or Rioja.

Pigeon Lively reds: Savigny, Chambolle-Musigny; Crozes-Hermitage, Chianti Classico, Argentine Malbec, or California Pinot. Or try Franken Silvaner Spätlese. See also Squab.

Pork, roast A good rich, neutral background to a fairly light red or rich white. It deserves ★★ treatment – Médoc is fine. Portugal's suckling pig is eaten with Bairrada Garrafeira, Chinese is good with Pinot N.

with prunes Can take a big New World Cab Sauv.

Pot au feu, bollito misto, cocido Rustic red wines from the region of origin; Sangiovese di Romagna, Chusclan, Lirac, Rasteau, Portuguese Alentejo or Yecla and Jumilla from Spain.

Quail As for squab. Carmignano, Rioja Reserva, mature claret, Pinot N.

Rabbit Lively medium-bodied young Italian red or Aglianico del Vulture; Chiroubles, Chinon, Saumur-Champigny, or Rhône rosé.

    with prunes Bigger, richer, fruitier red.

Satay Australia's McLaren Vale Shiraz, or Alsace or New Zealand Gewürz.

Sauerkraut (German) Lager or Pils. (But see also Choucroute garni.)

Sausages See also Charcuterie, Frankfurters, Salami. The British banger requires a young Malbec from Argentina (a red wine, anyway), or British ale.

Shepherd's pie Rough-and-ready red seems most appropriate, e.g. Sangiovese di Romagna, but beer or dry cider is the real McCoy.

Squab Fine white or red Burgundy, Alsace Ries Grand Cru or mature claret. See also Pigeon.

Steak

    au poivre A fairly young Rhône red or Cab Sauv.

    filet or tournedos Any red (but not old wines with Béarnaise sauce: top New World Pinot N or Californian Chard is better).

    Fiorentina (bistecca) Chianti Classico Riserva or Brunello. The rarer the meat, the more classic the wine; the more well done, the more you need New World, fruit-driven wines. Argentina Malbec is the perfect partner for steak Argentine style, i.e. cooked to death.

    Korean Yuk Whe (the world's best steak tartare) Sake.

    tartare Vodka or light young red: Beaujolais, Bergerac, Valpolicella.

    T-bone Reds of similar bone structure: Barolo, Hermitage, Australian Cab Sauv or Shiraz.

Steak and kidney pie or pudding Red Rioja Reserva, Douro red, or mature Bordeaux.

Stews and casseroles Burgundy such as Chambolle-Musigny or Bonnes-Mares if fairly simple; otherwise lusty full-flavoured red: young Côtes du Rhône, Toro, Corbières, Barbera, Shiraz, Zin, etc.

Sweetbreads A grand dish, so grand wine: Rhine Ries or Franken Silvaner Spätlese, Alsace Grand Cru Pinot Gr, or Condrieu, depending on sauce.

Tagines These vary enormously, but fruity young reds are a good bet: Beaujolais, Tempranillo, Sangiovese, Merlot, Shiraz.

Tandoori chicken Riesling or Sauv Bl, or young red Bordeaux or light north Italian red served cool. Also Cava and NV Champagne.

Thai dishes Ginger and lemongrass call for pungent Sauv Bl (Loire, Australia, New Zealand, South Africa) or Ries (Spätlese or Australian).

    coconut milk Hunter Valley and other ripe, oaked Chards; Alsace Pinot Bl for refreshment; Gewürz or Verdelho. And, of course, Cava or NV Champagne.

Tongue Good for any red or white of abundant character, especially Italian. Also Beaujolais, Loire reds, Tempranillo, and full dry rosés.

Tripe Red (e.g. Corbières, Roussillon) or rather sweet white (e.g. German Spätlese). Better: Western Australian Sem/Chard, or cut with pungent dry white such as Pouilly-Fumé or fresh red such as Saumur-Champigny.

Veal, roast A good neutral background for any fine old red which may have faded with age (e.g. a Rioja Reserva) or a German or Austrian Ries or Vouvray, or Alsace Pinot Gr.

Venison Big-scale reds, including Mourvèdre, solo as in Bandol, or in blends. Rhône, Bordeaux or California Cab Sauv of a mature vintage; or rather rich white (Pfalz Spätlese or Alsace Pinot Gr). With a sharp berry sauce, try a German Grosses Gewächs Riesling, or a New World Cab Sauv.

Vitello tonnato Full-bodied whites, especially Chard; or light reds (e.g. Valpolicella) served cool.

Wild boar Serious red: top Tuscan or Priorat.

Vegetarian dishes (see also First courses)

Baked pasta dishes Pasticcio, lasagne and cannelloni with elaborate vegetarian fillings and sauces: an occasion to show off a grand wine, especially finest Tuscan red, but also claret and burgundy. Also Gavi from Italy.

Cauliflower cheese Crisp aromatic white: Sancerre, Ries Spätlese, Muscat, English Seyval Bl, or Schönburger.

Couscous with vegetables Young red with a bite: Shiraz, Corbières, Minervois; or well-chilled rosé from Navarra or Somontano; or a robust Moroccan red.

Fennel-based dishes Sauv Bl: Pouilly-Fumé or one from New Zealand; English Seyval Bl or young Tempranillo.

Grilled Mediterranean vegetables Brouilly, Barbera, Tempranillo, or Shiraz.

Lentil dishes Sturdy reds such as southern French, or Zin or Shiraz.

Mushrooms (in most contexts) Fleshy red, e.g. Pomerol, California Merlot, Rioja Reserva, top Burgundy, or Vega Sicilia. On toast , your best claret. Ceps/porcini are best for Ribera del Duero, Barolo or Chianti Rufina, or top claret: Pauillac or St-Estèphe.

Onion/leek tart Fruity off-dry or dry white: Alsace Pinot Gr or Gewürz, Canadian or New Zies Ries, English whites, Jurançon, Australian Ries. Or Loire red.

Peppers or aubergines (eggplant), stuffed Vigorous red wine: Nemea, Chianti, Dolcetto, Zin, Bandol, Vacqueyras.

Pumpkin/squash ravioli or risotto Full-bodied fruity dry or off-dry white: Viognier or Marsanne, demi-sec Vouvray, Gavi, or South African Chenin.

Ratatouille Vigorous young red: Chianti, New Zealand Cabernet , Merlot, Malbec, Tempranillo; young red Bordeaux, Gigondas, or Coteaux du Languedoc.

Spanacopitta Valpolicella (its bitterness helps); Greco di Molise, or white Sicilian/Sardinian.

Spiced vegetarian dishes See under Indian dishes, Thai dishes.

Watercress, raw This makes every wine on earth taste revolting. Soup is slightly easier, but doesn't require wine.

Desserts

Apple pie, strudel or tarts Sweet German, Austrian, or Loire white, Tokáji Aszú, or Canadian Ice Wine.

Apples, Cox's Orange Pippins Vintage port (and sweetmeal biscuits).

Bread-and-butter pudding Fine 10-yr-old Barsac, Tokáji Azsú or Australian botrytized Sem.

Cakes and gâteaux See also Chocolate, Coffee, Ginger, Rum. Bual or Malmsey madeira, oloroso or cream sherry.

Cheesecake Sweet white: Vouvray, Anjou, or fizz – refreshing, nothing special.

Chocolate Generally only powerful flavours can compete. Bual, California Orange Muscat, Tokay Azsú, Australian Liqueur Muscat, 10-yr-old tawny port; Asti for light, fluffy mousses. Experiment with rich, ripe reds: Syrah, Zin, even sparkling Shiraz. Banyuls for a weightier partnership. Médoc can match bitter black chocolate. Or a tot of good rum.

Christmas pudding, mince pies Tawny port, cream sherry, or liquid Christmas pudding itself, Pedro Ximénez sherry. Asti or Banyuls.

Coffee desserts Sweet Muscat, Australia Liqueur Muscats, or Tokáji Aszú.

Creams, custards, fools, syllabubs See also Chocolate, Coffee, Ginger, and Rum. Sauternes, Loupiac, Ste-Croix-du-Mont, or Monbazillac.

Crème brûlée Sauternes or Rhine Beerenauslese, best madeira or Tokáji. (With concealed fruit, a more modest sweet wine.)

Crêpes Suzette Sweet Champagne, Orange Muscat or Asti.

Fruit

blackberries vintage port.

dried fruit (and compotes) Banyuls, Rivesaltes, Maury.

flans and tarts Sauternes, Monbazillac, sweet Vouvray or Anjou.

fresh Sweet Coteaux du Layon or light sweet Muscat.

poached, i.e. apricots, pears, etc. Sweet Muscatel: try Muscat de Beaumes-de-Venise, Moscato di Pantelleria, or Spanish dessert Tarragona.

salads, orange salad A fine sweet sherry or any Muscat-based wine.

Ginger flavours Sweet Muscats, New World botrytized Ries and Sém.

Ice-cream and sorbets Fortified wine (Australian liqueur Muscat, Banyuls); sweet Asti or sparkling Moscato. Pedro Ximenez, Amaretto liqueur with vanilla; rum with chocolate.

Lemon flavours For dishes like Tarte au Citron, try sweet Ries from Germany or Austria, or Tokay Aszú; very sweet if lemon is very tart.

Meringues Recioto di Soave, Asti or Champagne doux.

Mille-feuille Delicate sweet sparkling white, such as Moscato d'Asti or demi-sec Champagne.

Nuts Finest oloroso sherry, madeira, vintage or tawny port (nature's match for walnuts), Tokáji Aszú, Vin Santo or Setúbal Moscatel.

Orange flavours Experiment with old Sauternes, Tokáji Aszú or California Orange Muscat.

Panettone Jurançon moelleux, late-harvest Ries, Barsac, Tokáji Aszú.

Pears in red wine A pause before the port. Or try Rivesaltes, Banyuls or Ries Beerenauslese.

Pecan pie Orange Muscat or liqueur Muscat.

Raspberries (no cream, little sugar) Excellent with fine reds which themselves taste of raspberries: young Juliénas, Regnié.

Rum flavours (baba, mousses, ice-cream) Muscat – from Asti to Australian liqueur, according to weight of dish.

Strawberries and cream Sauternes or similar sweet Bordeaux, Vouvray moelleux or Jurançon Vendange Tardive.

Strawberries, wild (no cream) Serve with red Bordeaux (most exquisitely Margaux) poured over.

Summer pudding Fairly young Sauternes of a good vintage.

Sweet soufflés Sauternes or Vouvray moelleux. Sweet (or rich) Champagne.

Tiramisú Vin Santo, young tawny port, Muscat de Beaumes-de-Venise, Sauternes, or Australian Liqueur Muscat.

Trifle Should be sufficiently vibrant with its internal sherry.

Zabaglione Light-gold marsala or Australian botrytized Sem, or Asti.

Wine & cheese

The notion that wine and cheese were married in heaven is not borne out by experience. Fine red wines are slaughtered by strong cheeses: only sharp or sweet white wines survive. Principles to remember, despite exceptions, are first: the harder the cheese the more tannin the wine can have. And second: the creamier the cheese is the more acidity needed in the wine. Cheese is classified by its texture and the nature of its rind, so its appearance is a guide to the type of wine to match it. Individual cheeses mentioned below are only examples taken from hundreds sold in good cheese shops that could bear more research. I try to keep a glass of white wine to drink with my cheese.

Fresh, no rind – cream cheese, crème fraîche, Mozzarella
Light crisp white – Simple Bordeaux Blanc, Bergerac, English unoaked whites; or rosé – Anjou, Rhône; or very light, very young, very fresh red such as Bordeaux, Bardolino, or Beaujolais.

Hard cheeses, waxed or oiled, often showing marks from cheesecloth – Gruyère family, Manchego and other Spanish cheeses, Parmesan, Cantal, Comté, old Gouda, Cheddar and most "traditional" English cheeses
Particularly hard to generalize here; Gouda, Gruyère, some Spanish, and a few English cheeses complement fine claret or Cab Sauv and great Shiraz/Syrah wines. But strong cheeses need less refined wines, preferably local ones. Sugary, granular old Dutch red Mimolette or Beaufort are good for finest mature Bordeaux. Also for Tokáj Aszú. But try white wines too.

Blue cheeses Roquefort can be wonderful with Sauternes, but don't extend the idea to other blues. It is the sweetness of Sauternes, especially old, that complements the saltiness. Stilton and port, preferably tawny, is a classic. Intensely flavoured old oloroso, amontillado, madeira, marsala, and other fortified wines go with most blues.

Natural rind (mostly goat's cheese) with bluish-grey mould (the rind becomes wrinkled when mature), sometimes dusted with ash – St-Marcellin
Sancerre, Valençay, light fresh Sauv Bl, Jurançon, Savoie, Soave, Italian Chard, lightly oaked English whites.

Bloomy rind soft cheeses, pure white rind if pasteurized, or dotted with red: Brie, Camembert, Chaource, Bougon (goat's milk 'Camembert')
Full dry white burgundy or Rhône if the cheese is white and immature; powerful, fruity St-Emilion, young Australian (or Rhône) Shiraz/ Syrah or Grenache if it's mature.

Washed-rind soft cheeses, with rather sticky orange-red rind – Langres, mature Epoisses, Maroilles, Carré de l'Est, Milleens, Munster
Local reds, especially for Burgundy cheeses; vigorous Languedoc, Cahors, Côtes du Frontonnais, Corsican, southern Italian, Sicilian, Bairrada. Also powerful whites, especially Alsace Gewurz and Muscat.

Semi-soft cheeses, grey-pink thickish rind – Livarot, Pont l'Evêque, Reblochon, Tomme de Savoie, St-Nectaire
Powerful white Bordeaux, Chard, Alsace Pinot Gr, dryish Ries, southern Italian and Sicilian whites, aged white Rioja or dry oloroso sherry. But the strongest of these cheeses kill most wines.

Wine with food

Why drink wine?

Or, to be more specific, why drink wine with food? It's not obligatory, even for wine lovers. Most of us would blanch at the thought of wine with pickled herring, for example, and would prefer aquavit; with Japanese food we might welcome green tea, or sake. Cider can replace light white wine with many dishes, and beer aficionados are as exacting in their views on which beer goes best with which dish as the most fervent wine drinker. Wine is no longer the only option with food.

It does, however, offer more choices than anything else. At the risk of serious attack from beer lovers, I will state firmly that no other alcoholic drink has the range of textures and weights that wine can offer. White wine varies from barely-there fragility to thought-provoking complexity; red from lollipop lightness to punchy muscularity. And that's before one looks at flavours: every flower, fruit and herb under the sun, plus smoke, tar, chocolate, coffee, toast, earth, flint...

Wine also offers digestibility – and its alcoholic strength is usually such that you can drink it in sufficient volumes to quench your thirst without getting drunk.

Age plays its part, too, and it's a major part when it comes to matching wine with food. A good red will suit some dishes when it is young, others when it is fully mature or ageing. Mature vintage Champagne is a very different food proposition from young non-vintage. Sometimes a great vintage of a given wine, with all the concentration and complexity that that implies, is the best choice with a given dish; sometimes a lesser vintage will flatter more, by being less obtrusive.

A minefield, then? Only if you see all this as a problem. Food and wine matching is about enjoyment. It's not an exam. The pages that follow are designed to amuse, stimulate and, just possibly, make you look at your wine rack in a new light. At the very least, one might have a glass of wine while thinking about it.

To start: which comes first, food or wine?

It should be the wine, shouldn't it? We should all be thinking, Ah, here we are in the hills of Tuscany, Rioja, or Adelaide, watching the sun dip below the horizon; let's look at the wine list and find something local, unknown and wonderful to drink, and then let's ask the sommelier what he, or she, would recommend that we eat with it.

Or should it be the food? Should we say, I went to the fishmonger's today and the scallops looked marvellous. So we're having scallops. What is there in the cellar?

Wine, as we know, offers a multitude of choices – of colour, flavour, weight and maturity. Food in practice offers a more urgent choice – what is in the fridge that must be eaten or thrown away. But food is flexible as well: add a different flavour or texture and it will go with a different wine. An earthy bean purée will bridge the gap between those scallops and a light red. Roast guinea fowl served with ratatouille will be happy with a substantial white; with pommes dauphinoise, caramelized shallots and a rich jus, one would think in terms of red. There is always something one can do to adapt what needs to be eaten to what is in the cellar.

Your cellar probably reflects what you eat anyway. If you love game you'll have a lot of Pinot Noir and Syrah stashed away; if you're a fish fanatic you'll have Chardonnay, but also Gewurztraminer, Pinot Noir, and Riesling.

Just occasionally, though, there'll be a special bottle around which the food will be designed. Roast lamb for a special claret, perhaps, or a faultlessly pink grouse for a top red burgundy. These are the ideal, classic matches for which no adjustments are necessary. Simplicity as perfection. (See pp 319–20 for some further suggestions.)

Matching wine and food

Flavours

The world used to be a simpler place. Think back to what our grandparents ate: classic dishes, classically prepared.

Nowadays every ingredient is available to us. In our kitchens we can knock up a Thai curry involving lime leaves, lemon grass, shrimp paste, and fish sauce. Chefs make their name by reinventing food from the ground up. Every month sees a new ingredient – a cheese, perhaps, matured for three years and five days precisely, made from the milk of Albanian ewes that lambed under a waning moon; oil made from a seed which, until that moment, you had no idea could produce oil. We even have a new flavour – umami – to add to the old roster of sweet and sour, bitter and salty. It's no wonder that the old rule of red wine with red meat, white wine with white meat and fish, begins to look a little inadequate.

And that's before one looks at the expansion of wine flavours. One used to think confidently of Mosel Riesling with, say, trout – but what about a lime-flavoured South Australian Riesling? Or a more floral New Zealand one? Suddenly it's a different equation. Will a soft, toffeeish Chilean Merlot go with the same dishes that Pomerol will match? What about Carmenère, a grape that had disappeared off the radar until the Chileans found it had been masquerading as Merlot? What about Italian Pecorino, suddenly a grape variety as well as a cheese? What about the vast store of indigenous Portuguese grapes, or Greek?

Enough questions; it's time for some answers. And the first answer is that in order to match modern food with modern wine we must do what good contemporary painters do: learn the traditional rules, and then abandon them. (The results, in both food and painting, are very different from not knowing the rules in the first place.)

Think of how one plans a menu: by starting off with an ingredient, and building on it. Lamb, say, a delicately flavoured, sweetish meat. Add another ingredient to flatter it: black olives? Aubergines and tomatoes? Garlic and rosemary? Haricot beans and pesto? Now start thinking of the wine – but don't start by thinking in terms of wine names, start with flavours and move on from there. Black olives have, for example, an uncanny knack of softening tannins; aubergines, even with tomatoes, go very well with rich, solid, sweetish reds; sweet, caramelized garlic flatters most reds, and rosemary will be happy with most; pesto would normally suggest a white, but the beans will pull the whole thing together with a red. With the black olives, then, perhaps a northern Rhône? Or a northern Italian? Not a blockbuster, but something with some grip. With the aubergines, a Zinfandel? With garlic and rosemary – well, lots of things. A classic match of Cabernet, perhaps. And with the pesto, something earthy but with a bite of acidity. A Portuguese red could perhaps be interesting.

The lamb might be the main ingredient, but everything you add to it modifies it, as does the way you cook it. Roasting adds sweet, caramelized notes, while rare meat is very good at handling tannins. That's what makes it so perfect for flattering special, classic bottles. Do the Greek and Italian trick of squeezing some lemon over roast meat, however, and you'll need a wine with more acidity – Chianti, perhaps, or, yes, a Greek red. Deglaze the juices with something sweet, like redcurrant jelly or balsamic vinegar, and you're tilting the balance towards something richer and fruitier.

Must acidity balance acidity, and sweetness sweetness? Yes. Sauternes and strawberries are good together because each has sweetness and acidity. Tarte au citron is a demon to match because it has too much of both; even a Beerenauslese Riesling can be overwhelmed. Fish with lemon juice demands a crisp, high-acidity white; without, but with a creamy sauce, it will settle happily with a good, lower-acidity Chardonnay, either oaked or unoaked.

Matching the flavours of food and wine is all about building bridges between them. You've got a blockbuster New World Cabernet and can't think what to eat with it? Up the ante with powerfully flavoured vegetables – grilled radicchio, broccoli with garlic perhaps – and rich, creamy pommes dauphinoise to coat the mouth. Or, say, you're cooking for somebody who'll drink nothing but white, but you hate fish? Roast a chicken, getting the skin good and brown, and serve it with just the natural juices – and perhaps some peas. Roast chicken, and peas, are high in savoury umami, the so-called fifth taste. (See page 308.) Lay off all other vegetables. And serve it with vintage Champagne, one of the most umami-friendly of all wines. Those eating will practically lick the plate.

Weight and texture

Matching wine with food is no mystery if you think in terms of one flavour balancing another across the spectrum of the dish. The same goes for weight and texture: think of the wine in exactly the same way as you do of the food. Just as you would play with textures on the plate – something firm, something crisp, something soft – so you can play with the texture and weight of the wine. You want something soft and unctuous to meld with roasted root vegetables? Or something crisp and light to match the texture of a salad?

Pinning down weight and texture in wine is, however, slightly less easy than pinning down flavours. Weight is simple enough: it comes (technically speaking) from alcohol, tannin, and dry extract; less technically, you know it when you see it. Barolo is weightier than Valpolicella. Grand Cru Chablis is weightier than simple Chablis. Accordingly, you might drink simple Chablis with some plain grilled fish, but select the Grand Cru if the fish is monkfish wrapped in proscuitto in a sauce of olive oil and saffron. Of course that is partly flavour, but it's weight as well. If you think of German Riesling, you

wouldn't match a Mosel Kabinett with the same food that would match a Pfalz Grosses Gewächs. The flavours are similar, but the Pfalz has more power and could even handle, perhaps, wild boar with a cranberry sauce, with sweetness and acidity providing the flavour match. The Mosel, on the other hand, one would keep for dressed crab.

Texture, likewise, comes from alcohol, tannins, and glycerine (or from a prickle on the palate). Alcohol gives fatness in the mouth; tannins – of the best, modern, ripe but not over-extracted variety – give velvety richness and smoothness. You know that seductive silkiness Pinot Noir can have? Or the silkiness of a fine Margaux? Or the richness of an Argentine Malbec? That's the sort of thing. As for glycerine – think of Sauternes, thick and unctuous. Why does Sauternes go so well with Rocquefort? Partly because of flavour –

you need sweetness with blue cheese; partly because of weight; but also because it has the fatness in the mouth to match the creaminess of the cheese.

Sauternes, Selection des Grains Nobles Gewurztraminer, and Tokaji handle foie gras so well because their texture, dense and smooth, matches perfectly. But put them with hot foie gras, with its lighter texture, and they will overwhelm it. Here the best match known to man is very good old vintage Champagne: the bubbles work magic.

The bubbles in sparkling wines can make a huge difference. Put a glass of Asti, all fresh, crunchy grapiness, with Christmas pudding and suddenly you feel much less like going to sleep afterwards: a Sauternes, however, matching weight for weight and sweetness for sweetness, is exhausting. Asti, light and bubbly, is refreshing. Champagne goes surprisingly well with meringue, whereas anything with matching sweetness is too heavy. The bubbles are the reason that Champagne goes so much better with scrambled eggs at a celebration breakfast than any still Chardonnay, however good: they lighten the mouth-coating texture of the eggs.

Texture is probably the least considered of all wine qualities when we think of matching wine with food. Weight we tend to deal with almost subconsciously. But texture has been a big preoccupation of winemakers for the last 10 years. It's all about getting tannins really ripe and silky, so that wines can be drunk younger, which is what we mostly want to do these days. And it's had the side-effect of making red wines much more food-friendly. Whereas before the only thing to do with a chunky red was to throw a lump of rare meat at it, now you can sit it down with an earthy vegetable dish and it'll behave itself. Silky tannins have made life more interesting for vegetarian wine drinkers, and for lovers of Indian and even Korean food. Beefy southern European reds would, in the past, have given a jarring tannic clash with such dishes; now they're still beefy, but they're civilized.

Alcohol, one of the key components of both weight and texture, can provide problems, however. Too much alcohol fights with food and usually wins: a 16% red is going to be very difficult to match. Even if you found the perfect dish, are you ever going to want that much weight, that much power? Putting fortified wines with food is difficult for the same reason: they have so much of everything. What the most powerful fortifieds need is food with equal intensity, but in small quantities. A glass of vintage Port with a piece of Stilton, for example, or a fine old amontillado with some aged parmesan. Fino, coming in at around 16% yet with an ethereal lightness, can be good with oily fish, which needs both lightness and substance. Smoked salmon is a classic match, but grilled sardines can be as good.

Dip into my list of wine and food pairings (p. 293 *et seq.*) to continue your exploration of matching wine and food. In the end one of the key words to bear in mind is "refreshing". Food and wine matches should not be tiring, or cloying. If they are, then it's time to lighten up – be it in flavour, weight, or texture.

Must you drink local wine with local food?

There is a theory, frequently aired, that the best match for any given food is its local wine, and vice versa. Look at *crottins*, those little goat's cheeses from the Loire, goes this theory, don't they go perfectly with the local Sauvignon Blanc? And what would you drink with Alsace choucroute if not Alsace Riesling? And the marvellous vegetable stew of Rioja – menestra – goes so perfectly with Rioja that you'd be mad to drink anything else with it.

All these things are true, and unarguable. But the idea that may lurk behind this theory – that food and wine flavours grew up together in each region, and adapted to suit each other over the centuries, is another matter, and extremely arguable. It suggests that to split up such close siblings is at best thoughtless and at worst criminal; and that even in today's world, where we partner a Sauvignon Blanc as readily with a Thai green curry as with goat's cheese, we should take into account the roots of our food and wine when considering what to put with what.

But the question is: should we? In reality most of us live in both worlds, the global world and the local one. We would be unlikely to order burgundy in a brasserie in Bordeaux, or French wine in Italy – although the wine shops of southern Italy are these days full of the wines of the north, which southerners would ordinarily regard as another country. (Many Italian winemakers have cellars full of French wine.) Australian winemakers, too, have wine delivered from all over

the world, while visitors to Australia want only to drink local wine. What is local, and what is global, changes with each shift in perspective. Dining at home we may mix and match; dining abroad in a wine region, our loyalties will be fiercely local.

Why do local foods tend to go with local wines? Well, rustic foods and rustic wines tend to go together, because poor, isolated regions tended to produce both. The need was for food and wine that would last through the winter: beans were dried, fish was dried and salted, and every scrap of meat was preserved. Winemaking in such regions was probably primitive and produced gutsy flavours – oxidized, yes; infected with every sort of bacterial taint, yes; vinegary, probably; but without a doubt gutsy.

Then there were other regions, usually richer, where wine was exported. Everybody wanted to export wine if they could: it brought in good money. One of the reasons that monasteries were so keen to plant vines and improve the quality of their wine was that it produced a healthy income. And what was planted and made was tailored to what the market wanted, whether the market was in other cities, as it was for Burgundy, or other countries, as it was for Bordeaux. Rich customers, ordering from their wine merchant, wanted the best: Pinot Noir rather than Gamay, for example. If it hadn't been for the pressures of wealthy and perhaps distant customers, who knows how much Gamay there might now be on the Côte d'Or?

Wine styles could thus evolve in either a local or a global context. Food, too, was both local and global, though the global influences on food (in Europe, at least) consisted of new ingredients arriving, rather than local produce being exported. Tomatoes and lemons are not indigenous to the Mediterranean, nor potatoes to northern Europe.

Food and wine have evolved over the centuries and continue to do so, sometimes though not necessarily in parallel. Look at Pacific Rim cuisine, derived in part from countries with no native wine-growing tradition, and now encouraging the production of some lighter, more elegant wines in California and Australia. By contrast, what one might dub "Bullimenthal" food – molecular cuisine, as pioneered by El Bulli in Spain and by Heston Blumenthal at The Fat Duck in Britain – can occasionally prove very difficult to match with wine, and sometimes very easy. Either way, the wine is secondary; it is not what this food is about.

When food is completely international, what does one drink? Local tastes still intrude. Red Bordeaux is the most international of wines, but the British still like it more mature than, say, the French. In China they're apt to drink it very young indeed. And while in Europe we've got used to the idea that we can't afford First Growths any more, and so we drink lesser wines (most of us, anyway), in the Far East, in Russia, and in many so-called emerging markets, it's only the top wines that find a ready audience. You may not feel that Mouton 2005 is the perfect match for some spice-and-chilli-laden dish, but that's what they want on the table.

Tell us you care: do top chefs really love wine?

Sometimes even asking the question can seem subversive. Of course chefs care about wine. They work in restaurants, don't they? Restaurants care about wine. QED.

Except that it's not always that simple. If you want to taste some really bad matches of food and wine – matches where the two do not just fail to flatter each other but actively clash – the best place to go is a top restaurant for a lunch or dinner hosted by an equally top wine producer. What the chef will want to produce is his signature dishes, which are what made him a star. And if they don't go with the wine – well, too bad.

A famous German grower cites an extreme example of this: he was giving a wine dinner at a leading restaurant and rang in advance to discuss it with the chef. But the chef refused to tell him what he was going to cook, and when he asked what wines he should bring, the chef said, "bring anything".

Why this lack of interest, even antagonism? Partly it's because the professions of chef and sommelier are separate; it's the sommelier's job to look after the wine, not the chef's. Partly it's a question of ego: chefs want their food to play the starring role, and they don't want to waste their time cooking the sort of simple food that flatters wine best. They like complicated food, food that is difficult to copy, food that makes them famous. And very complicated flavours mean that perhaps one in 200 wines will go, rather than, say, one in 30. The famous kitchen machismo also plays a part. It is not so unusual for kitchen staff to view sommeliers as a lesser breed, only out there to talk to the customers because they lack the testosterone to survive life in the kitchen. Chefs and sommeliers do not always love each other.

One should not, however, imply that chefs are never interested in wine; many are, especially among the younger generation of chefs. That same German grower also recalls working with young Italian chefs who produced brilliantly inventive dishes to flatter old Rieslings. And there are many top restaurants where the chef will stand back and let the wine take centre stage; and very many more where food and wine are equals. But shouldn't it always be like that?

Six sommeliers' choices

Six highly regarded sommeliers from around the world share some food and wine pairings that make their mouths water.

Andreas Larsson

Andreas won the important Meilleur Sommelier du Monde competition in 2007. He is creative head sommelier, PM & Vänner, in Vaxjo in Sweden.

"As an overall wine style Riesling is my great weapon, because of its impeccable freshness, purity, and because it ranges from dry to sweet.

It is not rocket science to pair a red wine with meat; the most interesting combinations are always those with white wines. The elegant nature of most "white wine" dishes is flattered by a great and fresh white wine; the combination is even more transparent. And speaking of Riesling, it is ideal for a lot of flavours in modern cuisine, where one bumps into a variety of sweet-sour combinations, spicy flavours, or the naturally sweet elements found in shellfish, crab, and vegetables.

A specific example that we are now serving at PM & Vänner, and one that I adore, is a tartare of elk with dried apples, parsnips, and cottage cheese with chanterelle mushrooms. These are very nutty and autumnal flavours that I pair with a complex and completely dry Amontillado, La Sacristia de Sanchez Romate, which is just wonderful with the dish thanks to its dryness, power, elegance, and complexity. The digestable nature of sherry is also helpful with raw meat, whilst the maturity is enhanced by the mushrooms. In short, it's darn good!"

Nathalie Reymond

Chef Jacques Reymond is a personal favourite of eminent Australian wine writer James Halliday. Jacques' daughter Nathalie is sommelier at their acclaimed family-run restaurant.

"We make our own Pinot Noir with Bass Philip, and one of my favourite matches is Bass Philip Pinot with steak and chips on Sunday night at home with the family. It's a sentimental kind of match: we have a Burgundy background, and Bass Philip is burgundian in style. Yes, theoretically we should be having Cabernet.

A lovely match in our restaurant is lacquered Tasmanian petuna ocean trout with a fennel and vanilla purée and some oriental mushrooms, which I serve with 2006 Fire Rising Pinot Noir from Geelong in Victoria. The trout is lacquered with a paste, and has sweet and sour flavours and a soya glaze with a bit of miso – there's also some palm sugar and some mirin (Japanese sweet rice wine). This dish works better with a red, and especially Pinot. A lot depends on the structure of the Pinot, though; this wine has a firm structure, which makes the match work."

Gérard Basset

A Master of Wine, Gérard was runner-up in the Meilleur Sommelier du Monde competition in Rhodes in 2007. He is chef-proprietor of Hotel TerraVina, in Hampshire, UK.

"I would pick a classic match and something a bit different. For the classic match, blue cheese and sweet wine: perhaps a Rocquefort. A good Rocquefort is fantastic with a glass of Sauternes, perhaps Château Climens 2001. You have the perfect balance between the richness of the cheese and the sweetness of the wine, and the saltiness of the cheese and the sweetness of the wine. It's a wonderful match. It's classic, but sometimes classics work...

For something different; well, I love sushi with a bit of soy sauce; it has a strong character, so I'd put it with an Austrian Grüner Veltliner from Hirtzberger – Axpoint, his top cru. You have the purity of the fish and the slight spice of the soy sauce, so you need a wine that is bone dry but with the depth of flavour and character of a top Grüner Veltliner from the Wachau."

Hendrik Thoma

Hendrik is a hugely respected sommelier with an international following. He is master sommelier at Hotel Louis C. Jacob in Hamburg, Germany.

"One of the most astonishing food and wine pairings I have ever had is Sauternes and oysters. This is not regarded as a normal match, though it occurs in some old books, and it was a favourite dish in the 1800s and 1900s. I learnt it from Alexandre de Lur-Saluces (of Château de Fargues in Sauternes; his family owned, and he used to run, Yquem until its sale in 1999). You have the saltiness of the oysters, as you have in Rocquefort, and a nuttiness, especially in the oysters from Bordeaux, and they are enhanced by the sweetness of the Sauternes, and by the noble rot. The Sauternes has to be chilled, and the oysters have to have a rich, creamy texture. You can use a lighter style of Sauternes, or even Cérons or Loupiac, but it must be nicely chilled so that you get the acidity.

Another remarkable dish is simple pasta and white truffles – the pasta tossed in butter, not in olive oil – and Barolo. It works wonderfully well. You would think that butter, red wine and white pasta wouldn't go, but the truffle pulls it all together. The only thing is that you need an older wine. It can be Barolo or Barbaresco, or even a simple Nebbiolo, if it's a good one.

I was doing a tasting with Ben Glaetzer [of Glaetzer Wines, in Australia's Barossa Valley] of his icon red, Amon-Ra, which is super-concentrated. We had it with some bitter chocolate and a cassis sauce – we have a very good pâtissier at the hotel, and he chose the particular type of chocolate. It was a wonderful combination. Some people didn't like it, but others thought it was great."

Pamela S Busch

Pamela has "the best palate on the West Coast and knows how to take it to food", according to one authority. Pamela is proprietor/wine director, CAV Wine Bar & Kitchen in San Francisco, USA.

"Memorable food and wine pairings are often the ones that are unexpected; like, and no joke here, Mount Eden Chardonnay and a peanut butter and jelly sandwich. However, one of my all-time favourites is the Olive Oil Poached Black Cod that is on our current menu. The fish has a delicate, buttery texture and is accented by melted leeks, toasted pumpkin seeds and crushed caper berries that enliven without shocking the palate. The 2006 Anheuser de Noir, Pauly Anheuser, from the Nahe, a white wine made from Pinot Noir, is the perfect complement. In spite of its colour, it has hints of strawberry fruit which, combined with vanilla cream and spiced apple flavours, accentuate and contrast with the dish. Even though the fish is not rich, it benefits from the acidity in the wine. As this dish is so outrageously good it works with numerous white wines and some rosés, but with the Anheuser de Noir it's an absolutely ethereal match."

Silvano Giraldin

Silvano can be found at Le Gavroche, one of London's finest French restaurants. He is senior consultant at the Albert Roux Consultancy.

"One of my favourite dishes is Poulet aux Morilles with a red burgundy; you have white meat, cream, morels and the velvet of Pinot,

perhaps an Echezeaux from Jayer, if you want to go for the best, or just a humble Chambolle-Musigny. It's always the best combination.

Staying with meat, if you have a fillet steak and some red wine sauce and a bordeaux, that is fantastic. Choose a vintage that is drinking very well now, like 1985, 1988 or 1989, not necessarily a First Growth but a Forts de Latour, which is a bit robust, or Cos d'Estournel. Have foie gras on top, to make it Tournedos Rossini. It's a classic.

Another great dish is Lièvre à La Royale, which you call jugged hare: hare off the bone, with the liver of the hare and some foie gras, slowly cooked in red wine and finished with the blood. Have it with Côte Rôtie. The flavours are delicious: I dream of it."

Food and finest wines

With very special bottles the wine guides the choice of food rather than the other way around. The following suggestions are based largely on the gastronomic conventions of the wine regions producing these treasures, plus much diligent research. They should help bring out the best in your best wines.

Red wines
Red Bordeaux and other Cabernet Sauvignon-based wines (very old, light and delicate: e.g. pre-1959, with exceptions such as 45)
  Leg or rack of young lamb, roast with a hint of herbs (but not garlic); entrecôte; roast partridge or grouse, sweetbreads; or cheese soufflé after the meat has been served.
Fully mature great vintages (e.g. Bordeaux 59 61 82)
  Shoulder or saddle of lamb, roast with a touch of garlic, roast ribs, or grilled rump of beef.
Mature but still vigorous (e.g. 89 90)
  Shoulder or saddle of lamb (including kidneys) with rich sauce. Fillet of beef *marchand de vin* (with wine and bone-marrow). Avoid Beef Wellington: pastry dulls the palate.
Merlot-based Bordeaux (Pomerol, St-Emilion)
  Beef as above (fillet is richest) or well-hung venison.
Côte d'Or red burgundy Consider the weight and texture, which grow lighter/more velvety with age. Also the character of the wine: Nuits is earthy, Musigny flowery, great Romanées can be exotic, Pommard renowned for its four-squareness. Roast chicken, or capon, is a safe standard with red burgundy; guinea-fowl for

A little learning...

A few technical words

The jargon of laboratory analysis is often seen on back-labels. It creeps menacingly into newspapers and magazines. What does it mean? This hard-edged wine-talk, unsympathetic as it is to most lovers of wine, is very briefly explained below.

Alcohol content (mainly ethyl alcohol) is expressed in per cent by volume of the total liquid. (Also known as "degrees".) Table wines are usually between 12.5° and 14.5°, though up to 16° is increasingly seen.

Acidity is both fixed and volatile. Fixed acidity consists principally of tartaric, malic and citric acids, all found in the grape, and lactic and succinic acids, produced during fermentation. Volatile acidity consists mainly of acetic acid, which is rapidly formed by bacteria in the presence of oxygen. A small amount of volatile acidity is inevitable and even attractive. With a larger amount the wine becomes "pricked" – to use the Shakespearian term. It turns to vinegar. Acidity may be natural, in warm regions it may also be added.

Total acidity is fixed and volatile acidity combined. As a rule of thumb, for a well-balanced wine it should be in the region of one gram per thousand for each 10° Oechsle (see above).

Barriques Vital to modern wine, either in ageing and/or for fermenting in barrels (the newer the barrel the stronger the influence) or from the addition of oak chips or – at worst – oak essence. Newcomers to wine can easily be beguiled by the vanilla-like scent and flavour into thinking they have bought something luxurious rather than something cosmetically flavoured. But barrels are expensive; real ones are only used for wines with the inherent quality to benefit long-term. French oak is classic and most expensive. American oak has a strong vanilla flavour.

Malolactic fermentation is often referred to as a secondary fermentation, and can occur naturally or be induced. The process involves converting tart malic acid into softer lactic acid. Unrelated to alcoholic fermentation, the "malo" can add complexity and flavour to both red and white wines. In hotter climates where natural acidity may be low canny operators avoid it.

Micro-oxygenation is a widely used technique that allows the wine controlled contact with oxygen during maturation. This mimics the effect of barrel-ageing, reduces the need for racking, and helps to stabilize the wine.

pH is a measure of the strength of the acidity: the lower the figure the more acid. Wine usually ranges from pH 2.8 to 3.8. High pH can be a problem in hot climates. Lower pH gives better colour, helps stop bacterial spoilage and allows more of the SO_2 to be free and active as a preservative.

Residual sugar is that left after fermentation has finished or been stopped, measured in grams per litre. A dry wine has virtually none.

Sulphur dioxide (SO_2) is added to prevent oxidation and other accidents in winemaking. Some of it combines with sugars etc and is "bound". Only the "free" SO_2 is effective as a preservative. Total SO_2 is controlled by law according to the level of residual sugar: the more sugar, the more SO_2 is needed.

Tannins are the focus of attention for red-winemakers intent on producing softer, more approachable wines. Later picking, and picking by tannin ripeness rather than sugar levels gives riper, silkier tannins.

Toast refers to the burning of the inside of the barrel. "High toast" gives the wine caramel-like flavours.